# AUDITING CASES

Eighth Edition

**Michael C. Knapp**
*University of Oklahoma*

Australia • Brazil • Japan • Korea • Mexico • Singapore • Spain • United Kingdom • United States

**Auditing Cases, Eighth Edition**
Michael C. Knapp

VP/Editorial Director: Jack W. Calhoun
Editor-in-Chief: Rob Dewey
Acquisition Editor: Matt Filimonov
Developmental Editor: Lauren Athmer
Corrections Coordinator: Nancy Stamper
Marketing Manager: Natalie King
Production Manager: Jennifer Ziegler
Senior Art Director: Stacy Jenkins Shirley
Senior Permissions Acquisition Manager/Image: Deanna Ettinger
Permissions Acquisition Manager/Text: Mardell Glinski Schultz
Manufacturing Buyer: Doug Wilke
Content Project Manager: Karunakaran Gunasekaran
Production House: Pre-PressPMG
Internal Designer: Pre-PressPMG
Cover Designer: Patti Hudepohl
Photo Credits:
B/W Image: Getty Images/Rubberball
Color Image: Shutterstock images/Haywiremedia
Cover Image: Shutterstock



Library of Congress Control Number: 2009939709

International Student Edition ISBN 13: 978-0-538-46680-6
International Student Edition ISBN 10: 0-538-46680-4

**Cengage Learning International Offices**

**Asia**
cengageasia.com
tel: (65) 6410 1200

**Australia/New Zealand**
cengage.com.au
tel: (61) 3 9685 4111

**Brazil**
cengage.com.br
tel: (011) 3665 9900

**India** 10 0614472X
cengage.co.in
tel: (91) 11 30484837/38

**Latin America**
cengage.com.mx
tel: +52 (55) 1500 6000

**UK/Europe/Middle East/Africa**
cengage.co.uk
tel: (44) 207 067 2500

**Represented in Canada by Nelson Education, Ltd.**
nelson.com
tel: (416) 752 9100/(800) 668 0671

For product information: **www.cengage.com/international**
Visit your local office: **www.cengage.com/global**
Visit our corporate website: **www.cengage.com**

Printed in Canada
1 2 3 4 5 6 7 13 12 11 10

# DEDICATION

To my parents
William Jackson Knapp and
Orebel DeBurger Knapp

# BRIEF CONTENTS

# CONTENTS

**SECTION 1 Comprehensive Cases** 1

**Case 1.1** Enron Corporation 3

*Arthur Edward Andersen established a simple motto that he required his subordinates and clients to invoke: "Think straight, talk straight." For decades, that motto served Arthur Andersen & Co. well. Unfortunately, the firm's association with one client, Enron Corporation, abruptly ended Andersen's long and proud history in the public accounting profession.*

KEY TOPICS: history of the public accounting profession in the United States, scope of professional services provided to audit clients, auditor independence, and retention of audit workpapers.

**Case 1.2** Just for FEET, Inc. 23

*In the fall of 1999, just a few months after reporting a record profit for fiscal 1998, Just for FEET collapsed and filed for bankruptcy. Subsequent investigations by law enforcement authorities revealed a massive accounting fraud that had grossly misrepresented the company's reported operating results. Key features of the fraud were improper accounting for "vendor allowances" and intentional understatements of the company's inventory valuation allowance.*

KEY TOPICS: applying analytical procedures, identifying inherent risk and control risk factors, need for auditors to monitor key developments within the client's industry, assessing the health of a client's industry, and receivables confirmation procedures.

**Case 1.3** AMRE, Inc. 37

*AMRE's chief financial officer arranged a secret meeting with the company's independent auditors in a subtle but unsuccessful effort to focus their attention on a fraudulent scheme masterminded by his superiors.*

KEY TOPICS: hiring of former auditors by audit clients, client-imposed audit scope limitations, auditors' responsibility for unaudited quarterly financial data, and auditing large and suspicious write-offs by clients.

**Case 1.4** ESM Government Securities, Inc. 47

*The ESM scandal rocked the international financial markets and resulted in one state imposing the first "banking holiday" in the United States since the Depression.*

KEY TOPICS: performance pressure exerted on auditors, the use of audit confirmation procedures, quality control in an auditing practice, and discovery of financial statement errors following the issuance of an audit report.

**Case 1.5** United States Surgical Corporation 59

*An SEC investigation revealed that officials of this company went to great lengths to conceal pervasive irregularities in the company's accounting records from its independent auditors.*

KEY TOPICS: the use of analytical procedures, accounting for revenue and capital expenditures, implications of the imbalance of power in the auditor-client relationship, and evaluation of conflicting audit evidence.

**Case 1.6** The Fund of Funds, Ltd. 69

*Bernie Cornfeld, John McCandish King, and Robert Vesco were among the parties associated with this once high-flying mutual fund.*

KEY TOPICS: detection of fraud, client confidentiality, materiality of financial statement errors, and auditors' legal exposure under the Securities Exchange Act of 1934.

**Case 1.7** Crazy Eddie, Inc. 83

*"Crazy Eddie" Antar oversaw a profitable chain of consumer electronics stores on the East Coast during the 1970s and 1980s. After new owners discovered that the company's financial data had been grossly misrepresented, Antar fled the country, leaving behind thousands of angry stockholders and creditors.*

KEY TOPICS: auditing inventory, inventory control activities, management integrity, the use of analytical procedures, and the hiring of former auditors by audit clients.

**Case 1.8** ZZZZ Best Company, Inc. 93

*Barry Minkow, the "boy wonder" of Wall Street, created a $200,000,000 company that existed only on paper.*

KEY TOPICS: identification of key management assertions, limitations of audit evidence, importance of candid predecessor-successor auditor communications, client confidentiality, and client-imposed audit scope limitations.

**Case 1.9** Gemstar-TV Guide International, Inc. 107

*In 2000,* U.S. News and World Report *predicted that Henry Yuen, the chief executive of Gemstar-TV Guide International, would become the "Bill Gates of television" thanks to the innovative business model that he had developed for his company. When that business model proved to be a "bust," Yuen used several accounting gimmicks to embellish his company's reported operating results.*

KEY TOPICS: conditions commonly associated with "audit failures," revenue recognition principle, quantitative and qualitative materiality assessments, and "legal" vs. "ethical" conduct.

**Case 1.10** New Century Financial Corporation 119

*The collapse of New Century Financial Corporation in April 2007 signaled the beginning of the subprime mortgage crisis in the United States, a crisis that would destabilize securities and credit markets around the globe. A federal bankruptcy examiner has maintained that New Century's independent audits were inadequate.*

KEY TOPICS: auditing loan loss reserves, Section 404 audit procedures, material internal control weaknesses, auditor independence, and audit staffing issues.

**Case 1.11** Madoff Securities 137

*As an adolescent, Bernie Madoff dreamed of becoming a "key player" on Wall Street. Madoff realized his dream by overseeing the world's largest and possibly longest running Ponzi scheme. Madoff's auditor pleaded guilty to several criminal charges for his role in that fraud.*

KEY TOPICS: factors common to financial frauds, regulatory role of Securities and Exchange Commission (SEC), nature and purpose of peer reviews, appropriate audit procedures for client investments, and the importance of the independent audit function.

**SECTION 2 Audits of High-Risk Accounts 147**

**Case 2.1** Doughtie's Foods, Inc. 149

*Inadequate inventory observation procedures prevented this company's auditors from discovering a materially overstated inventory balance.*

**Case 2.2** Golden Bear Golf, Inc. 153

*Jack Nicklaus, the "Golden Bear," endured public embarrassment and large financial losses when key subordinates misapplied the percentage-of-completion accounting method to numerous golf course development projects.*

**Case 2.3** Happiness Express, Inc. 161

*To compensate for flagging sales of their Mighty Morphin Power Rangers toys, this company's executives booked millions of dollars of bogus sales. Deficiencies in the audit procedures applied by Happiness Express's auditors resulted in the bogus sales and receivables going undetected.*

**Case 2.4** SmarTalk Teleservices, Inc. 169

*In recent years, "restructuring" reserves have been a controversial subject in the financial reporting domain. This case examines accounting and auditing issues stemming from a large restructuring reserve booked by SmarTalk.*

**Case 2.5** Dollar General Stores, Inc. 175

*An IBM employee came up with a creative solution to an "accounting problem" that was impeding a major purchase of IBM equipment by Dollar General. That solution resulted in both companies being sanctioned by the SEC.*

**Case 6.2** Bill DeBurger, In-Charge Accountant 293

*To "sign off" or "not sign off" was the issue facing Bill DeBurger after he completed the audit procedures for a client's most important account. An angry confrontation with the audit engagement partner made Bill's decision even more difficult.*

**Case 6.3** David Myers, WorldCom Controller 297

*This case provides a poignant chronological history of the WorldCom scandal from the perspective of David Myers, the company's former controller.*

**Case 6.4** Tommy O'Connell, Audit Senior 303

*A new audit senior is quickly exposed to the challenging responsibilities of his professional work role when he is assigned to supervise a difficult audit engagement. During the audit, the senior must deal with the possibility that a staff accountant is not completing his assigned audit procedures.*

**Case 6.5** Avis Love, Staff Accountant 307

*Auditors sometimes develop close friendships with client personnel. Such friendships can prove problematic for auditors, as demonstrated in this case.*

**Case 6.6** Charles Tollison, Audit Manager 311

*Audit managers occupy an important role on audit engagements and are a critical link in the employment hierarchy of public accounting firms.*

**Case 6.7** Hamilton Wong, In-Charge Accountant 315

*"Eating time," or underreporting time worked on audit engagements, has serious implications for the quality of audit services and for the quality of auditors' work environment. Hamilton Wong came face-to-face with these issues when a colleague insisted on understating the hours she worked on her assignments.*

**SECTION 7 Professional Issues 319**

**Case 7.1** Ligand Pharmaceuticals 321

*Ligand's auditor was the first Big Four firm sanctioned by the Public Company Accounting Oversight Board (PCAOB).*

**Case 7.2** HealthSouth Corporation 327

*In recent years, scores of large companies have paid their independent auditors huge amounts for a wide range of non-audit services, which prompted the SEC to begin requiring public companies to disclose such payments. HealthSouth Corporation was criticized for allegedly misrepresenting the nature of non-audit services provided by its independent audit firm, Ernst & Young.*

*impacted Japan's accounting profession and independent audit function. An accounting and auditing scandal involving a large cosmetics and apparel company, Kanebo Limited, posed the first major challenge of that new regulatory framework.*

**Case 8.4** Registered Auditors, South Africa 407

*The South African economy was rocked in recent years by a series of financial reporting scandals. To restore the credibility of the nation's capital markets, the South African Parliament passed a controversial new law, the Auditing Profession Act (APA). The APA established a new auditing regulatory agency and a new professional credential for independent auditors. The APA also mandated that independent auditors immediately disclose to the new auditing agency any "reportable irregularities" committed by an audit client.*

**Case 8.5** *Zuan Yan* 419

*The Big Four accounting firms view China as one of the most lucrative markets for accounting and auditing services worldwide. However, those firms face major challenges in that market. Among these challenges are an increasing litigation risk and the difficulty of coping with the often heavy-handed tactics of China's authoritarian central government.*

**Case 8.6** Kaset Thai Sugar Company 431

*This case focuses on the 1999 murder of Michael Wansley, a partner with Deloitte Touche Tohmatsu. Wansley was supervising a debt-restructuring engagement in a remote region of Thailand when he was gunned down by a professional assassin.*

**Case 8.7** Australian Wheat Board 435

*During the United Nations (U.N.) embargo imposed on Iraq following that nation's invasion of Kuwait, this large Australian company paid $300 million in bribes to secure lucrative Iraqi wheat contracts administered through the U.N. Oil-for-Food program. After the bribes were discovered in 2005 by a U.N. task force, two major international accounting firms became involved in the ensuing controversy.*

**Case 8.8** OAO Gazprom 445

Business Week *referred to the huge Gazprom debacle as "Russia's Enron." For the first time in the history of the new Russian republic, a Big Four accounting firm faced a lawsuit for allegedly issuing improper audit opinions on a Russian company's financial statements.*

**Case 8.9** Tata Finance Limited 459

*A financial reporting fraud involving this large Indian company became known as "India's Enron." Company executives retained one of India's most prominent accounting firms to investigate the fraud. The report filed by that accounting firm implicated those same executives. Shortly after the report was released, the accounting firm retracted the report and fired the three partners responsible for it.*

# PREFACE

The past decade has arguably been the most turbulent and traumatic in the history of the accounting profession and the independent audit function. Shortly after the turn of the century, the Enron and WorldCom fiascoes focused the attention of the investing public, the press, Wall Street, and, eventually, Congress on our profession. Those scandals resulted in passage of the Sarbanes-Oxley Act of 2002 (SOX) and the creation of the Public Company Accounting Oversight Board (PCAOB). Next came the campaign to replace U.S. generally accepted accounting principles (GAAP) with International Financial Reporting Standards (IFRS). That campaign stalled in 2008 when the subprime mortgage crisis in the United States caused global stock markets to implode and global credit markets to "freeze." Many parties insisted that fair value accounting and inadequate audits were major factors that led to the onset of the most severe global economic downturn since the Great Depression.

As Congress and regulatory authorities struggled to revive the U.S. economy in late 2008, news of the largest Ponzi scheme in world history grabbed the headlines. Investors worldwide were shocked to learn that Bernie Madoff, an alleged "wizard of Wall Street," was a fraud. Law enforcement authorities determined that as much as $65 billion in client investments supposedly being held by Madoff's company, Madoff Securities, did not exist. The business press was quick to report that for decades Madoff Securities' financial statements had been audited by a New York accounting firm and had received unqualified audit opinions each year from that firm.

As academics, we have a responsibility to help shepherd our profession through these turbulent times. Auditing instructors, in particular, have an obligation to help restore the credibility of the independent audit function that has been adversely impacted by the events of the past decade. To accomplish this latter goal, one strategy we can use is to embrace the litany of reforms recommended several years ago by the Accounting Education Change Commission (AECC). Among the AECC's recommendations is that accounting educators employ a broader array of instructional resources, particularly experiential resources, designed to stimulate active learning by students. In fact, the intent of my casebook is to provide auditing instructors with a source of such materials that can be used in both undergraduate and graduate auditing courses.

This casebook stresses the "people" aspect of independent audits. If you review a sample of recent "audit failures," you will find that problem audits seldom result from inadequate audit technology. Instead, deficient audits typically result from the presence of one, or both, of the following two conditions: client personnel who intentionally subvert an audit and auditors who fail to carry out the responsibilities assigned to them. Exposing students to problem audits will help them recognize the red flags that often accompany audit failures. An ability to recognize these red flags and the insight gained by discussing and dissecting problem audits will allow students to cope more effectively with the problematic situations they are certain to encounter in their own careers. In addition, this experiential approach provides students with context-specific situations that make it much easier for them to grasp the relevance of important auditing topics, concepts, and procedures.

The cases in this text also acquaint students with the work environment of auditors. After studying these cases, students will better appreciate how client pressure, peer pressure, time budgets, and related factors complicate the work roles of independent auditors. Also embedded in these cases are the ambiguity and lack of structure that auditors face each day. Missing documents, conflicting audit evidence, auditors' dual obligations to the client and to financial statement users, and the lack of definitive professional standards for many situations are additional aspects of the audit environment that are woven into these cases.

The eighth edition of my casebook contains the following eight sections of cases: Comprehensive Cases, Audits of High-Risk Accounts, Internal Control Issues, Ethical Responsibilities of Accountants, Ethical Responsibilities of Independent Auditors, Professional Roles, Professional Issues, and International Cases. This organizational structure is intended to help adopters readily identify cases best suited for their particular needs.

In preparing this edition, I retained those cases that have been most popular with adopters. You will find that many of the "returning" cases have been updated for relevant circumstances and events that have occurred since the publication of the previous edition.

**New To This Edition** This edition also features new cases, most of which are included in the international section. Easily the most dramatic trend in the business world over the past few decades has been the "globalization" of markets, including the market for professional accounting services. Business schools have responded to this dramatic trend by establishing new international majors, study-abroad programs, and a slew of international courses across all business disciplines. Accounting may very well be the business discipline that has been the slowest to "internationalize" its curriculum. The international cases in this edition provide auditing instructors with an efficient and cost-effective way to introduce their students to a wide range of important issues within the global accounting profession that will have far-reaching implications for their careers.

The *Societe Generale* case provides an opportunity for students to compare and contrast the independent audit functions of France and the United States. In France, large public companies are generally required to have "joint" audits, meaning that two accounting firms collaborate to audit those companies. Instructors can also use the *Societe Generale* case to examine key differences between IFRS and U.S. GAAP. A "loophole" in IFRS allowed *Societe Generale*, one of France's largest banks, to "backdate" a large loss that it suffered on unauthorized securities trades by an employee. The loss actually occurred in 2008 but the bank recorded the loss in 2007.

The *Shari'a* case presents another opportunity to compare and contrast U.S. auditing practices with those in another region of the world. Large companies in Islamic countries are generally required to have two audits each year: a standard financial statement audit and a *Shari'a* compliance audit. Islamic religious law or *Shari'a* prohibits Islamic companies from engaging in certain transactions. For example, Islamic banks are not allowed to pay interest on depositors' funds or to charge interest to borrowers. Islamic religious scholars review or "audit" a company's financial records to ensure that the company's transactions are *Shari'a*-compliant. Big Four accounting firms have recently begun offering *Shari'a* audit services to gain broader access to the rapidly growing Islamic sector of the global economy.

The Republic of Sudan and *Tae Kwang Vina* cases revolve around two important social issues that have impacted the accounting profession recently. In 2004, the SEC began requiring domestic and foreign registrants to disclose any operations or other connections they have with so-called "state sponsors of terrorism" (SSTs). Principal among these countries is the Republic of Sudan whose central government is allegedly responsible for genocidal attacks on residents of the Darfur region of that nation. In 2007, the SEC created a webpage on its EDGAR website that listed all registrants reporting a link to one or more SSTs. This new policy created a storm of controversy. Companies appearing on the SEC's SST "blacklist" insisted that they were being singled out unfairly by the federal agency. This controversy, in turn, sparked a debate over the regulatory mandate of the SEC. A principal focus of this debate was the SEC's materiality standard that it relies on to determine what information must be disclosed by public companies in their periodic registration statements.

During the 1990s, the major international accounting firms began offering a wide range of nontraditional services to generate new revenue streams. Among the new services developed by these firms were environmental and labor practices audits. Nike, Wal-Mart, and many other large U.S. companies required such audits to rebut allegations that they were using foreign "sweatshops" to produce many of their products. Social activists responsible for those allegations attacked Ernst & zYoung when the firm's environmental and labor practices audit of a large Nike factory in Vietnam failed to disclose major problems existing at that factory. The *Tae Kwang Vina* case demonstrates the challenges and problems that accounting firms may confront when they offer services outside of their traditional areas of expertise.

The final new international case involves an ethical dilemma faced by an internal auditor employed by the U.S. embassy of the United Arab Emirates (UAE) in Washington, D.C. Shortly after coming to the United States, Mohamed Salem El-Hadad, an Egyptian citizen, discovered that his superior and the individual at the UAE embassy who had hired him as an internal auditor was embezzling from that organization. Not long after reporting the embezzlement scheme, El-Hadad experienced recriminations from UAE government officials in Dubai. El-Hadad was eventually fired and subsequently found it impossible to obtain another accounting position in the United States or his native Egypt where he was forced to return. Instructors can use this case to point out the challenging circumstances that accountants and auditors may encounter when they become involved in a whistle blowing incident.

Three new cases in this edition can be used to acquaint students with the massive economic crisis that the U.S. and global economies have recently faced and the role that the accounting profession has played in that crisis. These cases are New Century Financial Corporation, Madoff Securities, and American International Group (AIG), Inc. New Century was one of the nation's largest subprime mortgage companies when it collapsed in 2007 and triggered the chain of events that would eventually result in the meltdown of global securities and credit markets. A federally-appointed bankruptcy examiner claims that New Century's audit firm overlooked numerous red flags that foreshadowed the company's collapse.

The accounting profession faced more criticism in early 2009 when preliminary results of the investigation of Bernie Madoff's massive Ponzi scheme were publicly released. Regulatory authorities revealed that the one-man audit firm for Madoff's company had issued unqualified opinions on its annual financial statements throughout the time frame that the fraud was being perpetrated. Those same authorities also disclosed that Madoff's auditor and several of his family members had maintained investment accounts with Madoff's company that violated the profession's auditor independence rules.

AIG has been tagged as the "poster child" of the federal bailout program that Congress used to stymie the crisis that engulfed the U.S. economy in late 2008 and early 2009. In fact, AIG received more federal bailout funds than any other company. The new AIG case focuses on a series of events that predates the 2008–2009 economic crisis. In 2001, AIG began marketing a new financial services product that involved developing customized special purpose entities (SPEs) for large corporations. The intent of the new service was to help such companies improve their apparent financial condition by transferring troubled assets and related liabilities to an unconsolidated SPE—a strategy popularized by Enron. Surprisingly, one of the Big Four firms agreed to partner with AIG in developing and marketing this controversial new service.

One of the new comprehensive cases, Gemstar-TV Guide International, Inc. (GTGI), revolves around a small sliver of everyday life in American culture, namely, the ubiquitous television scroll that many of us check numerous times per day. When a new business model developed for GTGI proved to be a bust, its management relied on accounting machinations to embellish the company's financial statements. The SEC charged that "repeated audit failures" prevented the company's audit firm from detecting the fraud.

This casebook can be used in several different ways. Adopters can use the casebook as a supplemental text for the undergraduate auditing course or as a primary text for a graduate-level seminar in auditing. The instructor's manual contains a syllabus for a graduate auditing course organized around this text. This casebook can also be used in the capstone professional practice course incorporated in many five-year accounting programs. Customized versions of this casebook are suitable for a wide range of accounting courses as explained later.

**Organization of Casebook** Listed next are brief descriptions of the eight groups of cases included in this text. The casebook's Table of Contents presents an annotated description of each case.

*Comprehensive Cases* Most of these cases deal with highly publicized problem audits performed by large, international accounting firms. Each of these cases addresses a wide range of auditing, accounting, and ethical issues.

*Audits of High-Risk Accounts* In contrast to the cases in the prior section, these cases highlight contentious accounting and auditing issues posed by a single account or group of accounts.

*Internal Control Issues* In recent years, leading authorities in the public accounting profession have emphasized the need for auditors to thoroughly understand their clients' internal control policies and procedures. The cases in this section introduce students to control issues in a variety of contexts.

*Ethical Responsibilities of Accountants* Integrating ethics into an auditing course requires much more than simply discussing the AICPA's *Code of Professional Conduct*. This section presents specific scenarios in which accountants or future accountants have been forced to deal with perplexing ethical dilemmas. By requiring students to study actual situations in which important ethical issues have arisen, they will be better prepared to resolve similar situations in their own professional careers.

*Ethical Responsibilities of Independent Auditors* The cases in this section highlight ethical dilemmas encountered by independent auditors. Consider the situation faced in the Koger Properties case by Michael Goodbread, an audit partner with a major accounting firm. His firm acquires an audit client in which he has a small but direct financial interest. What should he do? No doubt, any auditing textbook will provide the easy answer to that question. But auditors in public practice don't always "go by the book."

*Professional Roles* Cases in this section examine specific work roles in the accounting profession. These cases explore the responsibilities associated with those roles and related challenges that professionals occupying them commonly encounter. The Tommy O'Connell case involves a young auditor recently promoted to audit senior. Shortly following his promotion, Tommy finds himself assigned to supervise a small but challenging audit. Tommy's sole subordinate on that engagement happens to be a young man whose integrity and work ethic have been questioned by seniors he has worked for previously. Two cases in this section spotlight the staff accountant work role, which many of your students will experience firsthand following graduation.

*Professional Issues* The dynamic nature of the public accounting profession continually impacts the work environment of public accountants and the nature of the services they provide. The cases in this section explore this changing work environment.

*International Cases* The purpose of these cases is to provide your students with an introduction to important issues facing the global accounting profession and auditing discipline. After studying these cases, students will discover that most of the technical, professional, and ethical challenges facing U.S. practitioners are shared by auditors and accountants across the globe. Then again, some of these cases document unique challenges that must be dealt with by auditors and accountants in certain countries or regions of the world. For example, the Chinese case (*Zuan Yan*) demonstrates the problems that an authoritarian central government can pose for independent auditors and accounting practitioners. Likewise, the Kaset Thai Sugar Company case vividly demonstrates that auditors and accountants may be forced to cope with hostile and sometimes dangerous working conditions in developing countries where their professional roles and responsibilities are not well understood or appreciated.

**Customize Your Own Casebook** To maximize your flexibility in using these cases, Cengage Learning/South-Western has included *Auditing Cases* in its customized publishing program, Make it Yours. Adopters have the option of creating a customized version of this casebook ideally suited for their specific needs. At the University of Oklahoma a customized selection of my cases is used to add an ethics component to the undergraduate managerial accounting course. In fact, since the cases in this text examine ethical issues across a wide swath of different contexts, adopters can develop a customized ethics casebook to supplement almost any accounting course.

This casebook is ideally suited to be customized for the undergraduate auditing course. For example, auditing instructors who want to add a strong international component to their courses can develop a customized edition of this text that includes a series of the international cases. Likewise, to enhance the coverage of ethical issues in the undergraduate auditing course, instructors could choose a series of cases from this text that highlight important ethical issues. Following are several examples of customized versions of this casebook that could be easily integrated into the undergraduate auditing course.

> *International Focus: Kansayaku* (8.3), Registered Auditors, South Africa (8.4), *Zuan Yan* (8.5), Australian Wheat Board (8.7), OAO Gazprom (8.8), Institute of Chartered Accountants of India (8.10). This custom casebook would provide your students with an in-depth understanding of the current state of the auditing discipline in four of the world's most important countries. This series of cases would also acquaint your students with the controversial "reportable irregularities" rule in South Africa and expose them to several important issues related to the Foreign Corrupt Practices Act that are dealt with in the Australian case.

> *Ethics Focus (I)*: Suzette Washington, Accounting Major (4.3), Leigh Ann Walker, Staff Accountant (6.1), Avis Love, Staff Accountant (6.5), Hamilton Wong, In-Charge Accountant (6.7). The first three of these cases give your students an opportunity to discuss and debate ethical issues directly pertinent to them as accounting majors. The final three cases expose students to important ethical issues they may encounter shortly after graduation if they choose to enter public accounting.

> Staff Accountant (6.1), Avis Love, Staff Accountant (6.5), Hamilton Wong, In-Charge Accountant (6.7). The first case gives your students an opportunity to discuss and debate ethical issues directly pertinent to them as accounting majors. The final three cases expose students to important ethical issues they may encounter shortly after graduation if they choose to enter public accounting.

> *Ethics Focus (II)*: Creve Couer Pizza, Inc. (4.1), F&C International, Inc. (4.2), Thomas Forehand, CPA (4.4), Koger Properties, Inc. (5.5). This selection of cases is suitable for auditing instructors who have a particular interest in covering a variety of ethical topics relevant to the AICPA's *Code of Professional Conduct*, several of which are not directly or exclusively related to auditing.

> *Applied Focus:* Enron Corporation (1.1), ZZZZ Best Company, Inc. (1.8), Golden Bear Golf, Inc. (2.2), Cardillo Travel Systems, Inc. (5.1), Livent, Inc. (8.1). This

series of cases will provide students with a broad-brush introduction to the *real world* of independent auditing. These cases raise a wide range of technical, professional, and ethical issues in a variety of different client contexts.

*Professional Roles Focus:* Leigh Ann Walker, Staff Accountant (6.1), Bill DeBurger, In-Charge Accountant (6.2), Tommy O'Connell, Audit Senior (6.4), Avis Love, Staff Accountant (6.5), Charles Tollison, Audit Manager (6.6). This custom casebook would be useful for auditing instructors who choose to rely on a standard textbook to cover key technical topics in auditing—but who also want to expose their students to the everyday ethical and professional challenges faced by individuals occupying various levels of the employment hierarchy within auditing firms.

*High-Risk Accounts Focus:* Each of the cases in Section 2, Audits of High-Risk Accounts. This series of cases will provide your students with relatively intense homework assignments that focus almost exclusively on the financial statement line items that pose the greatest challenges for auditors.

Of course, realize that you are free to choose any "mix" of my cases to include in a customized casebook for an undergraduate auditing course that you teach. For more information on how to design your customized casebook, please contact your Cengage Learning/South-Western sales representative or visit the textbook website: www.cengage.com/custom/makeityours/knapp.

**Acknowledgements** I greatly appreciate the insight and suggestions provided by the following reviewers of earlier editions of this text: Alex Ampadu, University at Buffalo; Barbara Apostolou, Louisiana State University; Sandra A. Augustine, Hilbert College; Jane Baird, Mankato State University; James Bierstaker, Villanova University; Ed Blocher, University of North Carolina; Susan Cain, Southern Oregon University; Kurt Chaloupecky, Southwest Missouri State University; Ray Clay, University of North Texas; Jeffrey Cohen, Boston College; Mary Doucet, University of Georgia; Rafik Elias, California State University, Los Angeles; Ruth Engle, Lafayette College; Diana Franz, University of Toledo; Chrislynn Freed, University of Southern California; Carolyn Galantine, Pepperdine University; Soha Ghallab, Brooklyn College; Michele C. Henney, University of Oregon; Laurence Johnson, Colorado State University; Donald McConnell, University of Texas at Arlington; Heidi Meier, Cleveland State University; Don Nichols, Texas Christian University; Marcia Niles, University of Idaho; Robert J. Ramsay, Ph.D., CPA, University of Kentucky; John Rigsby, Mississippi State University; Edward F. Smith, Boston College; Dr. Gene Smith, Eastern New Mexico University; Rajendra Srivastava, University of Kansas; Richard Allen Turpen, University of Alabama at Birmingham; T. Sterling Wetzel, Oklahoma State University; and Jim Yardley, Virginia Polytechnic University. This project also benefitted greatly from the editorial assistance of my sister, Paula Kay Conatser, my wife, Carol Ann Knapp, and my son, John William Knapp. I would also like to thank Glen McLaughlin for his continuing generosity in funding the development of instructional materials that highlight important ethical issues. Finally, I would like to acknowledge the contributions of my students, who have provided invaluable comments and suggestions on the content and use of these cases.

Michael C. Knapp
McLaughlin Chair in Business
Ethics and Professor of Accounting
*University of Oklahoma*

# AUDITING CASES

Eighth Edition

SECTION 1

# COMPREHENSIVE CASES

## CASE 1.1

# Enron Corporation

John and Mary Andersen immigrated to the United States from their native Norway in 1881. The young couple made their way to the small farming community of Plano, Illinois, some 40 miles southwest of downtown Chicago. Over the previous few decades, hundreds of Norwegian families had settled in Plano and surrounding communities. In fact, the aptly named Norway, Illinois, was located just a few miles away from the couple's new hometown. In 1885, Arthur Edward Andersen was born. From an early age, the Andersens' son had a fascination with numbers. Little did his parents realize that Arthur's interest in numbers would become the driving force in his life. Less than one century after he was born, an accounting firm bearing Arthur Andersen's name would become the world's largest professional services organization with more than 1,000 partners and operations in dozens of countries scattered across the globe.

### Think Straight, Talk Straight

Discipline, honesty, and a strong work ethic were three key traits that John and Mary Andersen instilled in their son. The Andersens also constantly impressed upon him the importance of obtaining an education. Unfortunately, Arthur's parents did not survive to help him achieve that goal. Orphaned by the time he was a young teenager, Andersen was forced to take a fulltime job as a mail clerk and attend night classes to work his way through high school. After graduating from high school, Andersen attended the University of Illinois while working as an accountant for Allis-Chalmers, a Chicago-based company that manufactured tractors and other farming equipment. In 1908, Andersen accepted a position with the Chicago office of Price Waterhouse. At the time, Price Waterhouse, which was organized in Great Britain during the early nineteenth century, easily qualified as the United States' most prominent public accounting firm.

At age 23, Andersen became the youngest CPA in the state of Illinois. A few years later, Andersen and a friend, Clarence Delany, established a partnership to provide accounting, auditing, and related services. The two young accountants named their firm Andersen, Delany & Company. When Delany decided to go his own way, Andersen renamed the firm Arthur Andersen & Company.

In 1915, Arthur Andersen faced a dilemma that would help shape the remainder of his professional life. One of his audit clients was a freight company that owned and operated several steam freighters that delivered various commodities to ports located on Lake Michigan. Following the close of the company's fiscal year but before Andersen had issued his audit report on its financial statements, one of the client's ships sank in Lake Michigan. At the time, there were few formal rules for companies to follow in preparing their annual financial statements and certainly no rule that required the company to report a material "subsequent event" occurring after the close of its fiscal year—such as the loss of a major asset. Nevertheless, Andersen insisted that his client disclose the loss of the ship. Andersen reasoned that third parties who would use the company's financial statements, among them the company's banker, would want to be informed of the loss. Although unhappy with Andersen's position, the client eventually acquiesced and reported the loss in the footnotes to its financial statements.

Two decades after the steamship dilemma, Arthur Andersen faced a similar situation with an audit client that was much larger, much more prominent, and much more profitable for his firm. Arthur Andersen & Co. served as the independent auditor for the giant chemical company, du Pont. As the company's audit neared completion one year, members of the audit engagement team and executives of du Pont quarreled over how to define the company's operating income. Du Pont's management insisted on a liberal definition of operating income that included income earned on certain investments. Arthur Andersen was brought in to arbitrate the dispute. When he sided with his subordinates, du Pont's management team dismissed the firm and hired another auditor.

Throughout his professional career, Arthur E. Andersen relied on a simple, four-word motto to serve as a guiding principle in making important personal and professional decisions: "Think straight, talk straight." Andersen insisted that his partners and other personnel in his firm invoke that simple rule when dealing with clients, potential clients, bankers, regulatory authorities, and any other parties they interacted with while representing Arthur Andersen & Co. He also insisted that audit clients "talk straight" in their financial statements. Former colleagues and associates often described Andersen as opinionated, stubborn, and, in some cases, "difficult." But even his critics readily admitted that Andersen was point-blank honest. "Arthur Andersen wouldn't put up with anything that wasn't complete, 100% integrity. If anybody did anything otherwise, he'd fire them. And if clients wanted to do something he didn't agree with, he'd either try to change them or quit."[1]

As a young professional attempting to grow his firm, Arthur Andersen quickly recognized the importance of carving out a niche in the rapidly developing accounting services industry. Andersen realized that the nation's bustling economy of the 1920s depended heavily on companies involved in the production and distribution of energy. As the economy grew, Andersen knew there would be a steadily increasing need for electricity, oil and gas, and other energy resources. So he focused his practice development efforts on obtaining clients involved in the various energy industries. Andersen was particularly successful in recruiting electric utilities as clients. By the early 1930s, Arthur Andersen & Co. had a thriving practice in the upper Midwest and was among the leading regional accounting firms in the nation.

The U.S. economy's precipitous downturn during the Great Depression of the 1930s posed huge financial problems for many of Arthur Andersen & Co.'s audit clients in the electric utilities industry. As the Depression wore on, Arthur Andersen personally worked with several of the nation's largest metropolitan banks to help his clients obtain the financing they desperately needed to continue operating. The bankers and other leading financiers who dealt with Arthur Andersen quickly learned of his commitment to honesty and proper, forthright accounting and financial reporting practices. Andersen's reputation for honesty and integrity allowed lenders to use with confidence financial data stamped with his approval. The end result was that many troubled firms received the financing they needed to survive the harrowing days of the 1930s. In turn, the respect that Arthur Andersen earned among leading financial executives nationwide resulted in Arthur Andersen & Co. receiving a growing number of referrals for potential clients located outside of the Midwest.

During the later years of his career, Arthur Andersen became a spokesperson for his discipline. He authored numerous books and presented speeches throughout the nation regarding the need for rigorous accounting, auditing, and ethical standards for the emerging public accounting profession. Andersen continually urged his

1. R. Frammolino and J. Leeds, "Andersen's Reputation in Shreds," *Los Angeles Times* (online), 30 January 2002.

fellow accountants to adopt the public service ideal that had long served as the underlying premise of the more mature professions such as law and medicine. He also lobbied for the adoption of a mandatory continuing professional education (CPE) requirement. Andersen realized that CPAs needed CPE to stay abreast of developments in the business world that had significant implications for accounting and financial reporting practices. In fact, Arthur Andersen & Co. made CPE mandatory for its employees long before state boards of accountancy adopted such a requirement.

By the mid-1940s, Arthur Andersen & Co. had offices scattered across the eastern one-half of the United States and employed more than 1,000 accountants. When Arthur Andersen died in 1947, many business leaders expected that the firm would disband without its founder, who had single-handedly managed its operations over the previous four decades. But, after several months of internal turmoil and dissension, the firm's remaining partners chose Andersen's most trusted associate and protégé to replace him.

Like his predecessor and close friend who had personally hired him in 1928, Leonard Spacek soon earned a reputation as a no-nonsense professional—an auditor's auditor. He passionately believed that the primary role of independent auditors was to ensure that their clients reported fully and honestly regarding their financial affairs to the investing and lending public. Spacek continued Arthur Andersen's campaign to improve accounting and auditing practices in the United States during his long tenure as his firm's chief executive. "Spacek openly criticized the profession for tolerating what he considered a sloppy patchwork of accounting standards that left the investing public no way to compare the financial performance of different companies."[2] Such criticism compelled the accounting profession to develop a more formal and rigorous rule-making process. In the late 1950s, the profession created the Accounting Principles Board (APB) to study contentious accounting issues and develop appropriate new standards. The APB was replaced in 1973 by the Financial Accounting Standards Board (FASB). Another legacy of Arthur Andersen that Leonard Spacek sustained was requiring the firm's professional employees to continue their education throughout their careers. During Spacek's tenure, Arthur Andersen & Co. established the world's largest private university, the Arthur Andersen & Co. Center for Professional Education located in St. Charles, Illinois, not far from Arthur Andersen's birthplace.

Leonard Spacek's strong leadership and business skills transformed Arthur Andersen & Co. into a major international accounting firm. When Spacek retired in 1973, Arthur Andersen & Co. was arguably the most respected accounting firm not only in the United States, but worldwide as well. Three decades later, shortly after the dawn of the new millennium, Arthur Andersen & Co. employed more than 80,000 professionals, had practice offices in more than 80 countries, and had annual revenues approaching $10 billion. However, in late 2001, the firm, which by that time had adopted the one-word name "Andersen," faced the most significant crisis in its history since the death of its founder. Ironically, that crisis stemmed from Andersen's audits of an energy company, a company founded in 1930 that, like many of Arthur Andersen's clients, had struggled to survive the Depression.

## The World's Greatest Company

Northern Natural Gas Company was founded in Omaha, Nebraska, in 1930. The principal investors in the new venture included a Texas-based company, Lone Star Gas Corporation. During its first few years of existence, Northern wrestled with the

2. *Ibid.*

problem of persuading consumers to use natural gas to heat their homes. Concern produced by several unfortunate and widely publicized home "explosions" caused by natural gas leaks drove away many of Northern's potential customers. But, as the Depression wore on, the relatively cheap cost of natural gas convinced increasing numbers of cold-stricken and shallow-pocketed consumers to become Northern customers.

The availability of a virtually unlimited source of cheap manual labor during the 1930s allowed Northern to develop an extensive pipeline network to deliver natural gas to the residential and industrial markets that it served in the Great Plains states. As the company's revenues and profits grew, Northern's management launched a campaign to acquire dozens of its smaller competitors. This campaign was prompted by management's goal of making Northern the largest natural gas supplier in the United States. In 1947, the company, which was still relatively unknown outside of its geographical market, reached a major milestone when its stock was listed on the New York Stock Exchange. That listing provided the company with greater access to the nation's capital markets and the financing needed to continue its growth-through-acquisition strategy over the following two decades.

During the 1970s, Northern became a principal investor in the development of the Alaskan pipeline. When completed, that pipeline allowed Northern to tap vast natural gas reserves it had acquired in Canada. In 1980, Northern changed its name to InterNorth, Inc. Over the next few years, company management extended the scope of the company's operations by investing in ventures outside of the natural gas industry, including oil exploration, chemicals, coal mining, and fuel-trading operations. But the company's principal focus remained the natural gas industry. In 1985, InterNorth purchased Houston Natural Gas Company for $2.3 billion. That acquisition resulted in InterNorth controlling a 40,000-mile network of natural gas pipelines and allowed it to achieve its long-sought goal of becoming the largest natural gas company in the United States.

In 1986, InterNorth changed its name to Enron. Kenneth Lay, the former chairman of Houston Natural Gas, emerged as the top executive of the newly created firm that chose Houston, Texas, as its corporate headquarters. Lay quickly adopted the aggressive growth strategy that had long dominated the management policies of InterNorth and its predecessor. Lay hired Jeffrey Skilling to serve as one of his top subordinates. During the 1990s, Skilling developed and implemented a plan to transform Enron from a conventional natural gas supplier into an energy-trading company that served as an intermediary between producers of energy products, principally natural gas and electricity, and end users of those commodities. In early 2001, Skilling assumed Lay's position as Enron's chief executive officer (CEO), although Lay retained the title of chairman of the board. In the management letter to shareholders included in Enron's 2000 annual report, Lay and Skilling explained the metamorphosis that Enron had undergone over the previous 15 years:

> *Enron hardly resembles the company we were in the early days. During our 15-year history, we have stretched ourselves beyond our own expectations. We have metamorphosed from an asset-based pipeline and power generating company to a marketing and logistics company whose biggest assets are its well-established business approach and its innovative people.*

Enron's 2000 annual report discussed the company's four principal lines of business. Energy Wholesale Services ranked as the company's largest revenue producer. That division's 60 percent increase in transaction volume during 2000 was fueled by the rapid development of EnronOnline, a B2B (business-to-business) electronic

**EXHIBIT 1**

ENRON CORPORATION 2000 ANNUAL REPORT FINANCIAL HIGHLIGHTS TABLE (IN MILLIONS EXCEPT FOR PER SHARE AMOUNTS)

| | 2000 | 1999 | 1998 | 1997 | 1996 |
|---|---|---|---|---|---|
| Revenues | $100,789 | $40,112 | $31,260 | $20,273 | $13,289 |
| Net Income: | | | | | |
| Operating Results | 1,266 | 957 | 698 | 515 | 493 |
| Items Impacting Comparability | (287) | (64) | 5 | (410) | 91 |
| Total | 979 | 893 | 703 | 105 | 584 |
| Earnings Per Share: | | | | | |
| Operating Results | 1.47 | 1.18 | 1.00 | .87 | .91 |
| Items Impacting Comparability | (.35) | (.08) | .01 | (.71) | .17 |
| Total | 1.12 | 1.10 | 1.01 | .16 | 1.08 |
| Dividends Per Share: | .50 | .50 | .48 | .46 | .43 |
| Total Assets: | 65,503 | 33,381 | 29,350 | 22,552 | 16,137 |
| Cash from Operating Activities: | 3,010 | 2,228 | 1,873 | 276 | 742 |
| Capital Expenditures and Equity Investments: | 3,314 | 3,085 | 3,564 | 2,092 | 1,483 |
| NYSE Price Range: | | | | | |
| High | 90.56 | 44.88 | 29.38 | 22.56 | 23.75 |
| Low | 41.38 | 28.75 | 19.06 | 17.50 | 17.31 |
| Close, December 31 | 83.12 | 44.38 | 28.53 | 20.78 | 21.56 |

marketplace for the energy industries created in late 1999 by Enron. During fiscal 2000 alone, EnronOnline processed more than $335 billion of transactions, easily making Enron the largest e-commerce company in the world. Enron's three other principal lines of business included Enron Energy Services, the company's retail operating unit; Enron Transportation Services, which was responsible for the company's pipeline operations; and Enron Broadband Services, a new operating unit intended to be an intermediary between users and suppliers of broadband (Internet access) services. Exhibit 1 presents the five-year financial highlights table included in Enron's 2000 annual report.

The New Economy business model that Enron pioneered for the previously staid energy industries caused Kenneth Lay, Jeffrey Skilling, and their top subordinates to be recognized as skillful entrepreneurs and to gain superstar status in the business world. Lay's position as the chief executive of the nation's seventh-largest firm gave him direct access to key political and governmental officials. In 2001, Lay served on the "transition team" responsible for helping usher in the administration of President-elect George W. Bush. In June 2001, Skilling was singled out as "the No. 1 CEO in the entire country," while Enron was hailed as "America's most innovative company."[3]

3. K. Eichenwald and D. B. Henriques, "Web of Details Did Enron In as Warnings Went Unheeded," *The New York Times* (online), 10 February 2002.

Enron's chief financial officer (CFO) Andrew Fastow was recognized for creating the financial infrastructure for one of the nation's largest and most complex companies. In 1999, *CFO Magazine* presented Fastow the Excellence Award for Capital Structure Management for his "pioneering work on unique financing techniques."[4]

Throughout their tenure with Enron, Kenneth Lay and Jeffrey Skilling continually focused on enhancing their company's operating results. In the letter to shareholders in Enron's 2000 annual report, Lay and Skilling noted that "Enron is laser-focused on earnings per share, and we expect to continue strong earnings performance." Another important goal of Enron's top executives was increasing their company's stature in the business world. During a speech in January 2001, Lay revealed that his ultimate goal was for Enron to become "the world's greatest company."[5]

As Enron's revenues and profits swelled, its top executives were often guilty of a certain degree of chutzpah. In particular, Skilling became known for making brassy, if not tacky, comments concerning his firm's competitors and critics. During the crisis that gripped California's electric utility industry during 2001, numerous elected officials and corporate executives criticized Enron for allegedly profiteering by selling electricity at inflated prices to the Golden State. Skilling brushed aside such criticism. During a speech at a major business convention, Skilling asked the crowd if they knew the difference between the state of California and the Titanic. After an appropriate pause, Skilling provided the punch line: "At least when the Titanic went down, the lights were on."[6]

Unfortunately for Lay, Skilling, Fastow, and thousands of Enron employees and stockholders, Lay failed to achieve his goal of creating the world's greatest company. In a matter of months during 2001, Enron quickly unraveled. Enron's sudden collapse panicked investors nationwide, leading to what one *Newsweek* columnist described as the "the biggest crisis investors have had since 1929."[7] Enron's dire financial problems were triggered by public revelations of questionable accounting and financial reporting decisions made by the company's accountants. Those decisions had been reviewed, analyzed, and apparently approved by Andersen, the company's independent audit firm.

## Debits, Credits, and Enron

Throughout 2001, Enron's stock price drifted lower. Publicly, Enron executives blamed the company's slumping stock price on falling natural gas prices, concerns regarding the long-range potential of electronic marketplaces such as EnronOnline, and overall weakness in the national economy. By mid-October, the stock price had fallen into the mid-$30s from a high in the lower $80s earlier in the year. On October 16, 2001, Enron issued its quarterly earnings report for the third quarter of 2001. That report revealed that the firm had suffered a huge loss during the quarter. Even more problematic to many financial analysts was a mysterious $1.2 billion reduction in Enron's owners' equity and assets that was disclosed seemingly as an afterthought in the earnings press release. This write-down resulted from the reversal of previously recorded transactions involving the swap of Enron stock for notes receivable. Enron had acquired the notes receivable from related third parties who had invested in limited partnerships organized and sponsored by the company. After studying those transactions in more depth, Enron's accounting staff and its Andersen auditors

4. E. Thomas, "Every Man for Himself," *Newsweek*, 18 February 2002, 25.
5. Eichenwald and Henriques, "Web of Details."
6. *Ibid.*
7. N. Byrnes, "Paying for the Sins of Enron," *Newsweek*, 11 February 2002, 35.

concluded that the notes receivable should not have been reported in the assets section of the company's balance sheet but rather as a reduction to owners' equity.

The October 16, 2001, press release sent Enron's stock price into a free fall. Three weeks later on November 8, Enron restated its reported earnings for the previous five years, wiping out approximately $600 million of profits the company had reported over that time frame. That restatement proved to be the death knell for Enron. On December 2, 2001, intense pressure from creditors, pending and threatened litigation against the company and its officers, and investigations initiated by law enforcement authorities forced Enron to file for bankruptcy. Instead of becoming the nation's greatest company, Enron instead laid claim to being the largest corporate bankruptcy in U.S. history, imposing more than $60 billion of losses on its stockholders alone. Enron's "claim to fame" would be eclipsed the following year by the more than $100 billion of losses produced when another Andersen client, WorldCom, filed for bankruptcy.

The massive and understandable public outcry over Enron's implosion during the fall of 2001 spawned a mad frenzy on the part of the print and electronic media to determine how the nation's seventh-largest public company, a company that had posted impressive and steadily rising profits over the previous few years, could crumple into insolvency in a matter of months. From the early days of this public drama, skeptics in the financial community charged that Enron's earnings restatement in the fall of 2001 demonstrated that the company's exceptional financial performance during the late 1990s and 2000 had been a charade, a hoax orchestrated by the company's management with the help of a squad of creative accountants. Any doubt regarding the validity of that theory was wiped away—at least in the minds of most members of the press and the general public—when a letter that an Enron accountant had sent to Kenneth Lay in August 2001 was discovered. The contents of that letter were posted on numerous websites and lengthy quotes taken from it appeared in virtually every major newspaper in the nation.

Exhibit 2 contains key excerpts from the letter that Sherron Watkins wrote to Kenneth Lay in August 2001. Watkins' job title was vice president of corporate development, but she was an accountant by training, having worked previously with Andersen, Enron's audit firm. The sudden and unexpected resignation of Jeffrey Skilling as Enron's CEO after serving in that capacity for only six months had prompted Watkins to write the letter to Lay. Before communicating her concerns to Lay, Watkins had attempted to discuss those issues with one of Lay's senior subordinates. When Watkins offered to show that individual a document that identified significant problems in accounting decisions made previously by Enron, Watkins reported that he rebuffed her. "He said he'd rather not see it."[8]

Watkins was intimately familiar with aggressive accounting decisions made for a series of large and complex transactions involving Enron and dozens of limited partnerships created by the company. These partnerships were so-called SPEs or special purpose entities that Enron executives had tagged with a variety of creative names, including Braveheart, Rawhide, Raptor, Condor, and Talon. Andrew Fastow, Enron's CFO who was involved in the creation and operation of several of the SPEs, named a series of them after his three children.

SPEs—sometimes referred to as SPVs (special purpose vehicles)—can take several legal forms but are commonly organized as limited partnerships. During the 1990s, hundreds of large corporations began establishing SPEs. In most cases, SPEs were used to finance the acquisition of an asset or fund a construction project or related activity.

8. T. Hamburger, "Watkins Tells of 'Arrogant' Culture; Enron Stifled Staff Whistle-Blowing," *The Wall Street Journal* (online), 14 February 2002.

**EXHIBIT 2**

SELECTED EXCERPTS FROM SHERRON WATKINS' AUGUST 2001 LETTER TO KENNETH LAY

Dear Mr. Lay,

Has Enron become a risky place to work? For those of us who didn't get rich over the last few years, can we afford to stay?

Skilling's abrupt departure will raise suspicions of accounting improprieties and valuation issues. Enron has been very aggressive in its accounting—most notably the Raptor transactions and the Condor vehicle. . . .

We have recognized over $550 million of fair value gains on stocks via our swaps with Raptor, much of that stock has declined significantly. . . . The value in the swaps won't be there for Raptor, so once again Enron will issue stock to offset these losses. Raptor is an LJM entity. It sure looks to the layman on the street that we are hiding losses in a related company and will compensate that company with Enron stock in the future.

I am incredibly nervous that we will implode in a wave of scandals. My 8 years of Enron work history will be worth nothing on my resume, the business world will consider the past successes as nothing but an elaborate accounting hoax. Skilling is resigning now for "personal reasons" but I think he wasn't having fun, looked down the road and knew this stuff was unfixable and would rather abandon ship now than resign in shame in 2 years.

Is there a way our accounting gurus can unwind these deals now? I have thought and thought about how to do this, but I keep bumping into one big problem—we booked the Condor and Raptor deals in 1999 and 2000, we enjoyed a wonderfully high stock price, many executives sold stock, we then try and reverse or fix the deals in 2001 and it's a bit like robbing the bank in 1 year and trying to pay it back 2 years later. . . .

I realize that we have had a lot of smart people looking at this and a lot of accountants including AA & Co. have blessed the accounting treatment. None of this will protect Enron if these transactions are ever disclosed in the bright light of day. . . .

The overriding basic principle of accounting is that if you explain the "accounting treatment" to a man on the street, would you influence his investing decisions? Would he sell or buy the stock based on a thorough understanding of the facts?

My concern is that the footnotes don't adequately explain the transactions. If adequately explained, the investor would know that the "Entities" described in our related-party footnote are thinly capitalized, the equity holders have no skin in the game, and all the value in the entities comes from the underlying value of the derivatives (unfortunately in this case, a big loss) AND Enron stock and N/P. . . .

The related-party footnote tries to explain these transactions. Don't you think that several interested companies, be they stock analysts, journalists, hedge fund managers, etc., are busy trying to discover the reason Skilling left? Don't you think their smartest people are pouring [sic] over that footnote disclosure right now? I can just hear the discussions—"It looks like they booked a $500 million gain from this related-party company and I think, from all the undecipherable 1/2 page on Enron's contingent contributions to this related-party entity, I think the related-party entity is capitalized with Enron stock." . . . "No, no, no, you must have it all wrong, it can't be that, that's just too bad, too fraudulent, surely AA & Co. wouldn't let them get away with that?"

Regardless, the underlying motivation for creating an SPE was nearly always "debt avoidance." That is, SPEs provided large companies with a mechanism to raise needed financing for various purposes without being required to report the debt in their balance sheets. *Fortune* magazine charged that corporate CFOs were using SPEs as scalpels "to perform cosmetic surgery on their balance sheets."[9] During the early 1990s, the Securities and Exchange Commission (SEC) and the FASB had wrestled with the contentious accounting and financial reporting issues posed by SPEs. Despite intense debate and discussions, the SEC and the FASB provided little in the way of formal guidance for companies to follow in accounting and reporting for SPEs.

The most important guideline that the authoritative bodies implemented for SPEs, the so-called 3 percent rule, proved to be extremely controversial. This rule allowed a company to omit an SPE's assets and liabilities from its consolidated financial statements as long as parties independent of the company provided a minimum of 3 percent of the SPE's capital. Almost immediately, the 3 percent threshold became both a technical minimum and a practical maximum. That is, large companies using the SPE structure arranged for external parties to provide exactly 3 percent of an SPE's total capital. The remaining 97 percent of an SPE's capital was typically contributed by loans from external lenders, loans arranged and generally collateralized by the company that created the SPE.

Many critics charged that the 3 percent rule undercut the fundamental principle within the accounting profession that consolidated financial statements should be prepared for entities controlled by a common ownership group. "There is a presumption that consolidated financial statements are more meaningful than separate statements and that they are usually necessary for a fair presentation when one of the companies in the group directly or indirectly has a controlling financial interest in the other companies."[10] *Business Week* chided the SEC and FASB for effectively endorsing the 3 percent rule.

> *Because of a gaping loophole in accounting practice, companies can create arcane legal structures, often called special-purpose entities (SPEs). Then, the parent can bankroll up to 97 percent of the initial investment in an SPE without having to consolidate it. . . . The controversial exception that outsiders need invest only 3 percent of an SPE's capital for it to be independent and off the balance sheet came about through fumbles by the Securities and Exchange Commission and the Financial Accounting Standards Board.*[11]

Throughout the 1990s, many companies took advantage of the minimal legal and accounting guidelines for SPEs to divert huge amounts of their liabilities to off-balance sheet entities. Among the most aggressive and innovative users of the SPE structure was Enron, which created hundreds of SPEs. Unlike most companies, Enron did not limit its SPEs to financing activities. In many cases, Enron used SPEs for the sole purpose of downloading underperforming assets from its financial statements to the financial statements of related but unconsolidated entities. For example, Enron would arrange for a third party to invest the minimum 3 percent capital required in an SPE and then sell assets to that SPE. The SPE would finance the purchase of those assets by loans collateralized by Enron common stock. In some cases, undisclosed side agreements made by Enron with an SPE's nominal owners insulated those individuals

---

9. J. Kahn, "Off Balance Sheet—And Out of Control," *Fortune*, 18 February 2002, 84.

10. *Accounting Research Bulletin No. 51*, "Consolidated Financial Statements" (New York: AICPA, 1959).

11. D. Henry, H. Timmons, S. Rosenbush, and M. Arndt, "Who Else Is Hiding Debt?" *Business Week*, 28 January 2002, 36–37.

from any losses on their investments and, in fact, guaranteed them a windfall profit. Even more troubling, Enron often sold assets at grossly inflated prices to their SPEs, allowing the company to manufacture large "paper" gains on those transactions.

Enron made only nominal financial statement disclosures for its SPE transactions and those disclosures were typically presented in confusing, if not cryptic, language. One accounting professor observed that the inadequate disclosures that companies such as Enron provided for their SPE transactions meant that, "the nonprofessional [investor] has no idea of the extent of the [given firm's] real liabilities."[12] *The Wall Street Journal* added to that sentiment when it suggested that Enron's brief and obscure disclosures for its off-balance sheet liabilities and related-party transactions "were so complicated as to be practically indecipherable."[13]

Just as difficult to analyze for most investors was the integrity of the hefty profits reported each successive period by Enron. As Sherron Watkins revealed in the letter she sent to Kenneth Lay in August 2001, many of Enron's SPE transactions resulted in the company's profits being inflated by unrealized gains on increases in the market value of its own common stock. In the fall of 2001, Enron's board of directors appointed a Special Investigative Committee chaired by William C. Powers, dean of the University of Texas Law School, to study the company's large SPE transactions. In February 2002, that committee issued a lengthy report of its findings, a document commonly referred to as the Powers Report by the press. This report discussed at length the "Byzantine" nature of Enron's SPE transactions and the enormous and improper gains those transactions produced for the company.

> *Accounting principles generally forbid a company from recognizing an increase in the value of its capital stock in its income statement. . . . The substance of the Raptors [SPE transactions] effectively allowed Enron to report gains on its income statement that were . . . [attributable to] Enron stock, and contracts to receive Enron stock, held by the Raptors.*[14]

The primary motivation for Enron's extensive use of SPEs and the related accounting machinations was the company's growing need for capital during the 1990s. As Kenneth Lay and Jeffrey Skilling transformed Enron from a fairly standard natural gas supplier into a New Economy intermediary for the energy industries, the company had a constant need for additional capital to finance that transformation. Like most new business endeavors, Enron's Internet-based operations did not produce positive cash flows immediately. To convince lenders to continue pumping cash into Enron, the company's management team realized that their firm would have to maintain a high credit rating, which, in turn, required the company to release impressive financial statements each succeeding period.

A related factor that motivated Enron's executives to window dress their company's financial statements was the need to sustain Enron's stock price at a high level. Many of the SPE loan agreements negotiated by Enron included so-called price "triggers." If the market price of Enron's stock dropped below a designated level (trigger), Enron was required to provide additional stock to collateralize the given loan, to make significant cash payments to the SPE, or to restructure prior transactions with the SPE.

---

12. *Ibid.*

13. J. Emshwiller and R. Smith, "Murky Waters: A Primer on the Enron Partnerships," *The Wall Street Journal* (online), 21 January 2002.

14. W. C. Powers, R. S. Troubh, and H. S. Winokur, "Report of Investigation by the Special Investigative Committee of the Board of Directors of Enron Corporation," 1 February 2002, pp. 129–130.

In a worst-case scenario, Enron might be forced to dissolve an SPE and merge its assets and liabilities into the company's consolidated financial statements.

> *What made Enron's stock price so important was the fact that some of the company's most important deals with the partnerships [SPEs] run by Mr. Fastow—deals that had allowed Enron to keep hundreds of millions of dollars of potential losses off its books—were financed, in effect, with Enron stock. Those transactions could fall apart if the stock price fell too far.*[15]

As Enron's stock price drifted lower throughout 2001, the complex labyrinth of legal and accounting gimmicks underlying the company's finances became a shaky house of cards. Making matters worse were large losses suffered by many of Enron's SPEs on the assets they had purchased from Enron. Enron executives were forced to pour additional resources into many of those SPEs to keep them solvent. Contributing to the financial problems of Enron's major SPEs was alleged self-dealing by Enron officials involved in operating those SPEs. Andrew Fastow realized $30 million in profits on his investments in Enron SPEs that he oversaw at the same time he was serving as the company's CFO. Several of his friends also reaped windfall profits on investments in those same SPEs. Some of these individuals "earned" a profit of as much as $1 million on an initial investment of $5,800. Even more startling was the fact that Fastow's friends realized these gains in as little as 60 days.

By October 2001, the falling price of Enron's stock, the weight of the losses suffered by the company's large SPEs, and concerns being raised by Andersen auditors forced company executives to act. Enron's management assumed control and ownership of several of the company's troubled SPEs and incorporated their dismal financial statement data into Enron's consolidated financial statements. This decision led to the large loss reported by Enron in the fall of 2001 and the related restatement of the company's earnings for the previous five years. On December 2, 2001, the transformed New Age company filed its bankruptcy petition in New Age fashion—via the Internet. Only six months earlier, Jeffrey Skilling had been buoyant when commenting on Enron's first-quarter results for 2001. "So in conclusion, first-quarter results were great. We are very optimistic about our new businesses and are confident that our record of growth is sustainable for many years to come."[16]

As law enforcement authorities, Congressional investigative committees, and business journalists rifled through the mass of Enron documents that became publicly available during early 2002, the abusive accounting and financial reporting practices that had been used by the company surfaced. Enron's creative use of SPEs became the primary target of critics; however, the company also made extensive use of other accounting gimmicks. For example, Enron had abused the mark-to-market accounting method for its long-term contracts involving various energy commodities, primarily natural gas and electricity. Given the nature of their business, energy-trading firms regularly enter into long-term contracts to deliver energy commodities. Some of Enron's commodity contracts extended over periods of more than 20 years and involved massive quantities of the given commodity. When Enron finalized these deals, company officials often made tenuous assumptions that inflated the profits booked on the contracts.

> *Energy traders must book all the projected profits from a supply contract in the quarter in which the deal is made, even if the contract spans many years. That means companies can inflate profits by using unrealistic price forecasts, as Enron has been accused of doing. If a company contracted to buy natural gas through 2010 for $3 per thousand*

15. Eichenwald and Henriques, "Web of Details."

16. *Ibid.*

*cubic feet, an energy-trading desk could aggressively assume it would be able to supply gas in each year at a cost of just $2, for a $1 profit margin.*[17]

The avalanche of startling revelations regarding Enron's aggressive business, accounting, and financial reporting decisions reported by the business press during the early weeks of 2002 created a firestorm of anger and criticism directed at Enron's key executives, principally Kenneth Lay, Jeffrey Skilling, and Andrew Fastow. A common theme of the allegations leveled at the three executives was that they had created a corporate culture that fostered, if not encouraged, "rule breaking." *Fortune* magazine observed that, "[i]f nothing else, Lay allowed a culture of rule breaking to flourish,"[18] while Sherron Watkins testified that Enron's corporate culture was "arrogant" and "intimidating" and discouraged employees from reporting and investigating ethical lapses and questionable business dealings.[19] Finally, a top executive of Dynegy, a company that briefly considered merging with Enron during late 2001, reported that "the lack of internal controls [within Enron] was mindboggling."[20]

Both Kenneth Lay and Andrew Fastow invoked their Fifth Amendment rights against self-incrimination when asked to testify before Congress in early 2002. Jeffrey Skilling did not. While being peppered by Congressional investigators regarding Enron's questionable accounting and financial reporting decisions, Skilling replied calmly and repeatedly: "I am not an accountant." A well-accepted premise in the financial reporting domain is that corporate executives and their accountants are ultimately responsible for the integrity of their company's financial statements. Nevertheless, frustration stemming from the lack of answers provided by Enron insiders to key accounting and financial reporting-related questions eventually caused Congressional investigators, the business press, and the public to focus their attention, their questions, and their scorn on Enron's independent audit firm, Andersen. These parties insisted that Andersen representatives explain why their audits of Enron had failed to result in more transparent, if not reliable, financial statements for the company. More pointedly, those critics demanded that Andersen explain how it was able to issue unqualified audit opinions on Enron's financial statements throughout its 15-year tenure as the company's independent audit firm.

## Say It Ain't So Joe

Joseph Berardino became Andersen's chief executive shortly before the firm was swamped by the storm of criticism surrounding the collapse of its second-largest client, Enron Corporation. Berardino launched his business career with Andersen in 1972 immediately after graduating from college and just a few months before Leonard Spacek ended his long and illustrious career with the firm. Throughout its history, the Andersen firm had a policy of speaking with one voice, the voice of its chief executive. So, the unpleasant task of responding to the angry and often self-righteous accusations hurled at Andersen following Enron's demise fell to Berardino, although he had not been a party to the key decisions made during the Enron audits.

A common question directed at Berardino was whether his firm had been aware of the allegations Sherron Watkins made during August 2001 and, if so, how had Andersen responded to those allegations. Watkins testified before Congress that shortly after she communicated her concerns regarding Enron's questionable accounting and financial reporting decisions to Kenneth Lay, she had met with a

17. P. Coy, S. A. Forest, and D. Foust, "Enron: How Good an Energy Trader?" *Business Week*, 11 February 2002, 42–43.

18. B. McLean, "Monster Mess," *Fortune*, 4 February 2002, 94.

19. Hamburger, "Watkins Tells of 'Arrogant' Culture."

20. N. Banjeree, D. Barboza, and A. Warren, "At Enron, Lavish Excess Often Came before Success," *The New York Times* (online), 26 February 2002.

member of the Andersen firm with whom she had worked several years earlier. In an internal Andersen memorandum, that individual relayed Watkins' concerns to several colleagues, including the Enron audit engagement partner, David Duncan. At that point, Andersen officials in the firm's Chicago headquarters began systematically reviewing previous decisions made by the Enron audit engagement team.

In fact, several months earlier, Andersen representatives had become aware of Enron's rapidly deteriorating financial condition and become deeply involved in helping the company's executives cope with that crisis. Andersen's efforts included assisting Enron officials in restructuring certain of the company's SPEs so that they could continue to qualify as unconsolidated entities. Subsequent press reports revealed that in February 2001, frustration over the aggressive nature of Enron's accounting and financial reporting decisions caused some Andersen officials to suggest dropping the company as an audit client.[21]

On December 12, 2001, Joseph Berardino testified before the Committee on Financial Services of the U.S. House of Representatives. Early in that testimony, Berardino freely admitted that members of the Enron audit engagement team had made one major error while analyzing a large SPE transaction that occurred in 1999. "We made a professional judgment about the appropriate accounting treatment that turned out to be wrong."[22] According to Berardino, when Andersen officials discovered this error in the fall of 2001, they promptly notified Enron's executives and told them to "correct it." Approximately 20 percent of the $600 million restatement of prior earnings announced by Enron on November 8, 2001, was due to this item.

The remaining 80 percent of the earnings restatement involved another SPE that Enron created in 1997. Unknown to Andersen auditors, one-half of that SPE's minimum 3 percent "external" equity had been effectively contributed by Enron. As a result, that entity did not qualify for SPE treatment, meaning that its financial data should have been included in Enron's consolidated financial statements from its inception. When Andersen auditors discovered this violation of the 3 percent rule in the fall of 2001, they immediately informed Enron's accounting staff. Andersen also informed the company's audit committee that the failure of Enron officials to reveal the source of the SPE's initial funding could possibly be construed as an illegal act under the Securities Exchange Act of 1934. Berardino implied that the client's lack of candor regarding this SPE exempted Andersen of responsibility for the resulting accounting and financial reporting errors linked to that entity.

Berardino also explained to Congress that Andersen auditors had been only minimally involved in the transactions that eventually resulted in the $1.2 billion reduction of owners' equity reported by Enron on October 16, 2001. The bulk of those transactions had occurred in early 2001. Andersen had not audited the 2001 quarterly financial statements that had been prepared following the initial recording of those transactions—public companies are not required to have their quarterly financial statements audited.

Berardino's testimony before Congress in December 2001 failed to appease Andersen's critics. Over the next several months, Berardino continually found himself defending Andersen against a growing torrent of accusations. Most of these accusations centered on three key issues. First, many critics raised the controversial and longstanding "scope of services" issue when criticizing Andersen's role in the Enron debacle. Over the final few decades of the twentieth century, the major

21. S. Labaton, "S.E.C. Leader Sees Outside Monitors for Auditing Firms," *The New York Times* (online), 18 January 2002.

22. J. Kahn and J. D. Glater, "Enron Auditor Raises Specter of Crime," *The New York Times* (online), 13 December 2001.

accounting firms had gradually extended the product line of professional services they offered to their major audit clients. A research study focusing on nearly 600 large companies that released financial statements in early 1999 revealed that for every $1 of audit fees those companies had paid their independent auditors, they had paid those firms $2.69 for nonaudit consulting services.[23] These services included a wide range of activities such as feasibility studies of various types, internal auditing, design of accounting systems, development of e-commerce initiatives, and a varied assortment of other information technology (IT) services.

In an interview with *The New York Times* in March 2002, Leonard Spacek's daughter revealed that her father had adamantly opposed accounting firms providing consulting services to their audit clients. "I remember him ranting and raving, saying Andersen couldn't consult and audit the same firms because it was a conflict of interest. Well, now I'm sure he's twirling in his grave saying, 'I told you so.'"[24] In the late 1990s, Arthur Levitt, the chairman of the SEC, had led a vigorous, one-man campaign to limit the scope of consulting services that accounting firms could provide to their audit clients. In particular, Levitt wanted to restrict the ability of accounting firms to provide IT and internal audit services to their audit clients. An extensive and costly lobbying campaign that the Big Five firms carried out in the press and among elected officials allowed those firms to defeat the bulk of Levitt's proposals.

Public reports that Andersen earned approximately $52 million in fees from Enron during 2000, only $25 million of which was directly linked to the 2000 audit, caused the scope of services issue to resurface. Critics charged that the enormous consulting fees accounting firms earned from their audit clients jeopardized those firms' independence. "It's obvious that Andersen helped Enron cook the books. Andersen's Houston office was pulling in $1 million a week from Enron—their objectivity went out the window."[25] These same critics reiterated an allegation that had widely circulated a few years earlier, namely, that the large accounting firms had resorted to using the independent audit function as "a loss leader, a way of getting in the door at a company to sell more profitable consulting contracts."[26] One former partner of a Big Five accounting firm provided anecdotal evidence corroborating that allegation. This individual revealed that he had been under constant pressure from his former firm to market various professional services to his audit clients. So relentless were his efforts that at one point a frustrated client executive asked him, "Are you my auditor or a salesperson?"[27]

A second source of criticism directed at Andersen stemmed from the firm's alleged central role in Enron's aggressive accounting and financial reporting treatments for its SPE-related transactions. The Powers Report released to the public in February 2002 spawned much of this criticism. That lengthy report examined in detail several of Enron's largest and most questionable SPE transactions. The Powers Report pointedly and repeatedly documented that Andersen personnel had been deeply involved in those transactions. Exhibit 3 contains a sample of selected excerpts from the Powers Report that refers to Andersen's role in "analyzing" and "reviewing" Enron's SPE transactions.

---

23. N. Byrnes, "Accounting in Crisis," *Business Week*, 28 January 2002, 46.

24. D. Barboza, "Where Pain of Arthur Andersen Is Personal," *The New York Times* (online), 13 March 2002.

25. *SmartPros.com*, "Lawsuit Seeks to Hold Andersen Accountable for Defrauding Enron Investors, Employees," 4 December 2001.

26. J. Kahn, "One Plus One Makes *What*?" *Fortune*, 7 January 2002, 89.

27. I. J. Dugan, "Before Enron, Greed Helped Sink the Respectability of Accounting," *The Wall Street Journal* (online), 14 March 2002.

**EXHIBIT 3**

SELECTED EXCERPTS FROM THE POWERS REPORT REGARDING ANDERSEN'S INVOLVEMENT IN KEY ACCOUNTING AND FINANCIAL REPORTING DECISIONS FOR ENRON'S SPE TRANSACTIONS

Page 5: In virtually all of the [SPE] transactions Enron's accounting treatment was determined with the extensive participation and structuring advice from Andersen, which reported to the Board.

Page 17: Various disclosures [regarding Enron's SPE transactions] were approved by one or more of Enron's outside [Andersen] auditors and its inside and outside counsel. However, these disclosures were obtuse, did not communicate the essence of the transactions completely or clearly, and failed to convey the substance of what was going on between Enron and the partnerships.

Page 24: The evidence available to us suggests that Andersen did not fulfill its professional responsibilities in connection with its audits of Enron's financial statements, or its obligation to bring to the attention of Enron's Board (or the Audit and Compliance Committee) concerns about Enron's internal controls over the related-party [SPE] transactions.

Page 24: Andersen participated in the structuring and accounting treatment of the Raptor transactions, and charged over $1 million for its services, yet it apparently failed to provide the objective accounting judgment that should have prevented these transactions from going forward.

Page 25: According to recent public disclosures, Andersen also failed to bring to the attention of Enron's Audit and Compliance Committee serious reservations Andersen partners voiced internally about the related-party transactions.

Page 25: The Board appears to have reasonably relied upon the professional judgment of Andersen concerning Enron's financial statements and the adequacy of controls for the related-party transactions. Our review indicates that Andersen failed to meet its responsibilities in both respects.

Page 100: Accountants from Andersen were closely involved in structuring the Raptors [SPE transactions]. . . . Enron's records show that Andersen billed Enron approximately $335,000 in connection with its work on the creation of the Raptors in the first several months of 2000.

Page 107: Causey [Enron's chief accounting officer] informed the Finance Committee that Andersen "had spent considerable time analyzing the Talon structure and the governance structure of LJM2 and was comfortable with the proposed [SPE] transaction."

Page 126: At the time [September 2001], Enron accounting personnel and Andersen concluded (using qualitative analysis) that the error [in a prior SPE transaction] was not material and a restatement was not necessary.

Page 129: Proper financial accounting does not permit this result [questionable accounting treatment for certain of Enron's SPE transactions]. To reach it, the accountants at Enron and Andersen—including the local engagement team and, apparently, Andersen's national office experts in Chicago—had to surmount numerous obstacles presented by pertinent accounting rules.

Page 132: It is particularly surprising that the accountants at Andersen, who should have brought a measure of objectivity and perspective to these transactions, did not do so. Based on the recollections of those involved in the transactions and a large collection of documentary evidence, there is no question that Andersen accountants were in a position to understand all the critical features of the Raptors and offer advice on the appropriate accounting treatment. Andersen's total bill for Raptor-related work came to approximately $1.3 million. Indeed, there is abundant evidence that Andersen in fact offered Enron advice

(*continued*)

**EXHIBIT 3—*continued***

SELECTED EXCERPTS FROM THE POWERS REPORT REGARDING ANDERSEN'S INVOLVEMENT IN KEY ACCOUNTING AND FINANCIAL REPORTING DECISIONS FOR ENRON'S SPE TRANSACTIONS

at every step, from inception through restructuring and ultimately to terminating the Raptors. Enron followed that advice.

Page 202: While we have not had the benefit of Andersen's position on a number of these issues, the evidence we have seen suggests Andersen accountants did not function as an effective check on the disclosure approach taken by the company. Andersen was copied on drafts of the financial statement footnotes and the proxy statements, and we were told that it routinely provided comments on the related-party transaction disclosures in response. We also understand that the Andersen auditors closest to Enron Global Finance were involved in drafting of at least some of the disclosures. An internal Andersen e-mail from February 2001 released in connection with recent Congressional hearings suggests that Andersen may have had concerns about the disclosures of the related-party transactions in the financial statement footnotes. Andersen did not express such concerns to the Board. On the contrary, Andersen's engagement partner told the Audit and Compliance Committee just a week after the internal e-mail that, with respect to related-party transactions, "'[r]equired disclosure [had been] reviewed for adequacy,' and that Andersen would issue an unqualified audit opinion on the financial statements."

Source: W. C. Powers, R. S. Troubh, and H. S. Winokur, "Report of Investigation by the Special Investigative Committee of the Board of Directors of Enron Corporation," 1 February 2002.

Among the parties most critical of Andersen's extensive involvement in Enron's accounting and financial reporting decisions for SPE transactions was former SEC Chief Accountant Lynn Turner. During his tenure with the SEC in the 1990s, Turner had participated in the federal agency's investigation of Andersen's audits of Waste Management Inc. That investigation culminated in sanctions against several Andersen auditors and in a $1.4 billion restatement of Waste Management's financial statements, the largest accounting restatement in U.S. history at that time. Andersen eventually paid a reported $75 million in settlements to resolve various civil lawsuits linked to those audits and a $7 million fine to settle charges filed against the firm by the SEC.

In an interview with *The New York Times*, Turner suggested that the charges of shoddy audit work that had plagued Andersen in connection with its audits of Waste Management, Sunbeam, Enron, and other high-profile public clients was well-deserved. Turner compared Andersen's problems with those experienced several years earlier by Coopers & Lybrand, a firm for which he had been an audit partner. According to Turner, a series of "blown audits" was the source of Coopers' problems. "We got bludgeoned to death in the press. People did not even want to see us at their doorsteps. It was brutal, but we deserved it. We had gotten into this mentality in the firm of making business judgment calls."[28] Clearly, the role of independent auditors does not include "making business judgments" for their clients. Instead, auditors have a responsibility to provide an objective point of view regarding the proper accounting and financial reporting decisions for those judgments.

Easily the source of the most embarrassment for Berardino and his Andersen colleagues was the widely publicized effort of the firm's Houston office to shred a large quantity of documents pertaining to various Enron audits. In early January 2002, Andersen officials informed federal investigators that personnel in the Houston office had "destroyed a significant but undetermined number of documents relating to the

28. F. Norris, "From Sunbeam to Enron, Andersen's Reputation Suffers," *The New York Times* (online), 23 November 2001.

company [Enron] and its finances."[29] That large-scale effort began in September 2001 and apparently continued into November after the SEC revealed it was conducting a formal investigation of Enron's financial affairs. The report of the shredding effort immediately caused many critics to suggest that Andersen's Houston office was attempting to prevent law enforcement authorities from obtaining potentially incriminating evidence regarding Andersen's role in Enron's demise. Senator Joseph Lieberman, chairman of the U.S. Senate Governmental Affairs Committee that would be investigating the Enron debacle, warned that the effort to dispose of the Enron-related documents might be particularly problematic for Andersen.

> *It [the document-shredding] came at a time when people inside, including the executives of Arthur Andersen and Enron, knew that Enron was in real trouble and that the roof was about to collapse on them, and there was about to be a corporate scandal. . . . [This] raises very serious questions about whether obstruction of justice occurred here. The folks at Arthur Andersen could be on the other end of an indictment before this is over. This Enron episode may end this company's history.*[30]

The barrage of criticism directed at Andersen continued unabated during the early months of 2002. Ironically, some of that criticism was directed at Andersen by Enron's top management. On January 17, 2002, Kenneth Lay issued a press release reporting that his company had decided to discharge Andersen as its independent audit firm.[31]

> *As announced on Oct. 31, the Enron Board of Directors convened a Special Committee to look into accounting and other issues relating to certain transactions. While we had been willing to give Andersen the benefit of the doubt until the completion of that investigation, we can't afford to wait any longer in light of recent events, including the reported destruction of documents by Andersen personnel and the disciplinary actions against several of Andersen's partners in its Houston office.*[32]

Throughout the public relations nightmare that besieged Andersen following Enron's bankruptcy filing, a primary tactic employed by Joseph Berardino was to insist repeatedly that poor business decisions, not errors on the part of Andersen, were responsible for Enron's downfall and the massive losses that ensued for investors, creditors, and other parties. "At the end of the day, we do not cause companies to fail."[33] Such statements failed to generate sympathy for Andersen. Even the editor-in-chief of *Accounting Today*, one of the accounting profession's leading publications, was unmoved by Berardino's continual assertions that his firm was not responsible for the Enron fiasco. "If you accept the audit and collect the fee, then be prepared to accept the blame. Otherwise you're not part of the solution but rather, part of the problem."[34]

---

29. K. Eichenwald and F. Norris, "Enron Auditor Admits It Destroyed Documents," *The New York Times* (online), 11 January 2002.

30. R. A. Oppel, "Andersen Says Lawyer Let Its Staff Destroy Files," *The New York Times* (online), 14 January 2002.

31. Kenneth Lay resigned as Enron's chairman of the board and CEO on January 23, 2002, one day after a court-appointed "creditors committee" had requested him to step down.

32. M. Palmer, "Enron Board Discharges Arthur Andersen in All Capacities," *Enron.com*, 17 January 2002.

33. M. Gordon, "Labor Secretary to Address Enron Hearings," *Associated Press* (online), 6 February 2002.

34. B. Carlino, "Enron Simply Newest Player in National Auditing Crisis," *The Electronic Accountant* (online), 17 December 2001.

## Ridicule and Retrospection

As 2001 came to a close, *The New York Times* reported that the year had easily been the worst ever for Andersen, "the accounting firm that once deserved the title of the conscience of the industry."[35] The following year would prove to be an even darker time for the firm. During the early months of 2002, Andersen faced scathing criticism from Congressional investigators, enormous class-action lawsuits filed by angry Enron stockholders and creditors, and a federal criminal indictment stemming from the shredding of Enron-related documents.

In late March 2002, Joseph Berardino unexpectedly resigned as Andersen's CEO after failing to negotiate a merger of Andersen with one of the other Big Five firms. During the following few weeks, dozens of Andersen clients dropped the firm as their independent auditor out of concern that the firm might not survive if it was found guilty of the pending criminal indictment. The staggering loss of clients forced Andersen to lay off more than 25 percent of its workforce in mid-April. Shortly after that layoff was announced, U.S. Justice Department officials revealed that David Duncan, the former Enron audit engagement partner, had pleaded guilty to obstruction of justice and agreed to testify against his former firm. Duncan's plea proved to be the death knell for Andersen. In June 2002, a federal jury found the firm guilty of obstruction of justice. That conviction forced the firm to terminate its relationship with its remaining public clients, effectively ending Andersen's long and proud history within the U.S. accounting profession.

Three years later, the U.S. Supreme Court unanimously overturned the felony conviction handed down against Andersen. In an opinion written by Chief Justice William Rehnquist, the high court ruled that federal prosecutors did not prove that Andersen had *intended* to interfere with a federal investigation when the firm shredded the Enron audit workpapers. The Supreme Court's decision was little consolation to the more than 20,000 Andersen partners and employees who had lost their jobs when the accounting firm was forced out of business by the felony conviction.

Numerous Enron officials faced criminal indictments for their roles in the Enron fraud, among them Andrew Fastow, Jeffrey Skilling, and Kenneth Lay. Fastow pleaded guilty to conspiracy to commit securities fraud as well as to other charges. The former CFO received a 10-year prison term, which was reduced to 6 years after he testified against Skilling and Lay. Fastow was also required to forfeit nearly $25 million of personal assets that he had accumulated during his tenure at Enron. Largely as a result of Fastow's testimony against them, Skilling and Lay were convicted on multiple counts of fraud and conspiracy in May 2006. In September 2006, Skilling was sentenced to 24 years in prison. Kenneth Lay, who was to be sentenced at the same time, died of a massive heart attack in July 2006. Three months later, a federal judge overturned Lay's conviction since Lay was no longer able to pursue his appeal of that conviction.

The toll taken on the public accounting profession by the Enron debacle was not limited to Andersen, its partners, or its employees. An unending flood of jokes and ridicule directed at Andersen tainted and embarrassed practically every accountant in the nation, including both accountants in public practice and those working in the private sector. The Enron nightmare also prompted widespread soul-searching within the profession and a public outcry to strengthen the independent audit function and improve accounting and financial reporting practices. Legislative and regulatory authorities quickly responded to the public's demand for reforms.

The FASB imposed stricter accounting and financial reporting guidelines on SPEs as a direct result of the Enron case. Those new rules require most companies to

---

35. F. Norris, "From Sunbeam to Enron."

include the financial data for those types of entities in their consolidated financial statements. In 2002, Congress passed the Sarbanes-Oxley Act to strengthen financial reporting for public companies, principally by improving the rigor and quality of independent audits. Among other requirements, the Sarbanes-Oxley Act limits the types of consulting services that independent auditors can provide to their clients and requires public companies to prepare annual reports on the quality of their internal controls. The most sweeping change in the profession resulting from the Enron fiasco was the creation of a new federal agency, the Public Company Accounting Oversight Board, to oversee the rule-making process for the independent audit function.

Among the prominent individuals who commented on the challenges and problems facing the accounting profession was former SEC Chairman Richard Breeden when he testified before Congress in early 2002. Chairman Breeden observed that there was a simple solution to the quagmire facing the profession. He called on accountants and auditors to adopt a simple rule of thumb when analyzing, recording, and reporting on business transactions, regardless of whether those transactions involved "New Economy" or "Old Economy" business ventures. "When you're all done, the result had better fairly reflect what you see in reality."[36]

In retrospect, Commissioner Breeden's recommendation seems to be a restatement of the "Think straight, talk straight" motto of Arthur E. Andersen. Andersen and his colleagues insisted that their audit clients adhere to a high standard of integrity when preparing their financial statements. An interview with Joseph Berardino by *The New York Times* in December 2001 suggests that Mr. Berardino and his contemporaries may have had a different attitude when it came to dealing with cantankerous clients such as Enron: "In an interview yesterday, Mr. Berardino said Andersen had no power to force a company to disclose that it had hidden risks and losses in special-purpose entities. 'A client says: 'There is no requirement to disclose this. You can't hold me to a higher standard.'"[37]

Berardino is certainly correct in his assertion. An audit firm cannot force a client to adhere to a higher standard. In fact, even Arthur Edward Andersen did not have that power. But Mr. Andersen did have the resolve to tell such clients to immediately begin searching for another audit firm.

## Questions

1. The Enron debacle created what one public official reported was a "crisis of confidence" on the part of the public in the accounting profession. List the parties who you believe are most responsible for that crisis. Briefly justify each of your choices.
2. List three types of consulting services that audit firms have provided to their audit clients in recent years. For each item, indicate the specific threats, if any, that the provision of the given service can pose for an audit firm's independence.
3. For purposes of this question, assume that the excerpts from the Powers Report shown in Exhibit 3 provide accurate descriptions of Andersen's involvement in Enron's accounting and financial reporting decisions. Given this assumption, do you believe that Andersen's involvement in those decisions violated any professional auditing standards? If so, list those standards and briefly explain your rationale.

---

36. R. Schlank, "Former SEC Chairmen Urge Congress to Free FASB," *AccountingWeb* (online), 15 February 2002.

37. F. Norris, "The Distorted Numbers at Enron," *The New York Times* (online), 14 December 2001.

4. Briefly describe the key requirements included in professional auditing standards regarding the preparation and retention of audit workpapers. Which party "owns" audit workpapers: the client or the audit firm?
5. Identify and list five recommendations that have been made recently to strengthen the independent audit function. For each of these recommendations, indicate why you support or do not support the given measure.
6. Do you believe that there has been a significant shift or evolution over the past several decades in the concept of "professionalism" as it relates to the public accounting discipline? If so, explain how you believe that concept has changed or evolved over that time frame and identify the key factors responsible for any apparent changes.
7. As pointed out in this case, the SEC does not require public companies to have their quarterly financial statements audited. What responsibilities, if any, do audit firms have with regard to the quarterly financial statements of their clients? In your opinion, should quarterly financial statements be audited? Defend your answer.

**CASE 1.2**

# Just for FEET, Inc.

*Life is so fragile. A single bad choice in a single moment can cause a life to turn irrevocably 180 degrees.*

*U.S. District Judge C. Lynwood Smith, Jr.*

In 1971, 25-year-old Thomas Shine founded a small sporting goods company, Logo 7, that would eventually become known as Logo Athletic. Shine's company manufactured and marketed a wide range of shirts, hats, jackets, and other apparel items that boldly displayed the logos of the Minnesota Vikings, New York Islanders, St. Louis Cardinals, and dozens of other professional sports teams. In 2001, Shine sold Logo to Reebok and became that company's senior vice president of sports and entertainment marketing. In that position, Shine wined and dined major sports stars with the intent of persuading them to sign exclusive endorsement contracts with Reebok.

During his long career, Thomas Shine became one of the most well-known and respected leaders of the sporting goods industry. Shine's prominence and credibility in that industry took a severe blow in February 2004 when he pleaded guilty to a criminal indictment filed against him by the U.S. Department of Justice. The Justice Department charged that Shine had signed a false audit confirmation sent to him in early 1999 by one of Logo's largest customers. The confirmation indicated that Logo owed that customer approximately $700,000. Although Shine knew that no such debt existed, he signed the confirmation and returned it to the customer's independent audit firm, Deloitte & Touche, after being pressured to do so by an executive of the customer. As a result of his guilty plea, Shine faced a possible sentence of five years in federal prison and a fine of up to $250,000.

## Out of South Africa

At approximately the same time that Thomas Shine was launching his business career in the retail industry in the United States, Harold Ruttenberg was doing the same in South Africa. Ruttenberg, a native of Johannesburg, paid for his college education by working nights and weekends as a sales clerk in an upscale men's clothing store. After graduation, he began importing Levi's jeans from the United States and selling them from his car, his eventual goal being to accumulate sufficient capital to open a retail store. Ruttenberg quickly accomplished that goal. In fact, by the time he was 30, he owned a small chain of men's apparel stores.

Mounting political and economic troubles in his home country during the early and mid-1970s eventually convinced Ruttenberg to move his family to the United States. South Africa's strict emigration laws forced Ruttenberg to leave practically all of his net worth behind. When he arrived in California in 1976 with his spouse and three small children, Ruttenberg had less than $30,000. Despite his limited financial resources and unfamiliarity with U.S. business practices, the strong-willed South African was committed to once again establishing himself as a successful entrepreneur in the retailing industry.

Ruttenberg soon realized that the exorbitant rents for commercial retail properties in the major metropolitan areas of California were far beyond his reach. So, he moved his family once more, this time to the more affordable business environment of

Birmingham, Alabama. Ruttenberg leased a vacant storefront in a Birmingham mall and a few months later opened Hang Ten Sports World, a retail store that marketed children's sportswear products. Thanks largely to his work ethic and intense desire to succeed, Ruttenberg's business prospered over the next decade.

In 1988, Ruttenberg decided to take a gamble on a new business venture. Ruttenberg had come to believe that there was an opportunity to make large profits in the retail shoe business. At the time, the market for high-priced athletic shoes—basketball shoes, in particular—was growing dramatically and becoming an ever-larger segment of the retail shoe industry. The principal retail outlets for the shoes produced by Adidas, Nike, Reebok, and other major athletic shoe manufacturers were relatively small stores located in thousands of suburban malls scattered across the country, meaning that the retail athletic shoe "subindustry" was highly fragmented. The five largest retailers in this market niche accounted for less than 10 percent of the annual sales of athletic shoes.

Ruttenberg realized that the relatively small floor space of retail shoe stores in suburban malls limited a retailer's ability to display the wide and growing array of products being produced by the major shoe manufacturers. Likewise, the high cost of floor space in malls with heavy traffic served to limit the profitability of shoe retailers. To overcome these problems, Ruttenberg decided that he would build freestanding "Just for FEET" superstores located near malls. To lure consumers away from mall-based shoe stores, Ruttenberg developed a three-pronged business strategy focusing on "selection," "service," and "entertainment."

The business plan that Ruttenberg developed for his superstores involved a stores-within-a-store concept; that is, he intended to create several mini-stores within his large retail outlets, each of which would be devoted exclusively to the products of individual shoe manufacturers. He believed this store design would appeal to both consumers and vendors. Consumers who were committed to one particular brand would not have to search through store displays that included a wide assortment of branded products. Likewise, his proposed floor design would provide major vendors an opportunity to participate in marketing their products. Ruttenberg hoped that his planned floor design would spur the major vendors to compete with each other in providing so-called vendor allowances to his superstores to make their individual displays more attractive than those of competitors.

Customer service was the second major element of Ruttenberg's business plan for his shoe superstores. Ruttenberg planned to staff his stores so that there would be an unusually large ratio of sales associates to customers. Sales associates would be required to complete an extensive training course in "footwear technology" so that they would be well equipped to answer any questions posed by customers. When a customer chose to try on a particular shoe product, he or she would have to ask a sales associate to retrieve that item from the "back shop." Sales associates were trained to interact with customers in such a way that they would earn their trust and thus create a stronger bond with them.

Just for Feet's 1998 Form 10-K described the third feature of Harold Ruttenberg's business plan as creating an "Entertainment Shopping Experience." Rock and roll music and brightly colored displays greeted customers when they entered the superstores. When they tired of shopping, customers could play a game of "horse" on an enclosed basketball half-court located near the store's entrance or sit back and enjoy a multiscreen video bank in the store's customer lounge. Frequent promotional events included autograph sessions with major sports celebrities such as Bart Starr, the former Green Bay Packers quarterback who was also on the company's board of directors.

Ruttenberg would eventually include two other key features in the floor plans of his superstores. Although Just for Feet did not target price-conscious customers, Ruttenberg added a "Combat Zone" to each superstore where such customers could rummage through piles of discontinued shoe lines, "seconds," and other discounted items. For those customers who simply wanted a pair of shoes and did not have a strong preference for a given brand, Ruttenberg developed a "Great Wall" that contained a wide array of shoes sorted not by brand but rather by function. In this large display, customers could quickly compare and contrast the key features of dozens of different types of running shoes, walking shoes, basketball shoes, and cross-trainers.

## Quite a FEET

Just for Feet's initial superstore in Birmingham proved to be a huge financial success. That success convinced Harold Ruttenberg to open similar retail outlets in several major metropolitan areas in the southern United States and to develop a showcase superstore within the glitzy Caesar's Forum shopping mall on the Las Vegas Strip. By 1992, Just for Feet owned and operated five superstores and had sold franchise rights for several other stores. The company's annual sales were approaching $20 million, but that total accounted for a nominal proportion of the retail shoe industry's estimated $15 billion of annual sales.

To become a major force in the shoe industry, Ruttenberg knew that he would have to expand his retail chain nationwide, which would require large amounts of additional capital. To acquire that capital, Ruttenberg decided to take his company public. On March 9, 1994, Just for Feet's common stock began trading on the NASDAQ exchange under the ticker symbol FEET. The stock, which sold initially for $6.22 per share, would quickly rise over the next two years to more than $37 per share.

Ruttenberg used the funds produced by Just for Feet's initial public offering (IPO) to pursue an aggressive expansion program. The company opened dozens of new superstores during the mid-1990s and acquired several smaller competitors, including Athletic Attic in March 1997 and Sneaker Stadium in July 1998. For fiscal 1996, which ended January 31, 1997, the company reported a profit of $13.9 million on sales of $250 million. Two years later, the company earned a profit of $26.7 million on sales of nearly $775 million. By the end of 1998, Just for Feet was the second largest athletic shoe retailer in the United States with 300 retail outlets.

During the mid-1990s, Just for Feet's common stock was among the most closely monitored and hyped securities on Wall Street. Analysts and investors tracking the stock marveled at the company's ability to consistently outperform its major competitors. By the late 1990s, market saturation and declining profit margins were becoming major concerns within the athletic shoe segment of the shoe industry. Despite the lackluster profits and faltering revenues of other athletic shoe retailers, Harold Ruttenberg continued to issue press releases touting his company's record profits and steadily growing sales. Most impressive was the company's 21 straight quarterly increases in same-store sales through the fourth quarter of fiscal 1998.

In November 1997, Delphi Investments released a lengthy analytical report focusing on Just for Feet's future prospects. In that report, which included a strong "buy" recommendation for the company's common stock, Delphi commented on the "Harold Ruttenberg factor." The report largely attributed the company's financial success and rosy future to "the larger-than-life founder and inventor of the Just for Feet concept."

In frequent interviews with business journalists, Harold Ruttenberg was not modest in discussing the huge challenges that he had personally overcome to establish himself as one of the leading corporate executives in the retail apparel industry. Nor was Ruttenberg reluctant to point out that he had sketched out the general framework of Just for Feet's successful business plan over a three-day vacation in the late 1980s. After being named one of 1996's Retail Entrepreneurs of the Year, Ruttenberg noted that Just for Feet had succeeded principally because of the unique marketing strategies he had developed for the company. "Customers love our stores because they are so unique. We are not a copycat retailer. Nobody does what we do, the way we do it. The proof is in our performance."[1] In this same interview, Ruttenberg reported that he had never been tempted to check out a competitor's stores. "I have nothing to learn from them. I'm certainly not going to copy anything they are doing."[2] Finally, Ruttenberg did not dispute, or apologize for, his reputation as a domineering, if not imposing, superior. "I can be a very demanding, difficult boss. But I know how to build teams. And I have made a lot of people very rich."[3]

Ruttenberg realized that one of his primary responsibilities was training a new management team to assume the leadership of the company following his retirement. "As the founder, my job is to put the right people in place for the future. I'm preparing this company for 25 years down the road when I won't be here."[4] One of the individuals who Ruttenberg handpicked to lead the company into its future was his son, Don-Allen Ruttenberg, who shared his father's single-minded determination and tenacious business temperament. In 1997, at the age of 29, Don-Allen Ruttenberg was named Just for Feet's Vice President of New Store Development. Two years later, the younger Ruttenberg was promoted to the position of Executive Vice President.

Similar to most successful companies, Just for Feet's path to success was not without occasional pitfalls. In 1995, Wall Street's zeal for Just for Feet's common stock was tempered somewhat by an accounting controversy involving "store opening" costs. Throughout its existence, Just for Feet had accumulated such costs for each new store in an asset account and then amortized the costs over the 12-month period following the store's grand opening. A more common practice within the retail industry was to expense such costs in the month that a new store opened. Criticism of Just for Feet's accounting for store opening costs goaded company management to adopt the industry convention, which resulted in the company recording a $2.1 million cumulative effect of a change in accounting principle during fiscal 1996.

In the summer of 1996, Wall Street took notice when Harold Ruttenberg, his wife, Pamela, and their son, Don-Allen, sold large blocks of their Just for Feet common stock in a secondary offering to the general public. Collectively, the three members of the Ruttenberg family received nearly $49.5 million from the sale of those securities. Major investors and financial analysts questioned why the Ruttenbergs would dispose of much of their Just for Feet stock while, at the same time, the senior Ruttenberg was issuing glowing projections of the company's future prospects.

## Clay Feet

No one could deny the impressive revenue and profit trends that Just for Feet established during the mid- and late 1990s. Exhibits 1 and 2, which present the company's primary financial statements for the three-year period fiscal 1996 through fiscal 1998, document those trends. However, hidden within the company's financial data for that three-year period was a red flag. Notice in the statements of cash flows shown

1. *Chain Store Age*, "Retail Entrepreneurs of the Year: Harold Ruttenberg," December 1996, 68.
2. *Ibid.*
3. *Ibid.*
4. *Ibid.*

in Exhibit 2 that despite the rising profits Just for Feet reported in the late 1990s, the company's operating cash flows during that period were negative. By early 1999, these negative operating cash flows posed a huge liquidity problem for the company. To address this problem, Just for Feet sold $200 million of high-yield or so-called "junk" bonds in April 1999.

A few weeks after selling the junk bonds, Just for Feet issued an earnings warning. This press release alerted investors that the company would likely post its first-ever quarterly loss during the second quarter of fiscal 1999. One month later, Just for Feet shocked its investors and creditors when it announced that it might default on its first interest payment on the $200 million of junk bonds. Investors received more disturbing news in July 1999 when Harold Ruttenberg unexpectedly resigned as Just for Feet's CEO. The company replaced Ruttenberg with a corporate turnaround specialist,

**EXHIBIT 1**

JUST FOR FEET, INC., 1996–1998 BALANCE SHEETS

**JUST FOR FEET, INC.**
**BALANCE SHEETS (000s omitted)**

| | | January 31, | |
|---|---|---|---|
| | 1999 | 1998 | 1997 |
| Current assets: | | | |
| Cash and cash equivalents | $ 12,412 | $ 82,490 | $138,785 |
| Marketable securities available for sale | — | — | 33,961 |
| Accounts receivable | 18,875 | 15,840 | 6,553 |
| Inventory | 399,901 | 206,128 | 133,323 |
| Other current assets | 18,302 | 6,709 | 2,121 |
| Total current assets | 449,490 | 311,167 | 314,743 |
| Property and equipment, net | 160,592 | 94,529 | 54,922 |
| Goodwill, net | 71,084 | 36,106 | — |
| Other | 8,230 | 6,550 | 6,169 |
| Total assets | $689,396 | $448,352 | $375,834 |
| Current liabilities: | | | |
| Short-term borrowings | $ — | $ 90,667 | $100,000 |
| Accounts payable | 100,322 | 51,162 | 38,897 |
| Accrued expenses | 24,829 | 9,292 | 5,487 |
| Income taxes payable | 902 | 1,363 | 425 |
| Current maturities of long-term debt | 6,639 | 3,222 | 2,105 |
| Total current liabilities | 132,692 | 155,706 | 146,914 |
| Long-term debt and obligations | 230,998 | 24,562 | 10,364 |
| Total liabilities | $363,690 | $180,268 | $157,278 |
| Shareholders' equity: | | | |
| Common stock | 3 | 3 | 3 |
| Paid-in capital | 249,590 | 218,616 | 190,492 |
| Retained earnings | 76,113 | 49,465 | 28,061 |
| Total shareholders' equity | 325,706 | 268,084 | 218,556 |
| Total liabilities and shareholders' equity | $689,396 | $448,352 | $375,834 |

Helen Rockey. Upon resigning, Ruttenberg insisted that Just for Feet's financial problems were only temporary and that the company would likely post a profit during the third quarter of fiscal 1999.

Harold Ruttenberg's statement did not reassure investors. The company's stock price went into a freefall during the spring and summer of 1999, slipping to near $4 per share by the end of July. In September, the company announced that it had lost $25.9 million during the second quarter of fiscal 1999, a much larger loss than had been expected by Wall Street. Less than two months later, on November 2, 1999, the company shocked its investors and creditors once more when it filed for Chapter 11 bankruptcy protection in the federal courts.

Just for Feet's startling collapse over a period of a few months sparked a flurry of lawsuits against the company and its executives. Allegations of financial mismanagement and accounting irregularities triggered investigations of the company's financial affairs by state and federal law enforcement authorities, including the Alabama Securities Commission, the FBI, the Securities and Exchange Commission (SEC), and the U.S. Department of Justice. In May 2003, the Justice Department announced that a former Just for Feet executive, Adam Gilburne, had pleaded guilty to conspiracy

**EXHIBIT 2**

JUST FOR FEET, INC., 1996–1998 INCOME STATEMENTS AND STATEMENTS OF CASH FLOWS

**JUST FOR FEET, INC.**
**CONSOLIDATED STATEMENTS OF EARNINGS (000s omitted)**

| | Year Ended January 31, | | |
|---|---|---|---|
| | 1999 | 1998 | 1997 |
| Net sales | $774,863 | $478,638 | $256,397 |
| Cost of sales | 452,330 | 279,816 | 147,526 |
| Gross profit | 322,533 | 198,822 | 108,871 |
| Other revenues | 1,299 | 1,101 | 581 |
| Operating expenses: | | | |
| Store operating | 232,505 | 139,659 | 69,329 |
| Store opening costs | 13,669 | 6,728 | 11,240 |
| Amortization of intangibles | 2,072 | 1,200 | 180 |
| General and administrative | 24,341 | 18,040 | 7,878 |
| Total operating expenses | 272,587 | 165,627 | 88,627 |
| Operating income | 51,245 | 34,296 | 20,825 |
| Interest expense | (8,059) | (1,446) | (832) |
| Interest income | 143 | 1,370 | 4,750 |
| Earnings before income taxes and cumulative effect of change in accounting principle | 43,329 | 34,220 | 24,743 |
| Provision for income taxes | 16,681 | 12,817 | 8,783 |
| Earnings before cumulative effect of a change in accounting principle | 26,648 | 21,403 | 15,960 |
| Cumulative effect on prior years of change in accounting principle | — | — | (2,041) |
| Net earnings | $ 26,648 | $ 21,403 | $ 13,919 |

**EXHIBIT 2—** *continued*

JUST FOR FEET, INC., 1996–1998 INCOME STATEMENTS AND STATEMENTS OF CASH FLOWS

**JUST FOR FEET, INC.**
**CONSOLIDATED STATEMENTS OF CASH FLOWS (000s omitted)**

| | Year Ended January 31, | | |
|---|---|---|---|
| | 1999 | 1998 | 1997 |
| **Operating activities:** | | | |
| Net earnings | $ 26,648 | $ 21,403 | $ 13,919 |
| Adjustments to reconcile net earnings to net cash used by operating activities: | | | |
| Cumulative effect of a change in accounting principle | — | — | 2,041 |
| Depreciation and amortization | 16,129 | 8,783 | 3,971 |
| Deferred income taxes | 12,100 | 2,194 | (744) |
| Deferred lease rentals | 2,655 | 2,111 | 1,456 |
| Changes in assets and liabilities providing (using) cash, net of effects of acquisitions: | | | |
| (Increase) decrease in accounts receivable | (2,795) | (8,918) | (3,143) |
| (Increase) decrease in inventory | (170,169) | (56,616) | (76,685) |
| (Increase) decrease in other assets | (8,228) | (5,643) | 271 |
| Increase (decrease) in accounts payable | 34,638 | 7,495 | 16,628 |
| Increase (decrease) in accrued expenses | 7,133 | 2,264 | 2,709 |
| Increase (decrease) in income taxes payable | (181) | 543 | (2,506) |
| Net cash used by operating activities | (82,070) | (26,384) | (42,083) |
| **Investing activities:** | | | |
| Purchases of property and equipment, net of disposals | (78,984) | (43,446) | (33,206) |
| Acquisitions, net of cash acquired | (199) | (25,548) | — |
| Purchases of marketable securities | — | (14,726) | (44,778) |
| Maturities and sales of marketable securities | — | 51,653 | 63,132 |
| Net cash used for investing activities | (79,183) | (32,067) | (14,852) |
| **Financing activities:** | | | |
| Borrowings (repayments) under credit facilities, net | (90,667) | (9,333) | 45,000 |
| Borrowings of long-term obligations | 291,076 | 12,739 | 479 |
| Principal payments on long-term obligations | (132,290) | (2,054) | (1,335) |
| Proceeds from issuance of common stock, net | 20,000 | — | 52,900 |
| Proceeds from exercise of options | 3,056 | 804 | 1,822 |
| Net cash provided by financing activities | 91,175 | 2,156 | 98,866 |
| Net increase (decrease) in cash and equivalents | (70,078) | (56,295) | 41,931 |
| Cash and equivalents, beginning of year | 82,490 | 138,785 | 96,854 |
| Cash and equivalents, end of year | $ 12,412 | $ 82,490 | $138,785 |

to commit wire and securities fraud. Gilburne, who had served in various executive positions with Just for Feet, revealed that he and other members of the company's top management had conspired to inflate the company's reported earnings from 1996 through 1999.

> *The information [testimony provided by Gilburne] alleges that beginning in about 1996, Just for Feet's CEO [Harold Ruttenberg] would conduct meetings at the end of every quarter in which he would lay out analysts' expectations of the company's earnings, and then draw up a list of "goods"—items which produced or added income—and "bads"—those which reduced income. The information alleges that the CEO directed*

*Just for Feet's employees to increase the "goods" and decrease the "bads" in order to meet his own earnings expectations and those of Wall Street analysts.*[5]

Approximately two years following Gilburne's guilty plea, the SEC issued a series of enforcement releases that documented the three key facets of the fraudulent scheme perpetrated by Just for Feet's management team. "Just for Feet falsified its financial statements by (1) improperly recognizing unearned and fictitious receivables from its vendors, (2) failing to properly account for excess inventory, and (3) improperly recording as income the value of display booths provided by its vendors."[6]

As noted earlier, the stores-within-a-store floor plan developed by Harold Ruttenberg provided an opportunity for Just for Feet's vendors to become directly involved in the marketing of their products within the company's superstores. Each year, Just for Feet received millions of dollars of "vendor allowances" or "advertising co-op" from Adidas, Converse, Nike, Reebok, and its other major suppliers. These allowances were intended to subsidize Just for Feet's advertising expenditures for its superstores.

Despite the large size of the vendor allowances, there was typically not a written agreement that documented the conditions under which Just for Feet was entitled to an allowance. Instead, an account manager of each vendor generally had considerable discretion in determining the size and timing of the allowances to be granted to Just for Feet. After Just for Feet had run a series of advertisements or other promotional announcements for a vendor's product, copies of the advertising materials would be submitted to the vendor. The vendor would then pay Just for Feet an allowance based largely upon the amount of the advertised products that the company had purchased.

Generally accepted accounting principles (GAAP) dictated that vendor allowances not be offset against advertising expense until the given advertisements had been run or other promotional efforts had been completed. However, Just for Feet began routinely recording *anticipated* vendor allowances as receivables and advertising expense offsets well before the related advertising or promotional programs had been completed. Just for Feet's management team was particularly aggressive in "front-loading" vendor allowances during fiscal 1998. At the end of fiscal 1997, Just for Feet had slightly more than $400,000 of outstanding vendor allowance receivables; twelve months later, at the end of fiscal 1998, that total had soared to almost $29 million.[7]

During fiscal 1998, Just for Feet's merchandise inventory nearly doubled, rising from $206 million on January 31, 1998, to almost $400 million on January 31, 1999. Although Just for Feet had a large amount of slow-moving inventory, the company's management team refused to properly apply the lower of cost or market rule in arriving at a year-end valuation reserve for that important asset. As a result, at the end of both fiscal 1997 and fiscal 1998, the company's allowance for inventory obsolescence stood at a nominal $150,000.

The major athletic shoe vendors frequently erected promotional displays or booths in the Just for Feet superstores. These booths were maintained by sales representatives of the vendors and were the property of those vendors. In early 1998, Don-Allen Ruttenberg concocted a fraudulent scheme to produce millions of dollars of "booth

5. U.S. Department of Justice, "Former 'Just for Feet, Inc.' Executive Pleads Guilty to Conspiracy to Commit Wire, Securities Fraud," www.usdoj.gov, 12 May 2003.

6. U.S. Securities and Exchange Commission, "SEC Charges Deloitte & Touche and Two of Its Personnel for Failures in Their Audits of Just for Feet," www.sec.gov, 26 April 2005.

7. Although technically receivables, the vendor allowances purportedly due to Just for Feet were netted against the given vendor's accounts payable balance, which explains why these receivables do not appear explicitly in the company's balance sheets shown in Exhibit 1.

income" for Just for Feet. Without the knowledge of its vendors, Just for Feet began recording in its accounting records monthly booth income amounts allegedly earned from those vendors. The offsets to these revenue amounts for accounting purposes were booked (debited) to a booth assets account.[8] By the end of fiscal 1998, Just for Feet had recorded $9 million of bogus assets and related revenues as a result of this scheme. More than 80 percent of these bogus transactions were recorded during the final two quarters of fiscal 1998, ostensibly to allow Just for Feet to reach its previously announced earnings targets for those two periods.

An important feature of the Just for Feet accounting fraud was Don-Allen Ruttenberg's close relationship with key executives of the major athletic shoe vendors. Since Just for Feet was among the largest customers of each of those vendors, the company had a significant amount of economic leverage on their executives. The younger Ruttenberg used this leverage to persuade those executives to return false confirmations to Just for Feet's independent audit firm, Deloitte & Touche. Those confirmations were sent to Just for Feet's vendors to confirm bogus receivables that were a product of the company's fraudulent accounting scheme. In most cases, the bogus receivables resulted from inflated or otherwise improper vendor allowances booked by Just for Feet. One of the five vendor executives who capitulated to Don-Allen Ruttenberg's demands was Thomas Shine, the senior executive of Logo Athletic. Executives of four Just for Feet vendors steadfastly refused to provide false confirmations to Deloitte. Those executives were employed by Asics-Tiger, New Balance, Reebok, and Timberland. Ironically, in 2001, Thomas Shine became an executive of Reebok when that company purchased Logo Athletic.

## Footing & Cross-Footing

Deloitte & Touche served as Just for Feet's independent audit firm from 1992 through early December 1999, one month after the company filed for Chapter 11 bankruptcy. Deloitte issued unqualified audit opinions each year on Just for Feet's financial statements, including the financial statements in the S-1 registration statement the company filed with the SEC when it went public in 1994.

Steven Barry served as Just for Feet's engagement partner for the fiscal 1998 audit. Barry was initially an employee of Touche Ross & Co. and was promoted to partner with that firm in 1988. The next year, Barry became a Deloitte & Touche partner following the merger of Touche Ross with Deloitte, Haskins, & Sells. In 1996, Barry was promoted to managing partner of Deloitte's Birmingham, Alabama office. Barry's principal subordinate on the 1998 Just for Feet audit was Karen Baker, who had been assigned to the company's audit engagement team since 1993. Initially the audit senior on that engagement team, she became the engagement audit manager after being promoted to that rank in 1995.

Deloitte assigned a "greater than normal" level of audit risk to the fiscal 1998 Just for Feet audit during the planning phase of that engagement. To help monitor high-risk audit engagements, Deloitte had established a "National Risk Management Program." In both 1997 and 1998, Just for Feet was included in that program. Each client involved in this program was assigned a "National Review Partner." This partner's duties included "discussing specific risk areas and plans to respond to them . . . reviewing the audit workpapers concerning risk areas of the engagement, and reviewing the financial statements and Deloitte's audit reports with an emphasis

---

8. This fraudulent scheme actually replaced a similar but smaller-scale scam that the younger Ruttenberg had used since December 1996 to inflate Just for Feet's operating results.

on the identification of specific risk areas as well as the adequacy of the audit report and disclosures regarding these risk areas."[9]

The audit workpapers for the fiscal 1997 audit identified several specific audit risk factors. These factors included "management accepts high levels of risk," "places significant emphasis on earnings," and "has historically interpreted accounting standards aggressively." Another 1997 workpaper noted that the company's management team placed a heavy emphasis on achieving previously released earnings targets, expressed an "excessive" interest in maintaining the company's stock price at a high level, and engaged in "unique and highly complex" transactions near fiscal year-end. A summary 1997 workpaper entitled "Risk Factors Worksheet" also noted that Harold Ruttenberg exercised "one-man rule (autocrat)" rule over Just for Feet and that the company practiced "creative accounting."

For both the 1997 and 1998 audit engagements, Deloitte personnel prepared a "Client Risk Profile." This workpaper for those two audits identified vendor allowances and inventory valuation as key audit risk areas. In 1996, Deloitte's headquarters office had issued a firm-wide "Risk Alert" informing practice offices that vendor allowances should be considered a "high-risk area" for retail clients.

During the 1998 audit, the Deloitte engagement team identified several factors that, according to the SEC, should have caused both Barry and Baker to have "heightened professional skepticism" regarding Just for Feet's vendor allowances. The most important of these factors was the huge increase in the vendor allowance receivables between the end of fiscal 1997 and fiscal 1998. In the final few weeks of fiscal 1998, Just for Feet recorded $14.4 million of vendor allowances, accounting for almost one-half of the year-end balance of that account. Deloitte was never provided with supporting documentation for $11.3 million of those vendor allowances, although a Just for Feet executive had promised to provide that documentation. Deloitte completed its fieldwork for the fiscal 1998 audit on April 23, 1999, almost three months following the fiscal year-end. As of that date, Just for Feet had not received any payments from its suppliers for the $11.3 million of undocumented vendor allowances.

In March 1999, Deloitte mailed receivables confirmations to 13 of Just for Feet's suppliers. Collectively, those vendors accounted for $22 million of the $28.9 million of year-end vendor allowances. Again, Don-Allen Ruttenberg persuaded executives of five Just for Feet vendors to sign and return confirmations to Deloitte even though the vendor allowance receivables listed on those confirmations did not exist or were grossly inflated. The confirmations returned by the other eight vendors were generally "nonstandard," according to the SEC. That is, these confirmations included caveats, disclaimers, or other statements that should have alerted Deloitte to the possibility that the given receivable balances were unreliable. "Five vendors returned non-standard letters that, instead of unambiguously confirming amounts owed to Just for Feet at the *end* of the fiscal 1998 year, as requested by the auditors, provided ambiguous information on amounts of co-op [vendor allowances] that the Company had earned, accrued, or had available *during* the year" [emphasis added by SEC]. Another of the returned confirmations explicitly noted that "no additional funds" were due to Just for Feet.

The eight nonstandard confirmations accounted for approximately $16 million of the $22 million of vendor allowance receivables that Deloitte attempted to confirm at year-end. "Despite these and other flaws, the Respondents [Deloitte, Barry, and Baker]

9. Securities and Exchange Commission, *Accounting and Auditing Enforcement Release No. 2238*, 26 May 2005. Unless noted otherwise, the remaining quotations in this case were taken from this source.

nonetheless accepted these letters as confirming approximately $16 million in receivables claimed by Just for Feet." The SEC's investigation of Deloitte's Just for Feet audits revealed that although Barry and Baker accepted these flawed confirmations, two subordinates assigned to the 1998 engagement team continued to investigate the obvious discrepancies in those confirmations well after the completion of that audit. These two individuals, who were audit seniors, twice contacted a Just for Feet executive in the months following the completion of the 1998 audit in an attempt to obtain plausible explanations for the eight nonstandard and suspicious confirmations. That executive did not respond to the audit seniors and neither Barry, nor Baker, apparently, insisted that he provide appropriate documentation and/or explanations regarding the amounts in question.

Just for Feet's large increase in inventory during fiscal 1998 raised several important issues that the Deloitte auditors had to address during the 1998 audit, the most important being whether the client's reserve for inventory obsolescence was sufficient. The primary audit procedure used by Deloitte during the 1998 audit to assess the reasonableness of the client's inventory valuation reserve was to obtain and test an inventory "reserve analysis" prepared by a company vice president. This latter document was supposed to include the three classes of inventory items to which company policy required the lower of cost or market rule to be applied: (1) shoe styles for which the company had four or fewer pairs, (2) shoes and other apparel that were selling for less than cost, and (3) any inventory styles for which no items had been sold during the previous 12 months. The reserve analysis for 1998, however, excluded those inventory styles for which no sales had been made during the previous 12 months, an oversight that the Deloitte auditors never questioned or investigated. The Deloitte auditors also discovered that a large amount of inventory included in a Just for Feet warehouse had been excluded from the reserve analysis prepared by the company vice president. Again, the auditors chose not to question client personnel regarding this oversight.

After completing their inventory audit procedures, the Deloitte auditors concluded that Just for Feet's year-end reserve for inventory obsolescence was significantly understated. The SEC noted that this conclusion was reached by the Deloitte auditors despite the obvious deficiencies in audit procedures applied to Just for Feet's reserve for inventory obsolescence:

> *Even using the flawed inventory analysis provided by the Vice President and the deficient inventory information that excluded the goods from the New Jersey warehouse, the Respondents concluded that Just for Feet's obsolescence reserve should have been in the range of $441,000 to over $1 million.*

The Deloitte audit team proposed an audit adjustment to increase the reserve for inventory obsolescence by more than $400,000; however, the client rejected that audit adjustment, meaning that the year-end balance of that account remained at a meager $150,000.

Although not specifically identified as a "key audit risk area" during the 1998 audit, the Deloitte auditors focused considerable attention on Just for Feet's accounting decisions for the approximately $9 million of "booth income" the company recorded during that year. The Deloitte auditors discovered the monthly booth income journal entries recorded by Just for Feet during fiscal 1998 and prepared a workpaper documenting those entries. "An analysis at the end of the workpaper, which Baker reviewed, showed that the net effect of Just for Feet's booth-related journal entries was to increase assets with a corresponding increase in income. The Respondents [Deloitte, Barry, and Baker] performed no further analysis to determine the basis and propriety of these journal entries." Instead of independently investigating these entries, the Deloitte auditors accepted the representation of a Just for Feet executive who insisted that the entries had no effect on the company's net income. According to this executive, the monthly booth income amounts were offset by preexisting "co-op" or advertising credits that had been granted to Just for Feet by its major vendors. In other words, instead of using those advertising credits to reduce reported advertising expenses, Just for Feet was allegedly converting those credits into booth income or revenue amounts.

By the end of 1998, the bogus booth income journal entries had produced $9 million of nonexistent "booth assets" in Just for Feet's accounting records. Since "neither the Company nor the auditors had internal evidence supporting the recording of $9 million of booth assets," the Deloitte engagement team decided to corroborate the existence and ownership assertions for those assets by obtaining confirmations from the relevant Just for Feet vendors. These confirmations were prepared with the assistance of certain Just for Feet executives who were aware of the fraudulent nature of the booth income/booth assets amounts. Apparently, these executives contacted the vendor representatives to whom the confirmations were mailed and told them how to respond to the confirmations. The booth assets confirmations returned by the vendors to Deloitte were replete with errors and ambiguous statements. A frustrated audit senior who reviewed the confirmations brought this matter to the attention of both Barry and Baker.

> *An audit senior reviewed these confirmations and informed Barry and Baker that she was in some cases sending multiple confirmation requests to the vendors because many of their initial requests came back in forms different from that requested. The Respondents failed to discover from these indications that Just for Feet might not actually . . . [own] . . . the booths as claimed.*

---

## EPILOGUE

In February 2000, after realizing that Just for Feet was no longer salvageable, Helen Rockey began the process of liquidating the company under Chapter 7 of the federal bankruptcy code. Over the next few years, settlements were announced to a number of large lawsuits linked to the Just for Feet accounting fraud and the company's subsequent bankruptcy. Just for Feet's former executives and Deloitte were among the principal defendants in those lawsuits. One of those cases, a class-action lawsuit filed by Just for Feet's former stockholders, was settled for a reported $32.4 million in 2002.

Several of Just for Feet's former executives pleaded guilty to criminal charges for their roles in the company's massive accounting fraud. Among these individuals was Don-Allen Ruttenberg. In April 2005, a federal judge sentenced Ruttenberg to 20 months in federal prison and fined him $50,000. At the same time that the younger Ruttenberg's sentence was announced, a Department of Justice official reported that Harold Ruttenberg, who was gravely ill with brain cancer, would not be charged in the case. In January 2006, Harold Ruttenberg died at the age of 63.

Five executives of Just for Feet's former vendors also pleaded guilty to various criminal charges for providing false confirmations to the company's auditors. Most of these individuals, including Thomas Shine, received probationary sentences. An exception was Timothy McCool, the former director of apparel sales for Adidas, who received a four-month "noncustodial" sentence. While sentencing McCool, U.S. District Judge C. Lynwood Smith, Jr., noted, "Life is so fragile. A single bad choice in a single moment can cause a life to turn irrevocably 180 degrees. I think that is where you find yourself."[10]

Arguably, the party to the Just for Feet scandal that received the most condemnation from the courts and the business press was Deloitte. In April 2005, the SEC berated the prominent accounting firm for the poor quality of its Just for Feet audits in *Accounting and Auditing Enforcement Release No. 2238*. In that same enforcement release, the SEC fined Deloitte $375,000 and suspended Steven Barry from serving on audit engagements involving SEC registrants for two years; Karen Baker received a one-year suspension.

On the same date that the SEC announced the sanctions that it had imposed on Deloitte for its Just for Feet audits, the federal agency also revealed the sanctions that Deloitte received for its allegedly deficient audits of a large telecommunications company, Adelphia Communications. Similar to Just for Feet, the once high-flying Adelphia had suddenly collapsed in 2002 following revelations that its previously issued financial statements that had been audited by Deloitte were riddled with errors. The SEC stunned the public accounting profession by fining Deloitte $50 million for its role in the huge Adelphia scandal, which was easily the largest fine ever imposed on an accounting firm by the federal agency.

Shortly after the SEC announced the sanctions that it had levied on Deloitte for its Just for Feet and Adelphia Communications audits, James Quigley, Deloitte's CEO, issued a press release responding to those sanctions. Quigley noted in his press release that, "Among our most significant challenges is the early detection of fraud, particularly when the client, its management and others collude specifically to deceive a company's auditors."[11] This statement infuriated SEC officials. An SEC spokesperson responded to Quigley's press release by stating that, "Deloitte was not deceived in this case. The findings in the order show that the relevant information was right in front of their eyes. Deloitte just didn't do its job, plain and simple. They didn't miss red flags. They pulled the flag over their head and claimed they couldn't see."[12]

The SEC also suggested that Quigley's press release violated the terms of the agreement that the agency had reached with Deloitte in settling the Just for Feet and Adelphia cases. Under the terms of that agreement, Deloitte was not required to "admit" to the SEC's findings, nor was it allowed to "deny" those findings. Deloitte subsequently rescinded Quigley's press release and issued another that eliminated some, but not all, of the statements that had offended the SEC.

## Questions

1. Prepare common-sized balance sheets and income statements for Just for Feet for the period 1996–1998. Also compute key liquidity, solvency, activity, and profitability ratios for 1997 and 1998. Given these data, comment on what you believe were the high-risk financial statement items for the 1998 Just for Feet audit.
2. Just for Feet operated large, high-volume retail stores. Identify internal control risks common to such businesses. How should these risks affect the audit planning decisions for such a client?

10. *The Associated Press State & Local Wire*, "Adidas America Executive Sentenced in Just for Feet Case," 22 March 2004.

11. S. Laub, "Deloitte Statement Irks SEC," *CFO.com*, 28 April 2005.

12. S. Hughes, "SEC Rebukes Deloitte over Spin of Adelphia Audit," *The Associated Press State & Local Wire*, 27 April 2005.

3. Just for Feet operated in an extremely competitive industry, or sub-industry. Identify inherent risk factors common to businesses facing such competitive conditions. How should these risks affect the audit planning decisions for such a client?
4. Prepare a comprehensive list, in a bullet format, of the audit risk factors present for the 1998 Just for Feet audit. Identify the five audit risk factors that you believe were most critical to the successful completion of that audit. Rank these risk factors from least to most important and be prepared to defend your rankings. Briefly explain whether or not you believe that the Deloitte auditors responded appropriately to the five critical audit risk factors that you identified.
5. Put yourself in the position of Thomas Shine in this case. How would you have responded when Don-Allen Ruttenberg asked you to send a false confirmation to Deloitte & Touche? Before responding, identify the parties who will be affected by your decision.

**CASE 1.3**

# AMRE, Inc.

In the popular movie *The Tin Men* released in 1987, Richard Dreyfus and Danny DeVito portray aluminum siding salesmen during the early 1960s. The two competitors use every means possible to obtain an unfair advantage over each other. Like other aluminum siding salesmen, the key to success for Dreyfus and DeVito is obtaining and vigorously pursuing "leads," or indications of interest from potential customers. Leads are not only a key success factor for home siding companies but also figure prominently in many of these firms' accounting and control systems. Take the case of AMRE, Inc., a firm that for nearly two decades sold home siding and interior refurnishing products such as cabinet countertops. AMRE, short for American Remodeling, began operations in 1980 in Irving, Texas, home of the Dallas Cowboys. Within a few years, the fast-growing firm ranked as the largest company in the home siding industry, an industry historically dominated by small businesses that market their services in one metropolitan area. In 1987, AMRE went public and listed its common stock on the New York Stock Exchange.

AMRE's principal operating expenses were advertising costs incurred to identify potential leads via direct mail and television commercials. Throughout the 1980s, AMRE charged a portion of its advertising costs each year to a deferred expense account. AMRE justified this accounting treatment by maintaining that these advertising costs benefited future periods. Each accounting period, AMRE divided its total advertising costs by the number of new leads generated that period. AMRE then multiplied the resulting "cost per lead" by the total number of "unset leads," that is, new leads that had not yet been pursued, to determine the amount of advertising costs to defer. The firm charged the remaining advertising costs for that period to its advertising expense account.

AMRE created a computer-based "lead bank" during the mid-1980s. When a potential customer contacted AMRE, a clerk collected and then entered information in the lead bank that could be used to develop an appropriate sales pitch for that individual. This information included variables such as age, income, home market value, and length of residency. Data for each sales presentation were also entered in the lead bank. This information allowed AMRE to evaluate each salesperson's performance by computing measures such as sales as a percentage of appointments, cancellation rate, and average dollar sales per appointment. The control functions and data provided by AMRE's computerized lead bank contributed significantly to the company's early success in the intensely competitive home siding industry.

## Accounting for "Leads" Leads to Trouble

When AMRE went public in February 1987, the company's top officers gave optimistic revenue and profit projections to financial analysts tracking the firm. (At the time, AMRE's fiscal year ran from May 1 of one year until April 30 of the next. The company's first fiscal year as a public company, fiscal 1988, ended April 30, 1988.) As the end of AMRE's first quarter as a public company approached, July 31, 1987, the net income projected for that quarter earlier in the year was clearly unattainable.

Robert Levin, an AMRE executive and major stockholder, feared that AMRE's stock price would drop sharply if the company failed to reach its forecasted earnings for the first quarter of fiscal 1988. Levin, a CPA since 1972, served as the company's principal financial officer and held the titles of executive vice-president, treasurer, and chief operating officer. To inflate AMRE's net income for the first quarter of fiscal 1988, Levin instructed the company's chief accounting officer, Dennie D. Brown, to overstate the number of unset leads in AMRE's computerized lead bank.[1] Brown, in turn, instructed Walter W. Richardson, the company's vice-president of data processing who had served as AMRE's controller in the early 1980s, to enter fictitious unset leads in the lead bank. Entering the fictitious leads in the lead bank caused a disproportionate amount of AMRE's advertising costs for the first quarter of 1988 to be deferred rather than expensed. This accounting scam allowed AMRE to overstate its pretax income for that quarter by approximately $1 million, or by nearly 50 percent.

Once corporate executives misrepresent their firm's operating results for one accounting period, the temptation to manipulate its operating results in later periods becomes difficult to resist. In the second quarter of fiscal 1988, AMRE's executives again inflated the company's unset leads to understate the firm's advertising expenses.

During the third and fourth quarters of fiscal 1988, AMRE's actual operating results again fell far short of expectations. At this point, Levin decided to expand the scope of the accounting fraud. In addition to overstating unset leads, Levin instructed his subordinates to overstate AMRE's ending inventory for the third and fourth quarters of fiscal 1988. Richardson complied by entering fictitious inventory in AMRE's computerized inventory records and by preparing bogus inventory count sheets that were later submitted to the company's Price Waterhouse auditors.

Levin also instructed AMRE's accounting personnel to overstate the company's revenue for the third and fourth quarters of fiscal 1988. AMRE used the percentage-of-completion method to recognize revenue on unfinished installation jobs at the end of an accounting period. To overstate the revenue booked on unfinished projects at the end of fiscal 1988, AMRE grossly overstated their percentage of completion. In fact, AMRE recognized revenue at the end of fiscal 1988 on customer projects that had not been started.

AMRE reported a pretax income of $12.2 million in its fiscal 1988 financial statements. A subsequent investigation by the Securities and Exchange Commission (SEC) revealed that AMRE's actual pretax income for that year was less than 50 percent of the reported figure. Before AMRE filed its 1988 10-K with the SEC, Levin met with AMRE's chief executive officer and chairman of the board, Steven D. Bedowitz. At this meeting, Levin admitted to Bedowitz for the first time that illicit accounting methods had been used to overstate AMRE's reported profit for 1988. According to the SEC's investigation, Bedowitz "concurred with these efforts to improperly increase AMRE's earnings."[2]

Bedowitz and Levin signed the "Letter to Shareholders" included in AMRE's 1988 annual report. That letter began with the following greeting: "We are proud

1. The information reported in this case was drawn principally from a series of enforcement releases issued by the Securities and Exchange Commission (SEC) in the early 1990s. The individuals involved in this case neither admitted nor denied the facts as represented by the SEC.

2. Securities and Exchange Commission, *Accounting and Auditing Enforcement Release No. 356*, 2 March 1992.

to announce that fiscal 1988 was another record year for AMRE in both earnings and revenues." In a subsequent AMRE annual report, Levin recalled how he had met Bedowitz in 1981, several years before Levin accepted an executive position with AMRE. At the time, Levin worked for a building materials company that was an AMRE supplier.

> *We discovered that we were very much alike. We both had a lot of energy, ambition, and dreams. Our partnership was inevitable.*[3]

Price Waterhouse issued an unqualified opinion on AMRE's financial statements for fiscal 1988. Nevertheless, a financial analyst for *The New York Times* questioned the credibility of those financial statements.[4] The analyst pointed out that AMRE's use of the percentage-of-completion accounting method seemed unusual. Businesses typically use the percentage-of-completion method to recognize revenue on projects that take several months, if not years, to complete. AMRE's installation jobs required only a few days to complete. Even more troubling to the analyst was the three weeks of "unbilled revenues" that AMRE had recognized on unfinished installation jobs near the end of 1988. That figure seemed excessive since AMRE's average time to complete an installation job was one week. The analyst also questioned AMRE's advertising expense figure by pointing out that the company's deferred advertising costs had been rising rapidly. In summary, the analyst bluntly challenged the integrity of AMRE's financial statements.

> *To short-sellers, it looks like a classic pattern of inflating revenues and understating expenses, a pattern that often ends in a write-off. Mr. Wesselman [an AMRE spokesperson] said the company's accounting practices were proper and were periodically reviewed with outside auditors.*[5]

## AMRE's 1989 Fiscal Year

During fiscal 1989, AMRE's executives became increasingly concerned that their indiscretions would be discovered. In the third quarter of that year, the conspirators decided to end the accounting fraud. The executives met regularly to discuss how best to terminate the fraud without raising the suspicions of the firm's Price Waterhouse auditors and other parties. One method the executives settled on was to transfer fictitious assets in AMRE's accounting records to the firm's Decks division. That division's principal line of business was building backyard decks on residential homes. Company officials had already decided to eliminate the Decks division. By transferring approximately $3 million of fictitious assets to that division, AMRE "buried" the write-offs of those assets in the discontinued operations section of its 1989 income statement. AMRE booked these write-offs principally during the third quarter of fiscal 1989.

Company executives wrote off approximately $5 million of additional fictitious assets as losses or expenses in the fourth quarter of fiscal 1989 via adjusting entries. These write-offs and those of the previous quarter resulted in AMRE reporting a net loss of nearly $6 million for 1989. Exhibit 1 summarizes key financial data included in AMRE's 1989 annual report for the five-year period 1985–1989.

---

3. AMRE, Inc., 1989 Annual Report, 11.
4. F. Norris, "AMRE Drawing Short Sellers," *The New York Times*, 19 December 1988, D8.
5. *Ibid.*

**EXHIBIT 1**

KEY FINANCIAL DATA FOR AMRE, INC., 1985–1989 (IN THOUSANDS)

| | Year Ended April 30, | | | | |
|---|---|---|---|---|---|
| | 1989 | 1988 | 1987 | 1986 | 1985 |
| Contract revenues | $183,885 | $121,033 | $72,187 | $39,575 | $22,451 |
| Contract costs | 64,702 | 41,369 | 25,017 | 15,275 | 9,259 |
| Gross profit | 119,183 | 79,664 | 47,170 | 24,300 | 13,192 |
| Operating income | 1,602 | 9,983 | 6,153 | 1,516 | 661 |
| Net income | (5,744) | 7,298 | 2,907 | 878 | 414 |
| Working capital | 11,719 | 15,307 | 13,236 | 40 | 175 |
| Total assets | 50,399 | 34,113 | 23,527 | 7,239 | 2,471 |
| Stockholders' equity | 27,174 | 23,565 | 16,895 | 1,334 | 456 |

## The Role of AMRE's New CFO in Terminating the Accounting Fraud

In March 1989, near the end of AMRE's fourth quarter of fiscal 1989, AMRE hired Mac M. Martirossian to serve as the company's chief accounting officer. Martirossian, a CPA since 1976, had more than 10 years of public accounting experience with the Dallas office of Price Waterhouse, which performed AMRE's annual audits. In July 1989, Martirossian assumed the title of chief financial officer (CFO). Levin, who had essentially served as AMRE's CFO for several years, retained the titles of executive vice-president, treasurer, and chief operating officer.

While becoming acquainted with AMRE's accounting system in his first few weeks with the firm, Martirossian discovered numerous accounting entries that lacked adequate documentation. Martirossian immediately began investigating this obvious internal control problem. No doubt, AMRE's top executives realized that the inquisitive accountant would eventually "put two and two together." So, they decided to reveal the fraud to Martirossian. (Recognize that by this point the executives had already begun terminating the fraud.)

The startling confession made by his new colleagues stunned Martirossian. On April 28, 1989, just two days before the end of fiscal 1989, Martirossian called a meeting with the executives involved in the fraud. At this meeting, he insisted that the misstatements remaining in the company's accounting records be immediately corrected. If the corrections were not made, Martirossian threatened to resign.

> *Martirossian further stated that he would hold himself responsible for the company's financial statements for periods after fiscal 1989, but that the scheme's participants would be responsible for correcting the misstatements in the periods to which they related, and for addressing any questions [from AMRE's independent auditors and other parties] arising from the corrections.*[6]

Bedowitz acquiesced to Martirossian's demands. Initially, the two men decided to correct AMRE's accounting records with a large prior period adjustment. In a matter of days, this plan backfired. Outside directors on AMRE's board became aware of the prior period adjustment and began questioning why it was necessary. At this point, AMRE's executives, including Martirossian, met to consider other alternatives for correcting the company's accounting records. The executives decided that the

6. Securities and Exchange Commission, *Accounting and Auditing Enforcement Release No. 394*, 30 June 1992.

remaining errors in AMRE's accounting records would be written off against the operating results of the fourth quarter of fiscal 1989 via period-ending adjusting entries, as discussed earlier.

Shortly after the end of fiscal 1989, Martirossian attended several meetings between AMRE's top executives and representatives of Price Waterhouse. At these meetings, the large accounting adjustments made by AMRE during the fourth quarter of fiscal 1989 were discussed. According to the SEC, Martirossian sat silently while other company executives provided false explanations to Price Waterhouse regarding the large adjustments.

The efforts of his colleagues to mislead the Price Waterhouse auditors troubled Martirossian. Before Price Waterhouse completed its 1989 audit of AMRE, Martirossian arranged a confidential meeting at a local hotel with key Price Waterhouse personnel assigned to the AMRE audit. Martirossian had become well acquainted with several of these individuals during the 10 years he worked for Price Waterhouse's Dallas office.

> *At this meeting, Martirossian expressed a high level of anxiety regarding the audit, and he specifically stated that a portion of the adjustments "did not pass the smell test." Further, he also posed questions to the auditors that linked seemingly unrelated audit issues and events to the adjustments in an attempt to direct the auditors to the undisclosed scheme [accounting fraud].*[7]

Although he hinted strongly to the auditors that AMRE's fourth-quarter write-offs were suspicious, Martirossian never revealed the true nature or purpose of those adjustments. Price Waterhouse ultimately accepted the large fourth-quarter adjustments before issuing an unqualified opinion on AMRE's 1989 financial statements.

Following the completion of the 1989 audit, Martirossian signed a letter of representations addressed to Price Waterhouse. This letter indicated that he and other key AMRE executives were not aware of any irregularities that would materially affect the accuracy of the company's financial statements.

During fiscal 1990, Martirossian undertook an extensive effort to improve AMRE's accounting and financial reporting functions. This effort included implementing several measures to strengthen the company's internal control system. Martirossian also searched the company's accounting records for any remaining errors and reviewed the company's accounting policies to ensure that they were being properly applied.

## The Fraud Is Disclosed Publicly

In 1990, the SEC revealed that it was investigating AMRE's financial statements for the previous few years. *The New York Times* article in late 1988 that challenged AMRE's financial data prompted that investigation. In early 1991, AMRE formed a special committee consisting of three outside members of its board to scrutinize the company's financial affairs. Following the report of this committee, AMRE publicly revealed that its financial statements for each year 1987 through 1990, but principally 1988 and 1989, contained material errors. AMRE restated its financial statements for each of those years. From early 1992 through mid-1994, the SEC issued several enforcement releases disclosing the results of its lengthy investigation of AMRE's accounting fraud.[8]

---

7. *Ibid.*

8. AMRE's financial condition continued to deteriorate during the mid-1990s. In 1997, the company ceased operations and filed for involuntary bankruptcy.

Each of the AMRE executives who actively participated in the fraud, including Bedowitz, Levin, Brown, and Richardson, agreed to an SEC consent order. The executives neither admitted nor denied their alleged roles in the fraud but pledged not to violate federal securities laws in the future. Levin and Brown also forfeited proceeds they had received from the sale of AMRE stock while the fraud was in progress. This feature of the agreement required Brown to pay approximately $16,000 to the federal government. Levin paid nearly $1.8 million to the federal government, including a $500,000 fine for violating the provisions of the Insider Trading Sanctions Act.

In November 1991, *The Wall Street Journal* reported that Bedowitz, Levin, and AMRE, Inc., had reached an agreement to settle a large class action lawsuit filed by AMRE's stockholders.[9] This agreement required the two former AMRE executives to contribute approximately $8.8 million to a settlement pool. AMRE, Inc., contributed another $5.9 million to that pool.

Martirossian reached an agreement with the SEC similar to the agreement made by the federal agency with the other AMRE executives. However, the federal agency issued a separate enforcement release describing Martirossian's role in the fraud. The SEC criticized Martirossian for not insisting that proper measures be taken to correct AMRE's accounting records and for not disclosing the fraud to Price Waterhouse.

*Martirossian's non-participation in the original fraudulent scheme cannot justify his actions in turning a blind eye to the methods utilized by AMRE to correct the material misstatements . . . Although he expressed concern and posed questions to AMRE's auditors in an attempt to expose the existence of the scheme to them, Martirossian's effort to discharge his duty to make accurate and complete disclosure to AMRE's auditors was ineffectual and misleading because he failed to provide the auditors all of the information he possessed.*[10]

## SEC Investigates Price Waterhouse's 1988 and 1989 AMRE Audits

After the SEC finished dealing with AMRE's executives, the federal agency turned its attention to the company's independent audit firm, Price Waterhouse. The SEC focused on the conduct of two members of the AMRE audit engagement team, Edward J. Smith and Joel E. Reed. Smith served as AMRE's audit engagement partner, while Reed was a senior audit manager assigned to the AMRE audits.

Among the SEC's complaints lodged against Price Waterhouse was that the audit firm failed to properly test AMRE's deferred advertising expenses. Recall that AMRE computed the advertising costs to be deferred for a given accounting period by multiplying the "cost per lead" for that period by the number of "unset leads" at the end of the period. One method AMRE used to inflate its reported profits was to create fictitious unset leads. Staff auditors of Price Waterhouse assigned to the AMRE engagement verified the cost-per-lead computation during the 1988 audit. However, the staff auditors failed to adequately test the number of unset leads reported by AMRE at the end of fiscal 1988. The auditors simply compared the number of unset leads on two client-prepared schedules.

9. K. Blumenthal, "AMRE, Ex-Officers Agree to Settlement of Stockholder Lawsuit," *The Wall Street Journal*, 12 November 1991, A13.

10. Securities and Exchange Commission, *Accounting and Auditing Enforcement Release No. 394*, 30 June 1992.

*The audit of the unset leads deferral was flawed because no procedures were performed to verify the integrity of the reports on which the audit relied. In fact, the reports were not supported by underlying data. Although the number of unset leads supposedly had increased during the year by over 200% (from 10,438 to 31,580), the audit relied on AMRE's summary reports.*[11]

Price Waterhouse's audit planning memorandum for the 1988 AMRE audit indicated that EDP audit procedures would be used to test the integrity of AMRE's lead bank. AMRE executives involved in the accounting fraud feared that these procedures would result in detection of the fictitious leads in the lead bank. These executives persuaded Smith and Reed to bypass the EDP tests.

AMRE also inflated its reported profits by overstating year-end inventory. During fiscal 1988, AMRE's inventory increased by 213 percent, while sales increased 68 percent and inventory purchases increased 66 percent. The 1988 AMRE audit planning memorandum identified the large increase in inventory as a key risk factor. The audit planning memorandum also pointed out that AMRE did not use a perpetual inventory system, meaning that the year-end inventory quantities would be determined by a physical count.

Price Waterhouse's initial audit plan for 1988 called for the observation of the client's physical inventory counts at 11 of 26 inventory sites. The previous year, Price Waterhouse had visited nine of 22 inventory sites during the physical counts. Client management complained that the increase in the number of inventory sites to be observed by Price Waterhouse would materially increase the cost of the 1988 audit. AMRE's executives convinced Price Waterhouse to allow AMRE accounting personnel to monitor the physical counts at three of the inventory sites that the auditors had selected for observation. According to the SEC's investigation, AMRE management inflated the year-end inventory of each of the 18 inventory sites not observed at year-end by Price Waterhouse. These inventory sites included the three sites where AMRE accounting personnel observed the physical counts. In total, AMRE overstated its 1988 year-end inventory by $1.4 million.

During the third and fourth quarters of fiscal 1989, AMRE began writing off its fictitious assets. Recall that AMRE's executives concealed several million dollars of such write-offs in the losses booked for the discontinued Decks division. The Price Waterhouse auditors reviewed the large losses stemming from the elimination of AMRE's Decks division during fiscal 1989. However, according to the SEC, the Price Waterhouse auditors accepted the client's explanations for these losses without applying any "meaningful audit procedures" to them.[12]

While writing off fictitious assets during the fourth quarter of 1989, AMRE purged 17,000 bogus unset leads from the computerized lead bank. The average cost of these leads was $108.33, meaning that the total loss related to their write-off exceeded $1.8 million. A Price Waterhouse staff auditor asked an AMRE accountant why the large number of unset leads was being dropped from the lead bank. The accountant responded that the unset leads had been improperly recorded due to an "accounting control weakness." In the audit workpapers, the staff auditor concluded, based on the AMRE accountant's statement, that this "weakness" was an "isolated incident" that did not require further investigation.[13] Smith and Reed concurred with the staff

---

11. Securities and Exchange Commission, *Accounting and Auditing Enforcement Release No. 554*, 26 April 1994.

12. *Ibid.*

13. *Ibid.*

auditor's assessment and did not require any further audit procedures to be applied to the large adjustment.

The SEC also questioned Price Waterhouse's review of the quarterly financial data included in AMRE's 1989 10-K registration statement. Near the end of the 1989 audit, Smith recommended that AMRE disclose in the 10-K the large period-ending accounting adjustments that were largely responsible for the company's net loss for fiscal 1989. AMRE's executives refused. After reconsidering the matter, Smith noted in the audit workpapers that the fourth quarter adjustments did not need to be disclosed separately.

> *Smith concluded that the adjustments did not require disclosure because "the quarterly data is not part of the financial statements and the disclosure is informative only . . . the magnitude of the adjustments is not sufficient to cause us to require them to do it [that is, disclose the adjustments]."*[14]

A key factor that reportedly influenced Smith and Reed's decisions to accept AMRE's questionable accounting treatments was their familiarity with Martirossian, a former colleague of theirs in the Dallas office of Price Waterhouse. According to the SEC, Smith and Reed "relied improperly on his [Martirossian's] unverified representations based upon their prior experience with him and his reputation for integrity within Price Waterhouse."[15]

In an enforcement release issued in April 1994, the SEC concluded that Smith and Reed had failed to comply with generally accepted auditing standards during the 1988 and 1989 AMRE audits. As a result, the SEC prohibited Smith and Reed from being assigned to audits of SEC registrants for nine months.

## Questions

1. Define the terms *ethics* and *professional ethics*. Using the following scale, evaluate the conduct of each individual involved in this case.

| −100 . . . . . . . . . 0 . . . . . . . . . 100 | |
|---|---|
| Highly Unethical | Highly Ethical |

2. Do you believe that the individuals who behaved unethically in this case were appropriately punished? Defend your answer.
3. Identify the alternative courses of action available to Martirossian when he became aware of the accounting fraud at AMRE. Assume the role of Martirossian. Which of these alternatives would you have chosen? Why?
4. Was AMRE's practice of deferring a portion of its advertising costs in an asset account appropriate? Defend your answer.

---

14. *Ibid.*
15. *Ibid.*

5. What key red flags, or audit risk factors, were present during the 1988 and 1989 AMRE audits? Did Price Waterhouse appropriately consider these factors in planning those audits? Why or why not?
6. Was Price Waterhouse justified during the 1988 audit in agreeing to allow client personnel to observe the physical counts at certain inventory sites? To what extent should an audit client be allowed to influence key audit planning decisions?
7. *SAS No. 31*, "Evidential Matter," identifies five management assertions that underlie a set of financial statements. Which of these assertions should have been of most concern to Price Waterhouse regarding the large period-ending adjustments AMRE recorded during the fourth quarter of fiscal 1989?
8. What responsibility do auditors have for quarterly financial information reported in the footnotes to a client's audited financial statements?

**CASE 1.4**

# ESM Government Securities, Inc.

Cuban-born Jose Gomez emigrated to Miami in 1961. Only thirteen at the time and fatherless, Gomez obtained a job sacking groceries in a neighborhood supermarket to help his mother pay the bills. The young man's work ethic and cheerful personality made him a favorite of his superiors and the store's customers. A few years later, Gomez landed a job as a grocery buyer, a job that he used to finance an accounting degree at the University of Miami. Following graduation, Gomez entered public accounting with the hopes of becoming a partner of a major accounting firm.

On August 1, 1979, Jose Gomez achieved his long-sought goal when he was named a partner with Alexander Grant & Company, the tenth largest CPA firm in the United States at the time. Only 31-years-old, Gomez was recognized by his fellow partners as an individual who would likely rise to the upper management ranks of Alexander Grant during his career. Gomez's bright future with Grant seemed even more assured when he was named the managing partner of the firm's Fort Lauderdale office while he was still in his early thirties. Unfortunately, Gomez never realized his potential. In March 1987, he began serving a 12-year sentence in a federal prison in Tallahassee, Florida, after pleading guilty to forgery and fraud charges.

Ironically, Gomez's fate was sealed just a few days following his promotion to partner. During a lunch with Alan Novick, an officer of his largest audit client, Gomez was startled by Novick's admission that the client's audited financial statements for the prior two years contained material errors. The client, ESM Government Securities, Inc., a Fort Lauderdale brokerage firm specializing in government securities, had several million dollars in losses that Novick had concealed from Gomez and his subordinates on the ESM audit team. Novick reminded Gomez that he had personally authorized the unqualified opinions on ESM's 1977 and 1978 financial statements. Disclosure of the large errors in those financial statements might jeopardize Gomez's career.

According to Gomez, Novick repeatedly goaded him with comments such as, "It's going to look terrible for you . . . and you just got promoted to partner."[1] Novick maintained that he could recoup the losses he had concealed from Alexander Grant if Gomez would not withdraw the audit opinions on ESM's 1977 and 1978 financial statements. If Gomez insisted on withdrawing the audit opinions, Novick warned him that ESM would fail and that several parties would suffer as a result, including Gomez and ESM's customers. Eventually, Gomez succumbed to Novick's persuasive arguments.[2]

When Novick made his startling confession to Gomez, he was aware that the audit partner was experiencing financial problems. Although Gomez earned a sizable salary as a partner of a major CPA firm, that salary was not sufficient to support his affluent lifestyle. After Gomez agreed to remain silent regarding the ESM fraud, Novick offered to help relieve his financial problems. In November 1979, Novick

---

1. M. Brannigan, "Auditor's Downfall Shows A Man Caught in Trap of His Own Making," *The Wall Street Journal*, 4 March 1987, 33.

2. Former colleagues at Alexander Grant maintain that Gomez's account of his involvement with Novick is not totally accurate. For instance, certain of Gomez's former colleagues suggest that he knew of the ESM fraud prior to 1979.

issued Gomez a $20,000 check to cover past-due credit card bills. The following year, after Gomez complained of his worsening financial condition, Novick gave him an additional $60,000. Court records document that during the seven-year ESM fraud, Gomez received approximately $200,000 from ESM officials. Gomez later acknowledged that his personal ambition and greed blinded him to the high ethical standards he had learned earlier in life.

> *I was a young man in a hurry. I needed more money than I was making. I wanted nice clothes for my wife. I had to have a nice home, be seen at the right places. Take a trip to the Super Bowl. Do whatever was necessary to further my career. Use the plastic, the credit cards. When the plastic limit was reached, borrow and pay off the balances. Then use the plastic again.*[3]

If Gomez actually believed, as he later alleged, that ignoring the misrepresentations in ESM's financial statements was the best alternative for all parties concerned, he was wrong. The relatively small unreported losses in the 1977 and 1978 ESM financial statements ballooned to collective losses of more than $300 million by the spring of 1985. Most financial scandals affect only the stockholders and creditors of one company. Not so with the ESM scandal. Public disclosure of the ESM fraud was the first domino to topple in a series of events that eventually rocked both the national and international financial markets.

ESM owed its largest customer, Home State Savings, an Ohio bank, approximately $145 million when the brokerage firm ceased operations in March 1985. Home State Savings happened to be the largest of the more than 70 banks in Ohio whose deposits were not insured by the Federal Deposit Insurance Corporation. These banks had formed their own private deposit insurance fund into which each paid annual premiums. Home State's collapse following ESM's closure caused panic-stricken depositors to trigger runs on the other privately insured Ohio banks. Within a matter of days, the governor of Ohio was forced to close all of the state's privately insured banks while state and federal regulatory authorities worked around the clock to contain the economic fallout from the ESM scandal. The closure of the Ohio banks and a growing loss of confidence in the government securities market destabilized all of the nation's capital markets. At the peak of the crisis, the U.S. dollar plunged 14 percent in value in the international markets in one day as foreign investors became concerned that the entire U.S. banking system might be jeopardized.

The impact of the ESM scandal was not restricted to the state of Ohio and the financial markets. Besides Home State Savings, ESM's major customers included municipalities scattered across the nation. Collectively, ESM owed these municipalities more than $100 million. When the news of the ESM insolvency broke, the credit ratings of those municipalities plummeted, and many were forced to take immediate and drastic measures to remain solvent. One example was the city of Beaumont, Texas, which laid off approximately 15 percent of its municipal employees following ESM's closure.

Among the parties most victimized by the ESM fraud were Gomez's colleagues, his fellow partners at Alexander Grant. A proud and respected firm nationwide, Alexander Grant suddenly became the focus of intense and adverse publicity. The poor judgment of one partner cost the firm much of the credibility and prestige it had earned over its 60-year history. Alexander Grant, its successor firm, Grant Thornton, and the company that provided the firms' malpractice insurance eventually absorbed $200 million of legal judgments and out-of-court settlements stemming from the ESM debacle.

3. J. Russell, "Pride Led to Fall, ESM Auditor Says," *The Miami Herald*, 15 February 1987, 1A.

## History of ESM Government Securities

Ronnie Ewton, Bobby Seneca, and George Mead founded ESM Government Securities, Inc., in November 1975 with a total capitalization of $75,000. ESM's principal line of business was buying and selling for customer accounts debt securities issued by the federal government and its various agencies. Ewton, who had a long and checkered career with several brokerage firms, was ESM's principal executive. Ewton hired a close friend, Steve Arky, to serve as the firm's legal counsel, and Alan Novick, a Wall Street investment banker who later corrupted Jose Gomez, to be the firm's principal securities trader.[4]

In the mid-1970s, the U.S. government securities market was subject to minimal regulatory oversight, although it was, and still is today, the world's largest securities market. Until the mid-1970s, large brokerage firms accounted for nearly all of the daily sales volume of U.S. government securities. The tremendous growth in the national debt during the Carter and Reagan administrations forced the U.S. Treasury Department to begin working with so-called secondary dealers to raise the funds necessary to operate the federal government. Secondary dealers are generally small brokerage houses that trade federal debt securities for the accounts of small to moderately sized banks and municipalities. Prior to legislation enacted in the late 1980s, such brokers were subject only to the regulatory oversight of state securities commissions. These state agencies tend to be severely underfunded and relatively ineffective as a result.

An intriguing aspect of the government securities markets is the degree of leverage available to investors. The Federal Reserve Board establishes margin requirements for a wide range of securities investments. In recent years, the margin requirement for investments in most equity securities has been 50 percent, meaning that an investor must put up at least one dollar for every two dollars in stock purchased. Because of the huge amount of funds that the federal government must raise, the Federal Reserve Board establishes much more liberal margin requirements for the government securities market. An investor who purchases government securities is generally required to make a down payment equal to only 10 percent of the total cost of those securities. Because the market value of government securities may move several percentage points in any one day in response to fractional changes in market interest rates, an investor can easily have his or her initial cash investment in such securities wiped out in a few days. On the other hand, a lucky or skillful investor who successfully forecasts a change in interest rates may see the value of an initial investment in government securities increase dramatically over a short period of time.

Most of ESM's transactions were repurchase agreements, more commonly known as "repos." In a repo transaction, a government securities dealer sells a customer a block of federal securities and then simultaneously pledges to repurchase those securities at a later date at an agreed-upon price. The brokerage firm selling the securities hopes that their value will rise over the period of the repurchase agreement, which may be as short as 12 hours (overnight) or as long as 12 months. In substance, a repo transaction is a short-term loan from the customer to the securities dealer. ESM also engaged in a limited number of "reverse repos." In these transactions, ESM purchased government securities from a customer who simultaneously agreed to repurchase the securities at a later date at a predetermined price. Reverse repos were essentially loans made by ESM to another party.

In repo transactions, the purchaser should either take physical possession of the government securities or have a bonded third party assume physical possession. If the purchaser does not take physical possession of the securities, an unscrupulous

---

4. For an excellent and comprehensive history of the ESM scandal, see D.L. Maggin, *Bankers, Builders, Knaves and Thieves* (Chicago: Contemporary Books, 1989).

broker can sell them to another customer. Unfortunately, many of the banks and municipalities with which ESM did business were not familiar with the government securities market. These customers naively relied on ESM to retain the securities they purchased or asked the brokerage firm to transfer the securities to a segregated account with a trust company for the term of the repurchase agreement. Even when instructed to transfer customer securities to a trust company, ESM often retained the securities, which allowed ESM officials to use the securities for whatever purpose they chose.

Besides making securities trades with customers, ESM also engaged in purely speculative transactions in which it attempted to predict and profit from future changes in market interest rates. Soon after joining ESM, Novick convinced Ewton that he could earn millions of dollars in profits for ESM in speculative securities trades. Novick intended to produce these profits by making effective use of the considerable leverage afforded by the small margin requirements in the government securities market. Unfortunately, Novick was less than proficient in predicting future movements of interest rates. Over a short period in 1980, Novick lost more than $80 million when interest rates surged upward a few weeks after he had gambled that they would fall.

The trading losses suffered by Novick in 1980, when coupled with the much smaller pre-1980 trading losses he had rung up, easily wiped out the equity of ESM's three owners. At this point, the owners could either publicly admit that their firm was bankrupt or employ on a much larger scale a practice they had begun a few years earlier: using (stealing) customer securities for their own benefit. Sadly, Ewton and his colleagues chose the latter alternative.

Although ESM was insolvent by 1980, the firm managed to remain in business for several more years because of the huge sums of cash it acquired in repo transactions with customers. An accountant hired to reconstruct the history of the ESM fraud noted that cash flow, not profit, was the lifeblood of ESM. "The name of the game was cash flow. It had nothing to do with profit. As long as there was an ability to deliver enough cash, then whether or not the transactions made money was not relevant."[5] One of ESM's primary sources of cash was fraudulent sales of securities. The firm often sold large blocks of federal securities to several different customers, since most of its clients did not take physical possession of the securities they purchased. The positive cash flow produced by this and other fraudulent practices allowed Novick to continue "playing the market" in an increasingly desperate effort to recoup the millions he had gambled away on earlier trades.

## ESM's Bookkeeping Scam

In 1977, Ronnie Ewton delegated the responsibility for concealing ESM's unreported trading losses to Alan Novick. The key challenge Novick faced was designing a scheme that would prevent Jose Gomez and the other Alexander Grant auditors from discovering the unreported losses during the annual audits of ESM's financial records. ESM Government Securities was just one of several companies controlled by Ewton and his associates. The other companies were "shells" with no express business purpose and were not audited by Alexander Grant. Novick decided to use these nonoperating entities to hide ESM's unreported trading losses.

Novick devised a bookkeeping charade to transfer trading losses incurred by ESM to an affiliated company under the ESM corporate umbrella. Novick routinely recorded a "mirror" intercompany transaction for ESM's repo and reverse repo transactions.

5. Unless noted otherwise, this and subsequent quotations were taken from the following source: U.S. Congress, House, Subcommittee on Oversight and Investigations of the Committee on Energy and Commerce, *SEC and Corporate Audits, Part 2* (Washington, D.C.: U.S. Government Printing Office, 1985).

If the actual transaction with a customer was a repo, the mirror transaction would be a reverse repo, and vice versa. By covering both sides of a transaction, Novick could close out the "losing" side to the unaudited affiliate and close out the profitable side to ESM, ensuring that the latter appeared to be profitable. After this scam had gone on for several years, the cumulative trading losses transferred to the unaudited affiliate resulted in a huge receivable owed to ESM by that entity. This receivable did not appear explicitly on ESM's annual balance sheet.[6] The only reference that ESM made to the receivable and related mirror transactions was an oblique description of them in the footnotes accompanying the annual balance sheet. In 1984, the reference to these transactions was included in footnote D (see Exhibit 1).

Novick also used the unaudited affiliate to conceal thefts of ESM funds. Novick diverted these funds to himself, his colleagues, and to co-conspirators who were officers or employees of ESM's major customers. Many of these co-conspirators

**EXHIBIT 1**

ESM's 1984 BALANCE SHEET AND ACCOMPANYING FOOTNOTES

**ESM Government Securities, Inc.**
**(a wholly-owned subsidiary of ESM Group, Inc.)**
**STATEMENT OF FINANCIAL CONDITION**
**December 31, 1984**

**ASSETS**

| | |
|---|---|
| Cash | $ 421,000 |
| Deposits with clearing organizations and others (note B) | 182,000 |
| Receivable from brokers and dealers (note C) | 3,643,000 |
| Receivable from customers (note C) | 73,050,000 |
| Securities purchased under agreement to resell (notes A and D) | 2,945,953,000 |
| Accrued interest | 406,000 |
| Securities purchased not sold—at market (note A) | 26,059,000 |
| Due from parent | 2,550,000 |
| Other | 61,000 |
| | $3,052,325,000 |

**LIABILITIES AND STOCKHOLDERS' EQUITY**

| | |
|---|---|
| Short-term bank loans (note E) | $ 47,258,000 |
| Payable to brokers and dealers (note C) | 12,266,000 |
| Payable to customers | 9,304,000 |
| Securities sold under agreement to repurchase (notes A and D) | 2,945,953,000 |
| Accounts payable and accrued expenses | 799,000 |
| Commitments and contingencies (notes F and G) Stockholders' equity: | |
| Common stock—authorized, issued and outstanding; 1,000 shares, $1.00 par value | 1,000 |
| Additional contributed capital | 4,160,000 |
| Retained earnings | 32,584,000 |
| | $3,052,325,000 |

The accompanying notes are an integral part of this statement.

*(continued)*

6. Like many financial institutions, ESM issued only a balance sheet to external parties. ESM was not required by any regulatory body to issue a balance sheet but apparently chose to do so because many of its customers requested an audited balance sheet before they would transact business with the firm.

**EXHIBIT 1—*continued***

ESM'S 1984 BALANCE SHEET AND ACCOMPANYING FOOTNOTES

## NOTES TO STATEMENT OF FINANCIAL CONDITION
## December 31, 1984

### NOTE A—SIGNIFICANT ACCOUNTING POLICIES

A summary of the significant accounting policies applied in the preparation of the financial statements follows.

**Security Transactions**. Security transactions are recorded on a settlement date basis, generally the first business day following the transaction date.

Purchases of securities under agreements to resell and sales of securities under agreements to repurchase are considered financing transactions and represent the amount of purchases and sales which will be resold or reacquired at amounts specified in the respective agreements.

**Securities Purchased, Not Sold.** Securities inventory, which consists of marketable federal government or government agency securities, is carried at market value.

**Furniture and Equipment.** Furniture and equipment are stated at cost. Depreciation is provided in amounts sufficient to relate the cost of depreciable assets to operations over their estimated service lives, principally on a straight-line basis over five years.

**Income Taxes**. The company participates in the filing of a consolidated income tax return with its parent. Any tax liability of the affiliated group is allocated to each member company based on its contribution to taxable income.

### NOTE B—DEPOSITS WITH CLEARING ORGANIZATIONS AND OTHERS

The company has deposits of cash and securities with commodity brokers to meet margin requirements. The company also has cash escrow deposits with its securities clearing agent.

### NOTE C—BROKER, DEALER, AND CUSTOMER ACCOUNTS

Receivables from brokers, dealers, and customers at December 31, 1984, include outstanding securities failed to deliver. Payables to brokers, dealers and customers at December 31, 1984, include outstanding securities failed to receive. "Fails," all of which have been outstanding less than 30 days, represent the contract value of securities which have not been received or delivered by settlement date. Fails to receive and fails to deliver from brokers and customers were $7,291,426 and $9,993,081, respectively, at December 31, 1984.

### NOTE D—SECURITY TRANSACTIONS

The company entered into repurchase and resale agreements with customers whereby specific securities are sold or purchased for short durations of time. These agreements cover securities, the rights to which are usually acquired through similar purchase/ resale agreements. The company has agreements with an affiliated company for securities purchased under agreements to resell amounting to approximately $1,621,481,000 and securities sold under agreements to repurchase amounting to approximately $1,324,472,000 at December 31, 1984. Accrued interest receivable from and payable to the affiliated company at year-end were $11,174,000 and $64,410,000 respectively.

### NOTE E—SHORT-TERM BANK LOANS

Short-term bank loans at December 31, 1984, are collateralized by securities purchased not sold.

### NOTE F—RELATED PARTY TRANSACTIONS

Certain common expenses paid by the parent company, including depreciation, are allocated to the subsidiary companies based on transaction volume. The company paid a dividend of

**EXHIBIT 1—*continued***

ESM'S 1984 BALANCE SHEET AND ACCOMPANYING FOOTNOTES

$10 million to its parent company as of December 31, 1984. The company occupies premises leased by the parent company from a partnership of which one of the officers is a partner. Rent expense paid the partnership amounted to $112,000 for the year ended December 31, 1984 (note G).

**NOTE G—COMMITMENTS**

The company conducts its operations in leased facilities under noncancellable operating leases expiring at various dates through 2010. The minimum lease payment for one location has been calculated based on current transaction volume (note F) under a 30- year lease. The minimum rental commitments under the operating lease are as follows:

| Year ended December 31, | |
|---|---|
| 1985 | $ 162,900 |
| 1986 | 162,900 |
| 1987 | 141,900 |
| 1988 | 112,400 |
| 1989 | 112,400 |
| 1990 and thereafter | 2,332,400 |
| | $3,024,900 |

Rental expense charged to operations approximated $137,000 for the year ended December 31, 1984.

established personal trading accounts with ESM, into which Novick dumped millions of dollars of profits from repo and reverse repo transactions. In return, when Novick needed additional government securities, these individuals would supply ESM with securities from their own firms' vaults.[7] Over the course of the ESM scam, Novick, his colleagues, and their co-conspirators were the beneficiaries of more than $100 million of ESM funds, funds stolen from the banks and municipalities that were ESM's major customers. When these thefts were added to the trading losses incurred by Novick and ESM's other investment losses, the net deficit for the corporate ESM group exceeded $300 million by the spring of 1985.

Two events in late 1984 proved to be the downfall of ESM. First, Novick collapsed and died at his desk of a massive heart attack in November 1984. Novick, in his early forties at the time, had been under immense stress for several years, since he had been responsible for the day-to-day operations of the ESM scam. Ewton and Steve Arky, ESM's legal counsel, tried to persuade Gomez to leave Alexander Grant and assume Novick's position. Gomez refused. Apparently concerned that the increasingly nervous Gomez might blow the whistle on the entire operation, Ewton transferred $100,000 to Gomez's personal ESM account to keep him on board.

The second event that led to ESM's undoing was a major customer's insistence in late 1984 that ESM turn over the securities the customer had purchased in a long-term repo transaction. ESM no longer had those securities. After stonewalling the customer for several months, Ewton resigned from the firm and retained the services of a criminal defense attorney. Within a short time, the ESM fraud made the headlines of metropolitan newspapers nationwide.

---

7. These securities were allegedly additional collateral for loans that ESM had made previously to these customers. Court records documented that these loans were grossly overcollateralized and that the true purpose of these transfers of securities was simply to perpetuate the ESM fraud.

## Audit Issues Raised by the ESM Debacle

On February 28, 1985, Alexander Grant issued what would be its final audit opinion for ESM Government Securities (see Exhibit 2). Less than 24 hours later, after Gomez admitted his involvement in the ESM fraud to fellow partners, Alexander Grant hastily withdrew the unqualified opinion and announced that it should no longer be relied upon. After learning of Grant's withdrawal of its audit report, an attorney for Home State Savings (which was owed approximately $145 million by ESM) flew to Fort Lauderdale. This attorney demanded that ESM officials explain why the audit report had been rescinded. By this point, Ewton was nowhere to be found. Two of Ewton's subordinates referred the Home State attorney to a lawyer ESM had retained a few weeks earlier, following Steve Arky's resignation. The two attorneys then contacted a local accountant and asked him to meet them at ESM headquarters the following morning. By midmorning on March 2, 1985, only two hours after the accountant first obtained ESM's accounting records, he informed the attorneys that ESM was insolvent by at least $200 million.

The congressional subcommittee that investigated the ESM scandal was shocked that such a massive fraud could be detected in a matter of hours, when Alexander Grant had failed for seven years to detect the scam. Members of the subcommittee insisted that at least some of Gomez's 40 colleagues and subordinates who worked on the ESM audits must have been aware of the fraudulent scheme. Nevertheless, state and federal prosecutors never indicted any other Alexander Grant auditors.[8] In a subsequent civil suit, Gomez testified that little effort had been required on his part to divert his subordinates away from the fraudulent sections of ESM's financial records. "I thought about when my own audit people would come up with questions that I wouldn't be able to answer without forcing me to lie extensively. That never happened."[9]

The accountant who uncovered the ESM fraud on March 2, 1985, did not unravel the thousands of intercompany transactions Novick used to conceal the firm's losses.

**EXHIBIT 2**

ALEXANDER GRANT'S AUDIT REPORT ON ESM'S 1984 BALANCE SHEET

[Note: This audit report appeared on the letterhead of Alexander Grant & Company.]

Board of Directors
ESM Government Securities, Inc.

We have examined the statement of financial condition of ESM Government Securities, Inc. (a Florida corporation and wholly-owned subsidiary of ESM Group, Inc.) as of December 31, 1984. Our examination was made in accordance with generally accepted auditing standards and, accordingly, included such tests of the accounting records and such other auditing procedures as we considered necessary in the circumstances.

In our opinion, the statement referred to above presents fairly the financial condition of ESM Government Securities, Inc. at December 31, 1984, in conformity with generally accepted accounting principles applied on a basis consistent with that of the preceding year.

Alexander Grant & Company

[signed]
Fort Lauderdale, Florida
January 30, 1985

8. One individual on Alexander Grant's tax staff stumbled across a payment to Gomez entered in ESM's accounting records. Rather than bringing this matter to the attention of other partners, this individual took it directly to Gomez. Apparently, Gomez fabricated an explanation for the payment that satisfied the individual.

9. Maggin, *Bankers, Builders, Knaves and Thieves*, 215.

Instead, the accountant happened to compare the firm's audited balance sheets with the consolidated corporate tax returns filed for the ESM corporate group. ESM executives did not want to pay income taxes on the "profitable" securities trades booked by Novick to offset the huge trading losses actually suffered by the company. So, the executives provided Alexander Grant's tax staff with accurate financial data to prepare ESM's annual consolidated tax returns. These corporate tax returns clearly revealed that the collective ESM operation was consistently losing tens of millions of dollars each year. An attorney in the law firm appointed as ESM's receiver noted that the scam was immediately obvious when the tax returns and audited balance sheets were compared. "It's incredible because it's so plain. It did not take detective work to find this. You just compare the reported balance sheets and the tax returns and you see the whole thing."[10]

Members of the congressional subcommittee queried expert witnesses in the ESM hearings at length regarding the complex maze of bogus intercompany transactions that Novick entered in ESM's accounting records. Alexander Grant's apparent failure to audit these transactions thoroughly troubled the subcommittee.

MR. TEW [attorney for ESM receiver]: . . . *it is critical that auditors inspect interrelated or affiliated transactions, because [in such cases] the client is booking entries with itself. If you can book an entry with yourself, you can commit a massive fraud.*

CONGRESSMAN DINGELL: *And control both entries?*

MR. TEW: *Yes, sir. You have it on both sides. You can do what you want. If this company [ESM Government Securities] lost money on a term repo, they would record a reverse repo or a mirror transaction, and move the loss up to the parent company.*

Another issue raised by the congressional subcommittee was the failure of ESM's auditors and the auditors of ESM's customers to discover the constant shortage of securities that was a by-product of Novick's fraudulent scheme. Members of the subcommittee speculated that the most basic audit procedures should have uncovered this shortage.

MR. TEW: . . . *the first thing you do, one of the first and simplest things, is to do a box count of the securities or confirm that the actual securities are in the possession of the custodian.*

CONGRESSMAN DINGELL: *To make sure these securities and assets are (a) what they purport to be; and (b) are physically in the place that they are supposed to be; and (c) are in the custody of the people in whose custody they are supposed to be. Isn't that right?*

MR. TEW: *Correct on all counts. The fundamental confirmation technique is to cover all the issues you just raised.*

Auditors of ESM's major customers testified that they had performed confirmation procedures. Unfortunately, they directed their confirmations to Jose Gomez. This testimony incensed Representative Ron Wyden, the most severe critic of the auditors involved in the ESM case.

*The auditors tell us that they had no choice but to rely on second-party confirmations—in this case, the word of Mr. Gomez—that the collateral for these large loans did exist and did adequately secure their clients' interest. What disturbs me is that the system literally breeds this kind of buck-passing. If the auditors went as far as the system and the rules of their profession require in confirming the collateral, any reasonable person would conclude that once again the auditing system has failed . . . it is my view that the only watchdogs throughout this sorry spectacle were either asleep, forgot how to bark, or were taking handouts from the burglars.*

10. J. Sterngold, "ESM's Auditor Is Sued," *The New York Times*, 16 March 1985, 30.

Several members of Congress also questioned the adequacy of Alexander Grant's audit review process. These members suggested that Grant's review procedures should have uncovered the flaws in the firm's ESM audits that prevented the auditors from discovering Novick's fraudulent activities.

CONGRESSMAN LUKEN: *What is your [review] system?*

MR. KLECKNER [managing partner of Grant Thornton, the successor firm to Alexander Grant & Company]: *Every report that is issued by an office is required to receive what we call a basic review within that office. In certain circumstances, the report is required to receive what we call an in-depth review, and in other circumstances, a report is required to receive what we call a technical review, which normally involves people from outside that office.*

CONGRESSMAN LUKEN: *Would you say that the review system has broken down rather badly here since you say that Mr. Gomez passed the review system?*

MR. KLECKNER: *I think it's a key question.*

CONGRESSMAN SIKORSKI: *Can rendering an inaccurate audit opinion be the fault of only one person under your firm's quality control procedure?*

MR. KLECKNER: *I think it really depends upon the degree and the nature of the manipulation that was taking place.*

CONGRESSMAN SIKORSKI: *Well, your system allows that manipulation.*

MR. KLECKNER: *The system is based on a fundamental assumption. The fundamental assumption is that the audit partner is honest.*

CONGRESSMAN SIKORSKI: *That's right. What kind of system do you have set up to catch dishonest people?*

Mr. Kleckner: *I would have to admit that I don't think our system starts out to try to question the honesty and integrity of each partner.*

In a subsequent court case, testimony obtained by a plaintiff attorney further disparaged Alexander Grant's audit review process. "Garcia-Pedrosa [plaintiff counsel] got a review partner to admit that he only made cursory investigations of Gomez's ESM workpapers from 1977 to 1982. And there was no refutation of Jose Gomez's testimony that another review partner said, 'I don't understand this s____, so please tell me it's okay and I'll sign it.'"[11]

Congressman John Dingell asked the accountant retained by ESM's receiver to identify the key red flags that should have alerted Alexander Grant auditors that something was wrong at ESM. The first warning signal was the magnitude of the intercompany transactions between ESM and its unaudited affiliate. Even more important than the size of these transactions was the absence of an underlying business purpose for them. The inability of the auditors to follow these suspicious intercompany transactions from "cradle to grave," since the other party to the transactions was ESM's unaudited affiliate, could easily have been considered a material audit scope limitation. Ironically, the scheme used by Novick to hide the ESM losses was very similar to the bookkeeping scams used in several classic audit failures, including Continental Vending, Drysdale Securities, and Equity Funding.

Another warning signal apparently overlooked by the Alexander Grant auditors was the exorbitant lifestyles that ESM's key officers adopted and flaunted over the short history of their firm. As an example, Exhibit 3 lists the personal assets of Ewton that a bankruptcy judge froze following ESM's collapse.

Possibly the most important red flag disregarded by the Alexander Grant auditors was the personal background of ESM's chief executive, Ronnie Ewton. A thorough background investigation of Ewton would have revealed several suspicious incidents in his past. In 1973, the National Association of Securities Dealers censured Ewton.

---

11. Maggin, *Bankers, Builders, Knaves and Thieves*, 215.

**EXHIBIT 3**

PERSONAL ASSETS OF RONNIE EWTON FROZEN BY BANKRUPTCY COURT ORDER

| Asset | Estimated Value (net of any mortgage balance) |
|---|---|
| Residence in Boca Raton, Fla. | $1,650,000 |
| Residence in Greenwich, Conn. | 330,000 |
| 5,600-acre horse farm in Aiken, S.C. | Unknown |
| Polo pony stable and 17 horses | 700,000 |
| House and two vacant lots in Boone, N.C. | Unknown |
| Boat slip in Key Largo, Fla. | Unknown |
| House and 57 acres in Aiken, S.C. | Unknown |
| One-fifteenth ownership interest in Hounds Lake Country Club in Aiken, S.C. | Unknown |
| Five lots in Elk River Country Club in Linville, N.C. | Unknown |
| One Aston Martin Laconda (automobile) | 151,000 |
| One 1984 Chevrolet Corvette | 20,000 |
| One Mercedes Benz, one Cadillac, one Toyota, and several jeeps and trucks | Unknown |
| 70-foot yacht | 1,350,000 |
| Partnership interest in horse-breeding operation | Unknown |
| Account with Provident Securities | 400,000 |
| Letter of credit held by Provident Bank | 200,000 |
| Partnership interest in 5,600 acres of property in Jasper, Tenn. | Unknown |
| Partnership interest in Colee Hammock Building | 200,000 |
| Mortgages receivable | 1,995,279 |
| Partnership interest in Tampa Bay Bandits professional sports franchise | Unknown |
| Partnership interest in S-J Minerals Partnership | Unknown |
| Numerous partnership interests in oil and gas ventures and coal-mining projects | Unknown |

In that same case, prosecutors convicted two of Ewton's associates of falsifying financial records and using customer securities as collateral for personal loans. During the 12 months prior to forming ESM, Ewton had been employed by three different brokerage firms. Two of these firms had bilked investors out of millions of dollars. In each case, Ewton had avoided prosecution, although several of his co-workers received jail terms.

The Securities and Exchange Commission (SEC) investigated Ewton shortly after he formed ESM. Although the SEC had no direct regulatory oversight over ESM, it filed suit against the firm, alleging that Ewton had attempted to swindle an SEC-registered bank holding company. The SEC report on this investigation included the following observation: "The staff believes that it may have uncovered the tip of an iceberg involving the fraudulent trading of Ginnie Mae's and other securities issued by the United States and its agencies."[12] Unfortunately for ESM's future customers, Steve Arky, ESM's skillful legal counsel, thwarted the SEC charges, and Ewton escaped unscathed once again.[13]

12. *Ibid.*, 75.

13. Ewton relied on Steve Arky's legal expertise on several occasions to bail ESM out of desperate straits. In 1980, the wife of Bobby Seneca, one of ESM's co-founders, sued him for divorce. To avoid a large divorce settlement, Seneca provided ESM's financial records, including those of the firm's affiliates, to the judge presiding over the divorce trial. These records clearly demonstrated that the ESM corporate entity was bankrupt. Steve Arky's law firm convinced the judge that ESM's insolvent condition should be kept confidential following the trial, ostensibly to allow ESM to liquidate in an orderly manner.

# EPILOGUE

The principal conspirators in the ESM scandal were convicted of various crimes and sentenced to jail. Ewton, for example, received a 24-year sentence. Three months following ESM's collapse, Steve Arky committed suicide. Several months later, the bookkeeper who helped Alan Novick maintain the fraudulent accounting records of ESM's bogus affiliate committed suicide after being convicted and sentenced to prison.

Shortly after the ESM scandal began grabbing nationwide headlines, Alexander Grant & Company changed its name to Grant Thornton. In a negotiated settlement with the Florida Board of Accountancy in 1985, Grant received a 60-day suspension from accepting any new clients and agreed to submit to a peer review by a CPA firm selected by the state board.

## Questions

1. In an interview that he granted after confessing to his role in the ESM fraud, Jose Gomez suggested that new partners in major CPA firms are subject to considerable pressure from their superiors to attract and retain clients. What measures should audit firms take to ensure that such pressure does not become dysfunctional, as it did in the case of Jose Gomez?
2. Note A to ESM's 1984 balance sheet (see Exhibit 1) discusses the consolidated tax return filed for the ESM corporate group. What responsibility, if any, do auditors have to review a client's corporate tax return? If tax and audit services are provided to a client by a CPA firm, what responsibility, if any, do the tax practitioners have to communicate to the audit team any information they discover that may have financial statement implications?
3. During his testimony before the congressional subcommittee, Grant Thornton's managing partner noted that his firm's audit review process is based on the fundamental assumption that the engagement audit partner is honest. Should CPA firms rethink their basic quality control strategies, given what happened in the ESM case?
4. When Gomez informed his fellow partners of the ESM fraud, Alexander Grant immediately withdrew the audit opinion that had been issued on ESM's December 31, 1984, balance sheet. Was that the appropriate decision under the circumstances? Did Alexander Grant have a responsibility to take any other actions?
5. During the ESM congressional hearings, the auditors of ESM's major customers were questioned regarding the confirmation procedures they used for their clients' transactions with ESM. What would be the key objective or objectives of an auditor's confirmation procedures when a client has engaged in (a) repo transactions with a government securities broker and (b) reverse repo transactions with a government securities broker?
6. Because of the concept of joint and several liability, each partner of Alexander Grant was held financially responsible for the malfeasance of Jose Gomez. Is it appropriate for society to impose joint and several liability on the partners of large professional firms? Why or why not?
7. Congressional testimony disclosed that ESM officers had several million dollars in outstanding loans from ESM. These loans were not shown separately on the 1984 ESM balance sheet. Do technical standards require that such loans be reported separately in a client's financial statements? If so, why?

CASE 1.5

# United States Surgical Corporation

Leon Hirsch founded United States Surgical Corporation (USSC) in 1964 with very little capital, four employees, and one product: an unwieldy mechanical device that he intended to market as a surgical stapler. In his mid-thirties at the time and lacking a college degree, Hirsch had already tried several lines of business, including frozen foods, dry cleaning, and advertising, each with little success. In fact, the dry cleaning venture ended in bankruptcy. No doubt, few of Hirsch's friends and family members believed that USSC would become financially viable. Despite the long odds against him, in a little more than one decade Hirsch had built the Connecticut-based USSC into a large and profitable public company whose stock was traded on a national exchange. More importantly, the surgical stapler that Hirsch invented revolutionized surgery techniques in the United States and abroad.

During the early years of its existence, USSC dominated the small surgical stapling industry that Hirsch had established in the mid-1960s. By 1980, several companies were encroaching on USSC's domestic and foreign sales markets. USSC's principal competitor at the time was a company owned by Alan Blackman. Blackman's company sold its products primarily in foreign countries but was attempting to significantly expand its U.S. sales. Hirsch alleged that Blackman, who was a former friend and associate, had infringed on USSC's patents by "reverse- engineering" the company's products.

In the early 1980s, USSC began an aggressive counterattack to repel Blackman's intrusion into its markets. First, USSC adopted a worldwide litigation strategy to contest Blackman's right to manufacture and market his competing products. Second, the company embarked on a large research and development program to create a line of new products technologically superior to those being manufactured by Blackman. Each of these initiatives required multimillion-dollar commitments by USSC—commitments that threatened the company's steadily rising profits and Hirsch's ability to raise additional capital that USSC desperately needed to finance its rapid growth.

Hirsch overcame the major challenges facing his company. USSC maintained its dominant position in the surgical stapling industry, while continuing to report record profits and sales each year. Ironically, those record profits and sales eventually spelled trouble for the company. Mounting suspicion that USSC's reported operating results were too good to be true prompted the Securities and Exchange Commission (SEC) to launch an investigation of the company's financial affairs. In 1983, the SEC leveled several charges of misconduct against key USSC officers, including Leon Hirsch. Within a short time, USSC's audit firm, Ernst & Whinney, resigned and withdrew the unqualified audit opinions it had issued on the company's 1980 and 1981 financial statements. In 1985, the SEC released a report on its lengthy investigation of USSC. The SEC ruled that the company had used a "variety of manipulative devices to overstate its earnings in its 1980 and 1981 financial statements."[1] (Exhibit 1 contains USSC's original balance sheets and income statements for the period 1979 to 1981.)

**EXHIBIT 1**

UNITED STATES SURGICAL CORPORATION'S 1979–1981 FINANCIAL STATEMENTS

**U.S. Surgical Corporation**
**Consolidated Balance Sheets 1979–1981**
**(000s omitted)**

| | December 31, 1981 | 1980 | 1979 |
|---|---|---|---|
| Current Assets: | | | |
| Cash | $ 426 | $ 1,243 | $ 596 |
| Receivables (net) | 36,670 | 30,475 | 22,557 |
| Inventories: | | | |
| Finished Goods | 29,216 | 9,860 | 5,685 |
| Work in Process | 5,105 | 2,667 | 1,153 |
| Raw Materials | 20,948 | 18,806 | 7,365 |
| | 55,269 | 31,333 | 14,203 |
| Other Current Assets | 7,914 | 1,567 | 1,820 |
| Total Current Assets | 100,279 | 64,618 | 39,176 |
| Property, Plant, and Equipment: | | | |
| Land | 2,502 | 2,371 | 1,027 |
| Buildings | 32,416 | 18,511 | 13,019 |
| Molds and Dies | 32,082 | 15,963 | 8,777 |
| Machinery and Equipment | 40,227 | 23,762 | 12,362 |
| | 107,227 | 60,607 | 35,185 |
| Allowance For Depreciation | (14,953) | (9,964) | (6,340) |
| | 92,274 | 50,643 | 28,845 |
| Other Assets | 14,786 | 3,842 | 2,499 |
| Total Assets | $207,339 | $119,103 | $70,520 |
| Current Liabilities: | | | |
| Accounts Payable | $ 12,278 | $ 6,951 | $ 6,271 |
| Notes Payable | — | — | 1,596 |
| Income Taxes Payable | — | 1,685 | — |
| Current Portion of Long-Term Debt | 724 | 666 | 401 |
| Accrued Expenses | 5,673 | 5,130 | 5,145 |
| Total Current Liabilities | 18,675 | 14,432 | 13,413 |
| Long-Term Debt | 80,642 | 47,569 | 33,497 |
| Deferred Income Taxes | 7,466 | 2,956 | 1,384 |
| Stockholders' Equity: | | | |
| Common Stock | 1,081 | 930 | 379 |
| Additional Paid-in Capital | 72,594 | 34,932 | 10,736 |
| Retained Earnings | 32,665 | 20,881 | 13,189 |
| Translation Allowance | (1,086) | — | — |
| Deferred Compensation—from Issuance of Restricted Stock | (4,698) | (2,597) | (2,078) |
| Total Stockholders' Equity | 100,556 | 54,146 | 22,226 |
| Total Liabilities and Stockholders' Equity | $207,339 | $119,103 | $70,520 |

1. This and subsequent quotations, unless indicated otherwise, were taken from Securities and Exchange Commission, *Accounting and Auditing Enforcement Release No. 109A*, 6 August 1986.

**EXHIBIT 1—**
***continued***

UNITED STATES SURGICAL CORPORATION'S 1979–1981 FINANCIAL STATEMENTS

**U.S. Surgical Corporation**
**Consolidated Income Statements 1979–1981**
**(000s omitted)**

| | 1981 | December 31, 1980 | 1979 |
|---|---|---|---|
| Net Sales | $111,800 | $86,214 | $60,876 |
| Costs and Expenses: | | | |
| Cost of Products Sold | 47,983 | 32,300 | 25,659 |
| Selling, General, and Administrative* | 45,015 | 37,740 | 23,935 |
| Interest | 5,898 | 4,063 | 3,403 |
| | 98,896 | 74,103 | 52,997 |
| Income Before Income Taxes | 12,904 | 12,111 | 7,879 |
| Income Taxes | | | |
| Federal and Foreign | 795 | 3,406 | 2,279 |
| State and Local | 325 | 820 | 471 |
| | 1,120 | 4,226 | 2,750 |
| Net Income | $ 11,784 | $ 7,885 | $ 5,129 |
| Net Income per common share and common share equivalent | $ 1.13 | $ .89 | $ .68 |
| Average number of common shares and common share equivalents outstanding | | | |
| 1981 | 10,403,392 | | |
| 1980 | | 8,816,986 | |
| 1979 | | | 7,555,710 |

*Included in the amounts for this line item are the following research and development expenses: 1981—$1,337, 1980—$3,020, 1979—$2,289.

To settle the SEC charges, USSC officials signed an agreement with the federal agency that forced the company to reduce its previously reported earnings by $26 million. Additionally, senior executives of USSC agreed to return to the company large bonuses they had been paid during 1980 and 1981. Hirsch alone repaid more than $300,000 to USSC. Following the signing of the agreement with the SEC, Hirsch reported that the criticism of his company and his management decisions was undeserved. Hirsch implied that cost considerations motivated him to accept the SEC sanctions: "It was our opinion that the settlement [with the SEC] was preferable to long, costly and time-consuming litigation."[2]

## USSC's Abusive Accounting Practices

The enforcement release that disclosed the key findings of the SEC's investigation of USSC charged the company with several abusive accounting and financial reporting practices. A focal point of the SEC's investigation was an elaborate scheme that USSC executives implemented to charge inventoriable production costs to a long-term asset account, molds and dies. This scheme, which required the cooperation of several of USSC's vendors, was deliberately concealed from the company's audit firm, Ernst & Whinney.[3]

2. K. B. Noble, "U.S. Surgical Settlement to Restate Earnings," *The New York Times*, 28 February 1984, B2.

3. A subsequent section of this case discusses the details of this scheme, including the measures that USSC executives took to conceal it from Ernst & Whinney.

The SEC investigation also revealed that USSC recorded inventory shipments to its sales force as consummated sales transactions. Until the mid-1970s, USSC had marketed its products through a network of independent dealers. Historically, inventory shipments to these dealers had been treated as arm's length transactions and thus reportable as revenue. By 1980, the company marketed its products almost exclusively through a sales staff consisting of full-time employees working on a commission basis. Each member of the sales staff maintained an inventory of USSC products, which they transported from client to client. When USSC shipped products to a salesperson, the company recorded the inventory as having been sold, although employees could return unsold items for full credit.

In 1980 and 1981, USSC's management began intentionally shipping excessive amounts of inventory to its sales staff. A former USSC sales manager later testified regarding this practice. "It was nothing to come home and find $3,000 worth of product sitting in a box on your front porch from UPS and a note saying, 'We thought you needed a little more product.'"[4] According to the SEC, USSC's policy of recognizing inventory shipments to its sales staff as consummated sales transactions inflated the company's 1980 and 1981 pretax profits by $1,150,000 and $750,000, respectively.

The SEC also charged that USSC abused the accounting rule that permits the capitalization of legal expenditures incurred to develop and successfully defend a patent. In 1980, the company capitalized less than $1 million of such expenditures; the following year, that figure leaped to $5.8 million. The SEC investigation disclosed that a significant portion of the 1981 litigation expenditures stemmed from Australian lawsuits filed against Alan Blackman and his company. Because USSC did not have any registered patents in Australia, these expenditures should have been immediately charged to operations instead of being deferred in an asset account. Approximately $3.7 million of USSC's 1981 litigation expenditures involved efforts to defend the company's U.S. patents. However, USSC chose to amortize these costs over a 10-year period even though the 17-year legal life of most of the patents would expire in 1983 or 1984.

USSC leased, rather than sold, many of its surgical tools. The company's accounting staff recorded the cost of these assets in a subsidiary fixed asset ledger, leased and loaned assets. USSC periodically retired such assets and removed their accounts from the sub-ledger. However, SEC investigators discovered that in many cases the costs associated with these assets were not removed from the sub-ledger but instead debited to the accounts of other assets still in service. In 1981, USSC also understated depreciation expense on several fixed assets by arbitrarily extending their useful lives and establishing salvage values for them for the first time.

## Allegations of Audit Deficiencies

The SEC's investigation of USSC uncovered several alleged flaws in Ernst & Whinney's audits of the company, particularly the 1981 audit. An important risk factor present during the 1981 USSC audit that Ernst & Whinney may have overlooked was the company's strong incentive to reach targeted sales and profit goals. If those targeted figures were not reached, USSC would have had difficulty raising the additional capital needed for expansion purposes. A former USSC vice-president later revealed that Hirsch often made firm commitments to security analysts regarding the company's future sales and profits.[5] This individual maintained that many of USSC's abusive accounting practices sprang from Hirsch's efforts to deliver the promised sales and

4. N. R. Kleinfeld, "U.S. Surgical's Checkered History," *The New York Times*, 13 May 1984, F4.

5. *Ibid.*

earnings figures. USSC's management bonus plan provided another incentive for USSC officials to misrepresent the company's financial data.

> *Surgical's executive officers could earn bonuses ranging from 15% to 75% of their base salaries, if the earnings per share growth ranged from 15% to 30% over the previous year. Management therefore had powerful personal incentives to keep the earnings per share high.*

The SEC also suggested that Ernst & Whinney failed to make proper use of analytical procedures during the planning phase of the 1981 audit. Ernst & Whinney apparently overlooked the important implications for its 1981 audit of several material changes in USSC account balances between December 31, 1980, and December 31, 1981. For example, the balance of the molds and dies account more than doubled from the end of 1980 to the end of 1981. According to the SEC, "This unusually large increase should have caused the auditors to scrutinize carefully the nature and source of the additions, and whether certain costs were properly identified and capitalized under GAAP."

Research and development expenses and patents were two other USSC accounts whose balances changed materially from 1980 to 1981. USSC reported a greater than 50 percent decrease in research and development expenses in 1981 compared with the previous year. This decrease occurred even though USSC undertook a large product development campaign during 1981. USSC's accounting records for 1981 also reflected a significant increase in litigation expenditures that were deferred in its patents account. (USSC included the patents account in noncurrent "Other Assets" on its balance sheet. See Exhibit 1.) The SEC maintained that the unusually large changes in key USSC account balances between 1980 and 1981 should have placed Ernst & Whinney on alert that the 1981 USSC audit would have a higher-than-normal degree of risk associated with it. "The heightened audit attention was particularly important since the aggregate effect of the changes was material to Surgical's 1981 financial statements . . . [and] the changes all had the effect of increasing income."

According to the SEC, Ernst & Whinney made three critical errors when considering the question of whether USSC should be allowed to record inventory shipments to its sales staff as valid sales transactions. First, the SEC pointed out that Ernst & Whinney failed to recognize that "sales" of inventory to employees generally do not qualify as arm's length transactions. "Because the potential for abuse is so great when a 'sale' transaction is between a company and its employee, the presumption is that no 'true' sale has taken place." Second, the SEC maintained that USSC's repurchase of significant amounts of inventory from its salespeople during 1981 should have alerted Ernst & Whinney that the original inventory shipments to these employees were not bona fide sales transactions. This oversight by Ernst & Whinney particularly troubled the SEC since the audit firm's 1980 and 1981 workpapers clearly documented these repurchases.

Finally, the SEC criticized Ernst & Whinney for failing to investigate a client executive's assertion that USSC was not obligated to repurchase inventory from employees who resigned or were terminated. Ernst & Whinney's 1981 audit program included a procedure to obtain and review a copy of the employment contract signed by USSC's sales employees and to incorporate that contract in the permanent workpaper file. Although the Ernst & Whinney audit program indicated that this procedure had been completed, there was no evidence to this effect in the firm's 1981 workpapers. The SEC ruled that if the employment contract had been obtained and reviewed, Ernst & Whinney would have learned that USSC not only had a policy of repurchasing inventory from former employees but had a contractual obligation to do so.

The SEC reserved its harshest criticism of Ernst & Whinney for the firm's failure to prevent USSC from capitalizing a material amount of production expenses in the molds and dies account. During the last few months of 1980, USSC began systematically charging production costs to that noncurrent asset account, resulting in a significant overstatement of assets and a corresponding understatement of cost of goods sold. Company executives used several methods to conceal this illicit scheme. The most common of these methods was instructing the company's vendors, who did most of the production work on USSC's products, to describe generic production costs as capitalizable expenditures on invoices submitted for payment to USSC.

One of USSC's primary vendors was Lacey Manufacturing Company, a division of Barden Corporation—which also happened to be an Ernst & Whinney audit client. In late 1980, USSC officials instructed Barden Corporation to begin using the phrase "tooling modifications" to describe the work performed for USSC by Lacey Manufacturing. Previously, these invoices had described the expenditures incurred for USSC as generic production costs. This change in the description of the incurred costs was critical, since all tooling costs for new or redesigned products were capitalizable expenditures.

## Chronology of USSC-Ernst & Whinney Disagreement Regarding Capitalization of Alleged Tooling Costs

For many years, accounting educators have maintained that the imbalance of power in the auditor-client relationship impairs the quality of audits.[6] This imbalance of power favors the client, largely because client executives retain and compensate their company's independent auditors. When technical disputes arise during an audit, client executives may use their leverage on auditors to extract important concessions from them.

A classic example of an audit conflict arose during Ernst & Whinney's 1981 audit of USSC. This conflict stemmed from USSC's illicit scheme to charge production costs to the noncurrent asset account molds and dies. The following chronology lists the key events in this dispute:

1/27/82 The Ernst S& Whinney audit team completes its fieldwork on the USSC engagement.

2/2/82 Paul Yamont, senior vice-president and treasurer of Barden Corporation, makes an unsolicited telephone call to William Burke, the Ernst & Whinney audit engagement partner on the Barden audit. Yamont informs Burke that Barden accountants have discovered numerous USSC purchase orders and corresponding Barden invoices that do not accurately describe the work that Lacey Manufacturing (a division of Barden Corporation) has been performing for USSC. According to Yamont, these invoices and purchase orders, totaling approximately $1 million, indicate that the Lacey work for USSC has been for "tooling modifications." In fact, Lacey has simply been producing and assembling products for USSC. Burke immediately visits Barden to discuss this issue with Yamont.

2/3/82 Ernst & Whinney approves the issuance of a press release by USSC management that reports the company's sales and earnings for 1981. (At this

---

6. A. Goldman and B. Barlev, "The Auditor-Firm Conflict of Interests: Its Implications for Independence," *Accounting Review* 49 (October 1974), 707–718; D. R. Nichols and K. Price, "The Auditor-Firm Conflict: An Analysis Using Concepts of Exchange Theory," *Accounting Review* 51 (April 1976), 335–346; M. C. Knapp and B. H. Ward, "An Integrative Analysis of Audit Conflict: Sources, Consequences and Resolution," *Advances in Accounting* 4 (1987), 267–286.

point, Michael Hope, the USSC audit engagement partner, is unaware of the problem brought to William Burke's attention by Paul Yamont.)

2/5/82 Burke again visits Yamont to discuss the alleged mislabeled invoices.

2/8/82 Barden Corporation's board of directors votes to retain Ernst & Whinney to formally investigate the mislabeled invoices.

2/10/82 Burke contacts Norman Strauss, regional director of accounting and auditing for Ernst & Whinney's New York region, and informs him of Yamont's concerns. Strauss immediately informs Bruce Dixon, Ernst & Whinney partner in charge of the New York region, of the Barden situation. Shortly thereafter, Dixon calls Hope and instructs him not to sign off on the USSC audit until the questionable invoice charges have been fully investigated. Dixon also informs Robert Neary, Ernst & Whinney's chief technical partner, of the problem.

2/13/82 Burke sends an Ernst & Whinney audit manager to Barden Corporation to investigate the invoices and purchase orders in question.

2/15/82 Burke joins the Ernst & Whinney audit manager at Barden Corporation to tour the Lacey Manufacturing facility and to discuss the questionable invoices and purchase orders with Robert More, the Lacey general manager. More informs Burke that nearly all of the invoiced charges being reviewed were for generic production work performed for USSC rather than for tooling modifications.

2/18/82 Burke meets with the Barden board of directors and reports that the results of the Ernst & Whinney investigation demonstrate that the USSC purchase orders and the corresponding Barden invoices misrepresent the nature of the work performed by Lacey Manufacturing for USSC. The chairman of Barden's board of directors then reports that an independent investigation by an outside law firm has yielded the same conclusion. The Barden directors vote to require that all future work performed for USSC be properly described in invoices submitted for payment to the company.

2/20/82 Hope and Dixon are unsure how to proceed on the USSC (approx-audit, given the results of Burke's investigation. imately) Because of confidentiality concerns, Hope cannot raise the issue directly with USSC officers. Barden officers are concerned that if USSC perceives that Barden has brought the problem to the attention of Ernst & Whinney, USSC may terminate its relationship with Barden. Finally, Hope and Dixon decide to send a confirmation letter to Yamont and More that asks them to confirm that the disputed $1 million in charges was for tooling modifications. (Hope and Dixon realize that Yamont and More will refuse to sign the confirmation letter.)

2/25/82 Yamont contacts Hope and informs him that he cannot sign the confirmation letter since he is aware that the disputed charges are not for tooling modifications. Following the refusal of Yamont and, subsequently, More to sign the confirmation letter, Ernst & Whinney officials discuss the problem with the management of both USSC and Barden. Eventually, executives of each company agree to allow auditors from the two Ernst & Whinney teams to have mutual access to their company's accounting records.

3/3/82 Hope meets with top USSC executives and asks them to relate their understanding of the costs incurred by Lacey Manufacturing on behalf of USSC. The USSC officials inform Hope that in early 1981, they had instructed More, the Lacey general manager, to make certain tooling changes that would result in improved efficiency in the production of USSC products. The executives then provided an elaborate and confusing explanation as to why the tooling modifications were charged out on a per-unit basis. (Earlier, Ernst & Whinney representatives had noted that the disputed costs were billed to USSC based upon the number of units of product manufactured by Lacey. Intuitively, costs associated with tooling modifications should have been billed in one lump sum or in installments. The fact that the costs were billed on a per-unit basis suggested that they were production costs.)

Hope asks USSC's controller for purchase orders that the company had placed with outside contractors other than Barden (Lacey). Hope is searching for evidence of additional mislabeled costs. In the files that Hope is allowed to review, he finds charges billed to USSC that are similar to the disputed tooling modification costs billed to USSC by Barden. USSC officials assure Hope that the costs incurred on USSC's behalf by these vendors were, in fact, for tooling modifications.

3/5/82 Hope and Burke meet with senior USSC executives and More of Lacey Manufacturing. In More's presence, one of the USSC executives again explains that the disputed costs involved tooling changes requested by USSC in early 1981. More indicates that he agrees with that characterization of the costs. (Of course, More had previously maintained that the disputed amounts were production, not tooling, costs. More justifies his change in opinion by stating that earlier he "hadn't thought it through.")

3/10/82 Hope and Burke tour the Lacey Manufacturing facility to obtain a better understanding of the firm's production process. More is asked to act as a guide for the Ernst & Whinney partners on the tour. Shortly before the tour is scheduled to begin, a senior executive with USSC arrives unexpectedly at Lacey and asks permission to accompany the others on the tour. During the tour, More explains that production personnel charge their time to either tooling jobs or production jobs. He also notes that personnel often inadvertently charge tooling costs to production jobs.

3/11/82 During a conference call involving Hope, Burke, top technical partners of Ernst & Whinney, and the CPA firm's internal and external legal counsel, Hope explains the additional audit procedures performed to analyze the disputed tooling costs. He then reports his conclusion that the disputed costs involved tooling modifications, not generic production work. The other Ernst & Whinney personnel agree with Hope.

3/14/82 To support the conclusion that the disputed costs were (approx- for tooling modifications, Hope is instructed to obtain a imately) signed confirmation letter from Yamont of Barden Corporation to that effect. When asked to sign the letter, Yamont refuses, as he had done in late February.

3/15/82 Hope decides not to investigate further the questionable tooling costs that he discovered on March 3—tooling costs charged to USSC by vendors other than Lacey Manufacturing. Regarding these items, Hope makes the following entry in the USSC workpapers: "Discussed with [another audit partner] on 3/15/82. Although explanations are incomplete, amounts are immaterial."

3/16/82 More signs the Ernst & Whinney confirmation letter regarding the tooling modification costs that Yamont had refused to sign.

3/17/82 Hope signs Ernst & Whinney's unqualified audit opinion on USSC's 1981 financial statements, which are issued shortly thereafter.

The SEC's investigation of USSC's 1981 financial statements and Ernst & Whinney's audit of those financial statements revealed that Hope and the other Ernst & Whinney auditors had been lied to extensively by USSC personnel. The mislabeled purchase orders and invoices that Ernst & Whinney uncovered were elements of a fraudulent scheme USSC's management had concocted to make production expenditures appear to be capitalizable tooling costs. Apparently, the scheme originated in 1980 when USSC executives tried to force several vendors to take back a significant amount of inventory that had been rendered obsolete by technological changes. When the vendors refused, the USSC executives devised a "compromise." The executives would inflate the amount of future purchase orders for production work to include the cost of the obsolete inventory and then indicate in the purchase orders that these amounts were for tooling modifications rather than for production expenses. The USSC executives also instructed the vendors to describe these amounts on subsequent invoices as charges for tooling modifications. This agreement required USSC to pay for the obsolete inventory; however, the company benefited since the cost of that inventory was not expensed immediately but rather capitalized in the molds and dies account and depreciated over several years.[7]

Although the SEC's investigation revealed that USSC officials had lied repeatedly to Michael Hope, the federal agency still censured the audit partner.[8] The SEC ruled that Ernst & Whinney, and Hope in particular, had sufficient opportunity to discover, and should have discovered, that USSC executives were misrepresenting their firm's financial condition and results of operations.

> *The auditors failed to design proper audit procedures, test critical assertions, resolve material conflicts in the audit evidence, and reconcile with the other evidence what they should have recognized were implausible client representations, in violation of GAAS. The bulk of the evidence available to the auditors was so inconsistent with their client's position that the auditors should have realized the [disputed] billings were not properly capitalizable as tooling and that Surgical's representations were false and not made in good faith.*

## EPILOGUE

USSC recovered from the problems it experienced in the early 1980s. Impressive growth rates in revenues and earnings sent USSC's stock price spiraling upward during the latter part of that decade. By 1996, USSC reported a net income of $109 million on sales of $1.1 billion and total assets exceeding $1.5 billion. Leon Hirsch also recovered nicely from his close and unpleasant encounter with the SEC. Hirsch ranked as the third highest paid corporate executive in the nation in 1991, earning more than $23 million.[9] In September 1997, Hirsch's nearly five million shares of USSC stock had a market value surpassing $200 million.

Leon Hirsch made headlines once again in October 1997. In the midst of a takeover bid for a rival, Circon Corporation, Hirsch chastised certain executives of that company. Hirsch charged that the executives were not focusing sufficient attention on the economic interests of their stockholders and attempted to replace two of the company's directors with his own nominees

7. In some instances, the SEC found that USSC and its vendors simply fabricated phony purchase orders and invoices for tooling modifications to "convert" the obsolete inventory costs to capitalizable expenditures.

8. The SEC also filed a civil complaint against Barden Corporation and Robert More. The SEC alleged that Barden and More "provided substantial cooperation and assistance in furthering and concealing practices" that USSC employed to misrepresent its financial condition and results of operations. Barden and More settled the SEC complaint without admitting guilt or denying any wrongdoing by agreeing to abide by a court order prohibiting them from engaging in any future violations of federal securities laws.

9. *The New York Times*,"Executive Pay At New Highs," 11 May 1992, D5.

to Circon's board. Hirsch justified his action by stating that his nominees "can make some of the other [Circon] directors understand their responsibilities to shareholders."[10] A leading stockholder rights activist was apparently not convinced that Hirsch, given his prior history, was motivated by a desire to improve Circon's corporate governance. This activist bluntly stated that Hirsch "is like the devil of corporate governance."[11]

USSC withdrew its takeover bid for Circon in mid-1998 after announcing that it had agreed to be acquired by the large conglomerate, Tyco International Ltd. Analysts pegged the value of the takeover package at approximately $3.3 billion. Following the merger, Tyco executives reported that Leon Hirsch would continue to oversee USSC's operations.

## Questions

1. Identify audit procedures that, if employed by Ernst & Whinney during the 1981 USSC audit, might have detected the overstatement of the leased and loaned assets account that resulted from the improper accounting for asset retirements.
2. In 1981, USSC extended the useful lives of several of its fixed assets and adopted salvage values for many of these same assets for the first time. Are these changes permissible under generally accepted accounting principles? Assuming these changes had a material effect on USSC's financial condition and results of operations, how should the changes have been disclosed in the company's financial statements? How should these changes have affected Ernst & Whinney's 1981 audit opinion? (Assume that the current audit reporting standards were in effect at the time.)
3. Prepare common-sized financial statements for USSC for the period 1979–1981. Also compute key liquidity, solvency, activity, and profitability ratios for 1980 and 1981. Given these data, identify what you believe were the high-risk financial statement items for the 1981 USSC audit.
4. What factors in the auditor-client relationship create a power imbalance in favor of the client? Discuss measures that the profession could take to minimize the negative consequences of this power imbalance.
5. Regarding the costs incurred for USSC by Barden, identify (a) the evidence Hope collected that supported USSC's claim that the costs involved tooling modifications and (b) the audit evidence that supported the position that the costs were generic production expenses. What do generally accepted auditing standards suggest are the key evaluative criteria that auditors should consider when assessing audit evidence? Given these criteria, do you believe Hope was justified in deciding that the costs in question were for tooling modifications? Why or why not?
6. In your opinion, did Hope satisfactorily investigate the possibility that there were additional suspicious tooling charges being paid and recorded by USSC? If not, what additional steps should he have taken to further explore this possibility? If Hope believed there was some likelihood that his client had committed an illegal act, what additional audit procedures, if any, would have been appropriate? (Assume that current auditing standards were in effect at the time.)
7. When a CPA firm has two audit clients that transact business with each other, should the two audit teams be allowed to share information regarding their clients? Why or why not?

---

10. "U.S. Surgical's Rx for Circon: Corporate Governance," *The Wall Street Journal*, 6 October 1987, B4.
11. *Ibid.*

**CASE 1.6**

# The Fund of Funds, Ltd.

Bernie Cornfeld founded Investors Overseas Services (IOS) in 1956 with an initial investment of $300. Cornfeld, who was 29-years-old at the time, recognized that the large contingent of U.S. troops stationed in post-World War II Europe collectively had a huge amount of funds to invest but few investment opportunities. Cornfeld created 11 specialized mutual funds in which members of the U.S. military could invest as little as $25 per month. The most successful of these funds was The Fund of Funds, Ltd., an open-ended mutual fund that initially invested only in U.S.-based mutual funds. This fund's assets eventually approached $500 million.

Cornfeld was born in 1927 in Istanbul, Turkey, and emigrated with his parents to New York three years later. As a young man, Cornfeld became involved in the revolutionary Socialist Youth League and actively campaigned for socialistic political candidates. Trained as a social worker and employed for several years as a New York taxi driver, Cornfeld became disenchanted with politics while in his mid-twenties and turned his attention instead to the world of finance. Five-feet five-inches tall and shy by nature because of a speech impediment, Cornfeld rose from total obscurity at the time he founded IOS to international fame and an estimated net worth of $200 million only a decade later. At the height of IOS's financial success, Cornfeld lived in a castle in France; dated actress Victoria Principal; and could count as friends many international jet-setters, including his best friend, the acclaimed designer Oleg Cassini.

The Securities and Exchange Commission (SEC) disrupted Cornfeld's idyllic lifestyle in the mid-1960s with a lengthy investigation of IOS's financial affairs. As the IOS mutual funds, Fund of Funds in particular, grew dramatically in size during the early 1960s, the SEC became increasingly alarmed. By 1965, IOS transactions often accounted for 5 percent of the daily volume of activity on the New York Stock Exchange. The SEC feared that IOS portfolio managers might eventually be able to manipulate the stock market for their own benefit. Even more troubling to the SEC was the difficulty of imposing regulatory oversight on IOS, since the firm's corporate headquarters was in Geneva, Switzerland. After a two-year investigation, the SEC and Cornfeld reached an agreement. The SEC dropped its investigation of IOS. In exchange, Cornfeld agreed to abide by all SEC regulations and pledged not to allow IOS to obtain a controlling interest in any U.S. company.

A contemporary of Bernie Cornfeld in the international investment community of the 1960s was John McCandish King, a Denver-based speculator in the oil and gas industry. Cornfeld and King were the same age and both rose from obscurity to tremendous wealth in a short period of time. The similarities between the two men stopped there. At six-feet three-inches, the 250-pound King towered over the diminutive Cornfeld. A high school dropout, King was brash and overbearing and known for his expensive taste in cowboy boots, his 10-gallon cowboy hats, and his 3,000 pairs of cuff links. King's stretch limousine sported a custom-designed sunroof to accommodate his zealous interest in hunting. While still in his twenties, King became renowned for his seemingly innate ability to discover oil. In 1952, King invested $1,500, one-half of his net worth at the time, in an oil-drilling venture in Oklahoma. A string of wildcat wells in that venture allowed him to form King

Resources, which soon became one of the nation's largest and most profitable independent oil companies. By the mid-1960s, *Forbes* estimated King's wealth at $300 million, meaning that the towering Texan was well on his way to achieving his personal goal of becoming a billionaire.

In early 1968, Cornfeld decided to diversify Fund of Funds' investment portfolio. A mutual acquaintance arranged a meeting in April 1968 between Cornfeld and King to discuss the possibility of Fund of Funds investing in oil and natural gas properties owned by King Resources. Cornfeld then invited King to make a presentation during a Fund of Funds board of directors meeting in Acapulco, Mexico. Following that presentation, Cornfeld and King reached an agreement. Fund of Funds would establish a natural resources proprietary account (NRPA) for investments in oil and gas properties to be purchased from King Resources. Although the two men never signed a formal contract, the minutes of the Fund of Funds board of directors meeting documented the intended relationship between the two companies.

> *The role of King Resources with respect to the contemplated Natural Resources Proprietary Account would be that of a vendor of properties to the proprietary account, with such properties to be sold on an arm's length basis at prices no less favorable to the proprietary account than the prices charged by King to its 200-odd industrial and other purchasers.*[1]

A Fund of Funds executive later testified he understood that King Resources would sell natural resource properties to Fund of Funds at cost plus a "reasonable markup" of 7 to 8 percent.

Initially, Cornfeld agreed to purchase $10 million of oil and gas properties from King Resources. By the end of 1969, however, King had convinced Fund of Funds' officers to purchase more than $100 million of oil and gas properties from his company. Unfortunately for Fund of Funds' stockholders, King took unfair advantage of the mutual fund's executives, who knew little about the oil and gas industry. Court records later revealed that King often bought relatively inexpensive oil and gas properties and then immediately sold those properties to Fund of Funds at grossly inflated prices. King unloaded properties on Fund of Funds for as much as 50 times what he had paid for the properties just days earlier.

Within a few years, falling stock prices and the weight of the poor investments made for Fund of Funds by King forced the mutual fund into bankruptcy. Among the defendants in the tangle of civil lawsuits stemming from Fund of Funds' collapse was Arthur Andersen & Co., the audit firm of both Fund of Funds and King Resources. Arthur Andersen was sued by John Orr, a Touche Ross partner appointed to serve as Fund of Funds' bankruptcy trustee. Orr alleged that Arthur Andersen failed to inform the mutual fund's officers that they were being defrauded by King Resources. When the verdict in the subsequent trial was handed down, Andersen became the victim of the largest court-ordered judgment ever imposed on an accounting firm at the time.

## Arthur Andersen's Dual Relationship With Fund of Funds and King Resources

Three Arthur Andersen offices were involved in each annual audit of Fund of Funds. The Geneva office coordinated the audits of all the IOS mutual funds and paid particular attention to the Fund of Funds audit, given the size, prominence, and complexity

1. This and all subsequent quotations were taken from the following court opinion: *The Fund of Funds, Limited v. Arthur Andersen & Co.*, 545 F. Supp. 1314 (1982).

of that fund. The New York City office assumed primary responsibility for the Fund of Funds audit. Finally, Andersen's Denver office performed selected audit procedures each year on the Fund of Funds' NRPA. The Denver office also audited King Resources, which was headquartered in Denver. In fact, the partner in charge of the King Resources audit and the principal manager assigned to that audit supervised the audit procedures applied to Fund of Funds' NRPA.

A central issue in the suit filed against Arthur Andersen by the Fund of Funds bankruptcy trustee was Andersen's awareness of the excessive prices King Resources charged the mutual fund for oil and gas properties. Arthur Andersen's Fund of Funds workpapers noted that King Resources had "carte blanche authority to buy oil and gas properties" for the NRPA. The Denver office of Arthur Andersen also had complete access to King Resources' accounting data that documented the cost of the properties sold to Fund of Funds and the profit margins on those sales.

A closely related issue was exactly when Arthur Andersen discovered that Fund of Funds was being charged exorbitant prices for oil and gas properties by King Resources. Arthur Andersen issued its audit report on Fund of Funds' 1968 financial statements on February 5, 1969. Plaintiff counsel in the Fund of Funds litigation attempted to establish that Arthur Andersen knew when it prepared its 1968 audit report that King Resources was overcharging Fund of Funds for the oil and gas properties.

A final issue addressed at length in the Fund of Funds civil lawsuit was Arthur Andersen's involvement with several so-called revaluation transactions arranged by King Resources for Fund of Funds. Fund of Funds was required to establish a monetary value for its entire portfolio on a daily basis since it was an open-ended mutual fund. To compute its net asset value (NAV), Fund of Funds established a market value for each of its investments, including its natural resource properties. This collective market value was then divided by the number of outstanding mutual fund shares to arrive at the NAV. Mutual funds use their NAV to distribute proceeds to shareholders electing to redeem their shares. The illiquid nature of Fund of Fund's NRPA investments complicated the computation of its daily NAV. King Resources periodically sold parcels of natural resource properties owned by Fund of Funds to establish a fair market value for the residual portions of those properties retained by the mutual fund. On a few occasions, King Resources sold a portion of its own equity interest in such properties to establish a fair market value for Fund of Funds' NRPA investments.[2]

Evidence presented during the Fund of Funds trial demonstrated that many of the revaluation transactions arranged by King Resources were fraudulent. In at least two cases, King Resources found a third party that agreed to buy a small portion of either Fund of Funds' or King Resources' interest in an oil and gas property at a price considerably higher than its fair market value. Unknown to Fund of Funds' officials, King Resources made secret "side agreements" with the purchasers of these properties. These side agreements obligated King Resources to compensate the purchasers for any losses they subsequently incurred on these properties. Because of these side agreements, the revaluation transactions were not arm's length transactions and thus not a valid basis for establishing a fair market value for the given properties. King Resources arranged these fraudulent revaluation transactions to convince Fund of Funds' executives that the natural resource investments were profitable. Since

2. King Resources retained a 12.5 percent equity interest in most of the natural resource properties it sold to Fund of Funds.

these transactions grossly inflated the NAV of Fund of Funds' shares, the investors who redeemed their shares following these transactions profited from them. On the other hand, these transactions adversely affected those investors who retained their mutual fund shares indefinitely.

## Arthur Andersen's 1968 and 1969 Audits of Fund of Funds

Court records in the Fund of Funds trial documented that Arthur Andersen considered the IOS and Fund of Funds audits high-risk engagements. The highest-risk financial statement items in the 1968 and 1969 Fund of Funds audits were the large investments in natural resource properties. During the Fund of Funds trial, plaintiff counsel established that Arthur Andersen had "repeated serious difficulties with King as a client at least since 1961" and had expressed concern regarding several of King's questionable business practices. These prior difficulties with John King placed Arthur Andersen on notice that the Fund of Funds-King Resources transactions needed to be scrutinized closely.

During the 1968 Fund of Funds audit, Arthur Andersen personnel in the Denver office compiled King Resources' sales data for its natural resource properties. These data revealed that King Resources realized much higher gross profit margins on properties sold to Fund of Funds than it did on properties sold to other customers. The accounting firm documented the following gross profit percentages for five of the sales made by King Resources to Fund of Funds: 98.7, 98.6, 85.6, 58, and 56.7 percent. These gross profit percentages appeared particularly excessive since most of the properties had been owned only a short time by King Resources before being sold to Fund of Funds. The court reached the following conclusion regarding Arthur Andersen's knowledge of the prices charged Fund of Funds by King Resources: "It is reasonable to find that AA knew what FOF paid for the [natural resource] interests purchased in 1968, that AA knew what King Resources paid for them, and that AA knew King Resources' profits [on these transactions] prior to February 5, 1969, when the FOF audit report was filed."

During the trial in the Fund of Funds case, a lengthy debate ensued regarding the client confidentiality rule. That debate focused on whether the confidentiality rule precluded Arthur Andersen from using the sales data obtained from King Resources to audit Fund of Funds' natural resource investments. Clouding this issue was the close linkage between the Fund of Funds and King Resources audits.

> *The NRPA audit was performed by using the records of King Resources, and sometimes AA staffers would work on the King Resources and NRPA audits contemporaneously. Thus, AA's understanding of the ongoing business relationship between FOF and the King group can be determined from documents found in AA files for King Resources or NRPA and from testimony regarding the actual conduct of the audits.*

Another critical issue Arthur Andersen faced during the Fund of Funds audits was the validity of the revaluation transactions. In December 1968, John King arranged for Fund of Funds to sell 10 percent of a natural resource property to Fox-Raff, a Seattle brokerage firm audited by Arthur Andersen. This sale allowed Fund of Funds to recognize a $900,000 increase in the value of its investment portfolio. Arthur Andersen questioned this transaction, since Fund of Funds had owned the property a very short time and since there were no new geological data suggesting that the market value of the property had risen. Arthur Andersen also doubted whether the sale of a 10 percent interest in the property justified recognizing an increase in the remaining 90 percent interest retained by Fund of Funds.

In January 1969, Phil Carr, the Arthur Andersen partner in the Denver office responsible for the King Resources audit and for overseeing the limited audit procedures that his subordinates applied to Fund of Funds' NRPA investments, discovered that the Fox-Raff transaction was not a bona fide sale. King had provided Fox-Raff with the required down payment for the purchase transaction and relieved the brokerage firm of any commitment to pay the balance of the purchase price. Carr passed this information on to John Robinson of the New York City office of Arthur Andersen, the engagement audit partner for Fund of Funds.

According to court records, the Fox-Raff transaction was ultimately discussed at the "very highest partnership level" within Arthur Andersen. For undisclosed reasons, the accounting firm chose not to inform Fund of Funds' executives that the Fox-Raff sale was not an arm's length transaction. Arthur Andersen also decided that the revaluation of the Fund of Funds assets due to the Fox-Raff transaction had not materially affected the mutual fund's NAV. Shortly after this latter decision was made, Arthur Andersen issued an unqualified opinion on Fund of Funds' 1968 financial statements. (Because of the complexity of this case, Exhibit 1 provides a glossary of the principal parties involved, as well as a summary of certain of the key events.)

**EXHIBIT 1**

KEY PARTIES AND EVENTS IN THE FUND OF FUNDS CASE

**Blakely-Wolcott transaction.** A transaction involving the sale of an oil and gas property by King Resources to a third party. Arthur Andersen subsequently discovered that John King had negotiated an undisclosed and illicit "side agreement" with the purchaser of the property that invalidated the sale as an arm's length transaction. This discovery was significant because it cast doubt on the integrity of the audit evidence Arthur Andersen collected from John King to support Fund of Funds' 1969 financial statements.

**Phil Carr.** An Arthur Andersen partner assigned to the firm's Denver office. Carr supervised both the King Resources audit and the audit procedures applied to Fund of Funds' NRPA.

**Bernie Cornfeld.** The founder of Investors Overseas Services.

**Fox-Raff transaction.** A transaction in which Fund of Funds sold a small portion of an oil and gas property to a Seattle brokerage firm. John King arranged the transaction to establish a fair market value for the portion of the property retained by Fund of Funds. Arthur Andersen discovered, after the fact, that King had a "side agreement" with the brokerage firm.

**Investors Overseas Services (IOS).** An investment company founded by Bernie Cornfeld in 1956. One of the many mutual funds managed by IOS was The Fund of Funds, Ltd.

**John McCandish King.** The founder and principal owner of King Resources.

**King Resources.** An investment company specializing in natural resource properties. King Resources sold Fund of Funds more than $100 million of oil and gas properties during the late 1960s.

**John Mecom.** An investor who purchased a small percentage of a large oil and gas property owned by Fund of Funds. This transaction allowed Fund of Funds to increase the value of its residual interest in the property by $119 million.

**John Orr.** A Touche Ross partner who was appointed the bankruptcy trustee for Fund of Funds.

**John Robinson.** A New York partner with Arthur Andersen who served as the audit engagement partner for Fund of Funds.

While planning the 1969 Fund of Funds audit, Phil Carr developed a set of guidelines to be used in auditing subsequent revaluation transactions. Carr wanted to avoid a controversy similar to the one that arose following the discovery of the Fox-Raff transaction, in particular, because his audit team would play a much larger role in the 1969 Fund of Funds audit.

Court testimony disclosed that during the 1969 audit Arthur Andersen's Denver office was assigned "full audit responsibility for the investment [NRPA] account both as to cost and market value." During the 1968 engagement, the Denver office's role in the Fund of Funds audit had been primarily collecting and compiling information for the New York City audit team regarding the mutual fund's natural resource investments. The higher level of responsibility assigned to his audit team for the risky Fund of Funds audit troubled Carr. Also troubling to him was a stern warning he had been given by the IOS audit engagement partner in Geneva. That partner told Carr that it would not be appropriate simply to disclose the valuation method used by Fund of Funds for its natural resource properties if such disclosure "does not fairly present the facts."

In November 1969, Carr drafted a memo discussing the guidelines Arthur Andersen would follow in reviewing revaluation transactions. The memorandum, reproduced in Exhibit 2, was approved by the regional director of Arthur Andersen's West Coast

**EXHIBIT 2**

ARTHUR ANDERSEN MEMO DICTATING CONDITIONS FOR RECOGNIZING INCREASES IN THE VALUE OF FUND OF FUNDS' NATURAL RESOURCE PROPERTIES

November 7, 1969

Any significant increase in the value of natural resource properties over original cost to FOF must, for audit purposes, be supported by either:

(1) An appraisal report rendered by a competent, independent expert, or

(2) an arm's length sale of a sufficiently large portion of a property to establish a proportionate value for the portion retained.

Item 2 above is where we currently are not in clear agreement with the client. King Resources Company has been informed by FOF (purportedly Ed Cowett, Executive Vice President) that sale of a 10% interest in a property would be sufficient for FOF's purposes in ascribing a proportionate value to the 90% retained. This procedure was first used at December 31, 1968, when King Resources Company arranged, on behalf of FOF, for the sale of a 10% interest in an oil and gas drilling prospect and certain uranium claims and leases to Fox-Raff, Inc., a Seattle brokerage firm affiliate.

Since our responsibilities here in Denver with respect to the December 31, 1968, FOF audit consisted only of determining the basis on which King Resources determined the valuations (not auditing such values), we discussed this transaction with John Robinson and Nick Constantakis in New York but left any final audit decision up to them. It is our understanding that the King Resources valuations determined by the 10% sale were allowed to stand in the final FOF audit report

On the question of what constitutes adequate sales data for valuation purposes (i.e., the 10% question), we have proposed the following to King Resources:

(1) No unrealized appreciation would be allowed on sales of relatively small percentages of properties to private investors or others who do not have the necessary expertise to determine a realistic fair market value. By "relatively small," we envision approximately 50% as being a minimum level in this type of sale to establish proportionate values for the remaining interests. This would preclude any unrealized appreciation on sales such as

the December, 1968, sale to Fox-Raff, Inc. since it could not be reasonably sustained that a brokerage firm has the expertise necessary to evaluate primarily undeveloped resource interests.

(2) Appreciation would be allowed if supported by arm's length sales to knowledgeable outside parties. For example, if King Resources sold a 25% interest in the Arctic permits to Texaco or another major oil company, we believe it would be appropriate to ascribe proportionate value to the 75% retained. Just where to draw the line on the percentage has not been clearly established. We feel 10% would be a bare minimum and would like to see a higher number.

Drafted by: Phil Carr, Partner,

Denver Office of AA & Co.

**EXHIBIT 2—*continued***

ARTHUR ANDERSEN MEMO DICTATING CONDITIONS FOR RECOGNIZING INCREASES IN THE VALUE OF FUND OF FUNDS' NATURAL RESOURCE PROPERTIES

audit practice and by an executive partner in the firm's Chicago headquarters. Arthur Andersen gave copies of the memo to a Fund of Funds officer and to executives of King Resources.

In late 1969, King Resources began searching for a third party to purchase a small interest in a large natural resource property in the Arctic that Fund of Funds had previously acquired from King Resources. A revaluation transaction was needed to establish the property's fair market value. King Resources attempted to structure a revaluation transaction that would satisfy the key stipulations included in John Carr's memo shown in Exhibit 2. Eventually, King Resources arranged for a sale of slightly less than 10 percent of the Arctic property to John Mecom. Mecom was the principal owner of U.S. Oil of Louisiana, another Arthur Andersen audit client. At the time, Mecom was experiencing serious financial difficulties. In fact, Arthur Andersen's managing partner had met with Mecom and John King in February 1968 to help Mecom resolve his financial problems.

The Arctic revaluation transaction allowed Fund of Funds to recognize a more than 25 percent increase in the value of its total investment portfolio—an increase of approximately $119 million. Unknown to Arthur Andersen, John King had negotiated a side agreement with Mecom, similar to the agreement he had arranged with Fox-Raff the previous year. Because of this side agreement, the Mecom transaction failed to qualify as a valid arm's length sale, and thus was not a proper basis for increasing the value of Fund of Funds' residual interest in the Arctic property.

The impact of the Arctic revaluation transaction on Fund of Funds' investment portfolio alarmed Phil Carr. Carr discussed the transaction with the regional director of Arthur Andersen's West Coast audit practice. He informed the regional director that the Denver office's review of the revaluation transaction alone did not provide sufficient evidence to support the increased market value ascribed to Fund of Funds' investment in the Arctic property. The regional director supported Carr's position. Carr went on to argue that Arthur Andersen's headquarters office in Chicago should assume final responsibility for approving the valuation of Fund of Funds' natural resource investments.

Several executive partners of Arthur Andersen discussed the NRPA investments before the accounting firm issued its 1969 Fund of Funds audit opinion. This discussion focused on whether it was possible to reach a firm audit conclusion regarding the fair market value of those investments. The IOS audit engagement partner in Geneva was very concerned with the possibility of Fund of Funds' receiving a qualified audit

**EXHIBIT 3**

ARTHUR ANDERSEN'S AUDIT OPINION ON FUND OF FUNDS' 1969 FINANCIAL STATEMENTS

To the Shareholders and Board of Directors,

The Fund of Funds, Limited:

We have examined the consolidated statements of net assets and investments of The Fund of Funds, Limited (an Ontario, Canada, corporation) and subsidiary as of December 31, 1969, and the related consolidated statements of fund operations and changes in net assets for the year then ended. Our examination was made in accordance with generally accepted auditing standards, and accordingly included such tests of the accounting records and such other auditing procedures as we considered necessary in the circumstances. Investments owned by the Fund at December 31, 1969, were confirmed directly to us by the custodian or brokers. The position of investments sold short was confirmed directly to us by the custodian or brokers. Consistent with past practice, certain investments, in the absence of quoted market prices, have been valued by the Board of Directors as indicated in Note 9. These valuations have been reviewed by us to ascertain that they have been determined on the bases described, but since we are not competent to appraise these investments we do not express an opinion as to such valuations.

In our opinion, subject to the effect of certain investment valuations referred to in the preceding paragraph, the above-mentioned financial statements present fairly the financial position of The Fund of Funds, Limited and subsidiary as of December 31, 1969, and the results of their operations and the changes in their net assets for the year then ended, in conformity with generally accepted accounting principles applied on a basis consistent with that of the preceding year.

opinion. That individual remarked that a qualification would cause an "explosion" at Fund of Funds. Nevertheless, Arthur Andersen issued the audit report shown in Exhibit 3 on Fund of Funds' 1969 financial statements. In that audit report, Arthur Andersen declined to express an opinion on whether Fund of Funds' NRPA investments were properly valued. (Notice that the opinion paragraph of the audit report includes a "subject to" qualification relating to the proper valuation of the NRPA investments.)

Arthur Andersen's review of the 1969 Arctic revaluation transaction became a focal point of the trial in the Fund of Funds civil suit. In evaluating Arthur Andersen's review of that transaction, the judge in the Fund of Funds case focused on Andersen's awareness of what became known as the Blakely-Wolcott transaction—a transaction that accounted for nearly 40 percent of King Resources' 1966 net income. The Blakely-Wolcott transaction involved another sale of an oil and gas property by King Resources in which John King had negotiated an illicit and undisclosed side agreement with the purchaser of the property. Although similar to the Fox-Raff and Mecom transactions, the Blakey-Wolcott deal did not involve Fund of Funds. The audit workpapers for the 1966 King Resources audit documented that Arthur Andersen had questioned the validity of the transaction. In fact, the workpapers noted that the Blakely-Wolcott transaction was a "borderline case of simply writing up property." Nevertheless, Arthur Andersen accepted King Resources' accounting treatment for the transaction. Andersen made this decision only after obtaining a representation letter from John King in which he denied the existence of any side agreements related to the Blakely-Wolcott sale.

In early 1970, before signing off on the 1969 Fund of Funds audit, Arthur Andersen's Denver office uncovered concrete evidence indicating that the Blakely-Wolcott transaction was fraudulent. This discovery impugned the integrity of all of the audit evidence collected from John King and King Resources to support the 1969 Fund of

Funds financial statements. Most important, this discovery cast doubt on the audit evidence used to corroborate the large increase in the fair market value of the Arctic property. Nevertheless, as pointed out by the judge in the Fund of Funds case, Arthur Andersen still chose to rely heavily on evidence collected from John King and King Resources while completing the 1969 audit.

> *AA's audit thus continued after the December 1969 Arctic revaluation and after AA knew about Blakely-Wolcott. AA sought and obtained representation letters from King and [an associate] that the Arctic sale was bona fide. Although AA obtained representation letters from Mecom and [an associate] confirming the terms of the express purchase [Arctic] agreement, no inquiry was made of Mecom concerning side agreements as was made to King Resources.*

## *The Fund of Funds, Limited v. Arthur Andersen & Co.:* Allegations and Court Rulings

In the civil lawsuit filed against Arthur Andersen by the Fund of Funds bankruptcy trustee, the principal allegation was that Andersen allowed King Resources to defraud Fund of Funds. The trustee argued that Arthur Andersen should have disclosed to Fund of Funds the modest prices that King Resources had paid for properties later sold to the mutual fund. The trustee also alleged that Arthur Andersen should have disclosed to Fund of Funds its doubts regarding the validity of the Arctic revaluation transaction. According to the trustee, Fund of Funds would not have relied on the Arctic transaction to revalue its investment portfolio if Arthur Andersen had disclosed its concerns regarding the transaction's validity.

Finally, the trustee alleged that Arthur Andersen breached its contractual obligation to disclose to Fund of Funds' officers irregularities [fraud] discovered during the annual audits of the mutual fund. Exhibit 4 presents an excerpt from the engagement letter for the 1968 Fund of Funds audit. As indicated in the final paragraph of that excerpt, Arthur Andersen had agreed to disclose any irregularities discovered during the audit to Fund of Funds' officers.

**EXHIBIT 4**

EXCERPT FROM ARTHUR ANDERSEN'S ENGAGEMENT LETTER FOR 1968 FUND OF FUNDS AUDIT

Our audit work on companies for which we are responsible will consist of examination of the respective balance sheets and statements of net assets and investments as of December 31, 1968, and the related statements of income, surplus and changes in net assets for the year then ending in order to enable us to express an opinion on the financial position and the results of their operations. These examinations will be made in accordance with generally accepted auditing standards and will include all auditing procedures which we consider necessary in the circumstances. These procedures will include, among other things, review and tests of the accounting procedures and internal controls, tests of documentary evidence supporting the transactions recorded in the accounts and direct confirmation of certain assets and liabilities by correspondence with selected customers, creditors, legal counsel, banks, etc.

While certain types of defalcations and similar irregularities may be disclosed by this kind of an examination, it is not designed for that purpose and will not involve the audit of a sufficiently large portion of the total transactions to afford assurances that any defalcations and irregularities will be uncovered. Generally, primary reliance for such disclosure is placed on a company's system of internal control and effective supervision of its accounts and procedures. *Of course, any irregularities coming to our attention would be reported to you immediately*. [Emphasis added by court.]

Arthur Andersen responded to each allegation made by the Fund of Funds bankruptcy trustee. First, the accounting firm maintained that disclosing information obtained during audits of King Resources to Fund of Funds would have violated the client confidentiality rule.[3] Second, Arthur Andersen insisted that Fund of Funds' board of directors had the primary responsibility for determining whether the Arctic revaluation transaction justified restating the mutual fund's remaining equity interest in the Arctic property. Arthur Andersen went on to argue that there was no evidence available prior to that transaction, and very little afterwards, that suggested it was fraudulent. The accounting firm also stressed that the plaintiff had not proven that the transaction resulted in a material overstatement of the mutual fund's NAV. Finally, Arthur Andersen claimed that none of the transactions or activities discovered during the Fund of Funds audits qualified as irregularities and thus were not subject to being reported to client management.

The presiding judge in the Fund of Funds case ruled that Arthur Andersen knew that King Resources was defrauding the mutual fund. In the judge's opinion, Arthur Andersen had a responsibility to disclose to Fund of Funds the prices that King Resources paid to acquire the oil and gas properties ultimately sold to the mutual fund—even though Andersen collected this data during the audits of King Resources. The judge also ruled that Arthur Andersen should have disclosed to Fund of Funds its concerns regarding the Arctic revaluation transaction.

> *Moreover, AA knew all the facts which reasonably suggested that the methodology and result of the 1969 Arctic revaluation was a sham and yet AA persisted in the misleading and incomplete disclosures. . . . Although Fund of Funds management bears primary responsibility for business decisions, the auditor must inform the client when the basic terms of business dealings are so confused as to effectively prevent any conclusions as to the client's financial picture.*

The judge found that the Arctic revaluation transaction clearly had a material effect on Fund of Funds' NAV and, thus, had a "substantial likelihood" of influencing a reasonable investor. Because the Fund of Funds' trustee sued Arthur Andersen under the Securities Exchange Act of 1934, the trustee had to prove scienter, or intent to deceive, on the part of Arthur Andersen. The judge ruled that Arthur Andersen exhibited such a reckless disregard for the truth that the scienter standard was satisfied.[4]

Regarding the breach of contract allegation, the judge found that Arthur Andersen failed to satisfy its contractual commitment to report irregularities discovered during the Fund of Funds audits to the mutual fund's officers. In particular, the judge ruled that the Arctic revaluation transaction was fraudulent and thus an irregularity that should have been reported to Fund of Funds' management. The judge emphasized three points in making this ruling: (1) Arthur Andersen knew, prior to issuing its audit opinion on the 1969 Fund of Funds financial statements, that John King had engaged in a similar fraudulent sale in 1966, namely, the Blakely-Wolcott transaction;[5]

---

3. Plaintiff legal counsel argued that Arthur Andersen, at the very least, had a responsibility to resign from the Fund of Funds engagement after discovering that King Resources was charging the mutual fund exorbitant prices for the oil and gas properties. Arthur Andersen's attorneys maintained that even if their firm had resigned, Fund of Funds would not have benefited, since its management would still have been unaware of King Resources' pricing structure.

4. Another important issue in the Fund of Funds case was exactly what standards of conduct governed Arthur Andersen's performance during its audits of the large mutual fund. According to the judge in this case, "GAAS were relevant to but not determinative of AA's duties of inquiry and disclosure."

5. Recognize that at the time, Arthur Andersen was also aware that the 1968 Fox-Raff revaluation transaction, another transaction arranged by John King, was not legitimate.

(2) Arthur Andersen knew that John Mecom did not have the financial wherewithal to buy a 10 percent interest in the Arctic property; and (3) Arthur Andersen failed to ask Mecom whether the Arctic transaction included a side agreement with John King.

Two issues in the Fund of Funds case had particularly important implications for the public accounting profession. The first of these issues concerned the client confidentiality defense used by Arthur Andersen. According to Arthur Andersen, the client confidentiality rule had precluded it from disclosing to Fund of Funds executives the excessive prices King Resources was charging the mutual fund for oil and gas properties. The judge in the Fund of Funds case discredited this argument.

> *AA's invocation of the shield of client confidentiality conveniently disregards the fact that King Resources' and [an affiliated firm's] records were used for the NRPA audits and that on numerous occasions AA sought information about the King Resources/FOF relationship from the King group. Assuming that the duty of confidentiality applies in this instance . . . [the auditor] may: (1) strongly encourage one client to make the necessary disclosure; (2) disclose that it has relevant information not available to the other client; or (3) resign from one account. AA did none of these.*

A second important issue raised by the Fund of Funds case involved the profession's audit reporting standards. Arthur Andersen's audit report on Fund of Funds' 1969 financial statements contained a "subject to" qualification, as shown in Exhibit 3. The judge ruled that this qualification failed to adequately warn financial statement users that Arthur Andersen seriously questioned the valuation of Fund of Funds' NRPA. "The addition of the words 'subject to' in the 1969 FOF Annual Report was neither soon enough nor complete enough to avoid substantial damage to FOF." Several years later, the profession eliminated "subject to" qualifications.

## EPILOGUE

Following a two-month trial in the summer of 1981, the Fund of Funds bankruptcy trustee was awarded an $80.7 million judgment against Arthur Andersen. In July 1982, Judge Charles Stewart, who presided over the trial, reduced that judgment by approximately $10 million. Nevertheless, the huge size of the judgment raised concerns within the profession regarding the economic viability of accounting firms, particularly smaller national firms that might be forced into bankruptcy if required to pay such a large sum. Ironically, the Fund of Funds shareholders, who were the principal victims of the frauds perpetrated by John King, ultimately recovered the majority of their losses. The Arthur Andersen judgment alone allowed them to recoup a significant portion of their investments in the mutual fund. The shareholders received an even larger payoff following the discovery of oil on the large Arctic property that John King pawned off on the mutual fund in 1969.[6]

John King was convicted and sentenced to prison for the fraudulent transactions he arranged through King Resources. King spent less than two years in prison. Shortly after his release, he suffered a broken neck when he fell from his horse. King died a few months later. Bernie Cornfeld served nearly one year in a Swiss prison after being indicted for securities

6. Following the liquidation of Fund of Funds, its former shareholders received shares of stock in a company that was formed to assume ownership of the Arctic property.

fraud, although he was never convicted of that charge. In 1970, Cornfeld lost control of IOS to a prominent businessman and financier, Robert Vesco. Approximately three years later, the SEC filed suit against Vesco, charging him with stealing $224 million from the IOS funds. Vesco fled the United States and became one of the most sought-after fugitives in U.S. history. For more than two decades, Vesco lived in Havana under the protection of his friend, Fidel Castro. That friendship apparently ended in 1996 when a Cuban court convicted Vesco of defrauding investors in a venture intended to develop a wonder drug effective against cancer. Vesco received a 13-year prison sentence.

After being released from the Swiss prison, Bernie Cornfeld spent most of his remaining years in Acapulco. In 1992, Cornfeld resurfaced in the headlines of U.S. newspapers when he unsuccessfully attempted to purchase MGM Studios in Hollywood. During the last few years of his life, Cornfeld squandered his remaining fortune on a string of bad investments. He died in a London hospital of natural causes in 1995. Cornfeld's close friends established a memorial fund to pay his large hospital bill.

---

## Questions

1. Was it appropriate for Arthur Andersen's Denver office to audit King Resources and to be involved in the audit of Fund of Funds' NRPA investments? Identify the advantages and disadvantages of this arrangement for Arthur Andersen.
2. According to the judge in the Fund of Funds case, Arthur Andersen could have chosen to resign from the Fund of Funds engagement when it discovered the excessive prices being charged the mutual fund by King Resources. Arthur Andersen contended that resigning at that point would not have benefited Fund of Funds. Do you agree? Why or why not? Does the profession's *Code of Professional Conduct* recommend a course of action in this set of circumstances?
3. During the 1968 Fund of Funds audit, the engagement audit partner decided that the revaluation of the mutual fund's assets following the Fox-Raff transaction did not materially affect its NAV. Do you believe that was an appropriate decision? Defend your answer. What precedent, if any, did that decision establish for future audits of Fund of Funds?
4. Arthur Andersen maintained during the Fund of Funds trial that the client's board of directors was primarily responsible for reviewing and eventually approving revaluation transactions. Do you agree with that position? Why did the judge reject this argument?
5. During the 1966 audit of King Resources, Arthur Andersen placed significant reliance on the letter of representations signed by John King. That letter indicated that the Blakely-Wolcott sale was an arm's length transaction. What are the primary objectives an auditor hopes to accomplish by obtaining a letter of representations from client management? How competent is the audit evidence provided by a letter of representations?
6. What additional evidence could Arthur Andersen have obtained to evaluate the legitimacy of the Arctic revaluation transaction?
7. Discuss the general elements of proof a plaintiff must establish when filing a lawsuit under the Securities Exchange Act of 1934. Briefly discuss the evidence

that Fund of Funds' attorneys likely presented to the court to establish each of these elements of proof.

8. The judge in the Fund of Funds case criticized the qualified audit opinion Arthur Andersen issued on Fund of Funds' 1969 financial statements as being "neither soon enough nor complete enough to avoid substantial damage to Fund of Funds." Draft an audit report that would be appropriate for the 1969 Fund of Funds financial statements, given present audit reporting standards.

CASE 1.7

# Crazy Eddie, Inc.

In 1969, Eddie Antar, a 21-year-old high school dropout from Brooklyn, opened a consumer electronics store with 150 square feet of floor space in New York City.[1] Despite this modest beginning, Antar would eventually dominate the retail consumer electronics market in the New York City metropolitan area. By 1987, Antar's firm, Crazy Eddie, Inc., had 43 retail outlets, sales exceeding $350 million, and outstanding stock with a collective market value of $600 million. Antar personally realized more than $70 million from the sale of Crazy Eddie stock during his tenure as the company's chief executive.

A classic rags-to-riches story became a spectacular business failure in the late 1980s when Crazy Eddie collapsed following allegations of extensive financial wrongdoing by Antar and his associates. Shortly after a hostile takeover of the company in November 1987, the firm's new owners discovered that Crazy Eddie's inventory was overstated by more than $65 million. This inventory shortage had been concealed from the public in registration statements filed with the Securities and Exchange Commission (SEC). Subsequent investigations by regulatory authorities revealed that Eddie Antar and his subordinates had grossly overstated Crazy Eddie's reported profits throughout its existence.[2]

## Eddie Antar: The Man Behind the Legend

Eddie Antar was born into a large, closely knit Syrian family in 1947. After dropping out of high school at the age of 16, Antar began peddling television sets in his Brooklyn neighborhood. Within a few years, Antar and one of his cousins scraped together enough cash to open an electronics store near Coney Island. It was at this tiny store that Antar acquired the nickname "Crazy Eddie." When a customer attempted to leave the store empty-handed, Antar would block the store's exit, sometimes locking the door until the individual agreed to buy something—anything. To entice a reluctant customer to make a purchase, Antar first determined which product the customer was considering and then lowered the price until the customer finally capitulated.

Antar became well known in his neighborhood not only for his unusual sales tactics but also for his unconventional, if not asocial, behavior. A bodybuilder and fitness fanatic, he typically came to work in his exercise togs, accompanied by a menacing German shepherd. His quick temper caused repeated problems with vendors, competitors, and subordinates. Antar's most distinctive trait was his inability to trust anyone outside of his large extended family. In later years, when he needed someone to serve in an executive capacity in his company, Antar nearly always tapped a family member, although the individual seldom had the appropriate training or experience

1. This case was coauthored by Carol Knapp, Assistant Professor at the University of Oklahoma.

2. The facts of this case were drawn from numerous articles and SEC enforcement releases published over a period of several years. *The New York Times* and *The Wall Street Journal*, in particular, closely followed the colorful saga of Crazy Eddie and its founder, Eddie Antar. One of the more comprehensive investigative reports that documented the history of Crazy Eddie, Inc., is the following article: G. Belsky and P. Furman, "Calculated Madness: The Rise and Fall of Crazy Eddie Antar," *Crain's New York Business*, 5 June 1989, 21–33. That article provided much of the background information regarding Eddie Antar that is included in this case.

for the position. Eventually, Antar's father, sister, two brothers, uncle, brother-in-law, and several cousins would assume leadership positions with Crazy Eddie, while more than one dozen other relatives would hold minor positions with the firm.

## Crazy Eddie's Formula for Success

In the early 1980s, sales in the consumer electronics industry exploded, doubling in the four-year period from 1981 to 1984 alone. As the public's demand for electronic products grew at an ever-increasing pace, Antar converted his Crazy Eddie stores into consumer electronics supermarkets. Antar stocked the shelves of Crazy Eddie's retail outlets with every electronic gadget he could find and with as many different brands of those products as possible. By 1987, the company featured seven product lines. Following are those product lines and their percentage contributions to Crazy Eddie's 1987 sales.

| | |
|---|---|
| Televisions | 53% |
| Audio products and systems | 15 |
| Portable and personal electronics | 10 |
| Car stereos | 5 |
| Accessories and tapes | 4 |
| Computers and games | 3 |
| Miscellaneous items—including microwaves, air conditioners, and small appliances | 10 |
| Total | 100% |

Antar encouraged his salespeople to supplement each store's profits by pressuring customers to buy extended product warranties. Many, if not most, of the repair costs that Crazy Eddie paid under these warranties were recovered by the company from manufacturers that had issued factory warranties on the products. As a result, the company realized a 100 percent profit margin on much of its warranty revenue.

As his firm grew rapidly during the late 1970s and early 1980s, Antar began extracting large price concessions from his suppliers. His ability to purchase electronic products in large quantities and at cut-rate prices enabled him to become a "transhipper," or secondary supplier, of these goods to smaller consumer electronics retailers in the New York City area. Although manufacturers frowned on this practice and often threatened to stop selling to him, Antar continually increased the scale of his transhipping operation.

The most important ingredient in Antar's marketing strategy was large-scale advertising. Antar created an advertising "umbrella" over his company's principal retail market that included the densely populated area within a 150-mile radius of New York City. Antar blanketed this region with raucous, sometimes annoying, but always memorable radio and television commercials.

In 1972, Antar hired a local radio personality and part-time actor known as Doctor Jerry to serve as Crazy Eddie's advertising spokesperson. Over the 15 years that the bug-eyed Doctor Jerry hawked products for Crazy Eddie, he achieved a higher "recognition quotient" among the public than Ed Koch, the longtime mayor of New York City. Doctor Jerry's series of ear-piercing television commercials that featured him screaming "Crazy Eddie—His prices are insane!" brought the company national notoriety when they were parodied by Dan Akroyd on *Saturday Night Live*.

Crazy Eddie's discounting policy served as the focal theme of the company's advertising campaigns. The company promised to refund the difference between the selling price of a product and any lower price for that same item that a customer found within 30 days of the purchase date. Despite the advertising barrage intended to convince the public that Crazy Eddie was a deep-discounter, the company's prices on most products were in line with those of its major competitors. Customers drawn to Crazy Eddie outlets by "advertised specials" were routinely diverted by sales staff to higher-priced merchandise.

## Crazy Eddie Goes Public

In 1983, Antar decided to sell stock in Crazy Eddie to raise capital to finance his aggressive expansion program. The underwriting firm retained by Antar delayed Crazy Eddie's initial public offering (IPO) for more than one year after discovering that the company's financial records were in disarray. Among other problems uncovered by the underwriter were extensive related-party transactions, interest-free loans to employees, and speculative investments unrelated to the company's principal line of business. The underwriting firm was also disturbed to find that nearly all of the company's key executives were members of the Antar family. Certain of these individuals, including Antar's wife and mother, were receiving salaries approaching $100,000 for little or no work.

To prepare for the IPO, the underwriter encouraged Antar, Crazy Eddie's chairman of the board and president, to clean up the company's accounting records and financial affairs. The underwriter also urged Antar to hire a chief financial officer (CFO) who had experience with a public company and who was not a member of the Antar family. The underwriter warned Antar that investors would question the competence of Crazy Eddie's executives who were his relatives. Despite the underwriter's concern, Antar hired his first cousin, Sam E. Antar, to serve as Crazy Eddie's CFO.

The sale of Crazy Eddie's stock to the public was a tremendous success. Because the IPO was oversubscribed, the company's underwriter obtained permission from the SEC to sell 200,000 more shares than originally planned. Following the public offering, Antar worked hard to convince the investment community, particularly financial analysts, that his firm was financially strong and well managed. At every opportunity, Antar painted a picture of continued growth and increased market share for Crazy Eddie.

One tactic Antar used to convince financial analysts that the company had a rosy future was to invite them to a store and demonstrate in person his uncanny ability to "close" sales. Such tactics worked to perfection as analysts from prominent investment firms released glowing reports regarding Crazy Eddie's management team and the company's bright prospects. One analyst wrote, "Crazy Eddie is a disciplined, competently organized firm with a sophisticated management and a well-trained, dedicated staff."[1] Another analyst wrote that Antar is a "brilliant merchant surrounded by a deeply dedicated organization eager to create an important retail business."[2] Because of such reports and continued strong operating results (as reflected by the company's 1984–1987 financial statements shown in Exhibit 1 and Exhibit 2), the price of Crazy Eddie's stock skyrocketed. Many investors who purchased the company's stock in the IPO realized a 1,000 percent increase in the value of their investments.

## Crazy Eddie Goes ... Bust

Despite Crazy Eddie's impressive operating results during the mid-1980s and the fact that the company's stock was one of the hottest investments on Wall Street, all was not well within the firm. By 1986, the company was in deep trouble. By the latter part of

3. J. E. Tannenbaum, "How Mounting Woes at Crazy Eddie Sank Turnaround Effort," *The Wall Street Journal*, 10 July 1989, A1, A4.

4. G. Belsky and P. Furman, "Calculated Madness: The Rise and Fall of Crazy Eddie Antar," *Crain's New York Business*, 5 June 1989, 26.

**EXHIBIT 1**

1984–1987 BALANCE SHEETS OF CRAZY EDDIE

**CRAZY EDDIE, INC.**
**BALANCE SHEETS (000s omitted)**

| | March 1, 1987 | March 2, 1986 | March 3, 1985 | May 31, 1984 |
|---|---|---|---|---|
| Current assets: | | | | |
| Cash | $ 9,347 | $ 13,296 | $22,273 | $ 1,375 |
| Short-term investments | 121,957 | 26,840 | — | — |
| Receivables | 10,846 | 2,246 | 2,740 | 2,604 |
| Merchandise inventories | 109,072 | 59,864 | 26,543 | 23,343 |
| Prepaid expenses | 10,639 | 2,363 | 645 | 514 |
| Total current assets | 261,861 | 104,609 | 52,201 | 27,836 |
| Restricted cash | — | 3,356 | 7,058 | — |
| Due from affiliates | — | — | — | 5,739 |
| Property, plant and equipment | 26,401 | 7,172 | 3,696 | 1,845 |
| Construction in process | — | 6,253 | 1,154 | — |
| Other assets | 6,596 | 5,560 | 1,419 | 1,149 |
| Total assets | $294,858 | $126,950 | $65,528 | $36,569 |
| Current liabilities: | | | | |
| Accounts payable | $ 50,022 | $ 51,723 | $23,078 | $20,106 |
| Notes payable | — | — | — | 2,900 |
| Short-term debt | 49,571 | 2,254 | 423 | 124 |
| Unearned revenue | 3,641 | 3,696 | 1,173 | 764 |
| Accrued expenses | 5,593 | 17,126 | 8,733 | 6,078 |
| Total current liabilities | 108,827 | 74,799 | 33,407 | 29,972 |
| Long-term debt | 8,459 | 7,701 | 7,625 | 46 |
| Convertible subordinated debentures | 80,975 | — | — | — |
| Unearned revenue | 3,337 | 1,829 | 635 | 327 |
| Stockholders' equity: | | | | |
| Common stock | 313 | 280 | 134 | 50 |
| Additional paid-in capital | 57,678 | 17,668 | 12,298 | 574 |
| Retained earnings | 35,269 | 24,673 | 11,429 | 5,600 |
| Total stockholders' equity | 93,260 | 42,621 | 23,861 | 6,224 |
| Total liabilities and stockholders' equity | $294,858 | $126,950 | $65,528 | $36,569 |

that year, the boom days had ended for the consumer electronics industry. Although sales of consumer electronics were still increasing, the rate of growth had tapered off considerably as compared with the dramatic growth rates realized by the industry during the early 1980s. Additionally, the industry had become saturated with retailers, particularly in major metropolitan areas such as New York City, Crazy Eddie's home base. Increased competition meant smaller profit margins for Crazy Eddie and diminished Antar's ability to extract sweetheart deals from his suppliers.

Besides the problems posed by the increasingly competitive consumer electronics industry, Crazy Eddie faced a corporate meltdown in the late 1980s. The tripling of the company's annual sales volume between 1984 and 1987 and the more

**EXHIBIT 2**

1984–1987 INCOME STATEMENTS OF CRAZY EDDIE

CRAZY EDDIE, INC.
INCOME STATEMENTS (000s omitted)

| | Year Ended March 1, 1987 | Year Ended March 2, 1986 | Nine Months Ended March 3, 1985 | Year Ended May 31, 1984 |
|---|---|---|---|---|
| Net sales | $352,523 | $262,268 | $136,319 | $137,285 |
| Cost of goods sold | (272,255) | (194,371) | (103,421) | (106,934) |
| Gross profit | 80,268 | 67,897 | 32,898 | 30,351 |
| Selling, general and administrative expense | (61,341) | (42,975) | (20,508) | (22,560) |
| Interest and other income | 7,403 | 3,210 | 1,211 | 706 |
| Interest expense | (5,233) | (820) | (438) | (522) |
| Income before taxes | 21,097 | 27,312 | 13,163 | 7,975 |
| Pension contribution | (500) | (800) | (600) | — |
| Income taxes | (10,001) | (13,268) | (6,734) | (4,202) |
| Net income | $ 10,596 | $ 13,244 | $ 5,829 | $ 3,773 |
| Net income per share | $.34 | $.48 | $.24 | $.18 |

complex responsibilities associated with managing a public company imposed an enormous administrative burden on Crazy Eddie's executives. Complicating matters was the disintegration of Antar's inner circle of relatives, who had served as his principal advisers during the first 15 years of his company's existence. Antar forced many of his relatives to leave the firm after they sided with his former wife in a bitter divorce. Even as Crazy Eddie's internal affairs spiraled into chaos and the firm lurched toward financial disaster, Wall Street continued to tout the company's stock as a "can't miss" investment.

In late 1986, Eddie Antar resigned as company president, although he retained the title of chairman of the board. A few weeks later, he simply dropped out of sight. In the absence of Antar, Crazy Eddie's financial condition worsened rapidly. Poor operating results that the company reported for the fourth quarter of fiscal 1987—which ended March 1, 1987—sent Crazy Eddie's stock price into a tailspin from which it never recovered. In November 1987, a takeover group headed by two well-known financiers gained control of the company. A company-wide physical inventory taken by the new owners uncovered the $65 million shortage of inventory alluded to earlier. That inventory shortage, which was larger than the cumulative profits the company had reported since it went public in 1984, would eventually plunge Crazy Eddie into bankruptcy and send regulatory authorities in pursuit of Eddie Antar for an explanation.

## Charges of Accounting Irregularities

Extensive investigations of Crazy Eddie's financial records by the new owners and regulatory authorities culminated in fraud charges being filed against Eddie Antar and his former associates. The SEC alleged that after Crazy Eddie went public in 1984,

Antar became preoccupied with the price of his company's stock. Antar realized that Crazy Eddie had to keep posting impressive operating results to maintain the upward trend in the stock's price. An SEC investigation revealed that within the first six months after the company went public, Antar ordered a subordinate to overstate inventory by $2 million, resulting in the firm's gross profit being overstated by the same amount. The following year Antar ordered year-end inventory to be overstated by $9 million and accounts payable to be understated by $3 million. Court records documented that Crazy Eddie employees overstated year-end inventory by preparing inventory count sheets for items that did not exist. To understate accounts payable, employees prepared bogus debit memos from vendors and entered them in the company's accounting records.

As the economic fortunes of Crazy Eddie began to fade in the late 1980s, Antar became more desperate in his efforts to enhance the company's reported revenues and profits. He ordered company employees to include in inventory consigned merchandise and goods being returned to suppliers. Another fraudulent tactic Antar used to overstate inventory involved transhipping transactions, the large-volume transactions between Crazy Eddie and many of its smaller competitors.

Antar knew that financial analysts closely monitor the annual percentage change in "same-store" sales for retailers. A decline in this percentage is seen as a negative indicator of a retailer's future financial performance. As the consumer electronics industry became increasingly crowded, the revenues of Crazy Eddie's individual stores began to fall, although the firm's total revenues continued to climb due to new stores being opened each year. To remedy the drop in same-store sales, Antar instructed his employees to record selected transhipping transactions as retail sales of individual stores. For instance, suppose that Crazy Eddie sold 100 microwaves costing $180 each to another retailer at a per unit price of $200. The $20,000 in sales would be recorded as retail sales with a normal gross profit margin of 30 to 50 percent—meaning that inventory would not be credited for the total number of microwaves actually sold. This practice killed two birds with the proverbial stone. Same-store sales were inflated for selected operating units, and inventory was overstated with a corresponding increase in gross profit from sales.

## Where Were the Auditors?

"Where were the auditors?" was a question posed repeatedly by investors, creditors, and other interested parties when the public learned of the Crazy Eddie fraud. Four different accounting firms audited Crazy Eddie's financial statements over its turbulent history. Antar dismissed Crazy Eddie's first accounting firm, a local firm, before he took the company public. The underwriter that managed Crazy Eddie's IPO urged Antar to retain a more prestigious accounting firm to increase the public's confidence in the company's financial statements. As a result, Antar retained Main Hurdman to serve as Crazy Eddie's audit firm. Main Hurdman had a nationwide accounting practice with several prominent clients in the consumer electronics industry. In the mid-1980s, Peat Marwick became Crazy Eddie's audit firm when it merged with Main Hurdman. Following the corporate takeover of Crazy Eddie in 1987, the new owners replaced Peat Marwick with Touche Ross.

Much of the criticism triggered by the Crazy Eddie scandal centered on Main Hurdman and its successor, Peat Marwick. Main Hurdman charged Crazy Eddie comparatively modest fees for the company's annual audits. A leading critic of major accounting firms alleged that Main Hurdman had "lowballed" to obtain Crazy Eddie as an audit client, realizing that it could make up for any lost audit revenue by selling the company consulting services.

> *In one year, Main Hurdman charged only $85,000 to do a complete audit of Crazy Eddie—a business with hundreds of millions of dollars in reported revenues, dozens of retail stores, and two large warehouses. At the very same time that Main Hurdman was charging the bargain basement price of $85,000 for supposedly conducting an audit, its consulting division was charging Crazy Eddie millions of dollars to computerize Crazy Eddie's inventory system.*[3]

This same individual challenged Main Hurdman's ability to objectively audit an inventory system that it had effectively developed. Main Hurdman's independence was also questioned because many of Crazy Eddie's accountants were former members of that accounting firm. Critics charge that a company that hires one or more of its former auditors can more easily conceal fraudulent activities during the course of subsequent audits. That is, a former auditor may help his or her new employer undermine subsequent audits. In fact, Crazy Eddie's practice of hiring its former auditors is not unusual. Many accounting firms actually arrange such "placements" with audit clients.

> *You would think that if an auditor wanted to leave a public accounting firm, he or she would be discouraged from going to work for clients they had audited. Instead, just the opposite is true with big accounting firms encouraging their personnel to work for clients in the apparent belief that it helps cement the accountant—client relationship.*[4]

Most of the criticism directed at Crazy Eddie's auditors stemmed from their failure to uncover the huge overstatement of the company's inventory and the material understatement of accounts payable. Third parties who filed suit against the auditors accused them of "aiding and abetting" the fraud by failing to thoroughly investigate numerous suspicious circumstances they discovered. Of particular concern were several reported instances in which the auditors requested client documents, only to be told that those documents had been lost or inadvertently destroyed.

In Peat Marwick and Main Hurdman's defense, Antar and his associates engaged in a large-scale plan to deceive the auditors. For example, after determining which inventory sites the auditors would be visiting at year-end, Antar shipped sufficient inventory to those stores or warehouses to conceal any shortages. Likewise, Crazy Eddie personnel systematically destroyed incriminating documents to conceal inventory shortages from the auditors. Antar also ordered his employees to "junk" the sophisticated, computer-based inventory system designed by Main Hurdman and to return to the outdated manual inventory system previously used by the company. The absence of a computer-based inventory system made it much more difficult for the auditors to determine exactly how much inventory the firm had at any point in time.

A particularly disturbing aspect of the Crazy Eddie scandal was the involvement of several key accounting employees in the various fraudulent schemes. These parties included the director of the internal audit staff, the acting controller, and the director of accounts payable. Past audit failures demonstrate that a fraud involving the collusion of key accounting personnel is difficult for auditors to uncover.

---

5. M. I. Weiss, "Auditors: Be Watchdogs, Not Just Bean Counters," *Accounting Today*, 15 November 1993, 41.

6. *Ibid.*, 42.

# EPILOGUE

In June 1989, Crazy Eddie filed a Chapter 11 bankruptcy petition after losing its line of credit. Later that year, the company closed its remaining stores and liquidated its assets. Meanwhile, Eddie Antar was named as a defendant in several lawsuits, including a large civil suit filed by the SEC and a criminal indictment filed by a U.S. district attorney. In January 1990, a federal judge ordered Antar to repatriate $52 million that he had transferred to foreign bank accounts in 1987.

The following month, federal marshals began searching for Antar after he failed to appear in federal court. A judge had scheduled a hearing to force Antar to account for the funds he had transferred to overseas bank accounts. After Antar surrendered to federal marshals, the judge found him in contempt and released him on his own recognizance. Following this court appearance, Antar became a fugitive. For the next two years, Antar eluded federal authorities despite reported sightings of him in Brooklyn, Jerusalem, and South America.

On June 25, 1992, Israeli police arrested Eddie Antar. At the time, he was living in a small town outside Tel Aviv and posing as an Israeli citizen, David Jacob Levi Cohen. On December 31, 1992, Antar's attorney announced that an extradition agreement had been reached with the U.S. Department of Justice and Israeli authorities. After being extradited, Antar was convicted in July 1993 on 17 counts of financial fraud including racketeering, conspiracy, and mail fraud. In May 1994, a federal judge sentenced Antar to 12 1/2 years in federal prison and ordered him to pay restitution of $121 million to former stockholders and creditors.

A federal appeals court overturned Antar's fraud conviction in April 1995. The appeals court ruled that the judge who had presided over Antar's trial had been biased against him and ordered that a new trial be held under a different judge. In May 1996, Antar's attorneys and federal prosecutors arranged a plea bargain agreement to settle the charges outstanding against him. Under the terms of this agreement, Antar pleaded guilty to one federal charge of racketeering and publicly admitted, for the first time, that he had defrauded investors by manipulating his company's accounting records. Following his admission of guilt, one of the prosecuting attorneys commented that "Crazy Eddie wasn't crazy, he was crooked."[5]

In early 1997, Eddie Antar was sentenced to seven years in federal prison. Antar, who had remained in custody since being extradited to the United States in 1993, received credit for the time he had already spent in prison. As a result, he was required to serve only two years of his seven-year sentence.

Several of Antar's former cohorts have also been convicted or have pleaded guilty to fraud charges, including Sam E. Antar, Crazy Eddie's former CFO. After being released from prison, Sam E. Antar openly described and discussed his role in the fraud masterminded by his cousin. He revealed that Eddie had financed his college degree in accounting because the family needed an expert accountant to help design, manage, and conceal the company's fraudulent schemes. Sam graduated ***magna cum laude*** in accounting and passed the CPA exam on his first attempt. Upon joining Crazy Eddie, Sam confessed that he became a "thug" and a willing participant in the massive fraud:

> *Crazy Eddie was an empire built on deceit. The company was rotten to its core. Eddie Antar, his father, brothers, brother-in-law, me and others formed the nucleus of this massive criminal enterprise. In our day, we considered the humanity of others as weaknesses to be exploited in our efforts to commit our crimes. We simply gave investors, creditors, and many customers a raw deal. . . . We were nothing but cold-hearted and soulless criminals. We were two-bit thugs.*[6]

7. F. A. McMorris, "Crazy Eddie Inc.'s Antar Admits Guilt in Racketeering Conspiracy," *The Wall Street Journal*, 9 May 1996, B7.

8. Sam E. Antar, "Crazy Eddie Speaks, Cousin Sam E. Antar Responds," *White Collar Fraud* (http://whitecollarfraud.blogspot.com), 25 June 2007.

In March 1993, an agreement was reached to settle dozens of pending civil lawsuits spawned by the Crazy Eddie fraud. The contributions of the various defendants to the $42 million settlement pool were not disclosed; however, the defendants contributing to that pool included Peat Marwick and the local accounting firm used by Crazy Eddie before the company went public. Law enforcement authorities recovered more than $150 million from the parties that profited from the fraud. Those funds included more than $40 million that a federal judge ordered Sam Antar, Eddie Antar's father, to surrender in August 2002.

In the late 1990s, Eddie Antar's mother purchased the Crazy Eddie logo and the company's former advertising catch phrase, "Crazy Eddie—His prices are insane!" which had been sold in bankruptcy proceedings years earlier. In 1998, two nephews of Eddie Antar revived their uncle's business. The "new" Crazy Eddie operated principally as a mail-order and Internet-based retailer of consumer electronics. In June 2001, a New York business publication reported that the company had hired a former executive in the consumer electronics industry to serve as the "creative force" behind its marketing efforts.[9] That individual was none other than Crazy Eddie Antar.[10]

## Questions

1. Compute key ratios and other financial measures for Crazy Eddie during the period 1984–1987. Identify and briefly explain the red flags in Crazy Eddie's financial statements that suggested the firm posed a higher-than-normal level of audit risk.
2. Identify specific audit procedures that might have led to the detection of the following accounting irregularities perpetrated by Crazy Eddie personnel: (a) the falsification of inventory count sheets, (b) the bogus debit memos for accounts payable, (c) the recording of transhipping transactions as retail sales, and (d) the inclusion of consigned merchandise in year-end inventory.
3. The retail consumer electronics industry was undergoing rapid and dramatic changes during the 1980s. Discuss how changes in an audit client's industry should affect audit planning decisions. Relate this discussion to Crazy Eddie.
4. Explain what is implied by the term lowballing in an audit context. How can this practice potentially affect the quality of independent audit services?
5. Assume that you were a member of the Crazy Eddie audit team in 1986. You were assigned to test the client's year-end inventory cutoff procedures. You selected 30 invoices entered in the accounting records near year-end: 15 in the few days prior to the client's fiscal year-end and 15 in the first few days of the new year. Assume that client personnel were unable to locate 10 of these invoices. How should you and your superiors have responded to this situation? Explain.
6. Should companies be allowed to hire individuals who formerly served as their independent auditors? Discuss the pros and cons of this practice.

9. *Crain's New York Business*, "Week in Review," 11 June 2001, 34.

10. In 2004, the "new" Crazy Eddie failed. The company's trademarks were purchased by a Texas-based firm.

**CASE 1.8**

# ZZZZ Best Company, Inc.

On May 19, 1987, a short article in *The Wall Street Journal* reported that ZZZZ Best Company, Inc., of Reseda, California, had signed a contract for a $13.8 million insurance restoration project. This project was just the most recent of a series of large restoration jobs obtained by ZZZZ Best (pronounced "zee best"). Located in the San Fernando Valley of southern California, ZZZZ Best had begun operations in the fall of 1982 as a small, door-to-door carpet cleaning operation. Under the direction of Barry Minkow, the extroverted 16-year-old who founded the company and initially operated it out of his parents' garage, ZZZZ Best experienced explosive growth in both revenues and profits during the first several years of its existence. In the three-year period from 1984 to 1987, the company's net income surged from less than $200,000 to more than $5 million on revenues of $50 million.

When ZZZZ Best went public in 1986, Minkow and several of his close associates became multimillionaires overnight. By the late spring of 1987, the market value of Minkow's stock in the company exceeded $100 million, while the total market value of ZZZZ Best surpassed $200 million. The youngest chief executive officer in the nation enjoyed the "good life," which included an elegant home in an exclusive suburb of Los Angeles and a fire-engine red Ferrari. Minkow's charm and entrepreneurial genius made him a sought-after commodity on the television talk show circuit and caused the print and visual media to tout him as an example of what America's youth could attain if they would only apply themselves. During an appearance on *The Oprah Winfrey Show* in April 1987, Minkow exhorted his peers with evangelistic zeal to "Think big, be big" and encouraged them to adopt his personal motto, "The sky is the limit."

Less than two years after appearing on *Oprah*, Barry Minkow began serving a 25-year prison sentence. Tried and convicted on 57 counts of securities fraud, Minkow had been exposed as a fast-talking con artist who swindled his closest friends and Wall Street out of millions of dollars. Federal prosecutors estimate that, at a minimum, Minkow cost investors and creditors $100 million. The company that Minkow founded was, in fact, an elaborate Ponzi scheme. The reported profits of the firm were nonexistent and the large restoration contracts, imaginary. As one journalist reported, rather than building a corporation, Minkow created a hologram of a corporation. In July 1987, just three months after the company's stock reached a market value of $220 million, an auction of its assets netted only $62,000.

Unlike most financial frauds, the ZZZZ Best scam was perpetrated under the watchful eye of the Securities and Exchange Commission (SEC). The SEC, a large and reputable West Coast law firm that served as the company's general counsel, a prominent Wall Street brokerage firm, and an international public accounting firm all failed to uncover Minkow's daring scheme. Ultimately, the persistence of an indignant homemaker who had been bilked out of a few hundred dollars by ZZZZ Best resulted in Minkow being exposed as a fraud.

How a teenage flimflam artist could make a mockery of the complex regulatory structure that oversees the U.S. securities markets was the central question posed by a congressional subcommittee that investigated the ZZZZ Best debacle. That subcommittee was headed by Representative John D. Dingell, chairman of the U.S. House

Committee on Energy and Commerce. Throughout the investigation, Representative Dingell and his colleagues focused on the role the company's independent auditors played in the ZZZZ Best scandal.

> *The ZZZZ Best prospectus told the public that revenues and earnings from insurance restoration contracts were skyrocketing but did not reveal that the contracts were completely fictitious. Where were the independent auditors and the others that are paid to alert the public to fraud and deceit?*[7]

Like many other daring financial frauds, the ZZZZ Best scandal caused Congress to reexamine the maze of rules that regulate financial reporting and serve as the foundation of the U.S. system of corporate oversight. Daniel Akst, however, a reporter for *The Wall Street Journal* who documented the rise and fall of Barry Minkow, suggested that another ZZZZ Best was inevitable. "Changing the accounting rules and securities laws will help, but every now and then a Barry Minkow will come along, and ZZZZ Best will happen again. Such frauds are in the natural order of things, I suspect, as old and enduring as human needs."[8]

## The Early History of ZZZZ Best Company

Barry Minkow was introduced to the carpet cleaning industry at the age of 12 by his mother, who helped make ends meet by working as a telephone solicitor for a small carpet cleaning firm. Although the great majority of companies in the carpet cleaning industry are legitimate, the nature of the business attracts a disproportionate number of shady characters. There are essentially no barriers to entry: no licensing requirements, no apprenticeships to be served, and only a minimal amount of start-up capital is needed. A 16-year-old youth with a driver's license can easily become what industry insiders refer to as a "rug sucker," which is exactly what Minkow did when he founded ZZZZ Best Company.

Minkow quickly learned that carpet cleaning was a difficult way to earn a livelihood. Customer complaints, ruthless competition, bad checks, and nagging vendors demanding payment complicated the young entrepreneur's life. Within months of striking out on his own, Minkow faced the ultimate nemesis of the small businessperson: a shortage of working capital. Because of his age and the fact that ZZZZ Best was only marginally profitable, local banks refused to loan him money. Ever resourceful, the brassy teenager came up with his own innovative ways to finance his business: check kiting, credit card forgeries, and the staging of thefts to fleece his insurance company. Minkow's age and personal charm allowed him to escape unscathed from his early brushes with the law that resulted from his creative financing methods. The ease with which the "system" could be beaten encouraged him to exploit it on a broader scale.

Throughout his tenure with ZZZZ Best, Minkow recognized the benefits of having an extensive social network of friends and acquaintances. Many of these relationships he developed and cultivated at a Los Angeles health club. After becoming a friend of Tom Padgett, an insurance claims adjuster, Minkow devised a scheme to exploit that friendship. Minkow promised to pay Padgett $100 per week if he would simply confirm over the telephone to banks and any other interested third parties that ZZZZ Best was the recipient of occasional insurance restoration contracts. Ostensibly, Minkow had

1. This and all subsequent quotations, unless indicated otherwise, were taken from the following source: U.S. Congress, House, Subcommittee on Oversight and Investigations of the Committee on Energy and Commerce, *Failure of ZZZZ Best Co.* (Washington, DC: U.S. Government Printing Office, 1988).

2. D. Akst, *Wonder Boy, Barry Minkow—The Kid Who Swindled Wall Street* (New York: Scribner, 1990), 271.

obtained these contracts to clean and do minor remodeling work on properties damaged by fire, storms, or other catastrophes. Minkow convinced the gullible Padgett that the sole purpose of the confirmations was to allow ZZZZ Best to circumvent much of the bureaucratic red tape in the insurance industry.

From this modest beginning, the ZZZZ Best fraud blossomed. Initially, Minkow used the phony insurance restoration contracts to generate the paper profits and revenues he needed to convince bankers to loan him money. Minkow's phony financial statements served their purpose, and he expanded his operations by opening several carpet cleaning outlets across the San Fernando Valley. Minkow soon realized that there was no need to tie his future to the cutthroat carpet cleaning industry when he could literally dictate the size and profitability of his insurance restoration "business." Within a short period of time, insurance restoration, rather than carpet cleaning, became the major source of revenue appearing on ZZZZ Best's income statements.

Minkow's "the sky is the limit" philosophy drove him to be even more innovative. The charming young entrepreneur began using his bogus financial statements to entice wealthy individuals in his ever-expanding social network to invest in ZZZZ Best. Eventually, Minkow recognized that the ultimate scam would be to take his company public, a move that would allow him to tap the bank accounts of unsuspecting investors nationwide.

## Going Public with ZZZZ Best

Minkow's decision to take ZZZZ Best public meant that he could no longer completely control his firm's financial disclosures. Registering with the SEC required auditors, investment bankers, and outside attorneys to peruse ZZZZ Best's periodic financial statements.

ZZZZ Best was first subjected to a full-scope independent audit for the 12 months ended April 30, 1986. George Greenspan, the sole practitioner who performed that audit, confirmed the existence of ZZZZ Best's major insurance restoration contracts by contacting Tom Padgett. Padgett served as the principal officer of Interstate Appraisal Services, which reportedly contracted the jobs out to ZZZZ Best. By this time, Padgett was an active and willing participant in Minkow's fraudulent schemes. Minkow established Interstate Appraisal Services and Assured Property Management for the sole purpose of generating fake insurance restoration contracts for ZZZZ Best.

In testimony before the congressional subcommittee that investigated the ZZZZ Best scandal, Greenspan insisted that he had properly audited Minkow's company. Greenspan testified that while planning the 1986 audit he had performed various analytical procedures to identify unusual relationships in ZZZZ Best's financial data. These procedures allegedly included comparing ZZZZ Best's key financial ratios with industry norms. Regarding the insurance contracts, Greenspan testified that he had obtained and reviewed copies of all key documents pertaining to those jobs. However, Greenspan admitted that he had not inspected any of the insurance restoration sites.

Congressman Lent: *Mr. Greenspan, I am interested in the SEC Form S-1 that ZZZZ Best Company filed with the SEC. . . You say in that report that you made your examination in accordance with generally accepted auditing standards and accordingly included such tests of the accounting records and other auditing procedures as we consider necessary in the circumstances. . . . You don't say in that statement that you made any personal on-site inspections.*

Mr. Greenspan: *It's not required. Sometimes you do; sometimes you don't. I was satisfied that these jobs existed and I was satisfied from at least six different sources, including payment for the job. What could you want better than that?*

Congressman Lent: *Your position is that you are an honest and reputable accountant.*

Mr. Greenspan: *Yes, sir.*

Congressman Lent: *You were as much a victim as some of the investors in this company?*

Mr. Greenspan: *I was a victim all right. . . . I am as much aghast as anyone. And every night I sit down and say, why didn't I detect this damned fraud.*

## Retention of Ernst & Whinney by ZZZZ Best

Shortly after Greenspan completed his audit of ZZZZ Best's financial statements for fiscal 1986, which ended April 30, 1986, Minkow dismissed him and retained Ernst & Whinney to perform the following year's audit. Apparently, ZZZZ Best's investment banker insisted that Minkow obtain a Big Eight accounting firm to enhance the credibility of the company's financial statements. At approximately the same time, and for the same reason, Minkow retained a high-profile Los Angeles law firm to represent ZZZZ Best as its legal counsel.

The congressional subcommittee asked Greenspan what information he provided to Ernst & Whinney regarding his former client. In particular, the subcommittee wanted to know whether Greenspan discussed the insurance restoration contracts with the new auditors.

Congressman Wyden: *Mr. Greenspan, in September 1986, Ernst & Whinney came on as the new independent accountant for ZZZZ Best. What did you communicate to Ernst & Whinney with respect to the restoration contracts?*

Mr. Greenspan: *Nothing. I did—there was nothing because they never got in touch with me. It's protocol for the new accountant to get in touch with the old accountant. They never got in touch with me, and it's still a mystery to me.*

Representatives of Ernst & Whinney later testified that they did, in fact, communicate with Greenspan prior to accepting ZZZZ Best as an audit client. However, Ernst & Whinney did not comment on the nature or content of that communication. (Greenspan was not recalled to rebut Ernst & Whinney's testimony on this issue.)[9]

Exhibit 1 contains the engagement letter signed by Ernst & Whinney and Barry Minkow in September 1986. The engagement letter outlined four services that the audit firm intended to provide ZZZZ Best: a review of the company's financial statements for the three-month period ending July 31, 1986; assistance in the preparation of a registration statement to be filed with the SEC; a comfort letter to be submitted to ZZZZ Best's underwriters; and a full-scope audit for the fiscal year ending April 30, 1987. Ernst & Whinney completed the review, provided the comfort letter to ZZZZ Best's underwriters, and apparently assisted the company in preparing the registration statement for the SEC; however, Ernst & Whinney never completed the 1987 audit.

---

3. After a lengthy investigation, the American Institute of Certified Public Accountants ruled in 1998 that there was no "prima facie evidence" that Greenspan had violated the organization's *Code of Professional Conduct* during the time that ZZZZ Best was his client. A similar conclusion was reached by two state boards of accountancy with which Greenspan was registered to practice public accounting.

**EXHIBIT 1**

ERNST & WHINNEY'S ZZZZ BEST ENGAGEMENT LETTER

September 12, 1986

Mr. Barry Minkow
Chairman of the Board
ZZZZ Best Co., Inc.
7040 Darby Avenue
Reseda, California

Dear Mr. Minkow:

This letter is to confirm our understanding regarding our engagement as independent accountants of ZZZZ BEST CO., INC. (the Company) and the nature and limitations of the services we will provide.

We will perform the following services:

1. We will review the balance sheet of the Company as of July 31, 1986, and the related statements of income, retained earnings, and changes in financial position for the three months then ended, in accordance with standards established by the American Institute of Certified Public Accountants. We will not perform an audit of such financial statements, the objective of which is the expressing of an opinion regarding the financial statements taken as a whole, and, accordingly, we will not express an opinion on them. Our report on the financial statements is presently expected to read as follows:

> "We have made a review of the condensed consolidated balance sheet of ZZZZ BEST CO., INC. and subsidiaries as of July 31, 1986, and the related condensed consolidated statements of income and changes in financial position for the three-month period ended July 31, 1986, in accordance with standards established by the American Institute of Certified Public Accountants. A review of the condensed consolidated financial statements for the comparative period of the prior year was not made.
>
> A review of financial information consists principally of obtaining an understanding of the system for the preparation of interim financial information, applying analytical review procedures to financial data, and making inquiries of persons responsible for financial and accounting matters. It is substantially less in scope than an examination in accordance with generally accepted auditing standards, which will be performed for the full year with the objective of expressing an opinion regarding the financial statements taken as a whole. Accordingly, we do not express such an opinion. Based on our review, we are not aware of any material modifications that should be made to the condensed consolidated interim financial statements referred to above for them to be in conformity with generally accepted accounting principles."

Our engagement cannot be relied upon to disclose errors, irregularities, or illegal acts, including fraud or defalcations, that may exist. However, we will inform you of any such matters that come to our attention.

2. We will assist in the preparation of a Registration Statement (Form S-1) under the Securities Act of 1933 including advice and counsel in conforming the financial statements and related information to Regulation S-X.

3. We will assist in resolving the accounting and financial reporting questions which will arise as a part of the preparation of the Registration Statement referred to above.

4. We will prepare a letter for the underwriters, if required (i.e., a Comfort Letter), bearing in mind the limited nature of the work we have done with respect to the financial data.

(continued)

**EXHIBIT 1—*continued***

ERNST & WHINNEY'S ZZZZ BEST ENGAGEMENT LETTER

5. We will examine the consolidated financial statements of the Company as of April 30, 1987, and for the year then ended and issue our report in accordance with generally accepted auditing standards approved by the American Institute of Certified Public Accountants. These standards contemplate, among other things, that (1) we will study and evaluate the Company's internal control system as a basis for reliance on the accounting records and for determining the extent of our audit tests; and (2) that we will be able to obtain sufficient evidential matter to afford a reasonable basis for our opinion on the financial statements. However, it should be understood that our reports will necessarily be governed by the findings developed in the course of our examination and that we could be required, depending upon the circumstances, to modify our reporting from the typical unqualified opinion. We will advise you, as our examination progresses, if any developments indicate that we will be unable to express an unqualified opinion. Because our examination will be performed generally on a test basis, it will not necessarily disclose irregularities, if any, that may exist. However, we will promptly report to you any irregularities which our examination does disclose.

Our fees will be derived from our customary rates for the various personnel involved plus out-of-pocket expenses. Certain factors can have an effect on the time incurred in the conduct of our work. Among these are the general condition of the accounting records, the amount of assistance received from your personnel in the accumulation of data, the size and transaction volume of business, any significant financial reporting issues that arise in connection with the SEC's review of the S-1, as well as unforeseen circumstances. Based upon our current understanding of the situation, the amount of our proposed billing for the various services which we will be providing are estimated to be:

| | |
|---|---|
| Review of the July 31, 1986 financial statements | $ 5,000–$ 7,500 |
| Assistance in the preparation of the Registration Statement | 8,000–30,000 |
| Comfort Letter | 4,000–6,000 |
| Audit of financial statements as of April 30, 1987 | 24,000–29,000 |

We will invoice you each month for the time charges and expenses incurred in the previous month and such invoices are due and payable upon presentation.

Larry D. Gray, Partner, is the Client Service Executive assigned to the engagement. Peter Griffith, Audit Manager, and Michael McCormick, Tax Manager, have also been assigned.

We greatly appreciate your engagement of our firm; if you have any questions, we shall be pleased to discuss them with you. Please indicate your acceptance of the above arrangements by signing and returning the enclosed copy. This letter constitutes the full understanding of the terms of our engagement.

Very truly yours,
Ernst & Whinney
By Larry D. Gray, Partner
ACCEPTED:
ZZZZ BEST CO., INC.
Barry J. Minkow, Chairman of the Board (signed)
9/16/86

The audit firm resigned on June 2, 1987, amid growing concerns that ZZZZ Best's financial statements were grossly misstated.

The congressional subcommittee investigating the ZZZZ Best fraud questioned Ernst & Whinney representatives at length regarding the bogus insurance restoration contracts—contracts that accounted for 90 percent of ZZZZ Best's reported profits.

Congressional testimony disclosed that Ernst & Whinney repeatedly insisted on visiting several of the largest of these contract sites and that Minkow and his associates attempted to discourage such visits. Eventually, Minkow realized that the auditors would not relent and agreed to allow them to visit certain of the restoration sites, knowing full well that none of the sites actually existed.

To convince Ernst & Whinney that the insurance restoration contracts were authentic, Minkow plotted and carried out a series of sting operations that collectively cost millions of dollars. In the late fall of 1986, Larry Gray, the engagement audit partner for ZZZZ Best, told client personnel that he wanted to inspect a restoration site in Sacramento on which ZZZZ Best had reported obtaining a multimillion-dollar contract. Minkow sent two of his subordinates to Sacramento to find a large building under construction or renovation that would provide a plausible site for a restoration contract. Gray had visited Sacramento a few weeks earlier to search for the site that Minkow had refused to divulge. As chance would have it, the building chosen by the ZZZZ Best conspirators was the same one Gray had identified as the most likely site of the insurance restoration job.

Minkow's two confederates posed as leasing agents of a property management firm and convinced the supervisor of the construction site to provide the keys to the building one weekend on the pretext that a large, prospective tenant wished to tour the facility. Prior to the arrival of Larry Gray and an attorney representing ZZZZ Best's law firm, Minkow's subordinates visited the site and placed placards on the walls at conspicuous locations indicating that ZZZZ Best was the contractor for the building renovation. No details were overlooked by the two co-conspirators. They even paid the building's security officer to greet the visitors and demonstrate that he was aware in advance of their tour of the site and its purpose. Although the building had not been damaged and instead was simply in the process of being completed, the sting operation went off as planned. Exhibit 2 presents the memorandum Gray wrote describing his tour of the building—a memorandum included in Ernst & Whinney's ZZZZ Best workpapers.

Congressional investigators quizzed Gray regarding the measures he took to confirm that ZZZZ Best actually had a restoration contract on the Sacramento building. They were particularly concerned that he never discovered the building had not suffered several million dollars in damages a few months earlier, as claimed by ZZZZ Best personnel.

Congressman Lent: *. . . Did you check the building permit or construction permit?*

Mr. Gray: *No, sir. That wouldn't be necessary to accomplish what I was setting out to accomplish.*

Congressman Lent: *And you did not check with the building's owners to see if an insurance claim had been filed?*

Mr. Gray: *Same answer. It wasn't necessary. I had seen paperwork internally of our client, the support for a great amount of detail. So, I had no need to ask—to pursue that.*

Congressman Lent: *You understand that what you saw was not anything that was real in any sense of the word? . . . You are saying you were duped, are you not?*

Mr. Gray: *Absolutely.*

Before allowing Ernst & Whinney auditors to visit a bogus restoration project, Minkow insisted that the firm sign a standard confidentiality agreement. Exhibit 3 presents a copy of that agreement. Members of the congressional subcommittee were troubled by the following stipulation of the confidentiality agreement: "We will

**EXHIBIT 2**

ERNST & WHINNEY INTERNAL MEMO REGARDING VISIT TO ZZZZ BEST RESTORATION PROJECT

TO: ZZZZ Best Co., Inc. File

FROM: Larry D. Gray

RE: Visit to Sacramento Job

At our request, the Company arranged for a tour of the job site in Sacramento on November 23rd [1986]. The site (not previously identified for us because of the confidentiality agreement with their customer) had been informally visited by me on October 27. I knew approximately where the job was, and was able to identify it through the construction activity going on.

On November 23, Mark Morse accompanied Mark Moskowitz of Hughes Hubbard & Reed and myself to Sacramento. We visited first the offices of the Building Manager, Mark Roddy of Assured Property Management, Inc. Roddy was hired by the insurance company (at Tom Padgett's suggestion according to Morse) to oversee the renovation activities and the leasing of the space. Roddy accompanied us to the building site.

We were informed that the damage occurred from the water storage on the roof of the building. The storage was for the sprinkler systems, but the water was somehow released in total, causing construction damage to floors 17 and 18, primarily in bathrooms which were directly under the water holding tower, then the water spread out and flooded floors 16 down through about 5 or 6, where it started to spread out even further and be held in pools.

We toured floor 17 briefly (it is currently occupied by a law firm) then visited floor 12 (which had a considerable amount of unoccupied space) and floor 7. Morse pointed out to us the carpet, painting and clean up work which had been ZZZZ Best's responsibility. We noted some work not done in some other areas (and in unoccupied tenant space). But per Mark, this was not ZZZZ Best's responsibility, rather was work being undertaken by tenants for their own purposes.

Per Morse (and Roddy) ZZZZ Best's work is substantially complete and has passed final inspection. Final sign-off is expected shortly, with final payment due to ZZZZ Best in early December.

Morse was well versed in the building history and in the work scope for ZZZZ Best. The tour was beneficial in gaining insight as to the scope of the damage that had occurred and the type of work that the Company can do.

not make any follow-up telephone calls to any contractors, insurance companies, the building owner, or other individuals involved in the restoration contract." This restriction effectively precluded the auditors from corroborating the insurance restoration contracts with independent third parties.

## Resignation of Ernst & Whinney

Ernst & Whinney resigned as ZZZZ Best's auditor on June 2, 1987, following a series of disturbing events that caused the firm to question Barry Minkow's integrity. First, Ernst & Whinney was alarmed by a *Los Angeles Times* article in mid-May 1987 that revealed Minkow had been involved in a string of credit card forgeries as a teenager. Second, on May 28, 1987, ZZZZ Best issued a press release, without consulting or notifying Ernst & Whinney, that reported record profits and revenues. Minkow intended this

**EXHIBIT 3**

ERNST & WHINNEY'S CONFIDENTIALITY AGREEMENT WITH ZZZZ BEST REGARDING VISITS TO RESTORATION PROJECTS

Mr. Barry Minkow, President
ZZZZ Best Co., Inc.
7040 Darby Avenue
Reseda, California

Dear Barry:

In connection with the proposed public offering (the Offering) of Units consisting of common stock and warrants of ZZZZ Best Co., Inc. (the Company), we have requested a tour of the site of the Company's insurance restoration project in Sacramento, California, Contract No. 18886. Subject to the representations and warranties below, the Company has agreed to arrange such a tour, which will be conducted by a representative of Assured Property Management Inc. (the Representative), which company is unaffiliated with Interstate Appraisal Services. The undersigned, personally and on behalf of Ernst & Whinney, hereby represents and warrants that:

1. We will not disclose the location of such building, or any other information with respect to the project or the building, to any third parties or to any other members or employees of our firm;

2. We will not make any follow-up telephone calls to any contractors, insurance companies, the building owner, or other individuals involved in the restoration project;

3. We will obey all on-site safety and other rules and regulations established by the Company, Interstate Appraisal Services and the Representative;

4. The undersigned will be the only representative of this Firm present on the tour.

This Confidentiality Letter is also being furnished for the benefit of Interstate Appraisal Services, to the same extent as if it were furnished directly to such company.

press release to restore investors' confidence in the company--confidence that had been shaken by the damaging *Los Angeles Times* story. Third, and most important, on May 29, Ernst & Whinney auditors discovered evidence supporting allegations made several weeks earlier by a third-party informant that ZZZZ Best's insurance restoration business was fictitious.

The informant had contacted Ernst & Whinney in April 1987 and asked for $25,000 in exchange for information proving that one of the firm's clients was engaging in a massive fraud. Ernst & Whinney refused to pay the sum, and the individual recanted shortly thereafter, but not until the firm determined that the allegation involved ZZZZ Best. (Congressional testimony disclosed that the individual recanted because of a bribe paid to him by Minkow.) Despite the retraction, Ernst & Whinney questioned Minkow and ZZZZ Best's board of directors regarding the matter. Minkow insisted that he did not know the individual who had made the allegation. On May 29, 1987, however, Ernst & Whinney auditors discovered several cancelled checks that Minkow had personally written to the informant several months earlier.

Because ZZZZ Best was a public company, the resignation of its independent auditor had to be reported to the SEC in an 8-K filing. This requirement alerts investors and creditors of circumstances that may have led to the change in auditors. At the time, SEC registrants were allowed 15 days to file an 8-K auditor change announcement. After waiting the maximum permissible time, ZZZZ Best reported the change in auditors but, despite Ernst & Whinney's insistence, made no mention in the 8-K of the fraud allegation that had been subsequently recanted.

The SEC requires a former audit firm to prepare a letter to be filed as an exhibit to its former client's 8-K auditor change announcement. That exhibit letter must comment on the 8-K's accuracy and completeness. In 1987, former audit firms had 30 days to file an exhibit letter, which was the length of time Ernst & Whinney waited before submitting its exhibit letter to the SEC. In that letter, Ernst & Whinney revealed that ZZZZ Best's insurance contracts might be fraudulent.

The congressional subcommittee was alarmed that 45 days passed before the charges of fraudulent misrepresentations in ZZZZ Best's financial statements were disclosed to the public. By the time the SEC released Ernst & Whinney's exhibit letter to the public, ZZZZ Best had filed for protection from its creditors under Chapter 11 of the federal bankruptcy code. During the period that elapsed between Ernst & Whinney's resignation and the public release of its 8-K exhibit letter, ZZZZ Best obtained significant financing from several parties, including $1 million from one of Minkow's close friends. These parties never recovered the funds invested in, or loaned to, ZZZZ Best. As a direct result of the ZZZZ Best debacle, the SEC shortened the length of time that registrants and their former auditors may wait before filing auditor change documents.

The congressional subcommittee also quizzed Ernst & Whinney representatives regarding the information they disclosed to Price Waterhouse, the audit firm Minkow retained to replace Ernst & Whinney.[4] Congressman Wyden wanted to know whether Ernst & Whinney had candidly discussed its concerns regarding Minkow's integrity with Price Waterhouse.

Congressman Wyden: *I am going to insert into the record at this point a memo entitled "Discussion with successor auditor," written by Mr. Gray and dated June 9, 1987. Regarding a June 4 meeting, Mr. Gray, with Dan Lyle of Price Waterhouse concerning the integrity of ZZZZ Best's management, you stated that you had no reportable disagreements and no reservations about management integrity pending the results of a board of directors' investigation. Then you went on to say that you resigned because, and I quote here: "We came to a conclusion that we didn't want to become associated with the financial statements." Is that correct?*

Mr. Gray: *That is correct.*

Mr. Wyden: . . . *Mr. Gray, you told the committee staff on May 29, 1987, that when you uncovered evidence to support allegations of fraud that you decided to pack up your workpapers and leave the ZZZZ Best audit site. How did your leaving without telling anybody except the ZZZZ Best management and board of directors the reasons for leaving help the public and investors?*

A final twist to the ZZZZ Best scandal was an anonymous letter Ernst & Whinney received one week after the firm resigned as ZZZZ Best's auditor. At that time, no one other than Ernst & Whinney and ZZZZ Best's officers was aware of the firm's resignation. The letter, shown in Exhibit 4, contained several allegations suggesting that ZZZZ Best's financial statements were fraudulent. According to the congressional testimony, Ernst & Whinney forwarded this letter to the SEC on June 17, 1987.

4. Price Waterhouse never issued an audit report on ZZZZ Best's financial statements. ZZZZ Best was liquidated less than two months after Price Waterhouse was retained.

**EXHIBIT 4**

ANONYMOUS LETTER RECEIVED BY ERNST & WHINNEY REGARDING ZZZZ BEST

June 9, 1987

Mr. Guy Wilson
Ernst & Whinney
515 South Flower
Los Angeles, California 90021

Dear Mr. Wilson:

I am an individual having certain confidential information regarding the financial condition of ZZZZ Best Co., Inc. I have read the prospectus and your Review Report dated October 3, 1986 and recognize you have not done an examination in accordance with generally accepted auditing standards, but that such audit will be forthcoming by you.

I wish to make you aware of the following material facts which require you to confirm or disaffirm:

1. The electric generators which appear on the balance sheet under Note 6 as being purchased for $1,970,000 were purchased for scrap for less than $100,000 thru intermediaries of ZZZZ Best and resold to ZZZZ Best at the inflated value. The sole purpose was to boost the assets on the balance sheet. These generators have never been used and have no utility to the company.

2. Note 5 of the balance sheet discusses joint ventures and two restoration contracts. These contracts are fictitious as are the bookkeeping entries to support their validity. Interstate Appraisal Service [sic] did not let such contracts although they confirm their existence. The same is true for the alleged $7,000,000 Sacramento contract and the $40–100 million contracts with Interstate.

3. Further, checks made and passed between ZZZZ Best, its joint venturers and some of its vendors are no more than transactions among conspirators to support the validity of these restoration contracts.

4. Earnings reported by ZZZZ Best are being reported as Billings in excess of costs and estimated earnings on restoration contracts. These contracts do not exist nor do the earnings. This can be confirmed directly by contacting the alleged insurance carriers as well as physical inspections as to the existence and extent of the contracts.

5. Billings and Earnings for 1985 and 1986 were fabricated by the company before being presented to other accountants for certification.

Confirmation of these allegations can be accomplished by a careful due diligence. Such due diligence on your behalf is imperative for your protection.

Very truly yours,

B. Cautious
(Signed)

## Collapse of ZZZZ Best

The *Los Angeles Times* article published in mid-May 1987 that disparaged Barry Minkow ultimately doomed the young entrepreneur and his company. Several years earlier, a homemaker had fallen victim to Minkow's credit card forgeries. Minkow had added a fraudulent charge to a credit charge slip the woman had used to make a payment on her account. Despite her persistence, Minkow avoided repaying the small amount. The woman never forgot the insult and tracked down, and kept a record of, individuals who had been similarly harmed by Minkow. At the urging of this woman, a reporter for the *Los Angeles Times* investigated her allegations. The woman's diary eventually became the basis for the *Los Angeles Times* article that, for the first time, cast doubt on the integrity of the "boy wonder" who was the talk of Wall Street.

The newspaper article triggered a chain of events that caused ZZZZ Best to collapse and disappear less than three months later. First, a small brokerage firm specializing in newly registered companies with suspicious earnings histories began short-selling ZZZZ Best stock, forcing the stock's price into a tailspin. Second, Ernst & Whinney, ZZZZ Best's law firm, and ZZZZ Best's investment banker began giving more credence to the allegations and rumors of financial wrongdoing by Minkow and his associates. Third, and most important, the article panicked Minkow and compelled him to make several daring moves that cost him even more credibility. The most critical mistake was his issuance of the May 28, 1987, press release that boldly reported record profits and revenues for his firm.

## EPILOGUE

Among the parties most vilified for their role in the ZZZZ Best scandal was Ernst & Whinney. The transcripts of the congressional testimony focusing on the ZZZZ Best fraud included a list of 10 "red flags" that the audit firm had allegedly overlooked while examining ZZZZ Best's financial statements (see Exhibit 5). Ernst & Whinney officials flatly rejected assertions that their firm was even partially to blame for the ZZZZ Best fiasco. In his congressional testimony, Leroy Gardner, the West Coast director of accounting and auditing for Ernst & Whinney, maintained that when all the facts were revealed, his firm would be totally vindicated:

> *The ZZZZ Best situation proves at least one thing: a well-orchestrated fraud will often succeed even against careful, honest, hard-working people. . . . The facts that have begun to emerge establish that Minkow along with confederates both inside and outside ZZZZ Best went to extraordinary lengths to deceive Ernst & Whinney. For example, Thomas Padgett, an alleged conspirator, revealed in a recent televised interview that Minkow spent $4 million to deceive Ernst & Whinney during a visit to one of ZZZZ Best's job sites. . . . Ernst & Whinney never misled investors about the reliability of ZZZZ Best's financial statements. Ernst & Whinney never even issued an audit opinion for ZZZZ Best. . . . We are not part of the problem in this case. We were part of the solution.*

In one of the largest civil suits stemming from the ZZZZ Best fraud, a court ruled that Ernst & Whinney was not liable to a large California bank that had extended ZZZZ Best a multimillion-dollar loan in 1986. The bank alleged that in granting the loan, it had relied upon the review report issued by Ernst & Whinney on ZZZZ Best's financial statements for the three-month period ending July 31, 1986. An appellate judge, however, ruled that the bank was not justified in relying on the review report since Ernst & Whinney had expressly stated in the report that it was not issuing an opinion on the ZZZZ Best financial statements. "Ernst, because it issued only a review report, specifically declined to express an opinion on ZZZZ Best's financial statements. The report expressly disclaimed any right to rely on its content."[5]

In the late 1980s, ZZZZ Best's former stockholders filed a class-action lawsuit against Ernst & Whinney, ZZZZ Best's former law firm, and ZZZZ Best's former investment banker. An Internet publication reported in March 1996 that

5. "Ernst & Young Not Liable in ZZZZ Best Case," *Journal of Accountancy*, July 1991, 22.

**EXHIBIT 5**

TEN RED FLAGS THAT ZZZZ BEST'S AUDITORS ALLEGEDLY OVERLOOKED

1. The amounts called for by the insurance restoration contracts were unrealistically large.
2. The number of multimillion-dollar insurance restoration contracts reportedly obtained by ZZZZ Best exceeded the total number available nationwide during the relevant time period.
3. The purported contracts failed to identify the insured parties, the insurance companies, or the locations of the jobs.
4. The contracts consisted of a single page which failed to contain details and specifications of the work to be done, such as the square yardage of carpet to be replaced, which were usual and customary in the restoration business.
5. Virtually all of the insurance restoration contracts were with the same party.
6. A large proportion of the ZZZZ Best insurance restoration contracts occurred immediately, and opportunistically, prior to a planned offering of stock.
7. The purported contracts provided for payments to ZZZZ Best or Minkow alone rather than to the insured or jointly with ZZZZ Best and the insured, contrary to the practice of the industry.
8. The purported contracts provided for payments by the insurance adjustor contrary to normal practice in the industry under which payments are customarily made by the insurance company directly to its insured or jointly to its insured and the restorer.
9. ZZZZ Best's purported gross profit margins for its restoration business were greatly in excess of the normal profit margins for the restoration industry.
10. The internal controls at ZZZZ Best were grossly inadequate.

this lawsuit had been settled privately. The defendants reportedly paid the former ZZZZ Best stockholders $35 million. However, the contribution of each defendant to the settlement pool was not disclosed.[6]

Barry Minkow was released from prison in late 1994. Minkow secured the reduction in his 25-year prison sentence for "good behavior and efforts to improve himself."[7] These efforts included earning by correspondence bachelor's and master's degrees in religion from Liberty University. Shortly after being paroled, Minkow married a young woman introduced to him by a fellow inmate. That inmate was a former subordinate of Charles Keating, the principal architect of the massive Lincoln Savings and Loan fraud.

In early 1995, Minkow began serving as the associate pastor of an evangelical church in a community near his hometown of Reseda. Two years later, Minkow was appointed the senior pastor of a large nondenominational church in San Diego. Besides his pastoral duties, Minkow serves as the spokesperson for an Internet company, the Fraud Discovery Institute, which markets various fraud prevention and detection services.

Minkow regularly presents lectures and seminars across the United States that focus on his "experience" with corporate fraud. He has spoken to groups of CPAs, educational institutions, and, most notably, the FBI Academy at Quantico, Virginia. Minkow, who typically delivers his lectures while dressed in an orange prison jumpsuit, often chastises the accountants and auditors in his audience. During one presentation, Minkow noted that, "CPAs are creatures of habit. You're interested in making tick marks and footnotes,

6. C. Byron, "$26 Million in the Hole," *Worth Online*, March 1996.
7. M. Matzer, "Barry Minkow," *Forbes*, 15 August 1994, 134.

not in thinking outside the box."[8] Minkow also chides auditors for being overly willing to accept weak forms of audit evidence, such as client representations. He warns auditors, "Don't give up objectivity for convenience."[9]

Journalists frequently interview Minkow and ask for his views on corporate fraud and related issues. In January 2005, Minkow gave the following response when he was asked by *CFO Magazine* whether the Sarbanes-Oxley Act of 2002 would likely serve to mitigate or deter corporate fraud: "Let me tell you why this legislation is brilliant. Sarbox hit at a common denominator of corporate fraud: bypassing systems of internal control. I would not have been able to perpetrate the ZZZZ Best fraud if I had not been able to bypass the internal controls."[10]

## Questions

1. Ernst & Whinney never issued an audit opinion on financial statements of ZZZZ Best but did issue a review report on the company's quarterly statements for the three months ended July 31, 1986. How does a review differ from an audit, particularly in terms of the level of assurance implied by the auditor's report?
2. *SAS No. 106,* "Audit Evidence," identifies the principal "management assertions" that underlie a set of financial statements. The occurrence assertion was particularly critical for ZZZZ Best's insurance restoration contracts. ZZZZ Best's auditors obtained third-party confirmations to support the contracts, reviewed available documentation, performed analytical procedures to evaluate the reasonableness of the revenues recorded on the contracts, and visited selected restoration sites. Comment on the limitations of the evidence that these procedures provide with regard to the management assertion of occurrence.
3. In testimony before Congress, George Greenspan reported that one means he used to audit the insurance restoration contracts was to verify that his client actually received payment on those jobs. How can such apparently reliable evidence lead an auditor to an improper conclusion?
4. What is the purpose of predecessor-successor auditor communications? Which party, the predecessor or successor auditor, has the responsibility for initiating these communications? Briefly summarize the information that a successor auditor should obtain from the predecessor auditor.
5. Did the confidentiality agreement that Minkow required Ernst & Whinney to sign improperly limit the scope of the ZZZZ Best audit? Why or why not? Discuss general circumstances under which confidentiality concerns on the part of a client may properly affect audit planning decisions. At what point do client-imposed audit scope limitations affect the type of audit opinion issued?
6. What procedures, if any, do professional standards require auditors to perform when reviewing a client's pre-audit but post-year-end earnings press release?

---

8. T. Sickinger, "Ex-Con Artist Helps Find Fraud," *The Kansas City Star,* 18 October 1995, B1.
9. *Ibid.*
10. *CFO Magazine*, "Ten Questions for Barry Minkow," CFO.com, 1 January 2005.

CASE 1.9

# Gemstar-TV Guide International, Inc.

The United States prides itself in being first in a wide range of socioeconomic, scientific, and cultural "top ten" lists. One ranking that does nothing to bolster national pride among United States citizens, however, is the nation's claim to watching more television programming than any other country across the globe. In 2007, the *Economist*, an international business periodical, reported that the average U.S. household spends 8 hours and 11 minutes each day viewing television programming, far surpassing the runner-up, the typical Turkish household, which spends exactly five hours watching the boob tube. Rounding out the top five in this inauspicious list were the sedentary citizens of Italy, Belgium, and Japan, respectively.

Over the past two decades, surfing the World Wide Web has become an important pastime for many former couch potatoes. The increasing popularity of the Internet during the 1990s convinced several e-commerce companies, principal among them AOL and Yahoo!, to establish massive websites intended to serve as "portals" to the Internet. These Internet portals were designed to "capture" Internet users when they went online and then direct them to the specific entertainment, business, sports, or other sites that they wanted to visit. AOL, Yahoo!, and their competitors expected to produce huge revenue streams by selling advertising on their portal websites to the large number of companies that wanted to market their products and services to Internet users who typically have deeper pockets than the average consumer.

Several insightful business executives recognized that the portal concept could be even more lucrative if applied to the "old school" but still dominant electronic information and entertainment medium, namely, the television. Despite the far-reaching impact that the Internet has had on U.S. culture over the past two decades, television viewing remains much more prevalent in the United States than surfing the World Wide Web. The Nielsen Company reported recently that the typical Internet user in the United States spends only twenty minutes online each day, a small fraction of the time that individual spends glued to his or her television screen.

The most successful television "portal" to date has been the ubiquitous scrolling programming guide that millions of bleary-eyed television addicts scan each day to find an upcoming episode of *NYPD Blue*, *Seinfeld*, or *The Beverly Hillbillies*. During the 1990s, several companies struggled to gain control over that very low-tech but also very important television portal. That struggle eventually culminated in a large-scale financial fraud that imposed billions of dollars of losses on investors worldwide.

## From Shanghai to Fenway Park

Che-Chuen Yuen was born in 1948 in Shanghai during the bloody civil war that rocked China following the conclusion of World War II. After the Chinese civil war ended in 1949, Mao Zedung, the leader of the Communist forces that gained control of the country, established an authoritarian central government and renamed the nation the People's Republic of China. The new Communist government forced business owners, professionals, and other Chinese citizens who were perceived to be counterrevolutionaries to leave the country. Che-Chuen's father, a businessman, was among those banished. The elder Yuen moved his family, including his infant son, to Hong Kong, which had been a British colony since the mid-1800s. Fifteen years later, Che-Chuen immigrated to the United States where he assumed the name Henry.

After finishing his undergraduate degree in mathematics at the University of Wisconsin, the quiet and studious Yuen decided to pursue a doctorate in applied mathematics at the prestigious California Institute of Technology (CalTech) in Pasadena, California. Upon completing his doctorate, Yuen remained in southern California, working for fourteen years as a research scientist for TRW, a large conglomerate. Because he had always been fascinated by the U.S. legal system, Yuen spent several years attending law school on a part-time basis while employed by TRW. He eventually earned a law degree from Loyola Law School near downtown Los Angeles.

While working toward his doctorate at CalTech, Henry Yuen became close friends with Daniel Kwoh, a doctoral student in the university's physics department. Like Yuen, Kwoh accepted a research position with TRW after completing his doctorate. In addition to having the same employer, the two friends had a mutual interest in sports, an interest that would eventually prove to be extremely lucrative for both of them.

As a young man, Yuen had aspired to becoming a world class soccer player. When he failed to achieve that goal, he became a martial arts expert, specializing in Wing Chun, a form of martial arts that involves aggressive, close range combat. After coming to the United States, Yuen became a hardcore baseball fan—his favorite team was the Boston Red Sox. Yuen's full-time job at TRW and his evening law school classes typically prevented him from watching Red Sox games that were televised on the West Coast. So, he would program his VCR to record those games. Unfortunately, Yuen often came home to find that his VCR had failed to record a game, leaving him frustrated and angry. In his mind, if a research scientist with a doctorate from CalTech could not successfully use a VCR's recording technology, then there was something wrong with that technology.

In 1988, Yuen and Kwoh teamed together to develop a simplified method for programming VCRs that they referred to as VCR Plus. This technology became the flagship product of a small company they co-founded, Gemstar Development Corporation. Although Gemstar produced only modest revenues during its first few years of operation, the company's impressive technology and seemingly bright future persuaded *Business Week* to name Yuen and Kwoh as the nation's "best entrepreneurs" in 1990. Five years later, Yuen and Kwoh took their company public, listing its stock on the NASDAQ stock exchange. That exchange would eventually include Gemstar in the NASDAQ 100, the stock index used to track the performance of companies listed on the world's largest electronic securities exchange. In 1997, a reported "falling out" between the two men resulted in Kwoh leaving the company to become an independent venture capitalist.

During the first five years that Gemstar was a public company, its revenues steadily increased, rising from $42 million in 1995 to $167 million in 1999. After incurring operating losses from 1995 through 1997, the company posted its first profit of $39 million in 1998. The following year, the company's net income increased to $74 million.

Gemstar generated revenues by licensing the various generations of its VCR Plus product and related technologies that it developed to companies in the broadcasting and electronic communications industries. A major feature of Gemstar's business model was acquiring a wide range of patents that allowed the company to gain effective control of programming and search technologies vital to companies in those industries. Gemstar eventually acquired nearly one hundred such patents. Another feature of Gemstar's business model was closely monitoring the efforts of other companies to develop technologies similar to those that it had patented. When a potential infringement of a Gemstar patent was discovered, Yuen would immediately file a lawsuit or multiple lawsuits against the offending company. Yuen's legal background was a key factor that helped Gemstar prevail in most of these lawsuits.

## "Patent Terrorist"

Henry Yuen quickly earned a reputation as a ruthless competitor because of his litigious business strategy. So ruthless, in fact, that certain of his rivals referred to him as a "patent terrorist." During an interview with *Business Week*, an executive in the cable TV industry, who asked to remain anonymous, candidly admitted that, "[h]e scares the hell out of us."[1] Yuen defended his aggressive legal tactics and insisted that they were not improper or unethical. "I am no terrorist. A terrorist is someone who breaks the law. I am only doing what the U.S. Congress and patent law allow."[2]

A few of Yuen's competitors begrudgingly complimented the tactics he used to establish Gemstar as a significant player in the fiercely competitive and rapidly evolving broadcasting and electronic communications industries. Rupert Murdoch, the chairman and CEO of the Australia-based News Corporation, easily the largest media company worldwide, fought repeated legal battles with Yuen. Nevertheless, Murdoch often referred to Yuen as a brilliant strategist and "genius." Another competitor noted that Yuen was "the smartest guy in television."[3] *U.S. News and World Report* referred to Yuen, who was effectively unknown outside the inner circle of top executives in the broadcasting and electronic communications industries, as "the Bill Gates of television."[4]

Yuen was among the first corporate executives to envision the revenue streams that a television portal could produce. As the turn of the century approached, he believed that the television medium would change dramatically over the following decade. Yuen expected television to become a highly interactive medium, similar to the Internet, in which the viewing public would have hundreds of television channels, movies, games, and other entertainment options to choose from. When that happened, he was convinced that a company that controlled television information and navigation services would be a formidable force within the broadcasting and electronic communications industries.

Among the first companies to provide on-screen navigation guides was United Video, a small technology company based in Tulsa, Oklahoma. That company marketed the Prevue Network, a scrolling on-screen programming guide, to cable TV networks during the mid-1980s. United Video's executives surprised their much larger competitors in 1999 when they launched a successful takeover of TV Guide International, a company they purchased from Rupert Murdoch's News Corporation. Following the takeover, Murdoch was one of the largest shareholders of the new company, which assumed the name TV Guide, Inc. The new company planned to use its prominent brand name to market the on-screen programming guide that it renamed the TV Guide Network.

Following the merger of United Video and TV Guide International, the new company's management team began butting heads with Henry Yuen. By this time, Gemstar controlled most patents related to the use of what had become known as EPG—electronic programming guide—technology. Yuen blocked every effort made by TV Guide to

---

1. R. Grover, T. Lowry, and L. Armstrong, "Henry Yuen: TV Guy," *Business Week* (online), 12 March 2001.
2. *Ibid.*
3. *Ibid.*
4. F. Vogelstein, "Meet the Bill Gates of TV," *U.S. News and World Report*, 7 August 2000, 50.

upgrade its onscreen navigation guide. To solve this problem, Rupert Murdoch goaded TV Guide to launch a hostile takeover bid for Gemstar. But Murdoch and the TV Guide management team were no match for the crafty and hardnosed Yuen who turned the tables on them by forcing them to sell their company to him in 2000.

Financial analysts and other members of the investment community had high expectations for the new company. Those expectations caused the company's stock price to surge. Thanks to that surging stock price, Henry Yuen became the third wealthiest Asian-American in the United States, according to *Forbes* magazine. Yuen's net worth of $1.3 billion easily secured him a spot in the Forbes 400, the publication's annual compilation of the four hundred richest U.S. citizens. At the age of 51, the Chinese immigrant whose family had been forced to leave its homeland following the Communist takeover of that nation was among the most successful capitalists in the world and was proudly living the "American dream." But he wasn't satisfied. According to *The New York Times*, Yuen believed that his company's "on-screen guide would be the ultimate toll-keeper for the media [television] and told colleagues that Gemstar would someday be bigger than Microsoft."[5]

## A Rocky Start for GTGI

Following the $15 billion purchase of TV Guide by Gemstar, Henry Yuen and Rupert Murdoch, who had been fierce rivals, were the new company's largest and most influential stockholders. Yuen was also the company's chief executive officer (CEO) and chairman of the board of directors. Gemstar's former stockholders, led by Yuen, controlled 55 percent of the company's common stock, while TV Guide's former stockholders, led by Murdoch, controlled the remainder. To take advantage of TV Guide's brand name, Yuen decided that the newly-formed company would be named Gemstar-TV Guide International, Inc. (GTGI).

Yuen organized GTGI into three business segments. Easily the largest of these segments was the Media and Services Sector, which accounted for approximately 70 percent of GTGI's consolidated revenues. This sector produced the bulk of its revenues from the *TV Guide*, the largest weekly publication in the world at the time in terms of circulation and readership. The second business segment was the Technology and Licensing Sector that included the former operations of Gemstar International.

Following the acquisition of TV Guide, Yuen's principal strategic initiative was to use Gemstar's EPG patents and TV Guide's brand name to establish a product line of interactive information and navigation services for use by cable TV networks. This product line of services was included in GTGI's third and smallest business segment, the Interactive Platform Sector. Advertising was the principal revenue producer for this sector, which accounted for less than two percent of GTGI's total revenues for fiscal 2000. Yuen was convinced that over the years to come major retailers and service companies would allocate a large portion of their advertising budgets to ads placed on GTGI's electronic navigation guides, most notably the TV Guide Network. By 2000, the profit potential of the TV Guide Network seemed enormous since it reached more than fifty million U.S. households.

Despite Yuen's glowing forecasts for GTGI's business model, the company's financial performance worsened dramatically during 2001, its second year of operation. In 2001, GTGI reported a net loss of $600 million, three times greater than the net loss it reported the previous year. Yuen downplayed this disappointing news in earnings releases and

---

5. R. Siklos, "The Math Whiz vs. the Media Moguls in a Battle for Millions," *The New York Times*, 3 April 2006, 1.

conference calls by focusing the attention of analysts and investors on the rapidly growing revenues of the Interactive Platform Sector. In fiscal 2001, that sector's revenues increased by more than 400 percent. He attributed this large increase to "advertisers' growing acceptance" of the new advertising medium offered by that sector.[6]

Explaining GTGI's large loss during fiscal 2001 wasn't the only challenge that Yuen faced in early 2002. During the merger deliberations with TV Guide, Yuen had negotiated an incentive-laden compensation contract for himself. During 2001, that contract resulted in Yuen earning nearly $20 million, which was three times his compensation the previous year. Financial analysts, investors, and other parties berated Yuen for that huge pay increase in the face of GTGI's $600 million loss for the year. That criticism was met with indifference and silence by Yuen. Two years earlier, several Gemstar shareholders had also suggested that Yuen was being overpaid. Yuen had responded to that criticism by brusquely noting that, "I deserve every bit of it."[7]

## An Unhappy Marriage

When Yuen orchestrated the takeover of TV Guide, he realized that the newly created company would pose a wide range of challenging problems due to its size, the highly competitive nature of its principal lines of business, and the strong personalities—including his own—that would play key roles in overseeing its operations. The most intractable of the company's problems proved to be its schizoid personality. Yuen and his associates from Gemstar were intent on creating a New Age, high-technology company that would serve as a traffic cop for literally billions of television viewers around the world. The former executives and major stockholders of TV Guide, Inc., wanted to maintain and increase the revenues from the "old school" media empire that had revolved for decades around the *TV Guide*. Rupert Murdoch served as the principal spokesperson for the latter individuals.

Enhancing GTGI's "split" personality was the composition of the company's twelve-member board of directors. Six of those directors were former Gemstar executives, while the remaining six directors were former TV Guide executives or major stockholders. Most prominent among the latter individuals was Rupert Murdoch. The Gemstar-TV Guide merger agreement gave Yuen the right to cast the tie-breaking vote to resolve deadlocks between the two factions of the GTGI board. To counterbalance Yuen's powerful position on the GTGI board, Murdoch had a stipulation included in the merger agreement that allowed the former TV Guide directors to dismiss Yuen as GTGI's chairman of the board and CEO after five years. Yuen accepted that unusual stipulation of the merger agreement only after Murdoch and the remaining GTGI board members agreed that Yuen would receive a huge severance payment if he was dismissed.

The troubled relationship between Henry Yuen and Rupert Murdoch became even more problematic in the months following the merger of Gemstar and TV Guide. Yuen focused most of his attention on GTGI's Interactive Platform Sector since he was convinced that the electronic programming services it marketed would eventually become the company's principal revenue stream. The inordinate attention placed by Yuen on that sector angered and frustrated Murdoch. Particularly upsetting to Murdoch was Yuen's continual hyping of the Interactive Platform Sector to the business press each quarterly reporting period since that sector, despite its

6. *Securities and Exchange Commission v. Henry C. Yuen and Elsie M. Leung*, Case No. CV 03-4376 NM, U.S. District Court for the Central District of California, Western Division, 29 June 2003.

7. L. Armstrong, "What's on TV? Ask Henry Yuen," *Business Week*, 14 September 1998, 164.

impressive revenue growth, still accounted for just a small fraction of GTGI's total revenues each quarter.

Murdoch believed that the principal focus of GTGI's operations should be the company's Media and Services Sector that had been consistently profitable for decades because of *TV Guide's* popularity. During the first two years that Yuen oversaw GTGI's operations, *TV Guide's* circulation dropped dramatically, falling by approximately one million subscribers. *TV Guide's* declining circulation and advertising revenues was the principal factor responsible for the large loss that GTGI reported for fiscal 2001.

By early 2002, Murdoch was pressuring Yuen to resign as GTGI's CEO. Yuen resisted that pressure. When Murdoch initiated weekly management meetings to address GTGI's declining health, Yuen often skipped those meetings. When he did attend, Yuen reportedly refused to participate, choosing instead to carry on conversations in Cantonese with his longtime confidant, Elsie Leung, GTGI's chief financial officer (CFO). As Gemstar's financial condition continued to deteriorate, Yuen became increasingly "abrupt" and "secretive,"[8] further undercutting his ability to work with Murdoch and key GTGI executives. Years later, his personal attorney would defend Yuen's management style, while admitting that his interpersonal skills, a skill set so critical to top corporate executives, were sub-par. "I would not say of Henry that sweetness and diplomacy were his strong suit."[9]

## Re-Re-Restatements

In April 2002, Henry Yuen and GTGI faced a major crisis when certain financial analysts began questioning the company's revenue recognition policies. Those analysts pointed out two questionable accounting decisions documented in the company's 2001 Form 10-K. The two decisions involved $100 million of disputed licensing fees that GTGI had booked as revenue and $20 million of revenue from an unusual barter transaction. Another third party pointed out that these items had significantly enhanced the reported operating results of the company's Interactive Platform Sector, the business segment that Henry Yuen had been regularly touting. These news reports caused several investment rating services to downgrade GTGI's stock, which, in turn, caused the stock's price to decline more than forty percent in one day.

In an interview a few days later with a *USA Today* reporter, Yuen dismissed the concerns raised regarding Gemstar's revenue recognition policies by pointing out that Gemstar's auditor, KPMG, "had no problem with the accounting."[10] Another source reinforced Yuen's position by noting that the accounting decisions in question had been "blessed" by KPMG.[11] Two months later, in June 2002, *Business Week* revealed that Rupert Murdoch had been responsible for forcing Yuen to highlight the two questionable accounting decisions in GTGI's 2001 Form 10-K despite the fact that KPMG had "approved" them.[12]

The public controversy over GTGI's revenue recognition decisions prompted the company's audit committee to investigate the matter. In October 2002, GTGI released the results of that investigation. The audit committee's report revealed additional problems with the company's accounting and financial disclosure decisions over the previous two years, which resulted in the SEC launching its own investigation of GTGI.

8. Siklos, "The Math Whiz vs. The Media Moguls."

9. *Ibid.*

10. D. Lieberman, "Accounting Issue Dulls Gemstar Stock," *USA Today*, 3 April 2002, 1B.

11. M. Scanlon, "Gemstar Bitten by Accounting Bug," *BNET.com*, 8 April 2002.

12. R. Grover, "Gemstar Wars: Murdoch Strikes Back," *Business Week*, 3 June 2002, 42.

Shortly after the release of the audit committee's report, Henry Yuen was replaced as GTGI's CEO by one of Murdoch's top subordinates. GTGI also disclosed that Ernst & Young had been retained to replace KPMG as its independent audit firm. At the same time that it announced the change in auditors, GTGI disclosed that it would likely be required to restate its financial statements for the past several years. In fact, GTGI would subsequently issue multiple restatements of those financial statements. These restatements resulted in a more than $250 million reduction of the revenues that the company had previously reported for the period 1999 through 2001 and increased the company's previously reported losses for that period by nearly $200 million.

In June 2003, the SEC announced that it was filing securities fraud charges against Henry Yuen and Elsie Leung for their role in misrepresenting GTGI's financial statements. The federal agency subsequently filed similar charges against several other GTGI executives who were allegedly involved in the scheme and/or were aware of it. The SEC also charged the company, as a separate entity, with releasing materially misrepresented financial statements.

In June 2004, the SEC disclosed that it had settled the charges pending against GTGI. This settlement did not include Yuen, Leung, and the other GTGI executives allegedly involved in the fraudulent accounting scheme. The federal agency would deal with those officers on an individual basis in subsequent litigation or out-of-court settlements. The SEC's settlement with GTGI required the company to pay a $10 million fine and permanently enjoined it from future violations of federal securities laws. In the settlement agreement, the SEC disclosed a litany of accounting gimmicks that GTGI had used to misrepresent its financial statements, each of which involved intentional misapplications of the revenue recognition rule.

The methods used by GTGI to inflate its operating results included recognizing revenue under "expired, disputed, or non-existent" contracts. A significant portion of this revenue was recorded by the company's "highly touted" Interactive Platform Sector, according to the SEC.[13] GTGI also accelerated revenue recognized under certain long-term contracts and improperly recorded revenue for large non-monetary and barter transactions. The SEC also reported that certain revenues earned by GTGI's Media and Services Sector had been diverted for accounting purposes to the Interactive Platform Sector. Finally, GTGI used a series of "multiple-element" transactions to inflate the reported revenue of the Interactive Platform Sector.

## "Repeated Audit Failures"

The SEC issued multiple enforcement and litigation releases that documented the GTGI accounting fraud. One of these releases analyzed the "repeated audit failures" of KPMG, GTGI's independent audit firm during the course of that fraud. [14] The SEC's criticism of KPMG focused on three facets of the firm's GTGI audits.

According to the SEC, the GTGI audit engagement team should have contacted KPMG's technical staff in the firm's headquarters office when the auditors uncovered suspicious and unusual transactions recorded by the client. The federal agency believed that such consultation would almost certainly have resulted in more thorough investigations of those transactions and ultimately led to KPMG discovering their fraudulent nature. Although KPMG had a "consultation policy" at the time, the SEC

13. Securities and Exchange Commission, *Litigation Release No. 18760*, 23 June 2004.

14. Securities and Exchange Commission, "KPMG LLP and Four Auditors Sanctioned for Improper Professional Conduct in Connection with Gemstar-TV Guide International, Inc. Audits," www.sec.gov, 20 October 2004.

suggested that the policy was not sufficiently comprehensive or rigorous, which explained why the GTGI engagement team had failed to ask for the assistance of the firm's technical staff.

The SEC also faulted the "materiality determinations" of the GTGI audit engagement team. A key feature of the GTGI fraud was Henry Yuen's effort to inflate the operating results of the new Interactive Platform Sector. According to the SEC, the GTGI auditors should have been aware of that sector's disproportionate importance to not only Yuen but also to financial analysts and other parties tracking the company's financial performance. Because the KPMG auditors relied on quantitative measures of materiality, they failed to adequately investigate the relatively nominal operating results of the Interactive Platform Sector.

> *". . . the KPMG auditors . . . unreasonably determined that the [Interactive Platform Sector] revenues were immaterial to Gemstar's financial statements. The KPMG auditors' materiality determinations were unreasonable in that they only considered quantitative materiality (i.e., that the amount of revenue was not a large percentage of Gemstar's consolidated financial results) and failed to also consider qualitative materiality (i.e., that the revenue related to business lines that were closely watched by securities analysts and had a material effect on the valuation of Gemstar stock).*[15]

The bulk of the lengthy SEC enforcement release that examined the role of KPMG in the GTGI debacle focused on the audit firm's consideration of several large revenue transactions that the company used to inflate and distort its operating results. Listed next are the most important of these transactions and the SEC's related criticism of the GTGI audit engagement team.

### Licensing Agreement with AOL

In early April 2000, AOL, the large Internet service provider, paid GTGI a nonrefundable fee of $23.5 million in exchange for an eight-year license on a patented technology controlled by GTGI. Although the fee was paid "upfront," the agreement between the two companies required GTGI to provide AOL with technical assistance and support over the entire eight-year term of the contract. Despite these contractual terms, GTGI management convinced the KPMG auditors that the $23.5 million fee was "for transfer of the license and for 12 months of technical assistance and engineering support." Because the auditors did not challenge that assertion, they allowed GTGI to recognize the entire fee as revenue over a twelve-month period from April 2000 through March 2001.

The SEC maintained that the KPMG auditors "unreasonably failed to exercise professional care and skepticism in reviewing the [AOL-GTGI] contract and in testing Gemstar's representations regarding the purpose of the upfront nonrefundable fee." If the auditors had properly investigated that contract and management's related representations, they would have determined that the $23.5 million fee paid to GTGI by AOL should have been prorated for revenue recognition purposes over the eight-year term of the contract.

### Disputed Scientific-Atlanta Revenue

Scientific-Atlanta manufactures equipment used by cable TV networks, Internet service suppliers, and various other companies involved in the broadcasting and electronic communications industries. Gemstar Development Corporation, the

---

15. Unless noted otherwise, the remaining citations in this text were drawn from the following source: Securities and Exchange Commission, *Accounting and Auditing Enforcement Release No. 2125*, 20 October 2004.

predecessor of GTGI, had a three-year licensing agreement with Scientific-Atlanta. This agreement allowed Scientific-Atlanta to use certain patented technologies controlled by Gemstar. The agreement expired in 1999 and was not renewed. Following the expiration of that agreement, Gemstar sued Scientific-Atlanta, alleging that the company was infringing on patented technologies that were Gemstar's exclusive intellectual property.

During this ongoing litigation, Gemstar continued to record licensing revenue from Scientific-Atlanta as if it still had a contractual relationship with that company. Following the 2000 merger with TV Guide, GTGI's accounting staff did the same. From early 2000 through the first quarter of fiscal 2002, GTGI recorded more than $100 million of disputed licensing revenue from Scientific-Atlanta.

According to the SEC, there was no defensible basis for Gemstar and later GTGI to record revenue from Scientific-Atlanta after the contract with that company expired in 1999. The federal agency identified the following four conditions that precluded the recording of that revenue.

1) GTGI did not have a current contract with Scientific-Atlanta;
2) GTGI did not receive any payments of the disputed revenues;
3) Scientific-Atlanta was insisting that it did not owe the revenues to GTGI; and,
4) any subsequent receipt of the disputed revenues by GTGI was contingent on a favorable outcome to the litigation between it and Scientific-Atlanta.

Because KPMG "knew or reasonably should have known" of each of these conditions, the auditors should have refused to endorse their client's decision to record that revenue.

### *Improper Recording of Revenue from Multiple-Element Transactions*

During 2001, GTGI engaged in large "multiple-element" revenue transactions with Motorola, Inc., which manufactures various electronic products, and the Tribune Company, a broadcasting company whose flagship television station is Chicago-based WGN. In each of these transactions, Motorola and the Tribune Company purchased certain assets from GTGI's Media and Services Sector. GTGI executives negotiated payment terms for the two transactions that required Motorola and the Tribune Company to purchase large amounts of advertising revenue from the Interactive Platform Sector. Collectively, those payment terms produced more than $100 million of revenue for that sector. GTGI's segment disclosures in the notes to its audited financial statements did not disclose that a material portion of the Interactive Platform Sector's revenues resulted from the two multiple-element transactions.

The SEC ruled that GTGI did not have a sufficient basis for ascertaining the fair value of the advertising revenues that were a major component of the Motorola and Tribune Company transactions.

> *Gemstar did not have sufficient stand-alone IPG [Interactive Platform Sector] advertising revenue (i.e., revenue from advertising that was not part of a related-party, nonmonetary, or multi-element transaction) to provide a basis on which to fair value the Motorola and Tribune IPG [Interactive Platform Sector] advertising components of the multi-element transactions.*

In fact, GTGI had structured the Motorola and Tribune Company transactions to divert disproportionate amounts of the revenues from those transactions to the Interactive Platform Sector. GTGI executives also took explicit steps to conceal this fact from the public and other parties. For example, in the case of the Tribune Company transaction, a GTGI executive threatened to cancel the transaction if Tribune's management insisted on complete disclosure of its terms.

The SEC concluded that KPMG failed to adequately audit these multiple-element transactions. In particular, the SEC found that KPMG did not collect "sufficient competent evidence" to substantiate the fair value of the advertising revenues that were components of those two transactions. Instead, the KPMG auditors accepted management's representations that the advertising revenue component of each transaction was determined on an arm's length or fair value basis. The SEC also criticized KPMG for failing to insist that GTGI disclose that a major portion of the revenues reported by the Interactive Platform Sector was attributable to multiple-element transactions.

### *Improper Recording of Revenue from Barter Transactions*

In fiscal 2001, GTGI acquired certain intellectual property from another company, Fantasy Sports. In exchange for that property that was supposedly worth $20.75 million, GTGI gave Fantasy Sports $750,000 cash and $20 million of future advertising credits. Fantasy Sports used these advertising credits during fiscal 2001, which produced $20 million of advertising revenue for the Interactive Platform Sector that period. The SEC once again faulted KPMG for not recognizing that GTGI had insufficient "stand-alone IPG [Interactive Platform Sector] advertising revenue to provide a basis on which to fair value" the $20 million of advertising credits. Likewise, the SEC pointed out that GTGI's financial statements on which KPMG had issued an unqualified opinion did not provide adequate disclosure of this barter transaction.

After reviewing these and similar GTGI revenue transactions audited by KPMG, the SEC ruled that the accounting firm had failed to comply with generally accepted auditing standards. This lack of compliance had been manifested in the following ways, according to the federal agency:

1) Failure to exercise professional care and skepticism, failure to obtain sufficient competent evidential matter, and over-reliance on management representations.
2) Failure to take appropriate action to correct disclosure that did not comply with GAAP and/or was not consistent with Gemstar's financial statements.
3) Failure to render accurate reports.

## EPILOGUE

In June 2004, the SEC and KPMG reached an agreement to resolve the allegations that the firm's GTGI audits had been deficient. KPMG agreed to pay a $10 million fine, which at the time was the largest fine ever imposed on an independent audit firm by the SEC.[16] The SEC also censured KPMG and sanctioned four of the firm's auditors involved in the relevant GTGI audit engagements. The latter individuals included the engagement audit partner, co-engagement audit partner, review partner, and senior audit manager who had been assigned to one or more of those engagements. Each of these individuals was suspended from practicing before the SEC for one or more years.

In February 2006, Elsie Leung, GTGI's former CFO, agreed to pay $1.3 million to resolve pending SEC charges that she had participated in the fraudulent scheme to misrepresent GTGI's financial statements. Leung was also permanently barred from serving as an officer or director of a public company.

16. In 2005, the SEC would levy a $22.5 million fine on KPMG for allegedly deficient audits of Xerox Corporation.

After a three-year court battle in a civil case, a federal judge ruled in March 2006 that Henry Yuen was guilty of securities fraud, falsifying GTGI's accounting records, and lying to his former company's independent auditors. The judge ruled that Yuen had to pay the victims of the GTGI accounting fraud $22.3 million. To date, the only criminal complaint filed against Yuen has been for obstruction of justice. Yuen allegedly destroyed documents during the course of the federal investigation into the GTGI accounting fraud. Yuen resolved the obstruction charge by agreeing to a plea bargain deal offered by the U.S. Department of Justice. This deal required Yuen to pay approximately $1 million in fines and to serve six months of home detention.

In December 2007, GTGI was purchased by another company for $2.8 billion, an amount that was a small fraction of the company's total market value shortly after the merger with TV Guide International. To date, Yuen's much-hyped EPG technology has not lived up to its great expectations. According to a *New York Times* reporter, "Mr. Yuen's vision for the electronic programming guide as a major money maker has yet to materialize."[17]

---

## Questions

1. What fundamental principles dictate when a company should recognize or record revenue in its accounting records? Revenue recognition issues can be particularly complex for companies that sell software and/or license technology. Identify specific rules or concepts in the professional standards that accountants and auditors can rely on to make proper revenue recognition decisions for such companies.
2. The SEC charged KPMG with "repeated audit failures" in this case. Identify general conditions, specific circumstances, and other factors that are common causes of, or, at a minimum, commonly associated with, "audit failures." What quality control mechanisms can audit firms implement to minimize the likelihood of audit failures?
3. The SEC criticized KPMG for relying on "quantitative" measures in arriving at materiality judgments while ignoring important "qualitative" issues relevant to those judgments. Under what circumstances should auditors rely more heavily on quantitative measures rather than qualitative issues in making materiality judgments? Under what circumstances should auditors rely more heavily on qualitative issues rather than quantitative measures in making materiality judgments? Explain.
4. Do you agree with Henry Yuen's assertion that a businessperson who is complying with all applicable laws and regulations is, by definition, behaving "ethically"? Defend your answer.

---

17. Siklos, "The Math Whiz vs. the Medial Moguls."

## CASE 1.10

# New Century Financial Corporation

*It is well enough that people of the nation do not understand our banking and monetary system, for if they did, I believe there would be a revolution before tomorrow morning.*

*Henry Ford*

From 1962 to 1992, Ed McMahon served as the quintessential sidekick and straight man to Johnny Carson on the long-running and popular television program *The Tonight Show*. After leaving that program, McMahon stayed in the television spotlight for 12 years by serving as the host of *Star Search*, a syndicated talent show. McMahon's resume also included long stints as cohost of *TV Bloopers and Practical Jokes*, the annual Macy's Thanksgiving Day Parade, and the Jerry Lewis Labor Day Telethon and as commercial spokesperson for such companies as Budweiser and American Family Publishing.

McMahon's fifty-year-plus career in television made him one of the most recognized celebrities in that medium. Understandably then, the American public was shocked when press reports in June 2007 revealed that McMahon was more than $600,000 past due on his home mortgage payments. The $5 million mortgage on McMahon's Beverly Hills mansion was held by Countrywide Financial Corporation.

Unfortunately, millions of everyday Americans with mortgage balances only a fraction of Ed McMahon's have recently faced the unhappy prospect of losing their homes due to the worst financial crisis to strike the United States economy since the Great Depression. As that crisis quickly worsened and spread to the global economy, the search began for the parties responsible for it. Among the potential culprits identified by the press was the accounting profession, in particular, independent auditors.

## Mortgage Mess

Nearly one-half of recent mortgage foreclosure victims in the United States obtained their loans from so-called subprime lenders that became dominant forces in the mortgage industry over the past two decades. The largest of those lenders were Countrywide, HSBC, New Century Financial Corporation (New Century), and Wells Fargo, but more than a dozen other large companies provided loans to borrowers with suspect credit histories. The implosion of the lucrative but high-risk subprime sector of the mortgage industry in 2007 and 2008 ignited a financial crisis in the United States that would quickly engulf the global economy.

The origins of the subprime mortgage debacle in the United States can be traced to the collapse of New Century, the nation's second largest subprime lender. New Century was founded in 1995 by three friends who had previously worked together at a mortgage banking company. New Century, which was based in Irvine, California, grew dramatically over its brief existence. In 1996, New Century reported total revenues of $14.5 million and total assets of $4.4 million. Nine years later, the company reported total revenues of $2.4 billion and total assets of $26 billion.

During the heyday of subprime mortgage lending in 2005 and 2006, New Century funded $200 million of new mortgage loans on a typical business day. In early February 2007, just a few months after company executives insisted that New Century was financially strong, those same executives unsettled Wall Street when they revealed that the company would be restating previously released financial statements as a result of the misapplication of generally accepted accounting principles (GAAP).

Two months later, New Century declared bankruptcy. A court-appointed bankruptcy examiner summarized the far-reaching implications that New Century's downfall had for the global economy.

> *The increasingly risky nature of New Century's loan originations created a ticking time bomb that detonated in 2007. . . The demise of New Century was an early contributor to the subprime market meltdown. The fallout from this market catastrophe has been massive and unprecedented. Global equity markets were rocked, credit markets tightened, recession fears spread, and losses are in the hundreds of billions of dollars and growing.*[1]

In fact, New Century would be just the first of many high profile companies brought down by the turmoil in the United States's mortgage industry. Longtime stalwarts of the nation's financial services industry that fell victim to that turmoil included Bear Stearns, Lehman Brothers, and Merrill Lynch.

In September 2008, the federal government assumed control of the Federal National Mortgage Association and the Federal Home Loan Mortgage Company, two "government-sponsored" but publicly owned companies better known as Fannie Mae and Freddie Mac, respectively. At the time, the two organizations owned or guaranteed nearly one-half of the approximately $12 trillion of home mortgages in the United States. For decades, the federal government had used Fannie Mae and Freddie Mac to create an orderly and liquid market for homeowner mortgages, but the enormous losses each suffered in 2007 and 2008 undercut that role and forced the U.S. Department of the Treasury to take over their operations.

Angry investors lashed out at a wide range of parties who they believed bore some measure of responsibility for the massive financial crisis. Those parties included the major subprime mortgage lenders in the United States, such as New Century, and the politicians, regulatory authorities, ratings agencies, and independent auditors who had failed to prevent or rein in the imprudent business practices of those lending institutions.

Only a few years removed from the sweeping reforms prompted by the Enron and WorldCom scandals, the accounting profession was once again forced to defend itself from a wide range of angry and often self-righteous critics. Among these critics was *The New York Times.* The prominent newspaper castigated the auditors of subprime lenders for stamping those institutions' financial statements with the accounting profession's equivalent of the Good Housekeeping Seal of Approval. "While accounting firms don't exert legal or regulatory authority over their clients, they do bestow seals of approval, the way rating agencies do. People in the financial industry, as well as investors, have reason to believe that a green light from an auditor means that a company's accounting practices have passed muster."[2]

---

1. "Final Report of Michael J. Missal, Bankruptcy Court Examiner," In re: New Century TRS Holdings, Inc., a Delaware corporation, *et al.*, U.S. Bankruptcy Court for the District Delaware, Case No. 07-10416 (KJC), 29 February 2008. Unless indicated otherwise, the quotations appearing in this case were taken from this source.
2. V. Bajaj and J. Creswell, "A Lender Failed. Did Its Auditor?" *The New York Times* (online), 13 April 2008.

The following section of this case provides a historical overview of subprime mortgage lending in the United States. Next, the history and operations of New Century Financial Corporation are reviewed with a particular focus on the company's major role in the subprime mortgage fiasco. The case then examines the criticism of KPMG, New Century's longtime independent audit firm, by the federal bankruptcy examiner appointed to investigate the company's sudden collapse in early 2007.

## Subprime Lending: A Historical Perspective

Like all businesses, mortgage companies struggle to achieve a proper balance between "risk" and "return" in their operations. The principal risk historically faced by mortgage lenders is the possibility that their clients will be unable or unwilling to pay the principal and interest on their mortgage loans.

Prior to the 1980s, individuals who were poor credit risks effectively had only two choices for obtaining a mortgage to purchase a home. Those alternatives were obtaining a home loan insured by either the Federal Housing Administration (FHA) or the Department of Veteran Affairs (VA). Borrowers with good credit histories, so-called prime borrowers, would typically seek financing for a new loan directly from a bank, savings and loan, or other financial institutions.

The deregulation of the lending industry beginning in the 1980s made it much easier for subprime borrowers to obtain mortgage loans to finance the purchase of a new home. The Depository Institutions Deregulation and Monetary Control Act of 1980 did away with restrictions that imposed a ceiling on the interest rates lending institutions could charge on new mortgage loans. Subsequent legislation allowed mortgage lenders to create a wide array of financing alternatives to compete with the standard 30-year, fixed interest rate mortgage loan that had long been the industry's principal product. Most notably, these non-traditional mortgage loans included ARMs, or adjustable rate mortgages, that would become particularly popular with mortgage borrowers who had impaired or "subprime" credit histories or profiles.

Despite the deregulatory legislation of the 1980s, the subprime sector of the mortgage industry did not experience explosive growth until the "securitization" of mortgage loans became increasingly common following the turn of the century. Wikipedia defines securitization as "a structured finance process in which assets, receivables, or financial instruments [such as mortgage loans] are acquired, classified into pools, and offered as collateral for third-party investment."

The securitization option caused many mortgage lenders to adopt an "originate to distribute" business model. This new business model meant that the credit risk posed by new mortgages was no longer exclusively absorbed by lending institutions but rather was shared with investors worldwide who purchased so-called mortgage-backed securities or MBS. By 2006, nearly one-fourth of all new residential mortgage loans in the United States were made to subprime borrowers; three-fourths of those mortgages were securitized and sold to investors in the United States and around the world.

The insatiable demand for high-yield MBS among investors, particularly institutional investors such as large banks and hedge funds, caused subprime lenders to ratchet up their marketing efforts. To persuade individuals who were high credit risks to obtain mortgage loans, the subprime lenders developed new products designed specifically for that sector of the mortgage market.

Among the most popular mortgage products developed for the subprime lending market were "stated-income" and "interest-only" mortgages. An applicant for a stated-income loan was simply asked to report his or her annual income during the application process for the loan. The applicant's self-reported income was used by the lender to determine the size of the loan that the individual could afford. Not surprisingly, many applicants for stated-income loans, commonly known as "liars' loans" in the mortgage industry, grossly overstated their annual incomes so that they could purchase a larger home than was economically feasible given their actual annual incomes.

A borrower who obtained an interest-only or IO mortgage loan was required to pay only interest on his or her loan balance for a fixed period of the mortgage term. The IO feature of these loans typically extended over either the first 5 or the first 10 years of the mortgage term. Similar to other mortgage loans, the most common term of an IO loan was 30 years.

Housing prices in those regions of the country where subprime lending was particularly prevalent—such as Arizona; California; south Florida; and Las Vegas, Nevada—rose steeply during the late 1990s and into the early years of the new century. Many subprime borrowers in those housing markets purchased a home with the express intention of reaping a short-term windfall profit. An individual who obtained a 100 percent loan to acquire a $2 million home could realize a more than $400,000 "profit" on that home in two years if housing prices rose 10 percent each year. After two years, the borrower could extract that profit by refinancing his or her mortgage. That profit could then be used to make the monthly payments on the new mortgage. Or, that individual could sell the home and use the resulting profit to purchase a much larger home—with a much larger mortgage—that he or she could also "flip" in a few years.

Housing prices generally reached their peak in the United States in mid-2006, although they had been declining in some regions of the country over the previous twelve months. By late 2007, prices in several major regional housing markets had declined by 10 percent from their peak levels. By mid-2008, housing prices in those same markets had declined by 20 percent, or more, from their high water marks.

As housing prices steadily fell, a growing number of subprime borrowers began defaulting on their monthly mortgage payments. In fact, many of those individuals quickly became "upside down in their homes," that is, the unpaid balances of their mortgages exceeded the market values of their homes. By early 2008, an estimated 9 million U.S. homeowners had a negative equity in their homes.

The sharp downturn in the housing market had an immediate and drastic impact on mortgage lenders, particularly subprime mortgage lenders such as New Century. Many of the subprime loans originated and packaged for sale by New Century included repurchase clauses. If the default rate on those packages of loans exceeded a certain rate, New Century could be forced to repurchase those loans. As the housing market weakened, New Century and other subprime lenders were flooded with loan repurchase requests.

The financial problems facing the mortgage industry soon spread to other sectors of the economy because of the securitization of subprime mortgage loans. Many high profile companies in the financial services industry, such as Merrill Lynch, that had no direct connection to the large subprime lenders, suffered huge losses as the market value of MBS plunged. Making matters worse, a large proportion of MBS that originated in the United States was sold worldwide. As one observer of the mortgage market noted, the securitization process effectively "spread the cancer of subprime mortgages to investors throughout the U.S. and the rest of the world."[3]

3. K. Amadeo, "Understanding the Subprime Mortgage Crisis," *About.com* (online), 9 October 2008.

## New Century: Poster Child for Subprime Mortgage Lending

Bob Cole, Ed Gotschall, and Brad Morrice found themselves without jobs in 1995 when the company for which they had worked for several years, Plaza Home Mortgage, was purchased by a much larger competitor. The three friends decided to pool their resources and establish their own mortgage company, a company that would focus on the "low-end" or subprime sector of the mortgage market. Cole served as New Century Financial Corporation's chief executive officer (CEO), Gotschall was the company's chief financial officer, and Morrice oversaw New Century's lending operations as the company's chief operating officer (COO). Morrice would eventually replace Cole as New Century's CEO. In June 1997, the company went public by listing its stock on the NASDAQ—New Century's stock would be switched to the New York Stock Exchange in late 2004.

Cole, Gotschall, and Morrice earned relatively modest annual salaries throughout their tenure with the company. For example, in 2005, each of them received a salary of $569,250. New Century's incentive compensation plan, however, rewarded the three co-founders handsomely with significant bonuses and stock option grants when the company met or exceeded its financial goals. During 2005, the three executives received total compensation of approximately $15 million each. In addition, *The New York Times* reported that, collectively, they realized more than $40 million in trading profits on the sale of New Century stock between 2004 and 2006.[4]

New Century thrived from its inception thanks largely to three key factors. First, mortgage interest rates, which had spiked during the mid-1990s, stabilized and then generally trended downward for more than a decade. Second, the economic and regulatory environment at the time made subprime lending the most lucrative sector of the mortgage industry. Finally, the booming housing market in Orange County, California, where the company was located, gave New Century a large and easily accessible market to tap.

Once New Century was well established in Orange County, the company's ruling troika of Cole, Gotschall, and Morrice began pursuing expansion opportunities for their company in other "hot" real estate markets in the United States. At its zenith, New Century operated more than 200 retail mortgage offices in the United States from which company employees originated new mortgage loans. The company's wholesale division, which produced the bulk of its loan originations, operated through a far-flung network of more than 35,000 independent mortgage brokers.

New Century's 2003 Form 10-K filed with the Securities Exchange Commission (SEC) provided a concise summary of the company's business model.

> *We offer mortgage products designed for borrowers who generally do not satisfy the credit, documentation or other underwriting standards prescribed by conventional mortgage lenders and loan buyers, such as Fannie Mae and Freddie Mac. We originate and purchase loans on the basis of the borrower's ability to repay the mortgage loan, the borrower's historical pattern of debt repayment and the amount of equity in the borrower's property (as measured by the borrower's loan-to-value ratio, or LTV). We have been originating and purchasing these types of loans since 1996 and believe we have developed a comprehensive and sophisticated process of credit evaluation and risk-based pricing that allows us to effectively manage the potentially higher risks associated with this segment of the mortgage industry.*

In 2004, New Century's management reorganized the company as a real estate investment trust (REIT) so that it would qualify for favorable tax treatment under the

4. V. Bajaj, "Report Assails Auditor for Work at Failed Home Lender," *The New York Times* (online), 26 March 2008.

Internal Revenue Code. This organizational change had little impact on the company's operations or the underlying nature of its principal line of business, that is, originating subprime mortgage loans.

New Century experienced impressive growth from its founding in 1996 through 2001, however, a significant increase in subprime lending activity quadrupled New Century's revenues from fiscal 2002 to fiscal 2005. In the latter year, New Century originated or purchased more than $56 billion of mortgage loans and securitized $17 billion of those loans, resulting in net earnings of $411 million for the company.

The decision by New Century's management to focus the company's marketing efforts principally on stated-income and IO loans contributed significantly to its remarkable growth in revenues beginning in 2002. By 2005, approximately three-fourths of the company's loan originations involved one of those two products.

Throughout the period that New Century's revenues were increasing dramatically, company spokespeople repeatedly insisted in press releases and public filings with the SEC that the company had a strong and sophisticated system of internal controls. That contention was subsequently questioned by the bankruptcy examiner appointed to investigate the collapse of New Century.

> *Several interviewees told the Examiner that they thought New Century's information technology and data entry and processing systems were not "state of the art" and were not sufficient for a business of the size and nature of New Century's. In particular, New Century's loan production processes were apparently manual and people-intensive through the fall of 2005. Up until that time, New Century apparently used an outdated DOS-based loan underwriting and appraising operating system, which according to one Management interviewee, allowed users to "finagle anything."*

The bankruptcy examiner's report went on to note that the company's accounting system was particularly lax with regard to tracking "loan repurchase claims." According to the examiner, New Century did not develop an "automated system or protocol" for tracking such claims until late 2006. By that time, the company was being swamped by loan repurchase requests due to the weakening housing markets in the principal geographical areas that it served. Besides failing to properly track loan repurchase requests throughout most of its history, New Century "did not have a formal policy spelling out exactly how to calculate reserves"[5] for loans that it would be required to repurchase.

By late 2005, several members of New Century's board of directors were openly challenging top management's high-risk business strategies as well as questionable accounting and financial reporting decisions made by the company. The most vocal of these critics was Richard Zona, an outside director who also served on the company's audit committee.

Earlier in his long and distinguished career, Zona had been a senior partner with Ernst & Young (E&Y) and had served for a time as E&Y's National Director of Financial Services, a position in which he oversaw the firm's audit, tax, and management consulting services. In the late 1990s, Zona had also served on an advisory council to the Federal Reserve Board.

In late 2005, Zona drafted a resignation letter, which he addressed to New Century's board of directors. In that letter, Zona suggested that company management was manipulating reported earnings, employing "aggressive" revenue recognition methods, and failing to provide an adequate allowance for loan losses.[6] Excerpts from Zona's letter are included in Exhibit 1.

---

5. Bajaj and Creswell, "A Lender Failed."

6. Zona eventually rescinded the 2005 resignation letter and remained on the company's board until September 2007.

**EXHIBIT 1**

EXCERPTS FROM DRAFT OF 2005 RESIGNATION LETTER SUBMITTED BY RICHARD ZONA TO NEW CENTURY'S BOARD

At the October 25th and 26th [2005] Board meeting, Management informed the Board that its current forecast and analyst consensus for third quarter EPS of $2.24 per share could not be achieved unless Management reversed $.26 per share of loan loss reserves . . . Obviously, Management's desire to reverse reserves in the third quarter smacked of earnings manipulation.

Management use of off balance sheet gain on sale accounting substantially overstates earnings when compared to cash flows, thus generating extremely aggressive income recognition.

Our largest shareholder has questioned the appropriateness of our accounting for loan losses.

As to accounting for loan losses, it is a long standing accounting maxim that accounting should be designed and applied to match revenues with expenses. Management's methodology to provide for loan losses based upon their estimate of charge offs over the next 18 months does not accomplish that objective . . . Management's methodology does not result in a proper matching of revenues with costs, (loan loss provisions), because charge offs are back ended.

Source: "Final Report of Michael J. Missal, Bankruptcy Court Examiner," In re: New Century TRS Holdings, Inc., a Delaware corporation, *et al.*, U.S. Bankruptcy Court for the District Delaware, Case No. 07-10416 (KJC), 29 February 2008.

Throughout 2006, New Century's financial condition and operating results deteriorated rapidly. To quell concerns regarding the company's health, New Century management repeatedly assured Wall Street that the company was financially sound. In August 2006, New Century reported a significant increase in its earnings for the second quarter of the year compared with that for the same period of the prior year. A company spokesperson noted that those operating results were "evidence of the strength and stability of our franchise." New Century's third quarter earnings press release for 2006 admitted that subprime lenders faced "challenging" market conditions because of increasing loan delinquencies. Nevertheless, the press release assured the investing public that New Century was "adequately reserved for the expected higher level of loan losses."

On January 31, 2007, New Century's management team met with the company's board of directors and audit committee. At that meeting, management told the board and audit committee that New Century had understated its reserve for loan repurchase losses for each of the first three quarterly reporting periods of 2006. New Century's controller, David Kenneally, attributed those understatements to an "inadvertent oversight" in the method used to compute the reserve. Members of New Century's board and audit committee testified that they were "shocked" by this revelation and described the January 31 meeting as "ugly" and "very emotional."

On February 7, 2007, New Century filed a Form 8-K with the SEC, which publicly disclosed the prior understatements of the loan repurchase loss reserve. The 8-K indicated that the understatements were due to the company failing "to account for expected discounts upon the disposition of repurchased loans" and due to its failure to "properly consider the growing volume of repurchase claims outstanding that resulted from the increasing pace of repurchase requests." The 8-K filing did not disclose to what extent the loan repurchase loss reserve had been understated but instead simply indicated that the previously reported earnings for the first three quarters of 2006 "should no longer be relied upon."

**EXHIBIT 2**

FICTITIOUS LETTER SUPPOSEDLY WRITTEN BY FORMER NEW CENTURY CEO FOLLOWING THE COMPANY'S BANKRUPTCY FILING

Dear BankNet360 Readers:

Hi, my name is Brad Morrice and I've just bailed out of my sinking ship, the SS New Century Financial.

But don't feel bad for me; I'll be doing just fine. I may have bankrupt the company, treated mortgage underwriting like a bad cold, and helped cause more layoffs than a recession, but I should still bank about $25 million. To the creditors I say, "nanee-nanee billy goat."

Regrets? Sure, I've got some. I should have cashed in more of my options when the NEW stock was on a rocket ship fueled by option ARMs and I.O. loans from heaven. Ah, those were the days, when loans fell from the sky—and into the laps of subprime borrowers who can more easily discern Britney from J-Lo than understand all the conditions of their upcoming loan repricings.

You know, I wonder also how I can walk away from New Century with so much dough. This Chief Restructuring Officer, Holly Etlin, I don't know what planet she is from, but she can come over to my palace, er, place, anytime.

Oh, look at the time. That money's going to hit my account any moment now, and I've got shopping to do. Well, my regards to the subprime mortgage industry. All you Wall Street guys—hope you can handle the risk.

Sincerely yours,

Brad A. Morrice
Founder (ret.)
New Century Financial Corp. (bankrupt)

Source: BankNet360.com (http://www.banknet360.com/viewpoints/Discussion.do?discussion_id=191), 13 June 2007.

On March 2, 2007, New Century informed the SEC that its 2006 Form 10-K would be delayed and that it would eventually report a loss for the entire year. At the same time, New Century disclosed that KPMG was considering issuing a going-concern opinion on the company's 2006 financial statements—KPMG resigned as New Century's auditor a few weeks later without having issued an opinion on those financial statements. On April 2, 2007, New Century filed for bankruptcy in a U.S. federal court. At the time, New Century was the ninth largest company to file for bankruptcy in U.S. history.[7] In May 2008, company management announced that New Century's audited financial statements for 2005 should no longer be relied upon.

Within a few days of New Century's bankruptcy filing, the company's stock price fell to less than $1 per share, down from more than $30 per share two months earlier—the stock had reached its all-time high of $66 per share in 2004. Not surprisingly, stockholders and other parties were enraged by the company's sudden collapse that mimicked the downfall of Enron and WorldCom a few years earlier. Exhibit 2 presents a sarcastic commentary on New Century's collapse by one of the company's many critics. This commentary was in the form of a fictitious letter addressed to the readers of an online banking forum.

7. The five largest companies to file for bankruptcy in 2007 were mortgage lenders. Four of those five companies were subprime lenders.

## "Go-to Auditor"

*The New York Times* characterized KPMG as the "go-to auditor" for the subprime sector of the mortgage industry.[8] KPMG's audit clients in that sector included the largest subprime lenders, namely, Countrywide, HSBC, New Century, and Wells Fargo. KPMG served as New Century's auditor from the company's inception in 1995 until its resignation in April 2007.

New Century's bankruptcy filing resulted in heated criticism of KPMG. *The New York Times* drew a parallel between Arthur Andersen's audits of Enron Corporation that had failed to expose the huge energy company's aggressive accounting treatments and KPMG's audits of New Century. According to the newspaper, KPMG had failed to warn investors that New Century's "mortgage freight train was about to run off the rails."[9]

> *New Century's accounting methods let it prop up profits, charming investors and allowing the company to continue to tap a rich vein of Wall Street cash that it used to underwrite more mortgages. Without the appearance of a strong bottom line, New Century's financial lifeline could have been cut earlier than it was.*[10]

The federal bankruptcy examiner appointed for New Century carried out an exhaustive investigation of the large subprime lender's sudden failure. A major focus of that investigation was KPMG's 2005 audit of New Century and the accounting firm's reviews of the financial statements included in the company's Form 10-Qs for the first three quarters of 2006. KPMG was required to provide the bankruptcy examiner with nearly 2 million pages of documents relating to those engagements. Exhibit 3 presents KPMG's audit report on New Century's 2005 financial statements.

In his 560-page report, the bankruptcy examiner alleged that KPMG had failed to perform its New Century engagements "in accordance with professional standards." The examiner's specific allegations included charges that the 2005 New Century audit was improperly staffed and that the independence of certain KPMG auditors may have been impaired. The examiner also maintained that KPMG failed to adequately consider serious internal control problems evident in New Century's accounting and financial reporting system and failed to properly audit the company's critically important loan repurchase loss reserve.

### *Staffing Issues on the New Century Engagement*

In the spring of 2005, shortly after KPMG completed the 2004 audit of New Century, an almost entirely new team of auditors, approximately 15 KPMG employees in total, was assigned to that client. The only two members of the 2004 audit engagement team "held over" for the 2005 audit were two first-year associates. The two key members of the 2005 audit team, the audit engagement partner and the senior manager, had just joined the Los Angeles office of KPMG, the practice office responsible for servicing New Century.

John Donovan, the engagement partner for the 2005 New Century audit, had served for 17 years as an audit partner with Arthur Andersen prior to that firm being forced to disband in 2002. After Andersen's demise, Donovan became an audit partner with E&Y, which he left in early 2005 to take a similar position with KPMG.

---

8. Bajaj and Creswell, "A Lender Failed."

9. *Ibid.*

10. *Ibid.*

**EXHIBIT 3**

New Century Financial Corporation and Subsidiaries Report of Independent Registered Certified Public Accounting Firm

**KPMG's 2005 Audit Report on New Century's Financial Statements**

The Board of Directors

New Century Financial Corporation

We have audited the accompanying consolidated balance sheets of New Century Financial Corporation and subsidiaries as of December 31, 2005, and 2004, and the related consolidated statements of income, comprehensive income, changes in stockholders' equity, and cash flows for each of the years in the three-year period ended December 31, 2005. These consolidated financial statements are the responsibility of Company's Management. Our responsibility is to express an opinion on these consolidated financial statements based on our audits.

We conducted our audit in accordance with the standards of the Public Company Accounting Oversight Board (United States). Those standards require that we plan the audit to obtain reasonable assurance about whether the financial statements are free of material misstatement. An audit includes examining, on a test basis, evidence supporting the amounts and disclosures in the financial statements. An audit also includes assessing the accounting principles used and significant estimates made by management, as well as evaluating the overall financial statement presentation. We believe that our audits provide a reasonable basis for our opinion.

In our opinion, the consolidated financial statements referred to above present fairly, in all material respects, the financial position of New Century Financial Corporation and subsidiaries as of December 31, 2005 and 2004, and the results of their operations and their cash flows for each of the years in the three-year period ended December 31, 2005, in conformity with U.S. generally accepted accounting principles.

We have also audited, in accordance with the standards of the Public Company Accounting Oversight Board (United States), the effectiveness of the Company's internal control over financial reporting as of December 31, 2005, based on criteria established in Internal Control—Integrated Framework issued by the Committee of Sponsoring Organizations of the Treadway Commission (COSO), and our report dated March 15, 2006 expressed an unqualified opinion on management's assessment of, and the effective operation of, internal control over financial reporting.

KPMG LLP
Los Angeles, California
March 15, 2006

Source: New Century's 2005 10-K.

New Century's audit committee was unhappy with KPMG's decision to appoint Donovan as the audit engagement partner for the 2005 audit. Members of the audit committee believed that Donovan's lack of experience with the mortgage industry made him a poor choice to supervise that audit and asked KPMG to appoint another partner to oversee the engagement. When KPMG refused, the audit committee considered dismissing KPMG and retaining a different audit firm. "Ultimately, the Audit Committee determined that a switch to a new accounting firm would be tremendously disruptive and would send a bad signal to its lenders."

Mark Kim accepted a position with KPMG in May 2005, shortly before being assigned to serve as the senior manager on the 2005 New Century audit engagement. Kim had several years of prior experience as an auditor and had served for three years as the assistant controller of a small mortgage lending company.

During his tenure on the New Century audit team, Mark Kim complained to John Donovan that it was difficult to recruit a "good team" of auditors to work on the engagement. In an e-mail to Donovan, an exasperated Kim remarked, "We will never get a good team out here because of the reputation that the engagement has." Another e-mail sent by a New Century accountant to the company's controller, David Kenneally, seemed to corroborate Kim's opinion. This latter e-mail noted that KPMG had not assigned the "A team" to the New Century audit.

In fact, Kenneally, a former KPMG employee, was apparently the key reason that the New Century engagement had a negative reputation within KPMG's Los Angeles office. Evidence collected by the New Century bankruptcy examiner suggested that the company's accounting function was "weak" and was overseen by Kenneally who was "domineering" and "difficult, condescending, and quick-tempered." One KPMG subordinate on the New Century audit team testified that Kenneally often berated Donovan and Kim. In another e-mail sent by Kim to Donovan, the KPMG senior manager indicated that "Dave [Kenneally] seems to know the answers for everything and anything and the rest of the accounting department is on almost the same boat as the audit team is—little knowledge of what's going on. This intimidates everyone on the engagement team."

The tense relationship between the KPMG audit engagement team and New Century's management, particularly Kenneally, worsened as the 2005 audit neared completion. Two individuals with KPMG's FDR (Financial Derivatives Resource) Group were brought in to review New Century's accounting for certain hedges and other financial derivatives during the final phase of the audit. They requested various documents from New Century that were needed to complete their review of the aforementioned items. When New Century failed to provide that documentation, the two specialists refused to "sign off" on the company's relevant accounting decisions. This refusal prevented Donovan from releasing the opinion on New Century's financial statements that were to be included in the company's 2005 Form 10-K.

Hours before the SEC filing deadline for New Century's 2005 10-K, an angry Donovan e-mailed one of the FDR specialists. "I am very disappointed we are still discussing this. As far as I am concerned, we are done. The client thinks we are done. All we are going to do is p___ everybody off." Later that same day, a high-ranking KPMG partner in the firm's New York headquarters office told Donovan to release the unqualified opinion on New Century's 2005 financial statements. Donovan was instructed to release the opinion even though the two FDR specialists had not approved the company's accounting decisions for its financial derivatives.[11]

The following day, New Century's audit committee called a meeting with Donovan and Kim. In that meeting, members of the audit committee reportedly "yelled" and "screamed" at the two KPMG auditors. Later, Kenneally told the New Century bankruptcy examiner that he had been "furious" over the "near-disaster"—that is, the fact that New Century's filing of its 2005 10-K with the SEC had almost been delayed. Because of the incident, New Century's audit committee deferred the decision of whether to reappoint KPMG as the company's auditor for the 2006 fiscal year.

---

11. The FDR specialists were allowed to dissociate themselves from the decision to issue the audit opinion on New Century's 2005 financial statements in a "disagreement memorandum" included in the 2005 workpapers. The following month, New Century finally provided the documentation that had been requested by those specialists. A review of that documentation revealed that New Century had improperly accounted for certain of its derivatives, resulting in "a misstatement of several million dollars." However, KPMG ruled that those errors were immaterial, meaning that it was not necessary to restate the 2005 financial statements.

Donovan later testified that he had been concerned that the audit committee would dismiss KPMG.

Over the following two months, Donovan assured New Century's audit committee that "a situation like this will never happen again." After receiving that assurance, the audit committee reappointed KPMG as New Century's audit firm.

The bankruptcy examiner speculated that the 2005 10-K incident impaired KPMG's independence during the remainder of the firm's tenure with New Century. "In particular, it is possible that Donovan and Kim were not as skeptical as they might otherwise have been with regard to critical assumptions [underlying New Century's accounting decisions]." The examiner went on to suggest that "Donovan and Kim may have looked for ways to add unique value in order to salvage KPMG's reputation, such as by providing proactive (though erroneous) advice in connection with the repurchase reserve calculation methodology."

In a subsequent interview with *The New York Times*, the bankruptcy examiner further questioned KPMG's independence when he maintained that the New Century auditors had been eager to please the company's management team. "They acquiesced overly to the client, which in the post-Enron era seems mind-boggling."[12] In another interview with the Reuters news agency, the examiner expressed a similar point of view. "In the post-Enron era, one of the lessons should have been that accountants need to be skeptical, strong, and independent. You didn't have any of those attributes here."[13]

### *Inadequate Consideration of Internal Control Problems*

Section 404 of the Sarbanes-Oxley Act requires auditors of public companies to audit the effectiveness of their clients' internal controls over financial reporting.[14] In both 2004 and 2005, KPMG concluded that New Century maintained effective internal control over its financial reporting function.

During the 2004 internal control audit, the KPMG auditors identified five "significant deficiencies" in internal controls that they reported to New Century's audit committee. Since the KPMG auditors concluded that those deficiencies did not qualify as "material weaknesses," the audit firm was able to issue an unqualified opinion on New Century's internal controls for 2004. No significant deficiencies or material weaknesses in internal controls were identified by KPMG during the 2005 internal control audit.

New Century's bankruptcy examiner challenged KPMG's conclusion that the company's internal controls over financial reporting were effective during 2004 and 2005. The examiner pointed out that throughout its existence New Century did not have an "effective mechanism for tracking, processing and handling [loan] repurchase claims." This internal control weakness prevented the company from determining the magnitude of loan repurchase requests at any point in time, which, in turn, prevented the company from properly considering those requests in arriving at the period-ending balances of the loan repurchase loss reserve.

---

12. Bajaj, "Report Assails Auditor."

13. A. Beck, "KPMG Allowed Fraud at New Century, Report Says," *Reuters.com*, 27 March 2008.

14. KPMG's 2004 and 2005 audits of New Century were completed while PCAOB *Auditing Standard No. 2*, "An Audit of Internal Control Over Financial Reporting Performed in Conjunction with an Audit of Financial Statements" was in effect. That standard has subsequently been replaced by PCAOB *Auditing Standard No. 5*, "An Audit of Internal Control Over Financial Reporting That Is Integrated with an Audit of Financial Statements." The two standards are very similar.

A related internal control weakness was New Century's failure to adopt "formal policies and procedures" for calculating the loan repurchase loss reserve at the end of each accounting period. The lower-level accountants who were assigned the task of computing the reserve balance each reporting period testified that they simply followed the instructions passed down to them by the individual who had previously been responsible for the reserve computation.

During both the 2004 and 2005 audits, the KPMG auditors discovered the internal control weaknesses related to New Century's loan repurchase loss reserve. The bankruptcy examiner noted that those control weaknesses had particularly critical implications for New Century in 2005 when the volume of loan repurchase requests was increasing rapidly. Despite those implications, KPMG characterized those weaknesses as "inconsequential" during the 2005 audit. Since the internal control problems were not deemed significant deficiencies or material weaknesses, KPMG did not communicate them to New Century's audit committee.

The bankruptcy examiner insisted that for at least the 2005 audit, the inadequate accounting procedures for loan repurchase requests qualified as a material weakness in internal control that should have caused KPMG to issue an adverse opinion on New Century's internal controls. In fact, New Century's management reached a similar conclusion in early 2007.

> *The material weaknesses identified [by New Century's management in early 2007] were: (1) the failure to maintain effective controls over the interpretation and application of the accounting literature relating to the Company's critical accounting policies (specifically as to the calculation of repurchase reserves); and (2) the failure to maintain effective controls to provide reasonable assurances that the Company collected, analyzed, and used information relating to outstanding purchase claims when establishing the allowance for repurchase losses.*

Debbie Biddle was the KPMG audit senior principally responsible for the 2005 internal control audit. Similar to John Donovan and Mark Kim, Biddle had joined KPMG's Los Angeles office shortly before the 2005 New Century audit began. Biddle had transferred to the Los Angeles office from a KPMG affiliate in the United Kingdom. Prior to being assigned responsibility for the 2005 New Century internal control audit, Biddle had "virtually no experience auditing U.S. clients and no prior SOX experience."

The bankruptcy examiner reported that Biddle and her colleagues failed to thoroughly review the 2004 audit workpapers for New Century. As a result, they may have been unaware of the internal control problems discovered by KPMG auditors the prior year and thus failed to properly consider those problems in planning and carrying out the 2005 audit.

> *The Examiner found no evidence that the KPMG [2005] engagement team engaged in a formal process to compare year over year deficiency findings in connection with the 2005 SOX 404 audit. Conducting this analysis would have been prudent given the wholesale turnover in the KPMG engagement team. This failure is significant, as it impacted the planning for the 404 audit in 2005, the evaluation of findings in 2005, and the planning for the year-end audits.*

### Failure to Properly Audit New Century's Loan Repurchase Loss Reserve

In early 2005, the quality of New Century's loan portfolio, as measured by such objective criteria as delinquency and default rates, began declining rapidly. Internal data collected by New Century revealed that the delinquency rate on loans originated during 2005 was approximately double that of loans originated during the previous year. The delinquency rate continued to rise throughout 2006 as conditions within the housing market deteriorated.

The increasing delinquency and default rates on loans originated by New Century caused a large increase in the number of loan repurchase claims filed by investors that had purchased large blocks of those loans. Because of the inadequate accounting procedures and internal controls for loan repurchase claims, New Century's accounting staff failed to record the needed increases in the loan repurchase loss reserve throughout 2005 and beyond. For example, despite the large increase in loan repurchase requests in 2005, New Century's loan repurchase loss reserve actually declined from the end of 2004 to the end of 2005.

New Century's bankruptcy examiner estimated that the understatement of the loan repurchase loss reserve and errors in related accounts inflated New Century's reported pre-tax earnings for fiscal 2005 by 14.3 percent or approximately $64 million. The examiner determined that errors in those same accounts overstated New Century's reported pre-tax earnings for the first three quarters of 2006 by approximately $200 million or 59 percent.

New Century's accountants used a 90-day "look-back" period in determining the adequacy of the loan repurchase loss reserve each financial reporting period. That is, only repurchase requests for loans sold in the 90 days immediately preceding the balance sheet date were considered in arriving at the reserve balance. In fact, the company often received repurchase requests for loans sold more than three months earlier.

The bankruptcy examiner criticized KPMG for not insisting that New Century use a longer than 90-day "window" in computing the loan repurchase loss reserve. However, a KPMG workpaper suggested that policy was reasonable. "Based on the review of the Company's repurchase log and discussions with management, it appears reasonable that the most recent 3 months sales are at risk for repurchase." The bankruptcy examiner contested the assertion that KPMG had reviewed the log of loan repurchase requests since that accounting record indicated that loans were being reacquired by New Century as long as three years after the date they were sold. The examiner also uncovered evidence suggesting that a New Century executive had informed a KPMG auditor that a significant number of loans older than 90 days were being repurchased by the company.

KPMG's audit workpapers documented the ominous increase in loan repurchase requests received by New Century beginning in late 2004. In 2005, New Century repurchased $332 million of loans, compared with $135 million the prior year. Despite this large increase, the bankruptcy examiner reported that KPMG "failed to perform any increased procedures or testing of New Century's repurchase reserves" during the 2005 audit.

A secondary factor that contributed to the understatement of New Century's loan repurchase loss reserve was the company's failure to consider an "interest recapture" element in computing that reserve each reporting period. The bankruptcy examiner found this obvious oversight by the company's accountants "perplexing."

> *The failure to include Interest Recapture in the repurchase reserve calculation from the outset is perplexing because the Examiner understands that it was a long time requirement under loan repurchase agreements for New Century to pay investors the amount of interest that the borrower had failed to pay.*

In fact, the workpaper memorandum that summarized the audit tests KPMG applied during the 2005 audit to the loan repurchase loss reserve indicated that interest recapture was a component of the reserve.

> *A KPMG workpaper from January 2006 notes that estimated losses on future repurchases "include accrued interest the investor [loan purchaser] would have collected from the borrower, if the loan had performed, that New Century must pay to the investor at the time of repurchase."*

The evidence that KPMG relied on to reach that erroneous conclusion was a statement made by David Kenneally. The bankruptcy examiner criticized the KPMG auditors for not corroborating Kenneally's assertion with other audit evidence. "If KPMG had performed adequate tests and calculations, it would have determined that Interest Recapture was omitted from the repurchase reserve calculation."

During early 2006, New Century changed the method used to compute the period-ending balance of the loan repurchase loss reserve.[15] This change resulted in large increases in the understatements of that account at the end of each subsequent quarterly reporting period—by the third quarter the reserve was understated by approximately 1000 percent.

Kenneally testified that the change in accounting for the reserve account was recommended by Mark Kim, the KPMG senior audit manager. Kim would later testify that he did not explicitly remember making that recommendation. Nevertheless, evidence collected by the bankruptcy examiner caused him to conclude that a KPMG auditor "almost certainly" recommended the change in accounting for the reserve account.

> *At a time when KPMG was aware, as evidenced by its own workpapers, that market conditions were worsening and repurchases were increasing, KPMG made a recommendation to New Century to remove a component of the repurchase reserve that had the effect of decreasing the reserve . . . and then failed to inform the Audit Committee of the change in this critical accounting policy.*

In November 2006, New Century hired a new chief financial officer (CFO) who had 30 years of prior experience in the mortgage industry. The CFO immediately questioned the adequacy of the company's loan repurchase loss reserve and asked KPMG to provide him with a written statement that the reserve was properly stated. KPMG refused to provide that written assurance.

As a result of the new CFO's persistent inquiries, New Century's accounting staff eventually recognized that the accounting change made in early 2006 for the loan repurchase loss reserve had been improper and had materially understated the reserve for each of the first three quarterly reporting periods of 2006. That realization led to the February 7, 2007, 8-K filing in which New Century reported those understatements. That 8-K disclosure triggered the series of events that resulted in New Century filing for bankruptcy less than two months later.

## In Defense of KPMG

Representatives of KPMG responded forcefully to the allegations against their firm in the report prepared by New Century's bankruptcy examiner. Particularly galling to the large accounting firm was the suggestion that KPMG auditors had "deferred

---

15. The change in the method of computing the loss reserve involved deleting the "inventory severity" component of that reserve. That component involved those losses expected to be incurred by New Century on loans that had already been reacquired as of the given balance sheet date. Kim allegedly suggested dropping this component because he believed that it was considered by New Century in arriving at the balance of a related valuation account for the company's portfolio of outstanding loans. In fact, that was not the case.

excessively"[16] to client executives during the course of the New Century engagements. In response to that allegation, a KPMG spokesperson told a reporter with *The New York Times*, "[t]here is absolutely no evidence to support that contention."[17] In a subsequent interview with the *Times*, that same individual suggested that the bankruptcy examiner's report was unfair and "one-sided."

> *The examiner was appointed by the court to identify potential lawsuits in a bankruptcy case. Consistent with that charge, he has prepared an advocacy piece, which has many one-sided statements and significant omissions. In the end, the examiner concluded that the bankruptcy estate may be able to file a lawsuit against KPMG for negligence—a claim we strongly dispute—and a claim even the examiner notes in his report for which KPMG has strong defenses.*[18]

Several other parties also came to KPMG's defense. An accounting professor at the University of Chicago maintained that KPMG was not at fault in the New Century case and instead attributed the company's bankruptcy to its high-risk business model. "The business model of New Century depended on real estate values that would continue to go up and certainly not go down. The economic model here is what is at fault. It's the cause of what happened, not anything that KPMG did."[19]

At a minimum, the New Century bankruptcy report served to sustain a string of embarrassing public relations incidents for KPMG. In 2005, KPMG had faced potential criminal charges for a series of questionable tax shelters that it had marketed to well-heeled tax clients. In that same year, KPMG had agreed to pay the SEC $22.5 million to settle charges that audits of one of its largest clients, Xerox, had been flawed. Subsequent to that announcement, KPMG paid $80 million to settle civil litigation stemming from its Xerox audits.

Even before the New Century bankruptcy report was released, KPMG had been linked to the ongoing crises and scandals in the mortgage industry. Charges of large-scale earnings manipulation by Fannie Mae called into the question the quality of KPMG's audits of that organization, which for decades had played such a large role in the mortgage industry. Finally, in early January 2008, KPMG had been named a co-defendant in a large class-action lawsuit that charged Countrywide, another KPMG audit client, with perpetrating an accounting fraud.

## EPILOGUE

In August 2008, Ed McMahon revealed that he had finally found a buyer for his Beverly Hills mansion that would allow him to pay off his large mortgage.[20] Most individuals snared by the financial crisis that overwhelmed the mortgage industry and housing market in the United States did not share McMahon's good fortune. By the end of 2008, more than 1.5 million Americans would face foreclosure proceedings on their homes, easily the largest number of residential foreclosures in U.S. history.

16. Bajaj, "Report Assails Auditor."
17. *Ibid.*
18. Bajaj and Creswell, "A Lender Failed."
19. *Ibid.*
20. Unfortunately, Mr. McMahon passed away in June 2009.

In an effort to thwart the nationwide financial panic caused by the meltdowns in the mortgage and housing industries, the U.S. Congress passed a massive bailout plan in October 2008. The price tag for that rescue effort, intended to shore up the nation's crumbling financial infrastructure, was measured in hundreds of billions of dollars. Even if the rescue effort proved successful, most experts expected that the U.S. economy, as well as the global economy, would suffer adverse lingering effects for years, if not decades, to come.

## Questions

1. KPMG served as the independent audit firm of several of the largest subprime mortgage lenders. Identify the advantages and disadvantages of a heavy concentration of audit clients in one industry or sub-industry.
2. As noted in the case, there was an almost complete turnover of the staff assigned to the New Century audit engagement team from 2004 to 2005. What quality control mechanisms should accounting firms have in such circumstances to ensure that a high-quality audit is performed?
3. Section 404 of the Sarbanes-Oxley Act requires auditors of a public company to analyze and report on the effectiveness of the client's internal controls over financial reporting. Describe the responsibilities that auditors of public companies have to discover and report (a) *significant deficiencies* in internal controls and (b) *material weaknesses* in internal controls. Include a definition of each item in your answer. Under what condition or conditions can auditors issue an unqualified or clean opinion on the effectiveness of a client's internal controls over financial reporting?
4. One of New Century's most important accounts was its loan repurchase loss reserve. Each accounting period, New Century was required to estimate the ending balance of that account. What general principles or procedures should auditors follow when auditing important "accounting estimates"?
5. New Century's bankruptcy examiner charged that KPMG did not comply with applicable "professional standards" while auditing the company. List specific generally accepted auditing standards (GAAS) that you believe KPMG may have violated on its New Century engagements. Briefly defend each item you list.
6. Mortgage-backed securities (MBS) produced by New Century and other major subprime lenders have been a focal point of attention during the recent financial crisis. Many parties have maintained that the mark-to-market rule for securities investments such as MBS has contributed significantly to that crisis and that the rule should be modified, suspended or even eliminated. Briefly summarize the principal arguments of those parties opposed to the mark-to-market rule. Do you believe that those arguments are legitimate? Why or why not?
7. Identify what you consider to be the three most important "take-aways" or learning points in this case. Rank these items in order of importance (highest to lowest). Justify or defend each of your choices.

## CASE 1.11

# Madoff Securities

*Bernie wanted to be rich; he dedicated his life to it.*

*John Maccabee, longtime friend of Bernie Madoff*

Bernard Lawrence Madoff was born on April 29, 1938, in New York City. Madoff spent his childhood in a lower middle-class neighborhood in the borough of Queens. After graduating from high school, Madoff enrolled in the University of Alabama but transferred to Hofstra College, now known as Hofstra University, on Long Island at the beginning of his sophomore year. Three years later in 1960, he graduated with a political science degree from Hofstra.

According to a longtime friend, the driving force in Madoff's life since childhood was becoming wealthy. "Bernie wanted to be rich; he dedicated his life to it."[1] That compelling force no doubt accounted for Madoff's lifelong fascination with the stock market. As a teenager, Madoff frequently visited Wall Street and dreamed of becoming a "major player" in the world of high finance. Because he did not have the educational training or personal connections to land a prime job on Wall Street after he graduated from college, Madoff decided that he would set up his own one-man brokerage firm.

While in college, Madoff had accumulated a $5,000 nest egg by installing sprinkler systems during the summer months for wealthy New Yorkers living in the city's exclusive suburbs. In the summer of 1960, Madoff used those funds to establish Bernard L. Madoff Investment Securities LLC, which was typically referred to as Madoff Securities. Madoff operated the new business from office space that was provided to him by his father-in-law, who was a partner in a small accounting firm. For nearly five decades, Madoff served as the senior executive of Madoff Securities. During that time, the shy New Yorker, who had an occasional stammer and several nervous tics, would accumulate a fortune estimated at more than one billion dollars.

## Taking on Wall Street

Initially, Madoff's brokerage firm traded only securities of small over-the-counter companies, securities commonly referred to as "penny stocks." At the time, the securities of most large companies were traded on the New York Stock Exchange (NYSE). The rules of that exchange made it extremely difficult for small brokerage firms such as Madoff's to compete with the cartel of large brokerage firms that effectively controlled Wall Street. Madoff and many other small brokers insisted that the NYSE's rules were anticompetitive and inconsistent with a free market economy. Madoff was also convinced that the major brokerage firms kept securities transaction costs artificially high to produce windfall profits for themselves to the detriment of investors, particularly small investors.

Because of Madoff's resentment of the major Wall Street brokerage firms he made it his mission to "democratize" the securities markets in the United States while at the same time reducing the transaction costs of trading securities. "Bernie was the king of democratization. He was messianic about this. He pushed to automate the [securities trading] system, listing buyers and sellers on a computer that anyone could access."[2]

1. J. Maccabee, "Mom and Dad and Ruth and Bernie," *New York Magazine* (nymag.com), 22 February 2009.
2. S. Fishman, "The Monster Mensch," *New York Magazine* (nymag.com), 22 February 2009.

In fact, Madoff Securities was one of the first brokerage firms to utilize computers to expedite the processing of securities transactions. Bernie Madoff is also credited as one of the founders of the NASDAQ stock exchange that was organized in 1971. The NASDAQ was destined to become the world's largest electronic stock exchange and the largest global stock exchange in terms of trading volume. In the late 1980s and early 1990s, Madoff served three one-year terms as the chairman of the NASDAQ.

Madoff's leadership role in the development of electronic securities trading contributed significantly to his firm's impressive growth throughout the latter decades of the 20th century. By the early years of the 21st century, Madoff Securities was the largest "market maker" on the NASDAQ, meaning that the firm accounted for more daily transaction volume on that exchange than any other brokerage.[3] By that time, the firm was also among the largest market makers for the New York Stock Exchange, accounting for as much as five percent of its daily transaction volume. This market-making service was lucrative and low risk for Madoff Securities and reportedly earned the firm, which was privately owned throughout its existence, annual profits measured in the tens of millions of dollars.

In 1962, Madoff had expanded his firm to include investment advisory services. For several years, most of the individuals who set up investment accounts with Madoff Securities were referred to him by his father-in-law. Although the firm was a pioneer in electronic trading and made sizable profits from its brokerage operations, investment advisory services would prove to be its most important line of business. By late 2008, the total value of customer accounts that Madoff Securities managed had reached $65 billion.

The key factor that accounted for the incredible growth in the amount of money entrusted to Madoff's firm by investors worldwide was the impressive rates of return that the firm earned annually on the funds that it managed. For decades, those funds earned an average annual rate of return generally ranging from 10 to 15 percent. Although impressive, those rates of return were not spectacular. What *was* spectacular was the consistency of the returns. In 2001, *Barron's* reported that some of the Madoff firm's largest investment funds had never experienced a losing year despite significant stock market declines in several individual years.[4] Even when the stock market collapsed in late 2008, individual Madoff funds continued to report net gains for the year-to-date period.

Although Madoff would eventually serve as an investment adviser to dozens of celebrities, professional athletes, and other wealthy individuals, most of the money he managed came from so-called "feeder firms," which were large hedge funds, banks, and other investment companies. The individuals who had committed their funds to these feeder firms were typically unaware that those funds had been turned over to Madoff.

The reclusive Madoff and his subordinates disclosed as little as possible about the investment strategy responsible for their firm's success in the stock market. On one occasion, Madoff told an executive of a feeder firm, "It's no one's business what goes on here."[5] The *Wall Street Journal* reported that Madoff commonly "brushed off" skeptics

---

3. *Investopedia*, an online encyclopedia of business terms, provides the following description of a "market maker": "Broker-dealer firm that accepts the risk of holding a certain number of shares of a particular security in order to facilitate trading in that security. Each market maker competes for customer order flow by displaying buy and sell quotations for a guaranteed number of shares. Once an order is received, the market maker immediately sells from its own inventory or seeks an offsetting order."

4. *Barron's* (online), "What We Wrote About Madoff," 12 December 2008.

5. *Ibid.*

who questioned his firm's investment results by pointing out that those results had been audited and by insisting that his investment strategy "was too complicated for outsiders to understand."[6]

The only substantive information Madoff Securities provided regarding its investment policies was that it employed a "split-strike conversion" investment model. In simple terms, this strategy involved purchasing several dozen blue-chip stocks and then simultaneously selling both put options and call options on those securities. Supposedly, this strategy ensured a positive rate of return on those investments whether the stock market went up or down.

Competitors, financial analysts, and academics repeatedly attempted to replicate the success of Madoff Securities' investment strategy. None of those attempts were successful, which only added to Bernie Madoff's stature and mystique on Wall Street. As one industry insider noted in 2001, "[e]ven knowledgeable people can't really tell you what he's doing."[7] A CNN reporter observed that by the turn of the century Madoff was widely regarded as a stock market wizard and that "everyone" on Wall Street, including his closest competitors, was "in awe of him."[8]

## The Bubble Bursts

On December 10, 2008, Bernie Madoff told his two sons who worked at Madoff Securities to meet him at his apartment that evening. In this meeting, Madoff reportedly told his sons that the impressive returns earned for clients of his firm's investment advisory division over the previous several decades had been fraudulent. Those returns had been produced by an elaborate Ponzi scheme engineered and overseen by Madoff without the knowledge of any of his employees or family members.[9] The following day, an attorney representing Madoff's sons notified the SEC of their father's confession. That evening, FBI agents came to Madoff's apartment. One of the agents asked Madoff "if there was an innocent explanation" for the information relayed to the SEC from his sons.[10] Madoff replied, "There is no innocent explanation."[11] The agents then placed Madoff under arrest and within hours filed securities fraud charges against him.

The public announcement of Madoff's fraudulent scheme in December 2008 stunned investors worldwide. That announcement further undercut the stability of global stock markets that were already reeling from the subprime mortgage crisis in the United States, which had "frozen" the world's credit markets, caused stock prices to drop precipitously, and threatened to plunge the global economy into a deep depression. Politicians, journalists, and everyday citizens were shocked to learn that a massive investment fraud, apparently the largest in history, could go undetected for decades within the capital markets of the world's largest economic power. Even more disconcerting was the fact that the Madoff fraud went undetected for several years

6. G. Zuckerman, "Fees, Even Returns and Auditor All Raised Flags," *Wall Street Journal* (online), 13 December 2008.

7. *Ibid.*

8. A. Chernoff, "What Drove Bernie Madoff," *CNNMoney.com*, 5 January 2009.

9. *Investopedia* provides the following description of a "Ponzi scheme": "A fraudulent investing scam promising high rates of return with little risk to investors. The Ponzi scheme generates returns for older investors by acquiring new investors. This scam actually yields the promised returns to earlier investors, as long as there are more new investors. These schemes usually collapse on themselves when the new investments stop."

10. Fishman, "The Monster Mensch."

11. *Ibid.*

after the implementation of the far-reaching regulatory reforms mandated by the U.S. Congress in the wake of the Enron and WorldCom debacles.

News of the Madoff fraud caused a wide range of parties to angrily demand that the federal government and law enforcement authorities determine why the nation's "watchdog" system for the capital markets had failed once again. The accounting profession was among the first targets of the public's anger. On the day that Madoff's fraud was publicly reported, Floyd Norris, a *New York Times* reporter acquainted with Madoff, asked a simple question that was on the minds of many people, namely, "[w]ho were the auditors?"[12]

## "Rubber-stamped" Financial Statements

Business journalists quickly determined that the auditor of Madoff Securities was Friehling & Horowitz, an accounting firm located in the small New York City suburb of New City. Friehling & Horowitz had issued unqualified opinions on the financial statements of Madoff's firm since at least the early 1990s. Madoff had paid Friehling & Hororwitz nearly $200,000 in annual audit fees.

Further investigation revealed that Friehling & Horowitz had only one active accountant, one non-professional employee (a secretary), and operated from a tiny office occupying approximately two hundred square feet. The active accountant was David Friehling, who had performed the annual audits of Madoff's firm and signed off on the firm's unqualified audit opinions. Accounting and auditing experts interviewed by the Associated Press insisted that it was "preposterous" to conceive that any one individual could complete an audit of a company the size of Madoff Securities by himself.[13]

Friehling and his firm were members of the American Institute of Certified Public Accountants (AICPA). A spokesperson for that organization revealed that Friehling had reported to the AICPA each year that he did not perform any audits. As a result, Friehling's firm was not required to submit to the AICPA's peer review program for CPA firms. Friehling's firm was also not required to have a periodic peer review at the state level. At the time, New York was one of six states that did not have a mandatory peer review program for accounting firms.

In March 2009, *The New York Times* reported that Friehling had maintained dozens of investment accounts with Madoff Securities, according to documents obtained by the court-appointed trustee for that firm. Those same documents indicated that Friehling & Horowitz had another 17 investment accounts with Madoff's firm. In total, Friehling, his accounting firm, and his family members had nearly $15 million invested in funds managed by Madoff. Federal prosecutors noted that these investments had "flouted" the accounting profession's auditor independence rules and "disqualified" Friehling from serving as the auditor of Madoff Securities.[14]

David Friehling would be the second person arrested by federal law enforcement authorities investigating Madoff's fraud. On March 17, 2009, federal prosecutors charged Friehling with securities fraud and with aiding and abetting an investment fraud. The prosecutors did not allege that Friehling was aware of Madoff's fraudulent scheme but rather that he had conducted "sham audits" of Madoff Securities that had "helped foster the illusion that Mr. Madoff legitimately invested his clients' money."[15]

---

12. F. Norris, "Bernie Madoff," *New York Times* (online), 12 December 2008.

13. Associated Press (online), "Questions Surround Madoff Auditor," 17 December 2008.

14. New York State Society of Certified Public Accountants, "Madoff Auditor Charged for Role in Massive Fraud," 19 March 2009 (www.nysscpa.org/ezine/ETPArticles/ML31909a.htm).

15. L. Neumeister, "Federal Appeals Court to Hear Madoff Jail Argument," Associated Press (online), 19 March 2009.

News reports of Friehling's alleged sham audits caused him to be berated in the business press. A top FBI official observed that Friehling's "job was not to merely rubber-stamp statements that he didn't verify" and that Friehling had betrayed his "fiduciary duty to investors and his legal obligation to regulators."[16] An SEC official maintained that Friehling had "essentially sold his [CPA] license for more than 17 years while Madoff's Ponzi scheme went undetected."[17] Many parties found this and other denigrating remarks made by SEC officials concerning Friehling ironic since the federal agency was itself the target of scornful criticism for its role in the Madoff fiasco.

## Sir Galahad and the SEC

On at least eight occasions, the SEC investigated alleged violations of securities laws by Madoff Securities during the two decades prior to Bernie Madoff's startling confession. In each case, however, the investigation concluded without the SEC charging Madoff with any serious infractions of those laws. Most of these investigations resulted from a series of complaints filed with the SEC by one individual, Harry Markopolos.

On the March 1, 2009, edition of the CBS news program *60 Minutes*, investigative reporter Steve Croft observed that until a few months earlier Harry Markopolos had been an "obscure financial analyst and mildly eccentric fraud investigator from Boston." Beginning in 1999, Markopolos had repeatedly told the SEC that Bernie Madoff was operating what he referred to as the "world's largest Ponzi scheme." Between May 2000 and April 2008, Markopolos mailed or hand delivered documents and other evidence to the SEC that purportedly proved that assertion. Although SEC officials politely listened to Markopolos's accusations, they failed to vigorously investigate them.

One lengthy report that Markopolos sent to the SEC in 2005 identified 29 specific "red flags" suggesting that Madopff was perpetrating a massive fraud on his clients. Among these red flags was Madoff's alleged refusal to allow the Big Four auditor of an investment syndicate to review his financial records. Another red flag was the fact that Madoff Securities was audited by a one-man accounting firm, namely, Friehling & Horowitz. Also suspicious was the fact that Madoff, despite his firm's leadership role in electronic securities trading, refused to provide his clients with online access to their accounts, providing them instead with monthly account statements by mail.

Among the most credible and impressive evidence Markopolos gave to the SEC were mathematical analyses and simulations allegedly proving that Madoff's split-strike conversion investment strategy could not consistently produce the investment results that his firm reported. Markopolos noted that if such an investment strategy existed, it would be the "Holy Grail" of investing and eventually be replicated by other Wall Street investment advisors. Even if Madoff had discovered this Holy Grail of investing, Markopolos demonstrated there was not sufficient transaction volume in the options market to account for the huge number of options that his investment model would have required him to buy and sell for his customers' accounts.

In the months following the public disclosure of Madoff's fraud, Harry Markopolos reached cult hero status within the business press. Markopolos was repeatedly asked

16. W. K. Rashbaum and D. B. Henriques, "Accountant for Madoff Is Arrested and Charged With Securities Fraud," *New York Times* (online), 18 March 2009.

17. *Ibid.*

to comment on and explain the scope and nature of Madoff's scheme. Markopolos's dissection of Madoff's fraud suggested that three key factors accounted for it continuing unchecked for decades.

First, Madoff targeted investors who were unlikely to question his investment strategy. According to Markopolos, a large number of "smart" investors had refused to invest with Madoff despite his sterling record. "Smart investors would stick to their investment discipline and walk away, refusing to invest in a black-box strategy they did not understand. Greedy investors would fall over themselves to hand Madoff money."[18]

The second factor that allowed Madoff's fraud to continue for decades was his impeccable credentials. Even if his impressive investment results were ignored, Madoff easily qualified as a Wall Street icon. He was a pioneer of electronic securities trading and throughout his career held numerous leadership positions within the securities industry, including his three stints as NASDAQ chairman. Madoff's stature on Wall Street was also enhanced by his well-publicized philanthropy. He regularly contributed large sums to several charities.

The final and most important factor that allowed Madoff to sustain his fraudulent scheme was the failure of the regulatory oversight function for the stock market. In testimony before Congress and media interviews, Harry Markopolos has insisted that the Madoff debacle could have been avoided or at least mitigated significantly if federal regulators, particularly the SEC, had been more diligent in fulfilling their responsibilities. According to Markopolos, Madoff knew that the SEC's accountants, attorneys, and stock market specialists were "incapable of understanding a derivatives-based Ponzi scheme" such as the one he masterminded.[19] That knowledge apparently emboldened Madoff and encouraged him to continually expand the scope of his fraud.

Even after Markopolos explained the nature of Madoff's fraud to SEC officials, they apparently did not understand it. "I gift-wrapped and delivered the largest Ponzi scheme in history to them . . . [but the SEC] did not understand the 29 red flags that I handed them."[20] The outspoken SEC critic went on to predict that "[i]f the SEC does not improve soon, they risk being merged out of existence in the upcoming rewrite of the nation's regulatory scheme."[21]

Markopolos's pointed criticism of the SEC and additional harsh criticism by several other parties forced the agency's top officials to respond. An embarrassed SEC Chairman Christopher Cox admitted that he was "gravely concerned" by the SEC's failure to uncover the fraud.[22]

> *In an extraordinary admission that the SEC was aware of numerous red flags raised about Bernard L. Madoff Investment Securities LLC, but failed to take them seriously enough, SEC Chairman Christopher Cox ordered a review of the agency's oversight of the New York securities-trading and investment management firm.*[23]

---

18. D. Carrozza, "Chasing Madoff," *Fraud Magazine*, May/June 2009, 39.

19. *Ibid.*, 57.

20. J. Chung and B. Masters, "SEC 'Illiteracy' to Blame for Madoff Affair," *Financial Times* (online), 4 February 2009.

21. Carozza, "Chasing Madoff," 58.

22. A. Lucchetti, K. Scannell, and A. Efrati, "SEC to Probe Its Ties to Madoffs," *Wall Street Journal* (online), 17 December 2008.

23. *Ibid.*

## EPILOGUE

On March 12, 2009, Bernie Madoff appeared before Judge Denny Chin in a federal courthouse in New York City. After Judge Chin read the eleven counts of fraud, money laundering, perjury and theft pending against Madoff, he asked the well-dressed defendant how he pled. "Guilty," was Madoff's barely audible one-word reply. Judge Chin then told Madoff to explain what he had done. "Your honor, for many years up until my arrest on December 11, 2008, I operated a Ponzi scheme through the investment advisory side of my business."[24] Madoff then added, "I knew what I did was wrong, indeed criminal. When I began the Ponzi scheme, I believed it would end shortly and I would be able to extricate myself and my clients . . . [but a] s the years went by I realized this day, and my arrest, would inevitably come."[25]

Despite allegations that his two sons, his brother, and his wife were at least knowledgeable of his fraud and possibly complicit in it, Madoff refused to implicate any of them or any of his other subordinates. Madoff claimed that he alone had been responsible for the fraud and that the brokerage arm of his business, which had been overseen by his brother and his two sons, had not been affected by his Ponzi scheme. On June 29, 2009, Madoff appeared once more in federal court. After reprimanding Madoff for his actions, Judge Chin sentenced him to 150 years in federal prison, meaning that the 71-year-old felon would spend the rest of his life incarcerated.[26]

In November 2009, David Friehling, Madoff's longtime auditor, pleaded guilty to numerous charges in a Manhattan federal court. These charges included securities fraud, obstructing or impeding the administration of federal tax laws, and submitting false filings to the SEC. Friehling, who was to be sentenced in 2010, faced a prison sentence of more than 100 years. In March 2009, the AICPA announced that it had expelled Friehling for not cooperating with its investigation of his audits of Madoff Securities. The controversy over the failure of Friehling's firm to undergo any peer reviews prompted the New York state legislature to pass legislation in December 2008 requiring New York accounting firms that provide attest services to be peer reviewed every three years.[27]

Although none of the Big Four accounting firms were directly linked to Madoff Securities, legal experts speculated that those firms might face civil lawsuits in the wake of Madoff's fraud. This potential liability stems from the Big Four's audits of the large "feeder firms" that entrusted billions of dollars to Madoff. Lynn Turner, a former chief accountant of the SEC, contends that the auditors of the feeder firms had a responsibility to check out Madoff's auditor. "If they didn't, then investors will have to hold the auditors [of the feeder firms] accountable."[28]

In February 2009, KPMG became the first of the Big Four firms to be named as a defendant in a civil lawsuit triggered by the Madoff fraud. A California charity sued the prominent accounting firm to recover the millions of dollars it lost due to Madoff's scheme. KPMG had served as the independent auditor of a large hedge fund that had hired Madoff to invest the charity's

24. D. B. Henriques and J. Healy, "Madoff Goes to Jail After Guilty Plea," *New York Times* (online), 13 March 2009.

25. *Ibid.*

26. In August 2009, Frank DiPascali, Madoff Securities' former chief financial officer, pleaded guilty to complicity in Madoff's fraudulent scheme. During an appearance in federal court, DiPascali testified that, "It was all fake; it was all fictitious. It was wrong and I knew it at the time" (C. Bray and T. Lauricella, "'All Fake': Key Madoff Executive Admits Guilt," *Wall Street Journal* (online), 11 August 2009.)

27. Ironically, the New York law exempts accounting firms that have fewer than three professional accountants, meaning that Friehling & Horowitz would not have been required to undergo a peer review if the law had been in place during the time span covered by Madoff's fraud.

28. I. J. Dugan and D. Crawford, "Accounting Firms That Missed Fraud at Madoff May Be Liable," *Wall Street Journal* (online), 18 February 2009.

funds. A legal expert commented on the allegations pending against KPMG:

> *[t]he suit alleges that the [hedge] fund's auditor, KPMG, missed numerous red flags that should have alerted the auditor to Madoff's scheme. From financial returns that were too good to be true, to the fact that Madoff's multi-billion dollar operation was utilizing bookkeepers headquartered in an upstate strip mall, KPMG truly missed the elephant in the room.*[29]

In early 2009, President Obama appointed Mary Schapiro to replace Christopher Cox as SEC Chairman. In the aftermath of the Madoff fraud, Schapiro reported that her agency would revamp its oversight policies and procedures for investment advisers having physical custody of customer assets. Among the proposals announced by Schapiro were annual "surprise audits" of such firms to ensure that customer funds were being properly safeguarded. Schapiro also recommended that those firms be required to have internal control audits by independent accounting firms to determine whether they have "the proper controls in place."[30] Finally, Chairman Schapiro pledged that the SEC would implement specific measures to ensure that credible whistle-blowing allegations, such as those made by Harry Markopolos regarding Madoff's firm, would be investigated on a thorough and timely basis.

Regulatory and law enforcement authorities predict that it will be years before the total losses suffered by Madoff investors are known. Most estimates put those losses in the tens of billions of dollars. The large asset management firm Fairfield Greenwich Advisers alone had more than one-half of its investment portfolio of $14 billion invested with Madoff. Other companies and organizations that had significant funds in the custody of Madoff Securities include the large Dutch bank Fortis Bank, the large British bank HSBC, the International Olympic Committee, Massachusetts Mutual Life Insurance Company, New York University, Oppenheimer Funds, and Yeshiva University.

One media outlet reported that the list of individuals who had investments with Madoff reads like a lineup from "Lifestyles of the Rich and Famous," a popular television program of the 1980s. Those individuals include award-winning actors and actresses, Hollywood directors and screenwriters, media executives, prominent journalists, professional athletes, a Nobel Prize winner, and high-profile politicians. Among these individuals are Kevin Bacon, Zsa Zsa Gabor, Jeffrey Katzenberg, Henry Kaufman, Larry King, Sandy Koufax, Senator Frank Lautenberg, John Malkovich, Stephen Spielberg, Elie Wiesel, and Mort Zuckerman. To date, several suicides have been attributed to Madoff's massive fraud.

---

## Questions

1. Research recent developments involving this case. Summarize these developments in a bullet format.
2. Suppose that a large investment firm had approximately 10 percent of its total assets invested in funds managed by Madoff Securities. What audit procedures should the investment firm's independent auditors have applied to those assets?
3. Describe the nature and purpose of a "peer review." Would peer reviews of Friehling & Horowitz have likely resulted in the discovery of the Madoff fraud? Why or why not?

---

29. *USLaw.com*, "The Madoff Saga Continues as Pomerantz Files the First Derivative Suit Against an Auditor," 11 February 2009.

30. S. N. Lynch, "SEC to Consider Surprise Audits of Advisers," *Wall Street Journal* (online), 14 May 2009.

4. Professional auditing standards discuss the three key "conditions" that are typically present when a financial fraud occurs and identify a lengthy list of "fraud risk factors." Briefly explain the difference between a fraud "condition" and a "fraud risk factor" and provide examples of each.
5. In addition to the reforms mentioned in this case, recommend other financial reporting and auditing-related reforms that would likely be effective in preventing or detecting frauds similar to that perpetrated by Madoff.

# SECTION 2

# AUDITS OF HIGH-RISK ACCOUNTS

**CASE 2.1**

# Doughtie's Foods, Inc.

In the late 1970s, William Nashwinter accepted a position as a salesman with Doughtie's Foods, Inc., a publicly owned food products company headquartered in Portsmouth, Virginia.[1] The ambitious young salesman impressed his superiors with his hard work and dedication and was soon promoted to general manager of the Gravins Division of Doughtie's, a promotion that nearly doubled his salary. The Gravins Division was essentially a large warehouse that wholesaled frozen-food products to retail outlets on the East Coast.

Nashwinter quickly discovered that managing a large wholesale operation was much more complicated and stressful than working a sales route. Within a short time after accepting the promotion, Nashwinter found himself being maligned by corporate headquarters for his division's poor performance. After several rounds of scathing criticism for failing to meet what he perceived to be unrealistic profit goals, Nashwinter decided to take matters into his own hands. The young manager began fabricating fictitious inventory on his monthly performance reports to headquarters. By inflating his monthly inventory balance, Nashwinter lowered his division's cost of goods sold and thus increased its gross profit.

Several years later, Nashwinter insisted that he had never intended to continue his scheme indefinitely. Instead, he saw his actions simply as a solution to a short-term problem: "I always had in the back of my mind that the division would make enough legitimate profit one day to justify the fake numbers."[2] Unfortunately for Nashwinter, his division's actual operating results continued to be disappointing. With each passing year, Nashwinter had to fabricate larger amounts of fictitious inventory to reach his profit goals. Finally, in 1982, Nashwinter admitted to a superior that he had been filing false inventory reports to corporate headquarters for several years. Doughtie's management immediately fired Nashwinter and retained Price Waterhouse to determine the magnitude of the inventory errors in Gravins' accounting records and their impact on the company's consolidated financial statements. Price Waterhouse's study revealed that Nashwinter's scheme had overstated Doughtie's 1980 consolidated net income by 15 percent, while the company's 1981 net income had been overstated by 39 percent.[3]

Nashwinter used simple methods to misrepresent his division's inventory. In 1980, he inflated Gravins' inventory by including three pages of fictitious inventory items in the count sheets that summarized the results of the division's annual physical inventory. Nashwinter also changed the unit of measure of many inventory items. Rather than reporting fifteen single boxes of a given product, for example, Nashwinter changed the inventory sheet so that it reported 15 cases of

1. This case was developed primarily from Securities and Exchange Commission, *Accounting and Auditing Enforcement Release No. 30*, 21 May 1984.

2. R.L. Hudson, "SEC Charges Fudging of Corporate Figures Is a Growing Practice," *The Wall Street Journal*, 2 June 1983, 1, 19..

3. Nashwinter's scheme affected Doughtie's reported earnings for several earlier years, but Price Waterhouse was unable to determine the magnitude of those misstatements.

the product. In 1981, after Doughtie's acquired a computerized inventory system, Nashwinter simply input fictitious inventory items into his division's computerized inventory ledger.

In 1980 and 1981, the CPA firm of Goodman & Company audited Doughtie's. Thomas Wilson of Goodman & Company served as the audit manager on the 1980 audit and as the audit engagement partner the next year, after having been promoted to partner. In both years, Frank Pollard was the audit supervisor assigned to the Doughtie's engagement. Following the disclosure of Nashwinter's scheme to the Securities and Exchange Commission (SEC) by Doughtie's executives, the federal agency began investigating the 1980 and 1981 audits of the food distribution company. The SEC subsequently criticized Wilson and Pollard for their roles in those audits, particularly for their failure to rigorously audit Doughtie's inventory account.

The SEC maintained that Doughtie's inventory should have been considered a high-risk account and thus subject to a higher-than-normal degree of scrutiny by Wilson and Pollard during the 1980 and 1981 audits. First, inventory was the largest line item on the Doughtie's balance sheet, accounting for approximately 40 percent of the company's total assets. Second, Wilson and Pollard were aware of several weaknesses in Doughtie's internal controls for inventory, particularly within the Gravins Division. These weaknesses increased the likelihood of inventory errors. Finally, the SEC noted that Gravins' inventory increased rapidly during 1980 and 1981. The federal agency maintained that Wilson and Pollard should have considered the audit implications of this high growth rate and the closely related implications of the division's abnormally low inventory turnover.

The SEC also criticized Wilson and Pollard for failing to pursue problems that they or their subordinates uncovered during the 1980 and 1981 audits of Gravins' inventory. Following the completion of the physical inventory for Gravins in 1980, Nashwinter forwarded the three fictitious inventory count sheets to Wilson and Pollard. Nashwinter claimed that the Goodman & Company auditors had overlooked the three count sheets. After briefly reviewing these count sheets, Wilson and Pollard added the items on them to Gravins' inventory. Following the division's 1981 physical inventory, the audit senior on the Doughtie's engagement could not reconcile the quantities for numerous items listed on the inventory count sheets with the quantities shown on the computer printout that summarized the details of Gravins' year-end inventory balance. The senior notified Wilson of the problem and wrote Nashwinter a memo asking for an explanation. Wilson failed to follow up on the problem, and Nashwinter never responded to the memo. In his review of the senior's workpapers, Pollard either did not notice the numerous differences between the count sheets and the computer listing of Gravins' inventory or chose not to investigate those differences.

Nashwinter's testimony to the SEC was not complimentary of Goodman & Company's annual audits. Nashwinter testified that he often made up excuses to account for missing or misplaced inventory and that the auditors apparently never double-checked his explanations. He also testified that the auditors were lax when it came time to test count inventory items in Gravins' blast freezer: "A lot of times the auditors didn't want to stay in the freezer. It was too cold."[4]

---

4 Hudson, "Fudging of Corporate Figures," 19.

## EPILOGUE

For their roles in the Doughtie's case, the SEC required Wilson and Pollard to complete several professional education courses. The SEC also required that selected audits supervised by the two men in the future be subjected to peer reviews to determine that the appropriate audit procedures had been performed. Goodman & Company was not sanctioned by the SEC, since Wilson and Pollard had failed to comply with the firm's quality control standards. In 1983, Doughtie's dismissed Goodman & Company and retained Price Waterhouse as its audit firm.

To settle the charges filed against him by the SEC, William Nashwinter signed a consent decree in which he neither admitted nor denied the charges but agreed not to violate federal securities laws in the future. At last report, Nashwinter still worked in the food distribution industry.[5]

## Questions

1. What are the auditor's primary objectives when he or she observes the client's annual physical inventory? Identify the key audit procedures that an auditor would typically perform during and after the client's physical inventory.
2. What audit procedure or procedures might have prevented Nashwinter from successfully overstating the 1980 year-end inventory of the Gravins Division? What audit procedure or procedures might have prevented Nashwinter from overstating the division's 1981 year-end inventory?
3. In 1981, Gravins' inventory turnover was approximately one-half that of comparable divisions within the firm. How should this fact have affected the planning for the 1981 audit of Doughtie's? What audit procedures should Wilson and Pollard have performed to investigate Gravins' unusually low inventory turnover rate?
4. Nashwinter was under considerable pressure to improve his division's operating results. Discuss how this fact, if known to the auditors of Doughtie's, should have affected their assessment of audit risk for this client.

5. In 1999, Sysco Corporation purchased Doughtie's Foods for $25.5 million.

## CASE 2.2

# Golden Bear Golf, Inc.

Jack Nicklaus electrified sports fans worldwide in 1986 when he won the prestigious Masters golf tournament at the ripe old age of 46. Over the previous several years, the "Golden Bear" had been struggling to remain competitive with the scores of talented young players who had earned the right to play in the dozens of golf tournaments sponsored each year by the Professional Golfers' Association (PGA).

Regaining his golden touch on the golf course was not the only challenge that Nicklaus faced during the mid-1980s. In 1985, Richard Bellinger, an accountant employed by Golden Bear International, Inc. (GBI), the private company that oversaw the famous golfer's many business interests, mustered the courage to approach his employer. Bellinger told Nicklaus that his company was on the verge of bankruptcy. Nicklaus, who had allowed subordinates to manage his company's operations, was startled by the revelation. In a subsequent interview with *The Wall Street Journal*, Nicklaus admitted that after a brief investigation he realized that he had allowed his company to become a tangled knot of dozens of unrelated businesses. "We were an accounting nightmare . . . I didn't know what any of them did and neither did anyone else."[1]

Nicklaus immediately committed himself to revitalizing his company. The first step that he took to turn around his company was naming himself as its chief executive officer (CEO). Nicklaus then placed Bellinger in charge of GBI's day-to-day operations. Within a few years, the two men had returned GBI to a profitable condition by focusing its resources on lines of business that Nicklaus knew best, such as golf course design, golf schools, and the licensing of golf equipment.

In the late 1990s, however, Jack Nicklaus once again found himself coping with an "accounting nightmare." This time, Nicklaus could not blame himself for the predicament he faced. Instead, the responsibility for the new crisis rested squarely on the shoulders of two of Nicklaus's key subordinates who had orchestrated a fraudulent accounting scheme that jeopardized their employer's corporate empire.

### Player of the Century

Jack Nicklaus began playing golf as a young boy and had mastered the game by his mid-teens. After graduating from high school, the golf prodigy accepted a scholarship to play collegiately for Ohio State University in his hometown of Columbus. At the age of 21, Nicklaus joined the professional golf tour and was an instant success, racking up more than one dozen victories within a few years.

Shortly after joining the professional golf tour, the business-minded Nicklaus realized that winning golf tournaments was not the most lucrative way to profit from his enormous skills. At the time, the undisputed "king" of golf was Arnold Palmer, who endeared himself to the golfing public with his easy smile and affable manner on the golf course. Adoring legions of fans known as "Arnie's Army" tracked Palmer's every move during a tournament. Palmer's popularity with the public translated into a

1. R. Lowenstein, "A Golfer Becomes an Executive: Jack Nicklaus's Business Education," *The Wall Street Journal*, 27 January 1987, 34.

series of high-profile and profitable endorsement deals. On the other hand, golf fans generally resented Nicklaus's no-nonsense approach on the golf course. Those same fans resented Nicklaus even more when it became evident that the burly Ohioan with the trademark crew cut would likely replace Palmer as the world's best golfer, which he did. Nicklaus would ultimately win a record 18 major golf championships and edge out Palmer for the "Player of the Century" award in the golfing world.

With the help of a professional sports agent, Nicklaus worked hard to develop a softer, more appealing public image. By the mid-1970s, Nicklaus's makeover was complete and his popularity rivaled that of Palmer. As his popularity with the public grew, Nicklaus was able to cash in on endorsement deals and other business opportunities. Eventually, Nicklaus founded GBI to serve as the corporate umbrella for his business interests.

In 1996, Nicklaus decided to expand his business operations by spinning off a subsidiary from GBI via an initial public offering (IPO). Nicklaus named the new public company Golden Bear Golf, Inc. (Golden Bear). One of Golden Bear's principal lines of business would be the construction of golf courses. GBI would remain a privately owned company that would continue to manage Nicklaus's other business ventures. Because Nicklaus planned to retain more than 50 percent of Golden Bear's common stock, he and his subordinates would be able to completely control the new company's operations.

Nicklaus chose his trusted associate Richard Bellinger to serve as Golden Bear's CEO. Bellinger then appointed John Boyd and Christopher Curbello as the two top executives of Paragon International, Golden Bear's wholly owned subsidiary that would be responsible for the company's golf course construction business. Boyd became Paragon's president and principal operating officer, while Curbello assumed the title of Paragon's vice president of operations. On August 1, 1996, Golden Bear went public. The company's stock traded on the NASDAQ exchange under the ticker symbol JACK.

## Triple Bogey for Golden Bear

Shortly after Golden Bear's successful IPO, Paragon International's management team was inundated with requests to build Jack Nicklaus–designed golf courses. In a few months, the company had entered into contracts to build more than one dozen golf courses. Wall Street analysts, portfolio managers, and individual investors expected these contracts to translate into sizable profits for Golden Bear. Unfortunately, those profits never materialized.

Less than one year after Golden Bear's IPO, Boyd and Curbello realized that they had been much too optimistic in forecasting the gross profit margins Paragon would earn on its construction projects. Instead of earning substantial profits on those projects, Paragon would incur large losses on many of them. To avoid the embarrassment of publicly revealing that they had committed Paragon to a string of unprofitable construction projects, the two executives instructed Paragon's accounting staff to embellish the subsidiary's reported operating results.

A key factor that may have contributed to Boyd and Curbello's decision to conceal Paragon's financial problems was the incentive compensation package each had received when they signed on with the company. The two executives could earn sizable bonuses if Paragon met certain operating benchmarks. In addition, Boyd had been granted a large number of Golden Bear stock options.

Because Paragon's construction projects required considerably more than one year to complete, the company used percentage-of-completion accounting to recognize the revenues associated with those projects. Initially, Paragon applied the widely used "cost-to-cost" percentage-of-completion method that requires a company to determine the percentage of a project's total estimated construction costs incurred in a given accounting period. Then, the same percentage of the total revenue (and gross profit) to be earned on the project is booked that period.

During the second quarter of fiscal 1997, Boyd and Curbello determined that Paragon would have a large operating loss if the cost-to-cost method was used to recognize revenue on the golf course construction projects. At that point, the two executives instructed Paragon's controller to switch to what they referred to as the "earned value" percentage-of-completion accounting method. "In developing its percentage-of-completion estimates under the earned value method, Paragon relied not on objective criteria, such as costs incurred, but instead relied on management's subjective estimates as to its [a project's] progress."[2]

Throughout the remainder of fiscal 1997 and into fiscal 1998, Paragon's management routinely overstated the percentage-of-completion estimates for the company's golf course construction projects each quarter. To further enhance Paragon's operating results, the company's accounting staff inflated the contractual revenue amounts for most of the company's construction projects. These increased revenue amounts were allegedly attributable to "change orders" that amended the original construction contracts between Paragon and the company's clients. A final window-dressing scheme used by Paragon was recording revenue for *potential* construction projects.

> *In some cases, Paragon recognized revenue in connection with potential projects that Paragon had identified while looking for new work, even though Paragon had no agreements in connection with these projects. In other cases, Paragon recognized revenue in connection with projects where the project's owners were either entertaining bids from Paragon and other contractors or were negotiating with Paragon regarding a project yet to be awarded.*[3]

During the spring of 1998, John Boyd and several of his top subordinates, including Christopher Curbello, attempted to purchase Paragon International from Golden Bear. When that effort failed, Boyd and Curbello resigned their positions with Paragon. After their departure, Paragon's new management team quickly discovered that the subsidiary's operating results had been grossly misrepresented.

A subsequent investigation carried out jointly by Arthur Andersen & Co. (Paragon's audit firm), PricewaterhouseCoopers, and Golden Bear's external legal firm resulted in Golden Bear issuing restated financial statements in October 1998 for fiscal 1997 and for the first quarter of fiscal 1998. For fiscal 1997, Golden Bear had initially reported a $2.9 million net loss and golf course construction revenues of $39.7 million; the restated amounts included a $24.7 million net loss for fiscal 1997 and golf course construction revenues of only $21.8 million. For the first quarter of fiscal 1998, Golden Bear had reported an $800,000 net loss and golf course construction revenues of $16.0 million. Those amounts were restated to a $7.2 million net loss and golf course construction revenues of $8.3 million.

## "Audit Failures"

The Securities and Exchange Commission (SEC) launched its own investigation of Golden Bear shortly after the company issued the restated financial statements. A primary target of the SEC investigation was Michael Sullivan, the Arthur Andersen audit

---

2. Securities and Exchange Commission, *Accounting and Auditing Enforcement Release No. 1604*, 1 August 2002.

3. Securities and Exchange Commission, *Accounting and Auditing Enforcement Release No. 1603*, 1 August 2002.

partner who served as the Golden Bear engagement partner. Sullivan had been employed by Andersen since 1970 and had been a partner in the firm since 1984.

The SEC enforcement release that disclosed the results of its investigation of Andersen's Golden Bear audits included a section entitled "Sullivan's Audit Failures." According to the SEC, Sullivan was well aware that the decision to use the earned value method "accelerated revenue recognition by material amounts" for Paragon.[4] In fact, Sullivan was very concerned by Paragon's decision to switch from the cost-to-cost method to the "new and untested" earned value method. This concern prompted him to warn Paragon's management that he expected the earned value method to produce operating results approximately in line with those that would have resulted from the continued application of the cost-to-cost method. To monitor the impact of the earned value method on Paragon's operating results, Sullivan required the client's accounting staff to "provide detailed schedules showing Paragon's project-by-project results under both methods for each reporting period from the second quarter of 1997 through the first quarter of 1998."

By the end of fiscal 1997, the comparative schedules prepared by Paragon's accountants clearly revealed that the earned value method was allowing Paragon to book much larger amounts of revenue and gross profit on its construction projects than it would have under the cost-to-cost method. When Sullivan questioned Paragon's executives regarding this issue, those executives maintained that "uninvoiced" construction costs had caused the cost-to-cost method to significantly understate the stages of completion of the construction projects. To quell Sullivan's concern, in early fiscal 1998 Paragon's management recorded $4 million of uninvoiced construction costs in a year-end adjusting entry for fiscal 1997. These costs caused the revenue that would have been recorded under the cost-to-cost method to approximate the revenue that Paragon actually recorded by applying the earned value method. Unknown to Sullivan, the $4 million of uninvoiced construction costs booked by Paragon were fictitious.[5]

The SEC criticized Sullivan and his subordinates for failing to adequately investigate the $4 million of uninvoiced construction costs that materialized at the end of fiscal 1997. According to the SEC, Sullivan relied almost exclusively on management's oral representations to corroborate those costs.

> *Sullivan knew that Paragon booked costs for which no invoices had been received and which were not reflected in the company's accounts payable system, and that recording these uninvoiced costs would have substantially reduced the gap between the results produced by the two estimation methods . . . While procedures with respect to invoiced and paid costs were performed, Sullivan did not employ any procedures to determine whether the uninvoiced costs had actually been incurred as of year-end.*

Paragon's scheme to overstate its reported revenues and profits by applying the earned value method resulted in a dramatic increase in unbilled revenues by the end of 1997. Approximately 30 percent of the revenues reported in Golden Bear's 1997 income statement had not been billed to its customers. When Paragon's executives switched to the earned value method, they had assured Sullivan that they would bill

---

4. The remaining quotations in this case were taken from Securities and Exchange Commission, *Accounting and Auditing Enforcement Release No. 1676*, 26 November 2002.

5. Recognize that the $4 million of uninvoiced construction costs that were accrued in the adjusting entry did not reduce Golden Bear's gross profit that it had recognized for fiscal 1997 under the earned value method. The $4 million of construction costs simply replaced an equal amount of expenses that had been recorded to produce the "proper" amount of gross profit under the earned value method.

their customers on that basis. Despite that commitment, Paragon continued to bill their customers effectively on a cost-to-cost basis. (Paragon could not bill customers for the full amount of revenue that it was recording on the construction projects since those customers were generally aware of the *actual* stages of completion of those projects.)

The SEC maintained that Sullivan and his subordinates should have rigorously tested Paragon's large amount of unbilled revenues at the end of 1997. "A significant unbilled revenue balance requires adequate testing to determine the reason that the company is not billing for the work it reports as complete and whether unbilled amounts are properly recognized as revenue." Instead, the SEC charged that Sullivan relied "excessively" on oral representations from Paragon management to confirm the unbilled revenues and corresponding receivables.

In at least one case, the SEC reported that members of the Golden Bear audit team asked the owner of a Paragon project under construction to comment on the reasonableness of the $2 million unbilled receivable that Paragon had recorded for that project at the end of 1997. The owner contested that amount, alleging that Paragon had overestimated the project's stage of completion. "Despite this significant evidence that a third party with knowledge of the project's status disputed Paragon's estimated percentage-of-completion under the contract, the audit team did not properly investigate this project or otherwise expand Andersen's scope of testing of Paragon's unbilled revenue balances." According to the SEC, Sullivan did not believe the unbilled revenue posed major audit issues but instead was a "business issue" that Paragon had to resolve with its clients.

A second tactic Paragon used to inflate its reported profits was to overstate the total revenues to be earned on individual construction projects. During the 1997 audit, Andersen personnel selected 13 of Paragon's construction projects to corroborate the total revenue figures the company was using in applying the earned value percentage-of-completion accounting method to its unfinished projects. For 11 of the 13 projects selected, the Andersen auditors discovered that the total revenue being used in the percentage-of-completion computations by Paragon exceeded the revenue figure documented in the construction contract. Paragon's management attributed these differences to unsigned change orders that had been processed for the given projects "but could not produce any documents supporting these oral representations." Sullivan accepted the client's representations that the given revenue amounts were valid. "In each instance, Sullivan failed to properly follow up on a single undocumented amount; instead, Sullivan relied solely on Paragon management's oral representations that the estimated revenue amounts accurately reflected the economic status of the jobs."

Another scam used by Paragon to inflate its revenues and profits was to record revenue for nonexistent projects. In the enforcement release that focused on Sullivan's role in the Paragon scandal, SEC officials pointed out that the publication *AICPA Audit and Accounting Guide—Construction Contracts* is clearly relevant to the audits of construction companies such as Paragon. This publication recommends that auditors visit construction sites and discuss the given projects with project managers, architects, and other appropriate personnel. The purpose of these procedures is to assess "the representations of management (for example, representations about the stage of completion and estimated costs to complete)." Despite this guidance, the Andersen auditors did not visit any project sites during the 1997 audit.[6] Such visits

6. As a point of information, most of Paragon's golf construction projects were outside of the United States. During 1996, auditors employed by foreign affiliates of Andersen visited some of these sites.

may have resulted in Andersen discovering that some of Paragon's projects were purely imaginary. In addition, Andersen would likely have determined that Paragon was overstating the stages of completion of most of its existing projects.

The SEC reprimanded Andersen for not visiting any of Paragon's job sites or discussing those projects with knowledgeable parties. "Failing to discuss project status, including percentage-of-completion estimates, with project managers and other on-site operating personnel was, under the circumstances, a reckless departure from GAAS."

The SEC also criticized Sullivan for not insisting that Golden Bear disclose in its 1997 financial statements the change from the cost-to-cost to the earned value method of applying percentage-of-completion accounting. Likewise, the SEC contended that Sullivan should have required Golden Bear to disclose material related-party transactions involving Paragon and Jack Nicklaus, Golden Bear's majority stockholder.

Finally, the SEC noted that Sullivan failed to heed his own concerns while planning the 1997 Golden Bear audit. During the initial planning phase of that audit, Sullivan had identified several factors that prompted him to designate the 1997 Golden Bear audit a "high-risk" engagement. These factors included the subjective nature of the earned value method, Paragon's large unbilled revenues, the aggressive revenue recognition practices advocated by Golden Bear management, and severe weaknesses in Paragon's cost accounting system. Because of these factors, the SEC maintained that Sullivan and his subordinates should have been particularly cautious during the 1997 Golden Bear audit and employed a rigorous and thorough set of substantive audit procedures.

## EPILOGUE

In August 1998, angry Golden Bear stockholders filed a class-action lawsuit against the company, its major officers, and its principal owner, Jack Nicklaus. That same month, the NASDAQ delisted the company's common stock, which was trading for less than $1 per share, considerably below its all-time high of $20. Richard Bellinger resigned as Golden Bear's CEO two months later to "pursue other interests." In December 1999, Golden Bear announced that it had reached an agreement to settle the class-action lawsuit. That settlement required the company to pay its stockholders $3.5 million in total and to purchase their shares at a price of $0.75. In 2000, Golden Bear, by then a private company, was folded into Nicklaus Companies, a new corporate entity that Jack Nicklaus created to manage his business interests.

In November 2002, Michael Sullivan was suspended from practicing before the SEC for one year. Sullivan's employer, Andersen, had effectively been put out of business a few months earlier when a federal jury found it guilty of obstruction of justice for destroying audit documents pertaining to its bankrupt client Enron Corporation.[7] In August 2002, Paragon's former controller received a two-year suspension from practicing before the SEC. At the same time, the SEC sanctioned three former Golden Bear executives by ordering them to "cease and desist" from any future violations of the federal securities laws. One of those executives was Richard Bellinger. The SEC maintained that Bellinger approved Paragon's change from the cost-to-cost to the earned value method. Additionally, the SEC charged that Bellinger knew the change would materially increase Golden Bear's reported revenues and gross profit but failed to require that the change be disclosed in the company's financial statements.

7. As discussed in Case 1.1, Andersen's conviction was subsequently overturned by the U.S. Supreme Court.

Finally, in March 2003, a federal grand jury indicted John Boyd and Christopher Curbello on charges of securities fraud and conspiracy to commit securities fraud. Curbello was arrested in San Antonio, Texas, on March 14, 2003, while Boyd was apprehended in Bogota, Columbia, a few days later by Secret Service and FBI agents who immediately flew him to the United States. In June 2003, Curbello pleaded guilty to conspiracy to commit securities fraud and was sentenced to 3½ years in prison. A few months later, Boyd pleaded guilty to similar charges and was given a five-year prison sentence.

## Questions

1. *SAS No. 106*, "Audit Evidence," identifies the "management assertions" that commonly underlie a set of financial statements. Which of these assertions were relevant to Paragon's construction projects? For each of the assertions that you listed, describe an audit procedure that Arthur Andersen could have employed to corroborate that assertion.
2. The SEC referred to several "audit failures" that were allegedly the responsibility of Michael Sullivan. Define what you believe the SEC meant by the phrase "audit failure." Do you believe that Sullivan, alone, was responsible for the deficiencies that the SEC noted in Andersen's 1997 audit of Golden Bear? Defend your answer.
3. Sullivan identified the 1997 Golden Bear audit as a "high-risk" engagement. How do an audit engagement team's responsibilities differ, if at all, on a high-risk engagement compared with a "normal" engagement? Explain.
4. The AICPA has issued several *Audit and Accounting Guides* for specialized industries. Do auditors have a responsibility to refer to these guides when auditing clients in those industries? Do these guides override or replace the authoritative guidance included in *Statements on Auditing Standards*?
5. Was the change that Paragon made in applying the percentage-of-completion accounting method a "change in accounting principle" or a "change in accounting estimate"? Briefly describe the accounting and financial reporting treatment that must be applied to each type of change.

## CASE 2.3

# Happiness Express, Inc.

Executives in the multibillion-dollar toy industry constantly search for the next big "hit," a magical toy that will trigger a nationwide frenzy among youngsters comparable to the mania sparked in recent decades by the Cabbage Patch Kids and Tickle Me Elmo. In more "ancient" times, silly putty, the slinky, and the hoola hoop prompted shouting matches and elbow-to-elbow combat among small armies of short-tempered parents intent on acquiring the latest must-have and hard-to-find toy as a birthday gift or Christmas present for little Suzie or tiny Tommy.

During the mid-1990s, the popular television program that featured the Mighty Morphin Power Rangers produced a windfall of revenues and profits for Happiness Express, Inc., a small New York–based company. Happiness Express had purchased licensing rights that allowed the company to market a wide range of Mighty Morphin Power Rangers toys and other merchandise. Unfortunately, similar to most toy fads, the Power Rangers craze soon subsided. To find a replacement source of revenue for his company, Joseph Sutton, Happiness Express's chief executive officer (CEO), turned to a member of the British royal family, Sarah Ferguson, the Duchess of York.

Following her divorce from Prince Andrew, the second son of Queen Elizabeth II, the Duchess decided to try her hand at writing children's books. Among the characters she created was Budgie the Little Helicopter. Joseph Sutton acquired U.S. licensing rights for toys and other merchandise featuring Budgie. Sutton believed that Budgie would be a huge hit in the United States and generate large sales of toys and related merchandise linked to him and his small squadron of friends. In announcing his company's relationship with Sarah Ferguson, the ever-optimistic and buoyant Sutton proclaimed that, "Happiness is proud to represent Budgie the Little Helicopter and to help him make his flight to America."[1]

### "In Kids We Trust"

Joseph Sutton and his older brother, Isaac, worked for years as sales representatives for various toy manufacturers. In 1989, the two brothers organized their own toy company, which they named Happiness Express, Inc. Joseph assumed the title of CEO, while his brother became the company's chief operating officer (COO). Despite an initial investment of only $10,000, the Sutton brothers' company quickly gained a toehold in the fiercely competitive toy industry. Happiness Express catapulted from a few hundred thousand dollars of sales in its first year of operation to total revenues of more than $40 million for its fiscal year ended March 31, 1994.

The Suttons' business model involved identifying trendy characters introduced to children in the United States by television programs, major movies, books, and other publications. The brothers then purchased merchandise-licensing rights for those characters from Disney, Nickelodeon, Universal Studios, Warner Brothers, and major publishing companies. Licensed merchandise manufactured by Happiness Express included plastic figurines, stuffed dolls, shoelaces, battery-operated toothbrushes,

1. *Business Wire* (online), "Happiness Express Gets Product License for Her Royal Highness the Duchess of York's 'Budgie the Little Helicopter,'" 14 February 1994.

night-lights, bedside lamps, and a wide range of "back-to-school" items such as pencils, notebooks, and binders. Happiness Express marketed its merchandise to FAO Schwartz, J.C. Penney, Kmart, Target, Toys "R" Us, Wal-Mart, and other major retailers. Central to the early success of Happiness Express was the Suttons' heavy reliance on market research that tracked children's interest in new media characters and toys. In fact, Joseph Sutton coined the motto "In Kids We Trust" to express his company's commitment to the results of that research.

The Little Mermaid and Barney, the Purple Dinosaur, were two of the earliest characters for which the Suttons obtained licensing rights. The impressive sales spawned by those two lines of merchandise allowed Happiness Express to establish itself in the toy industry. To acquire the capital needed to expand the company's operations, the Suttons took Happiness Express public in July 1994 with an initial public offering (IPO) that was well received by Wall Street and individual investors. Within a few months, the company's stock price nearly doubled from its initial selling price of $10. In the spring of 1995, *Business Week* named Happiness Express the "#1 Hot Growth Company" in the United States and featured the company on its front cover. According to *Business Week*, over the previous three years Happiness Express had realized annual growth rates in sales, profits, and return on capital of 112 percent, 439 percent, and 68 percent, respectively.

For fiscal 1994, merchandise linked to Barney accounted for approximately 55 percent of Happiness Express's total revenues. In fiscal 1995, Barney-related revenues evaporated, accounting for less than five percent of the company's sales that year. Fortunately, the Mighty Morphin Power Rangers stepped into the vacuum created by the sudden decline in children's affection for Barney—or, at least, Barney-related merchandise. For fiscal 1995, Power Rangers merchandise produced 75 percent of Happiness's revenues.

Despite the gaudy financial results posted by Happiness Express during the mid-1990s, many Wall Street analysts questioned whether the company could sustain that level of financial performance. Those analysts doubted that the Sutton brothers could continue their phenomenal winning streak of identifying the next "hot" children's character. One financial analyst and self-appointed critic of Happiness Express asked Joseph Sutton, "What will replace Power Rangers when they fade?"[2] The self-assured Sutton replied: "We've proved to the industry that we know how to go where the action is."[3] In Sutton's mind, the coming "action" in the toy industry would revolve around Budgie the Little Helicopter and Dudley the Dragon, a Barney-type character that had his own children's television program. Sutton's enthusiasm for those two characters did not placate his critic, who pointed out that toy companies that become heavily dependent on one or a few lines of merchandise often experience severe financial problems due to sudden and unexpected shifts in children's taste for toys.

## Budgie Crashes, Dudley Is a Dud

In the spring of 1995, shortly before the close of Happiness Express's 1995 fiscal year, a Wall Street investment firm projected a "precipitous" drop in the company's earnings during fiscal 1996.[4] The firm predicted that declining interest in the Mighty Morphin Power Rangers television program would quickly translate into falling sales

2. L. Bongiorno, "Happiness Is a Hot Toy," *Business Week*, 22 May 1995, 70.

3. *Ibid.*

4. *Business Wire* (online), "Happiness Express 'Comfortable' with Fiscal 1995, '96 Projections," 7 March 1995.

of licensed merchandise featuring those characters. Joseph Sutton responded to that grim prediction by referring to another earnings forecast for Happiness Express released at approximately the same time by Donaldson, Lufkin & Jenrette (DLJ), a major investment banking firm. This latter forecast projected a sizable increase in revenues and profits for Happiness Express during fiscal 1996.

To support this second forecast, Sutton revealed that his firm's backlog of toy orders in the spring of 1995 was nearly three times larger than the company's backlog 12 months earlier. While admitting that sales of Power Rangers merchandise would likely decline in fiscal 1996, Sutton insisted that the company's new products would more than make up for those lost sales. Bolstering Sutton's point of view regarding his company's future were the record operating results that Happiness Express reported in the late spring of 1995 for the fiscal year ended March 31, 1995. The company's net income for fiscal 1995 of $7.5 million was nearly double the figure reported the previous year, while its 1995 revenues rose to $60 million, a 50 percent increase over the previous 12 months. Approximately one-half of the latter increase was attributable to Happiness Express's fourth-quarter sales. During the fourth quarter of fiscal 1994, the company reported sales of $2.3 million; that figure was dwarfed by the $12.8 million of sales the company reported for the fourth quarter of fiscal 1995.

Despite Joseph Sutton's rosy outlook for his company, fiscal 1996 proved to be a difficult year for Happiness Express. By the fall of 1995, sales of Power Rangers merchandise had fallen off drastically. Making matters worse for Happiness Express, Budgie the Little Helicopter failed to capture the imagination of children in the United States despite intense promotional efforts by the company and the Duchess of York. Likewise, children's response to Dudley the Dragon was underwhelming. In early September 1995, the price of Happiness Express common stock plunged when Joseph Sutton publicly admitted that DLJ's earnings forecast for fiscal 1996 had been too optimistic. The day following that announcement, the company was rocked by the filing of a large class-action lawsuit that named Happiness Express and its key officers as defendants. The lawsuit charged that Happiness Express's previous financial statements had been distorted by fraudulent misrepresentations and that certain company executives had engaged in "insider trading." As those executives were touting the company's promising prospects earlier in the year, they were allegedly selling large blocks of the company's stock that they owned.

As the end of fiscal 1996 approached, Happiness Express's sales continued to sag, which caused management to issue an earnings release indicating that the company would report a loss of $14 to $17 million for the year. That news sent the company's stock price plummeting to less than $2 per share. A few days later, a company spokesperson revealed that federal authorities, including representatives of the Securities and Exchange Commission (SEC), had seized certain accounting records and documents of Happiness Express and were launching an investigation of financial irregularities within the company. More bad news arrived on May 31, 1996, when Happiness Express's audit firm, Coopers & Lybrand, withdrew the audit opinion it had issued a few weeks earlier on the company's 1996 financial statements. Exhibit 1 presents the letter Coopers & Lybrand sent to Joseph Sutton to notify him of that decision.

Throughout the summer of 1996, the financial condition of Happiness Express worsened. On September 25, the company's board of directors filed for bankruptcy and fired Isaac Sutton; two days later, Joseph Sutton resigned as CEO. In May 1999, the SEC filed a criminal complaint against Joseph Sutton, Isaac Sutton, and Happiness Express's former chief financial officer (CFO), Michael Goldberg. The complaint also named Goldberg's close friend and Goldberg's former landlord as defendants.

**EXHIBIT 1**

COOPERS & LYBRAND LETTER RESCINDING 1996 AUDIT OPINION

May 31, 1996

Mr. Joseph Sutton
Chief Executive Officer
Happiness Express, Inc.
One Harbor Park Drive
Port Washington, NY 11050

Dear Mr. Sutton:

In connection with the investigation into the financial irregularities recently discovered with respect to the financial statements and accounting records of Happiness Express, Inc., certain information has come to our attention regarding the Company's financial statements as of and for the year ended March 31, 1996, that indicates a revision of those statements is necessary.

Please notify persons who are known to be relying or who are likely to rely on the financial statements and the related auditors' report that they should not be relied upon, and that revised financial statements and auditors' report will be issued upon completion of the investigation.

Also, you should discuss with the Securities and Exchange Commission, appropriate stock exchanges, and other regulatory authorities the disclosures to be made or other measures to be taken in the circumstances.

Very truly yours,

Coopers & Lybrand L.L.P.

The SEC charged the Suttons and Goldberg with inflating Happiness Express's sales and net income for fiscal 1995 and 1996. For fiscal 1995, the SEC revealed that the company had actually incurred a net loss of $1 million rather than the $7.5 million net income it had reported. Happiness Express's executives had apparently booked phony sales and receivables to conceal the company's deteriorating financial condition and operating results from Wall Street analysts, investors, and other parties. The primary source of the company's financial problems that had prompted the fraudulent scheme was the sudden drop in sales of Mighty Morphin Power Rangers merchandise.

The SEC alleged that Michael Goldberg had sold Happiness Express common stock during 1995 before the fraudulent scheme was revealed, allowing him to earn "illicit" trading profits of approximately $310,000. Additionally, the SEC's investigation indicated that Goldberg had provided "material nonpublic information concerning Happiness Express's poor financial condition" to two other individuals, his close friend and his landlord. Reportedly, the close friend had used this information to earn large trading profits by "shorting" the common stock of Happiness Express. The nonpublic information that the landlord received from Goldberg caused him to sell Happiness Express common stock that he owned before the company's true financial condition and operating results were publicly reported.

## Class-Action Lawsuit Targets Coopers & Lybrand

Coopers & Lybrand was the principal target of the multimillion-dollar, class-action lawsuit filed by Happiness Express's stockholders in the fall of 1995. Plaintiff attorneys in that lawsuit alleged that Coopers & Lybrand had recklessly audited Happiness Express's financial statements for fiscal 1995, which prevented the firm from uncovering millions of dollars of bogus sales and corresponding receivables in the company's accounting records. Approximately $6 million of the bogus revenues involved fictitious sales to Wow Wee International, Ltd. and West Coast Liquidators that had been booked by Happiness Express's accounting staff near the end of fiscal 1995.

The allegations included in the class-action lawsuit focused almost exclusively on the audit procedures Coopers & Lybrand had applied to Happiness Express's 1995 sales and to the company's 1995 year-end receivables. Plaintiff attorneys charged that the Coopers & Lybrand audit team had failed to obtain a thorough understanding of Happiness Express's operations and internal controls and, as a result, failed to properly plan the 1995 audit. For example, the plaintiff attorneys identified several red flags linked to Happiness Express's year-end receivables that the Coopers & Lybrand auditors had apparently overlooked or ignored. These red flags included a significant change in the nature of Happiness Express's accounts receivable between the end of 1994 and the end of 1995.

Historically, Happiness Express had "factored" most of its accounts receivable. A finance company typically approved or authorized Happiness Express's credit sales before shipments were made to given customers and then provided cash advances for the resulting receivables. This practice significantly reduced the credit risk that Happiness Express faced on its outstanding receivables. At the end of fiscal 1994, approximately 88 percent of Happiness Express's receivables were factored. Because of the bogus sales (and corresponding receivables) entered in the company's accounting records near the end of fiscal 1995, only 19 percent of its 1995 year-end receivables were factored. The Coopers & Lybrand auditors apparently never learned of this change in the nature of Happiness Express's accounts receivable, and, consequently, failed to make the appropriate modifications in their planned audit procedures for that important financial statement line item.

> *The allegation here is that Coopers was reckless when it relied on a previous year's information without bothering to independently assess the current year's data, which were vastly different. . . . Coopers' [fiscal 1995] workpapers are replete with inaccurate references to conditions which did not exist at March 31, 1995. For example, in assessing Happiness's controls over its revenues, Coopers noted in its workpapers that: "Accounts receivable are predominantly factored (credit risk is not an issue) and the Company obtains credit authorizations from the factor company prior to shipping."*[5]

Another red flag Coopers & Lybrand allegedly ignored in planning the 1995 audit was the suspicious nature of the large receivables from Wow Wee and West Coast Liquidators that resulted from credit sales recorded by Happiness Express in late fiscal 1995. In fact, Happiness Express booked $2.4 million of fictitious sales to Wow Wee, alone, on the final day of fiscal 1995. The majority of the bogus sales to West Coast Liquidators were recorded in the final month of fiscal 1995. In their civil complaint, the attorneys for Happiness Express's stockholders pointed out that Coopers & Lybrand's policy and procedures manual alerted the firm's personnel to the risk posed by such transactions. "Unusually large increases in year-end sales to a single or a few customers is an indicator of the risk of potential material misstatements in financial statements."

Plaintiff legal counsel also pointed out that Coopers & Lybrand should have doubted the integrity of *any* credit sales made to Wow Wee since that company was

---

5. This and all subsequent quotations, unless indicated otherwise, were taken from the following source: *Jacobs and Sbordone, et al. v. Coopers & Lybrand, et al.*, 1999 U.S. Dist. LEXIS 2102; Fed. Sec. L. Rep. (CCH) P90, 443.

a toy manufacturer and one of Happiness Express's largest suppliers. An audit procedure performed by Coopers & Lybrand involved obtaining and testing a Happiness Express report listing the company's "Top 25 Customers" for the period April 1, 1994-March 31, 1995. The $3.2 million of sales allegedly made to Wow Wee during fiscal 1995 should have placed that company among Happiness Express's five largest customers. However, Wow Wee did not appear on the "Top 25" list, nor did the Coopers & Lybrand auditors apparently question client personnel regarding this noticeable omission from that report.

During the fiscal 1995 audit, the Coopers & Lybrand auditors performed a sales cutoff test. Included in this test were the $2.4 million of bogus credit sales to Wow Wee recorded by Happiness Express on the final day of fiscal 1995. Plaintiff attorneys contended that carelessness on the part of the auditors caused them to overlook glaring irregularities evident in the accounting documents for those sales.

> *In the performance of the sales cutoff test, Coopers purportedly examined invoices and bills of lading associated with approximately $2.4 million of approximately $3.2 million of phony Wow Wee sales. However, the invoices and bills of lading purportedly examined by Coopers in the performance of this test were highly suspicious on their face. For example, none of these Wow Wee invoices contained customer purchase order numbers. In addition, at least one of the three bills of lading associated with the fictitious Wow Wee sales purportedly examined by Coopers in the performance of the sales cutoff test was, illogically, purportedly signed by the shipping company's representative on March 29, 1995, two days prior to the date of the bill of lading. Obviously, it would have been impossible for someone to sign a bill of lading before it was generated. Yet, Coopers did not question the legitimacy of the bill of lading.*

Coopers & Lybrand mailed accounts receivable confirmations to selected customers of Happiness Express at the end of fiscal 1995. The auditors informed Michael Goldberg that the Wow Wee receivable was included in the accounts chosen for confirmation. Because Goldberg provided the auditors with an incorrect address for Wow Wee, the confirmation was never returned to Coopers & Lybrand. After the auditors discussed this matter with Goldberg, he offered to contact the appropriate individual at Wow Wee to ensure that the confirmation was returned. The auditors accepted Goldberg's offer. Goldberg then forged a confirmation and had it faxed to Coopers & Lybrand. The auditors apparently accepted the confirmation without performing any follow-up procedures.

The large receivable from West Coast Liquidators accounted for approximately 13 percent of Happiness Express's accounts receivable at the end of fiscal 1995.[6] However, that receivable was not among the accounts Coopers & Lybrand selected for confirmation. In the civil complaint they filed against Coopers & Lybrand, plaintiff attorneys also pointed out that Coopers & Lybrand's sales cutoff test did not include any of the bogus sales to West Coast Liquidators during the final month of fiscal 1995. The attorneys maintained that even a cursory investigation of those transactions would have revealed that they were suspicious in nature.

> *In fact, had Coopers even performed the perfunctory procedure of examining Happiness's invoices associated with the year-end receivables from West Coast Liquidators, it would have discovered that they also were highly suspicious on their face. For example, such invoices representing $1,346,598 of purported sales to West Coast Liquidators did not contain any bills of lading or purchase order numbers.*

---

6. Happiness Express had total receivables of almost $11 million at the end of fiscal 1995, accounting for approximately one-third of the company's total assets.

## EPILOGUE

Coopers & Lybrand contested each of the allegations included in the class-action lawsuit. At one point, the firm's legal counsel charged that the allegations involved no more than "nitpicking attacks" by the plaintiff attorneys. U.S. District Judge Robert P. Patterson, however, ruled that the allegations were sufficient to allow the case to proceed to trial. In particular, the federal judge ruled that, if proven, the plaintiffs' allegations would support a finding of "scienter" under the federal securities laws.

> *Based on the facts as alleged, a trier of fact could find Coopers' audit so reckless that Coopers should have had knowledge of the underlying fraud and acted in blind disregard that there was a strong likelihood that Happiness was engaged in the underlying fraud. Proving this will be plaintiffs' burden at trial, but they have alleged facts sufficient to support a finding of scienter on the part of Coopers and so Coopers' motion to dismiss is denied.*

After several years of legal wrangling, an out-of-court settlement was reached to resolve the class-action lawsuit stemming from the Happiness Express fraud. In January 2002, the parties to the lawsuit filed a legal notice describing the details of the proposed settlement with the federal district court in which the case would have been tried. The proposed settlement required Coopers & Lybrand to contribute $1.3 million to a settlement fund. Happiness Express's former stockholders would receive $715,000, or 55 percent, of the settlement fund, while the stockholders' attorneys would receive the remaining $585,000.

In the legal notice filed with the federal court, the plaintiff attorneys were required to state why they supported the settlement. The attorneys noted that a major problem they would have to surmount in pursuing the case was proving that Coopers & Lybrand had a motive to issue a false audit opinion on Happiness Express's financial statements. Additionally, the plaintiff attorneys admitted that they would have to overcome the contention by Coopers & Lybrand that the Happiness Express auditors had no actual knowledge of the falsifications in the company's accounting records and financial statements. Finally, even if the jury ultimately ruled in favor of Happiness Express's former stockholders, the plaintiff attorneys pointed out that the jury might decide that Coopers & Lybrand was responsible for only a small portion of the losses suffered by the stockholders. As a result, the stockholders might receive only a nominal judgment from the accounting firm.[7]

The SEC settled the charges pending against Michael Goldberg by requiring him to pay a $150,000 civil fine and to forfeit the $310,000 of insider trading profits that he had earned while serving as Happiness Express's CFO. Goldberg also agreed not to violate federal securities laws in the future, although under the terms of the SEC settlement he neither admitted nor denied the charges that the SEC had filed against him. In February 2003, the SEC issued a litigation release that reported the settlement of the charges pending against Michael Goldberg's close friend who had received "material nonpublic information" from Goldberg regarding Happiness Express's deteriorating financial condition. Goldberg's friend was required to forfeit the $79,000 of trading profits he had earned by "shorting" Happiness Express's common stock and to pay a civil fine in the same amount. The SEC also announced that it had settled the insider trading claim filed previously against Goldberg's former landlord but did not reveal the nature of that settlement.

In 2003, Joseph Sutton pleaded guilty to conspiracy to commit bank fraud and securities fraud and was sentenced to 30 months in federal prison. His brother, Isaac, refused to plead guilty to similar charges pending against him and instead opted for a jury trial. On September 29, 2004, a New York jury found Isaac Sutton innocent of all the fraud charges filed against him by the SEC.

7. No further public comment or report regarding the proposed settlement was found. Most likely, the parties agreed to the proposed settlement. As a point of information, the settlement payment would have been made by the successor firm to Coopers & Lybrand, PricewaterhouseCoopers.

## Questions

1. Identify the primary audit objectives that auditors hope to accomplish by (a) confirming a client's year-end accounts receivable, (b) performing year-end sales cutoff tests.
2. Identify and briefly describe any mistakes or errors in judgment that Coopers & Lybrand may have made in its effort to confirm the Wow Wee receivable at the end of fiscal 1995. In your opinion, did these apparent mistakes or errors in judgment involve "negligence" on the part of the given auditors? Would you characterize the mistakes or errors as "reckless" or "fraudulent"? In each case, justify your answer.
3. Should the Coopers & Lybrand auditors have confirmed the receivable from West Coast Liquidators at the end of fiscal 1995? Why or why not? Should the auditors have included one or more sales to West Coast Liquidators in their year-end sales cutoff tests for fiscal 1995?
4. What alternative audit procedures can be applied to a large receivable of an audit client when a confirmation of that receivable cannot be obtained for whatever reason? Compare and contrast the evidence provided by these procedures with the evidence yielded by a confirmation.
5. The SEC charged certain executives of Happiness Express with "insider trading." Do auditors have a responsibility to consider or investigate the possibility that client executives have engaged in insider trading activities? Defend your answer.

**CASE 2.4**

# SmarTalk Teleservices, Inc.

Arthur Levitt served as the chairman of the Securities and Exchange Commission (SEC) from 1993 to 2001, the longest tenure of any head of that federal agency. Throughout his eight-year term with the SEC, Levitt campaigned against "earnings management" practices that public companies used to embellish their financial statements. "Restructuring reserves" were a principal target of Levitt's campaign. During the 1990s, many public companies established a large restructuring reserve after acquiring another company. The items credited to these reserves typically included post-acquisition "exit" expenditures, such as severance payments to laid-off employees, that the given companies would allegedly incur in future years to eliminate redundant operating units or activities.

Levitt claimed that many companies overstated restructuring reserves by including in them routine operating expenses of future reporting periods. This accounting scam caused these companies to take a "big bath" or earnings reduction in the current period but gave them an opportunity to post impressive "turnaround" profits in future periods. Because Wall Street analysts realized that restructuring reserves would augment a company's future earnings, they often reacted favorably to them. "One of the reasons for the popularity of restructuring charges may be that announcements of restructuring are often rewarded by Wall Street . . . Analysts quickly update future earnings estimates and a jump in the company's stock price often results."[1] Such favorable reactions prompted a growing number of corporate executives to use restructuring reserves to manage or manipulate their company's reported earnings. Hundreds of public companies, including many blue-chip firms, booked restructuring reserves during the 1990s. General Motors shocked its stockholders by recording a $3 billion restructuring reserve, a "record" that was easily topped by an $8.9 billion restructuring reserve announced by IBM. Among the most prolific users of restructuring reserves was AT&T, which established four such reserves in the late 1980s and early 1990s.

In the mid-1990s, regulatory authorities and rule-making bodies began taking measures to deal with the growing prevalence of restructuring reserves in corporate financial statements. In 1995, the SEC warned 300 public companies that their most recent financial statements had contained questionable restructuring reserves. A few months earlier, the Emerging Issues Task Force (EITF) of the Financial Accounting Standards Board (FASB) had issued EITF 94-3, "Liability Recognition for Certain Employee Termination Benefits and Other Costs to Exit an Activity (including Certain Costs Incurred in a Restructuring)." EITF 94-3 was the first of a series of technical pronouncements that clarified the conditions under which companies could establish restructuring reserves and the specific items that could be properly included in those reserves. Among other stipulations, EITF 94-3

1. *World Accounting Report* (online), "SEC Warning Over Restructuring Charges," 1 April 1994.

requires companies to have a definitive "exit plan" before establishing a restructuring reserve. This document "must specifically identify all significant actions to be taken to complete the exit plan, activities that will not be continued, including the method of disposition and location of those activities, and the expected date of completion."[2]

Despite EITF 94-3 and related pronouncements, public companies continued to include restructuring reserves in their financial statements during the late 1990s. One such company was Los Angeles-based SmarTalk Teleservices, Inc., a leading provider of prepaid calling services and prepaid wireless services. In 1997, SmarTalk acquired six other prepaid telephone card companies. SmarTalk's 1997 financial statements included a $25 million restructuring reserve for future expenditures that the company would incur to "exit certain activities." The largest item in SmarTalk's restructuring reserve was $13.5 million of "contract termination fees" that the company would absorb in 1998 for changing from one service carrier, WorldCom, to another, Frontier Communications. SmarTalk's projected exit expenditures also included inventory write-downs, severance benefits for employees who would be laid off, and various other 1998 expenditures that the company lumped into a "general reserve" component of its restructuring reserve.

A subsequent SEC investigation revealed that SmarTalk's 1997 restructuring reserve and the related restructuring charges were invalid since the company did not have a formal exit plan as required by EITF 94-3. In fact, the largest component of the restructuring reserve, the contract termination fees, did not involve an "exit activity." SmarTalk's decision to switch service carriers was not prompted by the six acquisitions the company made in 1997 but instead was simply a strategic business decision made by the company's top executives. The SEC also found fault with each of the other components of SmarTalk's restructuring reserve. For example, much of the inventory write-down included in that reserve involved prepaid calling cards that the company continued to sell well into 1998. Likewise, the SEC pointed out that GAAP expressly prohibit companies from booking "general reserves" under any circumstances.

The restructuring charges that SmarTalk included in its 1997 income statement contributed significantly to the nearly $62 million net loss that the company incurred for that year. Nevertheless, in SmarTalk's press release that reported its 1997 operating results, company management chose to stress the fact that SmarTalk's "earnings before one-time charges" for 1997 were nearly $2.8 million, reflecting a large increase from the comparable amount reported the prior year.[3] Wall Street also apparently chose to focus on SmarTalk's 1997 earnings before one-time charges. In late February 1998, shortly after SmarTalk reported its 1997 operating results, Credit Suisse First Boston Corporation, a major Wall Street investment firm, issued a "buy" recommendation

2. This and all remaining quotes in this case, unless indicated otherwise, were taken from Securities and Exchange Commission, *Accounting and Auditing Enforcement Release No. 1787*, 22 May 2003.

3. *Coven vs. SmarTalk Services, Inc., et al.*, United States District Court for the Eastern District of New York (1998). In addition to the $25 million of restructuring charges, SmarTalk's 1997 income statement also included a $39 million "acquisition-related charge."

on the company's stock. The end result of the positive "spin" placed on SmarTalk's 1997 earnings report was that the company sustained an impressive upward trend in its stock price. From mid-August 1997 through March 1998, SmarTalk's stock price nearly doubled, rising from less than $19 per share to more than $34 per share over that time frame.

The SEC's investigation of SmarTalk's 1997 financial statements was triggered by an August 10, 1998, press release issued by the company. That press release revealed that PricewaterhouseCoopers (PwC), SmarTalk's audit firm, was reviewing the company's 1997 restructuring reserve. PwC had issued an unqualified opinion on SmarTalk's 1997 financial statements in the spring of 1998.[4] However, over the next several months, the company's increasingly aggressive accounting and financial reporting decisions caused the relationship between PwC and SmarTalk's management to become "contentious." On July 18, 1998, PwC initiated a "post-audit review" of the 1997 SmarTalk audit workpapers for the purpose of deciding whether to remain the company's audit firm. The major focus of that review was the $25 million restructuring reserve. Complicating the review was the fact that Philip Hirsch, the audit partner who had supervised the 1997 SmarTalk audit, had left PwC shortly after completing that engagement.

Ironically, SmarTalk's August 10, 1998, press release also prompted the SEC to investigate PwC's 1997 audit of SmarTalk. As a result of that investigation, the SEC criticized Hirsch and his subordinates for failing to properly audit SmarTalk's restructuring reserve. The SEC charged that the PwC auditors should have discovered that the contract termination fees included in the reserve were not true "exit" costs. Likewise, the auditors were apparently aware that during 1998 SmarTalk continued to sell the prepaid calling cards that were the basis for the inventory write-down included in the 1997 restructuring reserve. The federal agency also pointed out that the PwC audit team should have realized that GAAP forbid the accrual of "general reserves." Finally, and most importantly, the SEC reported that Hirsch knew SmarTalk's management team had failed to "commit the enterprise to an exit plan" by the end of fiscal 1997. The absence of such a commitment meant that SmarTalk had been precluded from establishing a restructuring reserve for that year.

Despite the SEC's extensive criticism of PwC's 1997 audit of SmarTalk, the federal agency's harshest criticism of the accounting firm was reserved for its post-audit review of the 1997 audit workpapers. Shortly after that review was initiated, PwC learned of a large class-action lawsuit being filed by SmarTalk's stockholders. That lawsuit apparently prompted PwC to make "undocumented changes in" and "revisions to" the 1997 SmarTalk audit workpapers.

4. Technically, Price Waterhouse, not PwC, audited SmarTalk's 1997 financial statements. PwC was formed on July 1, 1998, when Price Waterhouse and Coopers & Lybrand merged. For purposes of clarity, the SEC referred to PwC as SmarTalk's auditor in the enforcement release that it issued for this case.

> *During the period from the end of July through early August 1998, with the knowledge of several PwC partners with firm-wide responsibilities, PwC made revisions to its [1997 SmarTalk] working papers. Those revisions were not documented. Language in the working papers was revised, added, and deleted. Documents were removed from the working papers and discarded, and documents were also added to the working papers. The post-audit revisions were not dated or otherwise distinguished to indicate that they had been made as part of a post-audit review and PwC discarded most of the notes containing a second post-audit reviewer's instructions.*[5]

The SEC contacted PwC in February 1999 and asked the firm to produce its 1997 SmarTalk audit workpapers. PwC complied but did not inform the SEC that those workpapers had been altered. PwC officials admitted that the workpapers had been altered after the SEC discovered that some of the workpaper files that were in an electronic format had been accessed by PwC personnel in August 1998.

In May 2003, the SEC sanctioned PwC and Philip Hirsch for engaging in "improper professional conduct." The SEC banned Hirsch from practicing before it for one year and fined PwC $1 million. In addition, the SEC required PwC to "establish and maintain policies and procedures to preserve working papers intact following the archiving of working papers and also during the course of, and following the conclusion of, any post-audit review." PwC was also required to retain an independent consultant to prepare and submit a report to the SEC and the Public Company Accounting Oversight Board confirming that such policies and procedures had been implemented.

Several months prior to announcing the penalties imposed on PwC, the SEC had sanctioned SmarTalk's former chief financial officer (CFO) who was the individual responsible for making the key accounting decisions for the $25 million restructuring reserve. In addition to ordering him to cease and desist from future violations of federal securities laws, the SEC fined the CFO $50,000.

The August 10, 1998, press release that revealed PwC's decision to review SmarTalk's restructuring reserve sent the company's stock price into a freefall from which it never recovered. In January 1999, SmarTalk filed for bankruptcy. A few days following that bankruptcy filing, SmarTalk ceased operations when AT&T purchased the company's remaining assets.[6]

## Questions

1. Suppose that you are supervising a future audit engagement involving a public company that has recently established a large restructuring reserve. What audit objectives would you establish for that reserve? For each audit objective you list, identify audit evidence that you would collect to help achieve that objective.

---

5. As a point of information, at the time that PwC altered the audit workpapers, the firm was not under investigation by the SEC for its 1997 SmarTalk audit.

6. PwC was eventually named as a co-defendant in the class-action lawsuit filed by SmarTalk's stockholders. In 2002, PwC agreed to pay $15 million to be dismissed from that lawsuit.

2. What is the role of the FASB's Emerging Issues Task Force? Are pronouncements issued by the EITF considered generally accepted accounting principles?
3. Federal prosecutors successfully convicted Arthur Andersen & Co. of "obstruction of justice" for destroying documents that pertained to that firm's audits of Enron Corporation. Why was PwC not charged with obstruction of justice in this case? What professional standards, if any, do you believe PwC violated by altering the SmarTalk audit workpapers during its post-audit review?

## CASE 2.5

# Dollar General Stores, Inc.

In 1955, James Luther Turner and his son, Cal, opened a small retail store in Scottsville, Kentucky. The Turners hoped to emulate (on a smaller scale) the business model of major discount retailers that had become well established in the United States in the decade following World War II. The Turners developed a unique marketing concept to differentiate their business from other discount retailers. Their store would sell only merchandise with a retail sales price of one dollar or less.

The Turners' business model was a financial success from its inception. Within three years, the Turners were operating more than two dozen Dollar General Stores in Kentucky and surrounding states. Under the leadership of three generations of the Turner family, Dollar General Corporation would become one of the most recognizable retail companies in the United States. The company would eventually own and operate more than 8,000 stores, produce annual sales approaching $10 billion, and have its stock listed on the New York Stock Exchange.[1]

In 1999, Cal Turner, Jr., Dollar General's CEO, decided that if his company was to remain a major player in the intensely competitive discount retailing industry, he had to update its outmoded information systems. To accomplish that goal, Turner retained IBM to revamp his company's technology infrastructure. For years, IBM had marketed itself as the provider of "solutions" to a wide range of information technology challenges faced by companies of all sizes.

The major feature of IBM's technology solution for Dollar General was the installation of state-of-the-art electronic sales registers for each of the company's retail stores. The new sales registers—manufactured by IBM—would collect and process a wide range of point-of-sale information. This information would allow Dollar General's management to quickly identify important trends that could potentially impact the company's profitability and competitive position.

Cal Turner was pleased with IBM's recommendation to replace the company's antiquated sales registers and decided to purchase the new registers over a several year period beginning in 2000. However, Kevin Collins, an IBM employee involved in the Dollar General consulting engagement, believed that Dollar General should acquire and install the new sales registers much sooner. Collins recommended that the installation of the new equipment be completed by the end of 2000.

Dollar General's executives agreed with Collins' assessment that their company would realize significant benefits by installing the new sales registers as quickly as possible. But the executives were also aware that decision would have a significant impact on their company's reported operating results for fiscal 2000. Since the thousands of old sales registers had no salvage value, the company would be forced to record a $10 million loss on their disposal. That loss, which was the approximate book value of the old sales registers, would reduce the company's 2000 net income by an estimated six to seven percent.

---

1. Although one of the U.S.'s leading discount retailers, Dollar General's annual sales are dwarfed by those of Wal-Mart, the world's largest discount retailer. A major feature of Dollar General's marketing strategy is to locate stores in small communities that are not served by Wal-Mart.

On November 29, 2000, Dollar General contacted Collins and told him that the accelerated roll-out of the new sales registers was unacceptable due to the "accounting problem" it presented the company. The following day, Collins called a Dollar General executive and told him that he could solve that problem. Collins proposed that IBM purchase Dollar General's old sales registers for an amount equal to their remaining book value even though Collins and his superiors at IBM knew that they were worthless. Under Collins' proposal, the book value of Dollar General's old sales registers would be added to the price of the new sales registers that Dollar General purchased from IBM. This arrangement would result in Dollar General paying about $20 million for the new sales registers, which was approximately double the original purchase price agreed to by the two parties.

Collins' proposal called for the two-way transaction to be consummated in the final few days of Dollar General's 2000 fiscal year. IBM would pay the $10 million for the old sales registers at that time. A few days later, in early fiscal 2001, Dollar General would pay one-half of the $20 million purchase price of the new sales registers. This $10 million payment would serve to reimburse IBM for the amount it had paid for the worthless sales registers. Dollar General would pay the remaining $10 million owed to IBM in several installments.

In an intra-company e-mail, Collins explained that his proposal would eliminate the "book loss issue" that was the major stumbling block to finalizing the Dollar General transaction. "A buyback of the Omron equipment [Dollar General's old sales registers] will erase the book loss issue, removing this as an obstacle to a more rapid roll-out."[2] In a subsequent e-mail, Collins pointed out that his proposal would provide significant benefits for IBM as well. "This would be a quite nice deal to put this much business this far forward at a time when IBM desperately needs to show revenue growth."[3]

In this e-mail, Collins failed to point out that his proposal would also benefit him personally. A significant portion of Collins' compensation resulted from his annual year-end bonus. The expedited closing and restructuring of the Dollar General transaction would increase Collins' 2000 year-end bonus by nearly 50 percent.[4]

## EPILOGUE

With a few minor modifications, the IBM-Dollar General transaction proposed by Kevin Collins was agreed to by both parties and completed shortly before the end of Dollar General's fiscal year 2000. A subsequent SEC investigation revealed the true nature of the transaction and resulted in the federal agency sanctioning Dollar General, IBM, four former Dollar General executives, and Kevin Collins.

In April 2007, the SEC charged Dollar General with engaging in a series of "fraudulent or improper accounting practices" during its 1998 through 2001 fiscal years.[5] These abusive accounting practices included the "sham

2. Securities and Exchange Commission, *Accounting and Auditing Enforcement Release No. 2226,* 7 April 2005.

3. *Ibid.*

4. Under Collins' proposal, he would receive credit—for bonus computation purposes—for the full amount of the inflated $20 million sales price of the new sales registers.

5. Securities and Exchange Commission, *Accounting and Auditing Enforcement Release No. 2623,* 25 June 2007.

sale" of the company's worthless sales registers to IBM during the fourth quarter of 2000. Several of the company's top executives allegedly authorized these and other violations of generally accepted accounting principles to "report earnings that met or exceeded analysts' expectations and to maintain employee bonuses."[6]

Dollar General agreed to pay a $10 million fine to settle the charges filed against the company by the SEC. Additionally, Cal Turner, Jr., who by this time had retired as Dollar General's CEO, and the company's former chief financial officer agreed to pay civil fines and other penalties totaling more than $1 million each. Penalties levied on Dollar General's former president and controller totaled more than $100,000 each.[7]

In a June 2007 enforcement release, the SEC reported that IBM shared responsibility for the material misrepresentation of Dollar General's 2000 financial statements.

> *IBM knew the Omron purchase transaction was not a bona fide sale because the Omron equipment was worthless, would be destroyed, and that the purchase 'price' was really a loan from IBM to Dollar General that would be repaid through the inflated price for IBM's new equipment. In addition, IBM knew explicitly that it was an accounting impact on Dollar General's earnings that was the obstacle in completing the transaction—and IBM agreed to participate in a transaction that would solve that accounting problem. By engaging in the transaction with Dollar General, IBM was a cause of Dollar General's fraud.*[8]

In the same enforcement release, the SEC sanctioned IBM for other "numerous discrete incidents" during 2000 and 2001 that resulted in the company's revenues being significantly overstated for those two years. The SEC ordered IBM to cease and desist the improper revenue recognition practices and ordered the company to pay a $7 million fine. For his role in the Dollar General transaction, the SEC ordered Kevin Collins to forfeit the nearly $50,000 increase in his 2000 bonus that transaction produced for him. Collins was also assessed a fine of $25,000 by the SEC.[9]

---

## Questions

1. Identify audit procedures that might have detected the improper accounting treatment applied by Dollar General to the transaction with IBM.
2. Identify the accounting concepts or principles violated by Dollar General in this case. Defend each of your choices.
3. Under what circumstances, if any, are "earnings management" techniques acceptable under GAAP? Under what circumstances, if any, are such techniques ethical? Explain.
4. In addition to the parties identified in this case, what other parties bore some degree of responsibility for the improper accounting applied to the Dollar General–IBM transaction? Explain.

---

6. *Ibid.*

7. In early 2007, Dollar General announced that a private investment group would be purchasing all of the company's outstanding common stock. That transaction was finalized a few months later and resulted in Dollar General becoming a private company and no longer subject to the SEC's regulatory supervision.

8. Securities and Exchange Commission, *Accounting and Auditing Enforcement Release No. 2623.*

9. In the agreements reached to settle the charges pending against them, Collins and the four former Dollar General executives neither admitted nor denied the allegations of improper conduct included in those charges.

## CASE 2.6

# CBI Holding Company, Inc.

During the 1980s, CBI Holding Company, Inc., a New York–based firm, served as the parent company for several wholly owned subsidiaries, principal among them Common Brothers, Inc. CBI's subsidiaries marketed an extensive line of pharmaceutical products. The subsidiaries purchased these products from drug manufacturers, warehoused them in storage facilities, and then resold them to retail pharmacies, hospitals, long-term care facilities, and related entities. CBI's principal market area stretched from the northeastern United States into the upper Midwest.

In 1991, Robert Castello, CBI's president and chairman of the board, sold a 48 percent ownership interest in his company to Trust Company of the West (TCW), a diversified investment firm. The purchase agreement between the two parties gave TCW the right to appoint two members of CBI's board; Castello retained the right to appoint the three remaining board members. The purchase agreement also identified several so-called "control-triggering events." If any one of these events occurred, TCW would have the right to take control of CBI. Examples of control-triggering events included CBI's failure to maintain certain financial ratios at a specified level and unauthorized loans to Castello and other CBI executives.

Castello engaged Ernst & Young as CBI's independent audit firm several months before he closed the TCW deal. During this same time frame, Castello was named "Entrepreneur of the Year" in an annual nationwide promotion co-sponsored by Ernst & Young. From 1990 through 1993, Ernst & Young issued unqualified opinions on CBI's annual financial statements.

## Accounting Gimmicks

Castello instructed several of his subordinates to misrepresent CBI's reported operating results and financial condition for the fiscal years ended April 30, 1992 and 1993.[1] The misrepresentations allowed Castello to receive large, year-end bonuses to which he was not entitled for each of those fiscal years. CBI actively concealed the fraudulent activities from TCW's management, from TCW's appointees to CBI's board, and from the company's Ernst & Young auditors because Castello realized that the scheme, if discovered, would qualify as a control-triggering event under the terms of the 1991 purchase agreement with TCW. Several years later in a lawsuit prompted by Castello's fraud, TCW executives testified that they would have immediately seized control of CBI if they had become aware of that scheme.

Understating CBI's year-end accounts payable was one of the methods Castello and his confederates used to distort CBI's 1992 and 1993 financial statements. At any point in time, CBI had large outstanding payables to its suppliers, which included major pharmaceutical manufacturers such as Burroughs-Wellcome, Schering, and FoxMeyer. At the end of fiscal 1992 and fiscal 1993, CBI understated payables due to its large vendors by millions of dollars. Judge Burton Lifland, the federal magistrate who presided over the lawsuit stemming from Castello's fraudulent scheme, ruled that the intentional understatements of CBI's year-end payables were very material to the company's 1992 and 1993 financial statements.

1. Due to a change in CBI's fiscal year, the company's 1992 fiscal year was only 11 months.

## Ernst & Young's 1992 and 1993 CBI Audits

In both 1992 and 1993, Ernst & Young identified the CBI audit as a "close monitoring engagement." The accounting firm's audit manual defined a close monitoring engagement as "one in which the company being audited presents significant risk to E&Y . . . there is a significant chance that E&Y will suffer damage to its reputation, monetarily, or both."[2] Ernst & Young's workpapers for the 1992 and 1993 audits also documented several "red flags" suggesting that the engagements posed a higher-than-normal audit risk.

Control risk factors identified for the CBI audits by Ernst & Young included the dominance of the company by Robert Castello,[3] the absence of an internal audit function, the lack of proper segregation of duties within the company's accounting department, and aggressive positions taken by management personnel regarding key accounting estimates. These apparent control risks caused Ernst & Young to describe CBI's control environment as "ineffective." Other risk factors identified in the CBI audit workpapers included the possible occurrence of a control-triggering event, an "undue" emphasis by top management on achieving periodic earnings goals, and the fact that Castello's annual bonus was tied directly to CBI's reported earnings.

For both the 1992 and 1993 CBI audits, the Ernst & Young engagement team prepared a document entitled "Audit Approach Plan Update and Approval Form." This document described the general strategy Ernst & Young planned to follow in completing those audits. In 1992 and 1993, this document identified accounts payable as a "high-risk" audit area. The audit program for the 1992 audit included two key audit procedures for accounts payable:

a. Perform a search for unrecorded liabilities at April 30, 1992, through the end of field work.
b. Obtain copies of the April 30, 1992, vendor statements for CBI's five largest vendors and examine reconciliations to the accounts payable balances for such vendors as shown on the books of CBI.

The 1993 audit program included these same items, although that program required audit procedure "b" to be applied to CBI's 10 largest vendors.

During the 1992 audit, the Ernst & Young auditors discovered numerous disbursements made by CBI in the first few weeks of fiscal 1993 that were potential unrecorded liabilities as of April 30, 1992. The bulk of these disbursements included payments to the company's vendors that had been labeled as "advances" in the company's accounting records. CBI personnel provided the following explanation for these advances when questioned by the auditors: "When CBI is at its credit limit with a large vendor, the vendor may hold an order until they receive an 'advance.' CBI then applies the advance to the existing A/P balance."

In truth, the so-called advances, which totaled nearly $2 million, were simply payments CBI made to its vendors for inventory purchases consummated on, or prior to, April 30, 1992. Castello and his confederates had chosen not to record these transactions—their purpose being to strengthen key financial ratios of CBI at the end of fiscal 1992 and otherwise embellish the company's apparent financial condition.

---

2. This and all subsequent quotes were taken from the following court opinion: *In re CBI Holding Company, Inc., et al., Debtors; Bankruptcy Services, Inc., Plaintiff-against-Ernst & Young, Ernst & Young, LLP, Defendants;* 247 B.R. 341; 2000 Bankr. LEXIS 425.

3. The CBI audit engagement partner noted during the 1993 audit that the company's CFO appeared to be "afraid of his boss, Castello." When questioned by an auditor regarding an important issue, the CFO typically responded by telling the individual to "ask Castello." In the audit partner's view, this raised an "integrity red flag."

The conspirators developed the advances ruse because they feared that Ernst & Young would discover the material understatements of accounts payable at year-end.

Subsequent court testimony revealed that after reviewing internal documents supporting the advances explanation—documents that had been prepared to deceive Ernst & Young—the Ernst & Young auditors readily accepted that explanation and chose not to treat the items as unrecorded liabilities. This decision prompted severe criticism of Ernst & Young by Judge Lifland.

The federal judge pointed out that the auditors had failed to rigorously investigate the alleged advances and to consider the veracity of the client's explanation for them. For example, the auditors did not investigate the "credit limit" feature of that explanation. The Ernst & Young auditors neglected to determine the credit limit that the given vendors had established for CBI or whether CBI had "maxed out" that credit limit in each case as maintained by client personnel. Nor did the auditors attempt to analyze the given vendors' payable accounts or contact those vendors directly to determine if the alleged advances applied to specific invoice amounts, particularly invoice amounts for purchases made on or before April 30, 1992. Instead, the auditors simply chose to record in their workpapers the client's feeble explanation for the advances, an explanation that failed to address or resolve a critical issue. "The advance explanation recorded in E&Y's workpapers, even if it were true, did not tell the E&Y auditor the essential fact as to whether the merchandise being paid for by the advance had been received before or after April 30, 1992."

Because of the lack of any substantive investigation of the advances, the Ernst & Young auditors failed to determine "whether a liability should have been recorded for each such payment as of fiscal year-end, and whether, in fact, a liability was recorded for such payment as of fiscal year-end." This finding caused Judge Lifland to conclude that Ernst & Young had not properly completed the search for unrecorded liabilities. The judge reached a similar conclusion regarding the second major audit procedure for accounts payable included in the 1992 audit program for CBI.

The 1992 audit program required the Ernst & Young auditors to obtain the year-end statements sent to CBI by the company's five largest vendors and to reconcile the balances in each of those statements to the corresponding balances reported in CBI's accounting records. Ernst & Young obtained year-end statements mailed to CBI by five of the company's several hundred vendors and completed the reconciliation audit procedure. However, the vendors involved in this audit test were not the company's five largest suppliers. In fact, Ernst & Young never identified CBI's five largest vendors during the 1992 audit. The federal judge scolded Ernst & Young for this oversight and maintained that the "minimal" amount of testing applied by Ernst & Young to the small sample of year-end vendor statements was "not adequate."

The audit procedures that Ernst & Young applied to CBI's year-end accounts payable for fiscal 1993 suffered from the same flaws evident during the firm's 1992 audit. Similar to the previous year, CBI's management attempted to conceal unrecorded liabilities at year-end by labeling subsequent payments of those amounts as "advances" to the given vendors. Once more, Judge Lifland noted that the "gullible" auditors readily accepted the explanation for these advances that was relayed to them by CBI personnel. As a result, the auditors failed to require CBI to prepare appropriate adjusting entries for approximately $7.5 million of year-end payables that the client's management team had intentionally ignored.

The 1993 audit program mandated that Ernst & Young obtain the year-end statements for CBI's 10 largest vendors and reconcile the balances in those statements to the corresponding accounts payable balances in CBI's accounting records. Again, Ernst & Young failed to identify CBI's largest vendors and apply this procedure to their year-end payable balances. Instead, the auditors simply applied the reconciliation procedure to a sample of 10 CBI vendors.[4]

One of CBI's 10 largest vendors was Burroughs-Wellcome. If the Ernst & Young auditors had reconciled the balance due Burroughs-Wellcome in its year-end statement with the corresponding account payable balance in CBI's accounting records, the auditors would have discovered that a $1 million "advance" payment made to that vendor in May 1993 was actually for an inventory purchase two weeks prior to April 30, 1993. This discovery would have clearly established that the $1 million amount was an unrecorded liability at year-end.

## Ernst & Young Held Responsible for CBI's Bankruptcy

In March 1994, Ernst & Young withdrew its opinions on CBI's 1992 and 1993 financial statements after learning of the material distortions in those statements that were due to Castello's fraudulent scheme. Almost immediately, CBI began encountering difficulty obtaining trade credit from its principal vendors. A few months later in August 1994, the company filed for bankruptcy. In early 2000, Judge Lifland presided over a 17-day trial in federal bankruptcy court to determine whether Ernst & Young would be held responsible for the large losses that CBI's collapse inflicted on TCW and CBI's former creditors. Near the conclusion of that trial, Judge Lifland ruled that Ernst & Young's conduct during the 1992 and 1993 CBI audits was the "proximate cause" of those losses.

> *The demise of CBI was a foreseeable consequence of E&Y's failure to conduct its audits in fiscal 1992 and 1993 in accordance with GAAS, which was the cause of its failure to detect the unrecorded liabilities, which in turn foreseeably caused it to withdraw its opinions in March 1994. As direct and reasonably foreseeable consequences thereof, CBI's vendors restricted the amount of credit available, CBI's inventory and sales declined, its revenues declined, its value as a going concern diminished, and ultimately it filed for bankruptcy and was liquidated.*

Judge Lifland characterized Ernst & Young's conduct as either "reckless and/or grossly negligent" and identified several generally accepted auditing standards that the accounting firm violated while performing the 1992 and 1993 CBI audits. Although the bulk of the judge's opinion dealt with the audit procedures Ernst & Young applied to CBI's accounts payable, his harshest criticism focused on the firm's alleged failure to retain its independence during the CBI engagements.

Several circumstances that arose during Ernst & Young's tenure as CBI's audit firm called into question its independence. For example, Judge Lifland referred to an incident in 1993 when Robert Castello demanded that Ernst & Young remove the audit manager assigned to the CBI engagement. Apparently, Castello found the audit manager's inquisitive and probing nature disturbing. The CBI audit engagement partner "submissively acquiesced" to Castello's request and replaced the audit manager.

Shortly after the completion of the 1993 audit, Castello hired a new chief financial officer (CFO). This individual resigned eight days later. The CFO told members of the Ernst & Young audit team he was resigning because of several million dollars of "grey accounting" he had discovered in CBI's accounting records. Judge Lifland chided Ernst & Young for being slow to pursue this allegation. Nearly five months passed

4. The court opinion that provided the background information for this case did not indicate what criteria Ernst & Young used to select the vendor accounts to which the reconciliation procedure was applied in the 1992 and 1993 audits.

before the CBI audit engagement partner contacted the former CFO. By that point, Ernst & Young had already discovered Castello's fraudulent scheme and withdrawn its 1992 and 1993 audit opinions.

In February 1994, the audit engagement partner met with Castello to discuss several matters. Ernst & Young's unpaid bill for prior services provided to CBI was the first of those matters, while the second issue discussed was Ernst & Young's fee for the upcoming audit. The last topic on the agenda was the allegation by CBI's former CFO regarding the company's questionable accounting decisions. According to Judge Lifland, the audit partner "wanted to speak to [the former CFO] in order to ask him whether his leaving the post of chief financial officer and his allegations of 'grey accounting' had anything to do with the financial statements that E&Y had just certified; however, [the audit partner] obligingly allowed himself to be put off." In Judge Lifland's opinion, the Ernst & Young audit partner was "more concerned about insuring E&Y's fees than he was about speaking to [the former CFO]."

The final matter Judge Lifland discussed in impugning Ernst & Young's independence was the accounting firm's effort to retain CBI as an audit client after discovering that the 1992 and 1993 audits had been deficient. Judge Lifland charged that Ernst & Young officials realized when they withdrew the audit opinions on CBI's 1992 and 1993 financial statements that the CBI audits had been flawed. In the days prior to withdrawing those opinions, two individuals, a former CBI accountant and CBI's controller at the time, informed Ernst & Young that the "advances" discovered during the 1992 and 1993 audits had been for payment of unrecorded liabilities that existed at the end of CBI's 1992 and 1993 fiscal years. After investigating these admissions, Ernst & Young determined that they were true. Ernst & Young also determined that the CBI auditors "had failed to detect the unrecorded liabilities because they had failed to properly perform the search [for unrecorded liabilities]."

Ernst & Young failed to notify CBI's board of directors of the flaws in the 1992 and 1993 audits.[5] According to Judge Lifland, Ernst & Young did not inform the board members of those flaws because the accounting firm realized that doing so would lower, if not eliminate, its chance of landing the "reaudit" engagement for CBI's 1992 and 1993 financial statements. "E&Y's egocentric desire to get the reaudit work is illustrated by the fact that it prepared an audit program for the reaudit two days before E&Y met with the CBI board of directors and one day before they withdrew their opinion."

CBI's board ultimately selected Ernst & Young to reaudit the company's 1992 and 1993 financial statements. Given the circumstances under which Ernst & Young obtained that engagement, Judge Lifland concluded that the accounting firm's independence was likely impaired. "Thus, E&Y knew prior to agreeing to perform the reaudit work that it had not complied with GAAS. E&Y also knew that CBI's board of directors did not know of E&Y's failure to comply with GAAS. It is reasonable to infer that if CBI's board of directors knew of such failure, E&Y and CBI would be in adversarial positions."[6]

5. At this point, the TCW representatives on CBI's board were apparently the company's principal decision makers.

6. After ruling that Ernst & Young was principally responsible for the losses resulting from CBI's bankruptcy, Judge Lifland ordered that the trial be resumed on the issue of damages. The judgment imposed by Judge Lifland or the out-of-court settlement ultimately reached by the parties was not publicly reported.

## Questions

1. Most of Judge Lifland's criticism of Ernst & Young focused on the audit procedures Ernst & Young applied to CBI's accounts payable. Generally, what is an auditor's primary objective in auditing a client's accounts payable? Do you believe that the two principal audit tests applied to CBI's accounts payable would have accomplished that objective if those tests had been properly applied? Why or why not?
2. Do you believe that the Ernst & Young auditors should have used confirmations in auditing CBI's year-end accounts payable? Defend your answer. Briefly explain the differing audit objectives related to accounts receivable and accounts payable confirmation procedures and the key differences in how these procedures are applied.
3. In early 1994, Ernst & Young officials discovered that the CBI auditors had failed to determine the true nature of the "advances" they had uncovered during the 1992 and 1993 audits. In your view, did Ernst & Young have an obligation to inform CBI management of this oversight prior to seeking the "reaudit" engagement? More generally, does an auditor have a responsibility to inform client management of mistakes or oversights made on earlier audits?
4. Under what circumstances, if any, should an audit engagement partner acquiesce to a client's request to remove a member of the audit engagement team?
5. Ernst & Young officials believed that the CBI audits were high-risk engagements. Under what general circumstances should an audit firm choose not to accept a high-risk engagement?

**CASE 2.7**

# Flight Transportation Corporation

In January 1982, Charles Aune picked up his phone and called the Federal Bureau of Investigation (FBI).[1] Aune then proceeded to tell the FBI of a large-scale fraud being perpetrated by his former employer. Until 1981, Aune had worked for Flight Transportation Corporation (FTC), an aviation company based in Eden Prairie, Minnesota. FTC's principal line of business was executive and group air charters. In 1980 and 1981, the rapidly growing company reported revenues of $8 million and $24.8 million, respectively. FTC's dramatic growth caught the attention of investors nationwide. The company's strong operating results were particularly impressive since they were posted in the face of a recession gripping the country. Unfortunately for investors, most of FTC's revenues existed only in the minds of the company's executives. Similarly, several million dollars of assets reported in the company's 1980 and 1981 balance sheets were purely imaginary.

From 1979 through 1982, FTC executives used the company's bogus financial statements to raise more than $32 million of capital in three securities offerings to the public. The executives diverted much of these funds for their personal use. For example, the company's president financed his expensive hobby, collecting vintage cars, by tapping the company's bank accounts. In June 1982, FTC was preparing to sell an additional $24 million of securities. However, a secret six-month investigation by the FBI, prompted by Charles Aune's phone call, resulted in the Securities and Exchange Commission (SEC) shutting down the company's operations. A federal judge then appointed a receiver to take custody of the company's assets.

Over the next several months, press reports of the FTC fraud shocked investors who had purchased the company's securities on the basis of its impressive financial statements. Almost immediately, the underwriting firms that had managed FTC's securities offerings came under fire. An executive of one of these firms responded to this criticism. "I don't see this as embarrassing to our firm at all. Underwriters aren't auditors."[2] Predictably, the press then turned to FTC's auditors, Fox & Company, for an explanation. John Harrington, a senior partner with Fox & Company, served as the audit engagement partner on the 1980 and 1981 FTC audits. Harrington defended those audits, each of which concluded with an unqualified opinion issued on FTC's financial statements.

> *We're not the guardians of the world. It's the con artists who should be punished. Besides, if we go into every client's office with our eyes wide open, saying, "there's a crime in here somewhere," nobody is going to hire us.*[3]

---

1. Most of the facts of this case and the quotations, unless indicated otherwise, were drawn from the following source: Securities and Exchange Commission, *Accounting and Auditing Enforcement Release No. 81*, 5 December 1985.

2. K. Johnson, "How High-flying Numbers Fooled the Experts," *The New York Times*, 29 August 1982, Section 3, 9.

3. *Ibid.*

## Fox's 1980 Audit of FTC

The Minneapolis office of Fox & Company, the thirteenth-largest accounting firm in the nation at the time, acquired FTC as an audit client in March 1980. In prior years, a sole practitioner had audited the company. Besides Harrington, the audit engagement team assigned to the 1980 and 1981 FTC audits included an audit manager, Gregory Arnott, and three staff auditors. Arnott supervised the fieldwork for both audits. The 1980 FTC audit was the first engagement on which Arnott served as an audit manager, since he had been promoted to that position shortly before the audit began. In his previous eight years with Fox & Company, Arnott had worked on only one audit of a public company. Harrington had been a partner with Fox & Company since 1975 and had served for a time as the managing partner of Fox's Minneapolis office. During the early 1980s, Harrington oversaw the auditing practice of the Minneapolis office. He also reviewed and approved each SEC registration statement filed by clients of that office.

Harrington and Arnott met with FTC's top executives in early March 1980 to discuss the 1980 audit. An engagement letter, signed by Harrington and an FTC officer, documented the contractual details of that audit. The two auditors and client executives also discussed the staffing of the audit and timing issues during the March meeting. FTC's fiscal year ended on June 30. The company's president, William Rubin, insisted that the audited financial statements be ready for the printer by early August. Rubin wanted the audit completed quickly to expedite the filing of a registration statement with the SEC. FTC needed the SEC's approval of that registration statement to sell a large block of new securities to the public.

Like most large accounting firms, Fox & Company used a risk assessment questionnaire during the planning phase of each audit to document "special" audit risks. This questionnaire contained several items focusing on high-risk audit factors such as related party transactions. When asked whether FTC had engaged in any related party transactions during fiscal 1980, FTC officials responded with a blunt "no." However, shortly after the audit fieldwork began, a Fox auditor discovered that most of FTC's revenues stemmed from a contractual arrangement with International Air Systems (IAS), a company owned by William Rubin. Approximately two-thirds of FTC's 1980 consolidated revenues resulted from more than one hundred air charters that had been flown on IAS aircraft. To the staff auditor's surprise, he could find almost no documentary support for this $5.2 million of air charter revenues. There were no sales invoices, no entries in the sales journal, and no related expenses recorded for these revenues. The support for the revenues consisted almost entirely of handwritten entries made directly into FTC's general journal. Because of their unusual nature and the lack of documentation, the staff auditor prepared a list of the air charter revenues. He gave this list to Arnott.

Arnott asked FTC's controller to supply the documentation for the air charter revenues. The controller responded that the auditors would have to make arrangements with Rubin to obtain that documentation. Arnott then took the matter to Harrington, who contacted Rubin. After a brief conversation with Harrington, Rubin agreed to provide extensive documentation for the IAS-related revenues. This documentation was to include sales invoices, cash receipts and disbursements records, canceled checks, contracts, and computer runs listing the individual air charters. Despite Rubin's interest in completing the audit as quickly as possible, he repeatedly stonewalled the auditors when they asked for the documentation. Computer malfunctions served as Rubin's most popular excuse for failing to turn over the requested documents to the audit team.

**EXHIBIT 1**

ALLEGED CONTRACTUAL AGREEMENT BETWEEN FTC AND IAS

A. IAS shall provide FTC with large aircraft (727s and/or DC 8s) for charter to the Cayman Islands and Mexico.

B. All revenues earned by FTC will be recorded by IAS during the term of the agreement and provided to FTC at the conclusion of all flights along with the gross or net profit to be paid. Gross profit will be earned and paid if sufficient volume is attained. If volume is not high enough, only net profit will be paid to FTC.

C. This agreement covers the period from July 1, 1979, through June 30, 1980.

---

Source: Securities and Exchange Commission, *Accounting and Auditing Enforcement Release No. 81*, 5 December 1985.

A few days before the projected completion date for the 1980 audit, Rubin finally provided the Fox auditors with evidence to support the suspicious air charter revenues. Exhibit 1 presents the first of these documents, a brief and ambiguous one-page contract between IAS and FTC. The second item, another one-page document, listed the number of charter flights flown for FTC on IAS aircraft and the resulting revenues for FTC. When the auditors balked at accepting this documentation, Rubin took Harrington aside and told him that the air charter revenues were not FTC revenues at all. Instead, these revenues had been produced by IAS, which again, was owned by Rubin. Rubin explained to Harrington that "he was bored, had plenty of money, and wanted to use IAS to help FTC get into the charter business." Consequently, Rubin had "donated" the more than $5 million of IAS air charter revenues to FTC.

Harrington accepted Rubin's explanation for the IAS revenues booked in FTC's accounting records, an explanation that accounted for FTC's lack of documentation for those transactions. Harrington then explained to Arnott the true nature of the air charter revenues. He also informed Arnott that, in his opinion, no additional evidence would be needed to support those revenues. Arnott disagreed with Harrington initially but then changed his mind after the two men discussed the matter further. Arnott eventually indicated in the 1980 audit workpapers that the $5.2 million of air charter revenues were "appropriately included" in FTC's 1980 financial statements.

During a subsequent SEC investigation, Arnott testified that he never believed sufficient competent audit evidence had been obtained to support the air charter revenues. An SEC representative then questioned Arnott regarding his awareness of Fox's "disagreement procedure." This policy allowed a subordinate member of an audit team to express disagreement with a decision rendered on an audit engagement. Such a disagreement was to be documented in a written memorandum included in the audit workpapers. This memorandum effectively dissociated the subordinate from the given decision. Arnott testified that he was aware of the disagreement procedure but did not take advantage of it for two reasons. First, he realized that as the audit engagement partner Harrington would make the final decision regarding the suspicious air charter revenues. Second, he was worried that his job with Fox & Company might be jeopardized if he followed that procedure.

The SEC also quizzed Harrington regarding his discussion of the air charter revenues with Arnott. Harrington testified that he could not recall Arnott ever disagreeing with the decision that sufficient competent evidence had been collected to support the air charter revenues.

## Fox's 1981 Audit of FTC

In July 1980, shortly after the beginning of FTC's 1981 fiscal year, the company established a subsidiary in the Cayman Islands. The reported purpose of this subsidiary was to operate an air charter business. During fiscal 1981, FTC recorded $13 million of nonexistent revenues through FTC Cayman Ltd., its Cayman Islands subsidiary. These revenues accounted for more than one-half of FTC's consolidated revenues for fiscal 1981. FTC's consolidated balance sheet as of June 30, 1981, the final day of the company's 1981 fiscal year, reported more than $6 million of nonexistent receivables, land, and other assets related to FTC Cayman.

In June 1981, Harrington and Arnott met with Rubin and other FTC officers in a planning conference for the 1981 audit. During this meeting, Rubin told Harrington and Arnott that FTC's new Cayman Island subsidiary produced most of FTC's 1981 revenues. Rubin also told the auditors that the documentation for these revenues was in the Cayman Islands but would be brought to Minnesota during the audit. Again, Rubin wanted the audit completed as quickly as possible. The parties agreed to a fieldwork completion date of July 31 and a projected audit report signing date of August 12.

When the 1981 audit began in early July, the only documentation made available to the Fox auditors was a trial balance and a computerized general ledger and general journal. On August 6, one week after the fieldwork was supposed to have been finished and less than one week before the audit report was to be signed, FTC officials gave the auditors the fiscal 1981 bank statements for FTC Cayman. Except for a few other minor items, these bank statements were the only externally prepared documents provided to the Fox auditors to support FTC Cayman's revenues. These bank statements were not obtained directly from the subsidiary's bank but instead were given to the Fox auditors by an FTC employee.

Rubin told Harrington and Arnott that they could verify the subsidiary's revenues by reviewing the deposits reported in its bank statements during fiscal 1981. A member of the audit engagement team did just that. A reconciliation of the revenues reported by FTC Cayman and the deposits reflected in the subsidiary's 1981 bank statements resulted in a small unlocated difference between the two amounts. Given this small difference, the auditors concluded that the subsidiary's 1981 revenues were materially accurate. In fact, the bank statements were forgeries.

The Fox auditors attempted to confirm $3 million of cash that FTC Cayman reportedly had on deposit in the Cayman Islands as of June 30, 1981. Throughout the audit, FTC executives tried to persuade the auditors that obtaining a confirmation for that cash balance would be difficult given the bank secrecy laws in the Cayman Islands. The auditors mailed a confirmation to the subsidiary's Cayman Islands bank using an address supplied by FTC. That confirmation was never returned. Eventually, Harrington agreed to accept a confirmation of the year-end cash balance that an employee of the subsidiary had allegedly obtained from the Cayman Islands bank. The SEC's subsequent investigation revealed that the employee forged the confirmation.

Harrington also arranged to speak with an official of the Cayman Islands bank to obtain an oral confirmation of the subsidiary's year-end cash balance. Rubin invited Harrington to come to his office to receive this confirmation over the telephone. After Rubin placed a call—allegedly to the bank—and had a brief conversation, he handed the telephone receiver to Harrington. The individual at the other end of the line then confirmed that FTC's subsidiary had the reported amount of cash on deposit as of June 30, 1981.

The Fox auditors also attempted to confirm a $2 million receivable of FTC Cayman at the end of fiscal 1981. The auditors mailed a confirmation for this amount to a tour group operator who allegedly organized most of the subsidiary's air charter flights. A confirmation was returned indicating that the receivable did exist. However, the confirmation returned was not the confirmation that had been mailed by the Fox auditors. The returned confirmation was a forgery that contained typographical errors not present in the original confirmation.

## EPILOGUE

The SEC investigation of the 1980 and 1981 FTC audits culminated in sanctions imposed on both John Harrington and Gregory Arnott. Harrington was permanently banned from practicing before the SEC. However, the SEC's disciplinary order allowed Harrington to apply for a repeal of this ban after five years. Arnott received a one-year suspension from the SEC. In commenting on Arnott's role in the FTC audits, the SEC stressed the need for members of an audit engagement team to maintain an independent state of mind even if that means jeopardizing their jobs.

*Arnott engaged in unprofessional conduct by abdicating his role as an independent professional to the audit partner. He properly recognized that the audit evidence was inadequate and took the appropriate step of informing the partner. However, he failed to act on his conviction and caused the workpapers to evidence incorrectly his agreement.*

Following a series of highly publicized problem audits by Fox & Company, including the 1980 and 1981 FTC audits, the SEC prohibited the firm from accepting new SEC clients for a six-month period beginning in 1983. The SEC also formed an independent committee to review Fox & Company's auditing practice and to recommend changes to improve the firm's quality control procedures. In 1985, Fox & Company merged with Alexander Grant & Company. The newly-created firm was named Grant Thornton.

In 1982, the SEC sanctioned William Rubin for his role in the FTC fraud. The SEC permanently enjoined Rubin from further violations of federal securities laws. Eventually, federal law enforcement authorities and private plaintiffs recovered more than $45 million from FTC and its executives, including almost $2 million from Rubin. FTC's court-appointed receiver distributed these funds to the company's bondholders, other creditors, and stockholders.

## Questions

1. Assume the role of Gregory Arnott during the 1980 FTC audit. Draft a memo to be included in the FTC workpapers that expresses your disagreement with John Harrington's decision that sufficient competent evidence had been collected to support the suspicious air charter revenues.
2. Identify measures accounting firms can adopt to lower the risk that auditors will capitulate to their superiors when technical disagreements arise during an audit.
3. Assume that you were the staff auditor who discovered the bogus air charter revenues during the 1980 audit. What responsibilities did you have regarding those revenues? For example, did you have a responsibility to write a memo dissociating yourself from Harrington's decision to accept those revenues? Make any assumptions you believe are necessary to respond to this question.

4. In your opinion, what additional audit procedures should the Fox auditors have applied to the 1981 FTC Cayman revenues?
5. Identify the flaws in the confirmation procedures applied by the Fox auditors. How did these flaws affect the competence and sufficiency of the audit evidence yielded by these procedures?
6. Besides the related party transactions, what other "special" audit risks were posed by the FTC audits? How should these factors have affected the planning decisions for these audits?
7. Identify specific measures audit firms can take to ensure that client-imposed pressure does not adversely affect the quality of an independent audit.

**CASE 2.8**

# CapitalBanc Corporation

In 1975, Carlos Cordova and several other investors founded Capital National Bank (CNB) in Bronx, New York.[1] Cordova was appointed the bank's chief executive officer (CEO) and chairman of the board. Over the next several years, the bank opened five branch offices in the New York City metropolitan area. CNB catered primarily to the banking needs of Hispanic-American and immigrant communities in New York City. In 1986, Cordova and the other owners of CNB formed CapitalBanc Corporation, a publicly owned bank holding company registered with the Securities and Exchange Commission (SEC). Throughout its entire existence, the principal operating entity controlled by CapitalBanc was CNB. Cordova assumed the titles of president, CEO, and chairman of the board of the new bank holding company.

In the fall of 1987, CapitalBanc retained Arthur Andersen & Co. as its independent audit firm. Andersen's first engagement for CapitalBanc was to audit the bank holding company's consolidated financial statements for the fiscal year ending December 31, 1987. Thomas Curtin, an Arthur Andersen partner since 1979, served as the engagement partner for the 1987 CapitalBanc audit. Curtin delegated the responsibility for much of the audit planning to James Lukenda, an audit manager with Arthur Andersen since 1983. Lukenda also supervised the staff auditors assigned to the CapitalBanc engagement.

On December 29, 1987, several Arthur Andersen staff auditors accompanied members of CNB's internal audit staff to the bank's 177th Street Branch. The Arthur Andersen auditors intended to observe and participate in a surprise count of the branch's cash funds by the internal auditors. Related audit objectives included testing CNB's compliance with certain control procedures and evaluating the competence of the bank's internal audit staff. The accounting personnel at each CNB branch maintained a "vault general ledger proof sheet" that reconciled the cash on hand to the balance of the branch's general ledger cash account. During the surprise cash count at the 177th Street Branch, the Arthur Andersen auditors discovered a $2.7 million reconciling item listed on the branch's proof sheet. That amount equaled 61 percent of the branch's general ledger cash balance and 45 percent of the branch's total cash funds that were supposed to be available on the date of the surprise count. When the staff auditors asked to count the $2.7 million of cash represented by the reconciling item, bank employees told them that Cordova had segregated those funds in a locked cabinet within the bank's main vault. Three keys were required to unlock the cabinet. Cordova, who was out of the country at the time, maintained custody of one of those keys.

Stymied temporarily, one of the staff auditors telephoned Lukenda. The staff auditor relayed to Lukenda the information regarding the $2.7 million of segregated cash. After considering the matter and discussing it with Curtin, Lukenda instructed the

1. The facts of this case were drawn from the 1987 annual report of CapitalBanc Corporation and the following source: Securities and Exchange Commission, *Accounting and Auditing Enforcement Release No. 458*, 28 June 1993.

staff auditor to count the cash upon Cordova's return. Lukenda also reportedly told the staff auditor that it would not be necessary to place audit seals on the doors of the cabinet or to secure it in any other way given the three-key security system used by the branch. Following the telephone conversation with Lukenda, the staff auditor advised bank personnel that Arthur Andersen auditors would count the cash on the date Cordova returned from his trip.

CNB's practice of segregating a large amount of cash in the locked cabinet was clearly not a normal banking procedure. In a subsequent investigation, the SEC commented on this practice:

> *It is an unusual circumstance for a substantial portion of a bank's cash to be inaccessible for an extended period of time. It is also unusual for a substantial portion of a bank's assets not to be invested and earning interest for an extended period of time.*[2]

In early January 1988, an employee of the 177th Street Branch notified Arthur Andersen that Cordova would return on January 14. On that date, the Arthur Andersen staff auditors arrived at the branch to complete their count of the cash funds. Cordova opened the locked cabinet in the main vault in the presence of the staff auditors. The auditors then proceeded to count the $2.7 million that had not been counted on December 29, 1987. All of the cash was present. None of the other cash funds of the 177th Street Branch or other CNB branches was counted by the Arthur Andersen auditors on January 14, 1988.

After counting the segregated cash, the staff auditors asked Cordova why he kept those funds in the locked cabinet. Cordova explained that a customer who had cashed a large certificate of deposit insisted on having the funds available on demand at all times. According to Cordova, the customer intended to use the funds to buy foreign currencies when market conditions became favorable. The volatility of the foreign currency market dictated that the customer have immediate access to the funds on a daily basis.

Near the completion of the 1987 CapitalBanc audit, Lukenda reviewed the workpaper that documented Cordova's explanation for the $2.7 million of segregated cash. Lukenda then discussed that explanation with Curtin. After considering the matter, Curtin instructed Lukenda to have the staff auditors confirm that there was an offsetting liability to the given customer in CNB's accounting records equal to the amount of the segregated funds. The staff auditors obtained the documentation for this liability directly from CNB personnel. This information was not confirmed with the customer or independently verified by the auditors in any other way. The staff auditors also did not obtain documentation confirming that the customer had cashed a large certificate of deposit. Finally, the staff auditors neglected to obtain any evidence to corroborate Cordova's assertion regarding the customer's planned use of the funds.

Following the completion of the CapitalBanc audit in March 1988, Arthur Andersen issued an unqualified opinion on the firm's 1987 financial statements. Those financial statements reported a net income of $701,000, total cash funds of $14.1 million, and total assets of $143.2 million. CapitalBanc included the audited financial statements in its 1987 Form 10-K registration statement filed with the SEC.

---

2. Securities and Exchange Commission, *Accounting and Auditing Enforcement Release No. 458*, 28 June 1993.

## EPILOGUE

In July 1990, the Office of the Comptroller of the Currency declared CapitalBanc Corporation insolvent and placed it under the control of the Federal Deposit Insurance Corporation (FDIC). The following year, Banco Popular de Puerto Rico purchased the assets of CNB from the FDIC.

In late 1991, Carlos Cordova pleaded guilty to three counts of bank fraud and conspiracy to commit bank fraud. Two of Cordova's associates pleaded guilty to similar charges. Earlier in 1991, Cordova had agreed to an order issued by the SEC that permanently banned him from serving as an officer or director of a public company. A federal investigation of CNB's financial affairs revealed that Cordova misappropriated at least $400,000 of the $2.7 million allegedly stored in the locked cabinet in the 177th Street Branch's main vault. Cordova, with the help of his subordinates, had intentionally concealed this shortage from the Arthur Andersen auditors during the 1987 audit. Cordova secretly returned to the 177th Street Branch on January 9, 1988, and placed cash obtained from other CNB branches in the locked cabinet to replace the funds that he had embezzled.

The description of the three-key security system relayed to the Arthur Andersen auditors by employees of the 177th Street Branch was a subterfuge. The fast-thinking employees conceived that hoax to deter the auditors from gaining access to the locked cabinet on the day of the surprise cash count. Cordova's explanation regarding why he kept the large amount of cash segregated in the locked cabinet was also a fabrication.

In 1993, the SEC reported the results of its investigation of Arthur Andersen's 1987 CapitalBanc audit, an investigation that focused on the audit of the 177th Street Branch's cash funds. In that report, the SEC disclosed the following sanctions imposed on Thomas Curtin and James Lukenda:

> *It is hereby ordered, that Respondents [Curtin and Lukenda] are censured and must be duly registered and in good standing as certified public accountants in the states in which they each reside or their principal office is located and they must each become a member of or be associated with a member firm of the SEC Practice Section of the AICPA's Division for CPA Firms as long as they practice before the Commission.*[3]

## Questions

1. When auditing cash, which of the management assertions discussed in *SAS No. 106*, "Audit Evidence," are of primary concern to an auditor? Why?
2. Identify audit procedures that should be applied to cash funds maintained by a client on its business premises.
3. Identify mistakes or oversights made by Arthur Andersen personnel while auditing the cash funds at the 177th Street Branch.

3. *Ibid.*

SECTION 3

# INTERNAL CONTROL ISSUES

**CASE 3.1**

# The Trolley Dodgers

In 1890, the Brooklyn Trolley Dodgers professional baseball team joined the National League. Over the following years, the Dodgers would have considerable difficulty competing with the other baseball teams in the New York City area. Those teams, principal among them the New York Yankees, were much better financed and generally stocked with players of higher caliber.

After nearly seven decades of mostly frustration on and off the baseball field, the Dodgers shocked the sports world by moving to Los Angeles in 1958. Walter O'Malley, the flamboyant owner of the Dodgers, saw an opportunity to introduce professional baseball to the rapidly growing population of the West Coast. More important, O'Malley saw an opportunity to make his team more profitable. As an inducement to the Dodgers, Los Angeles County purchased a goat farm located in Chavez Ravine, an area two miles northwest of downtown Los Angeles, and gave the property to O'Malley for the site of his new baseball stadium.

Since moving to Los Angeles, the Dodgers have been the envy of the baseball world: "In everything from profit to stadium maintenance . . . the Dodgers are the prototype of how a franchise should be run."[1] During the 1980s and 1990s, the Dodgers reigned as the most profitable franchise in baseball with a pretax profit margin approaching 25 percent in many years. In late 1997, Peter O'Malley, Walter O'Malley's son and the Dodgers' principal owner, sold the franchise for $350 million to media mogul Rupert Murdoch. A spokesman for Murdoch complimented the O'Malley family for the longstanding success of the Dodgers organization: "The O'Malleys have set a gold standard for franchise ownership."[2]

During an interview before he sold the Dodgers, Peter O'Malley attributed the success of his organization to the experts he had retained in all functional areas: "I don't have to be an expert on taxes, split-fingered fastballs, or labor relations with our ushers. That talent is all available."[3] Edward Campos, a longtime accountant for the Dodgers, was a seemingly perfect example of one of those experts in the Dodgers organization. Campos accepted an entry-level position with the Dodgers as a young man. By 1986, after almost two decades with the club, he had worked his way up the employment hierarchy to become the operations payroll chief.

After taking charge of the Dodgers' payroll department, Campos designed and implemented a new payroll system, a system that only he fully understood. In fact, Campos controlled the system so completely that he personally filled out the weekly payroll cards for each of the 400 employees of the Dodgers. Campos was known not only for his work ethic but also for his loyalty to the club and its owners: "The Dodgers trusted him, and when he was on vacation, he even came back and did the payroll."[4]

---

1. R. J. Harris, "Forkball for Dodgers: Costs Up, Gate Off," *The Wall Street Journal*, 31 August 1990, B1, B4.
2. R. Newhan, "Dodger Sale Heads for Home," *Los Angeles Times*, 5 September 1997, C1, C12.
3. Harris, "Forkball for Dodgers," B1.
4. P. Feldman, "7 Accused of Embezzling $332,583 from Dodgers," *Los Angeles Times*, 17 September 1986, Sec. 2, 1, 6.

Unfortunately, the Dodgers' trust in Campos was misplaced. Over a period of several years, Campos embezzled several hundred thousand dollars from his employer. According to court records, Campos padded the Dodgers' payroll by adding fictitious employees to various departments in the organization. In addition, Campos routinely inflated the number of hours worked by several employees and then split the resulting overpayments fifty-fifty with those individuals.

The fraudulent scheme came unraveled when appendicitis struck down Campos, forcing the Dodgers' controller to temporarily assume his responsibilities. While completing the payroll one week, the controller noticed that several employees, including ushers, security guards, and ticket salespeople, were being paid unusually large amounts. In some cases, employees earning $7 an hour received weekly paychecks approaching $2,000. Following a criminal investigation and the filing of charges against Campos and his cohorts, all the individuals involved in the payroll fraud confessed.

A state court sentenced Campos to eight years in prison and required him to make restitution of approximately $132,000 to the Dodgers. Another of the conspirators also received a prison sentence. The remaining individuals involved in the payroll scheme made restitution and were placed on probation.

## Questions

1. Identify the key audit objectives for a client's payroll function. Comment on objectives related to tests of controls and substantive audit procedures.
2. What internal control weaknesses were evident in the Dodgers' payroll system?
3. Identify audit procedures that might have led to the discovery of the fraudulent scheme masterminded by Campos.

**CASE 3.2**

# Howard Street Jewelers, Inc.

Lore Levi was worried as she scanned the March 1983 bank statement for the Howard Street Jewelers.[1] For more than four decades, she and her husband, Julius, had owned and operated the small business that they had opened after fleeing Nazi Germany during World War II. Certainly the business had experienced ups and downs before, but now it seemed to be in a downward spiral from which it could not recover. In previous times when sales had slackened, the Levis had survived by cutting costs here and there. But now, despite several measures the Levis had taken to control costs, the business's cash position continued to steadily worsen. If a turnaround did not occur soon, Lore feared that she and her husband might be forced to close their store.

Lore had a theory regarding the financial problems of Howard Street Jewelers. On more than one occasion, she had wondered whether Betty the cashier, a trusted and reliable employee for nearly 20 years, might be stealing from the cash register. To Lore, it was a logical assumption. Besides working as a part-time sales clerk, Betty handled all of the cash that came into the business and maintained the cash receipts and sales records. If anybody had an opportunity to steal from the business, it was Betty.

Reluctantly, Lore approached her husband about her theory. Lore pointed out to Julius that Betty had unrestricted access to the cash receipts of the business. Additionally, over the previous few years, Betty had developed a taste for more expensive clothes and more frequent and costly vacations. Julius quickly dismissed his wife's speculation. To him, it was preposterous to even briefly consider the possibility that Betty could be stealing from the business. A frustrated Lore then raised the subject with her son, Alvin, who worked side by side with his parents in the family business. Alvin responded similarly to his father and warned his mother that she was becoming paranoid.

Near the end of each year, the Levis met with their accountant to discuss various matters, principally taxation issues. The Levis placed considerable trust in the CPA who served as their accountant; for almost 40 years he had given them solid, professional advice on a wide range of accounting and business matters. It was only natural for Lore to confide in the accountant about her suspicions regarding Betty the cashier. The accountant listened intently to Lore and then commented that he had noticed occasional shortages in the cash receipts records that seemed larger than normal for a small retail business. Despite Julius's protestations that Betty could not be responsible for any cash shortages, the accountant encouraged the Levis to closely monitor her work.

Embezzlements are often discovered by luck rather than by design. So it was with the Howard Street Jewelers. In the spring of 1985, a customer approached the cash register and told Alvin Levi that she wanted to make a payment on a layaway item. Alvin, who was working the cash register because it was Betty's day off, searched the file of layaway sales tickets and the daily sales records but found no trace of the customer's layaway purchase. Finally, he apologized and asked the customer to return the next day when Betty would be back at work.

---

1. Most of the facts of this case were reconstructed from information included in several legal opinions. The following two articles served as additional sources for this case: *Securities Regulation and Law Report*, "Accounting & Disclosure: Accounting Briefs," Vol. 23, No. 21 (24 May 1991), 814; *Securities Regulation and Law Report*, "Accounting & Disclosure: Accounting Briefs," Vol. 24, No. 19 (8 May 1992), 708.

The following day, Alvin told Betty that he was unable to find the layaway sales ticket. Betty expressed surprise and said she would search for the ticket herself. Within a few minutes, Betty approached Alvin, waving the sales ticket in her hand. Alvin was stumped. He had searched the layaway sales file several times and simply could not accept Betty's explanation that the missing ticket had been there all along. Suspicious, as well, was the fact that the sale had not been recorded in the sales records—a simple oversight, Betty had explained.

As Alvin returned to his work, a troubling and sickening sensation settled into the pit of his stomach. Over the next several weeks, Alvin studied the daily sales and cash receipts records. He soon realized that his mother had been right all along. Betty, the trusted, reliable, longtime cashier of the Howard Street Jewelers, was stealing from the business. The estimated embezzlement loss suffered by Howard Street Jewelers over the term of Betty's employment approached $350,000.

## Questions

1. Identify the internal control concepts that the Levis overlooked or ignored.
2. When Lore informed the CPA of her suspicions regarding Betty, what responsibilities, if any, did the CPA have to pursue this matter? Alternately, assume that, in addition to preparing tax returns for Howard Street Jewelers, the CPA (a) *audited* the business's annual financial statements, (b) *reviewed* the annual financial statements, and (c) *compiled* the annual financial statements.
3. Assume that you have a small CPA firm and have been contacted by a husband and wife, John and Myrna Trubey, who are in the final stages of negotiating to purchase a local jewelry store. John will prepare jewelry settings, size jewelry for customers, and perform related tasks, while Myrna will be the head salesclerk. The Trubeys intend to retain four of the current employees of the jewelry store—two salesclerks, a cashier, and a college student who cleans the store, runs errands, and does various other odd jobs. They inform you that the average inventory of the jewelry store is $200,000 and that annual sales average $800,000, 30 percent of which occur in the six weeks prior to Christmas.

   The Trubeys are interested in retaining you as their accountant should they purchase the store. They know little about accounting and have no prior experience as business owners. They would require assistance in establishing an accounting system, monthly financial statements for internal use, annual financial statements to be submitted to their banker, and all necessary tax returns. John and Myrna are particularly concerned about control issues—given the dollar value of inventory that will be on hand in the store and the significant amount of cash that will be processed daily.

   You see this as an excellent opportunity to acquire a good client. However, you have not had a chance to prepare for your meeting with the Trubeys because they came in without an appointment. You do not want to ask them to come back later, since that may encourage them to check out your competitor across the street.

   **Required:** Provide the Trubeys with an overview of the key internal control issues they will face in operating a jewelry store. In your overview, identify at least five control activities you believe they should implement if they acquire the store. You have never had a jewelry store as a client but you have several small retail clients. Attempt to impress the Trubeys with your understanding of internal control issues for small retail businesses.

## CASE 3.3

# United Way of America

In 1887, several of Denver's community and religious leaders established the Charity Organization Society. During its first year of operation, that organization raised a little more than $20,000, which it then distributed to several local charities. The charity-of-charities fundraising concept spread across the United States over the following decades. After several name changes, the original Denver-based organization adopted the name United Way in 1963.

United Way grew rapidly during the latter decades of the twentieth century, eventually becoming the nation's largest charitable organization. In 2006, United Way raised four billion dollars, more than double the charitable donations received that year by the Salvation Army, the nation's second largest charitable organization. Each year, approximately 40,000 charities across the United States receive cash distributions from United Way.

For more than two decades beginning in the early 1970s, William Aramony served as the president of United Way of America. The Virginia-based United Way of America serves as the umbrella organization for the almost 1,400 local United Way chapters scattered across the United States. An alliance that Aramony negotiated with the National Football League (NFL) resulted in huge nationwide exposure for the United Way during every Sunday afternoon and Monday night NFL game. That exposure was largely responsible for the explosive growth that United Way realized during Aramony's tenure as president.

In recent years, United Way has faced two major challenges that threaten its leadership position in the charitable sector. Over the past several decades, the number of charitable and other not-for-profit organizations in the United States has skyrocketed. Currently, there are nearly two million registered tax-exempt organizations in the United States, the large majority of which are charities. Collectively, these organizations employ one of every ten working Americans. Registered charities alone raise more than $300 billion each year in donations from the public and private sector. The intense and growing competition for Americans' charitable donations has made it increasingly difficult for United Way to sustain the impressive growth that it realized under William Aramony's leadership.

The second major challenge facing United Way is a loss of credibility suffered by the organization due to a series of embarrassing and highly publicized embezzlement schemes. In the early 1990s, federal prosecutors indicted William Aramony for allegedly embezzling and otherwise misusing millions of dollars of United Way funds. In 1995, a federal jury found Aramony guilty of more than two dozen of the individual fraud charges that had been filed against him. Aramony was later sentenced to serve seven years in federal prison. Testimony during Aramony's trial revealed that he had squandered United Way funds on lavish trips to Las Vegas, Europe, Africa, and other destinations. The sixty-eight-year-old Aramony reportedly used United Way funds to finance multiple romantic relationships as well.

Shortly before Aramony went to trial, another United Way executive in Westchester, New York admitted to embezzling several hundred thousand dollars of her chapter's funds. This individual, Evol Sealy, who oversaw the Westchester chapter's accounting and finance functions, was later sentenced to a three-year prison term. In 2003,

Jacquelyn Allen-MacGregor, the former vice president of finance of a United Way chapter in East Lansing, Michigan, pleaded guilty to stealing $1.9 million from the organization. Allen-MacGregor revealed that she had used the stolen funds to support her hobby, namely, horses—over the course of her embezzlement scheme she purchased more than seventy quarter horses. In June 2004, Allen-MacGregor was sentenced to four years in prison to be followed by three years of supervised probation.

In 2004, Aramony's friend and former associate, Oral Suer, who served for almost three decades as the president of a large United Way chapter in Washington, D.C., pleaded guilty to embezzling $1.5 million of United Way funds. The evidence collected by federal prosecutors against Suer included testimony documenting that Suer and Aramony had spent time together at a local racetrack. That evidence also documented that Suer used cash taken from his chapter to make good on the generous and well-publicized personal contribution pledges that he made during annual United Way fundraising campaigns. At his sentencing hearing, a contrite Suer told the presiding judge, "This is a very sad day for me, for the community and for the United Way. What I feel is embarrassment, shame, and guilt."[1] The judge then handed Suer a three-year prison sentence, the maximum permissible under federal sentencing guidelines.

United Way's reported theft losses have had a chilling effect on the organization's fundraising efforts nationwide in recent years. Not surprisingly, individual chapters impacted directly by the embezzlement losses have experienced dramatic declines in their annual receipts. For example, adverse publicity resulting from the embezzlement loss at the United Way chapter in the Washington, D.C., area caused that chapter's annual donations to plummet from $45 million to $18 million.

In recent years, many large charities in addition to United Way have suffered large losses due to embezzlements and other fraudulent activities perpetrated by organizational insiders. In 1989, former television evangelist Jim Bakker was sentenced to eighteen years in federal prison. Bakker was convicted of diverting millions of dollars for his personal use from the PTL Club, a religious broadcasting network that he and his wife, Tammy Faye, founded in the 1970s. The Bakkers had used passionate and persistent televised fundraising campaigns to convince the faithful and mostly shallow-pocketed viewers of their network to send them donations. In 1997, John G. Bennett, the founder of the New Era Philanthropy Foundation, was sentenced to twelve years in prison after embezzling an estimated $8 million from that charitable organization. In California, seven employees of Goodwill Industries, all of whom were related, operated a large-scale "fencing" operation from the early 1970s through 1998 in which they sold furniture, clothing, and other goods donated to that charity. Law enforcement authorities estimate that the seven relatives stole more than $25 million from that organization over the course of the fraudulent scheme.

To date, the largest fraud impacting a charity was a Ponzi scheme that involved the Baptist Foundation of Arizona. In 2006, William Crotts, the chief executive of that charitable religious organization, received an eight-year prison sentence for defrauding an estimated 10,000 individuals of nearly $160 million. Making matters worse, most of the victims of Crotts' fraud were elderly individuals, many of whom lost a sizable portion of their retirement nest eggs as a result of the fraud.

Empirical research has confirmed that fraud is a major problem plaguing the charitable sector. A recent study by four accounting professors estimates that approximately one of every eight dollars contributed to charitable organizations in the United States

1. J. Markon, "Ex-Chief of Local United Way Sentenced," *Washington Post* (online), 15 May 2004.

is stolen each year, resulting in annual losses to those organizations of $40 billion.[2] That study found that 95 percent of the losses suffered by charities result from the theft of cash and that the culprits are typically involved in the charity's financial functions. "They're usually done by someone in the financial area—the treasurer, the bookkeeper, the signer of checks—who knows how to avoid getting caught."[3]

A common theme of the frauds that have plagued charities in recent years has been inadequate or nonexistent internal controls. Understandably, charitable organizations make every effort to minimize their administrative expenses, including their accounting and control-related expenditures. For example, an internal study by United Way of America in 2002 found that fewer than 15 percent of the organization's local chapters had invested the time and other resources to develop written policies to address fundamental accounting and control issues.[4] No doubt, the porous nature of charities' internal control systems not only encourages opportunistic individuals to take advantage of those organizations but also makes it difficult to detect ongoing frauds.

In 2004, PricewaterhouseCoopers released a 200-page report that detailed the results of a seven-month investigative audit of the embezzlement loss suffered by the East Lansing, Michigan, chapter of United Way. That report castigated United Way for failing to implement some of the most rudimentary control procedures intended to prevent thefts by organizational insiders. "The audit, more than seven months in the making, gives a scathing review, depicting the charity as a place where top managers were permitted to dip into the millions of dollars in public donations with little or no oversight."[5]

According to *The New York Times*, the individual who embezzled the funds from the East Lansing chapter "did not need to be a criminal mastermind to succeed in the theft."[6] Instead, that individual took advantage of the chapter's lack of proper internal controls and stole the funds at will. "She simply wrote checks to herself, forging the signatures of the required cosigners and destroying the canceled checks when the bank mailed them back. No one noticed this because she also kept the organization's books."[7]

Similar to the other United Way fraudsters, the executive who embezzled several hundred thousand dollars from the Westchester, New York, United Way chapter used a simple scam to "rip off" her organization. The executive endorsed checks made payable to United Way from local donors and then deposited those checks in her personal bank account. The fraud was uncovered when a bank teller reported her to local authorities. In commenting on the embezzlement scheme, the local district attorney noted, "There was most certainly a total lack of supervision which permitted this to occur."[8] The president of that chapter expressed a different point of view. "As in the case of virtually any organization, our system of internal control procedures, no matter how strong, is based on trust."[9]

Compounding the weakness of the internal control systems of charities such as United Way is the absence of strong regulatory oversight for the charitable sector.

---

2. S. Strom, "Report Sketches Crime Costing Billions: Theft From Charities," *The New York Times* (online), 29 March 2008.
3. *Ibid.*
4. S. Strom, "Questions Arise on Accounting at United Way," *The New York Times* (online), 19 November 2002.
5. J. Salmon and P. Whoriskey, "Audit Excoriates United Way Leadership," *Washington Post* (online), 25 June 2004.
6. S. Strom, "Guilty Plea Due Today in Big United Way Theft," *The New York Times* (online), 6 February 2003.
7. *Ibid.*
8. J. Steinberg, "United Way Accountant Admits $282,500 Theft," *The New York Times* (online), 19 May 1992.
9. *Ibid.*

The regulatory infrastructure for charities is weak and enforcement is inconsistent. Unlike public companies that are overseen by the Securities and Exchange Commission (SEC), charitable organizations are not subject to direct oversight by a federal agency. Federal oversight of charities involves principally an annual information filing with the Internal Revenue Service (IRS).

Similar to other tax-exempt organizations, most charities are required to submit a Form 990 to the IRS each year. Among many other required disclosures in Form 990, charities must report their total annual revenues and the principal sources of those revenues, fundraising expenses, the salaries of highly paid executives, and losses due to theft, embezzlement, and other fraudulent activities. The latter disclosure was added to Form 990 beginning in 2008 as a direct consequence of the mounting theft losses being incurred by charities. A searchable database of the approximately two million Form 990s filed each year with the IRS is available at www.guidestar.org.

Although there is no federal agency with a direct responsibility to regulate charities, many states have established such an agency. Nevertheless, these state agencies tend to be underfunded and ineffectual as a result. "While most states have agencies [overseeing charitable organizations], most are inactive, ineffective or significantly understaffed."[10]

Following the passage of the Sarbanes-Oxley Act in 2002, some charities adopted internal control reforms and other provisions included in that federal statute. Not satisfied, prominent members of the philanthropic community have lobbied state and federal legislators to pass legislation that would require charities to implement a comprehensive reform agenda similar to that mandated by Sarbanes-Oxley. "The American government can no longer make a plausible argument that charities don't deserve the type of scrutiny that the for-profit sector warrants. Quite simply, the charitable sector is much too large to warrant the continued disinterest our government has shown it."[11]

One proponent of regulatory reform has suggested that charities be required to obtain a "seal of approval" of some type to reassure donors that their contributions are not being misused.[12] In fact, a common measure included in proposed regulatory reforms for charities is a requirement that they be subject to an annual independent audit by an accounting firm.

> *Only a few states currently require annual financial audits of nonprofit corporations . . . Independent financial audits have become such a fundamental and essential test of the financial soundness of any corporate enterprise that all best practice codes of nonprofit governance require that every nonprofit corporation with substantial assets or annual revenue should be audited annually by an independent auditing firm.*[13]

California and Massachusetts are examples of states that have passed legislation in recent years to require certain charities to be audited annually. California's Nonprofit Integrity Act of 2004 requires charities with annual gross revenues exceeding $2 million to be audited. The comparable state statute in Massachusetts requires charities with annual revenues exceeding $500,000 or total assets greater than

---

10. A. Rothschild, "Public Scrutiny of Exempt Organizations," www.abanet.org/rppt/publications/estate/2004/2/Rothschild-PublicScr.pdf.

11. T. Stamp, "Why Does Our Government Ignore Charities?" *Charity Navigator* (online), 14 October 2002.

12. W. Muller, "Charities and Anti-Money Laundering: Is a 'Seal of Approval' the answer?" *Trusts and Trustees* 14 (May 2008): 259–271.

13. T. Silk, "Good Governance Practices for 501 (c)(3) Organizations: Should the IRS Become Further Involved?" *International Journal of Not-for-Profit Law*, 2007 (Vol. 10), 40.

$5 million to be audited. These same charities are also required by the Massachusetts law to establish an audit committee.

Not all charity reform advocates believe that mandatory independent audits would remedy the problems facing the charitable sector. These parties point out that several of the charities that suffered large losses due to embezzlement and other fraudulent schemes had been audited by accounting firms. One such charity was United Way of America, which was audited by Arthur Andersen during the time frame that Aramony was embezzling from the organization. Andersen was widely criticized for failing to detect Aramony's fraud. The managing partner of the Andersen office that audited the organization responded to that criticism by insisting that United Way officials had intentionally concealed the fraudulent activities from the auditors.[14]

The auditors of the East Lansing, Michigan, United Way chapter that suffered an embezzlement loss of $1.9 million were also criticized for failing to uncover that fraud. The audit partner who supervised the annual audits of that chapter staunchly defended himself and his subordinates. "This [embezzlement scheme] went on prior to our being engaged in 1999, and when you have fraud going on a long time, it's hard to find because it has become the norm [within the organization]."[15]

## Questions

1. Identify and briefly describe fundamental and cost-effective internal controls that charitable organizations could implement to reduce their exposure to theft losses.
2. Do CPA firms have a responsibility to perform audits of charitable organizations for reduced or lower than normal audit fees? Defend your answer. Other than audit fees, what other benefits do accounting firms accrue by auditing a charity?
3. Identify unique or uncommon audit risk factors posed by a charity. How should accounting firms modify their audits to address these risk factors?

14. J. Garnatz, "United Way Cleaning House Nationally, Doing Well Locally," *St. Petersburg Times*, 17 April 1992, 11.

15. Strom, "Guilty Plea Due Today," *The New York Times*.

**CASE 3.4**

# Triton Energy Ltd.

Bill Lee retired in the mid-1990s from Triton Energy after leading the Dallas-based oil and gas exploration firm through three turbulent decades. During Lee's tenure, Triton discovered large oil and gas deposits in several remote sites scattered around the globe. Although adept at finding oil, Triton's small size hampered the company's efforts to exploit its oil and gas properties. Major oil firms, large metropolitan banks, and other well-heeled investors often refused to participate in the development of promising oil and gas properties discovered by Triton. Why? Because they were unnerved by Bill Lee's reputation as a run-and-gun, devil-may-care "wildcatter."

To compensate for Triton's limited access to deep-pocketed financiers, Lee resorted to less conventional strategies to achieve his firm's financial objectives. In the early 1980s, Triton struck oil in northwestern France at a site overlooked by many major oil firms. To expedite its drilling efforts and to gain an advantage over competitors that had begun snapping up leases on nearby properties, Triton formed an alliance with the state-owned petroleum firm, *Compagnie Francaise des Petroles*. This partnership proved very beneficial for Triton since it gave the firm ready access to the governmental agency that regulated France's petroleum industry. A business journalist commented on Triton's political skills as a key factor in its successful French venture. "Triton's success is due not just to sound geology but also to good politics. It has established a close relationship with the all-powerful French energy administration, which issues all new drilling permits."[1]

Triton's policy of working closely with government agencies and bureaucrats landed the company in trouble with U.S. authorities during the 1990s. Charges that Triton bribed foreign officials to obtain favorable treatment from governmental agencies led to investigations of the company's overseas operations by the U.S. Department of Justice and the Securities and Exchange Commission (SEC). These investigations centered on alleged violations of the Foreign Corrupt Practices Act of 1977, including the accounting and internal control stipulations of that federal statute.

## A Brief History of a Texas Wildcatter

L. R. Wiley founded Triton Energy Corporation, the predecessor of Triton Energy Ltd., in 1962. At the time, industry analysts estimated that there were approximately 30,000 businesses involved in oil and gas exploration, most of which were small "Mom and Pop" operations. The volatile ups and downs of the petroleum industry dramatically thinned the ranks of oil and gas producers during the 1960s and 1970s. The oil bust of the 1980s wiped out most of the surviving firms in the industry. Fewer than 20 significant "independent" oil and gas producers remained in business by 1985.[2] Triton Energy was one of those firms.

Bill Lee joined Triton in the early 1960s and was promoted to chief executive officer (CEO) in 1966. Under Lee, Triton competed in the rough-and-tumble business

1. P. Kemezis and W. Glasgall, "A Texas Wildcatter Cashes In on French Oil," *Business Week*, 13 May 1985, 106–107.

2. The dominant companies in the oil and gas industry include such firms as ExxonMobil and ConocoPhillips. These firms are often referred to as the "majors" or simply as "Big Oil."

of oil and gas exploration by employing a rough-and-tumble business strategy. Lee recognized that the large domestic oil firms in the U.S. had already identified the prime drilling sites in this country. So, Lee decided that Triton should focus its exploration efforts in other oil-producing countries, particularly in regions of those countries largely overlooked by "Big Oil." During Lee's tenure with Triton, the company launched exploration ventures in Argentina, Australia, Canada, Colombia, France, Indonesia, Malaysia, New Zealand, and Thailand.

In the early 1970s, Triton discovered a large oil and gas field in the Gulf of Thailand. Recurring disagreements and confrontations with the Thai government stymied Triton from developing that field for more than 10 years. Lee's experience with the Thai government taught him an important lesson: If Triton's exploration ventures were to be successful in foreign countries, the company had to foster good relationships with key governmental officials in those countries.

Lee created Triton Indonesia, Inc., a wholly owned subsidiary of Triton Energy, to develop an oil field that the company acquired in Indonesia in 1988. This oil field, located on the island of Sumatra and known as the Enim Field, belonged to a Dutch firm in the 1930s. At the time, Sumatra was a protectorate of the Netherlands. When the Japanese invaded Indonesia during World War II, retreating Dutch soldiers dynamited the Enim Field to render it useless to Japan. Over the next four decades, the dense jungles of Sumatra reclaimed the oil field. In the mid-1980s, Lee learned of the potential oil reserves still buried in the Enim Field. A small Canadian company owned the drilling rights for those reserves. Triton wrested control of the drilling rights from that company in a protracted legal battle. After investing several million dollars and several years of hard work in the Enim Field, Triton began pumping thousands of barrels each day from the long dormant oil reservoir.

Triton's strategy of working closely with officials of the Indonesian government contributed greatly to the success of the Enim Field project. To strengthen Triton's ties to those officials, the company hired a French citizen, Roland Siouffi, as a consultant. Siouffi, who had resided in Indonesia for nearly three decades, served as Triton's liaison with Indonesian tax authorities and with governmental agencies that oversaw the country's oil and gas industry.

In 1991, Triton struck black gold again, this time in Colombia. Several large firms had drilled exploratory wells in the foothills of the Andes Mountains that stretch across Colombia. Those wells came up dry. Nevertheless, geological reports convinced Lee and other Triton executives that the region contained large but well-hidden oil reservoirs. Lee and his colleagues were right. In 1991, Triton pinpointed huge oil and gas deposits trapped in complex geological structures lying beneath the Colombian jungles. These reservoirs were the largest discovered in the western hemisphere since the 1968 Prudhoe Bay discovery in Alaska. Again, Triton established close working relationships with governmental officials, this time in Colombia, to develop the new oil field.

On the strength of Triton's Indonesian and Colombian oil strikes, the company's stock skied from a few dollars per share in the late 1980s to more than $50 per share in 1991.[3] Triton's common stock ranked as one of the 10 best performing stocks on the New York Stock Exchange in 1991. Despite the company's obvious knack for finding oil, many Wall Street analysts refused to recommend Triton's common stock. Rumors of the bribing of foreign officials, allegations of creative accounting methods, and intimations of other corporate wrongdoings soured these analysts on Triton. One Wall

3. D. Galant, "The Home Runs of 1991," *Institutional Investor*, March 1992, 51–56.

Street portfolio manager succinctly summed up his view of Triton. "Bill Lee is not a guy I'd like to see running an oil company I had invested in."[4]

The allegations of abusive management practices and creative accounting caught up with Triton in the mid-1990s. Those allegations persuaded the U.S. Department of Justice and the SEC to probe Triton's ties to government officials in foreign countries. The principal focus of this investigation was the relationships that Triton executives had cultivated with Indonesian officials during the development of the Enim Field.

The central issue addressed by federal authorities while investigating Triton was whether the company had violated a seldom-enforced federal statute, the Foreign Corrupt Practices Act of 1977 (FCPA). The FCPA was a by-product of the scandal-ridden Watergate era of the 1970s. During the Watergate investigations, the Office of the Special Prosecutor uncovered numerous bribes, kickbacks, and other payments made by U.S. corporations to officials of foreign governments to initiate or maintain business relationships. Widespread public disapproval compelled Congress to pass the FCPA, which criminalizes most such payments. The FCPA also requires U.S. companies to maintain internal control systems that provide reasonable assurance of discovering improper foreign payments.

> *The accounting provisions [of the FCPA] were enacted by Congress along with the anti-bribery provisions because Congress concluded that almost all bribery of foreign officials by American corporations was covered up in the corporations' books and that the requirement for accurate records and adequate internal controls would deter bribery.*[5]

Exhibit 1 summarizes the FCPA's key anti-bribery and internal control requirements.

**EXHIBIT 1**

KEY PROVISIONS OF THE FOREIGN CORRUPT PRACTICES ACT

**Anti-Bribery Provisions:**

Section 30 (A) of the Securities Exchange Act, the anti-bribery provision of the FCPA, prohibits any issuer . . . or any officer, director, employee, or agent of an issuer from making use of instruments or interstate commerce corruptly to pay, offer to pay, promise to pay, or to authorize the payment of any money, gift, or promise to give, anything of value to any foreign official for purposes of influencing any act or decision of such foreign official in his official capacity, or inducing such foreign official to do or omit to do any act in violation of the lawful duty of such official, or inducing such foreign official to use his influence with a foreign government or instrumentality thereof to affect or influence any act or decision of such government or instrumentality, in order to assist such issuer in obtaining or retaining business for or with, or directing business to, any person.

**Recordkeeping and Internal Control Provisions:**

Section 13(b)(2) of the Securities Exchange Act is comprised of two accounting provisions referred to as the "books and records" and "internal controls" provisions. These accounting provisions were enacted as part of the FCPA to strengthen the accuracy of records and to "promote the reliability and completeness of financial information that issuers are required to file with the Commission or disseminate to investors pursuant to the Securities Exchange Act." Section 13(b)(2)(A) requires issuers to make and keep books, records, and accounts that accurately and fairly reflect the transactions and dispositions of their assets. Section 13(b)(2)(B) requires issuers to devise and maintain a system of internal accounting controls sufficient

4. T. Mack, "Lucky Bill Lee," *Forbes*, 14 October 1991, 50.

5. This quotation and the remaining quotations in this case, unless indicated otherwise, were drawn from the following source: Securities and Exchange Commission, *Accounting and Auditing Enforcement Release No. 889*, 27 February 1997.

**EXHIBIT 1—*continued***

KEY PROVISIONS OF THE FOREIGN CORRUPT PRACTICES ACT

to provide reasonable assurances that, among other things, transactions are executed in accordance with management's general or specific authorization and that transactions are recorded as necessary to permit presentation of financial statements in conformity with GAAP and to maintain accountability for assets.

Source: Securities and Exchange Commission, *Accounting and Auditing Enforcement Release No. 889*, 27 February 1997.

## Indonesian Charges

Triton Energy's former controller sued the company in 1991, claiming that he had been fired in 1989 after refusing to sign off on the company's Form 10-K registration statement. The controller refused to sign off on the 1989 10-K because it failed to disclose "bribery, kickbacks and payments to government officials, customs officials, auditors, inspectors and other persons in positions of responsibility in Indonesia, Columbia, and Argentina."[6] The controller acknowledged that Triton's senior management had not authorized the payments but insisted that the FCPA required such payments to be disclosed in the company's 10-K. Before the case went to trial, Triton officials dismissed the charges, suggesting that they were "totally without merit."[7] During the trial, considerable evidence surfaced supporting the controller's allegations. A memo written by Triton's former internal audit director contained the most damaging of this evidence.

In late 1989, Triton management sent the company's new internal audit director to review and report on Triton Indonesia's operations. Upon returning, the internal audit director filed a lengthy memorandum with several Triton executives, including the company's president and at least two key vice presidents. Exhibit 2 presents selected excerpts from that memo. The memo documented extensive wrongdoing by employees and officials of Triton Indonesia. At one point, the frustrated internal audit director complained that the subsidiary's accounting records were so misleading it was impossible "to tell a real transaction from one that has been faked."[8] After reading the memo, the alarmed Triton executives ordered that all copies be collected and destroyed. Despite these instructions, one copy of the memo survived and became a key exhibit in the lawsuit filed against Triton by its former controller.

**EXHIBIT 2**

SELECTED EXCERPTS FROM THE INTERNAL AUDIT MEMO REGARDING OPERATIONS OF TRITON INDONESIA

"In Indonesia, I found myself in a country of state supported corruption."

"I was told that we pay between $1,000 and $1,900 per month just to get our invoice to Pertamina [the state-owned Indonesian oil company] paid."

"We must pay people in customs in order to get our equipment off the dock so that it can be used in operations."

"What is worse, and this is extremely confidential, is that we paid the auditors in order to have their audit exceptions taken care of. . . . This part is particularly bad to me. I had hoped that at least the Indonesian auditors were honest."

Source: A. Zipser, "Crude Grab?" *Barron's*, 25 May 1992, 12–15.

6. A. Zipser, "Crude Grab?" *Barron's*, 25 May 1992, 15.
7. Mack, "Lucky Bill Lee."
8. A. Zipser, "Trials of Triton," *Barron's*, 26 July 1993, 14–15.

Another former Triton accountant also corroborated many of the former con ler's allegations. This individual, who had previously served as a Price Waterho auditor, joined Triton Indonesia's accounting staff in early 1989. Almost immediat the accountant discovered serious internal control deficiencies in the subsidiary's erations. Inadequate segregation of key accounting and control responsibilities ( ated an environment in which individuals could easily perpetrate and then conc fraudulent transactions. The accountant's most serious charge regarding his former employer involved an admission made by his superior. The superior told the accountant that auditors from Pertamina, the state-owned Indonesian oil firm, had been "bought" by Triton. Among other responsibilities, these auditors regularly reviewed Triton Indonesia's tax records. "I understood the words 'buy the audit' to mean bribe Pertamina auditors. To me, it represented an illegal transaction, the proposal of an illegal transaction."[9]

Co-workers reportedly shunned the accountant after he objected to such conduct. A few weeks later, the accountant resigned. Because he was concerned that his brief tenure with Triton Indonesia might blight his professional career, the accountant filed a 37-page report with the U.S. embassy in Indonesia. That report documented questionable transactions, events, and circumstances he had encountered during his employment with Triton Indonesia. In the report, the accountant described his former superiors as "unprincipled, unethical liars."[10]

Peat Marwick served as Triton Energy's audit firm over a span of more than two decades beginning in 1969. During the planning phase for the 1991 audit, Peat Marwick learned of the memorandum written by Triton's former internal audit director. A Peat Marwick auditor questioned client management concerning the unlawful activities allegedly documented in that memo. Company officials convinced Peat Marwick that all copies of the memo had been destroyed. A Triton executive then prepared a memo responding to Peat Marwick's inquiries. This second memo omitted many key details of questionable activities documented by the internal audit director. At a subsequent meeting with Peat Marwick representatives, Triton management directly refuted the principal allegation reportedly included in the internal audit memo. Several Triton officials told Peat Marwick that there was no evidence Triton Indonesia officers or employees had bribed Indonesian auditors.[11]

In the summer of 1992, the jury that heard the lawsuit filed by Triton's former controller ruled in his favor and awarded him a $124 million judgment. That judgment ranks as one of the largest wrongful termination awards ever handed down by a U.S. court.[12] Following the trial, the surviving copy of the memo written by Triton's former internal audit director became a road map for federal authorities to follow while investigating Triton's abusive management and accounting practices.

## "Dirty" Payments

Triton Indonesia negotiated a contract with the Indonesian government for the right to develop the Enim Field. This contract made the nation's state-owned oil company,

---

9. Zipser, "Crude Grab?"

10. *Ibid.*, 14.

11. In 1992, Triton Energy retained Price Waterhouse to serve as its audit firm, replacing Peat Marwick.

12. The judgment was subsequently reduced in a private, out-of-court settlement involving the former controller, Triton, and Triton's insurer. The former controller received approximately $10 million from Triton and an undisclosed additional sum from Triton's insurer. Shortly before the jury verdict was announced, the former controller had offered to settle the case for $5 million.

Pertamina, a partner in the project. The agreement gave the Triton subsidiary operational and financial control over the joint venture but allowed Pertamina to review and override all-important decisions involving the project. Another feature of the agreement required Triton Indonesia to transport oil recovered from the Enim Field through Pertamina's pipelines. Finally, the agreement obligated Triton Indonesia to pay significant taxes to the Indonesian government on the basis of the Enim Field's production.

Two Indonesian audit teams periodically examined Triton Indonesia's accounting and tax records. Pertamina auditors reviewed the accounting records to ensure that the Triton subsidiary complied with its contractual obligations to Pertamina. Auditors from the Indonesian Ministry of Finance and Pertamina auditors inspected the tax records to ensure that the proper taxes were being paid to the Indonesian government. The Ministry of Finance auditors were known as the "BPKP" auditors since they worked for the agency's audit branch, *Badan Pengawasan Keuangan Dan Pembangunan.*

Pertamina and BPKP auditors concluded a joint tax audit of a Triton Indonesia operating unit in May 1989. The audit revealed that the unit owed approximately \$618,000 of additional taxes. Of this total, \$385,000 involved taxes levied by Pertamina auditors, while the remaining \$233,000 were taxes assessed by BPKP auditors. Two officers of Triton Indonesia discussed this matter with Roland Siouffi, the longtime Indonesian resident hired the year before to serve as a liaison with government officials. Siouffi then met with two key members of the Pertamina audit team. Siouffi arranged to pay these two individuals \$160,000 to eliminate the additional tax assessment of \$385,000 proposed by the Pertamina auditors. Triton Indonesia paid \$165,000 to a company controlled by Siouffi in August 1989.[13] A few weeks later, that company paid \$120,000 and \$40,000, respectively, to the two Pertamina auditors. Triton Indonesia's controller prepared false documentation for the payment made to Siouffi's company. The documentation indicated that the payment was for seismic data purchased for the Enim Field.

In August 1989, a BPKP auditor reminded Triton Indonesia officials that their firm still owed \$233,000 of taxes. An executive of Triton Indonesia discussed this matter with Siouffi. After meeting with the BPKP auditor, Siouffi told Triton Indonesia's management that in exchange for \$20,000 the auditor would reduce the \$233,000 tax bill to \$155,000. Triton Indonesia processed a \$22,500 payment to another company controlled by Siouffi, who then paid the BPKP auditor \$20,000. Triton Indonesia's controller prepared false documentation indicating that the payment to Siouffi's company was for equipment repairs at the Enim Field made by Siouffi's employees. Following the payments made to the Pertamina and BPKP auditors by Siouffi, Triton Indonesia received letters from the two audit teams indicating that they had resolved the issues raised during the tax audit.

Throughout 1989 and 1990, Triton Indonesia continued to channel improper payments to various government officials through Roland Siouffi. Triton Indonesia fabricated false documentation to "sanitize" each payment for accounting purposes. The SEC identified \$450,000 of such payments recorded in Triton Indonesia's accounting records.

Triton Indonesia officers periodically briefed key members of Triton Energy's management regarding the payoffs funneled through Siouffi. In these briefings, the Triton Energy officers also learned of the false accounting entries and documentation prepared to conceal the true nature of the payments. "The Triton Energy officers expressed concern about such practices which they had neither directed nor authorized, but failed to require Triton Indonesia to discontinue those practices." At one point, a Triton Indonesia officer directly told Triton Energy's president that illicit payments were

13. Triton Indonesia paid Siouffi a "commission" for the illegal payments he funneled to government officials. In this case, the commission was \$5,000.

In February 1997, the Company and the Securities and Exchange Commission (SEC) concluded a settlement of the SEC's investigation of possible violations of the Foreign Corrupt Practices Act in connection with Triton Indonesia, Inc.'s former operations in Indonesia. The investigation was settled on a "consent decree" basis in which the Company neither admitted nor denied charges made by the SEC that the Company violated the Securities Exchange Act of 1934 when Triton Indonesia, Inc. made certain payments in 1989 and 1990 to a consultant advising Triton Indonesia, Inc. on its relations with the Indonesian state oil company and tax authority, misbooked the payments and failed to maintain adequate internal controls. Under the terms of the settlement, the Company's subsidiary, TEC, was permanently enjoined from future violations of the books and records and internal control provisions of the Securities Exchange Act of 1934 and paid a civil monetary penalty of $300,000. In 1996, the Company was advised that the Department of Justice had concluded a parallel inquiry without taking any action.

**EXHIBIT 3**

TRITON ENERGY'S DISCLOSURE OF SEC SETTLEMENT IN 1996 FINANCIAL STATEMENT FOOTNOTES

being made to Siouffi. The president responded "that he had worked in another foreign country and understood that such things had to be done in certain environments."[14]

## SEC Sends a Message

In 1997, the SEC climaxed a four-year investigation of Triton Indonesia and its parent company by issuing a series of enforcement releases. Those releases charged Triton and its executives with violating the anti-bribery, accounting, and control requirements of the FCPA. Without admitting or denying these charges, six officers of Triton Energy and Triton Indonesia signed consent decrees that prohibited them from violating federal securities laws in the future. The consent decrees also imposed a $300,000 fine on Triton Energy and fines of $35,000 and $50,000 on two former Triton Indonesia officers. Exhibit 3 presents the footnote appended to Triton Energy's 1996 financial statements that described the company's settlement with the SEC.

Although Triton Energy did not authorize the improper payments and the bogus accounting for the payments, the SEC sharply criticized two executives who were aware of the practices and allowed them to continue unchecked.

> *The senior management of Triton Energy, ______ and ______, simply acknowledged the existence of such practices and treated them as a cost of doing business in a foreign jurisdiction. The toleration of such practices is inimical to a fair business environment and undermines public confidence in the integrity of public corporations.*

The SEC publicly conceded that it intended the Triton case to send a "message" to corporate managers. SEC officials noted that the case "underscored the responsibilities of corporate management in the area of foreign payments"[15] and impressed upon U.S. companies that "it's not O.K. to pay bribes as long as you don't get caught."[16]

Prior to the Triton case, more than 10 years had elapsed since the SEC had filed FCPA-related charges against a public company. During the late 1990s, frequent allegations of improper foreign payments by U.S. corporations prompted the SEC to initiate several FCPA investigations. The SEC attributed the apparent increase in such

---

14. Apparently, the attention drawn to the illicit payments by the lawsuit filed by Triton Energy's former controller caused Triton Indonesia to stop making those payments.

15. *Securities Regulation and Law Report*, "SEC Official Predicts More FCPA Cases in Near Future," Vol. 29, No. 18 (2 May 1997), 607.

16. L. Eaton, "Triton Energy Settles Indonesia Bribery Case for $300,000," *The New York Times*, 28 February 1997, D2.

payments to the increasingly global nature of U.S. corporations.[17] Each year, additional U.S. companies attempt to establish footholds in emerging markets. Funneling unlawful payments to officials of foreign countries is often the most effective method of breaking down entry barriers to those markets.

The growing sophistication of illicit foreign payment schemes complicates the SEC's efforts to rigorously enforce the FCPA. In fact, critics of the FCPA suggest that it is practically unenforceable except in the most blatant cases. As one journalist noted, the days of "bulky cash payments in large sealed envelopes" are long past.

> *Now the bribes, kickbacks, and "facilitating payments," such as those described in Triton Energy's internal memorandum, more often get channeled through expensive "consultants," dummy charities, and construction projects that never seem to materialize.*[18]

Many corporate executives have lobbied against enforcement of the FCPA. These executives maintain that the federal law places U.S. multinational companies at a significant competitive disadvantage relative to other multinational firms. A member of President Clinton's administration supported this point of view when he observed that the U.S. is the only country that has "criminalized bribery of foreign officials."[19, 20]

## EPILOGUE

Bill Lee was never directly implicated in the Indonesian payments scandal and retired as Triton Energy's CEO in January 1993. Thomas Finck, who came to Triton after the Indonesian scandal, replaced Lee as Triton's CEO. In 1996, a journalist noted that Triton's new CEO seemed to be employing some of his predecessor's "old tricks."[21] One of Finck's first major decisions was to reorganize Triton Energy as a subsidiary of an offshore holding company headquartered in the Cayman Islands. Finck reported that moving Triton's headquarters to the Cayman Islands would significantly reduce the company's tax burden. Critics placed a different spin on the decision. They suggested that the company's desire "to avoid scrutiny under the U.S. Foreign Corrupt Practices Act" likely motivated the move to the Caymans.[22]

Triton Energy sold its Indonesian subsidiary in 1996 but under Finck continued its high-risk strategy of searching for obscure and overlooked oil fields across the globe. Depressed oil prices caused the value of Triton's sizable oil reserves to fall dramatically during the 1990s, leaving the company in a financial lurch in early 1998. Company officials announced that Triton was for sale and retained an investment banking firm to find a potential buyer. When a buyer could not be found, Triton announced plans to restructure its operations and to continue as an independent entity. That announcement caused Triton's stock to plummet to its lowest level in several years and prompted Thomas Finck to resign as the company's CEO. A few years later, in the summer of 2001, Triton Energy's tumultuous history as an independent firm ended when Amerada Hess purchased the company for a reported $2.7 billion.

17. *Securities Regulation and Law Report*, "SEC Official Predicts More FCPA Cases."

18. A. Zipser, "A Rarely Enforced Law," *Barron's*, 25 May 1992, 14.

19. *Ibid.*

20. The FCPA was initially unclear regarding whether or not so-called "facilitating payments" qualified as bribes and thus were illegal under that federal statute. Generally, bribes are significant amounts paid to foreign governmental officials to secure or retain business, while facilitating payments are relatively modest and routine payments typically made to lower-ranking governmental officials to expedite or "facilitate" business transactions. In 1988, the FCPA was amended to address that issue. As amended, facilitating payments made to encourage "routine governmental action" are not covered by the FCPA.

21. A. Zipser, "New Management, Old Tricks as Oil Firm Heads for Caymans," *Barron's*, 25 March 1996, 10.

22. *Ibid.*

## Questions

1. Identify the key factors that complicate the audit of a multinational company.
2. Identify specific control activities that Triton Energy could have implemented for Triton Indonesia and its other foreign subsidiaries to minimize the likelihood of illegal payments to government officials. Would these control activities have been cost-effective?
3. Does an audit firm of a multinational company have a responsibility to apply audit procedures intended to determine whether the client has complied with the FCPA? Defend your answer.
4. If a company employs a high-risk business strategy, does that necessarily increase the inherent risk and control risk components of audit risk for the company? Explain.
5. What responsibility, if any, does an accountant of a public company have when he or she discovers that the company has violated a law? How does the accountant's position on the company's employment hierarchy affect that responsibility, if at all? What responsibility does an auditor of a public company have if he or she discovers illegal acts by the client? Does the auditor's position on his or her firm's employment hierarchy affect this responsibility?
6. If the citizens of certain foreign countries believe that the payment of bribes is an acceptable business practice, is it appropriate for U.S. companies to challenge that belief when doing business in those countries? Defend your answer.

**CASE 3.5**

# Goodner Brothers, Inc.

"Woody, that's $2,400 you owe me. Okay? We're straight on that?"

"Yeah, yeah. I got you."

"And you'll pay me back by next Friday?"

"Al. I said I'd pay you back by Friday, didn't I?"

"Just checkin'."

Borrowing money from a friend can strain even the strongest relationship. When the borrowed money will soon be plunked down on a blackjack table, the impact on the friendship can be devastating.

Woody Robinson and Al Hunt were sitting side by side at a blackjack table in Tunica, Mississippi. The two longtime friends and their wives were spending their summer vacations together as they had several times. After three days of loitering in the casinos that line the banks of the Mississippi River 20 miles south of Memphis, Woody found himself hitting up his friend for loans. By the end of the vacation, Woody owed Al nearly $5,000. The question facing Woody was how he would repay his friend.[1]

## Two Pals Named Woody and Al

Woodrow Wilson Robinson and Albert Leroy Hunt lived and worked in Huntington, West Virginia, a city of 60,000 tucked in the westernmost corner of the state. The blue-collar city sits on the south bank of the Ohio River. Ohio is less than one mile away across the river, while Kentucky can be reached by making a 10-minute drive westward on Interstate 64. Woody and Al were born six days apart in a small hospital in eastern Kentucky, were best friends throughout grade school and high school, and roomed together for four years at college. A few months after they graduated with business management degrees, each served as the other's best man at their respective weddings.

Following graduation, Al went to work for Curcio's Auto Supply on the western outskirts of Huntington, a business owned by his future father-in-law. Curcio's sold lawnmowers, bicycles, and automotive parts and supplies, including tires and batteries, the business's two largest revenue producers. Curcio's also installed the automotive parts it sold, provided oil and lube service, and performed small engine repairs.

Within weeks of going to work for Curcio's, Al helped Woody land a job with a large tire wholesaler that was Curcio's largest supplier. Goodner Brothers, Inc., sold tires of all types and sizes from 14 locations scattered from southern New York to northwestern South Carolina and from central Ohio to the Delaware shore. Goodner concentrated its operations in midsized cities such as Huntington, West Virginia; Lynchburg, Virginia; Harrisburg, Pennsylvania; and Youngstown, Ohio, home to the company's headquarters. Founded in 1969 by two brothers, T. J. and Ross Goodner, nearly three decades later Goodner Brothers' annual sales approached $40 million. The Goodner family dominated the company's operations. T. J. served as the company's chairman of

1. The central facts of this case were drawn from a legal opinion issued in the 1990s. The names of the actual parties involved in the case and the relevant locations have been changed. Additionally, certain of the factual circumstances reported in this case are fictionalized accounts of background material disclosed in the legal opinion.

the board and chief executive officer (CEO), while Ross was the chief operating officer (COO). Four second-generation Goodners also held key positions in the company.

Goodner purchased tires from several large manufacturers and then wholesaled those tires to auto supply stores and other retailers that had auto supply departments. Goodner's customers included Sears, Wal-Mart, Kmart, and dozens of smaller retail chains. The company also purchased discontinued tires from manufacturers, large retailers, and other wholesalers and then resold those tires at cut-rate prices to school districts, municipalities, and to companies with small fleets of automobiles.

Goodner Brothers hired Woody to work as a sales representative for its Huntington location. Woody sold tires to more than 80 customers in his sales region that stretched from the west side of Huntington into eastern Kentucky and north into Ohio. Woody, who worked strictly on a commission basis, was an effective and successful salesman. Unfortunately, a bad habit that he acquired during his college days gradually developed into a severe problem. By the mid-1990s, a gambling compulsion threatened to wreck the young salesman's career and personal life.

Woody bet on any and all types of sporting events, including baseball and football games, horse races, and boxing matches. He also spent hundreds of dollars each month buying lottery tickets and lost increasingly large sums on frequent gambling excursions with his friend Al. By the summer of 1996 when Woody, Al, and their wives visited Tunica, Mississippi, Woody's financial condition was desperate. He owed more than $50,000 to the various bookies with whom he placed bets, was falling behind on his mortgage payments, and had "maxed out" several credit cards. Worst of all, two bookies to whom Woody owed several thousand dollars were demanding payment and had begun making menacing remarks that alluded to his wife, Rachelle.

## Woody Finds a Solution

Upon returning to Huntington in early July 1996, Woody struck upon an idea to bail him out of his financial problems: he decided to begin stealing from his employer, Goodner Brothers. Other than a few traffic tickets, Woody had never been in trouble with law enforcement authorities. Yet, in Woody's mind, he had no other reasonable alternatives. At this point, resorting to stealing seemed the lesser of two evils.

One reason Woody decided to steal from his employer was the ease with which it could be done. After several years with Goodner, Woody was very familiar with the company's sloppy accounting practices and lax control over its inventory and other assets. Goodner's executives preached one dominant theme to their sales staff: "Volume, volume, volume." Goodner achieved its ambitious sales goals by undercutting competitors' prices. The company's dominant market share in the geographical region it served came at a high price. Goodner's gross profit margin averaged 17.4 percent, considerably below the mean gross profit margin of 24.1 percent for comparable tire wholesalers. To compensate for its low gross profit margin, Goodner scrimped on operating expenses, including expenditures on internal control measures.

The company staffed its 14 sales outlets with skeletal crews of 10 to 12 employees. A sales manager supervised the other employees at each outlet and also worked a sales district. The remaining staff typically included two sales representatives, a receptionist who doubled as a secretary, a bookkeeper, and five to seven employees who delivered tires and worked in the unit's inventory warehouse. Goodner's Huntington location had two storage areas, a small warehouse adjacent to the sales office and a larger storage area two miles away that had previously housed a discount grocery store. Other than padlocks, Goodner provided little security for its tire inventory, which typically ranged from $300,000 to $700,000 for each sales outlet.

Instead of an extensive system of internal controls, T. J. and Ross Goodner relied heavily on the honesty and integrity of the employees they hired. Central to the company's employment policy was never to hire someone unless that individual could provide three strong references, preferably from reputable individuals with some connection to Goodner Brothers. Besides following up on employment references, Goodner Brothers obtained thorough background checks on prospective employees from local detective agencies. For more than two decades, Goodner's employment strategy had served the company well. Fewer than 10 of several hundred individuals employed by the company had been terminated for stealing or other misuse of company assets or facilities.

Each Goodner sales outlet maintained a computerized accounting system. These systems typically consisted of an "off-the-shelf" general ledger package intended for a small retail business and a hodgepodge of assorted accounting documents. Besides the Huntington facility's bookkeeper, the unit's sales manager and two sales representatives had unrestricted access to the accounting system. Since the large volume of sales and purchase transactions often swamped the bookkeeper, sales representatives frequently entered transactions directly into the system. The sales reps routinely accessed, reviewed, and updated their customers' accounts. Rather than completing purchase orders, sales orders, credit memos, and other accounting documents on a timely basis, the sales reps often jotted the details of a transaction on a piece of scrap paper. The sales reps eventually passed these "source documents" on to the bookkeeper or used them to enter transaction data directly into the accounting system.

Sales reps and the sales manager jointly executed the credit function for each Goodner sales outlet. Initial sales to new customers required the approval of the sales manager, while the creditworthiness of existing clients was monitored by the appropriate sales rep. Sales reps had direct access to the inventory storage areas. During heavy sales periods, sales reps often loaded and delivered customer orders themselves.

Each sales office took a year-end physical inventory to bring its perpetual inventory records into agreement with the amount of inventory actually on hand. One concession that T. J. and Ross Goodner made to the policy of relying on their employees' honesty was mandating one intra-year inventory count for each sales office. Goodner's management used these inventories, which were taken by the company's two-person internal audit staff, to monitor inventory shrinkage at each sales outlet. Historically, Goodner's inventory shrinkage significantly exceeded the industry norm. The company occasionally purchased large shipments of "seconds" from manufacturers; that is, tires with defects that prevented them from being sold to major retailers. The tires in these lots with major defects were taken to a tire disposal facility. A sales office's accounting records were not adjusted for these "throwaways" until the year-end physical inventory was taken.

## Selling Tires on the Sly

Within a few days after Woody hatched his plan to pay off his gambling debts, he visited the remote storage site for the Huntington sales office. Woody rummaged through its dimly lit and cluttered interior searching for individual lots of tires that apparently had been collecting dust for several months. After finding several stacks of tires satisfying that requirement, Woody jotted down their specifications in a small notebook. For each lot, Woody listed customers who could potentially find some use for the given tires.

Later that same day, Woody made his first "sale." A local plumbing supply dealer needed tires for his small fleet of vehicles. Woody convinced the business's owner that Goodner was attempting to "move" some old inventory. That inventory would be sold on a cash basis and at prices significantly below Goodner's cost. The owner agreed to purchase two dozen of the tires. After delivering the tires in his large pickup, Woody received a cash payment of $900 directly from the customer.

Over the next several months, Woody routinely stole inventory and kept the proceeds. Woody concealed the thefts in various ways. In some cases, he would charge merchandise that he had sold for his own benefit to the accounts of large volume customers. Woody preferred this technique since it allowed him to reduce the inventory balance in the Huntington facility's accounting records. When customers complained to him for being charged for merchandise they had not purchased, Woody simply apologized and corrected their account balances. If the customers paid the improper charges, they unknowingly helped Woody sustain his fraudulent scheme.

Goodner's customers frequently returned tires for various reasons. Woody completed credit memos for sales transactions voided by his customers, but instead of returning the tires to Goodner's inventory, he often sold them and kept the proceeds. Goodner occasionally consigned tires to large retailers for promotional sales events. When the consignees returned the unsold tires to Goodner, Woody would sell some of the tires to other customers for cash. Finally, Woody began offering to take throwaways to the tire disposal facility in nearby Shoals, West Virginia, a task typically assigned to a sales outlet's delivery workers. Not surprisingly, most of the tires that Woody carted off for disposal were not defective.

The ease with which he could steal tires made Woody increasingly bold. In late 1996, Woody offered to sell Al Hunt tires he had allegedly purchased from a manufacturer (by this time, Al owned and operated Curcio's Tires). Woody told Al that he had discovered the manufacturer was disposing of its inventory of discontinued tires and decided to buy them himself. When Al asked whether such "self-dealing" violated Goodner company policy, Woody replied, "It's none of their business what I do in my spare time. Why should I let them know about this great deal that I stumbled upon?"

At first reluctant, Al eventually agreed to purchase several dozen tires from his good friend. No doubt, the cut-rate prices at which Woody was selling the tires made the decision much easier. At those prices, Al realized he would earn a sizable profit on the tires. Over the next 12 months, Woody continued to sell "closeout" tires to his friend. After one such purchase, Al called the manufacturer from whom Woody had reportedly purchased the tires. Al had become suspicious of the frequency of the closeout sales and the bargain basement prices at which Woody supposedly purchased the tires. When he called the manufacturer, a sales rep told Al that his company had only one closeout sale each year. The sales rep also informed Al that his company sold closeout merchandise directly to wholesalers, never to individuals or retail establishments.

The next time Al spoke to Woody, he mentioned matter-of-factly that he had contacted Woody's primary supplier of closeout tires. Al then told his friend that a sales rep for the company indicated that such merchandise was only sold to wholesalers.

"So, what's the point, Al?"

"Well, I just found it kind of strange that, uh, that . . ."

"C'mon, get to the point, Al."

"Well, Woody, I was just wondering where you're getting these tires that you're selling."

"Do you want to know, Al? Do you really want to know, Buddy? I'll tell you if you want to know," Woody replied angrily.

After a lengthy pause, Al shrugged his shoulders and told his friend to "just forget it." Despite his growing uneasiness regarding the source of the cheap tires, Al continued to buy them and never again asked Woody where he was obtaining them.

## Internal Auditors Discover Inventory Shortage

On December 31, 1996, the employees of Goodner's Huntington location met to take a physical inventory. The employees treated the annual event as a prelude to their New Year's Eve party. Counting typically began around noon and was finished within three hours. The employees worked in teams of three. Two members of each team climbed and crawled over the large stacks of tires and shouted out their counts to the third member who recorded them on preformatted count sheets.

Woody arranged to work with two delivery workers who were relatively unfamiliar with Goodner's inventory since they had been hired only a few weeks earlier. Woody made sure that his team was one of the two count teams assigned to the remote storage facility. Most of the inventory he had stolen over the previous six months had been taken from that site. Woody estimated that he had stolen approximately $45,000 of inventory from the remote storage facility, which represented about 10 percent of the site's book inventory. By maintaining the count sheets for his team, Woody could easily inflate the quantities for the tire lots that he and his team members counted.

After the counting was completed at the remote storage facility, Woody offered to take the count sheets for both teams to the sales office where the total inventory would be compiled. On the way to the sales office, he stopped in a vacant parking lot to review the count sheets. Woody quickly determined that the apparent shortage remaining at the remote site was approximately $20,000. He reduced that shortage to less than $10,000 by altering the count sheets prepared by the other count team.

When the year-end inventory was tallied for Goodner's Huntington location, the difference between the physical inventory and the book inventory was $12,000, or 2.1 percent. That percentage exceeded the historical shrinkage rate of approximately 1.6 percent for Goodner's sales offices. But Felix Garcia, the sales manager for the Huntington sales office, did not believe that the 1996 shrinkage was excessive. As it turned out, neither did the accounting personnel and internal auditors at Goodner's corporate headquarters.

Woody continued "ripping off" Goodner throughout 1997. By midyear, Woody was selling most of the tires he stole to Al Hunt. On one occasion, Woody warned Al not to sell the tires too cheaply. Woody had become concerned that Curcio's modest prices and its increasing sales volume might spark the curiosity and envy of other Huntington tire retailers.

In October 1997, Goodner's internal audit team arrived to count the Huntington location's inventory. Although company policy dictated that the internal auditors count the inventory of each Goodner sales outlet annually, the average interval between the internal audit inventory counts typically ranged from 15 to 20 months. The internal auditors had last counted the Huntington location's inventory in May 1996, two months before Woody Robinson began stealing tires. Woody was unaware that the internal auditors periodically counted the entire inventory of each Goodner operating unit. Instead, he understood that the internal auditors only did a few test counts during their infrequent visits to the Huntington sales office.

After completing their inventory counts, the two internal auditors arrived at an inventory value of $498,000. A quick check of the accounting records revealed a book inventory of $639,000. The auditors had never encountered such a large difference between the physical and book inventory totals. Unsure what to do at this point, the auditors eventually decided to take the matter directly to Felix Garcia, the Huntington sales manager. The size of the inventory shortage shocked Garcia. He insisted that the auditors must have overlooked some inventory. Garcia, the two internal auditors, and three delivery workers spent the following day recounting the entire inventory.

The resulting physical inventory value was $496,000, $2,000 less than the original value arrived at by the auditors.

Following the second physical inventory, the two internal auditors and Garcia met at a local restaurant to review the Huntington unit's inventory records. No glaring trends were evident in those records to either Garcia or the auditors. Garcia admitted to the auditors that the long hours required "just to keep the tires coming and going" left him little time to monitor his unit's accounting records. When pressed by the auditors to provide possible explanations for the inventory shortage, Garcia erupted. "Listen. Like I just said, my job is simple. My job is selling tires. I sell as many tires as I can, as quickly as I can. I let you guys and those other suits up in Youngstown track the numbers."

The following day, the senior internal auditor called his immediate superior, Goodner's chief financial officer (CFO). The size of the inventory shortage alarmed the CFO. Immediately, the CFO suspected that the inventory shortage was linked to the Huntington unit's downward trend in monthly profits over the past two years. Through 1995, the Huntington sales office had consistently ranked as Goodner's second or third most profitable sales outlet. Over the past 18 months, the unit's slumping profits had caused it to fall to the bottom one-third of the company's sales outlets in terms of profit margin percentage. Tacking on the large inventory shortage would cause the Huntington location to be Goodner's least profitable sales office over the previous year and one-half.

After discussing the matter with T. J. and Ross Goodner, the CFO contacted the company's independent audit firm and arranged for the firm to investigate the inventory shortage. The Goodners agreed with the CFO that Felix Garcia should be suspended with pay until the investigation was concluded. Garcia's lack of a reasonable explanation for the missing inventory and the anger he had directed at the internal auditors caused Goodner's executives to conclude that he was likely responsible for the inventory shortage.

Within a few days, four auditors from Goodner's independent audit firm arrived at the Huntington sales office. Goodner's audit firm was a regional CPA firm with six offices, all in Ohio. Goodner obtained an annual audit of its financial statements because one was demanded by the New York bank that provided the company with a line of credit. Goodner's independent auditors had never paid much attention to the internal controls of the client's sales offices. Instead, they performed a "balance sheet" audit that emphasized corroborating Goodner's year-end assets and liabilities.

During their investigation of the missing inventory, the auditors were appalled by the Huntington unit's lax and often nonexistent controls. The extensive control weaknesses complicated their efforts to identify the source of the inventory shortage. Nevertheless, after several days, the auditors' suspicions began settling on Woody Robinson. A file of customer complaints that Felix Garcia kept in his desk revealed that over the past year an unusually large number of customer complaints had been filed against Woody. During that time, 14 of his customers had protested charges included on their monthly statements. Only two customers serviced by the other sales rep had filed similar complaints during that time frame.

When questioned by the auditors, Garcia conceded that he had not discussed the customer complaints with Woody or the other sales rep. In fact, Garcia was unaware that a disproportionate number of the complaints had been filed against Woody. When Garcia received a customer complaint, he simply passed it on to the appropriate sales rep and allowed that individual to deal with the matter. He maintained a file of the customer complaints only because he had been told to do so by the previous sales manager whom he had replaced three years earlier.

After the independent auditors collected other incriminating evidence against Woody, they arranged for a meeting with him. Also attending that meeting were

Goodner's CFO and Felix Garcia. When the auditors produced the incriminating evidence, Woody disclaimed any knowledge of, or responsibility for, the inventory shortage. Woody's denial provoked an immediate and indignant response from Goodner's CFO. "Listen, Robinson, you may have fooled the people you've been working with, but you're not fooling me. You'd better spill the beans right now, or else." At this point, Woody stood, announced that he was retaining an attorney, and walked out of the meeting.

## EPILOGUE

Goodner Brothers filed a criminal complaint against Woody Robinson two weeks after he refused to discuss the inventory shortage at the Huntington sales office. A few weeks later, Woody's attorney reached a plea bargain agreement with the local district attorney. Woody received a five-year sentence for grand larceny, four years of which were suspended. He eventually served seven months of that sentence in a minimum-security prison. A condition of the plea bargain agreement required Woody to provide a full and candid written summary of the fraudulent scheme that he had perpetrated on his employer.

Woody's confession implicated Al Hunt in his theft scheme. Over the 15 months that Woody had stolen from Goodner, he had "fenced" most of the stolen inventory through Curcio's Tires. Although the district attorney questioned Al Hunt extensively, he decided not to file criminal charges against him.[2]

Goodner Brothers filed a $185,000 insurance claim to recoup the losses resulting from Woody's thefts. The company's insurer eventually paid Goodner $130,000, which equaled the theft losses that Goodner could document. After settling the claim, the insurance company sued Curcio's Tires and Al Hunt to recover the $98,000 windfall that Curcio's allegedly realized due to Al Hunt's involvement in the theft ring. The case went to federal district court where a judge ordered Hunt to pay $64,000 to Goodner's insurer. Al Hunt then sued Woody Robinson to recover that judgment. The judge who presided over the earlier case quickly dismissed Al Hunt's lawsuit. According to the judge, Al Hunt's complicity in the fraudulent scheme voided his right to recover the $64,000 judgment from his former friend.

## Questions

1. List what you believe should have been the three to five key internal control objectives of Goodner's Huntington sales office.
2. List the key internal control weaknesses that were evident in the Huntington unit's operations.
3. Develop one or more control policies or procedures to alleviate the control weaknesses you identified in responding to Question 2.
4. Besides Woody Robinson, what other parties were at least partially responsible for the inventory losses Goodner suffered? Defend your answer.

2. Ironically, Woody's confession also implicated his wife, Rachelle. After Woody revealed that Rachelle had typically deposited the large checks written to him by Al Hunt, the district attorney reasoned that Rachelle must have been aware of Woody's fraudulent scheme and was thus an accessory to his crime. However, Woody insisted that he had told his wife the checks were for gambling losses owed to him by Al. After interrogating Rachelle at length, the district attorney decided not to prosecute her.

CASE 3.6

# Saks Fifth Avenue

Attracting customers and closing sales are challenges that face all retailers ranging from a Piggly Wiggly grocery in a small southern town to the Giorgio Armani boutique nestled among the elegant shops lining Rodeo Drive in Beverly Hills. Besides the never-ending need to produce revenues, retailers wrestle daily with many other challenges and problems that pose serious threats to their operations. Theft of cash and inventory by employees historically ranks as one of the most common threats to retail operations. Increasing numbers of employee lawsuits, lawsuits predicated on sexual harassment, racial discrimination, and related charges, also jeopardize the financial health of many retailers. Strong internal controls can significantly reduce the likelihood of losses stemming from employee theft and lawsuits filed by employees. Saks Fifth Avenue, an upscale merchandiser based in New York, learned that lesson firsthand in the late 1990s.

## Promotions, Pay Raises, and Pilfering

In late 1993, Joseph Fierro accepted a part-time sales position with a Saks Fifth Avenue store in New York City.[1] Fierro was assigned to the Men's Polo Department of that store, a department supervised by Robert Perley. Fierro's hard work and ingenuity produced sizable sales and impressed his superior. Within a few months, Perley hired Fierro as a full-time salesperson at an annual salary of $30,000. A few months later, Perley created a new position for Fierro, "Clothing Specialist," so that he could give his star employee a 20 percent raise. By early 1996, Fierro's annual salary had risen to $46,000 on the strength of strong performance appraisals consistently given to him by Perley.

In late August 1996, Joseph Fierro purchased a shirt from another department of the Saks store in which he worked. To obtain an employee discount for the shirt, a discount that he was not entitled to receive, Fierro forged two signatures on a document used to authorize employee sales discounts. The signatures he forged were those of Robert Perley and Donna Ruffman, a co-worker. Fierro also entered the transaction in one of his department's electronic cash registers using Ms. Ruffman's employee identification number. The discount saved Fierro $9.85.

Approximately one week later, two auditors from Saks' Loss Prevention Department reviewed the August transactions entered in the electronic cash registers of the Men's Polo Department. The auditors noticed the employee sales transaction entered by Ms. Ruffman. After examining the documentation for the transaction, they suspected that someone had forged the authorization signatures for the related discount. The auditors questioned several employees in the department regarding the suspicious sale, including Joseph Fierro. Fierro initially denied that he had entered the transaction in his department's cash register. When the auditors suggested that they could easily determine who initiated the transaction, Fierro recanted. He admitted originating the transaction and forging the signatures of both Perley and Ms. Ruffman. In a written statement, Fierro later apologized for the incident. "I realize it was wrong

1. The facts and quotations appearing in this case were drawn from the following legal opinion: *Fierro v. Saks Fifth Avenue*, 13 F.Supp. 2d 481 (1998).

to do this. I exercised poor judgment and I am truthfully sorry for what I did. I realize that something like this is wrong and it will never happen again."

After being questioned by the Loss Prevention auditors, Fierro returned to his department and discussed the matter with Perley. Perley told Fierro that he had no influence on the Loss Prevention Department's decisions but pledged to help him in any way he could. Perley later testified that he telephoned both the Loss Prevention Department and the Human Resources Department and appealed to them not to terminate Fierro.

On September 13, 1996, two representatives of Saks' Human Resources Department notified Fierro that he was being dismissed for violating company policy. They referred Fierro to Saks' employee handbook that lists specific examples of prohibited employee conduct. Listed next is the preface to that section of the employees' handbook. "The following list of prohibited conduct represents essential guidelines that are so fundamental to Saks Fifth Avenue's operations that such violations must result in immediate dismissal." Saks charged Fierro with engaging in the following three acts that mandated the dismissal of an employee.

> *1. Theft of Saks Fifth Avenue or another associate's merchandise, property, or services; 5. Forging a signature; 28. Ringing a transaction under another associate's number or on a dummy date line when doing so results in an unauthorized or unwarranted benefit to the associate ringing the transaction.*

Saks' Human Resources Department conducted an exit interview with Fierro on the date he was terminated. During this interview, Fierro again apologized for the poor judgment he had exercised. He also expressed disbelief that an "exceptional employee" could be fired for such a "trivial transgression."

## He Called Me Buttafucco!

After losing his job at Saks Fifth Avenue, Fierro searched for employment in the New York City area. Among the jobs he applied for was a position with a financial services company. This company insisted on contacting Fierro's former employers. Before the prospective employer contacted Saks, Fierro called a Saks employee in the Human Resources Department who had conducted his exit interview. This individual had allegedly indicated during the exit interview that the reason Fierro was dismissed would not be disclosed to prospective employers. However, when Fierro telephoned this individual, she informed him that if asked, she would reveal the circumstances that had led to his dismissal.

Shortly after Fierro's telephone conversation with the human resources employee, he filed a discrimination lawsuit against Saks Fifth Avenue with the Equal Employment Opportunity Commission (EEOC). Fierro filed the lawsuit pursuant to Title VII of the Civil Rights Act of 1964 and the New York Human Rights Law. In his lawsuit, Fierro claimed that he was subjected to a "hostile work environment" during his employment with Saks. Fierro also claimed that Robert Perley, his supervisor, discriminated against him because of his Italian-American heritage and that Perley fired him in retaliation for his decision to stand up to that discriminatory treatment.

Fierro predicated his charge of discriminatory treatment upon inappropriate remarks allegedly made to him by Perley. He claimed that Perley referred to him on occasion by a three-letter term commonly used as a slur against Italian-Americans.[2]

2. Perley testified that he was of English, Irish, and Scandinavian descent.

Fierro also claimed that Perley occasionally called him "Joey Buttafucco."[3] Finally, Perley allegedly made an insensitive racial remark alluding to Fierro's Hispanic wife. After Perley made the latter remark, Fierro told him that the remark was unacceptable. At that point, according to Fierro, Perley "commenced a plan to terminate him."

Fierro maintained that the discriminatory remarks allegedly made to him by Perley caused him to have low personal esteem and severely damaged his career. Those remarks also reportedly caused him to suffer "permanent psychological damage." Fierro insisted that he was haunted by images of the three-letter slur that Perley had used in referring to him: " . . . every time I look in the mirror I see those three letters above my head and it really hurts."

## District Court Settles Fierro's Lawsuit

Federal district judge Charles Brieant presided over Fierro's lawsuit against Saks Fifth Avenue. Judge Brieant quickly rejected Fierro's claim that Perley discriminated against him. The judge also dismissed the related allegation that Saks fired Fierro for "standing up" to Perley's discriminatory treatment. Evidence presented by both Fierro and Saks suggested that rather than discriminating against Fierro, Perley considered him a valued employee and gave him glowing job performance appraisals. The evidence reviewed by Judge Brieant also suggested that Perley was not involved in Fierro's dismissal. That decision apparently was made by the Human Resources Department with considerable input from the Loss Prevention Department. In fact, as noted earlier, Perley made two telephone calls to intercede on Fierro's behalf.

Judge Brieant concluded that Saks' dismissal of Fierro was not a discriminatory action but simply a consistent application of the company's zero tolerance policy for employee theft. The judge admitted that the theft loss Saks suffered was "relatively trivial." But, he went on to note that retailers have a "strong business interest in deterring employee pilfering." Neither the Civil Rights Act of 1964, nor the New York Human Rights Law, the judge observed, prohibit employers from being "overly rigid or even harsh" in punishing employee theft. Saks' employment records demonstrated that the company consistently punished employee theft with the harsh measure of termination. For example, Saks immediately dismissed a former co-worker of Fierro who was caught "booking credits to his own account."

Judge Brieant considered more seriously Fierro's claim that he was subjected to a hostile work environment. The judge invoked the following definition of a hostile work environment.

> *A hostile work environment exists when the workplace is permeated with discriminatory intimidation, ridicule, and insult, that is sufficiently severe or pervasive to alter the conditions of the victim's employment.*

An employer can assert several defenses in an employee lawsuit alleging a hostile work environment. Among the most credible defenses, Judge Brieant noted, is the existence of an explicit anti-harassment policy. Saks had such a policy during Fierro's employment. The company also had a related complaint procedure allowing employees to file a grievance against a superior or co-worker for engaging in "hostile" behavior. Judge Brieant noted that Fierro never filed a grievance against Perley or his co-workers during his three years with Saks. When asked why he did not take

3. Joey Buttafucco rose—or plunged—to infamy in the early 1990s for a highly publicized affair with an underage woman who later attempted to murder his wife. For several months, the travails of Buttafucco provided headline material for the tabloids and were the source of countless jokes for late night comedians.

such action, Fierro testified that "I was afraid of repercussions. If you start to conflict with your manager, before you know it it's not a very pleasant outcome."

Judge Brieant found Fierro's inaction unsatisfactory.

> *At some point, employees must be required to accept responsibility for alerting their employers to thepossibility of harassment. Without such a requirement, it is difficult to see how Title VII's deterrent purposes are to be served, or how employers can possibly avoid liability in Title VII cases. Put simply, an employer cannot combat harassment of which it is unaware.*

Fierro presented evidence supporting his contention that references to individuals' racial orientation, sexual orientation, and religious affiliation were common in his former department. However, his former co-workers testified that they intended such references to be humorous or self-deprecating. Perley denied participating "in this intended humor" by his subordinates. After reviewing the evidence presented in Fierro's lawsuit, Judge Brieant observed that Perley's department "did not adhere to the highest standards of decorum."[4] Nevertheless, he suggested that the department's work environment was not hostile but "merely offensive."

> *Conduct that is merely offensive and not severe enough to create an objectively hostile or abusive work environment—an environment that a reasonable person would find hostile or abusive—is beyond Title VII's purview. Thus for racist comments, slurs, and jokes to constitute a hostile workenvironment, there must be more than a few isolated incidents of racial enmity, meaning that instead of sporadicracial slurs, there must be a steady barrage of opprobrious racial comments.*

In July 1998, Judge Brieant dismissed Fierro's allegation that he was subjected to a hostile work environment at Saks Fifth Avenue. The judge noted that Fierro did not make such a claim during his employment with Saks or during his exit interview. Instead, that allegation and the related discrimination charges apparently originated near the time Saks refused to give Fierro a "clean" employment reference. Judge Brieant concluded that the timing of Fierro's allegations and Saks' refusal to provide the employment reference was "hardly a coincidence."

## Questions

1. In your opinion, was Saks' zero tolerance policy for employee theft reasonable? Was the policy likely cost-effective? Defend your answers.
2. Did Saks' anti-harassment policy and the related complaint procedure qualify as internal controls? Explain.
3. Identify five control activities that you would commonly find in a men's clothing department of a major department store. Identify the control objective associated with each of these activities.
4. Should a company's independent auditors be concerned with whether or not a client provides a non-hostile work environment for its employees? If your answer is "yes," identify the specific audit issues that would be relevant in this context.

---

4. Despite this observation, Judge Brieant complimented Perley for a department that "had an enviable record of diversity." The department included "men and women of African-American, Hispanic, Irish, Jewish, and Italian descent, as well as homosexuals."

# SECTION 4

# ETHICAL RESPONSIBILITIES OF ACCOUNTANTS

CASE 4.1

# Creve Couer Pizza, Inc.

Imagine this scenario: A few years after graduating from Alcorn State University, Bryant University, or College of Charleston with an accounting degree, you find yourself working as an audit senior with an international accounting firm. Your best friend, Rick, whom you have known since kindergarten, is a special agent with the Internal Revenue Service (IRS). Over lunch one day, Rick mentions the IRS's informant program.

"You know, Jess, you could pick up a few hundred dollars here and there working as a controlled informant for us. In fact, if you would feed us information regarding one or two of those large corporate clients of yours, you could make a bundle."

"That's funny, Rick. Real funny. Me, a double agent, spying on my clients for the IRS? Have you ever heard of the confidentiality rule?"

Sound farfetched? Not really. Since 1939, the IRS has operated an informant program. Most individuals who participate in this program provide information on a one-time basis; however, the IRS also retains hundreds of "controlled informants" who work in tandem with one or more IRS special agents on a continuing basis. Controlled informants provide the IRS with incriminating evidence regarding individuals and businesses suspected of cheating on their taxes. In the early 1990s, the IRS revealed that more than 40 of these controlled informants were CPAs.

Now consider this scenario. You, the audit senior, are again having lunch with your friend Rick, the IRS special agent. Rick knows that the IRS is investigating you for large deductions taken in recent years on your federal income tax returns for a questionable tax shelter scheme. The additional tax assessments and fines you face significantly exceed your net worth. Your legal costs alone will be thousands of dollars. To date, you have been successful in concealing the IRS investigation from your spouse, other family members, and your employer, but that will not be possible much longer.

"Jess, I know this investigation is really worrying you. But I can get you out of this whole mess. I talked to my supervisor. She and three other agents are working on a case involving one of your audit clients. I can't tell you which one right now. If you agree to work with them as a controlled informant and provide them with information that you can easily get your hands on, they will close the case on you. You will be off the hook. No questions. No fines or additional taxes. Case closed . . . permanently."

"Rick, come on, I can't do that. What if my firm finds out? I'd lose my job. I would probably lose my certificate."

"Yeah, but face these facts. If the IRS proves its case against you, you are going to lose your job and your certificate . . . and probably a whole lot more. Maybe even your marriage. Think about it, Jess. Realistically, the agency is looking at a maximum recovery of $50,000 from you. But if you cooperate with my supervisor, she can probably squeeze several million out of your client."

"You're sure they would let me off . . . free and clear?"

"Yes. Free and clear. Come on, Jess, we need you. More important, you need us. Plus, think of it this way. You made one mistake by becoming involved in that phony tax shelter scam. But your client has been ripping off the government, big time, for years. You would be doing a public service by turning in those crooks."

Returning to reality, consider the case of James Checksfield. In 1981, Checksfield, a Missouri CPA, became a controlled informant for the IRS. The IRS special agent who recruited Checksfield had been his close friend for several years and knew that Checksfield was under investigation by the IRS. Reportedly, Checksfield owed back taxes of nearly $30,000 because of his failure to file federal income tax returns from 1974 through 1977. At the same time the IRS recruited Checksfield, the federal agency was also investigating a Missouri-based company, Creve Couer Pizza, Inc. The IRS believed that the owner of this chain of pizza restaurants was "skimming receipts" from his business—that is, failing to report on his federal income tax returns the total sales revenue of his eight restaurants. Checksfield had served as Creve Couer's CPA for several years, although both the IRS and Checksfield denied that he was recruited specifically to provide information regarding that company.

From 1982 through 1985, Checksfield funneled information to the IRS regarding Creve Couer Pizza. Based upon this information, federal prosecutors filed a six-count criminal indictment against the owner of that business in 1989. This indictment charged the owner with underreporting his taxable income by several hundred thousand dollars. The owner faced fines of nearly $1 million and a prison term of up to 24 years if convicted of the charges. Meanwhile, the IRS dropped its case against Checksfield. Both the IRS and Checksfield maintained that there was no connection between the decision to drop the case against him and his decision to provide the IRS with information regarding Creve Couer Pizza.

Following the indictment filed against the owner of Creve Couer Pizza, the owner's attorneys subpoenaed the information that the IRS had used to build its case against him. As a result, the owner discovered the role played by his longtime friend and accountant in the IRS investigation. Quite naturally, the owner was very upset. "What my accountant did to me was very mean and devious. He sat here in my home with me and my family. He was like a member of the family. On the other hand, he was working against me."[1] In another interview, the owner observed, "A client has the right to feel he's getting undivided loyalty from his accountant."[2] Contributing to the owner's anger was the fact that he had paid Checksfield more than $50,000 in fees for accounting and taxation services during the time the CPA was working undercover for the IRS.

The print and electronic media reported the case of the "singing CPA" nationwide, prompting extensive criticism of the IRS. The case also caused many clients of CPAs to doubt whether they could trust their accountants to protect the confidentiality of sensitive financial information. When questioned concerning the matter, the IRS expressed no remorse for using Checksfield to gather incriminating evidence regarding the owner of Creve Couer Pizza. An IRS representative also rejected the contention that communications between accountants and their clients should be "privileged" under federal law similar to the communications between attorneys and their clients.

> *The IRS says the claim of a privileged [accountant-client] relationship is nonsense. "To the contrary," says Edward Federico of the IRS's criminal-investigation division in St. Louis, "the accountant has a moral and legal obligation to turn over information."*[3]

---

1. "Accountant Spies on Client for IRS," *Kansas City Star,* 18 March 1992, 2.
2. "The Case of the Singing CPA," *Newsweek*, 17 July 1989, 41.
3. *Ibid.*

The accounting profession was appalled by the Checksfield case and tried to minimize the damage it had done to the public's trust in CPAs. In particular, the profession condemned the actions of the IRS.

> *Rarely has there been such a case of prosecutorial zeal that violated rudimentary standards of decency. . . . Turning the client-accountant relationship into a secret tool for government agents is an abominable practice. It demeans the service. It erodes trust in the accounting profession.*[4]

## EPILOGUE

In August 1990, the Missouri State Board of Accountancy revoked James Checksfield's CPA license for violating a state law that prohibits CPAs from disclosing confidential client information without the client's permission. In November 1991, the U.S. Department of Justice suddenly announced that it was dropping the tax evasion charges against the owner of Creve Couer Pizza, although pretrial arguments had already been presented for the case. The Justice Department had little to say regarding its decision. Legal experts speculated that federal prosecutors dropped the charges because the judge hearing the case was expected to disallow the evidence that the IRS had collected with the assistance of Checksfield.

Despite the negative publicity produced by the Creve Couer case, the IRS continues to use accountants both in public practice and private industry as informants. In the late 1990s, *Forbes* magazine reported a case in which a disgruntled controller of a retail electronics chain got even with his boss.[5] Shortly before leaving the firm, the controller copied accounting and tax records documenting a large-scale tax fraud perpetrated by the chain's owner. Thanks to this information, the IRS collected a nearly $7 million fine from the owner and sent him to jail for 10 months. The former controller received a significant but undisclosed "finder's fee" from the IRS for his "cooperation."

## Questions

1. Do CPAs who provide accounting, taxation, and related services to small businesses have a responsibility to serve as the "moral conscience" of those clients? Explain.
2. In a 1984 opinion handed down by the U.S. Supreme Court, Chief Justice Warren Burger noted that "the independent auditor assumes a public responsibility transcending any employment relationship with the client." If this is true, do auditors have a moral or professional responsibility to turn in clients who are cheating on their taxes or violating other laws?
3. Assume that you were Jess in the second hypothetical scenario presented in this case. How would you respond to your friend's suggestion that you become a controlled informant for the IRS? Identify the parties that would be affected by your decision and the obligations you would have to each.

4. "IRS Oversteps with CPA Stoolies," *Accounting Today*, 6 January 1992, 22.
5. J. Novack, "Boomerang," *Forbes*, 7 July 1997, 42–43.

**CASE 4.2**

# F&C International, Inc.

Alex Fries emigrated to the United States from Germany in the early nineteenth century.[1] The excitement and opportunities promised by the western frontier fascinated thousands of new Americans, including the young German, who followed his dreams and the Ohio River west to Cincinnati. A chemist by training, Fries soon found a job in the booming distillery industry of southern Ohio and northern Kentucky. His background suited him well for an important need of distilleries, namely, developing flavors to make their often "sour" products more appealing to the public. Alex Fries eventually established his own flavor company. Thanks largely to Fries, Cincinnati became the home of the small but important flavor industry in the United States. By the end of the twentieth century, the flavor industry's annual revenues approached $5 billion.

Alex Fries' success in the flavor industry became a family affair. Two of his grandsons created their own flavor company, Fries & Fries, in the early 1900s. Several decades later, another descendant of Alex Fries, Jon Fries, served as the president and CEO of F&C International, Inc., a flavor company whose common stock traded on the NASDAQ stock exchange. F&C International, also based in Cincinnati, reigned for a time during the 1980s as Ohio's fastest-growing corporation. Sadly, the legacy of the Fries family in the flavor industry came to a distasteful end in the early 1990s.

## The Fraud

Jon Fries orchestrated a large-scale financial fraud that led to the downfall of F&C International. At least 10 other F&C executives actively participated in the scam or allowed it to continue unchecked due to their inaction. The methods used by Fries and his cohorts were not unique or even innovative. Fries realized that the most effective strategy for embellishing his company's periodic operating results was to inflate revenues and overstate period-ending inventories. Throughout the early 1990s, F&C systematically overstated sales revenues by backdating valid sales transactions, shipping customers product they had not ordered, and recording bogus sales transactions. To overstate inventory, F&C personnel filled barrels with water and then labeled those barrels as containing high-concentrate flavor products. The company also neglected to write off defective goods and included waste products from manufacturing processes in inventory. Company officials used F&C's misleading financial statements to sell equity securities and to obtain significant bank financing.

As F&C's fraud progressed, Jon Fries and his top subordinates struggled to develop appropriate sales and inventory management strategies since the company's accounting records were unreliable. To help remedy this problem, F&C created an imaginary warehouse, Warehouse Q.

1. The facts of this case were developed from several SEC enforcement releases and a series of articles that appeared in the *Cincinnati Enquirer*. The key parties in this case neither admitted nor denied the facts reported by the SEC. Those parties include Jon Fries, Catherine Sprauer, Fletcher Anderson, and Craig Schuster.

> *Warehouse Q became the accounting repository for product returned by customers for being below specification, unusable or nonexistent items, and items that could not be found in the actual warehouses.*[2]

Another baffling problem that faced Fries and his confederates was concealing the company's fraudulent activities from F&C's independent auditors. The executives continually plotted to divert their auditors' attention from suspicious transactions and circumstances uncovered during the annual audits. Subversive measures taken by the executives included creating false documents, mislabeling inventory counted by the auditors, and undercutting subordinates' attempts to expose the fraud.

The size and complexity of F&C's fraud eventually caused the scheme to unravel. Allegations that the company's financial statements contained material irregularities triggered an investigation by the Securities and Exchange Commission (SEC). The investigation revealed that F&C had overstated its cumulative pretax earnings during the early 1990s by approximately $8 million. The company understated its pretax net loss for fiscal 1992 alone by nearly 140 percent, or $3.8 million.

## The Division Controller

Catherine Sprauer accepted an accounting position with F&C International in July 1992, shortly after the June 30 close of the company's 1992 fiscal year. Sprauer, a CPA, drafted the Management's Discussion and Analysis (MD&A) section of F&C's 1992 Form 10-K registration statement. In October 1992, the 28-year-old Sprauer became the controller of F&C's Flavor Division. Following that promotion, Sprauer continued to help prepare the MD&A sections of F&C's periodic financial reports submitted to the SEC.

In early January 1993, an F&C employee told Sprauer that he saw company employees filling inventory barrels with water in the final few days of June 1992. This individual also advised Sprauer that he had documentation linking two F&C executives to that incident, which was apparently intended to overstate the company's year-end inventory for fiscal 1992. According to the SEC, Sprauer abruptly ended the conversation with this employee and did not discuss his allegations with anyone.

Later that same day, another F&C employee approached Sprauer and confessed that he was involved in the episode recounted to her earlier in the day. This individual told Sprauer that he had acted under the direct instructions of Jon Fries. The employee then attempted to hand Sprauer a listing of inventory items affected by the fraud. Sprauer refused to accept the list. The persistent employee placed the list in Sprauer's correspondence file. The document detailed approximately $350,000 of nonexistent inventory in F&C's accounting records. Sprauer reportedly never showed the list of bogus inventory to her superiors, to other F&C accountants, or to the company's independent auditors. However, she subsequently warned F&C's chief operating officer (COO), Fletcher Anderson, that the company had "significant inventory problems."

## The Chief Operating Officer

Fletcher Anderson became the COO of F&C International in September 1992 and joined the company's board of directors a few days later. On March 23, 1993, Anderson succeeded Jon Fries as F&C's president and CEO. During the fall of 1992, Anderson stumbled across several suspicious transactions in F&C's accounting records. In late

---

2. Securities and Exchange Commission, *Accounting and Auditing Enforcement Release No. 605*, 28 September 1994. All subsequent quotations are taken from this source.

September 1992, Anderson discovered sales shipments made before the given customers had placed purchase orders with F&C. He also learned that other sales shipments had been delivered to F&C warehouses rather than to customers. Finally, in early October 1992, Anderson uncovered a forged bill of lading for a customer shipment. The bill of lading had been altered to change the reported month of shipment from October to September. Each of these errors inflated F&C's reported earnings for the first quarter of fiscal 1993, which ended September 30, 1992.

More direct evidence that F&C's financial data were being systematically distorted came to Anderson's attention during the second quarter of 1993. In November, a subordinate told Anderson that some of the company's inventory of flavor concentrate was simply water labeled as concentrate. The following month, Anderson learned of Warehouse Q and that at least $1.5 million of the inventory "stored" in that warehouse could not be located or was defective.

Catherine Sprauer submitted her resignation to Fletcher Anderson in late January 1993. Among the reasons Sprauer gave for her resignation were serious doubts regarding the reliability of the company's inventory records. Anderson insisted that Sprauer not tell him why she believed those records were unreliable because he wanted to avoid testifying regarding her concerns in any subsequent litigation.

In February 1993, shortly before Anderson replaced Jon Fries as F&C's top executive, an F&C cost accountant warned him that the company had an inventory problem "in the magnitude of $3-4 million." Anderson later told the SEC that although the cost accountant had access to F&C's inventory records and its actual inventory, he believed the accountant was overstating the severity of the company's inventory problem.

## The Chief Financial Officer

Craig Schuster served as the chief financial officer (CFO) of F&C International during the early 1990s. As F&C's CFO, Schuster oversaw the preparation of and signed the company's registration statements filed with the SEC, including the company's Form 10-K reports for fiscal 1991 and 1992. Throughout 1992, Schuster became aware of various problems in F&C's accounting records, most notably the existence of Warehouse Q. In March 1992, Schuster learned that his subordinates could not locate many items listed in F&C's perpetual inventory records. A few months later, Schuster discovered that customer shipments were being backdated in an apparent attempt to recognize sales revenue prematurely. In late 1992, Schuster determined that approximately $1 million of F&C's work-in-process inventory was classified as finished goods.

On December 17, 1992, a frustrated Schuster prepared and forwarded to Fletcher Anderson a 23-page list of $1.5 million of inventory allegedly stored in Warehouse Q. The memo indicated that the inventory could not be located or was defective. The SEC's enforcement releases focusing on the F&C fraud did not reveal how or whether Anderson responded to Schuster's memo.

Because he supervised the preparation of F&C's financial reports filed with the SEC, Schuster knew that those reports did not comment on the company's inventory problems. On January 1, 1993, Craig Schuster resigned as the CFO of F&C International. The final F&C registration statement Schuster signed was the company's Form 10-Q for the first quarter of fiscal 1993, which ended September 30, 1993.

## The Rest of the Story

In a September 28, 1994, enforcement release, the SEC criticized Catherine Sprauer, Fletcher Anderson, and Craig Schuster for failing to ensure that F&C's financial reports "filed with the Commission and disseminated to the investing public were accurate."

The federal agency also chastised the three individuals for not disclosing in F&C's financial reports "significant accounting problems of which they were aware." Finally, the SEC scolded Anderson and Schuster for not establishing adequate internal controls to provide for the proper recognition of revenue and the proper valuation of inventory. In an agreement reached with the SEC to settle the allegations pending against them, the three former F&C executives pledged to "permanently cease and desist" from committing or causing violations of federal securities laws.

A second enforcement release issued by the SEC on September 28, 1994, contained a series of allegations directed at Jon Fries and seven other senior F&C executives. The SEC charged that these executives were primarily responsible for F&C's fraudulent earnings scheme. To settle these charges, each executive pledged not to violate federal securities laws in the future. The settlement agreement permanently banned Jon Fries from serving as an officer or director of a public company. Several of the individuals agreed to forfeit proceeds received from earlier sales of F&C securities. Fries relinquished more than $2 million he had realized from the sale of F&C common stock. Finally, the SEC imposed civil fines on four of the executives that ranged from $11,500 to $20,000.

F&C International filed for bankruptcy in April 1993 shortly after the fraud became public. The following year, a competitor purchased F&C's remaining assets. In March 1995, Jon Fries began serving a 15-month sentence in a federal prison for his role in the F&C fraud.

## Questions

1. Jon Fries (CEO), Fletcher Anderson (COO), Craig Schuster (CFO), and Catherine Sprauer (division controller) were the four central figures in this case. Identify the key responsibilities associated with the professional roles these individuals occupied. Briefly describe the type and extent of interaction each of these individuals likely had with F&C's independent auditors.

2. Using the scale shown below, evaluate the conduct of the four key individuals discussed in this case. Be prepared to defend your answers.

   −100 . . . . . . . . . 0 . . . . . . . . . 100
   Highly Unethical — Highly Ethical

3. For a moment, step into the shoes of Catherine Sprauer. What would you have done during and following each of the confrontations she had with the two employees who insisted that F&C executives were involved in a fraudulent scheme to misrepresent the company's financial statements?

4. Craig Schuster resigned as F&C's CFO on January 1, 1993. Apparently, Schuster did not reveal to any third parties the concerns he had regarding F&C's accounting records and previous financial statements. In your opinion, did Schuster have a responsibility to inform someone of those concerns following his resignation? Defend your answer.

5. Assume that you, rather than Fletcher Anderson, were F&C's COO in December 1992. What would you have done upon receiving the list of Warehouse Q inventory from Craig Schuster?

## CASE 4.3

# Suzette Washington, Accounting Major

Suzette Washington financed her college education by working as an inventory clerk for Bertolini's, a clothing store chain located in the southeastern United States.[1] Bertolini's caters primarily to fashion-conscious young men and women. The company's stores carry a wide range of clothing, including casual wear, business suits, and accessories. The Bertolini's store for which Suzette worked is located a few blocks from the campus of the large state university that she attended. Except for management personnel, most of Bertolini's employees are college students. Suzette's best friend and roommate, Paula Kaye, worked for Bertolini's as a sales clerk. Paula majored in marketing, while Suzette was an accounting major.

During Suzette's senior year in college, Bertolini's began experiencing abnormally high inventory shrinkage in the store's three departments that stocked men's apparel. Suzette's supervisor, an assistant store manager, confided in her that he believed one or more of the sales clerks were stealing merchandise. Over lunch one day in the student union, Suzette casually mentioned the inventory problem to Paula. Paula quickly changed the subject by asking Suzette about her plans for the weekend.

"Paula, rewind for just a second. Do you know something that I don't?"

"Huh? What do you mean?"

"Missing inventory . . . shrinkage . . . theft?"

After a few awkward moments, Paula stopped eating and looked squarely into her friend's eyes. "Suzette, I don't know if it's true, but I've heard a rumor that Alex and Matt are stealing a few things each week. Polo shirts, silk ties, jeans. Occasionally, they take something expensive, like a hand-knit sweater or sports jacket."

"How are they doing it?"

"I've heard—and don't repeat any of this now—I've heard that a couple of times per week, Alex stashes one or two items at the bottom of the trash container beneath the number two cash register. Then Matt, you know he empties the trash every night in the dumpster out in the alley, takes the items out and puts them in his car."

"Paula, we can't let them get away with this. We have to tell someone."

"No 'we' don't. Remember, this is just a rumor. I don't know that it's true. If you tell a manager, there will be questions. And more questions. Maybe the police will be brought in. You know that eventually someone's going to find out who told. And then . . . slashed tires . . . phone calls in the middle of the night."

"So, don't get involved? Don't do anything? Just let those guys keep stealing?"

"Suze, you work in inventory. You know the markup they put on those clothes. They expect to lose a few things here and there to employees."

"Maybe the markup wouldn't be so high if theft wasn't such a problem."

Now, there was no doubt in Paula's mind that Suzette was going to report the alleged theft scheme to management. "Two months, Suze. Two months till we graduate.

---

1. This case was developed from information provided by a former college student who is now a CPA. The names, location, and certain other background facts have been changed.

Can you wait till then to spill the beans? Then we can move out of state before our cars are spray-painted."

One week following Suzette and Paula's conversation, a Bertolini's store manager received an anonymous typed message that revealed the two-person theft ring rumored to be operating within the store. Bertolini's immediately retained a private detective. Over a four-week period, the detective documented $500 of merchandise thefts by Alex and Matt. After Bertolini's notified the police, the local district attorney filed criminal charges against the two young men. A plea bargain agreement arranged by their attorneys resulted in suspended prison sentences for Alex and Matt. The terms of that agreement included making restitution to Bertolini's, completing several hundred hours of community service, and a lengthy period of probation.

## Questions

1. What would you do if you found yourself in a situation similar to that faced by Suzette in this case?
2. Do you believe that it was appropriate for Suzette to report the alleged theft ring to a store manager? Would it have been unethical for Suzette *not* to report the rumored theft ring?
3. Accounting majors are preparing to enter a profession recognized as having one of the strongest and most rigorously enforced ethical codes. Given this fact, do you believe that accounting majors have a greater responsibility than other business majors to behave ethically?
4. Briefly discuss internal control activities that might have prevented the theft losses suffered by Bertolini's.

**CASE 4.4**

# Thomas Forehand, CPA

## Act I

Thomas Forehand spent the early years of his professional career in a large city working on the auditing staff of a major accounting firm and then serving as an assistant controller for a municipal hospital.[1,2] In 1995, Forehand and his wife decided they wanted a different lifestyle for themselves and their three young children. After several months of searching for a new job, Forehand decided to accept an offer made to him by a CPA with whom he had become acquainted at local professional meetings. Forehand agreed to purchase the CPA's accounting practice that was located in a small suburb approximately 30 miles from the downtown business district where Forehand had worked for more than a decade. The purchase agreement required the former sole practitioner to remain with the firm during a three-year transitional period to minimize client turnover. In 1998, when Forehand assumed complete ownership of the firm, he had six full-time employees, including a receptionist and five accountants, three of whom were CPAs. Tax, compilation, and bookkeeping services accounted for the bulk of Forehand's revenues.

Computer manufacturers, e-commerce start-ups, and other high-tech businesses dominated the greater metropolitan area in which Forehand's firm was located. As a result, the economy of that area was hit hard by the recession that rocked the nation's high-tech sector shortly after the turn of the century. In a span of 18 months, Forehand lost nearly one-third of his clients, forcing him to lay off two of his professional employees. Making matters worse, over that same time frame, Forehand lost more than 80 percent of his personal savings. He had invested those funds in the stocks of major e-commerce firms whose prices "tanked" in late 2000 and early 2001.

On a late Friday afternoon in June 2001, while Forehand sat at his desk contemplating his seemingly bleak future, his receptionist brought a potential client to his door. "Hello, Mr. Forehand. I'm John Jones." Jones was a tall man with a sturdy physique and a firm handshake. He was wearing a starched white shirt, blue jeans, and a frayed baseball cap. Immediately catching Forehand's attention were large, diamond-encrusted rings in the shape of a horseshoe that Jones wore on the pinkie finger of each hand.

"What can I do for you, Mr. Jones?"

"I'm looking for some accounting help."

"Well, you certainly came to the right place. I am the most helpful accountant you will find in this area."

1. This case was originally published by the American Accounting Association in *Issues in Accounting Education*, Vol. 19, November 2004, 529–538. The case was co-authored by Carol A. Knapp. I would like to thank Tracey Sutherland, Executive Director of the American Accounting Association, for granting permission to include this case in this edition of *Contemporary Auditing: Real Issues and Cases*. An instructional grant provided by Glen McLaughlin funded the development of this case. I would like to thank Mr. McLaughlin for his generous and continuing support of efforts to integrate ethics into business curricula.

2. The central facts of this case were drawn from a recent legal opinion. The names of the actual parties involved in the case have been changed. Additionally, key factual circumstances reported in this case are fictionalized accounts of background material disclosed in the legal opinion.

Jones proceeded to tell Forehand that he had recently inherited "a good deal of money" from his grandmother and planned to set up a business in his hometown that was some 60 miles away, on the other side of the metropolitan area. When Forehand seemed surprised that Jones was searching for an accounting firm a considerable distance from his proposed business, Jones quickly added that he planned to visit several accounting firms in the metropolitan area before choosing one.

Because he had worked several years for an electrical contractor, Jones believed that he had sufficient experience and contacts in that field to quickly develop a profitable electrical contracting business. "Coleman Services" was the name he intended to use for his new company. Jones had settled on the generic name—Coleman was his grandmother's maiden name—because he hoped to expand into other lines of business in the future.

As soon as Jones paused, an anxious Forehand seized the opportunity to "sell" his firm to the prospective client. Forehand described the types of services he could offer a new business, including taxation, bookkeeping, and general consulting services. He also stressed the importance of a new entrepreneur having a close relationship with his accountant. Because of his firm's small size, Forehand assured Jones that he would receive prompt and personalized service.

Jones listened politely to Forehand's sales pitch, put the business card Forehand offered him in his shirt pocket, and then excused himself. As Jones walked out the door, Forehand decided that he would likely never see him again. Since Jones had failed to ask any questions about Forehand's services or fees, he had obviously been unimpressed with the small accounting firm. Forehand realized that Jones had likely sensed that he was desperate to acquire new clients, which he was. A few minutes later, the disconsolate Forehand told his employees they could begin their weekend early—there was little for them to do anyway.

## Act II

When Thomas Forehand walked into his office the following Monday morning, he had a voice mail message waiting for him. John Jones had selected his firm over several others. In the brief message, Jones told Forehand that he would drop by the office that afternoon "to get the ball rolling."

During their conversation later that day, it soon became apparent to Forehand that Jones had little understanding of what steps were necessary to set up a new business. Most of the questions Forehand directed to Jones produced either a blank stare or an indifferent shrug of the shoulders. Finally, Forehand decided to take the initiative.

"John, I think we should start by developing a business plan for you." Jones seemed bored by the lengthy explanation of the nature and purpose of a business plan and only glanced momentarily at the example that Forehand spread out on his desk.

When Forehand attempted to goad him into talking about the specific services his business would provide, the restless Jones finally spoke. "We don't need to talk about that. What you really need to know is that I want to put together a business big enough to clear about $20,000 per month."

Forehand was surprised by the naïve nature of Jones' remark. "I'm not sure what you mean, John. Do you mean $20,000 of revenues per month or $20,000 of profits per month or $20,000 of net cash flow per month?"

"I mean $20,000 of cash, cash money, each month. I expect to operate on a cash basis and I want to know how much business I have to bring in every month to clear that much cash."

Even more confused now, Forehand responded, "You mean you aren't going to extend credit to your customers?"

"No. No credit. Just cash. I'm going to make them pay hard, cold cash."

Now, Forehand was just as frustrated as Jones, but for a different reason. Over the previous few minutes, Forehand had realized that this promising new client was not so promising after all. Clearly, Jones had no idea what was involved in operating a business, any type of business.

"Are you sure that you have the background necessary to start a business, John?"

"Yep. All I know is that the key to having a successful business is having customers willing to pay cash. And I have a lot of customers lined up who are willing to pay me cash."

Forehand put down his pen and leaned back in his chair for several moments before responding. "Well, exactly what do you want me to do to help you? I'll have to rely on you to tell me because I have to admit, I'm a little confused at this point."

"Okay, that's fair. Why don't we start like this." Finally, Jones seemed interested in the proceedings. "Over the next couple of days, you can set up a business on paper that would produce $20,000 of cash, or what did you say, 'net cash flow' per month. Why don't you fix up a set of financial statements or whatever you call them for a company that size that does electrical contracting work. And, I think you should put together a list of documents that the company would need to have and the types of reports that it would have to file with the IRS and any other of those government-type organizations."

"Aren't you going about this backward? Shouldn't we . . ."

Jones cut off Forehand in mid-sentence. "Now wait a minute. You asked me what I wanted, didn't you?" Forehand reluctantly nodded, which prompted Jones to speak again. "Somewhere, you can find information on a typical electrical contracting business. And you already know what types of documents and reports that a business like that would have to prepare every year. Soon as you get all of that information put together, then we can go from there."

"Go? Go where?" a flustered Forehand asked.

"Go about gettin' the business started," Jones shot back quickly. "Now, what's so hard about that? You said you're a CPA. I know you can put together all of that stuff."

"Well . . . you're right. I can do what you asked. I just hope that is what you really need."

"Good," the suddenly upbeat Jones replied. "Now, what do you charge for your services?"

"Well, for this type of work . . . I would have to charge $100 an hour." Forehand expected that the first mention of his hourly fee would stop Jones in his tracks and possibly bring their awkward discussion to an abrupt conclusion.

"Sounds fair to me," Jones replied nonchalantly. "How about I start out by paying you $2,500 up front. It's called a retainer, isn't it?"

As Forehand sat dumbfounded and silent at his desk, Jones stood and reached into his right front pocket and extracted a large roll of crisp $100 bills. He then counted out 25 of the bills and laid them in a neat pile in front of Forehand. "There you are. I'll be back on Friday afternoon around one to get that report." Without offering to shake Forehand's hand, Jones turned and left, leaving his newly hired accountant gawking at the stack of money in front of him.

## Act III

The always prompt Jones returned to Forehand's office at 1 p.m. on Friday. "Thomas, do you have my report?"

"Yes I do. Here you are."

Jones spent several minutes thumbing through the 15-page report after Forehand had completed his explanation of the key items included in it. He then shook his head and tossed the report on the corner of Forehand's desk. "Whew, I didn't know that starting a business involved this much stuff."

"It gets more complicated all the time," Forehand responded.

After taking off his baseball cap and scratching his head for several moments, Jones stood and closed the door to Forehand's office. Jones then sat down and leaned forward as he began speaking in a forceful and unapologetic tone. "Listen here, Thomas. I'm going to come clean with you." Over the next several minutes, Jones explained that the money he had inherited from his grandmother had been in the form of cash—cash that she had literally hidden under a mattress, buried in cans in her backyard, and stashed in remote corners of remote cubbyholes of her large home. "Dang it, she had told me where it was all hid. But, I may have forgotten some of the spots. I spent the better part of two days tearing that old house apart. I just hope I got it all." After a brief pause, Jones shook his head and smiled. "That old lady was quite a hoot. Didn't trust bankers a lick."

Forehand was too shocked to interrupt his new client or to provide any commentary on the sudden and unexpected revelation.

"Anyway, why don't we just forget about you helping me set up the business. I think I can do that myself. And, I really don't need an accountant. My brother has a friend who knows how to keep the books for a cash business." Jones paused for a moment as if to allow Forehand to recover. "Are you with me now? Thomas, you with me?" Forehand's gape-mouthed expression didn't change, but when he blinked his eyes and took a breath, Jones continued. "What I really need to do is run my money through a business. Any business. Here's my plan."

The "plan" was for Forehand to loan Jones $120,000 on a one-year promissory note. Jones would use the cash flow from his "business" to make 12 monthly payments of $11,000, meaning that Forehand would earn approximately 10 percent interest on the loan. The loan agreement would indicate that the assets of Jones' business would serve as the collateral for the loan. But, to persuade Forehand to go along with the plan, Jones would give him cash of $135,000 as the true collateral for the loan. When the loan was paid off, Forehand would return only $120,000 of the cash; he would keep the remaining $15,000 as a "loan origination fee."

By the time Jones had finished laying out his proposal, Forehand felt like he had been struck by a tidal wave. His head was spinning. Finally, he mustered enough breath to speak. "John, I can't go along with this . . ."

"C'mon, Thomas. There's nothing wrong here. Uncle Sam will be taken care of since I'll be paying a lot of taxes on my money. And, you are going to make out like a bandit. You'll get $12,000 in interest plus another $15,000. For what? For nothing. You're not taking any risk whatsoever. If I don't pay off the loan, you keep the cash collateral." Again, Jones waited to allow Forehand's brain to catch up. "And then, after one year, we can do it all over again. You'll be making nearly $30,000 a year for the next several years. I know you can use it. I know your business isn't doing well. You basically admitted that the other day."

During the tedious pause that followed, Forehand stared blankly at the wall to his left. He then leaned forward, propped his elbows on his desk, and clasped his hands together as if he were seeking divine guidance. At that point, Jones stood and took his wad of $100 bills out of his pocket. He slowly, deliberately counted out 50 of the bills. "Here you are, Thomas. Here's a bonus for doing the deal. That's $5,000. Now. Do we have a deal?"

After studying the large stack of bills for several moments, Thomas Forehand extended his right hand to John Jones and meekly said, "Deal."

## Act IV

Thomas Forehand liquidated his remaining investments and borrowed $25,000 from his parents to finance the $120,000 "loan" to John Jones. True to his word, Jones delivered a large bundle of $100 bills held together with rubber bands as collateral for the loan. For nine months, Jones made the monthly payments on the first day of each month. But, in the spring of 2002, two FBI agents arrived at Forehand's firm to tell him that Jones would not be making any further payments on the loan since he had been arrested for selling a variety of illegal drugs including marijuana and methamphetamines. The agents then informed Forehand that he was being charged with conspiracy to commit money laundering and aiding and abetting money laundering. Forehand was then handcuffed, read his Miranda rights, and taken to the local county courthouse to be arraigned.

The principal witness against Forehand during his criminal trial was John Jones. With the coaxing of federal prosecutors, Jones recounted the series of meetings between himself and Forehand that had eventually led to the loan agreement between the two men. Under cross-examination by Forehand's legal counsel, Jones testified that he had never told Forehand the actual source of his cash "inheritance." When given the opportunity to testify on his own behalf, Forehand insisted repeatedly that he did not know or suspect that Jones was attempting to launder money from an illicit drug operation but did admit that he had failed to report the receipt of more than $10,000 in cash to the IRS as required by a federal statute. Forehand's denials had little impact on the jury. Forehand was convicted on both federal charges filed against him. He was sentenced to six years in federal prison, fined $19,000, and was required to forfeit $70,000 of cash he had received from Jones that had been confiscated by law enforcement authorities.

## Questions

1. What professional standards are relevant to client acceptance decisions? What general principles do these standards suggest accounting firms should apply in arriving at client acceptance decisions? Identify specific measures that accounting firms should take before deciding to accept a potential client.
2. Assume that you were Thomas Forehand. How would you have responded to the "loan" proposition laid out by John Jones? Do CPAs have a professional or moral responsibility to report illegal acts committed by clients or potential clients?
3. Identify the parties who were affected by Forehand's decision to cooperate with John Jones. What responsibility, if any, did Forehand have to each of those parties? Indicate how each of those parties was affected by Forehand's decision.
4. Thomas Forehand did not intend to become involved in criminal activity when he met John Jones. Instead, Jones goaded Forehand into becoming an active participant in his money-laundering scheme. What strategies can CPAs and businesspeople use to prevent themselves from stepping onto a "slippery slope" that may eventually result in them becoming involved in unethical, immoral, and possibly criminal conduct?

**CASE 4.5**

# Oak Industries, Inc.

Oak Industries began operations in the early 1930s as a manufacturer of car radio components. The California-based company struggled financially through its first few years but managed to emerge from the Depression, unlike many of its competitors. In the late 1960s, Oak expanded into the cable television industry. Technological innovations developed by the company contributed to the tremendous growth of that industry during the past few decades. In 1977, Oak began marketing subscription television services. Within four years, Oak ranked as the largest operator of subscription television systems in the United States. Oak's subscription television subsidiary also generated the majority of the company's annual revenues by the early 1980s.

## Rainy Day Reserves

Exhibit 1 presents selected financial data for Oak Industries for the period 1978-1981. Oak established new sales and profit records each successive year during this period. In fact, in both 1980 and 1981 the company's *actual* net income eclipsed the figure reported by the company. In 1980, Oak's top executives became concerned that the company could not indefinitely sustain its impressive growth rate in annual profits. To help the company maintain this trend, the executives began creating reserves that could be used to boost Oak's reported profits in later years.

> *To report a smooth upward earnings trend and to provide a "cushion" of profits to be used in periods of lower actual earnings, Oak implemented a policy during 1980 and 1981 of establishing unneeded reserves to be released (reversed) in later periods, if needed.*[1]

These "rainy day reserves" included overstatements of the company's allowances for inventory obsolescence and uncollectible receivables.

**EXHIBIT 1**

OAK INDUSTRIES, INC., SELECTED FINANCIAL DATA, 1978–1981

**Oak Industries, Inc.**
**Selected Financial Data, 1978–1981**

| | 1981 | 1980 | 1979 | 1978 |
|---|---|---|---|---|
| Net Sales* | $507,119 | $385,586 | $281,348 | $192,181 |
| Gross Profit | 168,437 | 125,163 | 86,060 | 51,402 |
| Net Income | 30,350 | 20,082 | 11,170 | 4,850 |
| Earnings Per Share | 2.23 | 1.85 | 1.36 | .72 |

* Net sales, gross profit, and net income are expressed in thousands of dollars
Source: Oak Industries, Inc., 1982 Form 10-K filed with the Securities and Exchange Commission.

1. Securities and Exchange Commission, *Accounting and Auditing Enforcement Release No. 63*, 25 June 1985.

Unfortunately, Oak needed to "dip" into its rainy day reserves much sooner than expected. In 1981, Oak established subscription television operations in the Dallas-Fort Worth and Phoenix metropolitan areas. Almost immediately, the company began encountering major financial problems in these new operations due principally to unexpectedly low sales. Based upon its sales forecasts for these two new market areas, Oak had stockpiled a large quantity of television decoder boxes. Because of the significant shortfall in subscribers, much of this inventory was not needed. To make matters worse, rapid technological changes soon rendered the excess inventory obsolete. Oak also had an unusually high rate of sales returns for a new model of a decoder box that it sold to new subscribers. Quality control problems in Oak's manufacturing processes caused this model to be unreliable. Finally, Oak experienced a higher than normal rate of uncollectible receivables in the Dallas-Fort Worth and Phoenix market areas.

## Reversal of the Rainy Day Reserves

In the first quarter of fiscal 1982, Oak's senior executives instructed the company's accountants to "release" several million dollars of the reserves established during 1980 and 1981. The reversal of these reserves significantly reduced Oak's reported expenses and allowed the company to sustain its smooth upward earnings trend by reporting a record quarterly profit. If the reserves had not been reversed, the company's net income for the first quarter of 1982 would have been nearly 50 percent lower than the reported figure of $7.5 million. Oak's top executives boasted in the company's financial report for the first three months of 1982 that "First quarter sales and net income were greater than in any first quarter in the Company's history."

As fiscal 1982 progressed, Oak's financial problems worsened. At year-end, the management of Oak's subscription television subsidiary notified corporate headquarters of $40 million of asset write-offs and increases in loss reserves needed for that subsidiary. Oak's senior executives realized that if they booked the $40 million of additional expenses, the company's consolidated income statement for 1982 would reflect a large loss. Instead of reporting that loss, the executives decided to report earnings per share of $.25 for 1982, which translated to a net income of approximately $4.1 million.

To "manufacture" the desired net income for fiscal 1982, Oak's senior executives turned to the company's chief financial officer (CFO), who oversaw the company's accounting department. The senior executives instructed the CFO to take the necessary steps to produce the target earnings figure. In response to that directive, the CFO instructed the firm's controller to determine how much of the $40 million of unrecorded expenses could be booked if the company were to report earnings per share of $.25 for 1982. After the controller arrived at that figure, the CFO instructed him to arbitrarily allocate that amount between the company's reserves for bad debts and inventory obsolescence. The controller complied, resulting in Oak reporting the management-mandated $.25 earnings per share for 1982.

## SEC Investigation Focuses on Oak's Controller

The SEC investigation that uncovered the illicit accounting methods used by Oak Industries in the early 1980s focused on the firm's controller. Particularly disturbing to the SEC were the controller's impressive credentials. In addition to being a CPA, the controller had an extensive accounting background, including several years of experience with Arthur Andersen & Co., Oak's independent audit firm.

The SEC discovered that Oak's controller often questioned his superiors' judgment, at least initially, when they instructed him to misrepresent the company's financial data. For example, the controller recommended disclosing in Oak's financial statements for the first quarter of 1982 that the company had reversed several million dollars of the illicit rainy day reserves. When the firm's senior executives rejected the controller's recommendation, he relented and subsequently helped prepare the misleading financial statements for the first quarter of 1982.

Later in 1982, Oak's controller received a series of memos from the CFO of the firm's subscription television subsidiary. Among other financial problems being experienced by that unit, these memos notified the controller that the subsidiary's inventory obsolescence reserve was significantly understated. At the end of the fourth quarter of 1982, the subsidiary's CFO reported that his unit's inventory should be written down by nearly $10 million. Nevertheless, according to the SEC, the controller "accepted senior management's judgment and failed to take steps necessary to cause Oak to record the necessary reserves."[2]

The SEC also reported that Oak's controller knew that key accounting documents were being withheld from the company's independent auditors, Arthur Andersen & Co. Oak often prepared two sets of loss exposure analyses: one set to be used for internal decision-making purposes and another set to be forwarded to Arthur Andersen. The loss exposure analyses given to the independent auditors understated the severity of Oak's inventory obsolescence and bad debt problems. During Oak's 1982 audit, the firm's controller received a memorandum written by one of the company's internal auditors. This memorandum suggested that the independent auditors be given an "edited version" of an earlier memo that analyzed the status of Oak's reserve for uncollectible receivables. This edited version of the earlier memo significantly understated Oak's estimated uncollectible receivables at the end of 1982.

> *We [the internal audit staff] would like to issue the edited version of the . . . memo to Arthur Andersen to avoid any additional suspicions on their part as to the content. We believe the revised memo has been toned down sufficiently to be issued to them.*

The controller apparently did not prevent the internal audit staff from forwarding the misleading memo to the independent auditors. As a result, Oak's independent auditors received an inaccurate analysis of the year-end status of the client's uncollectible receivables.

Near the end of Arthur Andersen's 1982 audit of Oak Industries, the company's controller signed a letter of representations addressed to the audit firm. Among other assertions, this letter indicated that company officials had provided all of Oak's financial records and related information to Arthur Andersen. The letter of representations also stated that Oak's financial statements had been prepared in accordance with GAAP.

---

2. This and subsequent quotations, unless indicated otherwise, are taken from Securities and Exchange Commission, *Accounting and Auditing Enforcement Release No. 93*, 26 March 1986.

## EPILOGUE

In June 1985 and March 1986, the SEC issued enforcement releases documenting Oak Industries' abusive accounting and financial reporting practices. These releases also reported the sanctions imposed on the company and its executives involved in the fraudulent scheme. The SEC permanently banned Oak's chief executive officer from serving as an officer or director of a publicly owned firm. Four other Oak officers, including its CFO and controller, settled charges filed against them by agreeing not to violate federal securities laws in the future. The terms of the agreement also required Oak to establish an audit committee that would assume an active role in the company's accounting and financial reporting function. In early 1985, Oak voluntarily reissued its financial statements for 1982 and 1983. Collectively, these financial statements reduced Oak's previously reported net income for those years by approximately $44 million, or $2.70 per share. The company also disclosed in early 1985 that it would be discontinuing its subscription television operations.

One of the SEC's enforcement releases in the Oak Industries case focused exclusively on the firm's controller. In this release, the SEC noted that the controller clearly was not a "primary decision-maker" within the firm or a member of its senior management. As a result, the controller was not directly responsible for the company's earnings manipulation scheme. Nevertheless, the SEC maintained that the controller neglected his professional responsibilities when he became aware of that scheme. This was true despite the controller often challenging his superiors' questionable decisions.

> *Although [the controller] may have made the appropriate recommendations to his corporate supervisors, when those recommendations were rejected, [he] acted as the "good soldier," implementing their directions which he knew or should have known were improper.*

The SEC's refusal to recognize the "good soldier" defense as a valid justification for questionable conduct by mid-level corporate executives was debated by the business press following the public disclosure of the Oak Industries fraud. Most parties who commented on this issue supported the SEC's position. However, one individual warned, "It's unrealistic to place a burden on mid-level [corporate] managers to discharge obligations that they're not in a position to discharge."[3]

Often complicating the role of a corporate controller is the fact that his or her immediate superior lacks an accounting background. This was true in the Oak Industries case. Oak's controller was a CPA, but his immediate superior, the company's CFO, was not. The chief accountant of the SEC's enforcement division at the time, Robert Sack, observed that "added pressure" is often placed on a controller when his or her superior is not a CPA.[4] Sack recommended that in such cases a controller develop a relationship with the firm's board of directors, legal counsel, and independent auditors. These parties can serve as useful allies for the controller if his or her superior makes unreasonable demands at some point regarding accounting or financial reporting issues.

3. K. Victor, "Tough-Minded SEC Takes Aim At Corporate 'Good Soldiers'," *Legal Times*, 7 April 1986, 1.

4. *Securities Regulation and Law Reports*, "Internationalization Raising Questions on SEC Disclosure System, Peters Says," 12 December 1986, 1773.

## Questions

1. Is it unethical for a company to intentionally understate its earnings? Why or why not?
2. Should auditors be equally concerned with potential understatements and potential overstatements of a client's revenues and expenses? Identify audit techniques that may be particularly helpful in uncovering understatements of revenues and overstatements of expenses.
3. Place yourself in the position of Oak's controller when the company's senior executives rejected his recommendation to disclose the reversal of the rainy day reserves. What would you have done at that point?
4. What responsibilities does a company's controller and other accounting employees have when interacting with the firm's independent auditors? Do these responsibilities conflict with other job-related responsibilities of a company's accounting employees? Explain.
5. Should the SEC and other regulatory bodies hold corporate accountants who are CPAs to a higher standard of conduct than corporate accountants who are not CPAs? Defend your answer.

## CASE 4.6

# Laurel Valley Estates

In 1978, two California businessmen, Claude Trout and Harry Moore, formed a real estate development company, which they named Laurel Valley Estates.[1] The partnership agreement signed by Trout and Moore stated that the two partners would make equal capital contributions to the new firm and would share equally in its profits. Trout's initial capital contribution was a 400-acre parcel of undivided land appraised at $640,000; Moore contributed an equal amount of cash. From 1978 through the end of 1981, Trout supervised the subdivision of the 400-acre property into residential lots and the addition of improvements. During that same period, Moore negotiated with several construction companies to build expensive tract homes on the property.

Near the end of 1981, Moore became restless with the slow progress being made in developing the Laurel Valley property. Moore questioned whether Trout was properly managing the partnership's dwindling cash funds and whether those funds would be depleted before the completion of the project. To allay his concerns, Moore decided to retain Newby & Company, an accounting firm that he had employed in previous business ventures, to review the partnership's books. After learning of Moore's decision, Trout told Moore that he had no objection to Newby & Company's reviewing the partnership's accounting records. In fact, Trout offered to engage Newby & Company as the partnership's permanent accounting firm. Moore accepted Trout's offer. A few days later, Trout notified Douglas & Michaels, the partnership's accounting firm since its inception in 1978, of the decision to switch to Newby & Company.

In early December 1981, Jay Kent Newby, a staff accountant with Newby & Company and the son of the firm's founder, arrived at the Laurel Valley offices to review the partnership's books. Newby asked Trout for a listing of all tangible assets held in the partnership's name, as well as the partnership's general ledger, cash receipts and cash disbursements journals, and check register.

Late in the afternoon of his second day on the Laurel Valley engagement, a visibly upset Newby stormed into Trout's office, interrupting a conversation between Trout and his secretary. Newby told Trout that he had uncovered major problems in the partnership's financial records. The most serious problem involved the property that Trout had allegedly contributed to the partnership. That property was listed as an asset in the firm's general ledger; however, Trout had never transferred the legal title of the property to Laurel Valley Estates. Newby implied that Trout intended to claim, at some point in the future, that the property was his alone. Newby also charged that over the past three years, Trout had squandered most of the cash invested in the partnership by Moore. According to Newby, Trout had paid exorbitant amounts to contractors he had retained to develop the Laurel Valley property. Newby even suggested that some of the contractors were likely close friends or relatives of Trout. Newby concluded his tirade by informing Trout, in the presence of Trout's secretary, that the partnership's records were fraudulent, that Trout owed hundreds of thousands of dollars to the partnership, and that Trout "could be looking at jail."

---

1. This case was developed from a legal opinion written in the 1980s. The names of the actual parties involved in the case have been changed. In addition, certain of the factual circumstances reported in this case are fictionalized accounts of the actual facts disclosed in the legal opinion.

Newby's allegations stunned Claude Trout. Trout insisted that he had made every effort to conserve the partnership's cash, had not diverted any funds to friends or relatives, and had been unaware that he was required to deed the Laurel Valley property to the partnership. Trout then told Newby that he would immediately make the necessary change in the title of the property. Newby cut off Trout in mid-sentence, telling the elderly gentleman that "it was too late" to transfer the property to the partnership. Within minutes, Newby had packed his briefcase and was on his way out the door when Trout stopped him. "What can I do to clear this up?" Trout asked. After a brief pause, Newby replied sarcastically, "Pray."

Early the next morning, Harry Moore telephoned Trout and asked that he drive to Sacramento to meet with him, Jay Kent Newby, and Newby's father in the accounting firm's office. Trout agreed to make the short trip to Sacramento. Jay Kent Newby presided over the meeting that afternoon among the four men. Newby reported that he had devised a plan for resolving the situation without any legal action being taken against Trout. Because Trout was obviously "crooked and dishonest," Newby suggested that Moore be allowed to withdraw immediately from the partnership. Newby's plan called for Trout to return Moore's initial cash investment in the partnership and to pay Moore interest on his investment for the prior three years. When Trout asked Moore if that was what he wanted, Moore, who had yet to speak during the meeting, nodded affirmatively.

Trout agreed to the settlement arranged by Jay Kent Newby and then apologized for the mistake he had made. He insisted once more that he had been unaware of the need to transfer the title of the 400-acre property to the partnership. Trout also told Moore, a longtime friend, that he not been irresponsible in managing the funds committed to the partnership by Moore. Again, Moore remained silent.

Within two weeks, Trout borrowed approximately $900,000 to liquidate Moore's ownership interest in Laurel Valley Estates.

Following the dissolution of the partnership, Trout lost interest in completing the development of the Laurel Valley property and sold it, incurring a large loss. Over the following several months, Trout's health deteriorated, and he was eventually forced to seek psychiatric help. Trout attributed his physical and mental deterioration to the dissolution of his partnership with Moore and to Jay Kent Newby's allegation that he was "crooked and dishonest."

In late 1982, Trout told Jim Hardy, a partner of Laurel Valley Estates' original accounting firm, of the problem that had led to the breakup of his partnership with Moore. Hardy immediately informed Trout that state law did not require him to deed the Laurel Valley property to the partnership. According to Hardy, the stated intentions of partners dictate whether personal assets of individual partners have been contributed to the partnership. Because the Trout and Moore partnership agreement clearly specified that Trout's initial capital contribution would be the 400-acre property, that property was legally a partnership asset although the title remained in Trout's name. In fact, Hardy had researched that specific question when he set up the books for Laurel Valley Estates shortly after the partnership's formation in 1978.

Trout was livid after learning that he had not been required to transfer the title of the 400-acre property to Laurel Valley Estates, as Jay Kent Newby had insisted. Trout immediately sued Newby & Company, charging the accounting firm with professional malpractice, fraud, and the intentional infliction of emotional distress. The judge who presided over the initial hearing in the case decided there was no basis for any of the charges and dismissed Trout's suit. A few days later, Claude Trout died of a heart attack.

Several months following Trout's death, the executor of his estate appealed the dismissal of the lawsuit against Newby & Company. The appellate court ruled that considerable evidence existed supporting Trout's allegation of professional malpractice by Newby & Company but agreed with the lower court's decision to dismiss the charges of fraud and infliction of emotional distress. The appellate judge who wrote the legal opinion in the case stated that Jay Kent Newby should have researched more thoroughly the legal question regarding Trout's initial capital contribution to the partnership before rendering any professional advice to Trout. The judge also ruled that a jury trial should decide whether the accounting firm's actions caused Trout's damages. Finally, the judge observed that although Newby & Company could not be sued for the intentional infliction of emotional distress because of legal technicalities, plaintiff counsel might be able to prove that Jay Kent Newby had slandered Trout.

A few days before the trial was to begin in the civil lawsuit involving Newby & Company and Trout's executor, the accounting firm offered to make a sizable payment to Trout's estate to settle the case. Trout's executor accepted the offer only after Newby & Company's partners extended a personal apology to members of the Trout family for the unfortunate incident involving Jay Kent Newby and Claude Trout.

## Questions

1. What professional responsibilities did Jay Kent Newby fail to fulfill in his interaction with Claude Trout? Identify specific ethical rules and other professional standards that he violated. Would your answer be affected by the fact that Newby was not a CPA at the time? Given this additional fact, what other parties, if any, violated one or more of the public accounting profession's ethical rules or standards?
2. The controversy in this case focused on the legal question of whether Trout was required to deed the 400-acre property to the partnership. Are auditors required to be competent in such legal matters? If you had been in Jay Kent Newby's position, what would you have done when you discovered that the property had not been deeded to the partnership?
3. Trout was technically a client of Newby & Company when that firm reviewed the partnership's accounting records in late 1981. When Trout sued Newby & Company for professional malpractice, he filed a tort action against the accounting firm. Identify the general elements of proof that a client must establish when suing an accounting firm for professional malpractice. What other type of lawsuit could Trout have filed against Newby & Company, given that he was in privity with the accounting firm?

**CASE 4.7**

# Rocky Mount Undergarment Company, Inc.

Employees involved in the accounting and control functions of organizations often face ethical dilemmas. Typically, at some point in each of these dilemmas an employee must decide whether he or she will "do the right thing." Consider the huge scandal involving Equity Funding Corporation of America in the early 1970s. In that scandal, dozens of the life insurance company's employees actively participated in a fraudulent scheme intended to grossly overstate Equity Funding's revenues and profits. These employees routinely prepared phony insurance applications, invoices, and other fake documents to conceal the fraud masterminded by the firm's top executives. When questioned by a reporter following the disclosure of the fraud, one of Equity Funding's employees meekly observed, "I simply lacked the courage to do what was right."[1]

In early 1986, several employees of Rocky Mount Undergarment Co., Inc. (RMUC), came face to face with an ethical dilemma. RMUC, a North Carolina-based company, manufactured undergarments and other apparel products. Approximately one-half of the company's annual sales were to three large merchandisers: K-Mart (29 percent), Wal-Mart (11 percent), and Sears (9 percent). RMUC employed nearly 1,300 workers in its production facilities and another forty individuals in its administrative functions. Between 1981 and 1984, RMUC realized steady growth in revenues and profits. In 1981, RMUC reported a net income of $378,000 on net sales of $17.9 million. Three years later, the company reported a net income of $1.5 million on net sales of $32 million.

Unfortunately, RMUC failed to sustain its impressive profit trend in 1985 as reflected by the financial data presented for the firm in Exhibit 1. Disproportionately high production costs cut sharply into the company's profit margin during that year. These high production costs resulted from cost overruns on several large customer orders and from significant training and other start-up costs linked to the opening of a new factory.

A subsequent investigation by the Securities and Exchange Commission (SEC) revealed that the company's senior executive and another high-ranking officer had refused to allow the firm to report its actual net income of $452,000 for 1985. To inflate the company's 1985 net income, these executives instructed three RMUC employees to overstate the firm's year-end inventory and thereby understate its cost of goods sold. Initially, the employees were reluctant to participate in the scheme. The two executives warned the employees that unless they cooperated, the company might "cease operations and dismiss its employees."[2] After much prodding, the three employees capitulated and began systematically overstating the firm's 1985 year-end inventory.

1. H. Anderson, "12 More Ex-Equity Officials Get Jail, Fine or Probation," *Los Angeles Times,* 25 March 1975, Section 3, 9 & 11.

2. This and all subsequent quotes were taken from Securities and Exchange Commission, *Accounting and Auditing Enforcement Release No. 212,* 9 January 1989.

**EXHIBIT 1**

RMUC, INC., SELECTED FINANCIAL DATA, 1981–1985

**RMUC, Inc.**
**Selected Financial Data, 1981–1985 (000s omitted)**

| | 1985 | 1984 | 1983 | 1982 | 1981 |
|---|---|---|---|---|---|
| Net Sales | $39,505 | $32,167 | $25,697 | $21,063 | $17,851 |
| Cost of Sales | 32,415 | 24,199 | 19,700 | 16,590 | 4,358 |
| Selling, General & Administrative Expenses | 5,791 | 4,523 | 3,405 | 2,694 | 2,454 |
| Net Income | 452 | 1,529 | 1,153 | 756 | 378 |
| Total Assets | 24,808 | 14,745 | 11,134 | 6,916 | 5,529 |
| Stockholders' Equity | 11,263 | 6,999 | 3,510 | 3,469 | 2,714 |
| Current Assets | 20,924 | 12,678 | 9,648 | 5,779 | 4,639 |
| Accounts Receivable | 7,115 | 4,725 | 3,734 | 2,608 | 1,290 |
| Inventory | 12,158 | 7,507 | 5,694 | 2,869 | 3,045 |
| Current Liabilities | 7,302 | 6,999 | 3,510 | 3,469 | 2,714 |

*Following [the two executives'] specific instructions, the three RMUC employees inflated quantity figures on selected count sheets by adding numerals to the accurate quantity figures per item which had been previously recorded thereon during the physical inventory count.*

*The three RMUC employees then multiplied the inflated quantity figures per item on the count sheets by the actual unit cost per item and recorded the resulting false and inflated cost figures on the count sheets.*

While the three employees were overstating RMUC's inventory, the two company executives who concocted the scheme periodically telephoned them to check on their progress. At one point, the employees indicated that they were unwilling to continue falsifying RMUC's year-end inventory quantities. Additional coaxing and cajoling by the two executives convinced the employees to resume their fraudulent activities. Eventually, the employees "manufactured" more than $900,000 of bogus inventory. After RMUC's senior executive reviewed and approved the falsified inventory count sheets, the count sheets were forwarded to the company's independent audit firm.

To further overstate RMUC's December 31, 1985, inventory, the company's senior executive instructed another RMUC employee to obtain a false confirmation letter from Stretchlon Industries, Inc. Stretchlon supplied RMUC with most of the elastic needed in its manufacturing processes. At the time, RMUC had an agreement to purchase 50 percent of Stretchlon's common stock at net book value. On December 31, 1985, Stretchlon had in its possession only a nominal amount of RMUC inventory. Nevertheless, a Stretchlon executive agreed to supply a confirmation letter to RMUC's independent auditors indicating that his firm held approximately $165,000 of RMUC inventory at the end of 1985. As a condition for providing the confirmation, the Stretchlon executive insisted that RMUC prepare and forward to him a false shipping document to corroborate the existence of the fictitious inventory. After receiving this shipping document, the Stretchlon executive signed the false confirmation and mailed it to RMUC's independent audit firm.

**EXHIBIT 2**

FOOTNOTE DISCLOSURE OF RMUC'S INVENTORY FRAUD

> Subsequent to the issuance of its financial statements for the year ended December 31, 1985, the Company determined that inventory as reported was misstated. The accompanying financial statements have been restated to reflect correction of such misstatement. The significant effects of restatement were to reduce inventories $1,076,000, increase cost of sales $1,140,000, increase selling, general and administrative expenses $40,000, and reduce net income $607,000 from the amounts previously reported.

The fraudulent schemes engineered by RMUC's executives overstated the firm's December 31, 1985, inventory by approximately $1,076,000. Instead of reporting inventory of $12,158,000, in its original December 31, 1985, balance sheet, RMUC reported inventory of $13,234,000. The overstatement of inventory boosted RMUC's reported net income for 1985 to $1,059,000, which was more than $600,000 higher than the actual figure.

Near the completion of the 1985 audit, RMUC's auditors asked the company's senior executive to sign a letter of representations. Among other items, this letter indicated that the executive was not aware of any irregularities [fraud] involving the company's financial statements. The letter also stated that RMUC's financial statements fairly reflected its financial condition as of the end of 1985 and its operating results for that year. Shortly after receiving the signed letter of representations, RMUC's audit firm issued an unqualified opinion on the firm's 1985 financial statements.

Following the SEC's discovery of the fraudulent misrepresentations in RMUC's 1985 financial statements, the federal agency filed civil charges against the firm's two executives involved in the fraud. The SEC eventually settled these charges by obtaining a court order that prohibited the executives from engaging in any further violations of federal securities laws. RMUC also issued corrected financial statements for 1985. Exhibit 2 presents a footnote included in those financial statements. That footnote describes the inventory-related misstatements in the company's original 1985 financial statements.

## Questions

1. Did the overstatement of RMUC's inventory at the end of 1985 materially affect the company's reported financial data for that year? Defend your answer.
2. What audit procedures might have prevented or detected the overstatements of RMUC's inventory quantities at the end of 1985?
3. How did RMUC's buyout option for Stretchlon affect the quality of the evidence provided by the inventory confirmation letter, if at all? Explain.
4. Refer to Exhibit 2. In your view, did the footnote included in that exhibit adequately describe the misrepresentations in RMUC's original financial statements for 1985? Why or why not?
5. How would you have reacted if you had been one of the employees pressured by RMUC's executives to misrepresent the company's 1985 year-end inventory? Before responding, identify the alternative courses of action that would have been available to you.

# SECTION 5

# ETHICAL RESPONSIBILITIES OF INDEPENDENT AUDITORS

**CASE 5.1**

# Cardillo Travel Systems, Inc.

*If virtue is not its own reward,*
*I don't know any other stipend attached to it.*

*Lord Byron*

## ACT 1

Russell Smith knew why he had been summoned to the office of A. Walter Rognlien, the 74-year-old chairman of the board and chief executive officer (CEO) of Smith's employer, Cardillo Travel Systems, Inc.[1] Just two days earlier, Cardillo's in-house attorney, Raymond Riley, had requested that Smith, the company's controller, sign an affidavit regarding the nature of a transaction Rognlien had negotiated with United Airlines. The affidavit stated that the transaction involved a $203,000 payment by United Airlines to Cardillo but failed to disclose why the payment was being made or for what specific purpose the funds would be used. The affidavit included a statement indicating that Cardillo's stockholders' equity exceeded $3 million, a statement that Smith knew to be incorrect. Smith also knew that Cardillo was involved in a lawsuit and that a court injunction issued in the case required the company to maintain stockholders' equity of at least $3 million. Because of the blatant misrepresentation in the affidavit concerning Cardillo's stockholders' equity and a sense of uneasiness regarding United Airlines' payment to Cardillo, Smith had refused to sign the affidavit.

When Smith stepped into Rognlien's office on that day in May 1985, he found not only Rognlien but also Riley and two other Cardillo executives. One of the other executives was Esther Lawrence, the firm's energetic 44-year-old president and chief operating officer (COO) and Rognlien's wife and confidante. Lawrence, a long-time employee, had assumed control of Cardillo's day-to-day operations in 1984. Rognlien's two sons by a previous marriage had left the company in the early 1980s following a power struggle with Lawrence and their father.

As Smith sat waiting for the meeting to begin, his apprehension mounted. Although Cardillo had a long and proud history, in recent years the company had begun experiencing serious financial problems. Founded in 1935 and purchased in 1956 by Rognlien, Cardillo ranked as the fourth-largest company in the travel agency industry and was the first to be listed on a national stock exchange. Cardillo's annual revenues had steadily increased after Rognlien acquired the company, approaching $100 million by 1984. Unfortunately, the company's operating expenses had increased more rapidly. Between 1982 and 1984, Cardillo posted collective losses of nearly $1.5 million. These poor operating results were largely due to an aggressive franchising strategy implemented by Rognlien. In 1984 alone that strategy more than doubled the number of travel agency franchises operated by Cardillo.

Shortly after the meeting began, the overbearing and volatile Rognlien demanded that Smith sign the affidavit. When Smith steadfastly refused, Rognlien showed him the

1. The events discussed in this case were reconstructed principally from information included in Securities and Exchange Commission, *Accounting and Auditing Enforcement Release No. 143*, 4 August 1987. All quotations appearing in this case were taken from that document.

first page of an unsigned agreement between United Airlines and Cardillo. Rognlien then explained that the $203,000 payment was intended to cover expenses incurred by Cardillo in changing from American Airlines' Sabre computer reservation system to United Airlines' Apollo system. Although the payment was intended to reimburse Cardillo for those expenses and was refundable to United Airlines if not spent, Rognlien wanted Smith to record the payment immediately as revenue.

Not surprisingly, Rognlien's suggested treatment of the United Airlines payment would allow Cardillo to meet the $3 million minimum stockholders' equity threshold established by the court order outstanding against the company. Without hesitation, Smith informed Rognlien that recognizing the United Airlines payment as revenue would be improper. At that point, "Rognlien told Smith that he was incompetent and unprofessional because he refused to book the United payment as income. Rognlien further told Smith that Cardillo did not need a controller like Smith who would not do what was expected of him."

## ACT 2

In November 1985, Helen Shepherd, the audit partner supervising the 1985 audit of Cardillo by Touche Ross, stumbled across information in the client's files regarding the agreement Rognlien had negotiated with United Airlines earlier that year. When Shepherd asked her subordinates about this agreement, one of them told her of a $203,000 adjusting entry Cardillo had recorded in late June. That entry, which follows, had been approved by Lawrence and was apparently linked to the United Airlines-Cardillo transaction:

| | | |
|---|---|---|
| Dr Receivables—United Airlines | $203,210 | |
| Cr Travel Commissions and Fees | | $203,210 |

Shepherd's subordinates had discovered the adjusting entry during their second-quarter review of Cardillo's Form 10-Q statement. When asked, Lawrence had told the auditors that the entry involved commissions earned by Cardillo from United Airlines during the second quarter. The auditors had accepted Lawrence's explanation without attempting to corroborate it with other audit evidence.

After discussing the adjusting entry with her subordinates, Shepherd questioned Lawrence. Lawrence insisted that the adjusting entry had been properly recorded. Shepherd then requested that Lawrence ask United Airlines to provide Touche Ross with a confirmation verifying the key stipulations of the agreement with Cardillo. Shepherd's concern regarding the adjusting entry stemmed from information she had reviewed in the client's files that pertained to the United Airlines agreement. That information suggested that the United Airlines payment to Cardillo was refundable under certain conditions and thus not recognizable immediately as revenue.

Shortly after the meeting between Shepherd and Lawrence, Walter Rognlien contacted the audit partner. Like Lawrence, Rognlien maintained that the $203,000 amount had been properly recorded as commission revenue during the second quarter. Rognlien also told Shepherd that the disputed amount, which United Airlines paid to Cardillo during the third quarter of 1985, was not refundable to United Airlines under any circumstances. After some prodding by Shepherd, Rognlien agreed to allow her to request a confirmation from United Airlines concerning certain features of the agreement.

Shepherd received the requested confirmation from United Airlines on December 17, 1986. The confirmation stated that the disputed amount was refundable through 1990 if certain stipulations of the contractual agreement between the two parties were not fulfilled.[2] After receiving the confirmation, Shepherd called Rognlien and asked him to explain the obvious difference of opinion between United Airlines and Cardillo regarding the terms of their agreement. Rognlien told Shepherd that he had a secret arrangement with the chairman of the board of United Airlines. "Rognlien claimed that pursuant to this confidential business arrangement, the $203,210 would never have to be repaid to United. Shepherd asked Rognlien for permission to contact United's chairman to confirm the confidential business arrangement. Rognlien refused. In fact, as Rognlien knew, no such agreement existed."

A few days following Shepherd's conversation with Rognlien, she advised William Kaye, Cardillo's vice president of finance, that the $203,000 amount could not be recognized as revenue until the contractual agreement with United Airlines expired in 1990. Kaye refused to make the appropriate adjusting entry, explaining that Lawrence had insisted that the payment from United Airlines be credited to a revenue account. On December 30, 1985, Rognlien called Shepherd and told her that he was terminating Cardillo's relationship with Touche Ross.

In early February 1986, Cardillo filed a Form 8-K statement with the Securities and Exchange Commission (SEC) notifying that agency of the company's change in auditors. SEC regulations required Cardillo to disclose in the 8-K statement any disagreements involving accounting, auditing, or financial reporting issues with its former auditor. The 8-K, signed by Lawrence, indicated that no such disagreements preceded Cardillo's decision to dismiss Touche Ross. SEC regulations also required Touche Ross to draft a letter commenting on the existence of any disagreements with Cardillo. This letter had to be filed as an exhibit to the 8-K statement. In Touche Ross's exhibit letter, Shepherd discussed the dispute involving the United Airlines payment to Cardillo. Shepherd disclosed that the improper accounting treatment given that transaction resulted in misrepresented financial statements for Cardillo for the six months ended June 30, 1985, and the nine months ended September 30, 1985.

In late February 1986, Raymond Riley, Cardillo's legal counsel, wrote Shepherd and insisted that she had misinterpreted the United Airlines-Cardillo transaction in the Touche Ross exhibit letter filed with the company's 8-K. Riley also informed Shepherd that Cardillo would not pay the $17,500 invoice that Touche Ross had submitted to his company. This invoice was for professional services Touche Ross had rendered prior to being dismissed by Rognlien.

## ACT 3

On January 21, 1986, Cardillo retained KMG Main Hurdman (KMG) to replace Touche Ross as its independent audit firm. KMG soon addressed the accounting treatment Cardillo had applied to the United Airlines payment. When KMG personnel discussed the payment with Rognlien, he informed them of the alleged secret arrangement with United Airlines that superseded the written contractual agreement. According to Rognlien, the secret arrangement precluded United Airlines from demanding a refund of the $203,000 payment under any circumstances. KMG refused to accept this explanation. Roger Shlonsky, the KMG audit partner responsible for the Cardillo

---

2. Shepherd apparently never learned that the $203,000 payment was intended to reimburse Cardillo for expenses incurred in switching to United Airlines' reservation system. As a result, she focused almost exclusively on the question of when Cardillo should recognize the United Airlines payment as revenue. If she had been aware of the true nature of the payment, she almost certainly would have been even more adamant regarding the impropriety of the $203,000 adjusting entry.

engagement, told Rognlien that the payment would have to be recognized as revenue on a pro rata basis over the five-year period of the written contractual agreement with United Airlines.[3]

Cardillo began experiencing severe liquidity problems in early 1986. These problems worsened a few months later when a judge imposed a $685,000 judgment on Cardillo to resolve a civil suit filed against the company. Following the judge's ruling, Raymond Riley alerted Rognlien and Lawrence that the adverse judgment qualified as a "material event" and thus had to be reported to the SEC in a Form 8-K filing. In the memorandum he sent to his superiors, Riley discussed the serious implications of not disclosing the settlement to the SEC: "My primary concern by not releasing such report and information is that the officers and directors of Cardillo may be subject to violation of rule 10b-5 of the SEC rules by failing to disclose information that may be material to a potential investor."

Within 10 days of receiving Riley's memorandum, Rognlien sold 100,000 shares of Cardillo stock in the open market. Two weeks later, Lawrence issued a press release disclosing for the first time the adverse legal settlement. However, Lawrence failed to disclose the amount of the settlement or that Cardillo remained viable only because Rognlien had invested in the company the proceeds from the sale of the 100,000 shares of stock. Additionally, Lawrence's press release underestimated the firm's expected loss for 1985 by approximately 300 percent.

Following Lawrence's press release, Roger Shlonsky met with Rognlien and Lawrence. Shlonsky informed them that the press release grossly understated Cardillo's estimated loss for fiscal 1985. Shortly after that meeting, KMG resigned as Cardillo's independent audit firm.

## EPILOGUE

In May 1987, the creditors of Cardillo Travel Systems, Inc., forced the company into involuntary bankruptcy proceedings. Later that same year, the SEC concluded a lengthy investigation of the firm. The SEC found that Rognlien, Lawrence, and Kaye had violated several provisions of the federal securities laws. These violations included making false representations to outside auditors, failing to maintain accurate financial records, and failing to file prompt financial reports with the SEC. In addition, the federal agency charged Rognlien with violating the insider trading provisions of the federal securities laws. As a result of these findings, the SEC imposed permanent injunctions on each of the three individuals that prohibited them from engaging in future violations of federal securities laws. The SEC also attempted to recover from Rognlien the $237,000 he received from selling the 100,000 shares of Cardillo stock in April 1986. In January 1989, the two parties resolved this matter when Rognlien agreed to pay the SEC $60,000.

3. Cardillo executives also successfully concealed from the KMG auditors the fact that the United Airlines payment was simply an advance payment to cover installation expenses for the new reservation system.

## Questions

1. Identify the accountants in this case who faced ethical dilemmas. Also identify the parties who would be potentially affected by the outcome of each of these dilemmas. What responsibility did the accountant in each case owe to these parties? Did the accountants fulfill these responsibilities?
2. Describe the procedures an auditor should perform during a review of a client's quarterly financial statements. In your opinion, did the Touche Ross auditors who discovered the $203,000 adjusting entry during their 1985 second-quarter review take all appropriate steps to corroborate that entry? Should the auditors have immediately informed the audit partner, Helen Shepherd, of the entry?
3. In reviewing the United Airlines-Cardillo agreement, Shepherd collected evidence that supported the $203,000 adjusting entry as booked and evidence that suggested the entry was recorded improperly. Identify each of these items of evidence. What characteristics of audit evidence do the profession's technical standards suggest auditors should consider? Analyze the audit evidence that Shepherd collected regarding the disputed entry in terms of those characteristics.
4. What are the principal objectives of the SEC's rules that require Form 8-K statements to be filed when public companies change auditors? Did Shepherd violate the client confidentiality rule when she discussed the United Airlines-Cardillo transaction in the exhibit letter she filed with Cardillo's 8-K auditor change statement? In your opinion, did Shepherd have a responsibility to disclose to Cardillo executives the information she intended to include in the exhibit letter?
5. Do the profession's technical standards explicitly require auditors to evaluate the integrity of a prospective client's key executives? Identify the specific measures auditors can use to assess the integrity of a prospective client's executives.

CASE 5.2

# American International Group, Inc.

Cornelius Vander Starr wanted to see the world. In 1918, the twenty-six year-old Californian emptied his bank account to purchase a one-way ticket to the Far East on a steamship. After "bumming around" Japan for several months, Vander Starr traveled to Shanghai, China, where he landed a job working for an insurance company. Within a short period of time, Vander Starr realized that selling insurance was a low overhead business that was ideally suited for a young entrepreneurial type like himself so he quit his job and set up his own insurance agency, American Asiatic Underwriters. Vander Starr's business grew rapidly. By the time of his death in the late 1960s, Starr's one-man firm had become a multi-billion dollar international conglomerate with operating units in Europe, Latin America, the Middle East, and the United States. The Starr Foundation that he created before his death ranks among the world's largest philanthropic organizations.

In 1948, the Chinese civil war forced Vander Starr to relocate his company's headquarters from Shanghai to New York City. As he neared retirement, Vander Starr chose his protégé, Maurice "Hank" Greenberg, to replace him as his company's chief executive officer. During the early 1960s, Greenberg had revamped the company's business model. Instead of focusing on selling life insurance and other insurance products for individuals, Greenberg convinced Starr that the company's principal line of business should be insurance and other financial services products designed for large corporations. In 1969, Greenberg took the company, which had been renamed American International Group, Inc. (AIG), public by listing its stock on the New York Stock Exchange.

Greenberg would serve as AIG's top executive for nearly four decades. Under his leadership, the company became known worldwide for the new and innovative financial services products that it continually developed and the aggressive methods that it used to market those products. These efforts produced impressive financial results for the company. By the turn of the century, AIG was one of the ten largest companies in the United States and among the twenty largest companies worldwide.

In early 2001, a group of AIG executives came up with an idea for a new financial service that they believed would appeal to a wide range of large corporations. This service would involve AIG creating customized "special purpose entities" or SPEs for such companies. An SPE is typically a limited partnership that two or more companies join together to form. Since an SPE is an unconsolidated subsidiary, a company can download or transfer underperforming assets and related liabilities to that entity to improve its apparent financial condition. This "balance sheet management feature" of SPEs was the principal selling point that AIG intended to use in marketing its new service.

In fact, many large corporations were already using SPEs "to perform cosmetic surgery on their balance sheets."[1] Enron Corporation, a large Houston-based energy company, was among the most prolific users of SPEs.[2] Enron had significantly improved its apparent financial condition by "hiding" distressed assets and much of

1. J. Kahn, "Off Balance Sheet—And Out of Control," *Fortune*, 18 February 2002, 84.

2. See *Enron Corporation*, Case 1.1.

its outstanding debt in hundreds of SPEs that it had created. AIG's management was convinced that, unlike Enron, most companies did not have the in-house expertise to develop their own SPEs.

AIG's executives realized that their new SPE service, which was effectively an accounting mechanism, would be more credible if one of the major accounting firms was involved in its development and marketing. For that reason, AIG retained Michael Joseph, a partner in the national office of Ernst & Young (E&Y) and a "nationally recognized expert on the accounting for structured financial vehicles and SPEs,"[3] to help develop and market the new service. "To assist AIG in its marketing" of the new SPE service "Joseph caused E&Y to issue reports pursuant to *Statement on Auditing Standards No. 50*, 'Reports on the Application of Accounting Principles.'"[4] These *SAS No. 50* reports indicated that the "nonconsolidation accounting treatment" for the assets and liabilities transferred to an SPE that had been designed by AIG "was an appropriate application of GAAP." In promoting its new SPE service, "AIG referred to E&Y's advice in its marketing materials and referred potential buyers directly to Joseph to answer accounting-related questions."

Among the first companies to express an interest in purchasing AIG's SPE service was PNC Financial Services Group, Inc. (PNC), a large financial services firm that operated the fifth-largest bank in the United States. During the negotiations with AIG, PNC consulted with its independent auditors to determine whether the accounting treatment for AIG's SPE product complied with GAAP. In fact, PNC's audit firm was E&Y, which meant that the company's auditors contacted Joseph to determine whether PNC's proposed SPE would be GAAP-compliant.

Joseph gave the PNC auditors a copy of a *SAS No. 50* report that he had written for AIG. The auditors relied on that report "without performing any meaningful separate analysis" in deciding that the accounting treatment for the proposed SPE was acceptable. Joseph billed the time that he spent interacting with the PNC auditors to the PNC audit engagement.

During July 2001, PNC transferred nearly $100 million of nonperforming loans to an SPE that was created by AIG. A few months later, the company downloaded more than $100 million of additional nonperforming loans to another AIG-created SPE. In an earnings press release in late 2001, PNC reported that it had $361 million of nonperforming loans. That figure did not include more than $200 million of such loans that had been transferred to its SPEs.

Federal Reserve officials contacted PNC in November 2001 and inquired regarding the company's nonperforming loans. When those officials reviewed the transactions that had resulted in $207 million of PNC's nonperforming loans being transferred to SPEs, they questioned whether those transfers were appropriate. At this point, PNC executives asked Michael Joseph to intercede on their behalf with the Federal Reserve. Joseph discussed the matter with the Federal Reserve and defended the accounting and financial reporting treatment for the loans that had been transferred to SPEs. The Federal Reserve disagreed with Joseph and in January 2002 ordered PNC to reverse the SPE transactions and include the $207 million of nonperforming loans in the company's consolidated financial statements.

3. Securities and Exchange Commission, *Accounting and Auditing Enforcement Release No. 2523*, 11 December 2006. Unless indicated otherwise, subsequent quotes in this case were taken from this source.

4. Accounting firms typically prepare *SAS No. 50* reports to provide a third party, other than an audit client, with technical guidance on how "existing accounting principles apply to new transactions and financial products" (AU 625.01).

The Federal Reserve's decision to force PNC to reverse its SPE transactions triggered an investigation of the company by the Securities Exchange Commission (SEC). In reviewing PNC's SPE transactions, the SEC discovered that they were not in compliance with GAAP. GAAP dictates that for a company to treat an SPE as an unconsolidated subsidiary, an external entity must have a minimum capital investment of 3 percent in the SPE. The external entity that had invested in PNC's SPEs was AIG. However, AIG's investments in the SPEs had not met the required 3 percent threshold, meaning that the financial data for PNC's SPEs should have been included in the company's consolidated financial statements.

## EPILOGUE

In July 2002, PNC executives agreed to cease and desist from any future violations of federal securities laws to settle charges pending against the company by the SEC. One year later, PNC agreed to pay $115 million to settle related fraud charges filed against the company by the U.S. Justice Department.

In December 2006, the SEC issued an accounting and auditing enforcement release focusing on Michael Joseph's role in PNC's SPE transactions. In this release, the SEC reported that "Joseph was a cause of PNC's violations" of federal securities laws. The SEC maintained that Joseph should have known that PNC's SPE transactions were not in compliance with GAAP. In this same enforcement release, the SEC alleged that Joseph's dual role with AIG and PNC had been improper and had posed a conflict of interest for him.

> *Joseph was involved in the development and marketing of the AIG [SPE] accounting product. He advised AIG on the structure, he prepared several SAS 50 letters used in marketing the product, he participated in conference calls with potential purchasers . . . Consequently, Joseph was invested both financially and reputationally in the success of the [SPE] product and therefore had a conflict of interest when he later evaluated the accounting for the product by E&Y's audit client, PNC.*

The SEC went on to observe that Joseph's conduct was "highly unreasonable" and undermined the independence of E&Y's PNC audit engagement team. An accounting professor interviewed by the *Los Angeles Times* used an analogy to describe the likely impact that Joseph's conduct had on the PNC audit engagement team. "Did it bias the individual auditors in this particular case? It's like asking whether 40 years of smoking led to someone's lung cancer."[5]

The SEC suspended Joseph for three years from being involved with audits of public companies. In March 2007, the SEC fined E&Y $1.6 million for the firm's independence violations stemming from Joseph's conduct. The following month, E&Y agreed to pay approximately $9 million to settle a class-action lawsuit filed against it for its role in the PNC accounting scandal.

In late 2004, AIG agreed to pay $126 million in fines and restitution for its involvement in PNC's improper SPE accounting. That amount would be dwarfed by the $1.6 billion fine that AIG agreed to pay in late 2005 to settle charges that it had intentionally misrepresented its own accounting records. Among many other allegations, AIG had reportedly recorded bogus sales of insurance policies to inflate its earnings and understated its loss reserves. In addition to the huge fine, Hank Greenberg was forced to resign as AIG's chief executive as a result of the massive accounting fraud.[6]

5. *Los Angeles Times* (online), "Ernst & Young in SEC Probe of PNC's Books," 8 December 2004.

6. In August 2009, Greenberg agreed to pay a $15 million fine to settle civil fraud charges filed against him by the SEC. The settlement also prohibited Greenberg from serving as an officer of a public company for three years.

AIG was front and center in news headlines once more in late 2008 when the largest economic crisis since the Great Depression erupted in the United States and quickly spread around the globe. In September 2008, the federal government seized control of AIG to prevent the company from collapsing. The company had such an extensive role in global credit and insurance markets that financial experts maintained that its collapse would cause a worldwide economic calamity. In exchange for approximately $85 billion of capital, the federal government received an eighty percent equity interest in the company. In the following months, tens of billions of dollars of additional federal "bailout" money was invested in AIG to keep the company afloat. AIG would ultimately receive more federal bailout funds than any other U.S. company.

## Questions

1. Is it ethical for a CPA or CPA firm to help companies "manage" their reported earnings and financial condition? In responding to this question, first assume that the CPA or CPA firm is serving as a consultant, and then assume that the CPA or CPA firm is serving as the given entity's independent auditor. Defend your answers.
2. When a dispute arises between an audit client and its auditor regarding the proper accounting treatment for a transaction or other item, the audit client will sometimes retain another accounting firm to issue a *SAS No. 50* report on the proper accounting treatment for the given item. Identify the potential ethical dilemmas posed by allowing accounting firms to issue *SAS No. 50* reports to non-audit clients.

CASE 5.3

# The PTL Club

Jim and Tammy Faye Bakker founded the PTL (Praise the Lord) Club, a religious broadcasting organization, in 1974. A little more than one decade later, the PTL Club claimed more than 500,000 members and boasted annual revenues of almost $130 million. Bakker and his close associates came under intense scrutiny in 1987 following a revelation that they used PTL funds to pay a former church secretary to remain silent concerning a brief liaison between herself and Bakker. That disclosure triggered a series of investigations of PTL's finances. Key agencies involved in those investigations included the Internal Revenue Service, the Federal Bureau of Investigation, and the U.S. Postal Service. In March 1987, Bakker resigned as PTL's chairman. Two years later, a federal jury convicted him of fraud and conspiracy charges. A federal judge then fined Bakker $500,000 and sentenced him to forty-five years in prison.[1]

The Bakker scandal spurred a nationwide debate focusing on the issue of whether the financial affairs of religious broadcasting companies should be subject to regulatory oversight. The investigations of PTL revealed that Bakker and his associates received huge salaries and bonuses from funds raised via the organization's televised appeals. In 1986, PTL paid the Bakkers almost $2 million. During the first three months of 1987, while PTL struggled to cope with severe cash flow problems, the couple received $640,000. Critics also chastised the Bakkers for their flamboyant lifestyle. Tammy Faye Bakker decorated PTL's executive suites in Fort Mill, South Carolina, in opulent style, including gold-plated bathroom fixtures and extravagant chandeliers. The Bakkers enjoyed a rambling Palm Springs ranch house on their many trips to the West Coast, a $600,000 condominium in Highland Beach, Florida, and a fleet of luxury automobiles, including Rolls-Royces.

Before 1987, Jim Bakker's critics persistently called for more extensive financial disclosures by PTL. Bakker resisted these demands. He repeatedly insisted that such disclosures were not necessary since PTL maintained strong financial controls. In addition, Bakker often reminded his critics that PTL "had excellent accountants and that it had external audits by reputable [CPA] firms."[2] The subsequent investigations of PTL failed to support Bakker's claims. Those investigations revealed that the organization's internal controls were extremely weak, and nonexistent in many cases. Investigators found that Bakker's subordinates issued paychecks to individuals not employed by PTL and paid large sums to consultants who never provided any services to the organization. Additionally, investigators could not locate documentation for millions of dollars of construction costs recorded in PTL's accounting records.

---

1. In early 1991, a federal appeals court upheld Bakker's conviction on the fraud and conspiracy charges but voided Bakker's 45-year sentence, as well as the $500,000 fine, and ordered that a new sentencing hearing be held. According to the appeals court, the trial judge who imposed the lengthy sentence on Bakker may have allowed his personal religious predispositions to influence his sentencing decision. Following the re-sentencing hearing in August 1991, Bakker received an 18-year sentence. In 1994, Bakker was paroled after serving nearly five years in federal prison.

2. L. Berton, "Laventhol & Horwath Beset by Litigation, Runs into Hard Times," *The Wall Street Journal*, 17 May 1990, A1, A10.

One of the most troubling weaknesses uncovered in PTL's accounting system involved a secret payroll account used to disburse funds to Bakker and his closest aides. This account was so secretive that the organization's chief financial officer was not informed of the expenses funneled through it, while PTL's board of directors was totally unaware of its existence. Surprisingly, during the mid-1980s a partner of Laventhol & Horwath, PTL's independent audit firm, maintained the secret payroll account, including overseeing the preparation of the checks issued on that account.[3] Even more surprisingly, that same partner also supervised PTL's annual audits.

Laventhol was widely criticized for its role in the PTL scandal and eventually named as a co-defendant in a $757 million class action lawsuit filed by PTL contributors. The suit alleged that Laventhol assisted Bakker in misrepresenting PTL's financial condition and facilitated Bakker's efforts to embezzle millions of dollars from PTL through the secret payroll account. Among several other parties named as co-defendants in the lawsuit were Bakker and PTL's former audit firm, Deloitte, Haskins & Sells. PTL had dismissed Deloitte as its audit firm in 1985 for undisclosed reasons and retained Laventhol as its new audit firm.

Laventhol's decision to accept PTL as a client was apparently linked to an aggressive marketing strategy adopted by the firm in the late 1970s. From 1980 to 1986 alone, Laventhol's nationwide revenues increased 300 percent. This phenomenal growth resulted in part from Laventhol's acceptance of high-risk audit clients that other audit firms hesitated or refused to consider as clients. A former Laventhol employee bluntly observed that the firm "took too many risky clients like PTL--a strategy that, ironically, accountants often advise their clients to avoid."[4] Critics charged that the large fees Laventhol received from PTL influenced the accounting firm's decisions regarding that client. In the civil lawsuit that named Laventhol as a co-defendant, the plaintiffs maintained that the CPA firm permitted the questionable payments from the secret payroll account "because PTL was the largest client for its [Laventhol's] Charlotte office."[5]

In the fall of 1990, Laventhol, the seventh-largest CPA firm in the United States at the time, filed for bankruptcy. Attorneys for PTL's contributors subsequently dropped the accounting firm as a co-defendant in the $757 million class action lawsuit.[6] Two months later, the jury hearing that case rendered a $130 million judgment against Jim Bakker to be paid to the plaintiffs. The jury ruled that Deloitte & Touche, the successor firm of Deloitte, Haskins & Sells, was not guilty of any malfeasance in the case. In commenting on the jury's verdict, a Deloitte official noted that the suit was "a well-financed and well-executed attempt to recover enormous damages from an innocent accounting firm for the alleged wrongdoing of others."[7,8]

---

3. Although Laventhol prepared the checks written on this account, the accounting firm forwarded the checks to a PTL executive to be signed.

4. Berton, "Laventhol & Horwath Beset by Litigation," A1.

5. M. Isikoff and A. Harris, "PTL Contributors Sue Ministry's Accounting Firms," *Washington Post*, 19 November 1987, C10, C16.

6. Laventhol's partners and former partners did not escape financial responsibility for the firm's role in the PTL scandal. In a subsequent bankruptcy plan approved in 1992 by the U.S. Bankruptcy Court of New York, Laventhol's partners and former partners contributed approximately $47 million to a settlement pool to liquidate outstanding claims against Laventhol. This pool was to be divided among Laventhol's creditors and several parties that had sued the firm, including PTL's contributors. Individual payments made by Laventhol partners to this settlement pool reportedly ranged as high as $700,000.

7. "Deloitte Victorious in PTL Case," *Public Accounting Report*, 31 January 1991, 5.

8. An excellent and comprehensive summary of the accounting and auditing issues involved in the PTL scandal can be found in *Anatomy of A Fraud* (New York: Wiley, 1993), by Gary Tidwell.

## Questions

1. Identify the ethical questions raised by the maintenance of PTL's secret payroll account by the Laventhol partner. Does the fact that PTL was a private organization not registered with the Securities and Exchange Commission affect the propriety of the partner's actions? Explain.
2. What procedures should an audit firm perform before accepting an audit client, particularly a high-risk client such as PTL?
3. Briefly define the so-called "deep pockets theory" as it relates to the litigation problems of large public accounting firms in recent years. What measures can these firms take to protect themselves from large class action lawsuits predicated upon false or largely unfounded allegations?

**CASE 5.4**

# Zaveral Boosalis Raisch

Law enforcement authorities and officials of regulatory agencies frequently receive anonymous "hot tips." The shy tipsters typically charge that an individual or organization has violated one or more laws or regulatory directives and demand that the "guilty" party be brought to justice. When such allegations have some measure of credibility, the appropriate authorities have a responsibility to investigate the alleged wrongdoer.

In the late 1990s, the Colorado State Board of Accountancy received an anonymous letter that accused a Colorado-based accounting firm, Zaveral Boosalis Raisch, of various improprieties. The alleged indiscretions involved audit, accounting, and taxation services provided by Zaveral to two Colorado casinos. The informant charged that Zaveral had violated professional accounting and auditing standards in completing those engagements, was responsible for the clients' failure to remit federal withholding taxes and state unemployment taxes to the appropriate agencies, and caused the clients to submit improper information to the Colorado Gaming Commission.

After reviewing the allegations, the State Board launched an investigation. Among the first actions taken by the State Board was obtaining a subpoena to compel Zaveral to provide its investigative team with all relevant tax returns, financial statements, workpapers, correspondence with the two clients, reports filed with the Colorado Gaming Commission, and "all other documentation used or prepared in connection with these engagements."[1]

To the surprise of the State Board, Zaveral refused to comply with the subpoena. Instead, Zaveral filed a motion with a state court demanding to know whether the State Board had contacted the two clients and received their permission to obtain the requested documents from Zaveral. The accounting firm pointed out in its court filing that Colorado state law provides for privileged communications between CPAs and their clients. As a result, unless a client specifically waives that right, a CPA cannot be compelled to provide confidential information regarding the client even if a third party obtains a subpoena calling for the release of that information. In fact, Zaveral knew that its two clients had already invoked the CPA-client privilege, meaning that the clients had refused to grant the accounting firm the right to provide the subpoenaed information to the State Board. By invoking that privilege, the clients triggered a contentious court battle between Zaveral and the Colorado State Board of Accountancy.

To provide for an orderly society and the fair and expedient resolution of civil and criminal litigation, democratic nations generally impose a "duty to testify" on their citizens. However, democracies have also long recognized the need for their citizens to have a right to privileged or private communications with certain professionals. The concept of privileged communications is most often associated with attorney-client relationships. Although CPA-client communications are not privileged in cases

1. Unless indicated otherwise, the facts and quotes included in this case were taken from the following legal opinion: *The Colorado State Board of Accountancy v. Zaveral Boosalis Raisch*, 960 P.2d 102; 1998 Colo. LEXIS 427; 1998 Colo. J. C.A.R. 2651.

that originate in the federal courts, thirty states have enacted laws that protect the confidentiality of CPA-client communications in litigation initiated in their courts.[2] Colorado is one of those states. A Colorado state court explained that by protecting the confidentiality of CPA-client communications, the state legislature intended to encourage "full and frank communication between CPAs and their clients so that professional advice may be given on the basis of complete information, free from the consequences or the apprehension of disclosure."[3]

Most state statutes that grant privileged status to CPA-client communications include various exceptions that identify specific circumstances in which this privilege is voided. The most common of these exceptions involves "accountancy board investigations." In 27 of the 30 states that recognize the CPA-client privilege, CPAs must turn over to the state board of accountancy documents requested by that agency in connection with a disciplinary or other official investigation. The three states whose enabling statutes for the CPA-client privilege do not include such an exception are Colorado, Missouri, and Tennessee. Both the Missouri and Tennessee state laws provide for other exceptions to the CPA-client privilege rule. Colorado stands alone as the only state that provides an absolute CPA-client privilege. Because of the rigorous CPA-client privilege rule in Colorado, Zaveral believed that the State Board's effort to compel it to turn over the requested information regarding the two casino clients would be rejected by the state courts.

When Zaveral refused to comply with the State Board's subpoena, the State Board filed a motion in a Colorado state court to force the accounting firm to turn over the requested documents. To support the State Board, the American Institute of Certified Public Accountants (AICPA) filed an *amicus curiae* or friend of the court brief with the Colorado state court. In that legal brief, the AICPA encouraged the state court to force Zaveral to comply with the previously issued subpoena since state boards cannot rigorously carry out their oversight role for the public accounting profession without the ability to access and review CPAs' workpapers and related work product. The AICPA noted that, "at the center of almost any state board investigation into a CPA engagement will be the CPA's workpapers, for it is only through careful review of the workpapers that practice quality may be effectively assessed."

The Colorado state court that presided over the dispute between Zaveral and the Colorado State Board of Accountancy agreed with the AICPA's position. "The district court reasoned that requiring the Board to obtain client consent to a CPA subpoena would 'severely hamper' the ability of the board to carry out its statutory investigatory and disciplinary duties." As a result, the state court ordered Zaveral to provide the State Board with the client documents covered by the previously issued subpoena. Zaveral appealed this decision. The appellate court that heard the appeal reversed the lower court's ruling. In reaching this decision, the appellate court noted that it could not imply an exception to the CPA-client privilege rule since the statute that created this rule contained no exceptions, that is, the statute failed to identify any circumstances in which CPAs were *not* entitled to have privileged communications with their clients.

---

2. Recognize that the "privilege" rests with the client not the CPA. That is, only clients can invoke this statutory right. For example, if a client waives this right in response to a legally enforceable subpoena or other court order, the given CPA is obligated to produce the requested client-related documents and/or testify regarding communications with that client.

3. *Neusteter v. District Court*, 675 P.2d 1, 5 (Colo. 1984).

Not to be outdone by its feisty opponent, the State Board appealed the appellate court's ruling to the highest court in Colorado, the Supreme Court of Colorado, which would ultimately issue the final ruling in the case. In reviewing the case, the supreme court immediately realized that it faced a dilemma. "This case presents for our review a privilege statute which is absolute on its face and a state licensing statute granting an absolute and unqualified subpoena power to the Board." The court went on to observe that its responsibility was to review the statutes that created the mutually opposing and conflicting legal principles in an effort to determine the "legislative intent" underlying those statutes.

The Colorado state law that created the CPA-client privilege was adopted by the state legislature in 1929. According to that law, the state should provide for "inviolate" confidentiality between, or among, the parties to certain relationships.

> *A certified public accountant shall not be examined without the consent of his client as to any communication made by the client to him in person or through the media of books of account and financial records or his advice, reports, or working papers given or made thereon in the course of professional employment; nor shall a secretary, stenographer, clerk or assistant of a certified public accountant be examined without the consent of the client concerning any fact, the knowledge of which he has acquired in such capacity.*

Three decades later, in 1959, the Colorado state legislature passed a law creating the Colorado State Board of Accountancy "to insure that persons who hold themselves out as possessing professional qualifications as accountants are, in fact, qualified to render accounting services of a professional nature." That statute granted the State Board the power and duty to investigate CPAs accused of professional negligence or other malfeasance. To fulfill this responsibility, the legislature gave "the board or any member thereof" the power to "issue subpoenas to compel the attendance of witnesses and the production of documents . . . in connection with any investigation." The State Board subsequently issued a rule requiring Colorado CPAs to comply with legally enforceable subpoenas that mandate the production of client documents and other confidential information. This rule explicitly indicates that complying with such a subpoena will not subject a CPA to a violation of the State Board's client confidentiality rule.

After studying the statute that created the CPA-client privilege and the statute that created the State Board of Accountancy, the Supreme Court of Colorado then reviewed Colorado statutes that established privileged communications rules for other professional groups within the state. The supreme court found that the statutes creating privileged communications between medical examiners, nurses, and their respective clients included specific exceptions. Among these exceptions was the right of each group's state board to subpoena information needed in pursuing investigations of their licensees without first obtaining the consent of the given clients. Finally, the supreme court also noted that the Uniform Accountancy Act (UAA) recommends an "express" exception to the CPA-client privilege rule for state board investigations. The UAA is a legislative proposal sponsored by the AICPA and the National Association of State Boards of Accountancy that encourages state legislatures to adopt a uniform regulatory framework to oversee the practice of public accounting in each state.

Following its extensive study of the legal issues and statutes relevant to the Zaveral case, the Supreme Court of Colorado ruled in favor of Zaveral and refused to compel the accounting firm to produce the documents subpoenaed by the State Board of Accountancy. In reaching this decision, the supreme court observed that, "Unless and until the General Assembly [state legislature] chooses to provide the exception [to the CPA-client privilege rule for state board investigations] recommended by the Uniform Act and adopted by the vast majority of other states, the Board must obtain client consent for disclosure of information otherwise privileged by the accountant-client relationship."[4]

## Questions

1. A Colorado court opinion cited in this case suggests that in the absence of a CPA-client privilege, communications between those parties might be influenced by the "consequences or the apprehension of disclosure." Provide specific examples of how CPA-client communications might be adversely affected in the absence of a CPA-client privilege. In your opinion, why do the federal courts choose not to recognize a CPA-client privilege in litigation that originates in the federal courts?
2. Identify the parties who you believe benefit from Colorado's absolute CPA-client privilege rule and the parties who are disadvantaged by that rule. Briefly explain your reasoning for each party you identified.
3. Do you believe the Supreme Court of Colorado made the appropriate decision in this case? Defend your answer.

4. According to a conversation with an administrative official of the Colorado State Board of Accountancy, since the resolution of the Zaveral case the State Board has attempted to persuade the state legislature to modify the CPA-client privilege rule to include an exception for investigations initiated by regulatory agencies. To date, those efforts have been unsuccessful. The official went on to observe that Colorado's strict CPA-client privilege rule has "hamstrung" the State Board's ability to investigate alleged misconduct by Colorado CPAs.

**CASE 5.5**

# Koger Properties, Inc.

Becoming a partner with one of the large international accounting firms easily ranks among the most common career goals of accounting majors.[1] Michael Goodbread staked out that career goal four decades ago. After graduating from college, Goodbread made the first step toward reaching his objective when he accepted an entry-level position with Touche Ross & Company. In February 1973, Goodbread received his CPA license in the state of Florida after passing the CPA exam. Eight years later, the partners of Touche Ross selected Goodbread to join their ranks.

In December 1989, Goodbread accomplished his career goal a second time by becoming a partner with Deloitte & Touche, the firm created by the merger of Deloitte, Haskins & Sells and Touche Ross. Before the merger, Goodbread served as an audit partner in the Jacksonville, Florida, office of Touche Ross. Goodbread assumed an identical position with the newly formed Jacksonville office of Deloitte & Touche following the merger.

The impressive salaries earned by partners of large international accounting firms provide them ample discretionary funds for investment purposes. Like many investors, Goodbread often considered local companies when making investment decisions. One local firm that caught Goodbread's attention during the late 1980s was Koger Properties, Inc., a real estate development company headquartered in Jacksonville. Koger's claim to fame was originating the concept of an office park. According to a Koger annual report, the company opened the nation's first office park in 1957 in Jacksonville. By the early 1990s, Koger operated nearly 40 office parks in two dozen metropolitan areas scattered across the southern United States.

In December 1988, Goodbread purchased 400 shares of Koger's common stock at a price of $26 per share. At the time, Koger had approximately 25 million shares of common stock outstanding.

Following the December 1989 merger that created Deloitte & Touche, one of Goodbread's first assignments with his new firm was supervising the audit of Koger Properties for its fiscal year ending March 31, 1990. Koger had previously been an audit client of Deloitte, Haskins & Sells. In his role as audit engagement partner, Goodbread oversaw all facets of the Koger audit. On February 21, 1990, Goodbread signed the "audit planning memorandum" that laid out the general strategy Deloitte & Touche intended to follow in completing the Koger audit. Several months later, on June 27, 1990, Goodbread signed the "audit report record" for the Koger engagement. At the time, the signing of that document by the audit engagement partner formally completed a Deloitte & Touche audit.

Goodbread signed Koger's unqualified audit opinion on June 11, 1990. Almost exactly one month earlier, on May 10, 1990, Goodbread had sold the 400 shares of Koger stock that he had owned since December 1988. Goodbread sold the stock at a price of $20.75 per share.

The Securities and Exchange Commission (SEC) eventually learned that Goodbread had held an ownership interest in Koger Properties while he supervised the

1. The events discussed in this case were reconstructed principally from information included in Securities and Exchange Commission, *Accounting and Auditing Enforcement Release No. 861*, 10 December 1996.

company's 1990 audit. The SEC charged that Goodbread's ownership interest in Koger violated its independence rules, the *Code of Professional Conduct* of the American Institute of Certified Public Accountants (AICPA), and generally accepted auditing standards. Most important, the SEC charged that Goodbread caused Deloitte & Touche to issue an improper opinion on Koger's 1990 financial statements. Instead of the unqualified opinion Deloitte & Touche issued on those financial statements, the SEC maintained that a disclaimer of opinion had been required given the circumstances. Following its investigation of the matter, the SEC publicly censured Goodbread.

The embarrassing revelation of Michael Goodbread's ownership interest in Koger Properties marked the beginning of a long series of problems that Deloitte & Touche encountered with that audit client. In September 1991, Koger filed for bankruptcy. A short time earlier, Koger's stockholders had filed a class-action lawsuit against Deloitte & Touche. The suit alleged that the 1989 Koger audit performed by Deloitte, Haskins & Sells and the 1990 Koger audit completed by Deloitte & Touche were deficient. Those deficient audits allegedly contributed to the subsequent decline in Koger's stock price.

A federal jury agreed with the Koger stockholders and ordered Deloitte to pay the plaintiffs $81.3 million to compensate them for damages suffered because of the 1989 and 1990 audits. In July 1997, the U.S. Court of Appeals reversed the lower court's ruling and voided the huge judgment awarded to Koger's stockholders. The appellate court ruled that the stockholders failed to prove that any errors made by Deloitte during the 1989 and 1990 Koger audits caused the losses they subsequently incurred.[2]

Another of the megafirms created by a merger of two large international accounting firms encountered an independence problem similar to that experienced by Deloitte & Touche in the Koger Properties case. However, PricewaterhouseCoopers' "problem" was much more severe and embarrassing. In 1999, that firm agreed to be censured by the SEC for dozens of alleged violations of the profession's independence rules.

> *Without admitting or denying wrongdoing, PricewaterhouseCoopers has agreed to be censured by federal regulators over a dispute that ownership of client stock had compromised its independence as an auditor. The Big Five firm agreed to pay $2.5 million to establish education programs for the profession designed to improve auditor compliance. . . . The Securities and Exchange Commission claims it turned up 70 instances from 1996 to 1998 in which some of the partners and managers of the firm purchased client stock.*[3]

The problems experienced by Deloitte & Touche and PricewaterhouseCoopers apparently stemmed from unfamiliarity with the profession's auditor independence rules. In the late 1990s, a top SEC official revealed that personnel from the large international accounting firms frequently contacted the federal agency to inquire about its most basic ethical rules for independent auditors. According to this official, these inquiries commonly included questions regarding "such fundamental issues as the prohibition against owning stock in companies they audit."[4]

In recent years, the major accounting firms have continued to be plagued by embarrassing independence violations by their partners. In October 2008, Deloitte & Touche announced that it was suing its former vice chairman for allegedly using

2. *Securities Regulation and Law Report*, "Investors' 10b-5 Claims Against Deloitte Fail in CA for Lack of Loss Causation," 18 July 1997, 1018.

3. *Accounting Today*, "PwC Censured for Owning Client Stock," 8–21 February 1999, 3.

4. E. MacDonald, "Levitt Says Wave of Accounting Mergers Could Affect Independence of Auditors," *The Wall Street Journal*, 21 October 1997, A2, A4.

insider information obtained from at least twelve of the firm's audit clients to trade in the securities of those companies.[5] In May 2009, a federal jury convicted a former Ernst & Young partner of securities fraud for his role in a similar insider trading scheme that involved several of his firm's clients.[6]

## Questions

1. The SEC charged that Goodbread violated its independence rules, the AICPA's *Code of Professional Conduct*, and generally accepted auditing standards. Explain the SEC's rationale in making each of those allegations.
2. In your opinion, did Goodbread's equity interest in Koger Properties likely qualify as a "material" investment for him? Was the materiality of that investment a relevant issue in this case? Explain.
3. Given that Goodbread purchased stock of Koger Properties in 1988, under what conditions, if any, could he have later served as the audit engagement partner for that company?
4. During much of the 19th century in Great Britain, independent auditors were not only allowed to have an equity interest in their clients but were required to invest in their clients in certain circumstances. Explain the rationale likely underlying that rule. Would such a rule "make sense" in today's business environment in the United States? Defend your answer.

5. Reuters.com, "Deloitte Sues Vice Chairman for Client Securities Trades," 7 November 2008.
6. C. Bray, "Ex-Ernst & Young Partner Guilty of Six Fraud Counts," *Wall Street Journal* (online), 15 May 2009.

## CASE 5.6

# Ryden Trucking, Inc.

Jermell Marshall graduated with an accounting degree from the University of Washington in 1980 and immediately accepted a job with a regional accounting firm based in Seattle.[1] After spending four and one-half years on the auditing staff of that firm, Marshall decided he had worked for someone else long enough and resigned to establish his own accounting practice. Fifteen years later, Marshall's firm included two other partners, fifteen professional employees, and a support staff of ten paraprofessionals and clerical workers. Marshall served as the managing partner of his firm and supervised most audit, accounting services, and consulting engagements. The firm's audit and accounting services clients were primarily small to moderately sized companies in the Seattle area that required annual audits or reviews of their financial statements for their banks or other lenders.

In August 1999, Marshall hired Lola Rojas, a 28-year-old accountant who had recently moved to Seattle from southern California to be near her ailing mother. Four years earlier, Rojas had earned an accounting degree but after five attempts had yet to pass the CPA exam. During those four years, Rojas had held three different jobs, two as a staff accountant with small CPA firms and one as an entry-level accountant with a bank. Before hiring Rojas, Marshall had asked for letters of recommendation from two of her former employers. Each of those recommendation letters indicated that the cheerful and outgoing Rojas had been a dependable, competent, and hard-working employee.

During her first six months with the firm, Marshall assigned Rojas to several audit and accounting services engagements that he supervised. He was very pleased with her performance on those assignments. She was typically the first individual to arrive for work each morning, quickly established friendships with her peers, and was well liked by client personnel. Marshall's impression of Rojas changed abruptly in March 2000 when he received a phone call from Carson Caddell, the principal owner of Ryden Trucking, Inc., a trucking firm that serviced agricultural businesses in Washington and neighboring states. Ryden was easily the largest client of Marshall's firm. Caddell informed Marshall that one of his bookkeepers had discovered compelling evidence that Lola Rojas had embezzled approximately $32,000 during the three weeks she had spent in Ryden's office in early 2000.

Since establishing his firm, Marshall had dealt with several "problem" employees, but a client had never accused one of his employees of theft. Extremely upset, Marshall called Rojas into his office and informed her of the alleged theft reported by Carson Caddell. Within moments, Rojas began weeping and confessed to embezzling the funds. She explained that she needed the cash to pay for the medical expenses incurred over the prior year by her terminally ill mother who had no health insurance. Rojas then pleaded with Marshall to help her. She insisted that she had intended to somehow repay the stolen funds. If Marshall or Caddell reported her to law enforcement authorities, there would be no one to take care of her mother.

1. This case was developed from a recent legal opinion. The names of the actual parties involved in the case and the location of the events discussed in the case have been changed. In addition, certain of the factual circumstances reported in this case are fictionalized accounts of the actual facts disclosed in the legal opinion.

For more than one hour, Marshall discussed the situation with Rojas. Gradually, Marshall's anger subsided and he began to feel sorry for the emotionally distraught Rojas. In his mind, here was a young lady who had faced an unfortunate set of circumstances and made a foolhardy decision that stood to wreck her personal life and professional career. Finally, Marshall told Rojas that he wanted to discuss the matter with an attorney. In the meantime, he told her that he had no choice but to terminate her employment immediately since he could no longer trust her. Later that same day, Marshall drove to the law office of Andrew Tao. The two men had been friends since high school and fraternity brothers in college. After explaining the situation to Tao, Marshall asked if there was any way that the matter could be resolved without Rojas facing criminal charges. Tao responded that the decision of whether or not to file charges against Rojas rested with Carson Caddell.

The following morning, Marshall and Tao met with Caddell. During that meeting, Caddell repeatedly insisted that Rojas should be reported to law enforcement authorities. Even after Marshall explained the sad circumstances facing Rojas, Caddell was unmoved. "You can't let something like this slide, Jermell. Come on, she stole more than $30,000 from us. She deserves what she gets." Marshall made one last attempt to change Caddell's mind. He offered to repay one-half of the stolen funds immediately and sign a promissory note obligating him to repay the remainder within two years if Caddell would agree not to press charges. After several moments, Caddell responded by indicating that he "would think about it."[2]

Three days later, Marshall and Tao met with Lola Rojas. When Marshall told Rojas of his offer to reimburse Ryden Trucking for the embezzlement loss, she burst into tears and promised to repay him. After she regained her composure, Marshall reminded Rojas that Carson Caddell had not yet accepted his offer. Before Rojas left Marshall's office a few minutes later, he asked her how she expected to support herself over the coming weeks. Rojas told Marshall that, thanks to a recommendation from a friend, she had found a bookkeeping job with a small manufacturing firm located in a nearby Seattle suburb. She was scheduled to begin the job the following Monday.

Over the next few weeks, Marshall had two telephone conversations with Carson Caddell regarding Lola Rojas. During each of those conversations, Caddell indicated that he appreciated Marshall's offer but still firmly believed that Rojas should be held accountable for her actions. The day following the second conversation with Caddell, Marshall was surprised when Lola Rojas walked into his office and told him that she had convinced an uncle to loan her the $32,000 to repay Ryden Trucking. She then handed Marshall an envelope that contained a cashier's check in that amount. Marshall told Rojas that he would give the check to Carson Caddell but warned her that Caddell was still likely to insist on pressing charges. Nevertheless, he promised to talk with Caddell one more time and try to persuade him to change his mind.

The following day, Marshall, accompanied by Tao once more, delivered the cashier's check to Caddell. As Marshall had expected, the check did not change Caddell's mind. But, after Marshall made one final, heartfelt plea that Rojas deserved a second chance, Caddell agreed to drop the matter in exchange for Rojas pleading guilty to a misdemeanor. A few days later, Marshall, Tao, and Rojas met with an assistant district

2. As a point of information, the legal opinion from which this case was developed did not indicate whether Ryden Trucking had insurance that would reimburse the company for the embezzlement loss.

attorney and explained the series of events that had transpired over the past several weeks. After reviewing the matter and discussing it with his superiors, the assistant district attorney refused to accept Rojas's misdemeanor plea, explaining that the substantial size of the embezzlement warranted that she be charged with more than a misdemeanor.

A frazzled and frustrated Marshall reported the decision of the assistant district attorney to Carson Caddell. On hearing the news, an equally frazzled and frustrated Caddell told Marshall, "Let's just forget the whole mess right now. I am sick and tired of this. I just hope that she has learned her lesson and that she doesn't rip off anyone else in the future."

Less than one month after Carson Caddell decided not to press criminal charges against Lola Rojas, the young accountant was back in court—in handcuffs. Rojas was arrested for embezzling approximately $41,000 from her new employer. Rojas had used the bulk of that amount to repay the funds she had embezzled from Ryden Trucking.

## EPILOGUE

The insurance company that reimbursed Rojas's second victim for the $41,000 embezzlement loss filed a lawsuit against Jermell Marshall to recover the payment. That lawsuit included various charges of negligence and gross negligence against Marshall. But, the central premise of the lawsuit was that Marshall had been negligent in failing to warn Rojas's new employer of her prior criminal activity.[3]

The judge who presided over this lawsuit referred to several broad legal principles in reaching his decision, including his jurisdiction's definition of what constitutes negligence: the doing of that which an ordinarily prudent person would not have done under the same or similar circumstances, or the failure to do that which an ordinarily prudent person would have done under the same or similar circumstances. A second legal principle central to the case was the general rule that a person has no legal duty to protect another from the criminal acts of a third party. However, the judge noted that this latter rule is not absolute. For example, employers who can *reasonably foresee* that an employee *under their control* may commit criminal acts harming third parties generally have a responsibility to warn those parties of the impending criminal behavior.

After a brief trial, the judge ruled, and an appellate court later concurred, that Jermell Marshall had not been negligent in failing to warn Rojas's future employer of her prior criminal behavior. According to the judge, Marshall could not have foreseen or predicted that Lola Rojas would embezzle from future employers. In fact, it was just as likely, reasoned the judge, that Rojas "had learned her lesson" and thus was very unlikely to commit a similar act in the future. Additionally, once Marshall dismissed Rojas as an employee, he had no control over her future conduct. The appellate judge who reviewed the lower court opinion did suggest, however, that despite not having a legal responsibility to warn Rojas's new employer of her prior criminal conduct, Marshall may have been "morally obligated" to do so.

3. This lawsuit also named Lola Rojas and Andrew Tao as co-defendants, although the complaints filed against them differed from those filed against Jermell Marshall.

## Questions

1. The legal opinion in this case did not indicate how Lola Rojas actually used the funds she embezzled from Ryden Trucking. Suppose that Lola Rojas did use those funds to pay medical expenses of her mother. Given this assumption, would you describe her behavior as unethical? Defend your answer.
2. What factors may have motivated Jermell Marshall to go to such great lengths to help Lola Rojas? Do you believe that Marshall acted "prudently" in dealing with Rojas?
3. Although not mentioned in this case, the plaintiff that sued Marshall maintained that he had been negligent in supervising Lola Rojas while she was assigned to the Ryden engagement. That negligence, according to the plaintiff, had contributed to Rojas's decision to embezzle funds from Ryden. Briefly describe the supervisory responsibilities that professional auditing standards impose on senior personnel assigned to an audit or accounting services engagement. To what extent does a supervisor on such engagements have a responsibility to prevent his or her subordinates from engaging in criminal activity?
4. The judge who presided over the lawsuit in this case observed that Jermell Marshall may have been "morally obligated" to warn Rojas's new employer of her prior criminal conduct. Explain the difference between a "moral obligation" and a "legal obligation"? If someone fails to honor a moral obligation, has he or she behaved unethically?

SECTION 6

# PROFESSIONAL ROLES

**CASE 6.1**

# Leigh Ann Walker, Staff Accountant

Leigh Ann Walker graduated from a major state university in the spring of 1989 with a bachelor's degree in accounting.[1] During her college career, Walker earned a 3.9 grade point average and participated in several extracurricular activities, including three student business organizations. Her closest friends often teased her about the busy schedule she maintained and the fact that she was, at times, a little too "intense." During the fall of 1988, Walker interviewed with several public accounting firms and large corporations and received six job offers. After considering those offers, she decided to accept an entry-level position on the auditing staff of a Big Six accounting firm. Walker was not sure whether she wanted to pursue a partnership position with her new employer. But she believed that the training programs the firm provided and the breadth of experience she would receive from a wide array of client assignments would get her career off to a fast start.

Walker spent the first two weeks on her new job at her firm's regional audit staff training school. On returning to her local office in early June 1989, she was assigned to work on the audit of Saint Andrew's Hospital, a large sectarian hospital with a June 30 fiscal year-end. Walker's immediate superior on the Saint Andrew's engagement was Jackie Vaughn, a third-year senior. On her first day on the Saint Andrew's audit, Walker learned that she would audit the hospital's cash accounts and assist with accounts receivable. Walker was excited about her first client assignment and pleased that she would be working for Vaughn. Vaughn had a reputation as a demanding supervisor who typically brought her engagements in under budget. She was also known for having an excellent rapport with her clients, a thorough knowledge of technical standards, and for being fair and straightforward with her subordinates.

Like many newly hired staff auditors, Walker was apprehensive about her new job. She understood the purpose of independent audits and was familiar with the work performed by auditors but doubted that one auditing course and a two-week staff-training seminar had adequately prepared her for her new work role. After being assigned to work under Vaughn's supervision, Walker was relieved. She sensed that although Vaughn was demanding, the senior would be patient and understanding with a new staff auditor. More important, she believed that she could learn a great deal from working closely with Vaughn. Walker resolved that she would work hard to impress Vaughn and had hopes that the senior would mentor her through the first few years of her career.

Early in Walker's second week on the Saint Andrew's engagement, Jackie Vaughn casually asked her over lunch one day whether she had taken the CPA examination in May. After a brief pause, Walker replied that she had not but planned to study intensively for the exam during the next five months and then take it in November.[2]

1. This case is based upon a true set of facts; however, the names of the parties involved have been changed. An employee of a job placement firm provided much of the information incorporated in this case. This firm had been retained by the student identified in this case as Leigh Ann Walker.

2. At the time, the CPA examination was offered twice annually, in November and May. In most states, including Leigh Ann's home state, an individual who sat for the exam for the first time was required to take all four parts.

Vaughn indicated that was a good strategy and offered to lend Walker a set of CPA review manuals—an offer Walker declined. In fact, Walker had returned to her home state during the first week of May and sat for the CPA exam but she was convinced that she had failed it. Fear of failure, or, rather, fear of admitting failure, caused Walker to decide not to tell her co-workers that she had taken the exam. She realized that most of her peers would not pass all sections of the exam on their first attempt. Nevertheless, Leigh Ann wanted to avoid the embarrassment of admitting throughout the remainder of her career that she had not been a "first timer."

Walker continued to work on the Saint Andrew's engagement throughout the summer. She completed the cash audit within budget, thoroughly documenting the results of the audit procedures she applied. Vaughn was pleased with Walker's work and frequently complimented and encouraged her. As the engagement was winding down in early August, Walker received her grades on the CPA exam in the mail one Friday evening. To her surprise, she had passed all parts of the exam. She immediately called Vaughn to let her know of the impressive accomplishment. To Walker's surprise, Vaughn seemed irritated, if not disturbed, by the good news. Walker then recalled having earlier told Vaughn that she had not taken the exam in May. Walker immediately apologized and explained why she had chosen not to disclose that she had taken the exam. Following her explanation, Vaughn still seemed annoyed, so Walker decided to drop the subject and pursue it later in person.

The following week, Vaughn spent Monday through Wednesday with another client, while Walker and the other staff assigned to the Saint Andrew's engagement continued to wrap up the hospital audit. On Wednesday morning, Walker received a call from Don Roberts, the office managing partner and Saint Andrew's audit engagement partner. Roberts asked Walker to meet with him late that afternoon in his office. She assumed that Roberts simply wanted to congratulate her on passing the CPA exam.

The usually upbeat Roberts was somber when Walker stepped into his office that afternoon. After she was seated, Roberts informed her that he had spoken with Jackie Vaughn several times during the past few days and that he had consulted with the three other audit partners in the office regarding a situation involving Walker. Roberts told Walker that Vaughn was very upset by the fact that she (Walker) had lied regarding the CPA exam. Vaughn had indicated that she would not be comfortable having a subordinate on future engagements whom she could not trust to be truthful. Vaughn had also suggested that Walker be dismissed from the firm because of the lack of integrity she had demonstrated.

After a brief silence, Roberts told a stunned Walker that he and the other audit partners agreed with Vaughn. He informed Walker that she would be given 60 days to find another job. Roberts also told Walker that he and the other partners would not disclose that she had been "counseled out" of the firm if they were contacted by employers interested in hiring her.

## Questions

1. In your opinion, did Vaughn overreact to Walker's admission that she had been untruthful regarding the CPA exam? If so, how would you have dealt with the situation if you had been in Vaughn's position? How would you have dealt with the situation if you had been in Roberts' position?
2. Vaughn obviously questioned Walker's personal integrity. Is it possible that one can fulfill the responsibilities of a professional role while lacking personal integrity? Why or why not?

CASE 6.2

# Bill DeBurger, In-Charge Accountant

"Bill, will you have that inventory memo done by this afternoon?"

"Yeah, Sam, it's coming along. I should have it done by five, or so."

"Make it three . . . or so. Okay, Bub?"

Bill responded with a smile and a nod. He had a good relationship with Sam Hakes, the partner supervising the audit of Marcelle Stores.[1]

Bill DeBurger was an in-charge accountant who had 18 months of experience with his employer, a large national accounting firm. Bill's firm used the title "in-charge" for the employment position between staff accountant and audit senior. Other titles used by accounting firms for this position include "advanced staff" and "semi-senior." Typically, Bill's firm promoted individuals to in-charge after one year. An additional one to two years experience and successful completion of the CPA exam were usually required before promotion to audit senior. The title "in-charge" was a misnomer, at least in Bill's mind. None of the in-charges he knew had ever been placed in-charge of an audit, even a small audit. Based upon Bill's experience, an in-charge was someone a senior or manager expected to work with little or no supervision. "Here's the audit program for payables. Go spend the next five weeks completing the 12 program steps . . . and don't bother me," seemed to be the prevailing attitude in making work assignments to in-charges.

As he turned back to the legal pad in front of him, Bill forced himself to think of Marcelle Stores' inventory—all $50 million of it. Bill's task was to summarize in a two-page memo 900 hours of work that he, two staff accountants, and five internal auditors had done over the past two months. Not included in the 900 hours was the time spent on eight inventory observations performed by other offices of Bill's firm.

Marcelle Stores was a regional chain of 112 specialty stores that featured a broad range of products for do-it-yourself interior decorators. The company's most recent fiscal year had been a difficult one. A poor economy, increasing competition, and higher supplier prices had slashed Marcelle's profit to the bone over the past 12 months. The previous year, the company had posted a profit of slightly less than $8 million; for the year just completed, the company's pre-audit net income hovered at an anemic $500,000.

Inventory was the focal point of each audit of Marcelle's financial statements. This year, inventory was doubly important. Any material overstatement discovered in the inventory account would convert a poor year profit-wise for Marcelle into a disastrous year in which the company posted its first-ever loss.

Facing Bill on the small table that served as his makeshift desk were two stacks of workpapers, each two feet tall. Those workpapers summarized the results of extensive price tests, inventory observation procedures, year-end cutoff tests, an analysis of the reserve for inventory obsolescence, and various other audit procedures. Bill's task was to assimilate all of this audit evidence into a conclusion regarding Marcelle's

1. The source for this case was a former public accountant who is now a college instructor. The names of the parties involved in the case and certain other background facts have been changed.

inventory. Bill realized that Sam Hakes expected that conclusion to include the key catch phrase "presented fairly, in all material respects, in conformity with generally accepted accounting principles."

As Bill attempted to outline the inventory memo, he gradually admitted to himself that he had no idea whether Marcelle's inventory dollar value was materially accurate. The workpaper summarizing the individual errors discovered in the inventory account reflected a net overstatement of only $72,000. That amount was not material even in reference to Marcelle's unusually small net income. However, Bill realized that the $72,000 figure was little better than a guess.

The client's allowance for inventory obsolescence particularly troubled Bill. He had heard a rumor that Marcelle intended to discontinue 2 of the 14 sales departments in its stores. If that were true, the inventory in those departments would have to be sold at deep discounts. The collective dollar value of those two departments' inventory approached $6 million, while the client's allowance for inventory obsolescence had a year-end balance of only $225,000. Earlier in the audit, Bill had asked Sam about the rumored closing of the two departments. The typically easygoing partner had replied with a terse "Don't worry about it."

Bill always took his work assignments seriously and wanted to do a professional job in completing them. He believed that independent audits served an extremely important role in a free market economy. Bill was often annoyed that not all of his colleagues shared that view. Some of his co-workers seemed to have an attitude of "just get the work done." They stressed form over substance: "Tic and tie, make the workpapers look good, and don't be too concerned with the results. A clean opinion is going to be issued no matter what you find."

Finally, Bill made a decision. He would not sign off on the inventory account regardless of the consequences. He did not know whether the inventory account balance was materially accurate, and he was not going to write a memo indicating otherwise. Moments later, Bill walked into the client office being used by Sam Hakes and closed the door behind him.

"What's up?" Sam asked as he flipped through a workpaper file.

"Sam, I've decided that I can't sign off on the inventory account," Bill blurted out.

"What?" was Sam's stunned, one-word reply.

Bill stalled for a few moments to bolster his courage as he fidgeted with his tie. "Well . . . like I said, I'm not signing off on the inventory account."

"Why?" By this point, a disturbing crimson shade had already engulfed Sam's ears and was creeping slowly across his face.

"Sam . . . I just don't think I can sign off. I mean, I'm just not sure whether the inventory number is right."

"You're . . . *just not sure*?" After a brief pause, Sam continued, this time pronouncing each of his words with a deliberate and sarcastic tone. "You mean to tell me that you spent almost 1,000 hours on that account, and you're just not sure whether the general ledger number is right?"

"Well . . . yeah. Ya know, it's just tough to . . . to reach a conclusion, ya know, on an account that large."

Sam leaned back in his chair and cleared his throat before speaking. "Mr. DeBurger, I want you to go back into that room of yours and close the door. Then you sit down at that table and write a nice, neat, very precise and to-the-point inventory memo. And hear this: I'm not telling you what to include in that memo. But you're going to write that memo, and you're going to have it on my desk in two hours. Understood?" Sam's face was entirely crimson as he completed his short speech.

"Uh, okay," Bill replied.

Bill returned to the small conference room that had served as his work area for the past two months. He sat in his chair and stared at the pictures of his two-year-old twins, Lesley and Kelly, which he had taped to the wall above the phone. After a few minutes, he picked up his pencil, leaned forward, and began outlining the inventory memo.

## Questions

1. What conclusion do you believe Bill DeBurger reached in his inventory memo? Put yourself in his position. What conclusion would you have expressed in the inventory memo? Why?
2. Would you have dealt with your uncertainty regarding the inventory account differently than Bill did? For example, would you have used a different approach to raise the subject with Sam Hakes?
3. Evaluate Sam Hakes' response to Bill's statement that he was unable to sign off on the inventory account. In your view, did Sam deal with the situation appropriately? Was Sam's approach "professional"? Explain.
4. Is it appropriate for relatively inexperienced auditors to be assigned the primary responsibility for such critical accounts as Marcelle Stores' inventory? Explain.

## CASE 6.3

# David Myers, WorldCom Controller

Awaiting his court appearance to be charged with securities fraud, David Myers sat in a jail cell in 2002 and counted the cinder blocks again and again to distract himself.[1] In his pocket was a plastic red dog named Clifford, given to him by his young son. "He'll take care of you," the boy had said, according to his mother.

For Mr. Myers, the former controller of WorldCom Inc., the past four years have been a life-altering journey. It began when the prosperous businessman and father of three put aside his misgivings and agreed to go along with false accounting entries that eventually became part of an $11 billion fraud.

The scheme Mr. Myers participated in set off a chain of events that had a devastating impact on his company, his colleagues, and his family. The collapse of the telecommunications giant resulted in the loss of more than 17,000 jobs and billions of dollars in pensions and investments.

Hoping to win a lighter sentence, Mr. Myers, 47 years old, pleaded guilty and immersed himself in the government's investigation. He helped prosecutors identify false numbers in WorldCom's financial filings from 2000 to 2002. That evidence, and his court testimony, helped convict WorldCom Chief Executive Officer Bernard Ebbers last week for his role in one of the largest financial frauds in corporate history.

As the U.S. government rolls through a historic wave of prosecutions of business fraud, Mr. Myers is one of the executives watching a successful life come unglued. He and his family are now preparing for his sentencing set for June. Federal guidelines suggest he could serve more than 10 years in prison, though he is expected to receive a shorter sentence because of his cooperation.

"We don't know what is going to happen," says his wife, Lynn, 39. "I don't know if he's going to prison or for how long. I just want him home."

Raised in Jackson, Mississippi, Mr. Myers played basketball and was an honor student in high school. The son of civil servants, he earned degrees in marketing and accounting from the University of Mississippi. He married, had two children, and divorced in 1990.

In 1993, Mr. Myers married his second wife, Lynn, an interior designer and onetime cheerleader, who is also a Jackson native. The couple settled into a suburban life working in the yard and having dinners with friends. They had a son, Jack, now five. Mr. Myers joined WorldCom in 1995 as treasurer—just as the telecom upstart was about to hit a huge growth spurt.

As WorldCom's stock price rose through the late 1990s, the lifestyle [of the Myers family] grew richer. They moved to a house on the edge of a large, bass-filled lake. The couple began traveling to London, Paris, and Bermuda on WorldCom business trips. When WorldCom's share price peaked in 1999, the options held by the Myerses were valued at more than $15 million, though they cashed in only about $300,000 worth. "We had a good life and knowing the options were there was nice," says Mrs. Myers. The party ended in 2000 amid the bursting of the Internet bubble and a stiff price war among telecom companies. WorldCom's business began a sharp decline.

---

1. Reprinted by permission of *The Wall Street Journal*, Copyright © 2005 Dow Jones & Company, Inc. All Rights Reserved Worldwide. License number 2227610076255. This article originally appeared in *The Wall Street Journal* on March 24, 2005.

In January 2001, Mr. Myers and Buford Yates, an accountant who worked for him, met in the office of WorldCom's chief financial officer, Scott Sullivan, according to testimony from Mr. Myers. Knowing WorldCom wouldn't meet analyst expectations for the coming quarter, the three agreed, at Mr. Sullivan's behest, to reclassify some of the company's biggest expenses, according to Mr. Myers' testimony. This essentially moved expenses off WorldCom's income statement, erasing their effect on the bottom line. "I didn't think that was the right thing to do, but I had been asked by Scott to do it and I was asking him [Mr. Yates] to do it," Mr. Myers testified.

In an illustration of how huge ethical lapses often begin with small steps, he justified his actions to himself, thinking WorldCom's business would soon improve, people close to the case say. But rather than being a stopgap measure, the improper accounting continued. Mr. Myers helped direct false entries again and again. People close to Mr. Myers say he believed Mr. Sullivan's explanations that eventually the company's problems would be straightened out.

## Drawing Away

In the summer of 2001, Mr. Myers realized there was no end to the company's woes. He became depressed. He considered quitting, but realized the scandal would follow him because of what he had already done. On weekends, he withdrew, begging off on evenings out with his friends, blaming the stress of work. He grew increasingly irritable and distant.

Mrs. Myers sought the advice of Buddy Stallings, a priest from their Episcopal church. "She was worried about their life," says Father Stallings. "She felt things were spiraling out of control." He told her that she and Mr. Myers shouldn't be afraid to make changes in their life.

One warm evening in 2001, Mrs. Myers stood by the lake outside their house. When Mr. Myers joined her, she began crying. "You're somewhere else," she recalls telling him. "We have a baby. You work all the time. Why not quit?" Mr. Myers, whose annual salary was about $240,000 before options, told her he wanted to earn enough to start his own business and that he didn't want to quit, out of loyalty to Mr. Sullivan, the chief financial officer. But he didn't confide that he was also worried about the accounting at WorldCom.

Mr. Myers' thoughts turned to suicide, according to investigators. He began entertaining the idea of staging his own fatal car accident. Over a period of weeks, Mr. Myers began driving his BMW faster and faster through a turn on a highway underpass between Worldcom's Clinton, Mississippi, headquarters and his home, according to a person close to the situation. Trying to determine the speed at which his car would completely lose control, Mr. Myers pushed the speedometer higher each time, reaching 115 miles an hour one night. Eventually, Mr. Myers abandoned the idea.

Mrs. Myers says she urged her husband to see a doctor. He did, and began taking an antidepressant. His depression lifted. But he still didn't share the root of his troubles, Mrs. Myers says. "I knew something was wrong but I couldn't pull out of him what it was."

On a Sunday in June 2002, the phone rang at the [Myers family home]. Mr. Myers listened to a WorldCom employee who worked for Cynthia Cooper, head of internal audits. She was looking into accounting entries that she found suspicious. The employee said Ms. Cooper had focused in on certain large expense items—ones Mr. Myers knew would lead to his office.

Mr. Myers plopped on the stairs at the back of his house, watching his wife and son play in the yard. He mulled over the enormity of the problem. He vowed to come clean if Ms. Cooper confronted him.

On June 17, 2002, Ms. Cooper entered Mr. Myers' office. She peppered him with questions, according to regulatory filings. Did he know about the entries? Was there any support for them? Were other companies doing the same thing?

Mr. Myers confessed. He calmly explained that he knew about the entries but there was no support for them. An auditor accompanying Ms. Cooper asked what he had planned to tell the Securities and Exchange Commission if officials asked about the bookkeeping. He said he hoped they wouldn't ask. As the meeting broke up, Mr. Myers felt better than he had for months, as though a cloud over him had lifted, Mrs. Myers said he told her later.

Inside WorldCom, panic erupted as the company grappled with the explosive news that billions in profits had been manufactured through improper accounting. But initially, Mr. Myers was told by one WorldCom director that his job would probably be safe, people close to the situation say.

That changed a few days later, when he and Mr. Sullivan flew to Washington on the company plane for a meeting with the board's audit committee. The two men, seated at opposite ends of the plane, barely spoke. At one point, Mr. Sullivan offered Mr. Myers a chocolate-covered doughnut, telling him it was the only thing he could force himself to eat since the news broke. Mr. Myers declined.

It finally dawned on Mr. Myers that he was in trouble. He and Mr. Sullivan were excluded from a hastily called meeting of WorldCom's management and board. When Mr. Myers attempted to talk to a WorldCom lawyer, he was told he should hire his own lawyer and stop confiding in the WorldCom legal staff, people close to Mr. Myers say. On his way out that day, another WorldCom lawyer wished him the best. Mr. Myers knew he was going to lose his job.

Later that evening, Mr. Myers, staying at Embassy Suites hotel in Washington, got a call from a lawyer appointed for him by WorldCom; the lawyer told him that no one would believe Mr. Sullivan had pulled off the fraud alone. The board was offering him the chance to resign.

Mr. Myers, stricken, called his wife. He told her about his role in the bogus accounting entries. The usually restrained Mr. Myers cried as he asked what their friends and neighbors would say about him. Mrs. Myers, also crying, told him he was a good man and nothing would change that, she recalls. Mr. Myers later told her that he clung to those words in the weeks that followed. The next morning, he flew home and faxed in his letter of resignation.

In the days that followed, Mr. and Mrs. Myers drew the blinds, pulled the car in the garage and went into hiding, people close to them say. Because he had acted on orders, Mr. Myers still didn't think he would face personal liability for the fraud, Mrs. Myers says. When two agents with the Federal Bureau of Investigation showed up at the door and flashed their badges, Mrs. Myers let them in.

"I was shocked, but I thought they were there to talk about Bernie and Scott," she says. "I didn't think we were in trouble."

Mr. Myers led the agents to the sun porch. Mrs. Myers ran upstairs to call her father, a lawyer, who instructed her to tell Mr. Myers not to answer any questions without an attorney. As Mrs. Myers watched the agents drive away, she recalls thinking, "Oh my God, this is huge."

## "Helpless Feeling"

During a meeting with Richard Janis, the lawyer her husband later hired, Mrs. Myers recalls sobbing as he told them political pressure was high to make an example of WorldCom employees involved in the fraud. This was the first time she realized her husband might go to prison. "It was a helpless feeling," she says, realizing her husband could miss a big part of their son's childhood.

Mr. and Mrs. Myers moved to her parents' house in another part of Jackson to escape the media throng that had begun to gather at their own home. Once, when they saw a police car cruising the neighborhood, they froze, thinking the police might be looking for them, Mrs. Myers says. Mr. Myers began looking around when he took the trash out to see if anyone was watching him, Mrs. Myers says he told her.

On July 30, 2002, Mr. and Mrs. Myers prepared to go to New York, where he would be charged with securities fraud. Mrs. Myers cried as she kissed their son goodbye. "He didn't know why I was sad," she says. Jack, clutching a small plastic "Clifford" dog, handed the toy to his father, Mrs. Myers recalls. "That was his favorite toy and he gave it to David."

In New York, the couple met with Father Stallings, their former priest, who had relocated to a church on Staten Island. During a walk, Mr. Myers said he had been told he would have to turn over his shoelaces, belt and tie when he turned himself in the next day. Father Stallings gave Mr. Myers a pair of loafers so he wouldn't have to remove any laces. Afterward, he took the couple to the church and gave them communion. He thinks that gave Mr. Myers solace. "I believe it made a difference," he says.

The next day, Mr. Myers was fingerprinted in FBI offices in Manhattan and had his mug shot taken. He was led outside and handcuffed, in what is known as a "perp walk." Wearing a blue suit and a red tie, Mr. Myers appeared emotionless as he walked to a car waiting to take him to the federal courthouse. He wasn't allowed in the car for a few minutes, as an FBI agent sat inside with the door locked. Cameras flashed. The agent unlocked the door and Mr. Myers was let in.

Before returning home, the Myerses visited the World Trade Center site and Mr. Myers placed the plastic toy dog on an informal memorial there.

On September 25, 2002, Mr. Myers was the first of four WorldCom managers to plead guilty to securities fraud. Standing under an umbrella, his lawyer said: "Myers was a reluctant participant in the events that have led us here. . . . He recognizes that as a corporate officer, those facts do not relieve him of responsibility in this matter."

The Myerses returned to Jackson and tried to pick up their lives. Mr. Myers began volunteering as a bookkeeper at their church and worked on an archaeology dig nearby. Once, while on a treadmill at his gym, he looked up to see his own image in handcuffs on television. He put his head down and moved faster, Mrs. Myers says he told her. Driving around Jackson, he often thought he was recognized at stoplights, she says.

With the support of friends, the Myerses slowly began to emerge from their isolation. They received more than 200 letters from people who sympathized with their situation, Mrs. Myers says.

A turning point for Mr. Myers came in June 2003 when he borrowed a bicycle and signed up to chaperone a 500-mile bike ride with a group of youngsters, including some from troubled homes. Mr. Myers struggled to make the long rides each day. Often alone, he contemplated the future and his past actions, Mrs. Myers says. He strained to climb one particularly steep hill—and the exhilaration of riding down the other side made him believe good times still lay ahead, she says.

He returned home more optimistic. He bought a necklace with a cross on it at the gift shop of a Jackson church and began wearing it daily. Their priest reminded him that everyone makes mistakes but it's how a person deals with them that matters, Mrs. Myers says.

Anticipating a prison sentence, Mr. Myers began preparing. The family moved to a smaller house that shared a backyard with the couple's best friends. He started a real estate company with Mr. Yates, the accountant who worked for him and also pleaded guilty to securities fraud. They hoped the company, which buys residential real estate, would produce profits to help them tide their wives over if they were sent to prison.

Mr. Myers' work as a witness for the government increased. In December 2003, he spent most of a weekend in a New York hotel room, poring over WorldCom documents. Every five hours, he would take a break, walking across the street to grab some pizza and a soda. That Sunday, he handed prosecutors a computer disk detailing every false number he recognized in WorldCom's financial filings from 2000 to 2002.

Around that time, prosecutors were working to win a plea agreement from Mr. Sullivan, the former chief financial officer. Ultimately, they hoped to get Mr. Sullivan to testify against Mr. Ebbers, the chief executive.

On March 2, 2004, Mr. Sullivan pleaded guilty to three counts of securities fraud—and agreed to testify against Mr. Ebbers. In testimony, Mr. Sullivan said one of the reasons he decided to plead guilty was Mr. Myers' statements to investigators about him. The same day, Mr. Ebbers was indicted on fraud charges.

In January, Mr. Myers stood in the witness room at the courthouse in Manhattan, waiting to testify against Mr. Ebbers. Looking out the window at St. Andrew's church, he noticed an ornate cross on the rear peak of the roof, similar to the one he wears around his neck. As his testimony proceeded over the next several days, he often looked out at the cross at St. Andrew's, while holding the one around his neck, Mrs. Myers says.

On February 3, the day after Mr. Myers completed his testimony, the couple returned to Jackson. Their son was sleeping, and Mrs. Myers laid down beside him. He woke up and asked where his father was. He raced to the bedroom and jumped into the bed with Mr. Myers, crying "my Daddy," Mrs. Myers recalls.

Mrs. Myers says she hasn't told Jack his father may have to spend time in prison. "He doesn't understand what's going on," she says. "He loves his Daddy. What do you say when Daddy doesn't come home?"[2]

## Questions

1. Does the fact that David Myers' superior, Scott Sullivan, asked him to make the false accounting entries in WorldCom's accounting records diminish Myers' responsibility for his improper conduct? Defend your answer.
2. What punishment, if any, do you believe David Myers should have been given for his role in the WorldCom fraud?
3. Is it appropriate for federal law enforcement authorities "to make an example" of individuals involved in high-profile financial frauds, such as WorldCom and Enron? Explain.

2. On August 10, 2005, a federal judge sentenced David Myers to one year and one day in federal prison for his role in the WorldCom fraud. On October 10, 2005, Myers surrendered to federal authorities to begin serving his prison term at the federal correctional facility in Yazoo City, Mississippi. Because he received credit for good behavior while in prison, Myers was released in August 2006. One month earlier, the SEC had ruled that Myers should repay more than $1 million of bonuses that he had received from WorldCom over the course of the fraud. However, the federal agency subsequently waived that repayment when Myers demonstrated that he was incapable of making it. The SEC also permanently prohibited Myers from serving as an officer, director, or accountant of a public company.

## CASE 6.4

# Tommy O'Connell, Audit Senior

Tommy O'Connell had been a senior with one of the major international accounting firms for less than one month when he was assigned to the audit engagement for the Altamesa Manufacturing Company.[1] Tommy worked out of his firm's Fort Worth, Texas, office, while Altamesa was headquartered in Amarillo, the "capital" of the Texas Panhandle. The young senior realized that being assigned to the tough Altamesa engagement signaled that Jack Morrison, the Altamesa audit partner and the office managing partner, regarded his work highly. Serving as the audit senior on the Altamesa job would allow Tommy to become better acquainted with Morrison. Despite the challenges and opportunities posed by his new assignment, Tommy did not look forward to spending three months in Amarillo, a five-hour drive from Fort Worth. This would be his first assignment outside of Fort Worth since his marriage six months earlier. He dreaded breaking the news to his wife, Suzie, who often complained about the long hours his job required.

Altamesa manufactured steel girders used in the construction and renovation of bridges in West Texas, New Mexico, Colorado, and Oklahoma. The company's business was very cyclical and linked closely to the funding available to municipalities in Altamesa's four-state market area. To learn more about the company and its personnel, Tommy arranged to have lunch with Casi McCall, the audit senior on the Altamesa job the two previous years. According to Casi, Altamesa's management took aggressive positions regarding year-end expense accruals and revenue recognition. The company used the percentage-of-completion method to recognize revenue since its sales contracts extended over two to five years. Casi recounted several disputes with the company's chief accountant regarding the estimated stage of completion of jobs in progress. In an effort to "front-load" as much of the profit on jobs as possible, the chief accountant typically insisted that jobs were further along than they actually were.

Speaking with Casi made Tommy even more apprehensive about tackling the Altamesa engagement. But he realized that the job gave him an excellent chance to strengthen his fast-track image within his office. To reach his goal of being promoted to manager by his fifth year with the firm, Tommy needed to prove himself on difficult assignments such as the Altamesa engagement.

### An Unpleasant Surprise for Tommy

It was late May, just two weeks before Tommy would be leaving for Amarillo to begin the Altamesa audit—the company had a June 30 fiscal year-end. Tommy, Jack Morrison, and an audit manager were having lunch at the Cattleman's Restaurant in the Cowtown district of north Fort Worth.

"Tommy, I've decided to send Carl with you out to Amarillo. Is that okay?" asked Jack Morrison.

"Uhh . . . sure, Jack. Yeah, that'll be fine," Tommy replied.

1. This case is based upon an actual series of events. Names and certain background information have been changed to conceal the identities of the individuals involved in the case.

"Of all people," Tommy thought to himself, "he would send Carl Wilmeth to Amarillo with me." Carl was a staff accountant with only a few months' experience, having been hired in the middle of the just-completed busy season. Other than being auditors and approximately the same age, the two young men had little in common. Tommy was from Lockettville, a small town in rural West Texas, while Carl had been raised in the exclusive Highland Park community of north central Dallas. Texas Tech, a large state-supported university, was Tommy's alma mater. Carl had earned his accounting degree from a small private college on the East Coast.

Tommy did not appreciate Carl's cocky attitude, and his lack of experience made him a questionable choice in Tommy's mind for the Altamesa engagement. As he tried to choke down the rest of his prime rib, Tommy recalled the complaints he had heard about Carl's job performance. Over the past three months, Carl had worked on two audits. In both cases, he had performed admirably—too admirably, in fact, coming in well under budget on his assigned tasks. On one engagement, Carl had completed an assignment in less than 60 hours when the audit budget allotted 100 hours; the previous year, 110 hours had been required to complete that same task. Both seniors who had supervised Carl suspected that he had not completed all of his assigned audit procedures, although he signed off on those procedures on the audit program. The tasks assigned to Carl had been large-scale tests of transactions that involved checking invoices, receiving reports, purchase orders, and other documents for various attributes. Given the nature of the tests, the seniors would have had difficulty confirming their suspicions.

## "Boss" Tommy

Six weeks later, in early July, the Altamesa audit was in full swing. Carl had just finished his third assigned task on the job, in record time, of course. "Boss, here's that disbursements file," Carl said as he plopped a large stack of workpapers in front of Tommy. "Anything else you want me to do this afternoon? Since I'm way ahead of schedule, maybe I should take off and work on my tan out on the golf course."

"No, Carl. I think we have plenty to keep you busy right here." Tommy was agitated but he tried not to let it show. "Why don't you pull out the contracts file and then talk to Abby Littleton in the sales office. Get copies of any new contracts or proposals over the past year and put them in the contracts file."

At this point, Tommy simply did not have time to review Carl's cash disbursements workpapers. He was too busy trying to untangle Altamesa's complex method of allocating overhead costs to jobs in process. Later that afternoon, he had an appointment to meet with the chief accountant and a production superintendent to discuss the status of a large job. Tommy and the chief accountant had already butted heads on two occasions regarding a job's stage of completion. Casi had been right: the chief accountant clearly meant to recognize profit on in-progress jobs as quickly as possible. With four decades of experience, Scrooge—a nickname Casi had pinned on the chief accountant—obviously considered the young auditors a nuisance and did not appreciate their probing questions. Each time Tommy asked him a question regarding an important issue, the chief accountant registered his disgust by pursing his lips and running his hand through his thinning hair. He then responded with a rambling, convoluted answer intended to confuse rather than inform.

To comprehend Altamesa's accounting decisions for its long-term contracts, Tommy spent several hours of nonchargeable time each night in his motel room flipping through copies of job order worksheets and contracts. Occasionally, he referred to prior-year workpapers, his firm's policy and procedures manual, and even his tattered cost accounting textbook from his college days. Carl spent most of his evenings in the motel's club being taught the Texas Two-step and Cotton-eyed Joe by several new friends he had acquired.

During July and August, Tommy and Carl worked 50 to 60 hours per week on the Altamesa engagement. Several times Tommy wondered to himself whether it was worthwhile to work so hard to earn recognition as a "superstar" senior. He was also increasingly concerned about the impact of his fast-track strategy on his marriage. When he tried to explain to Suzie that the long hours and travel would pay off when he made partner, she was unimpressed. "Who cares if you make partner? I just want to spend more time with my husband," was her stock reply.

## To Tell or Not to Tell

Finally, late August rolled around and the Altamesa job was almost complete. Jack Morrison had been in Amarillo for the past three days combing through the Altamesa workpapers. Nothing seemed to escape Morrison's eagle eye. Tommy had spent 12 hours per day since Morrison had arrived, tracking down missing invoices, checking on late confirmations, and tying up dozens of other loose ends. Carl was already back in Fort Worth, probably working on his golf swing. Morrison had allowed Carl to leave two days earlier after he had finished clearing the review comments in his workpaper files.

"Tommy, I have to admit that I was a little concerned about sending a light senior out to run this audit. But, by golly, you have done a great job." Morrison did not look up as he signed off on the workpapers spread before him on Altamesa's conference table. "You know, this kid Carl does super work. I've never seen cleaner, more organized workpapers from a staff accountant."

Tommy grimaced as he sat next to Morrison at the conference table. "Yeah, right. They should look clean, since he didn't do half of what he signed off on," Tommy thought to himself. Here was his opportunity. For the past several weeks, Tommy had planned to sit down with Morrison and talk to him regarding Carl's job performance. But now he was reluctant to do so. How do you tell a partner that you suspect much of the work he is reviewing may not have been done? Besides, Tommy realized that as Carl's immediate supervisor, he was responsible for that work. Tommy knew that he was facing a no-win situation. He leaned back in his chair and remained silent, hoping that Morrison would hurry through the last few workpaper files so they could make it back to Fort Worth by midnight.

## EPILOGUE

Tommy never informed Jack Morrison of his suspicions regarding Carl's work. Thankfully, no problems—of a legal nature—ever arose on the jobs to which Carl was assigned. After passing the CPA exam on his first attempt, Carl left the accounting firm and enrolled in a prestigious MBA program. Upon graduation, Carl accepted a job on Wall Street with one of the large investment banking firms. Tommy reached his goal of being promoted to audit manager within five years. One year later, he decided that he was not cut out to be a partner and resigned from the firm to accept a position in private industry.

## Questions

1. Compare and contrast the professional roles of an audit senior and a staff accountant. In your analysis, consider the different responsibilities assigned to each role, the job-related stresses that individuals in the two roles face, and how each role contributes to the successful completion of an audit engagement. Which of these two roles is (a) more important and (b) more stressful? Defend your choices.
2. Assume that you are Tommy O'Connell and have learned that Carl Wilmeth will be working for you on the Altamesa audit engagement. Would you handle this situation any differently than Tommy did? Explain.
3. Again, assume that you are Tommy. Carl is badgering you for something to do midway through the Altamesa job. You suspect that he is not completing all of his assigned procedures, but at the time you are wrestling with an important accounting issue facing the client. What would you do at this point? What could you do to confirm your suspicions that Carl is not completing his assignments?
4. Now, assume that Jack Morrison is reviewing the Altamesa workpapers. To date, you (Tommy) have said nothing to Morrison about your suspicions regarding Carl. Do you have a professional responsibility to raise this matter now with Morrison? Explain.
5. Assume that at some point Tommy told Morrison that he suspected Carl was not completing his assigned tasks. The only evidence Tommy had to support his theory was the fact that Carl had come in significantly under budget on every major task assigned to him over a period of several months. If you were Jack Morrison, how would you have handled this matter?

## CASE 6.5

# Avis Love, Staff Accountant

"Oh no, not Store 51," Avis Love moaned under her breath. For the third time, Avis compared the dates listed in the cash receipts journal with the corresponding dates on the bank deposit slips. Avis shook her head softly and leaned back in her chair. There was no doubt in her mind now. Mo Rappele had definitely held open Store 51's cash receipts journal at the end of October.[1]

Avis Love was a staff accountant with the Atlanta office of a large international accounting firm. Several months earlier, Avis had graduated with an accounting degree from the University of Alabama at Birmingham. Although she did not plan to pursue a career in public accounting, Avis had accepted one of the several offers she had received from major accounting firms. The 22-year-old wanted to take a two- or three-year "vacation" from college, while at the same time accumulating a bankroll to finance three years of law school. Avis intended to practice law with a major firm for a few years and then return to her hometown in eastern Alabama and set up her own practice.

For the past few weeks, Avis had been assigned to the audit engagement for Lowell, Inc., a public company that operated nearly 100 retail sporting goods stores scattered across the South. Avis was nearing completion of a year-end cash receipts cutoff test for a sample of 20 Lowell stores. The audit procedures she had performed included preparing a list of the cash receipts reported in each of those stores' accounting records during the last five days of Lowell's fiscal year, which ended October 31. She had then obtained the relevant bank statements for each of the stores to determine whether the cash receipts had been deposited on a timely basis. For three of the stores in her sample, the deposit dates for the cash receipts ranged from three to seven days following the dates the receipts had been entered in the cash receipts journal. The individual store managers had apparently backdated cash receipts for the first several days of the new fiscal year, making it appear that the receipts had occurred in the fiscal year under audit by Avis's firm.

Avis had quickly realized that the objective of the store managers was not to overstate their units' year-end cash balances. Instead, the managers intended to inflate their recorded sales. Before Avis began the cutoff test, Teddy Tankersley, the senior assigned to the Lowell audit and Avis's immediate superior, had advised her that there was a higher-than-normal risk of cash receipts and sales cutoff errors for Lowell this year. The end of Lowell's fiscal year coincided with the end of a three-month sales promotion. This campaign to boost Lowell's sagging sales included bonuses for store managers who exceeded their quarterly sales quota. This was the first time that Lowell had run such a campaign and it was a modest success. Fourth-quarter sales for the fiscal year just ended topped the corresponding sales for the previous fiscal year by 6 percent.

When Avis uncovered the first instance of backdated cash receipts, she had felt a noticeable surge of excitement. In several months of tracing down invoices and receiving reports, ticking and tying, and performing other mundane tests, the young

1. This case was developed from an actual series of events. Names, locations, and certain other background information have been changed to conceal the identities of the individuals involved in the case.

accountant had occasionally found isolated errors in client accounting records. But this was different. This was fraud.

Avis had a much different reaction when she uncovered the second case of backdated cash receipts. She had suddenly realized that the results of her cutoff test would have "real world" implications for several parties, principally the store managers involved in the scheme. During the past few months, Avis had visited six of Lowell's retail stores to perform various interim tests of controls and to observe physical inventory procedures. The typical store manager was in his or her early 30s, married, with one or two small children. Because of Lowell's miserly pay scale, the stores were chronically understaffed, meaning that the store managers worked extremely long hours to earn their modest salaries.

No doubt, the store managers who backdated sales to increase their bonuses would be fired immediately. Clay Shamblin, Lowell's chief executive officer (CEO), was a hard-nosed businessman known for his punctuality, honesty, and work ethic. Shamblin exhibited little patience with subordinates who did not display those same traits.

When Avis came to the last store in her sample, she had hesitated. She realized that Mo Rappelle managed Store 51. Three weeks earlier, Avis had spent a long Saturday afternoon observing the physical inventory at Store 51 on the outskirts of Atlanta. Although the Lowell store managers were generally courteous and accommodating, Mo had gone out of his way to help Avis complete her tasks. Mo allowed Avis to use his own desk in the store's cramped office, shared a pizza with her during an afternoon break, and introduced her to his wife and two small children who dropped by the store during the afternoon.

"Mo, what a stupid thing to do," Avis thought to herself after reviewing the workpapers for the cutoff tests a final time. "And for just a few extra dollars." Mo had apparently backdated cash receipts for only the first two days of the new year. According to Avis's calculations, the backdated sales had increased Mo's year-end bonus by slightly more than $100. From the standpoint of Lowell, Inc., the backdated sales for Mo's store clearly had an immaterial impact on the company's operating results for the year just ended.

After putting away the workpapers for the cutoff test, a thought dawned on Avis. The Lowell audit program required her to perform cash receipts cutoff tests for 20 stores . . . any 20 stores she selected. Why not just drop Store 51 from her sample and replace it with Store 52 or 53 or whatever?

## EPILOGUE

Avis brooded over the results of her cutoff test the remainder of that day at work and most of that evening. The following day, she gave the workpaper file to Teddy Tankersley. Avis reluctantly told Teddy about the backdated cash receipts and sales she had discovered in three stores: Store 12, Store 24, and Store 51. Teddy congratulated Avis on her thorough work and told her that Clay Shamblin would be very interested in her findings.

A few days later, Shamblin called Avis into his office and thanked her for uncovering the backdated sales. The CEO told her that the company's internal auditors had tested the year-end cash receipts and sales cutoff for the remaining 72 stores and identified seven additional store managers who had tampered with their accounting records. As Avis was leaving the CEO's office, he thanked her once more and assured her that the store managers involved in the scam "would soon be looking for a new line of work . . . in another part of the country."

## Questions

1. Would it have been appropriate for Avis to substitute another store for Store 51 after she discovered the cutoff errors in that store's accounting records? Defend your answer.
2. Identify the parties potentially affected by the outcome of the ethical dilemma faced by Avis Love. What obligation, if any, did Avis have to each of these parties?
3. Does the AICPA's *Code of Professional Conduct* prohibit auditors from developing friendships with client personnel? If not, what measures can auditors take to prevent such friendships from interfering with the performance of their professional responsibilities?
4. Identify the key audit objectives associated with year-end cash receipts and sales cutoff tests.
5. What method would you have recommended that Avis or her colleagues use in deciding whether the cutoff errors she discovered had a material impact on Lowell's year-end financial statements? Identify the factors or benchmarks that should have been considered in making this decision.

## CASE 6.6

# Charles Tollison, Audit Manager

"No, that's okay, Bea. I'll write that memo this weekend and send it to Mr. Fielder. You go on home."[1]

"Are you sure, Chuck? I don't mind staying a while longer."

"Thanks, Bea, but you've already put in too much overtime this week."

After he sent his secretary home, Charles Tollison spent several minutes shuffling through the audit workpapers and correspondence stacked on his desk, trying to decide what work he would take home over the weekend. Finally, only one decision remained. Tollison couldn't decide whether to take the inventory file with him. Compulsive by nature, Tollison knew that if he took the inventory file home, he would have to complete his review of that file, which would increase his weekend workload from 6 hours to more than 12 hours. As he stewed over his decision, Tollison stepped to the window of his office and idly watched the rush-hour traffic on the downtown streets several stories below.

It was nearly 6:30 on a Friday evening in early August. Charles Tollison, an audit manager for a large international accounting firm, had suffered through a tough week. His largest audit client was negotiating to buy a smaller company within its industry. For the past two months, Tollison had supervised the fieldwork on an intensive acquisition audit of the competitor's accounting records. The client's chief executive officer (CEO) suspected that the competitor's executives had embellished their firm's financial data in anticipation of the proposed buyout. Since the client was overextending itself financially to acquire the other firm, the CEO wanted to be sure that its financial data were reliable. The CEO's principal concern was the valuation of the competitor's inventory, which accounted for 45 percent of its total assets.

The client's CEO had requested that Tollison be assigned to the acquisition audit because she respected Tollison and the quality of his work. Normally, an audit manager spends little time "in the trenches" supervising day-to-day audit procedures. Because of the nature of this engagement, however, Tollison had felt it necessary to spend 10 hours per day, six and seven days per week, poring over the accounting records of the takeover candidate with his subordinates.

As Tollison stared at the gridlocked streets below, he was relieved that the acquisition audit was almost complete. After he tied up a few loose ends in the inventory file, he would turn the workpapers over to the audit engagement partner for a final review.

Tollison's tough week had been highlighted by several contentious meetings with client personnel, a missed birthday party for his eight-year-old daughter, and an early breakfast Thursday morning with his office managing partner, Walker Linton. During that breakfast, Linton had notified Tollison that he had been passed over for promotion to partner—for the second year in a row. The news had been difficult for Tollison to accept.

For more than 13 years, Tollison had been a hardworking and dedicated employee of the large accounting firm. He had never turned down a difficult assignment, never complained about the long hours his work required, and made countless personal

1. This case was developed from information obtained from a CPA employed for many years with a large international accounting firm.

sacrifices, the most recent being the missed birthday party. After informing Tollison of the bad news, Linton had encouraged him to stay with the firm. Linton promised that the following year he would vigorously campaign for Tollison's promotion and "call in all favors" owed to him by partners in other offices. Despite that promise, Tollison realized that he had only a minimal chance of being promoted to partner the following year. Seldom were two-time "losers" ticketed for promotion.

Although he had been hoping for the best, Tollison had not expected a favorable report from the Partner Selection Committee. In recent weeks, he had gradually admitted to himself that he did not have the profile for which the committee was searching. Tollison was not a rainmaker like his friend and fellow audit manager, Craig Allen, whose name appeared on the roster of new partners to be formally announced the following week. Allen was a member of several important civic organizations and had a network of well-connected friends at the local country club. Those connections had served Allen well, allowing him to steer several new clients to the firm in recent years.

Instead of a rainmaker, Tollison was a technician. If someone in the office had a difficult accounting or auditing issue to resolve, that individual went first to Tollison, not to one of the office's six audit partners. When a new client posed complex technical issues, the audit engagement partner requested that Tollison be assigned to the job. One reason Tollison was a perfect choice for difficult engagements was that he micromanaged his jobs, insisting on being involved in every aspect of them. Tollison's management style often resulted in his "busting" time budgets for audits, although he seldom missed an important deadline. To avoid missing deadlines when a job was nearing completion, Tollison and the subordinates assigned to his engagements would work excessive overtime, including long weekend stints.

Finally, Tollison turned away from his window and slumped into his chair. As he sat there, he tried to drive away the bitterness that he was feeling. "If Meredith hadn't left the firm, maybe I wouldn't be in this predicament," Tollison thought to himself. Three years earlier, Meredith Oliveti, an audit partner and Tollison's closest friend within the firm, had resigned to become the chief financial officer (CFO) of a large client. Following Oliveti's resignation, Tollison had no one within the firm to sponsor him through the tedious and political partner selection process. Instead, Tollison had been "lost in the shuffle" with the dozens of other hardworking, technically inclined audit managers within the firm who aspired to a partnership position.

Near the end of breakfast Thursday morning, Walker Linton had mentioned to Tollison the possibility that he could remain with the firm in a senior manager position. In recent years, Tollison's firm had relaxed its "up or out" promotion policy. But Tollison was not sure he wanted to remain with the firm as a manager with no possibility of being promoted to partner. Granted, there were clearly advantages associated with becoming a permanent senior manager. For example, no equity interest in the firm meant not absorbing any portion of its future litigation losses. On the other hand, in Tollison's mind accepting an appointment as a permanent senior manager seemed equivalent to having "career failure" stenciled on his office door.

Ten minutes till seven, time to leave. Tollison left the inventory file lying on his desk as he closed his bulging briefcase and then stepped toward the door of his office. After flipping off the light switch, Tollison paused momentarily. He then grudgingly turned and stepped back to his desk, picked up the inventory file, and tucked it under his arm.

## Questions

1. Do you believe Charles Tollison was qualified for a partnership position with his firm? Explain.
2. Did Tollison's firm treat him "fairly"? Why or why not?
3. Identify the criteria you believe large international accounting firms should use when evaluating individuals for promotion to partner. In your opinion, which of these criteria should be most heavily weighted by these firms? Should smaller accounting firms establish different criteria for evaluating individuals for promotion to partner? Explain.
4. Discuss the advantages and disadvantages of the "up or out" promotion policy followed by many accounting firms.

CASE 6.7

# Hamilton Wong, In-Charge Accountant

After spending much of the previous three months working elbow-to-elbow with as many as six colleagues in a cramped and poorly ventilated conference room, Hamilton Wong was looking forward to moving on to his next assignment.[1] Wong was an in-charge accountant on the audit staff of the San Francisco office of a large international accounting firm, the firm that had offered him a job two years earlier as he neared completion of his accounting degree at San Jose State University. His current client, Wille & Lomax, Inc., a public company and the second largest client of Wong's office, owned a chain of retail stores in the western United States that stretched from Seattle to San Diego and as far east as Denver and Albuquerque.

Although Wille & Lomax's stores operated under different names in different cities, each stocked the same general types of merchandise, including briefcases and other leather goods, luggage and travel accessories, and a wide range of gift items, such as costume jewelry imported from Pacific Rim countries. The company also had a wholesale division that marketed similar merchandise to specialty retailers throughout the United States. The wholesale division accounted for approximately 60 percent of the company's annual sales.

A nondescript building in downtown San Francisco, just one block from bustling Market Street, served as Wille & Lomax's corporate headquarters. The company's fiscal year-end fell on the final Saturday of January. With the end of March just a few days away, Hamilton and his fellow "Willies"—the nickname that his office assigned to members of the Wille & Lomax audit engagement team—were quickly running out of time to complete the audit. Wong was well aware that the audit was behind schedule because he collected, coded, and input into an electronic spreadsheet the time worked each week by the individual Willies. He used the spreadsheet package to generate a weekly time and progress report that he submitted to Angela Sun, the senior who supervised the field work on the Wille & Lomax audit.

In addition to Wong and Sun, another in-charge accountant, Lauren Hutchison, and four staff accountants had worked on the Wille & Lomax audit since early January. Wong and Hutchison knew each other well. They shared the same start date with their employer and the past two summers had attended the same weeklong staff and in-charge training sessions at their firm's national education headquarters. Hutchison's primary responsibility on the current year's audit was the receivables account but she also audited the PP&E (property, plant, and equipment) and leases accounts. Besides his administrative responsibilities, which included serving as the engagement timekeeper and maintaining the correspondence file for the audit, Wong supervised and coordinated the audit procedures for inventory, accounts payable, and a few smaller accounts.

Hamilton was thankful that it was late Friday afternoon. In recent weeks, with the audit deadline looming, Angela Sun had required the Willie & Lomax crew to work until

1. This case is based upon the experiences of an individual previously employed by one of the major accounting firms. The names of the parties involved in this case and other background information, such as locations, have been changed.

at least 7 P.M. each weekday except Friday, when she allowed them to leave "early" at 5 P.M. The engagement team had spent three consecutive Saturdays in the client's headquarters and would be spending both Saturday and Sunday of the coming weekend hunched over their workpapers. Wong had just completed collecting and coding the hours worked during the current week by the other members of the engagement team. Now it was time for him to enter in the electronic spreadsheet his chargeable hours, which he dutifully recorded at the end of each work day in his little "black book."

Before entering his own time, Wong decided to walk across the hall and purchase a snack in the employees' break room. In fact, he was stalling, trying to resolve a matter that was bothering him. Less than 30 minutes earlier, Lauren Hutchison had told him that during the current week, which included the previous weekend, she had spent 31 hours on the receivables account, 18 hours on the leases account, and 3 hours on PP&E. What troubled Wong was the fact that he knew Hutchison had worked several additional hours on the Wille & Lomax audit during the current week.

This was not the first time Hutchison had underreported her hours worked. On several occasions, Wong had noticed her secretively slipping workpaper files into her briefcase before leaving for home. The next morning, those files included polished memos or completed schedules that had not existed the previous day. Wong was certain that Hutchison was not reporting the hours she spent working at home on her audit assignments. He was just as certain that each week she consciously chose to shave a few hours off the total number she had spent working at the client's headquarters. Collectively, Wong estimated that Hutchison had failed to report at least 80 hours she had worked on the audit.

"Eating time" was a taboo subject among auditors. Although the subject was not openly discussed, Wong was convinced that many audit partners and audit managers subtly encouraged subordinates to underreport their time. By bringing their jobs in near budget, those partners and managers enhanced their apparent ability to manage engagements. The most avid time-eaters among Wong's peers seemed to be the individuals who had been labeled as "fast-track" superstars in the office.

After Hutchison had reported her time to Wong that afternoon, he had nonchalantly but pointedly remarked, "Lauren, who are you trying to impress by eating so much of your time?" His comment had caused the normally mild-mannered Hutchison to snap back, "Hey, Dude, you are the timekeeper, not the boss. So just mind your own _____ business." Immediately, Wong regretted offending Hutchison, whom he considered his friend. But she stomped away before he could apologize.

Wong knew who Hutchison was trying to impress. Angela Sun would almost certainly be promoted to audit manager in the summer and then become the audit manager on the Wille & Lomax engagement, meaning that there would be a vacancy in the all-important senior position on the engagement team. Both Hutchison and Wong also anticipated being promoted during the summer. The two new seniors would be the most likely candidates to take over the job of overseeing the field work on the Wille & Lomax audit.

The in-charge accountant who handled the administrative responsibilities on the Wille & Lomax engagement was typically the person chosen to take over the senior's role when it came open. But Wong worried that the close friendship that had developed between Lauren Hutchison and Sun might affect his chances of landing the coveted assignment. Almost every day, Hutchison and Sun went to lunch together without extending even a token invitation to Wong or their other colleagues to join them. John Berardo, the audit engagement partner, would choose the new senior for the Wille & Lomax engagement, but Angela Sun would certainly have a major influence on his decision.

There was little doubt in Wong's mind that Hutchison routinely underreported the time she worked on the Wille & Lomax audit to enhance her standing with Sun and Berardo. Not that Hutchison needed to spruce up her image. She had passed the CPA exam shortly after joining the firm, had a charming personality that endeared her to her superiors and client executives, and, like both Sun and Berardo, was a Stanford graduate. Wong, on the other hand, had struggled to pass the CPA exam, was shy by nature, and had graduated from a public university.

What irritated Wong the most about his subtle rivalry with Hutchison was that during the past two weekends he had spent several hours helping her research contentious technical issues for Wille & Lomax's complex lease contracts on its retail store sites. Earlier in the engagement, Hutchison had also asked him to help analyze some tricky journal entries involving the client's allowance for bad debts. In each of those cases, Wong had not charged any time to the given accounts, both of which were Hutchison's responsibility.

Before entering his time for the week, Wong checked once more the total hours that he had charged to date to his major accounts. For both inventory and accounts payable, he was already over budget. By the end of the audit, Wong estimated that he would "bust" the assigned time budgets for those two accounts by 20 to 25 percent each. On the other hand, Hutchison, thanks to her superior "time management" skills, would likely exceed the time budget on her major accounts by only a few hours. In fact, she might even come in under budget on one or more of her accounts, which was almost unheard of, at least on the dozen or so audits to which Wong had been assigned.

After finishing the bag of chips he had purchased in the snack room, Wong reached for the computer keyboard in front of him. In a few moments, he had entered his time for the week and printed the report that he would give to Angela Sun the following morning. After briefly glancing at the report, he slipped it into the appropriate workpaper file, turned off the light in the empty conference room, and locked the door behind him as he resolved to enjoy his brief 16-hour "weekend."

## Questions

1. Place yourself in Hamilton Wong's position. Would you report all of your time worked on the Wille & Lomax audit? Why or why not? Do you believe that Lauren Hutchison behaved unethically by underreporting the time she worked on that engagement? Defend your answer.
2. Academic research suggests that underreporting time on audit engagements is a common practice. What are the key objectives of tracking hours worked by individual accounts or assignments on audit engagements? What implications does the underreporting of time have for individual auditors, their colleagues, and the overall quality of independent audits?
3. What measures can accounting firms take to ensure that time budgets do not interfere with the successful completion of an audit or become dysfunctional in other ways?
4. What measures can accounting firms take to reduce the likelihood that personal rivalries among auditors of the same rank will become dysfunctional?

# SECTION 7

# PROFESSIONAL ISSUES

## CASE 7.1

# Ligand Pharmaceuticals

In the late 1990s, James Fazio reached what many CPAs consider the pinnacle of success in the accounting profession, namely, partnership in one of the Big Four public accounting firms. For more than a decade, Fazio served as an audit partner with Deloitte & Touche in that firm's San Diego, California, practice office. Similar to his colleagues within Deloitte and the other major accounting firms, Fazio's professional life was disrupted by the Enron and WorldCom debacles. The sudden collapse of those two large companies following the turn of the century prompted a public outcry to impose more rigorous regulatory controls over the financial reporting function for publicly owned companies. The federal government's response to that outcry would further complicate the already complex and stressful nature of James Fazio's professional role as an audit partner with a Big Four accounting firm.

### Peek-A-Boo

In the summer of 2002, the U.S. Congress hurriedly passed the Sarbanes-Oxley Act (SOX). The SOX legislation contained the most far-reaching financial reporting reforms at the federal level since the passage of the Securities Act of 1933 and the Securities Exchange Act of 1934. Those reforms included a requirement that public companies have their internal controls over financial reporting audited by an independent accounting firm. That requirement, which became effective for most companies in 2004, forced U.S. companies to spend billions of dollars to rethink and, in many cases, completely overhaul their internal control systems.

The SOX legislation was an economic boon for Deloitte and the other Big Four accounting firms since those firms were ideally suited to provide the thousands of internal control audits mandated by SOX. To take full advantage of this large new revenue stream, these firms redesigned their audit processes, retooled their organizational structures, and hired a large number of new employees.

SOX also established a new regulatory structure for the independent audit function that had far-reaching implications for the major accounting firms. The role of the new Public Company Accounting Oversight Board (PCAOB) was to strengthen and improve the independent audit function for public companies and thereby minimize the likelihood of "audit failures." Many parties have alleged that the Enron and WorldCom fiascoes could have been avoided or at least mitigated if those companies' financial statements had been audited more rigorously.

Based in Washington, D.C., the PCAOB, commonly referred to as "Peek-a-boo" by auditing practitioners, falls under the regulatory purview of the Securities and Exchange Commission (SEC). The PCAOB's operations are overseen by five board members appointed by the SEC, has several hundred employees, and an annual operating budget exceeding $100 million. The agency's regulatory mandate includes registering and monitoring accounting firms that audit public companies required to file periodic financial statements with the SEC. Other responsibilities of the PCAOB include establishing auditing, ethical, and quality control standards for those firms and carrying out disciplinary investigations.

The years immediately following the passage of SOX presented exciting and profitable opportunities for the Big Four accounting firms but posed enormous challenges for them as well. No one knew exactly how the new regulatory agenda and infrastructure would impact the nature of financial reporting and the independent audit function in the United States. Despite the uncertainty they faced, James Fazio and other Big Four audit partners had more pressing concerns at the time, namely, the everyday "business" of, and professional responsibilities associated with, supervising the audits of their clients.

## Deloitte's 2003 Ligand Audit

In early 2004, the 43-year-old Fazio was overseeing the 2003 audit of Ligand Pharmaceuticals, a San Diego-based company whose stock was traded on the NASDAQ exchange. As the audit engagement partner for Ligand, Fazio had a wide range of responsibilities. The following excerpts from Deloitte's *Accounting and Auditing Practice Manual* at the time addressed the role and responsibilities of an audit engagement partner.

> *It is the responsibility of the Engagement Partner to form the audit opinion, or to disclaim an opinion, on the financial statements.*
>
> *The Engagement Partner has the final responsibility for the planning and performance of the audit engagement, including the assignment, on-the-job training, and audit work of professional staff, and the implementation of the decisions concerning matters that have been the subject of consultation . . .*
>
> *The knowledge and skills of an Engagement Partner should be matched with the needs and characteristics of the engagement.*

For several years, James Fazio had been involved in his office's "High Technology Group." Because of his experience with emerging growth companies, Fazio seemed well suited to serve as the audit engagement partner for Ligand, which was still in a developmental stage. In company press releases, Ligand described itself as an "emerging R&D and royalty-driven biotechnology company." The company's principal products included a painkiller and several cancer treatment drugs. The company also had several new products under development. Rising expectations for the company's future prospects had caused its stock price to soar from under $4 per share in early 2003 to nearly $24 per share in early 2004 despite the company never having reported an operating profit.

Deloitte requires each audit engagement team to assess the degree of "engagement risk" posed by a given audit.[1] Fazio and his subordinates concluded that the 2003 Ligand audit posed a "greater than normal" degree of engagement risk due to questions surrounding Ligand's accounting for sales returns. Ligand's distribution channel consisted principally of three large drug wholesalers. These wholesalers purchased Ligand's products and then marketed them to pharmacies and other healthcare facilities throughout the United States. Ligand recorded product shipments made to the three wholesalers as consummated sales transactions although the wholesalers had the right to return any products that they did not "sell through" to their customers. Because of this revenue recognition policy, Ligand was required to record a reserve (allowance) for expected future sales returns at the end of each accounting period.

---

1. At the time, Deloitte required "engagement risk" to be explicitly assessed for every audit engagement. The three levels of engagement risk that could be assigned to a given audit included normal, greater than normal, and much greater than normal.

By early 2004 when Deloitte was auditing Ligand's 2003 financial statements, the company had been marketing its major products for only a short period of time, which meant that Ligand's accountants had limited historical experience on which to base their estimates of future sales returns. Complicating matters was the difficulty Ligand had in obtaining sales and inventory data from its three wholesalers.

Ligand typically shipped product to those wholesalers twelve months before the expiration date of the given product. The wholesalers generally had the right to return product received from Ligand in a twelve-month window that extended six months on either side of a product's expiration date. To properly assess the quantity of future sales returns, Ligand's accounting staff needed up-to-date "sell-through" data from its wholesalers. However, the three wholesalers frequently failed to provide that data on a timely basis. In fact, Ligand often received large and unexpected shipments of product returns from the three wholesalers.

The limited sales returns data available to Ligand during 2003 suggested that the company was significantly underestimating its rate of product returns. For example, one product had experienced rates of return ranging from 13 percent to as high as 20 percent on "open lots."[2] Company management was convinced that those return rates were not representative of the overall return rate that product would eventually experience. As a result, management instructed the company's accountants to apply a much more modest 2.5 percent return rate when determining the product's 2003 year-end allowance for future sales returns.

Shortly before Deloitte completed the 2003 Ligand audit in early March 2004, Ligand received additional information from its wholesalers regarding the return rates being experienced by its major products. Although this information was available from the company's accounting staff, the Deloitte auditors did not review it. The updated sales returns data, similar to the earlier data that had been reviewed by the Deloitte auditors, indicated that the December 31, 2003, allowance for future sales returns was inadequate. In some cases, the returns received in early 2004 for products sold in 2003 exceeded those products' total 2003 year-end provision for sales returns.

Fazio was aware of the difficulty Ligand had in estimating its future sales returns and the fact that the projected return rates being applied by the company appeared insufficient given the actual sales returns data available from the company's wholesalers. Despite this knowledge, Fazio authorized the issuance of an unqualified opinion on Ligand's 2003 financial statements on March 10, 2004.

The following month, Fazio supervised Deloitte's interim review of Ligand's financial statements for the first quarter of 2004. During that engagement, Fazio and his subordinates obtained Ligand's sales returns data for the first two months of fiscal 2004. Those data alone demonstrated that the year-end allowance for sales returns was significantly understated. However, Ligand's accounting staff also provided forecast data to the auditors indicating that the company would experience a large amount of additional product returns from fiscal 2003 sales during the remaining months of 2004. Despite the considerable evidence that Ligand's 2003 year-end allowance for sales returns was materially understated, Fazio failed to recommend that the company recall and restate its 2003 financial statements.

---

2. Ligand used the term "lot" in reference to a given quantity of items of the same product that were manufactured at the same time and had the same expiration date. The term "open lot" referred to a product shipment for which the given wholesaler still had a right to return the unsold inventory from that shipment.

## The Trials and Tribulations of James Fazio

The contentious accounting issues posed by Ligand were not the only challenges that James Fazio faced during the 2003 audit of that company. Several months before that audit began, Fazio's immediate superior, the partner in charge of Deloitte's San Diego audit practice, asked to meet with him. During that meeting, Fazio was told that concerns were being expressed about his job performance. In fact, members of Deloitte's management had suggested that Fazio no longer be allowed to supervise audits of public companies.

In February 2004, during the course of the 2003 Ligand audit, Fazio's immediate superior met with him once more. During this meeting, Fazio was told that he was perceived as a "quality risk" and was "counseled to resign from the firm."[3] Several of Deloitte's top partners had been involved in the decision to ask for Fazio's resignation. These partners included the director of Deloitte's Risk Management Program, the Regional Audit Managing Partner for Deloitte's Pacific Southwest Region, and Deloitte's National Audit Managing Partner.

On March 5, 2004, the San Diego Audit Managing Partner and the Regional Audit Managing Partner met with Fazio. Following that meeting, the Regional Audit Managing Partner sent an e-mail to the National Audit Managing Partner that summarized the discussions that took place during the meeting. The e-mail documented the reasons why Fazio was being asked to resign from Deloitte.

> *Among the reasons given were the views of certain members of Deloitte's management that the Engagement Partner [Fazio] did not have the skills to adequately supervise public company engagements and other engagements with above-average risk profiles and that the Engagement Partner [Fazio] was not suited to handling complex or risky engagements.*[4]

Five days later, on March 10, 2004, Fazio signed the unqualified audit opinion issued by Deloitte on Ligand's 2003 financial statements. Fazio remained the audit engagement partner for Ligand following the issuance of that audit report.

On August 5, 2004, Deloitte resigned as Ligand's independent auditor. The price of Ligand's stock declined sharply following Deloitte's abrupt and unexpected resignation. From its high-water mark of nearly $24 per share in April 2004, the stock would eventually fall to under $1.50 per share by 2008.

---

## EPILOGUE

In May 2005, Ligand's management announced that the company would be restating its financial statements for 2002, 2003, and the first three quarters of 2004. Management reported that a joint investigation by the company's audit committee and new audit firm, BDO Seidman, had revealed material errors in those financial statements. The errors resulted principally from "improperly recognizing revenue on product shipments to distributors."[5] The financial restatement released by Ligand later in 2005 reduced the company's previously reported revenues for 2003 by 52 percent or $59 million in total. The company also increased its reported operating loss for 2003 by 250 percent.

---

3. PCAOB, "Order Instituting Disciplinary Proceedings, Making Findings and Imposing Sanctions: In the Matter of Deloitte & Touche LLP," *PCAOB Release No. 105-2007-005*, 10 December 2007, 7.

4. *Ibid.*

5. J. McEntee, "Ligand to Restate Financials Back to 2002," *sandiego.com*, 20 May 2005.

Ligand insisted that the joint investigation by its audit committee and BDO Seidman had "found no evidence of improper or fraudulent actions or practices by any member of management or that management acted in bad faith in adopting and administering the company's historical revenue recognition policies."[6] The company also reported that it intended to adopt a new revenue recognition model based upon sell-through accounting under which revenue would not be recognized until the company's wholesalers had sold Ligand's products to their customers.

On December 10, 2007, the PCAOB issued joint disciplinary releases announcing sanctions imposed on James Fazio and Deloitte & Touche stemming from Fazio's involvement in the 2003 Ligand audit.[7] The PCAOB barred James Fazio from being associated with a PCAOB-registered public accounting firm for two years. In a PCAOB press release also issued on December 10, 2007, an agency spokesperson reported that Fazio violated several professional auditing standards during the 2003 Ligand audit.

> *Mr. Fazio failed to perform appropriate and adequate audit procedures related to Ligand's reported revenue from sales of products for which a right of return existed and failed to supervise others adequately to ensure the performance of such procedures.*
>
> *Mr. Fazio neither performed nor ensured the performance of procedures that adequately took into account the existence of factors indicating that Ligand's ability to make reasonable estimates of product returns may have been impaired.*
>
> *Mr. Fazio neither performed nor ensured the performance of procedures that adequately took into account the extent to which Ligand had consistently and substantially underestimated its product returns.*
>
> *In auditing Ligand's reported revenues, Mr. Fazio failed to [exercise] . . . the due care and professional skepticism required under the circumstances.*
>
> *He also failed to identify and appropriately address issues concerning Ligand's policy of excluding certain types of returns from its estimates of future returns and the adequacy of Ligand's disclosure of this accounting policy.*[8]

The PCAOB publicly censured Deloitte and fined the firm $1 million for failing to take "meaningful steps to assure the quality of the audit work" on the 2003 Ligand audit engagement.[9] According to the PCAOB spokesperson, prior to and during the 2003 Ligand audit, "Certain members of Deloitte's management concluded that Mr. Fazio should be removed from public company audits" and that "he should be asked to resign from the firm."[10] The spokesperson went on to note that despite the grave concerns expressed regarding Mr. Fazio's competence, he was allowed to continue as the engagement partner for the 2003 Ligand audit.

The PCAOB's Director of Enforcement and Investigations issued a separate statement on the responsibility of registered accounting firms to ensure that their partners are competent to perform public company audits.

> *Registered public accounting firms must take reasonable steps to assure that their audit partners and other audit professionals are competent to conduct public audits. When concerns about an auditor's competency rise, a firm must act with dispatch to protect audit quality. The firm [Deloitte] failed to meet the Board's auditing standards in the audit led by Mr. Fazio.*[11]

6. *Ibid.*

7. Although the PCAOB issued the disciplinary reports in this case, SEC and PCAOB personnel were involved in the related investigations. In 2005, the SEC had announced that it was launching an independent investigation of Ligand. The federal agency apparently completed that investigation without imposing sanctions on Ligand or any Ligand executive or employee.

8. PCAOB, "PCAOB Issues Disciplinary Orders Against Deloitte & Touche LLP and a Former Audit Partner," www.pcaobus.org/News_and_Events/2007/12-10.aspx, 10 December 2007.

9. *Ibid.*

10. *Ibid.*

11. *Ibid.*

The sanctions imposed on Deloitte were the first levied on a Big Four accounting firm by the PCAOB. A former SEC official noted that the Ligand case was a milestone in the new agency's short regulatory history. "It shows that the PCAOB's Enforcement Division is fully mature and also that we should expect to see within a short period of time additional cases against not only other Big Four firms, but against the so-called second four firms as well."[12]

Deloitte issued a public statement responding to the sanctions imposed on it by the PCAOB. In that statement, a Deloitte official reported that the firm had "established and implemented changes to its quality-control policies that directly address the PCAOB's concerns."[13] The Deloitte spokesperson went on to insist that the firm was "confident that its audit policies and procedures were among the very best in the profession and that they meet or exceed all applicable standards."[14]

---

## Questions

1. Describe what you believe is implied by the term "engagement risk." What are the key factors likely considered by Deloitte and other audit firms when assessing engagement risk? How, if at all, are auditors' professional responsibilities affected when a client poses a higher than normal degree of engagement risk?
2. What quality control mechanisms should major accounting firms have in place to ensure that audit partners have the proper training and experience to supervise audit engagements?
3. Identify the accounting standards and concepts that dictate the proper accounting treatment for sales returns. How were these standards and concepts violated by Ligand?
4. During the review of Ligand's first-quarter financial statements for 2004, the Deloitte auditors learned that the company had significantly underestimated its future sales returns at the end of 2003. What responsibility, if any, did this discovery impose on the Deloitte auditors?
5. Since its inception, the PCAOB has been criticized by many parties. Summarize the principal complaints that have been directed at the PCAOB. Do you believe this criticism is justified? Explain. What measures could the PCAOB take to improve its effectiveness and efficiency as a regulatory body?

---

12. C. Johnson, "Deloitte Settles in Key Case Over Faulty Audit," *Washington Post*, 11 December 2007, D01.
13. F. Norris, "Deloitte Agrees to Pay $1 Million Fine," *The New York Times* (online), 11 December 2007.
14. *Ibid.*

**CASE 7.2**

# HealthSouth Corporation

"Full and fair disclosure" has long reigned as the motto of the Securities and Exchange Commission (SEC). The federal agency does not attempt to protect investors from unwise investment decisions. Instead, the agency's principal goal is to provide investors with the information they need to make fully informed investment decisions. That information includes the nature of the relationship between public companies and their independent auditors. Since the early 1970s, the SEC has required public companies to notify investors when they change their auditors. Among other requirements, the SEC's current auditor change disclosure rules require public companies to reveal whether they had any major disagreements with their former audit firm.

In the late 1990s, the SEC became concerned by the growing amount of consulting services audit firms were providing to SEC registrants. During a two-decade period stretching from the late 1970s to the late 1990s, the major accounting firms experienced a dramatic shift in their revenue mix. In 1976, audit fees accounted for approximately 70 percent of those firms' total revenues. Consulting had displaced auditing as the primary revenue source for major accounting firms by 1998, a year in which those firms generated only one-third of their total revenues from audit engagements.[1] The types of consulting services provided by auditors to public companies also concerned the SEC. Officials of the SEC believed that many nontraditional services supplied by accounting firms to their audit clients, such as internal auditing services, jeopardized auditors' objectivity and independence.

In early 2001, the SEC issued new rules that limited the consulting services accounting firms could market to publicly owned audit clients. Actuarial, brokerage, and legal services were among the ten types of services accounting firms were prohibited from providing to SEC registrants. The SEC's new rules also required public companies to disclose the following fees they paid to their independent auditors each year: fees for audit services, fees for financial information systems design and implementation services, and all other fees.[2] Exhibit 1 presents the fiscal 2000 audit fee disclosures that The Home Depot included in its annual shareholder proxy statement filed with the SEC. Notice that The Home Depot identified the specific types of "other" services provided by its auditor, KPMG, disclosures not required by the SEC.

The first wave of audit fee disclosures released by SEC registrants in early 2001 provided, for the first time, indisputable evidence that many public companies were paying their independent auditors enormous sums for non-audit services. Notice in Exhibit 1 that The Home Depot paid KPMG less than $1 million for its 2000 audit and more than $3.5 million for "all other" services. Dozens of large corporations reported an even greater disparity between their annual audit fee and the total fees paid for other services provided by their audit firm. Of the $62.3 million that Motorola paid KPMG in 2000, only $3.9 million of that amount was for KPMG's annual audit. Likewise, Sprint

1. J. Gardemal, "Stick to Auditing: Independence Concerns Led to SEC Rule Restricting Services by Accountants," *Legal Times*, 26 March 2001, 46.

2. SEC officials required separate disclosure of fees for "financial information systems design and implementation services" because they believed those types of services posed a particularly significant threat to the independence of auditors.

**EXHIBIT 1**

THE HOME DEPOT FISCAL 2000 AUDIT FEE DISCLOSURES

**General.** During fiscal 2000, the Company paid KPMG LLP fees in the aggregate amount of approximately $4,517,800. Of this amount, approximately $991,400 were fees for the fiscal 2000 audit and other audit services.

**Financial Information Systems Design and Implementation.** KPMG did not render any services related to financial information systems design and implementation during fiscal 2000.

**All Other Fees.** KPMG rendered other services consisting primarily of tax consulting, due diligence assistance, environmental consulting, litigation support and audits of the Company's employee benefit plans and other entities within the consolidated group for statutory filing purposes. Aggregate fees billed for all other services rendered by KPMG for fiscal 2000 were $3,526,400.

paid Ernst & Young $2.5 million to audit its 2000 financial statements and $61.3 million for various other services.

The SEC's new audit fee disclosures re-ignited the contentious debate over whether auditors were truly independent of their major clients. To quell this controversy, many corporate executives began insisting that the "other services" provided by accounting firms were typically "audit-related." "While the percentage of fees being paid to auditors for non-audit services is high, companies are quick to point out that most are 'audit-related.'"[3] In fact, some companies began reporting the amount of "other fees" paid to their independent auditors that were "audit-related." "Many companies, encouraged by their auditors, have tried to allay such [independence] concerns by voluntarily disclosing how much of their fees for 'other' services are 'audit-related.'"[4]

Among other companies, the large healthcare firm, HealthSouth Corporation, chose to voluntarily disclose "audit-related fees" in its annual audit fee disclosure filed with the SEC. Exhibit 2 presents that company's audit fee disclosures for 2000 and 2001.

Richard Scrushy, a 30-year-old physical therapist, founded HealthSouth in 1984 in Birmingham, Alabama, and eventually assembled a chain of 1,500 rehabilitation hospitals and clinics, making HealthSouth one of the nation's largest healthcare suppliers. Scrushy's world quickly crumbled in early 2003 when the SEC alleged that he and several of his former colleagues had engaged in a large-scale accounting and Medicare fraud that inflated HealthSouth's pre-tax earnings by nearly $3 billion over the three-year period 1999 through 2001. A few months later, a federal grand jury indicted Scrushy on 85 counts of conspiracy, securities fraud, and related charges. Scrushy was the first corporate executive to face a federal indictment filed under the criminal provisions of the Sarbanes-Oxley Act of 2002. Widespread public protest and indignation forced Scrushy and his top subordinates to resign their positions with HealthSouth.

3. *Corporate Governance Bulletin* (online), "Non-audit Fees Supersede Audit Fees, IRRC Finds," April 2001.

4. J. Weil, "'Audit-Related Fees' to Ernst Were for Janitorial Inspections," *The Wall Street Journal* (WSJ.com), 11 June 2003.

**EXHIBIT 2**

HEALTHSOUTH CORPORATION AUDIT FEE DISCLOSURES FOR FISCAL 2000 AND 2001

**Audit Fees [2000].** The aggregate fees billed to us for the fiscal year ended December 31, 2000, by Ernst & Young LLP for the fiscal year ended December 31, 2000, or related to its audit for such fiscal year were as follows:

| | |
|---|---|
| Audit Fees | $1,026,649 |
| All Other Fees: | |
| Audit-Related Fees | $2,583,854 |
| Non-Audit-Related Fees | 66,107 |

**Audit Fees [2001].** The aggregate fees billed to us for the fiscal year ended December 31, 2001, by Ernst & Young LLP for the fiscal year ended December 31, 2001, or related to its audit for such fiscal year were as follows:

| | |
|---|---|
| Audit Fees | $1,164,750 |
| All Other Fees: | |
| Audit-Related Fees | $2,387,676 |
| Non-Audit-Related Fees | 121,580 |

The fraud charges filed against HealthSouth immediately focused the attention of the business press on Ernst & Young, which had served as HealthSouth's audit firm since the company was founded. Because non-audit fees had been a "hot" topic over the past few years, business journalists accessed and reviewed HealthSouth's audit fee disclosures. As Exhibit 2 indicates, HealthSouth reported that more than 95 percent of the other fees paid to Ernst & Young in 2000 and 2001 had involved "audit-related" services. Not content with that assertion, Jonathan Weil, an investigative reporter for *The Wall Street Journal*, discovered that more than one-half of the "audit-related" fees HealthSouth paid to Ernst & Young had been for "pristine audits" or health inspections performed by representatives of the accounting firm.

Richard Scrushy had initiated the pristine audits in the late 1990s. Scrushy wanted to ensure that every HealthSouth facility was immaculately clean and aesthetic for the benefit of the company's customers. To achieve that objective, Scrushy developed a lengthy checklist of procedures to be completed by Ernst & Young personnel during an annual surprise visit to each HealthSouth facility. Those procedures included checking the cleanliness of toilets, making sure that all trash containers had linings, and determining that magazines in customer waiting rooms were displayed in an orderly fashion. During both 2000 and 2001, HealthSouth paid Ernst & Young approximately $1.3 million to perform the pristine audits, which was more than the company paid the accounting firm for its financial statement audit each of those years.

The HealthSouth management team that replaced Richard Scrushy and his subordinates insisted to Jonathon Weil that Ernst & Young's facility inspection audits had not involved "audit-related" services. Those officials also maintained that Ernst & Young had suggested that HealthSouth classify the fees paid for those inspections as audit-related in the annual audit fee disclosures filed with the SEC. When questioned regarding this issue, an Ernst & Young spokesperson defended the classification of the inspection fees. "E&Y believes that HealthSouth's [pristine audit] fees were properly classified."[5]

5. *Ibid.*

Ernst & Young's defense of HealthSouth's audit fee disclosures prompted angry rebuttals from two former SEC Chief Accountants, Lynn Turner and Walter Schuetze. Turner noted that, "E&Y arguing that checking the cleanliness of a facility is 'audit-related' goes well beyond the pale of sanity and common sense."[6] Schuetze was even more critical of the prominent accounting firm. "Calling that audit-related is false and misleading. Not only does it fly in the face of facts, it suggests that Ernst & Young was covering up the facts ... When Ernst & Young deliberately misclassifies something that is clearly on its face wrong, that undermines everything Ernst & Young says and does."[7]

The continuing controversy over the magnitude and nature of non-audit fees paid by large companies to their independent auditors caused the SEC to revise its audit fee disclosure rules in 2003. These new rules require SEC registrants to classify professional fees paid to their auditors into four categories: audit fees, audit-related fees, tax fees, and all other fees. According to the SEC, the category of "audit-related fees" should be reserved for fees paid for assurance and related services traditionally performed by audit firms. "More specifically, these services would include, among others: employee benefit plan audits, due diligence related to mergers and acquisitions, accounting consultations and audits in connection with acquisitions, internal control reviews, attest services that are not required by statue or regulation, and consultation concerning financial accounting and reporting standards."[8] Exhibit 3 presents the audit fee disclosures made by Pulte Homes, Inc., under the new rules issued by the SEC.

The SEC's revised audit fee disclosure rules failed to appease many critics who continued to question how auditors could retain their independence while providing a significant amount of non-audit services to their clients. For example, Institutional Shareholder Services, the "world's leading corporate governance agency and proxy voting advisory service," began encouraging stockholders not to ratify the appointment of independent auditors who provided "excessive" non-audit services to a company. Another organization, Citizens Funds, which oversees a group of "socially responsible mutual funds," called for major corporations to limit the amount of non-audit fees they paid to their audit firms. At a Microsoft annual stockholder meeting, that organization presented a resolution to limit the amount of non-audit fees Microsoft paid to its independent auditor, Deloitte & Touche, to an amount equal to 25 percent of the annual audit fee. Although Microsoft's stockholders rejected the resolution, Citizens Funds reported that it would continue presenting similar resolutions at annual stockholder meetings of major U.S. companies.

---

6. *Ibid.*

7. *Ibid.*

8. Securities and Exchange Commission, "Final Rule: Strengthening the Commission's Requirements Regarding Auditor Independence," 26 March 2003.

**EXHIBIT 3**

PULTE HOMES, INC. AUDIT FEE DISCLOSURES FOR FISCAL 2001 AND 2002

**Fees Paid to Independent Auditors.** Ernst & Young LLP are our independent auditors and our subsidiaries' independent auditors and have reported on our consolidated financial statements included in our Annual Report, which accompanies this proxy statement. Our independent auditors are ultimately accountable to our Audit Committee. Fees paid to Ernst & Young LLP for the years ended December 31, 2002 and 2001, are as follows:

| | 2002 | 2001 |
|---|---|---|
| Audit | $1,247,710 | $1,261,000 |
| Audit-Related | 81,500 | 462,000 |
| Tax | 839,997 | 1,464,500 |
| All Other | — | 900,500 |
| | $2,169,207 | $4,088,000 |

Fees for audit-related services include fees for employee benefit plan audits, due diligence services and accounting consultations. Fees for tax services include fees related to tax compliance and tax planning. Fees for all other services primarily include fees related to assistance with matters for the Del Webb merger.

We expect representative of Ernst & Young LLP to be present at the annual meeting of our shareholders, and they will have the opportunity to make a statement at the meeting. The representatives of Ernst & Young will also be available to respond to appropriate questions.

With the approval of the Audit Committee, Pulte has reengaged Ernst & Young LLP as our independent auditors for the year ending December 31, 2003.

## EPILOGUE

In April 2005, Ernst & Young filed a civil lawsuit against HealthSouth. The lawsuit charged HealthSouth with concealing a massive accounting fraud from Ernst & Young auditors and with damaging the large accounting firm's reputation and exposing it to significant litigation costs. In early June 2005, HealthSouth agreed to pay $100 million to settle securities fraud charges filed against the company by the SEC. The $100 million was to be distributed to investors who suffered losses following the announcement of the HealthSouth fraud. A few weeks later, on June 28, 2005, an Alabama jury found Richard Scrushy innocent of each of the criminal charges that had been filed against him two years earlier. In subsequent interviews, jurors in the case admitted that the prosecution team had clearly proven the existence of massive fraud within HealthSouth but insisted that the evidence linking Scrushy to that fraud was "ambiguous."

## Questions

1. A recent study found that companies that pay their auditors a disproportionately large amount of consulting fees relative to their annual audit fee are more likely than other companies to reach previously announced earnings targets. What does this finding imply about the independence of auditors that receive disproportionately large non-audit fees from their clients? Explain.
2. The study referred to in the prior question also suggested that investors "discount" the earnings of companies that have potential conflicts of interests with their independent auditors. Explain what is meant by investors "discounting earnings" in such circumstances. What implication does this finding have for the independent audit function?
3. Critics of major accounting firms have suggested that certain of those firms acquire new clients by quoting them "lowball" audit fees and then aggressively market lucrative (high profit-margin) non-audit services to those clients. How would such lowballing affect the independence of auditors, if at all? Explain.
4. Search online for two examples of recent audit fee disclosures made by public companies. (Those disclosures are included in annual shareholder proxy statements filed with the SEC by public companies and can be accessed from the SEC's website.) Print out those examples. Which of the two companies did a better job of satisfying the intent of the SEC's audit fee disclosure rules? Defend your choice.

**CASE 7.3**

# Baan Company, N.V.

In May 1998, Moret Ernst & Young Accountants resigned as the independent audit firm for Baan Company N.V., a software company headquartered in Barneveld, The Netherlands.[1] At the time, Baan, ranked among the leading worldwide suppliers of enterprise resource planning (ERP) software packages. Press reports provided conflicting accounts of why Moret Ernst & Young (Moret), the Dutch affiliate of the U.S. based accounting firm Ernst & Young, resigned as Baan's auditor. The *New York Times* reported that Baan management had been upset by Moret's insistence that the software maker include disclosures in its financial statement footnotes regarding certain large related party transactions.[2] A few days later, a press release issued by Baan reported that Moret resigned because of a planned "global software consultancy agreement" between Baan and Ernst & Young. In the years to follow, an investigation by the Securities and Exchange Commission (SEC) would reveal much more about the complicated nature of Baan's relationship with Moret and the circumstances that led to that relationship coming to an end.

## An Enterprising Software Company

The 1990s were a frenetic but blissful time for major software companies across the globe. A slew of Y2K (Year 2000) doomsayers warned multinational corporations, "Mom and Pop" businesses, charitable organizations, government agencies at all levels, and any other organization relying heavily on computers that those machines would likely shut down one nanosecond after midnight on January 1, 2000. The result would be disruption of practically every significant internal function of those organizations, not to mention worldwide chaos. Mounting concern caused by this doomsday scenario prompted organizations of all sizes to hire Y2K remediation experts to rid their computer code of the Y2K "bug." In the United States, businesses and government agencies spent an estimated $300 billion on Y2K remediation services. Citicorp, alone, reported spending $650 million on its Y2K project.

Opportunistic software companies and business consulting firms took advantage of the sudden and dramatic surge in IT (information technology) awareness to goad corporate executives to overhaul their organizations' IT systems. The punch line of these marketing efforts went something like this: "While we are solving your Y2K problem, why don't you allow us to revamp your IT systems to prepare your organization for the dynamic and hyper-competitive business environment of the 21st century?" Software vendors and business consultants promised to revolutionize business processes and make companies more efficient, more focused on their goals, and, most important, more profitable.

Such marketing efforts resulted in a huge increase in IT spending during the late 1990s and produced an array of new and impressive-sounding catch phrases. Review business archives for that period and you will find the following expressions

1. "N.V." is an abbreviation for "naamloze vennootschap." This phrase indicates that Baan Company was a limited liability company under Dutch federal law.

2. F. Norris, "An Audit Uncovers Soft Profits in Software," *The New York Times*, 10 May 1998, Section 3, 1.

and literally hundreds of similar ones bandied about in the business press: "business process reengineering," "mission-critical, customer-driven web applications," "digital document-management services," and "web-enabling software solutions." Among the most widely used, and possibly least understood, phrases coined in the late 1990s was "enterprise resource planning" (ERP). The following description of "ERP software" was provided by one major software vendor: "ERP software is generally used to automate and integrate corporate functions across the board, such as inventory control, procurement, manufacturing planning, distribution, sales forecasting, finance, human resources, EDI and project management."[3] Each of the major software companies developed and intensely marketed a broad product line of ERP software during the late 1990s. These companies included, among others, Oracle, PeopleSoft, Seibel Systems, and Baan Company.

Baan Company was founded in 1978 in The Netherlands. During the 1990s, the company's software engineers developed a family of products and services that they referred to as the "Orgware Solution." According to the company's promotional literature, these products and services were intended to help companies "depict organizational structure," "reduce the time to market," provide for "dynamic enterprise modeling," and "rapidly translate a business vision into improved business process."

To help market their products and services, each of the major software companies, including Baan, developed an extensive network of business partners that included the major firms in the financial services industries. Among the most valued of these business partners were the large international accounting firms. Software executives "covet connections to the Big Five firms because of those firms' access to the executives and decision makers at the thousands of companies that they audit."[4] Just as important, the auditing, taxation, and general business consulting services that the major accounting firms provided to their clients made them well aware of those companies' IT needs.

By the mid-1990s, each of the major software companies had aligned itself with at least one of the international accounting firms. For example, Oracle's principal Big Five partner was Arthur Andersen, while Microsoft had paired itself with Deloitte & Touche. Baan Company affiliated itself with both Ernst & Young and Coopers & Lybrand. In Europe, Baan developed a close working relationship with its independent audit firm, Moret.

## Bonding with Your Auditor

In May 1995, Baan Company went public with an initial public offering (IPO). The company's common stock traded on both the Amsterdam Stock Exchange and the NASDAQ exchange in the United States. For purposes of the Securities and Exchange Commission (SEC), Baan was a "foreign private issuer,"[5] a status that required the company to file an annual financial report with the SEC that included a complete

3. *Business Wire* (online), "Entrust Technologies Unveils Comprehensive Plan to Address Security Requirements of ERP Software Market," 23 November 1998.

4. M. Petersen, "Consulting by Auditors Stirs Concerns," *The New York Times*, 13 July 1998, D1.

5. The SEC defines a "foreign private issuer" as a registrant that meets the following four conditions: (1) 50% or less of its outstanding voting stock is held by U.S. residents; (2) the majority of the company's executive officers and directors are not U.S. citizens or residents; (3) 50% or more of the company's assets are located outside of the United States; and (4) the company's principal business operations are outside of the United States.

set of audited financial statements. Prior to Baan registering its securities for sale in the United States, the Moret partner who supervised the annual Baan audit engagement obtained a summary of the SEC's auditor independence rules from an audit partner with Ernst & Young, Moret's U.S. affiliate. The Moret partner was concerned that certain joint business relationships his firm had with Baan might violate the SEC's auditor independence rules.

From 1995 through 1997, Moret personnel worked closely with Baan to help the company market its software products, to complete software implementation projects, and to provide technical support to Baan's clients. In early 1995, Baan and Moret signed a "partner agreement" that created a "global alliance" between the two firms. "The agreement established guidelines for coordination of the global alliance, a joint structure for managing Baan's and Moret's activities, mutual indemnification between the parties, and prohibitions against the disclosure of confidential information."[6] A proposal for a consulting project that the Moret firm made to a potential client stressed the close relationship between the two firms. "Baan and Moret have a worldwide partnership. In this partnership both parties have made concrete arrangements of working together for clients. In practice this means that Baan and Moret operate as one party towards the client. Our activities are fully integrated with and steered by the Baan project management team."

During the late 1990s, Baan's IT software business grew dramatically, causing the company's stock price to spiral upward. Within two years of the company's IPO, its stock price had increased by ten-fold or 1000 percent. Because the firm was unable to hire sufficient software consultants to work on its growing backlog of customer projects, the firm "borrowed" Moret employees to help complete many of those projects. For example, in the fall of 1996, Moret assumed full responsibility for a large Baan software implementation project that was being completed for a Turkish company: "Moret consultants signed documents and made presentations on Baan's behalf, and Moret consultants were listed in project documents as being members of the Baan implementation team." Moret billed Baan more than $300,000 for the time its employees spent on that project.[7]

In another case, Moret provided employees to help Baan complete a software implementation project for a Finnish company that was Baan's third largest customer. One of those Moret employees served as the project director for a period of time. Moret billed Baan the equivalent of nearly $1 million for the work that its employees did on that project. Baan then added a 25 percent mark-up to the amounts billed to it by Moret when preparing the billing invoices submitted to the client. "Thus, in addition to directly helping Baan complete an implementation for an important company, Moret's furnishing of consultants contributed to Baan's profits."

From late 1996 through 1998, Moret loaned several of its professional employees to Baan to help staff the Baan Support Center, which provided technical support and assistance to the company's customers. While interacting with Baan customers in this facility, the Moret employees were required to identify themselves as Baan employees. Moret received $600,000 from Baan for the time that its employees spent working in the support center.

---

6. The remaining quotes in this case, unless indicated otherwise, were taken from Securities and Exchange Commission, *Accounting and Auditing Enforcement Release No. 1584*, 27 June 2002.

7. Because of a dispute over the amount of the bill, Moret was never paid for the time its employees spent working on this project.

These and other joint business relationships that Moret had with Baan clearly violated the SEC's auditor independence rule that precluded auditors of SEC registrants from having a "direct . . . business relationship [with an audit client], other than as a consumer in the normal course of business . . . [that] will adversely affect the accountant's independence with respect to the client." Despite their awareness of that rule, an awareness they had acquired from Ernst & Young, Moret personnel chose to ignore the rule and forge an increasingly close and profitable association with Baan.

## Ernst & Young's Dual Role at Baan USA

Baan Company had several international subsidiaries, including Baan USA. In 1995, Ernst & Young audited Baan USA's financial statements that were then incorporated into Baan's consolidated financial statements for that year. Ernst & Young resigned as the subsidiary's auditor in early 1996 to pursue joint business relationships with Baan USA, "including subcontracting on software implementations and submitting joint proposals with Baan [USA] for software sales and implementation business." Ernst & Young's resignation was prompted by the realization that the business relationships with Baan USA would cause the firm to violate the SEC's auditor independence rules.

To replace Ernst & Young, Baan retained a small accounting firm in California to audit Baan USA's 1996 financial statements. By the following year, Baan USA's explosive growth in revenues resulted in that subsidiary accounting for approximately 40 percent of Baan's total worldwide revenues. This development greatly concerned the Baan audit engagement partner. The partner was not comfortable with allowing the small accounting firm to take responsibility for such a large portion of the Baan annual audit. Moret officials discussed this issue with personnel in Ernst & Young's National Office in New York City. One alternative the parties considered was having Moret retain another major accounting firm to audit Baan USA's 1997 financial statements. That alternative was quickly rejected since each of those firms also had significant business relationships with Baan USA that would impair their independence while auditing the Baan subsidiary.

After considerable discussion, Moret and Ernst & Young reached an agreement that would allow the small California accounting firm to remain Baan USA's external auditor. The key feature of this agreement was that Ernst & Young would supply internal audit services to Baan USA, meaning that the subsidiary effectively outsourced its internal audit function to Ernst & Young. The Ernst & Young personnel assigned to Baan USA would work closely with the audit engagement team from the small accounting firm. This arrangement was intended to allay the concern of the Moret audit engagement partner regarding the small accounting firm's ability to successfully complete the 1997 audit of Baan USA. During the negotiations with Ernst & Young regarding the structure and nature of the 1997 Baan USA audit, the Moret audit engagement partner made it very clear that his firm intended to rely heavily on the work of the Ernst & Young internal auditors in deciding whether to accept the results of the Baan USA audit. "[Ernst & Young's procedures must] be adequate for us to use . . . for the external audit without having to supplement a lot of the work. So, they should be similar to a normal external audit plan, perhaps supplemented with some real internal audit stuff to further substantiate that this clearly is an internal audit."

The 1997 Baan audit went off as planned and resulted in Moret issuing an unqualified opinion on the company's consolidated financial statements. In their role as Baan USA's internal auditors, Ernst & Young personnel worked side by side with the audit engagement team from the small California accounting firm. According to the SEC, the California firm conducted a full scope audit of Baan USA. However, Moret "used and relied on E&Y's work" on that audit, "citing that work repeatedly in its audit working papers and using that work to confirm the accuracy and appropriate scope of the California firm's work."

## SEC Sanctions Moret

As noted earlier, Moret resigned as Baan's auditor in May 1998, following the completion of the 1997 audit. Again, two differing accounts of the reason for Moret's resignation were reported in the business press. An undisclosed factor that may have contributed to that resignation was tension between Ernst & Young's National Office and the Moret audit engagement partner. The SEC revealed that the two parties bickered over the role that the Ernst & Young auditors would play in the 1997 Baan USA audit. Ernst & Young officials resisted, and likely resented, the efforts of the Moret audit partner to pressure their firm into playing an increasingly important role in that audit. At one point, frustration prompted the Moret audit partner to consider not completing the engagement. "The Moret audit partner indicated that Moret might have to resign from the Baan audit if E&Y would not agree to perform internal audit work along the lines he wanted."

In 2002, the SEC issued *Accounting and Auditing Enforcement Release No. 1584* to report the results of its investigation of Moret's 1995 through 1997 audits of Baan Company. Because of the joint business relationships between Baan and Moret, the SEC ruled that Moret's independence had been impaired on each of those audits. The SEC also concluded that during the 1997 audit, "Moret improperly relied on the audit work of an affiliated firm, E&Y, which also lacked independence from Baan." According to the SEC, the Ernst & Young internal auditors assigned to Baan USA had "participated in a significant portion of the [external] audit" and been "an essential part of Moret's external audit team" at a time when they had "managerial responsibilities" with Baan USA.

The SEC fined Moret $400,000 for violating the federal agency's auditor independence rules during the 1995 through 1997 Baan audit engagements. This was the first time that the SEC had fined a foreign accounting firm and the first time that it had fined an accounting firm for having a significant business relationship with an audit client. The settlement agreement that the SEC reached with Moret required the firm to "develop and implement auditor independence policies for the firm." These policies were to include prohibitions on the types of business relationships that had impaired Moret's independence during the Baan audits. Among other stipulations, the SEC also required that Moret personnel assigned to any future audits involving SEC registrants "undergo training regarding auditor independence" at least once every twelve months.

# EPILOGUE

Similar to many software vendors and consulting companies that profited enormously from the late 1990s "IT revolution," Baan Company experienced a sudden and sharp drop in business activity following the turn of the century. In 2000, a British software company, Invensys, purchased Baan. Unfortunately, Baan's operating results continued to deteriorate and Invensys sold the company for a huge loss three years later.

The SEC did not sanction Ernst & Young for the role that it played in the 1997 Baan audit. But, Ernst & Young soon found itself the target of another SEC investigation involving a major software vendor, a case that was very reminiscent of the Moret-Baan debacle. From 1994 through 2000, Ernst & Young was a member of a network of business partners created by PeopleSoft. Twelve other financial services firms participated in the PeopleSoft Financials Implementation Partnership Program, including Deloitte & Touche and Price Waterhouse. Unlike the latter two accounting firms, Ernst & Young already had a relationship with PeopleSoft since it served as the large software company's independent auditor.

In June 2002, shortly before the SEC issued its enforcement release for the Moret-Baan case, the federal agency filed a complaint against Ernst & Young. This complaint charged the firm with violating auditor independence rules by maintaining a six-year joint business relationship with PeopleSoft while simultaneously serving as the company's independent auditor. "The SEC said that during the 1990s, E&Y developed and marketed a software product called EY/GEMS for PeopleSoft, which combined a PeopleSoft product with software that was used in E&Y's tax department."[8] According to the SEC, E&Y paid PeopleSoft a minimum $300,000 royalty for each sale of that joint product. PeopleSoft and Ernst & Young "closely coordinated" the marketing efforts for the software product, "including reciprocal endorsements of each other, links to each other's web sites, holding themselves out as 'business partners,' and sharing customer information, customer leads and 'target accounts.'"[9] As many as 1,000 Ernst & Young employees helped install the joint software product for hundreds of companies, including many that were Ernst & Young audit clients.

In July 2003, the SEC announced the sanctions it intended to impose on Ernst & Young for the dual and conflicting roles the accounting firm had maintained with PeopleSoft. Those sanctions required Ernst & Young to forfeit the nearly $2 million of audit fees it had received from PeopleSoft from 1994 through 2000. In addition, the SEC intended to prohibit Ernst & Young from accepting new SEC audit clients for a period of six months. In defending the harsh sanctions, the SEC noted that Ernst & Young was a repeat offender because the firm had been involved in a similar case in the mid-1990s. In an earlier discussion of the case, the SEC had made it very clear that auditor-client joint business relationships were totally inconsistent with, and undermined the credibility of, the independent audit function. "It is crucial that accountants [auditors] be independent; when they engage in joint business practices with clients, the entire audit process is subverted."[10]

---

8. N. Roland, "SEC Charges Ernst & Young with Conflicts: Ran Venture with PeopleSoft While Auditing Books," *National Post,* 21 May 2002, FP1.

9. S. Taub, "Will SEC Come Down Hard on E&Y Over PeopleSoft?" *CFO.com,* 14 November 2002.

10. S. Zuckerman, "Ernst & Young Faces Charges by SEC," *San Francisco Chronicle,* 21 May 2002, B1.

Ernst & Young officials reacted angrily to the charges that the SEC filed against their firm. Those officials pointed out that the federal agency did not allege, or even suggest, that Ernst & Young's joint business relationship with PeopleSoft had diminished the quality of its PeopleSoft audits. In addition, Ernst & Young maintained that the joint business relationship it had with PeopleSoft was "commonplace" among accounting firms and software vendors and that, "It did not affect our client, its shareholders, or the investing public."[11] Finally, Ernst & Young stated that since the sanctions proposed by the SEC were an "outrageous" overreaction by the federal agency, it would vigorously contest those sanctions in the federal courts. Despite such statements that the firm made repeatedly to the press, in April 2004, Ernst & Young relented and decided not to appeal the SEC sanctions.

> *While we are surprised and disappointed by the harsh sanctions, we accept them. The foundation of our profession depends on our independence and the objectivity of our auditors and advisors. We are committed to delivering quality in everything we do and this requires that our people never compromise their independence or objectivity, in perception or reality.*[12]

---

## Questions

1. Because Baan Company registered its common stock for sale in the United States, the SEC had regulatory authority over the company. Do the SEC's financial reporting requirements differ for foreign companies and domestic or U.S.-based companies? If so, briefly describe any such differences.
2. Provide specific examples of how the joint business relationships between Baan and Moret may have impaired the latter's independence while auditing Baan's annual financial statements.
3. Do you believe that the SEC should have sanctioned Ernst & Young for the role that it played in the 1997 Baan audit? Defend your answer.
4. Ernst & Young officials indicated that the joint business relationship with PeopleSoft "did not affect our client, its shareholders, or the investing public." Do you agree or disagree with that statement? Explain. Do you believe the sanctions that the SEC imposed on Ernst & Young were too harsh? Why or why not?

---

11. A. Rayner, "Ernst & Young Accused of Breaking SEC Rules," *The Times* (online), 22 May 2002.
12. B. Carlino, "E&Y Won't Challenge Client Ban," *Accounting Today*, May 19-June 6, 2004, 1.

## CASE 7.4

# *Hopkins v. Price Waterhouse*

In 1978, at the age of 34, Ann Hopkins faced a dilemma that a growing number of professional women are being forced to confront. Hopkins had to make a difficult choice involving her family and her career. Although comfortable with her position at Touche Ross & Company, for which she had worked several years, Hopkins realized that either she or her husband, also a Touche Ross employee, had to leave the firm because of its nepotism rules. Otherwise, neither would be considered for promotion to partner. Hopkins chose to make the personal sacrifice. She resigned from Touche Ross and within a few days accepted a position in the consulting division of Price Waterhouse.

Four years later, Hopkins was among the 88 individuals nominated for promotion to partner with Price Waterhouse. Hopkins, a senior manager in the firm's Washington, D.C., office, was the only woman in that group. Hopkins stood out from the other nominees in another respect. She had generated the most business for Price Waterhouse of all the partner candidates. Over the previous four years, clients obtained by Hopkins had produced $40 million of revenues for the firm. Because client development skills generally rank as the most important criterion in partnership promotion decisions, Hopkins appeared to be a shoo-in for promotion.

Strengthening Hopkins' case even more was the unanimous and strong backing her nomination received from the seven partners in the Washington, D.C., office. The extent of home office support for a candidate's nomination was another key factor Price Waterhouse considered in evaluating individuals for promotion to partner.

Much to her surprise, Hopkins was not awarded a partnership position. Instead, the senior manager was told that she would be considered for promotion the following year. A few months later, Hopkins was surprised again when her office managing partner informed her that she was no longer considered a viable candidate for promotion to partner. The firm's top executives did invite her to remain with Price Waterhouse in a nonpartner capacity. Disenchanted and somewhat bitter, Hopkins resigned from Price Waterhouse in January 1984 and accepted a position with the World Bank in Washington, D.C. Eventually, nagging uncertainty regarding her failure to make partner caused Hopkins to file a civil lawsuit against Price Waterhouse.

### Prior Criticism of Personnel Practices of Big Eight Firms

The lawsuit Ann Hopkins filed against Price Waterhouse drew attention to an issue simmering within the public accounting profession for years. During a 1976 investigation of the profession by a U.S. Senate subcommittee, several parties charged that Big Eight firms' personnel practices discriminated against females and minorities.[1] At one point during its hearings, the Senate subcommittee requested each of the Big Eight firms to disclose the average compensation of their partners and the number of females and nonwhite males in their partner ranks.

---

1. U.S. Congress, Senate Subcommittee on Reports, Accounting and Management of the Committee on Government Operations, *The Accounting Establishment* (Washington, DC: U.S. Government Printing Office, 1977).

The Senate subcommittee's request evoked uncooperative responses from several of the Big Eight firms. Exhibit 1 presents two of those responses. Exhibit 2 contains a letter that Senator Lee Metcalf, chairman of the investigative subcommittee, wrote to Ernst & Ernst after that firm questioned the Senate's authority to investigate the personnel practices of private partnerships. Eventually, six of the Big Eight firms provided the requested information regarding the number of females and minority males among their partners. Collectively, these firms had seven female partners and four partners who were African-American males out of a total of more than 3,500 partners.

**EXHIBIT 1**

SELECTED RESPONSES TO U.S. SENATE REQUEST FOR INFORMATION REGARDING BIG EIGHT FIRMS' PERSONNEL PRACTICES

June 11, 1976

The Honorable Lee Metcalf, Chairman
Subcommittee on Reports, Accounting, and Management
Committee on Government Operations
United States Senate
Washington, D.C. 20510

Dear Senator Metcalf:

I acknowledge receipt of your letter of June 7, 1976. As you know, this firm has responded and in considerable detail to the Committee's earlier requests. However, we consider the information sought in this letter to exceed the scope of the Committee's investigative authority. Moreover, the information sought includes data proprietary to this firm and its individual members. As a result, we respectfully decline to provide the requested data.

Very truly yours,

Russell E. Palmer
Managing Partner and
Chief Executive Officer
Touche Ross & Company

June 30, 1976

The Honorable Lee Metcalf, Chairman
Subcommittee on Reports, Accounting,
and Management
United States Senate
Washington, D.C. 20510

Dear Senator Metcalf:

This will acknowledge your letter of June 7 which was received during the period I was away from my office.

We find it difficult to understand why the compensation of our partners is a matter of valid interest to a subcommittee of the Committee on Government Operations. We are even more perplexed with the suggestion that this could be a matter of importance in an assessment of our professional performance.

Along with these reservations we also confess to a deep-rooted belief that members of a private partnership have a right to maintain privacy over such matters if they wish to do so. Therefore, absent an understanding of its justification, we respectfully decline to furnish the compensation information you have requested.

Two partners (.5% of the total number of our partners) are female. None of our partners are blacks.

Yours very truly,

William S. Kanaga
Arthur Young & Company

**EXHIBIT 2**

U.S. SENATE RESPONSE TO ERNST & ERNST'S RELUCTANCE TO PROVIDE REQUESTED PERSONNEL INFORMATION

June 28, 1976

Mr. R.T. Baker
Managing Partner
Ernst & Ernst
Union Commerce Building
Cleveland, Ohio 64115

Dear Mr. Baker:

In your letter of June 24, you question the authority of this subcommittee to request information from your firm on various subjects. You note that our authority is primarily directed to the accounting practices of Federal departments and agencies.

Our requests for information from your firm are based on the unusual and substantial relationship which has developed between certain Federal agencies and influential segments of the accounting profession. This relationship has led to official recognition by Federal agencies of judgments on binding standards which have been made entirely within the private sector. The Securities and Exchange Commission has even formalized its acceptance of private decision-making through Accounting Series Release 150. The Moss amendment to the Energy Policy and Conservation Act also contemplates Federal recognition of private decisions on the manner of uniform accounting to be developed for the oil and gas industry.

The substantial reliance by Federal agencies upon decisions made in the private sector represents a significant delegation of the statutory authority vested in those agencies. This arrangement involves important decisions affecting the policies of the Federal government and other segments of our society.

Decisions made by Federal agencies are subject to review by Congress and the public. Much progress has been made both in Congress and the Federal government in opening the processes of decision-making to public scrutiny. The public has a right to know the identity and interests of those who act under the public's authority to determine the directions which this nation shall take.

When public decision-making authority is delegated to the private sector, the public has an even greater interest in knowing who is directing important national policies. As you are well aware, little information is available to Congress or the public concerning the activities of accounting firms. That is why it is necessary for this subcommittee to request information on various activities of accounting firms.

Your firm is substantially involved in the private decision-making process which develops accounting standards that are recognized by Federal agencies. The information which has so far been requested by this subcommittee is only a small fraction of the information that is publicly available regarding the identity and interests of Federal officials, or even major corporate officials. Yet, the decision-making area in which your firm is involved influences public policy as much or more than do many companies for which the requested information is publicly available.

This subcommittee has a responsibility to ensure that Federal accounting practices are responsive to the public interest. We must be informed on matters which are relevant to Federal accounting practices. That is why your firm has been requested to provide information to this subcommittee.

Very truly yours,

Lee Metcalf, Chairman
Subcommittee on Reports,
Accounting, and Management

The criticism of the Big Eight firms' personnel practices spawned by the 1976 Senate investigation spurred academic researchers and the business press to begin monitoring the progress of women and minorities within Big Eight firms. By the late 1980s, when the Hopkins suit against Price Waterhouse was working its way through the courts, neither group had made significant inroads into the top hierarchy of the Big Eight firms. For instance, in 1988, women held approximately 3.5 percent of the partnership positions with Big Eight firms, although those firms had been hiring women in considerable numbers since the mid-1970s.[2]

Continued concern regarding the progress of women and minorities within Big Eight firms focused the accounting profession's attention on Ann Hopkins' civil suit against Price Waterhouse. Although the Hopkins case provides only anecdotal evidence regarding the personnel practices of large international accounting firms, it is noteworthy for several reasons. First, the case yielded revealing insights into the partnership selection process employed by large accounting firms. Second, the case pointed to the need to rid performance appraisal methods of gender-based criteria in all disciplines, including professional fields. Finally, *Hopkins v. Price Waterhouse* stimulated discussion of measures that professional firms could take to facilitate the career success of their female employees.

## Price Waterhouse's Consideration of Ann Hopkins for Promotion to Partner

During the 1980s, the partners of Price Waterhouse annually identified and then nominated for promotion to partner those senior managers whom they considered to be partner "material." Price Waterhouse's admissions committee collected these nominations and then provided a list of the nominees to each partner in the firm. The admissions committee invited partners to provide either a "long form" or "short form" evaluation of the individual candidates.

Typically, a partner well acquainted with a nominee provided a long form evaluation. Partners having had little or no contact with a given nominee submitted a short form evaluation or no evaluation at all. Both forms required the partners to assess the partnership potential of the nominees on several scaled dimensions, including client development abilities, interpersonal skills, and technical expertise. After responding to the scaled items, the partners indicated whether the given individual should be promoted, whether he or she should be denied promotion, or whether the promotion decision should be deferred for one or more years. The partners also provided a brief written explanation documenting the key reasons for their overall recommendation for each candidate.

After studying and summarizing the evaluations, the admissions committee prepared three lists of candidates: those recommended for admission to partnership, those not recommended for promotion, and those who had received a "hold" recommendation. These latter candidates typically included individuals having partner potential but also one or more weaknesses that needed to be addressed before they were considered again for promotion. The admissions committee submitted its recommendations to the firm's policy board, which reviewed them and selected the final slate of candidates to be voted on by the entire partnership.[3]

2. E. Berg, "The Big Eight," *The New York Times*, 17 December 1977, D1; "Women Comprise Half of 1986–87 Graduates," *Public Accounting Report*, 1 February 1988, 7.

3. This description of Price Waterhouse's partnership selection process was summarized from information presented in the 1985 court opinion *Hopkins v. Price Waterhouse*, 618 F. Supp. 1109 (D.C.D.C. 1985).

The admissions committee received 32 evaluation forms commenting on Ann Hopkins' nomination for partner. Thirteen partners submitted positive recommendations, eight recommended she not be promoted, three suggested she be held over for consideration the following year, and eight did not include a recommendation in their evaluation forms.

The most common criticism of Hopkins by partners who recommended she not be promoted was that she had poor interpersonal skills and an abrasive personality. These individuals criticized her for being too demanding of her subordinates, for using profanity, and for being generally harsh and overly aggressive. Two partners used gender-specific terms when commenting on Hopkins. One partner referred to her as "macho," while another observed that "she may have overcompensated for being a woman."[4]

After reviewing Hopkins' evaluations, the admissions committee recommended that she be held over for consideration, a recommendation accepted by the policy board. The admissions committee decided that her interpersonal skills needed to be strengthened to allow her to function effectively as a partner.

To improve her chances of promotion the following year, Hopkins agreed to undergo a "quality control review" to help her identify specific interpersonal and other job-related skills needing improvement. Subsequent to the quality control review, several partners indicated they would give her opportunities to demonstrate that she was remedying the deficiencies in her interpersonal skills. These partners never followed through on their commitments. Four months after Hopkins completed the quality control review, her office managing partner informed her that she would not be nominated for partner that year. Hopkins was also told that she probably would never be considered again for promotion to partner.

## Ann Hopkins' Civil Suit against Price Waterhouse

Ann Hopkins learned of the "hold" recommendation given to her nomination for partner in mid-1983. At that time, her office managing partner discussed with her some of the reservations partners expressed regarding her nomination. In particular, he told Hopkins that several partners believed her appearance and interpersonal manner were overtly masculine and that these traits caused her to be less appealing as a partner candidate.

The office managing partner suggested that she could improve her chances for promotion if she would "walk more femininely, wear make-up, have her hair styled, and wear jewelry." Following her resignation from Price Waterhouse, Hopkins recalled these suggestions and began to question why she had been denied promotion to partner. She began to suspect that Price Waterhouse had denied her promotion not because she was perceived as unqualified to be a partner with the firm but, rather, because she was perceived as unqualified to be a *female* partner with the firm.

Eventually, Hopkins concluded that Price Waterhouse, in fact, did apply different standards for promoting females and males to partner. This issue became the focal point of the civil trial in the *Hopkins v. Price Waterhouse* case. Hopkins included the following four specific allegations in the lawsuit she filed against Price Waterhouse:

1. The criticisms of her interpersonal skills were fabricated by the Price Waterhouse partners.

4. This and all subsequent quotations, unless indicated otherwise, were taken from *Hopkins v. Price Waterhouse*, 618 F. Supp. 1109 (D.C.D.C. 1985).

2. Even if the criticisms of her interpersonal skills were valid, Price Waterhouse had promoted male candidates to partner having similar deficiencies in their interpersonal skills.
3. The criticisms of her interpersonal skills resulted from sexual stereotyping by Price Waterhouse partners.
4. Price Waterhouse's partnership selection process did not discount the sexually discriminatory comments made regarding her candidacy.

The judge who presided over the civil trial dismissed Hopkins' first allegation. According to the judge, the defense counsel clearly proved that Hopkins did have poor interpersonal skills, particularly when dealing with subordinates. The judge ruled that Price Waterhouse was well within its rights to deny an individual a partnership position who did not possess adequate interpersonal skills. However, the judge then pointed to court testimony documenting that Price Waterhouse had previously promoted male partner candidates described as "crude, abrasive, and overbearing." These comments were very similar to criticisms of Hopkins' interpersonal skills made during the partner selection process.

A review of the firm's past promotion decisions also revealed that two earlier female partner candidates may have been denied admission to the partnership for reasons identical to those that cost Hopkins her promotion. Evaluation comments made for those candidates criticized them for acting like "Ma Barker" or for trying to be "one of the boys."

An earlier legal case established the precedent that an employer who evaluates a woman with an aggressive or abrasive personality differently than a man with similar personality traits is guilty of sex discrimination. After reviewing all of the evidence presented during the trial, the judge ruled that Price Waterhouse had evaluated Hopkins as a candidate for becoming a female partner rather than simply a partner with the firm.

> *[Female] candidates were viewed favorably if partners believed they maintained their femininity while becoming effective professional managers. To be identified as a "women's libber" was regarded as a negative comment. Nothing was done to discourage sexually biased evaluations. One partner repeatedly commented that he could not consider any woman seriously as a partnership candidate and believed that women were not capable of functioning as senior managers—yet the firm took no action to discourage his comments and recorded his vote in the overall summary of the evaluations.*

Although Hopkins was found to have been the victim of sex discrimination, the judge deemed that the discrimination was not overt or intentional. In fact, Hopkins freely admitted during the trial that she never perceived she was being discriminated against because of her gender while employed with Price Waterhouse. Instead, sexually discriminatory attitudes latent within the culture of Price Waterhouse victimized Hopkins' candidacy for partner. That is, the partners who made the sexually biased remarks regarding Hopkins were unaware that they were evaluating her unfairly relative to male candidates for partner. Nevertheless, the judge ruled that Price Waterhouse perpetuated an evaluation system that allowed sexual stereotypes to undermine the promotion opportunities of female employees.

> *There is no direct evidence of any determined purpose to maliciously discriminate against women but plaintiff appears to have been a victim of "omissive and subtle" discriminations created by a system that made evaluations based on "outmoded" attitudes. . . . Price Waterhouse should have been aware that women being evaluated by male partners might well be victims of discriminatory stereotypes. Yet the firm made no efforts . . . to discourage comments tainted by sexism or to determine whether they were influenced by stereotypes.*

## EPILOGUE

In May 1990, six years after Ann Hopkins filed suit against Price Waterhouse, a federal judge ordered the firm to pay her $400,000 of compensatory damages. More important, the judge ordered the CPA firm to offer Hopkins a partnership position. During a party to celebrate the court's decision, Hopkins maintained that she had no reservations joining a firm that had unfairly rejected her for partnership seven years earlier. She also joked with her male co-workers at the World Bank regarding several less-than-complimentary remarks made regarding her during the trial. In particular, she questioned the assertion of one Price Waterhouse partner that she needed to enroll in charm school. Moments later, Hopkins took a long and noisy slug of champagne—straight from the bottle.

In 1996, five years after rejoining Price Waterhouse, Ann Hopkins documented her difficult road to becoming a partner in a book published by the University of Massachusetts Press that was entitled "So Ordered: Making Partner the Hard Way." Despite the ordeal that she experienced, Hopkins insists that she has no "hard feelings" toward her fellow partners. In fact, Hopkins' daughter joined PricewaterhouseCoopers (PwC), the successor firm to Price Waterhouse, when she graduated from college in 1998.

Growing numbers of women have obtained partnership positions with the large international accounting firms since the resolution of the *Hopkins* case. But women still remain significantly underrepresented in the partnership ranks of those firms.[5] That fact was a key issue raised by Melissa Page, a former PwC tax manager, when she filed a lawsuit against PwC in July 2004 that was reminiscent of Ann Hopkins' lawsuit two decades earlier. In her complaint, Page alleged that the firm was guilty of "systematically discriminating" against women and suggested that an "old boy network" still pervaded PwC's culture.

> *[Page] claims her career was derailed by a corporate culture that kept women away from the very opportunities that led to partnership—including informal networking events, golf outings, and other activities that would have given her more access to clients and company executives.*[6]

Page's lawsuit prompted other women in the profession to speak out. One of those individuals was Barbara Hufsmith, who reported that she had chosen to establish her own accounting firm after being a victim of gender discrimination in a male-dominated accounting firm.

> *I too have been discriminated against in an old boys CPA firm. It has forced me to start my own firm, for which I am grateful, but it should not have been such a painful and expensive experience. I truly believe that only a couple of partners from my old firm knew what they were doing to me was not fair. The rest of the partners were blind, stupid, and arrogant. Hopefully, a case like Ms. Page will help change the industry to be more female-partner friendly.*[7]

## Questions

1. Do public accounting firms have a responsibility to facilitate the career success of female employees? Why or why not? Identify policies accounting firms could implement to increase the retention rate of female employees.

5. The results of a survey released by the *Public Accounting Report* in June 2009 indicated that approximately 18 percent of Big Four partners were women.

6. *AccountingWEB.com*, "PricewaterhouseCoopers Faces Discrimination Suit," 29 July 2004.

7. *Ibid.*

2. In business circles, one frequently hears references to the "old boy network." Many women in professional firms complain that their gender precludes them from becoming a member of the old boy network within their firm. Define, in your own terms, what is meant by the phrase *old boy network*. Should professional firms attempt to break down these networks?
3. Suppose that an audit client objects to a given auditor because of his or her gender or race. Identify the alternative courses of action the auditor's employer should consider taking in such a case. Which of these alternatives do you believe the accounting firm should take? Defend your answer.
4. The nepotism rules of many professional firms pose a major inconvenience for married couples who work for, or would like to work for, those firms. Discuss the costs and benefits of these rules in a public accounting setting. In practice, do you believe these rules are equally fair (or unfair) to both sexes?
5. Several of the large public accounting firms asked to provide information to the U.S. Senate during the 1976 investigation of the accounting profession claimed that the request was an invasion of their privacy. Do you agree or disagree with these firms' view? Why? Even if such disclosures are considered an invasion of privacy, are they justified from a public interest perspective?

## CASE 7.5

# Stock Option Mania

In the early 1990s, an avalanche of controversy blindsided the Financial Accounting Standards Board (FASB). This controversy stemmed from a proposed accounting rule calling for corporations to recognize compensation expense for certain stock options when they were granted to executives and employees. Shortly after the FASB circulated the proposal in an exposure draft, hundreds of letters flooded the rule-making body. Most of those letters sharply criticized the proposed change in accounting for stock options.

Even Congress and the President of the United States voiced opinions on the proposed stock option accounting rule. In early 1994, the Senate passed a resolution by a vote of 88-9 urging the FASB to drop the proposed standard. Two senators who seldom agree on important policy matters joined together to lead the debate against the proposal. Senator Barbara Boxer, a liberal Democrat from California, criticized the FASB for "pursuing an abstract theory" that will "damage the growth potential of many companies."[1] On the other side of the aisle, Senator Phil Gramm, a staunch Republican from Texas, bluntly observed, "The bottom line here is that this is a stupid proposal."[2] President Clinton expressed his concern that the stock option accounting standard might "undermine the competitiveness" of many of the nation's most important industries.[3]

By far, the most vocal critics of the FASB's stock option proposal were business executives of large public companies—the individuals who stood to lose the most if the standard were adopted. The 200-member Business Roundtable, composed of chief executive officers of large public companies, waged a public relations war against the FASB's efforts to overhaul accounting for stock options. These individuals realized that the new standard would likely cause many companies to stop issuing stock options, which for many years had been a lucrative source of income for corporate executives. The FASB's proposal so incensed the top executive of one computer firm that he suggested disbanding the rule-making body.

> *The arrogant, out-of-touch FASB bureaucracy should simply close its doors and stop damaging corporate America for the sake of accounting principles.*[4]

Numerous editorials in the business press criticized the proposed stock option rule. For example, an editorial in *Forbes* referred to the stock option proposal as "FASB's Folly."[5] The editorial noted that the proposed accounting rule ranked as one of the FASB's "most asinine, destructive proposals ever" and then added that "the idea is utterly illogical."[6]

Many prominent members of the accounting profession became involved in the controversy swirling around the proposed stock option rule. Eventually, the debate

1. K. Rankin, "Congress Rips FASB on Stock Options," *Accounting Today,* 1 November 1993, 1, 33.
2. *Ibid.*
3. C. Harlan, "Accounting Proposal Stirs Unusual Uproar in Executive Suites," *The Wall Street Journal,* 7 March 1994, A1, A8.
4. T. J. Rodgers, "New FASB Rule Is Ill-Conceived," *Business Credit,* June 1994, 20–21.
5. "FASB's Folly," *Forbes,* 31 January 1994, 26.
6. *Ibid.*

within the profession took on a nasty tone. Charges that certain accounting firms were lobbying against the proposal to appease their large audit clients were met with angry rebuttals. Nevertheless, these charges raised anew important issues that had faced the accounting profession over the past two decades. Among these issues was whether accounting firms undermined the integrity and credibility of the independent audit function when they lobbied on behalf of controversial positions supported by their audit clients. A related question was whether the authority for issuing accounting rules should remain in the private sector or be assumed by a governmental agency.

## Stock Options As Compensation Expense

Companies often include stock options as a component of their compensation plan for key executives and employees. In 1978, the financially troubled Chrysler Corporation wanted to hire Lee Iacocca as its chief executive, an individual who had enjoyed a successful career as a top executive of Ford Motor Company. Chrysler offered Iacocca a $1 annual salary and 400,000 stock options. The stock options gave Iacocca the right to purchase 400,000 shares of Chrysler common stock at a predetermined exercise price over a several-year period. If Iacocca succeeded in turning around Chrysler, the company's stock price would likely rise well above the exercise price of his stock options. He could then cash in those options by purchasing Chrysler's stock at the exercise price and reselling it at the higher market price. Within a few years, Iacocca masterminded one of the most celebrated corporate turnarounds in U.S. history. Iacocca was rewarded for that turnaround when he pocketed a $40 million profit on his stock options.

In recent years, executive stock option grants have become an important corporate strategy for newly formed companies. Compensatory stock option plans are particularly prevalent among emerging companies in high-technology industries. Developmental stage companies in these industries typically cannot afford to pay the large salaries commanded by the executives they want to hire. As a result, these companies often use the "Chrysler" strategy to attract those individuals.

In 1972, the Accounting Principles Board, the FASB's predecessor, issued *APB Opinion No. 25*, "Accounting for Stock Issued to Employees." Under *APB No. 25*, companies are generally not required to recognize compensation expense when they issue stock options to executives and employees if those options have an exercise price equal to or higher than the stock's market price on the date the options are granted. The FASB decided that this "nonaccounting" approach for out-of-the-money stock options was unreasonable and decided to change it. The FASB's position was very simple. Although stock options may have an exercise price equal to or above the current market price of a company's stock on the date granted, they still have an economic value on that date. This economic value arises from the opportunity the holders of the options may have to purchase the company's common stock at less than market value at some point over the term of the options. The FASB maintained that this economic value is a component of an entity's compensation expense and should be recognized as such in its accounting records.

One of the more difficult issues addressed by the FASB's stock option proposal was how companies should determine the economic or fair value of out-of-the-money stock options when they are granted. The FASB suggested that companies use option-pricing models for this purpose. Such models have long been employed by sophisticated investors to determine the economic value of publicly traded stock options. To compute the economic value of a stock option using an option-pricing model, several assumptions must be made. For example, the future volatility of the underlying common stock must be estimated. Small changes in these assumptions can result in wide fluctuations in the estimated value of a stock option.

## Criticism of FASB's Proposed Stock Option Rule

Opponents of the FASB's proposed change in accounting for stock options advanced two key arguments for rejecting the proposal, including the difficulty of establishing a reasonable estimate of stock options' economic value. The primary argument used to counter the FASB's proposal was that it would create financial problems for thousands of companies, particularly "start-up" companies.

Critics of the FASB's proposal maintained that because most new companies initially have minimal earnings, they could not offer stock options to executives they wanted to hire if the value of the options had to be expensed immediately. As a result, these companies would have difficulty attracting highly qualified personnel for their key management positions. Carrying this argument to its logical conclusion, fewer new companies would be formed if the FASB's proposal was adopted. The resulting implications for the national economy, according to an editorial in *Forbes*, would be dire. *Forbes* pointed out that in the mid-1980s, companies that had been in existence for only a few years accounted for 14 million of the nearly 19 million new jobs created nationwide.[7] A federal official denounced the FASB for stubbornly ignoring these negative economic consequences when considering the proposed stock option standard.

> *Faced with these arguments, the FASB's rebuttal is simple: When it comes to accounting principles, economic consequences be damned; the truth will set investors free.*[8]

Big Six accounting firms, both individually and jointly, also publicly registered strong disagreement with the stock option proposal. In commenting on the proposal, an Ernst & Young partner noted, "Why introduce an extremely subjective measure into financial statements?"[9] An 11-page analysis of the proposed rule by Arthur Andersen & Co. contained the following summary observation:

> *We believe it is in the best interests of the public, the financial community, and the FASB itself for the Board to address those issues that have a significant impact on improving the relevance and usefulness of financial reporting. In our view, employers' accounting for stock options and other stock compensation does not meet that test.*[10]

Coopers & Lybrand studied the proposal's potential impact on the earnings of 700 companies that issue stock options.[11] This study demonstrated that the proposed accounting rule would have a large negative impact on corporate earnings, particularly the earnings of new companies. In July 1994, the Big Six firms banded together and sent a joint letter to the FASB. In that letter, these firms strongly encouraged the FASB to drop the stock option proposal from its agenda.[12]

---

7. *Ibid.*

8. J. C. Beese, "A Rule That Stunts Growth," *The Wall Street Journal*, 8 February 1994, A18.

9. R. Khalaf, "If It Ain't Broke . . .," *Forbes*, 12 April 1993, 100.

10. Arthur Andersen & Co., *Arthur Andersen Accounting News Briefs*, "FASB Exposure Draft 'Accounting for Stock-based Compensation,'" August 1993, 8.

11. M. S. Akresh and J. Fuersich, "Stock Options: Accounting, Valuation, and Management Issues," *Management Accounting*, March 1994, 51–53.

12. P. B. W. Miller, "Ethics and Stock Options—An Update," *In The Public Interest*, Newsletter of The Public Interest Section of the American Accounting Association, October 1994, 3.

## Support for FASB's Stock Option Proposal

Supporters of the new accounting standard for stock options maintained that it was needed to recognize a very material expense of corporations that was going unrecorded. These same parties charged that the arguments used by opponents of the proposed standard were flimsy, at best. The proposal's defenders rejected the contention that compensation expense associated with newly issued stock options should not be booked simply because it is difficult to estimate. Warren Buffett, a billionaire investor and frequent critic of the FASB, noted that "It is both silly and cynical to say that an important item of cost should not be recognized simply because it can't be quantified with pinpoint accuracy."[13]

The "economic consequences" argument" articulated by opponents of the stock option proposal was widely belittled by the proposal's supporters. The FASB's vice-chairman, James Leisenring, insisted that the FASB had no mandate or responsibility to consider the economic consequences of new accounting standards such as their impact on job creation in the economy.[14] Likewise, Professor Paul Pacter of the University of Connecticut argued that the FASB must maintain a neutral attitude regarding the economic impact of new accounting standards.

> *Accounting standards seek to measure and report faithfully the economic events and transactions that have taken place. This objective applies equally to events and transactions that are favorable to the business and those that are unfavorable. Accounting standards are not and should not be designed to obscure or distort reality. If the reality is that stock options have value and are intended to motivate employees and to compensate them for their services, accounting should reflect that reality.*[15]

Supporters of the FASB's stock option proposal pointed to the fiasco in the savings and loan industry during the 1980s as a reminder of what can happen when economic considerations are allowed to dictate the choice of accounting methods. Regulatory authorities, including Congress, believed that the savings and loan industry's severe financial problems at the time would be short-lived. To mask the "temporary" bankrupt status of hundreds of insolvent savings and loans, Congress mandated that they be allowed to use accounting methods that overstated their assets and reported profits. This decision proved disastrous. Executives of many insolvent savings and loans made increasingly speculative investments, hoping to return them to a profitable condition. As a result, the losses of these savings and loans piled up at an ever-increasing rate. Finally, in the late 1980s when the savings and loan crisis threatened the health of the national economy, the federal government stepped in and spent several hundred billion dollars to bail out the industry.

Dennis Beresford, the chairman of the FASB and target of much of the criticism directed toward the stock option proposal, balked at the suggestion that his organization consider the economic consequences of new accounting rules. Beresford noted that the business community had often argued against new accounting standards because of their supposed negative economic consequences. In many of these cases, Beresford maintained, business executives simply wanted to avoid economic reality

13. Harlan, "Accounting Proposal Stirs Unusual Uproar," A8.
14. Rankin, "Congress Rips FASB," 33.
15. P. Pacter, "FASB's Stock Option Proposal: Correcting A Serious Flaw," *CPA Journal,* March 1994, 60–61.

by not accounting for certain expenses. *The New York Times*, which strongly supported the stock option proposal, reinforced that point of view.

> *For both pensions and post-retirement health benefits, companies resisted accounting reforms. . . . But when corporate boards were finally forced to look at reasonable estimates of the costs, companies began to control these costs.*[16]

Several parties alleged that the economic consequences argument used by business executives to denounce the FASB's stock option proposal served simply as a smoke screen to conceal their true motive in criticizing the proposal. For many years, corporate executives had been reaping windfall profits from the exercise of stock options, a job "perk" they did not want to see fall by the wayside because of the proposed accounting rule. Consider just two examples of enormous profits realized by corporate officers as a result of stock option grants. In 1992, two top executives of U.S. Surgical Corporation realized more than $80 million by cashing in stock options granted to them in prior years.[17] Topping that figure was a nearly $400 million profit on stock options realized by a Walt Disney Company executive in 1997.[18]

Of the hundreds of letters received by the FASB regarding the stock option proposal, one was a tongue-in-cheek correspondence from Mr. Beauregard T. Greede, the chairman of Sillicorp, Inc. Mr. Greede was quite upset with the FASB's suggestion that his firm record the expense associated with the stock options he had been granted.

> *Do you think my handpicked board of directors would have awarded me options on a gazillion shares of Sillicorp stock if they'd had to tell the stockholders what the options were worth? And expense 'em!*[19]

A financial analyst who supported the FASB's stock option proposal provided a more direct point of view on this matter.

> *To me, it doesn't make sense that you can give stock options to executives and not call it compensation. If it's compensation, it has to be accounted for. Right now, the companies have a free ride and they don't want to give it up. And that's what the uproar is about.*[20]

## The Debate Over Stock Options Turns Nasty

As the controversy over the stock option proposal escalated, the debate within the accounting profession became sidetracked. Instead of focusing on the soundness of the FASB's stock option proposal, accountants began debating whether accounting firms should lobby the FASB on proposed new standards. This debate centered on the Big Six accounting firms. Recall that in July 1994 the Big Six firms in a joint letter asked the FASB to drop the stock option proposal. An accounting professor questioned the motives of the Big Six firms in submitting this letter to the FASB.

---

16. F. Norris, "In Accounting, Truth Can Be Very Scary," *The New York Times*, 11 April 1993, Section 3, 1.

17. L. Berton and J. S. Lublin, "Executives Say Accounting Idea Is Poorly Timed," *The Wall Street Journal*, 4 December 1992, B1, B12.

18. "Eisner Uses Stock Option to Sell Shares," *The Norman Transcript*, 4 December 1997, 24.

19. G. M. Kang, "Hands Off My Stock Pile," *Business Week*, 12 April 1993, 28-30.

20. G. A. Cheney, "Stock Option Quest Sparks Questions About FASB's Future," *Accounting Today*, 10 October 1994, 10, 12.

> *This letter is dreadful in several respects. Its arguments are strictly political and advance the interests of corporate management. . . . When I weigh this letter on the ethics scales, I find it wanting. The economic world is waiting for and needs responsible behavior and more complete financial statements, but these people advocate the opposite.*[21]

Walter Schuetze, the Chief Accountant of the Securities and Exchange Commission (SEC), was the most prominent member of the profession to criticize the Big Six accounting firms' lobbying efforts against the stock option proposal. Schuetze pointed out that representatives of these firms initially supported the proposal when it appeared on the FASB's agenda in 1984. He suggested that the firms changed their position "in response to fear of losing clients or other forms of retaliation."[22] A former Big Six partner and former member of the FASB, Schuetze went on to suggest that the Big Six's lobbying efforts against the stock option proposal called into question the independence of these firms.

> *If public companies are pressuring their outside auditors . . . to take particular positions on financial accounting and reporting issues and outside auditors are subordinating their views to those of their clients, can the outside auditor community continue to claim to be independent?*[23]

Schuetze's criticism of Big Six accounting firms did not go unanswered. An editorial in the bimonthly publication *Accounting Today* chastised Schuetze for his disapproving remarks regarding the Big Six firms. The editorial noted that Schuetze was "unnecessarily shrill" in his criticism and suggested that he did the profession "a disservice by his intemperate remarks."[24] Philip Chenok, president of the American Institute of Certified Public Accountants, also berated Schuetze for his criticism of the dominant firms in the accounting profession. Chenok said he found it "offensive and inappropriate for the Chief Accountant of the SEC to suggest a loss of independence [by the major accounting firms] over the stock option matter."[25]

## Inviting Government Intervention?

In criticizing the Big Six firms for becoming "cheerleaders"[26] for their audit clients in the campaign against the stock option proposal, Walter Schuetze warned these firms that they might be damaging their own interests. Schuetze noted that such lobbying efforts could serve as an invitation for regulatory authorities "to regulate more heavily, and more directly, the auditing profession in particular and financial accounting and reporting in general."[27]

Schuetze's warning was not unfounded. During a 1970s investigation of the accounting profession, the U.S. Senate assailed the large accounting firms that dominate the profession.[28] Among the specific charges leveled at these firms was that

---

21. Miller, "Ethics and Stock Options," 3.

22. "Schuetze Wary Over CPA Independence on Stock Option Proposal," *Journal of Accountancy*, March 1994, 9–10.

23. *Ibid.*

24. "No Option Left," *Accounting Today*, 7 February 1994, 3.

25. "Accountants Are Chided Over Stock-Option Stance," *The Wall Street Journal*, 12 January 1994, A5.

26. *Ibid.*

27. "Schuetze Wary Over CPA Independence," 10.

28. U.S. Congress, Senate Subcommittee on Reports, Accounting and Management of the Committee on Government Operations, *The Accounting Establishment* (Washington, D.C.: U.S. Government Printing Office, 1977).

they routinely lobbied rule-making bodies to adopt accounting rules benefitting their largest audit clients. Like Schuetze, the Senate suggested that such lobbying efforts cast doubt on these firms' independence. Although never seriously considered, one recommendation spawned by the Senate's investigation was the creation of a federal agency to assume responsibility for the independent audit function.

A more credible recommendation that stemmed from the 1970s Senate investigation of the accounting profession was the creation of a federal agency to establish accounting standards. The heated controversy over the FASB's stock option proposal raised again the possibility of intervention in the profession's rule-making processes by the federal government. A former Chief Accountant of the SEC, John Burton, questioned whether the FASB could survive given the mounting pressure exerted on it by the business community.[29] In the early 1990s, two members of the FASB, both former partners of major international accounting firms, resigned from the rule-making body. In each case, these individuals cited as reasons for their resignation the pressure exerted on them by corporate interests opposed to one or more of the FASB's proposals.

## FASB Backs Off

In late 1994, the FASB rescinded its controversial stock option proposal. In its place, the FASB issued *Statement of Financial Accounting Standards No. 123*, "Accounting for Stock-Based Compensation," which became effective for fiscal years beginning after December 15, 1995. *SFAS No. 123 encourages* companies to recognize compensation expense for compensatory stock options that have an exercise price higher than the stock price on the grant date. However, this "fair value" method of accounting for stock options is not mandatory. Companies are permitted to simply disclose in their financial statement footnotes the compensation expense for newly-issued, out-of-the-money compensatory stock options. Not surprisingly, the great majority of companies chose the "disclosure" option for compensatory stock options when *SFAS No. 123* became effective.

The FASB's decision to adopt *SFAS No. 123* failed to placate those parties who insisted that companies should book compensation expense for out-of-the-money compensatory stock options. Once more, Warren Buffett, the billionaire investor, ranked among the most vocal of these critics.

> *In effect, accounting principles offer management a choice: Pay employees in one form and count the cost, or pay them in another form and ignore the cost. Small wonder then that the use of options has mushroomed. . . Whatever the merits of options may be, their accounting treatment is outrageous.*[30]

29. L. Berton, "FASB Finds That Criticism Increases Difficulty of Finding New Member," *The Wall Street Journal,* 18 January 1991, B3.

30. *1998 Annual Report,* Berkshire Hathaway, Inc., 13–14.

## EPILOGUE

During the late 1990s and into the new century, major stock indices in the United States rose sharply. Leading the huge run-up in stock prices was the NASDAQ, home of hundreds of dot-coms and other "New Economy" companies. Many of these firms relied on huge stock option grants to recruit "Old Economy" executives, which, in turn, fueled investors' expectations regarding the future prospects of these new firms. As the stock prices of high-tech companies crested higher and higher, Federal Reserve Chairman Alan Greenspan warned the public that the stock markets were being affected by "irrational exuberance."

The stock prices of high-tech companies began plummeting in the spring of 2000. In a little more than two years, the NASDAQ Composite Index declined by more than 75 percent from the all-time high it reached in March 2000. Over the same general timeframe, the Dow Jones Industrial Average declined by one-third. A key factor contributing to this sharp sell-off in stocks was a loss of investor confidence triggered by a series of accounting scandals involving several major high-tech companies, including Enron, WorldCom, Global Crossing, and Adelphia Commmunications.

Many business journalists charged that the stock option "mania" of the late 1990s was the root cause of these accounting scandals. Corporate executives who had received large stock option grants realized that to "cash in" their options, their company's stock price had to rise dramatically. No doubt, the easiest way to trigger a dramatic increase in a company's stock price is to inflate earnings with various accounting gimmicks. During his congressional testimony in early 2002, former Enron CEO Jeffrey Skilling admitted that stock options provided an "egregious" way for a large company to understate its expenses and thus inflate its earnings.[31] Skilling spoke from personal experience. During 2000, just months before Enron's sudden collapse, Skilling realized a gain of more than $60 million by cashing in a horde of stock options previously granted to him by Enron's board of directors.

The nationwide fit of anger prompted by the revelations of accounting irregularities underlying the collapse of Enron and several other major companies re-ignited the debate concerning the proper accounting treatment for stock options. Alan Greenspan, Warren Buffett, and several leading political figures, including Senator John McCain, led a campaign calling for the adoption of accounting standards that would result in more "transparent" corporate financial statements. The first target of these reformists was stock options. "While expensing stock options may not prevent a rogue executive from book cookery, it will provide more thorough disclosure about a company's performance and help lift a cloud of suspicion about the accuracy of financial statements."[32]

During the summer of 2002, the campaign to require the expensing of stock options gained momentum. U.S. Senator Carl Levin lobbied Congress to support a bill he had authored that would require public companies to expense stock options. A similar proposal was announced in July 2002 by the International Accounting Standards Board. At approximately the same time, the Council of Institutional Investors, which represents more than 130 pension funds with total assets exceeding $2 trillion, urged major companies to begin voluntarily expensing

31. G. Hitt and J. M. Schlesinger, "Stock Options Come Under Fire In the Wake of Enron's Collapse," *The Wall Street Journal* Online, 26 March 2002.

32. A. Elstein, "More Companies Are Jumping On Options-Expense Bandwagon," *The Wall Street Journal* Online, 8 August 2002.

stock options. As the pressure mounted on corporate executives, one by one dozens of large companies announced that in the future they would expense compensatory stock options. These companies included Coca-Cola, Procter & Gamble, Boeing, and the nation's largest company by stock market value, General Electric.

During the renewed public debate over accounting for options, several parties that had encouraged the FASB to not require the expensing of stock options during the mid-1990s remained curiously silent. Most notable among these parties were the four remaining members of the Big Six accounting firms.

## Questions

1. Identify the principal advantages and disadvantages of having the rule-making bodies in the accounting profession controlled by the private sector rather than the federal government.
2. Large accounting firms are among the parties most knowledgeable of accounting theory and the pragmatic or everyday problems of applying accounting standards. As such, these firms are well positioned to evaluate the soundness of proposed accounting rules. Should rule-making bodies make use of the expertise and insight of these firms when considering proposed accounting standards? Why or why not? If so, explain how this could be done while minimizing the risk that these firms would antagonize their clients or, conversely, be seen as catering to the economic interests of their clients.
3. Assume that you are the managing partner of an office of a large accounting firm. The chief executive officer of your office's largest client has contacted you and asked that you write a letter to the FASB, on behalf of your firm, criticizing a new accounting rule being considered by the FASB. What should you do at this point?
4. Should the FASB consider the economic consequences of proposed accounting standards when deciding whether to adopt these standards? Explain. Identify the key issues or factors the FASB should consider when deliberating on proposed accounting rules.

## CASE 7.6

# National Medical Transportation Network

San Diego-based National Medical Transportation Network (MedTrans) eventually became the largest ambulance services provider in the United States. Reaching that pinnacle was not an easy journey. In early 1992, MedTrans encountered cash flow problems that prompted the company's two owners to search for external financing. The co-owners located a company willing to invest $10 million in MedTrans. During negotiations with that company, MedTrans' auditor, Deloitte & Touche, uncovered problems in its client's accounting records. Those problems prevented Deloitte from issuing an unqualified opinion on MedTrans' 1992 financial statements. After several unpleasant confrontations with MedTrans' chief executive officer, Deloitte resigned as the company's audit firm.

Following Deloitte's resignation, the $10 million investment deal collapsed. Within a few months, MedTrans' two owners sold their firm to a large corporation. Unhappy with Deloitte's lack of "cooperation," MedTrans' former owners sued Deloitte to recover the sizable loss they incurred on the sale of their company. Among other charges, the former owners alleged that Deloitte acted negligently by "withdrawing prematurely" from the 1992 MedTrans audit engagement.

No doubt, Deloitte's legal counsel confidently tackled the MedTrans lawsuit. The allegation that Deloitte negligently withdrew from the 1992 MedTrans audit engagement seemed implausible since the client had adamantly refused to make several large and necessary adjustments to its 1992 financial statements. Threatening comments made to Deloitte auditors by one of MedTrans' co-owners provided even stronger justification for the audit firm's resignation. Imagine then the shock and disbelief of Deloitte's attorneys when the jury that heard the lawsuit agreed with MedTrans' former owners and imposed a multimillion-dollar judgment on the prominent accounting firm.

### MedTrans Seeks Help

MedTrans' two principal officers, Roberts and Morgan, served as the company's chief executive officer (CEO) and president, respectively, and each owned 50 percent of MedTrans' common stock. Deloitte audited the company's annual financial statements each year from 1988 through 1991—MedTrans' fiscal year ended March 31. Apparently, Deloitte encountered few problems during those audits and issued an unqualified opinion each year on MedTrans' financial statements.

By the late spring of 1992, MedTrans needed cash, and quickly. The company owed $2 million of payroll taxes and faced a $12 million repayment to its primary lender, which had suddenly and unceremoniously yanked MedTrans' line of credit. Making matters worse, MedTrans' chief financial officer (CFO) unexpectedly resigned in early June 1992. That resignation triggered a crisis between MedTrans and the company's audit firm. Deloitte was nearing completion of its 1992 MedTrans audit and had asked the CFO to sign a letter of representations indicating that the company's financial statements were materially accurate. The CFO told Gordon Johns, the Deloitte audit engagement partner, that he could not sign the letter of representations since he did not believe MedTrans' financial statements were reliable. A few days later, the CFO met with Johns to discuss the situation.

*At the meeting, Ensz [the CFO] alerted Johns to four or five matters relevant to the audit. Ensz said that upon informing Roberts [the CEO] that those matters were not properly entered in MedTrans's journals, Roberts told Ensz to leave the journals as they were and "let's see" if the auditors "find it." Questioning Roberts's character for honesty because of some things Roberts advocated in presenting financial information, Ensz also stated he lacked faith in the integrity of Roberts and MedTrans's financial statements.*[1]

The CFO's unsettling allegations caused Deloitte to approach the remainder of the 1992 MedTrans audit with extreme caution. By the end of June 1992, the Deloitte auditors concluded that their client's financial statements contained material errors. Those financial statements reported a net income of nearly $2 million for fiscal 1992, while Deloitte's audit suggested that MedTrans had suffered a loss of approximately $500,000. A large increase in MedTrans' allowance for bad debts proposed by Deloitte accounted for most of the difference between those two figures.

During June and July 1992, Roberts negotiated with William Blair & Company to obtain the additional capital needed by MedTrans. In exchange for a $10 million investment in MedTrans, Roberts and Morgan offered Blair a 50 percent ownership interest in the company. While mulling over this offer, Blair's executives reviewed MedTrans' unaudited financial statements for 1992. Based largely upon the $2 million profit reported in those financial statements, Blair forecasted that MedTrans' annual earnings would top $6 million by 1995. On July 27, Blair's executives tentatively agreed to invest in MedTrans. The agreement was contingent on MedTrans receiving an unqualified audit opinion on its 1992 financial statements.

Roberts's negotiations with Blair were periodically disrupted by an ongoing quarrel with Gordon Johns. Roberts and Johns feuded throughout the summer of 1992 over the large increase in the company's allowance for bad debts that Deloitte believed was necessary. During a July 9 meeting, Roberts warned Johns that MedTrans' audited financial statements would have a significant impact on whether the Blair transaction was consummated.

*A very focused Roberts vocally and explicitly emphasized the importance of MedTrans's pre-tax earnings because of the potential that Blair might invest in the company. . . . Johns [then] presented Roberts with about $2.5 million in suggested adjustments involving the accounts receivable reserve account. Roberts told Johns: "You better not propose any adjustment that will ______ my deal or you'll be sorry."*

Shortly after the July 9 meeting, Johns contacted an executive Deloitte partner in the firm's New York headquarters. The executive partner told Johns that "we should not be associated with companies that threaten us." Unless Roberts accepted the proposed adjustments, the executive partner recommended that Johns resign from the engagement. Johns told the executive partner that before raising the issue again with Roberts, he wanted to give him some time to analyze MedTrans' bad debt reserve and to reconsider the need for the proposed adjustments. On July 30, Roberts and Johns met again. During this meeting, Roberts reminded Johns of the impact Deloitte's audit would have on the proposed Blair deal. Roberts also gave Johns a memorandum prepared by MedTrans' personnel that presented a more favorable analysis of the company's bad debt reserve than the analysis developed by Deloitte.

Roberts and Johns met a final time on August 13, 1992, to discuss Deloitte's audit and the pending Blair transaction. At this meeting, Johns presented a memorandum containing a new set of proposed adjustments to MedTrans' 1992 financial statements.

---

1. This and all subsequent quotations were taken from the following court opinion: *National Medical Transportation Network v. Deloitte & Touche*, 62 Cal. App. 4th 412 (1998).

Collectively, these adjustments would have reduced MedTrans' pre-audit net income even more than the adjustments originally proposed by Deloitte.

> *During Johns's presentation, Roberts rose, threw down the memorandum and said very angrily: "You are finished." Although Johns thought he had been fired, Roberts told Johns not to construe the situation that way. However, after MedTrans's successive rejections of proposed adjustments to its unaudited financial statements, Johns believed the parties' mutually exclusive views of those statements indicated there was no longer a basis for a relationship. Thus, Johns told Roberts that if defendants [Deloitte] had not been fired, he was resigning. Roberts told Johns that "you're going to finish this regardless, under court order or otherwise." Johns believed such threat destroyed any ability to continue as an independent auditor. Johns also believed resignation was necessary because MedTrans bullied Deloitte's personnel and defendants were put at risk by MedTrans's lack of commitment to financial statements accurately depicting the difficulties the company experienced in fiscal 1992.*

Deloitte formally resigned from the MedTrans engagement shortly after the August 13 meeting between Johns and Roberts. Four days later, Roberts sent a letter to Deloitte reminding the firm that its resignation would have serious repercussions for the pending Blair deal. Roberts also insisted once more that Deloitte complete the 1992 audit. Deloitte refused to be swayed and remained MedTrans' "former" auditor.

## Desperately Seeking A Replacement Auditor

William Blair & Company learned of Deloitte's resignation in mid-August 1992. On August 25, a Blair representative told Roberts that his firm was indefinitely postponing the planned investment in MedTrans and would not reconsider that decision until MedTrans obtained an independent audit opinion on its 1992 financial statements. The Blair official suggested that MedTrans retain Blair & Company's audit firm, Ernst & Young. Roberts immediately contacted Ernst & Young. Within a few days, Roberts sent Deloitte a letter authorizing the firm to "discuss freely with E&Y the audit history of MedTrans with Deloitte, the details of Deloitte's proposed audit of MedTrans for fiscal 1992 and the facts and circumstances of Deloitte's withdrawal/resignation/ disengagement as MedTrans's auditor."

Gordon Johns met with representatives of Ernst & Young on September 3, 1992. During that meeting, Johns explained why Deloitte had resigned from the MedTrans engagement. Johns also revealed that he questioned the integrity of MedTrans' senior executives. Despite the information obtained from Johns, E&Y agreed to audit MedTrans' 1992 financial statements.

Roberts concluded during late September that Blair was unlikely to invest in MedTrans regardless of the outcome of E&Y's audit. At that point, Roberts began searching for another potential investor to bail MedTrans out of the financial crisis it faced. Within a few days, a company contacted by Roberts, American Medical Response, Inc. (AMR), expressed interest in acquiring MedTrans. Like MedTrans, AMR's principal line of business was providing ambulance services. When AMR executives recommended that MedTrans retain Peat Marwick, AMR's audit firm, to audit its 1992 financial statements, Roberts dismissed E&Y and contacted Peat Marwick. Roberts also contacted Deloitte and authorized the firm to discuss with Peat Marwick the circumstances surrounding its resignation from the MedTrans audit. After communicating with Deloitte, the San Diego office of Peat Marwick agreed to audit MedTrans' 1992 financial statements. One week after accepting the engagement, Peat Marwick resigned. Subsequent testimony revealed that a "directive" sent by Peat Marwick's headquarters office to the firm's San Diego office prompted that resignation. Peat Marwick's refusal to audit MedTrans apparently quelled AMR's interest in the company.

MedTrans finally retained another audit firm in late October 1992. This firm, identified only as "Silberman" in court transcripts, served as MedTrans' auditor during the mid-1980s. Before accepting the engagement, Silberman discussed with Deloitte the circumstances surrounding its resignation as MedTrans' auditor. In December 1992, Silberman issued an unqualified opinion on MedTrans' 1992 financial statements. Before issuing that opinion, Silberman persuaded MedTrans to accept the large adjustments proposed by Deloitte. MedTrans' 1992 income statement reported a loss of $480,000, which was approximately the figure Deloitte had arrived at several months earlier.

Laidlaw Medical Transportation, Inc., purchased MedTrans in June 1993. Roberts and Morgan netted $3 million from the sale of their company. Under Laidlaw's ownership, MedTrans soon became the largest provider of ambulance services in the nation.

## MedTrans Sues Deloitte

In August 1993, Roberts and Morgan sued Deloitte on behalf of their former company. The principal allegations against Deloitte centered on charges of professional negligence and breach of contract. Roberts and Morgan charged that Deloitte's malfeasance caused Blair not to consummate the $10 million investment deal arranged by Roberts. MedTrans' former co-owners requested damages equal to the difference between the amount they received from the sale of MedTrans and the amount the company allegedly would have been worth had Blair invested in the firm. The lawsuit was tried before a jury in a California state court in July 1995.

MedTrans' legal counsel succinctly summed up the key allegations against Deloitte in the following statement.

> *What is the negligence that we contend occurred? What is the breach that we contend occurred? Very simply: they [Deloitte] contracted over a course of years, and in connection with the year of 1992, to perform an audit and to render an opinion, they did neither, and walked away after getting payment for such services.*

Deloitte's defense team rebutted these allegations by insisting that the accounting firm had a right to resign from the 1992 audit when it "lost faith in the honesty of MedTrans's senior management." A CPA retained by Deloitte to serve as an expert witness testified that the firm was obligated to resign from the engagement after its independence was "compromised by Roberts' threats."

After a short trial, Judge Philip Sharp instructed the jurors on the legal matters they should consider during their deliberations. The jurors reached their decision quickly, ruling in favor of MedTrans on all key issues raised during the trial. The jury ruled that Deloitte acted negligently and breached its contractual obligations to MedTrans when it withdrew from the 1992 audit engagement. Additionally, the jury ruled that Deloitte "negligently interfered" with and "disrupted" MedTrans's economic relationships with Blair, Ernst & Young, and Peat Marwick. This latter ruling stemmed from charges that Deloitte made defamatory statements to E&Y and Peat Marwick concerning the integrity of MedTrans' former executives. Deloitte allegedly made these statements during the predecessor-successor auditor communications with those two firms following its resignation as MedTrans' auditor. After issuing their rulings on the specific complaints filed against Deloitte, the jurors awarded MedTrans' former owners a $9.9 million judgment against the accounting firm.

## Deloitte Appeals Jury Verdict

Deloitte quickly appealed the jury's verdict. The accounting firm insisted that the trial judge erred when he instructed the jury prior to its deliberations. Included in Judge

Sharp's instructions to the jury was the following statement concerning an auditor's right to resign from an engagement.

> *Once an accountant has undertaken to serve a client, the employment and duty as an accountant continues until ended by consent or request of the client or the accountant withdraws from the employment, if it does not unduly jeopardize the interest of the client, after giving the client reasonable opportunity to employ another accountant or the matter for which the person [accountant] was employed has been concluded.*

These instructions, Deloitte maintained, gave the jury only one alternative, namely, deciding the case in MedTrans' favor. The accounting firm argued that the phrase "if it [auditor's resignation] does not unduly jeopardize the interest of the client" implies that an auditor must consider the economic impact on a client before resigning. Deloitte demonstrated during the appeal that professional auditing standards do not require auditors to consider the potential economic impact on a client of a resignation decision. The jury instructions also suggested that an auditor must give a client "reasonable opportunity" to retain another audit firm before resigning. Again, Deloitte established that professional standards do not impose such a responsibility on independent auditors.

Deloitte argued before the appellate court that an accounting firm may resign from an audit engagement whenever it has "good cause" to do so. The firm also insisted that "good cause" in this context must be defined in reference to the professional standards of the auditing discipline. Deloitte then identified three reasons why it had good cause to resign from the 1992 MedTrans audit: MedTrans management's refusal to cooperate fully with the auditors, the auditors' loss of confidence in client management's integrity, and the threats that Roberts made to Johns. Deloitte claimed that Roberts' threats, alone, provided sufficient justification to resign since those threats undermined its independence. MedTrans' attorneys agreed that auditors could resign when they had "good cause" but attempted to persuade the appellate court to apply a more legalistic interpretation to that phrase, an interpretation independent of professional auditing standards.

Strengthening Deloitte's good cause argument was a "friend of the court" filing submitted by the American Institute of Certified Public Accountants (AICPA). In that filing, the AICPA reiterated Deloitte's assertion that Roberts' threats undermined the audit firm's independence. The AICPA noted that an auditor must decide as a "matter of professional judgment" whether he is independent. "An auditor's independence may be impaired whenever the member and the member's client company or its management are in threatened or actual positions of material adverse interests by reason of threatened or actual litigation." The AICPA went on to observe that "an auditor who believes independence has been impaired is forbidden from issuing an audit opinion."

After briefly contesting Deloitte's contention that it had "good cause" to resign from the 1992 audit, MedTrans' legal counsel adopted a second strategy during the appeal. MedTrans' attorneys argued that Deloitte forfeited its right to file an appeal predicated on the allegedly prejudicial jury instructions since the accounting firm had not offered the trial judge any alternate jury instructions. In fact, Deloitte initially challenged the jury instructions written by Judge Sharp. At that point, Judge Sharp offered to consider alternate instructions developed by Deloitte's legal counsel; however, the accounting firm never submitted revised jury instructions for the judge's consideration. Despite Deloitte's apparent oversight, the appellate court ruled that Deloitte did not forfeit its right to challenge the impact of Judge Sharp's jury instructions on the jury's verdict.

> *. . . where as here, the trial court gives a jury instruction which is prejudicially erroneous as given, i.e., which is an incorrect statement of law, the party harmed by the*

*instruction need not have objected to the instruction or proposed a correct instruction of his own in order to preserve the right to complain of the erroneous instruction on appeal.*

## Jury Verdict Overturned

In early 1998, the California Court of Appeal overturned the jury's verdict in the *MedTrans vs. Deloitte* civil case. The appellate court ruled that Judge Sharp's instructions predisposed the jury to rule in MedTrans' favor.

After overturning the jury's verdict, the appellate court addressed each of the major allegations made against Deloitte by MedTrans in the original trial. First, the appellate court rejected MedTrans' contention that Deloitte acted negligently when it withdrew from the 1992 audit. The court agreed with Deloitte that the auditing profession's standards are the primary authoritative source in this context. Applying those standards, the appellate court ruled that Deloitte clearly had a reasonable basis for resigning from the 1992 audit. Second, the appellate court discredited the breach of contract allegation lodged against Deloitte. Recall that MedTrans' management pressured Deloitte to issue an unqualified opinion on the company's original 1992 financial statements. The appellate court ruled that "Deloitte cannot be held liable to MedTrans in breach of contract for having declined to issue a false 'unqualified' audit report." The court also rejected MedTrans' claim that Deloitte's failure to issue an audit opinion of any kind constituted breach of contract. Finally, the appellate court dismissed MedTrans's assertion that Deloitte's communications with the company's successor auditors were defamatory.

*Defamation is an intentional tort. In any event, as discussed, the record contained ample evidence that defendants' communications with potential successor auditors about their reasons for resigning from their engagement with MedTrans complied with applicable professional standards requiring open communication with potential successor auditors and were consistent with MedTrans's written authorizations requesting defendants to speak freely with those potential successor auditors.*

## Questions

1. Following his resignation, MedTrans' former CFO met with Gordon Johns, the Deloitte audit engagement partner. Did the CFO have a responsibility to inform Johns of the errors in MedTrans' 1992 financial statements? Defend your answer.
2. What courses of action were available to Johns following his meeting with MedTrans' former CFO? Which of those options would you have selected? Why?
3. How did the threats Roberts made to Johns impair Deloitte's independence? The AICPA maintained that an audit firm is "forbidden" from issuing an audit opinion when it believes its independence has been impaired. Identify three circumstances, unrelated to this case, that would threaten an audit firm's independence.
4. Did Deloitte have a responsibility to be totally candid with MedTrans' prospective successor auditors? Explain. Under present auditing standards, what questions should a prospective successor auditor pose to a predecessor auditor?
5. The jury in the *MedTrans v. Deloitte* lawsuit ruled that the accounting firm negligently resigned from the 1992 audit, breached its contract with the client, and made defamatory statements regarding MedTrans' former executives during the predecessor-successor auditor communications. The appellate court reversed these rulings. Provide an example of each alleged type of misconduct for which an audit firm likely *would be* held legally responsible.

## SECTION 8

# INTERNATIONAL CASES

| | |
|---|---|
| Case 8.1 | Livent, Inc. |
| Case 8.2 | Royal Ahold, N.V. |
| Case 8.3 | *Kansayaku* |
| Case 8.4 | Registered Auditors, South Africa |
| Case 8.5 | *Zuan Yan* |
| Case 8.6 | Kaset Thai Sugar Company |
| Case 8.7 | Australian Wheat Board |
| Case 8.8 | OAO Gazprom |
| Case 8.9 | Tata Finance Limited |
| Case 8.10 | Institute of Chartered Accountants of India |
| Case 8.11 | *Societe Generale* |
| Case 8.12 | *Shari'a* |
| Case 8.13 | Republic of the Sudan |
| Case 8.14 | Mohamed Salem El-Hadad, Internal Auditor |
| Case 8.15 | *Tae Kwang Vina* |

## CASE 8.1

# Livent, Inc.

*The structure of a play is always the story of how the birds came home to roost.*

*Arthur Miller*

In 1995, Canadian native Maria Messina achieved one of the most sought-after career goals in the public accounting profession when she was promoted to partner with Deloitte & Touche, Chartered Accountants, the Canadian affiliate of the U.S.-based Deloitte & Touche, LLP. In an interview she granted to an accounting trade publication shortly after receiving that promotion, Ms. Messina noted that, "Becoming a partner is exciting because you are a part of everything."[1] Messina's promotion earned her the respect and admiration of her family, her friends, and her colleagues and catapulted her to a much higher tax bracket and a more comfortable standard of living. But another opportunity soon arose, an opportunity that promised even more intrinsic and extrinsic rewards for Messina.

Throughout the 1990s, Livent, Inc., was the only publicly owned company whose primary line of business was live theatrical productions. Livent's co-founder and the individual recognized as the creative genius responsible for the company's impressive string of Tony Award-winning shows was Garth Drabinsky. Livent's audit firm was Deloitte & Touche, Chartered Accountants. Maria Messina served as the engagement partner for the 1996 audit, after having been the audit manager on several prior audits of the company. Following the completion of the 1996 Livent audit, Drabinsky asked Messina to leave Deloitte & Touche and become Livent's chief financial officer (CFO). After carefully weighing the challenges, opportunities, and potential drawbacks of making the job change, Messina gave up the partnership position with Deloitte & Touche that she had coveted for years in exchange for a "back office" but high-paying and high-profile position in the glitzy and glamorous world of show business.

Within a few weeks of signing on with Livent, Maria Messina was questioning the wisdom of her decision. Time budgets, out-of-town travel, inexperienced subordinates, and an array of other common "stressors" faced by partners of major accounting firms had complicated Messina's professional and personal life when she was at Deloitte. But, at Livent, the pressures she faced were much more intense, much more difficult to manage and control, even physically debilitating at times. Each passing month imposed a heavier emotional burden on Messina. By the late summer of 1998, Messina's life was in complete disarray. A few months later, in January 1999, Messina pleaded guilty to a felony for her role in a massive financial fraud. Following that plea, the single mother of a 10-year-old daughter faced up to five years in prison and a $250,000 fine.

### There Is No Business Like Show Business

The entertainment industry had fascinated Garth Drabinsky from an early age. Unlike many of his colleagues in the industry, Drabinsky did not benefit from a network of family members and friends in show business. Instead, Drabinsky relied on his own drive, inspiration, and indomitable work ethic to claw his way to the top of the volatile and fickle entertainment industry. Born in Toronto in 1947, Drabinsky was struck

1. T. Frank, "Opportunity Knocks," *CA Magazine*, March 1997, 27.

down by polio at age three, leaving him with a severe limp for the remainder of his life. The young Canadian refused to allow his physical limitations prevent him from reaching his goals. In fact, Drabinsky freely admits that his physical problems and his modest upbringing—his father sold air conditioners—were key factors that motivated him to "aim for the stars."

During his college years, Drabinsky made his first foray into show business by publishing a free magazine that provided critiques of movies appearing in local theaters. After graduating from law school, where he concentrated his studies on the entertainment industry, Drabinsky became involved in real estate development. The young attorney hoped to accumulate a nest egg that he could use to begin producing movies and live plays. A successful condominium project provided him with the funds he needed to begin dabbling in motion pictures and Broadway productions. By age 30, Drabinsky had produced three feature-length movies and one Broadway musical, none of which were particularly well received by critics or the ticket-buying public.

In 1979, Drabinsky and a close friend, Myron Gottlieb, decided to enter the show business world via the "back door." The two young entrepreneurs persuaded a prominent Toronto businessman to invest nearly $1 million in a "cinema complex" project they had conceived.[2] This project involved converting the basement of a large shopping mall into a multiscreen theater. The design for the "cineplex" included plush interiors for each theater, luxurious seats, and cappuccino bars in the lobby. Drabinsky intended to make a trip to the local movie theater the captivating experience it had been several decades earlier in the halcyon days of Hollywood.

Most industry insiders predicted that Drabinsky's blueprint for his cineplex concept would fail, principally because the large overhead for his theaters forced his company to charge much higher ticket prices than competitors. But the critics were wrong. Toronto's moviegoers were more than willing to pay a few extra dollars to watch a film in Drabinsky's upscale theaters. Over the next several years, Drabinsky and Gottlieb expanded their company with the help of well-heeled investors whom they convinced to pony up large sums to finance the development of multiscreen theater complexes throughout Canada and the United States. By the mid-1980s, their company, Cineplex Odeon, controlled nearly 2,000 theaters, making it the second-largest theater chain in North America.

Several major investors in Cineplex Odeon eventually began complaining of Drabinsky's unrestrained spending practices. The company's rapid expansion and the increasingly sumptuous designs Drabinsky developed for new theaters required Cineplex Odeon to borrow enormous amounts from banks and other lenders. An internal investigation in 1989 uncovered irregularities in the company's accounting records that wiped out a large profit for the year and resulted in Cineplex Odeon reporting a significant loss instead. The controversy sparked by the discovery of the accounting irregularities gave Cineplex Odeon's major investors the leverage they needed to force Drabinsky and Gottlieb to resign. During the negotiations that led to their departure from the company, Drabinsky and Gottlieb acquired the Pantages Theatre, a large live production theater in Toronto, as well as the Canadian rights to certain Broadway plays.

Within a few weeks after severing their ties with Cineplex Odeon, Drabinsky and Gottlieb had organized Live Entertainment Corporation to produce Broadway-type shows in their hometown of Toronto. Drabinsky's concept for this new company,

2. The key financial amounts reported in this case are expressed in Canadian dollars.

which he coaxed several large investors and lenders to bankroll, was to bring "corporate management" to the notoriously freewheeling and undisciplined show business industry. Following a series of widely acclaimed productions, the company—renamed Livent, Inc.—went public in 1993.[3] In May 1995, Livent filed an application with the Securities and Exchange Commission (SEC) to sell its stock in the United States. The SEC approved that application and Livent's stock began trading on the NASDAQ stock exchange. Within two years, U.S. investors controlled the majority of Livent's outstanding stock.

By early 1998, Livent owned five live production theaters in Canada and the United States, including a major Broadway theater in New York. The company's productions, among them *Fosse, Kiss of the Spider Woman, Ragtime, Show Boat,* and *The Phantom of the Opera*, had garnered a total of more than 20 Tony Awards. Show business insiders attributed Livent's rapid rise to prominence to Garth Drabinsky. After organizing Livent, Drabinsky quickly developed a keen sense of what types of shows would appeal to the public. Even more important, he was able to identify and recruit talented directors, actors, set designers, and the array of other skilled artisans needed to produce successful Broadway shows. The single-minded and domineering Drabinsky micromanaged not only the creative realm of Livent's operations but every other major facet of the company's operations as well, although he relied heavily on his friend and confidant, Myron Gottlieb—who had an accounting background—to help him oversee the company's accounting and financial reporting functions.

Despite the artistic success enjoyed by several Livent productions and the company's increasing stature in the entertainment industry, Garth Drabinsky was dogged by critics throughout the 1990s. The enigmatic Drabinsky had a well-deserved reputation as flamboyant and charming with Wall Street analysts, metropolitan bankers, and fellow corporate executives. But critics were prone to point out that Drabinsky also had a darker side to his personality. "He is—by his own admission—complex and difficult, cranky and litigious, breathtakingly ambitious, singled-minded and self-centered."[4] According to company insiders, Drabinsky could be "tyrannical and abusive" to his subordinates, berating them when they failed to live up to his perfectionist standards or when they questioned his decisions.[5] Maria Messina subsequently revealed that Livent's accountants were common targets of verbal abuse by Drabinsky and other Livent executives. "They [Livent's accountants] were told on a very regular basis that they are paid to keep their [expletive] mouths shut and do as they are [expletive] told. They are not paid to think."[6]

Critics also charged that Drabinsky failed to live up to his pledge of bringing a disciplined style of corporate management to Broadway. In reality, Drabinsky was anything but disciplined in managing Livent's finances. Because he demanded that the company's live productions be "motion-picture perfect," most of Livent's shows,

3. Drabinsky and Gottlieb's company was not affiliated with the California-based Live Entertainment, Inc. Jose Menendez organized the latter company in 1988 but was murdered along with his wife, Kitty, in August 1989. In one of the many "trials of the century," the Menendez's sons, Lyle and Erik, were subsequently convicted of murdering their parents.

4. K. Noble, "The Comeback King: Garth Drabinsky Is Back, and Creating a Lot of Showbiz Buzz," *MacLean's* (online), 4 June 2001.

5. M. Potter and T. Van Alphen, "Livent Charges $7.5 Million Kickback Scam," *The Toronto Star* (online), 19 November 1998.

6. *Profit*, "Backstage at Livent," May 1999, 29.

particularly those that were box-office successes, incurred huge cost overruns. By 1998, Livent was buckling under the huge load of debt Drabinsky had incurred to finance the company's lavish productions. In early 1998, Roy Furman, a Wall Street investment banker and close friend, persuaded Drabinsky to accept a $20 million investment from former Disney executive Michael Ovitz to alleviate Livent's financial problems. A condition of Ovitz's investment was that he be granted sufficient common stock voting rights to allow him to control the company's board of directors.

During the 1980s, Ovitz had reigned as Hollywood's top talent agent. When he became chairman of the Creative Artists Agency, show business periodicals tagged him with the title of "Hollywood's most powerful man." In late 1995, Disney chief executive officer (CEO) Michael Eisner chose Ovitz to serve as his top lieutenant and gave him the title of company president. A little more than one year later, repeated personality clashes between the two Hollywood heavyweights resulted in Eisner dismissing Ovitz. No doubt, Ovitz hoped that Livent would provide him with an opportunity to refurbish his reputation in the entertainment industry, a reputation that had been tarnished during his brief and turbulent stint with Disney. Just as important, taking control of Livent would allow Ovitz to compete head-to-head with his former boss. At the time, Disney's *The Lion King* was a colossal hit on Broadway.

Before agreeing to invest in Livent, the cautious Ovitz retained the Big Five accounting firm KPMG to scrutinize the company's accounting records. After KPMG's "due diligence" investigation yielded a clean bill of health for Livent, Ovitz became the company's largest stockholder in early June of 1998 and took over effective control of the company. Ovitz took a seat on the company's board and became chairman of the board's executive committee, while Furman assumed Drabinsky's former titles of chairman of the board and CEO. Drabinsky was given the titles of vice chairman and chief creative director. In the latter role, Drabinsky continued to oversee the all-important creative facets of Livent's operations. To provide a second opinion on artistic matters, Ovitz appointed the noted producer and songwriter Quincy Jones to Livent's board.

Ovitz also demoted Myron Gottlieb to a vice president position. A former Disney executive who left that company along with Ovitz assumed Gottlieb's former position as Livent's president. Among other changes that Ovitz made in Livent's corporate management structure was hiring former KPMG audit partner Robert Webster to serve as an executive vice president of the company. Webster, who had supervised KPMG's due diligence investigation of Livent's accounting records, was given a broad range of responsibilities but his principal role was to monitor Livent's accounting and finance functions for Ovitz's new management team.

## Webster's Summer of Discontent

Like Maria Messina, Robert Webster quickly discovered that the work environment within Livent was much less than ideal. After joining Livent in the early summer of 1998, Webster found that the accounting staff, including Messina, who remained Livent's CFO, was reluctant to discuss accounting matters with him. Webster later testified that some of the Livent accountants "told him that Mr. Drabinsky had warned them not to provide certain financial information until [Drabinsky] had reviewed and approved it."[7] Even more troubling to Webster was Drabinsky's management style. Webster testified that, "I had never before experienced anyone with Drabinsky's

7. M. Petersen, "The Roar of the Accountants: The Strange Last Days of a Theater Impresario's Reign," *The New York Times* (online), 10 October 1998.

abusive and profane management style."[8] He was shocked to find that Livent's executives often screamed and swore at the company's accountants. Webster reported that after meeting with Drabinksy, Livent's accountants were often in tears or even nauseous. Following one such meeting, Webster recalled Messina "shaking like a leaf."[9]

When Webster demanded that Livent's accountants provide him with unrestricted access to the company's accounting records, the former KPMG partner became the target of Drabinsky's wrath. Drabinsky accused Webster of attempting to "tear the company" apart with his persistent inquiries and told him that he was there to "service his [Drabinsky's] requirements."[10] Webster refused to be deterred by Drabinsky's bullying tactics. In early August 1998, after Webster began asking questions regarding a suspicious transaction he had uncovered, Messina and four of her subordinates secretly met with him. The five accountants admitted to Webster that Livent's accounting records had been distorted by a series of fraudulent schemes initiated and coordinated by Drabinsky and other top Livent executives.

Webster relayed the disturbing revelations to Livent's board. On August 11, 1998, Roy Furman issued a press release announcing that "significant financial irregularities" adversely affecting Livent's financial statements for the past three years had been discovered. The press release also indicated that Drabinsky and Gottlieb had been indefinitely suspended pending the outcome of a forensic investigation by KPMG. During the fall of 1998, company officials issued successive press releases suggesting that the impact of the accounting irregularities would be more severe than initially thought. Adding to Livent's problems was the suspension of all trading in the company's stock and a series of large class-action lawsuits filed against the company and its officers. In August 1998 alone, 12 such lawsuits were filed.

On November 18, 1998, Livent's board announced that KPMG's forensic investigation had revealed "massive, systematic, accounting irregularities that permeated the company."[11] The press release issued by Livent's board also disclosed that Deloitte & Touche had withdrawn its audit opinions on the company's 1995–1997 financial statements. Finally, the press release reported that Drabinsky and Gottlieb had been dismissed and that Livent had simultaneously filed for bankruptcy in Canada and the United States. A few weeks later, a federal grand jury in New York issued a 16-count fraud indictment against Drabinsky and Gottlieb. When the former Livent executives failed to appear for a preliminary court hearing, a U.S. federal judge issued arrest warrants for the two Canadian citizens and initiated extradition proceedings.

## A "Pervasive and Multi-faceted" Fraud

Details of the fraud allegedly conceived by Garth Drabinsky and Myron Gottlieb were eventually revealed to the public by the SEC, the Ontario Securities Commission—a Canadian agency comparable to the SEC—and publicly available records of various court proceedings in civil lawsuits. In numerous enforcement and litigation releases, SEC officials repeatedly used the descriptive phrase "pervasive and multi-faceted" when referring to the Livent fraud. One of the earliest elements of the fraud was a large kickback scheme.

8. A. Clark, "An Epic from Livent: Executive Accuses Drabinsky of Bullying Tactics," *MacLean's* (online), 1 March 1999.

9. *Ibid.*

10. *Ibid.*

11. *In re Livent, Inc. Noteholders Securities Litigation*, 151 F. Supp. 2d 371 (2001).

"As early as 1990, and continuing through 1994, Drabinsky and Gottlieb operated a kickback scheme with two Livent vendors designed to siphon millions of dollars from the company directly into their own pockets."[12] Gottlieb reportedly instructed the two vendors to include in the invoices that they submitted to Livent charges for services that they had not provided to the company. After Livent paid the inflated invoice amounts, Drabinsky and Gottlieb received kickbacks equal to the payments for the bogus services. According to the SEC, over a four-year period in the 1990s, Drabinsky and Gottlieb received approximately $7 million in kickbacks from the two Livent vendors. The fake charges billed to Livent by the vendors were capitalized in "preproduction" cost accounts for the various shows being developed by the company. Legitimate costs charged to those accounts included expenditures to produce sets and costumes for new shows, costs that were amortized over a maximum period of five years.

By the mid-1990s, the kickback scheme and large losses being registered by several of Livent's plays made it increasingly difficult for the company to achieve quarterly earnings targets that Drabinsky and Gottlieb had relayed to Wall Street analysts. The two conspirators realized that if Livent failed to reach those earnings targets, the company's credit rating and stock price would fall, jeopardizing the company's ability to raise the additional capital needed to sustain its operations. Faced with these circumstances, the SEC reported that beginning in 1994 Drabinsky and Gottlieb directed Livent's accounting staff to engage in an array of "accounting manipulations" to obscure the company's financial problems.

These manipulations included such blatant subterfuges as simply erasing from the accounting records previously recorded expenses and liabilities at the end of each quarter. A particularly popular accounting scam within Livent was transferring preproduction costs from a show that was running to a show still in production. Such transfers allowed the company to defer, sometimes indefinitely, the amortization of those major cost items. To further reduce the periodic amortization charges for preproduction costs, Livent's accountants began charging such costs to various fixed asset accounts. These assets were typically depreciated over 40 years, compared with the five-year amortization period for preproduction costs. Eventually, the company's accountants began debiting salary expenses and other common operating expenses to long-term fixed asset accounts.

The SEC estimated that the accounting manipulations understated Livent's expenses by more than $30 million in the mid-1990s. Despite the resulting favorable impact on Livent's financial statements, Drabinsky and Gottlieb eventually realized that additional efforts were needed to embellish the company's financial data. So, beginning in 1996, Drabinsky and Gottlieb organized and carried out what the SEC referred to as a "fraudulent revenue-generating" scheme.

This new scam involved several multimillion-dollar transactions arranged by Drabinsky and Gottlieb. The specific details of these transactions varied somewhat but most of them involved the sale of production rights owned by Livent to third parties. For example, Livent sold the rights to produce *Ragtime* and *Show Boat* in various U.S. theaters to a Texas-based company. The contract for this transaction indicated that the $11.2 million fee paid to Livent by the Texas company was not refundable under any circumstances. However, a secret side agreement arranged by Livent's executives shielded the Texas company from any loss on this deal and, in fact, guaranteed it a reasonable rate of return on its large investment. Despite the considerable

12. Securities and Exchange Commission, *Accounting and Auditing Enforcement Release No. 1095*, 19 May 1999.

uncertainty regarding the actual profit, if any, that would ultimately be earned on this and similar transactions, Livent's accounting staff included at least $34 million of revenues on those transactions in the company's 1996 and 1997 income statements.

A final Livent scam documented by the SEC involved inflating reported box-office results for key productions. In late 1997, Livent opened *Ragtime* in a Los Angeles theater. The agreement with that theater allowed it to close the show if weekly ticket sales fell below $500,000. Livent's executives planned to open *Ragtime* on Broadway in January 1998. Those executives realized that if the show fared poorly in Los Angeles, its Broadway opening could be jeopardized. To inflate *Ragtime's* ticket sales during its Los Angeles run, Livent executives arranged to have two of the company's vendors—the same individuals involved in the fraudulent kickback scheme alluded to previously—purchase several hundred thousand dollars of tickets to the show. Livent reimbursed the vendors for these ticket purchases and charged the payments to various fixed asset accounts.

The fraudulent schemes engineered by Livent's executives caused the company's periodic financial statements to be grossly misrepresented. For example, in 1992, the company reported a pretax profit of $2.9 million when the actual figure was approximately $100,000. Four years later, Livent reported a pretax profit of $14.2 million, when it actually incurred a loss of more than $20 million. By 1997, the company's total fixed assets of $200.8 million were overstated by nearly $24 million due to the various accounting schemes.

SEC officials found two features of the Livent fraud particularly disturbing. As the scope of the fraud steadily grew throughout the 1990s, the company's accounting staff found it increasingly difficult to provide meaningful financial data to top management. "Because of the sheer magnitude and dollar amount of the manipulations, it became necessary for senior management to be able to track both the real and the phony numbers."[13] Gordon Eckstein, the company's senior vice president of finance and administration and Maria Messina's immediate superior, allegedly instructed a subordinate to develop computer software that would solve this problem. This software could be used to filter the bogus data out of the company's accounting records. The secret software also served a second purpose, namely, allowing Livent's accountants to record fraudulent transactions "without leaving a paper trail that Livent's outside auditors might stumble across."[14] The accountants processed in a batch mode the fraudulent changes in the accounting records demanded by Livent's executives. When these so-called "adjustments" were processed, they replaced the initial journal entries for the given transactions, making the adjustments appear as if they were the original transactions, thus duping the company's Deloitte auditors.

The second extremely troubling feature of the Livent fraud, according to the SEC, was the matter-of-fact manner in which the company's management team organized and carried out the fraud. Reportedly, Drabinsky, Gottlieb, and Robert Topol, Livent's chief operating officer (COO), regularly met with Eckstein, Messina, and other members of the company's accounting staff to discuss the details of the fraud. At these meetings, the three top executives reviewed preliminary financial reports prepared by the accounting staff and instructed the accountants on the "adjustments" needed to improve or embellish those reports. As suggested earlier, Livent's top executives relied on coercion and intimidation to browbeat their accountants, including

13. *Ibid.*

14. M. A. Hiltzik and J. Bates, "U.S. Indicts Stage Producer Drabinsky," *Los Angeles Times* (online), 14 January 1999.

Messina, into accepting these illicit changes. Once the adjustments were processed, "the bogus numbers were presented to Livent's audit committee, the auditors, investors, and eventually filed with the Commission [SEC]."[15]

## Keeping the Auditors in the Dark

Press reports of a large accounting fraud involving a public company often prompt scathing criticism of the company's independent audit firm. The disclosure of the Livent fraud in the late summer and fall of 1998 caused Deloitte & Touche to become a target of such criticism. A Canadian financial analyst observed that investors depend on auditors to clamp down on their clients and force them to prepare reliable financial reports. "They [auditors] are the only ones in a position to question the policies, to question the numbers, to make sure they're right."[16]

Critics could readily point to several red flags or fraud risk factors during Deloitte's tenure with Livent that should have placed the accounting firm on high alert regarding the possible existence of financial statement misrepresentations. Among those factors were an extremely aggressive, growth-oriented management team; a history of prior financial reporting indiscretions by Drabinsky and Gottlieb; a constant and growing need for additional capital; and the existence of related-party transactions. Regarding the latter, several of Livent's fraudulent "revenue-generating transactions" that were documented by the SEC involved companies or corporate executives affiliated with Livent or its management team.

In Deloitte's defense, a massive collusive fraud that involves a client's top executives and the active participation of its accountants is extremely difficult to detect. Making matters worse for Deloitte was the contemptuous attitude that Livent's executives had toward independent auditors. At one point, a top Livent officer told a subordinate that independent auditors were a "necessary evil and that it was no one's business how they [Livent's executives] ran their company."[17] Also complicating the Livent audits for Deloitte was the fact Maria Messina and Christopher Craib, two former members of the Livent audit engagement team, had accepted key accounting positions with the company. The personal relationships the auditors had with Messina and Craib may have impaired their objectivity during the Livent engagements.

Christopher Craib replaced Maria Messina as the audit manager assigned to the Livent audit engagement team following Messina's promotion to partner in 1995. After the 1996 audit was completed, Drabinsky hired Craib to serve as Livent's senior controller for budgeting. Not long after joining Livent, Craib, a chartered accountant, became involved in the ongoing effort to segregate Livent's "real" accounting data from its bogus data. In subsequent testimony, Craib recalled meeting with Gordon Eckstein to discuss Livent's schizoid accounting system. Eckstein explained to Craib why it was imperative to track both the real and bogus accounting data. "I have to keep all the lies straight. I have to know what lies I'm telling these people [outside auditors]. I've told so many lies to different people I have to make sure they all make sense."[18]

---

15. Securities and Exchange Commission, *Accounting and Auditing Enforcement Release No. 1095.*

16. J. McCarten, "Auditors Taking the Heat after Financial Scandals," *The Toronto Star* (online), 18 August 1998.

17. Securities and Exchange Commission, *Accounting and Auditing Enforcement Release No. 1096*, 19 May 1999.

18. *Ibid.*

Like Craib, Maria Messina realized that concealing the Livent fraud from the Deloitte auditors was among her primary responsibilities. During a meeting shortly after Messina joined Livent, she became aware of the adversarial attitude that Livent's top executives had toward the company's independent auditors. During this meeting, Topol became angry when Messina raised an issue involving what documents to turn over to Deloitte. Topol responded with an angry outburst. "[Expletive] you and your auditors . . . I don't care what they see or don't see."[19]

Despite the efforts of Livent officials to sabotage their independent audits, the company's Deloitte auditors focused considerable attention on several suspicious transactions that they uncovered. The Deloitte auditors became increasingly skeptical of Livent's accounting records in 1996 and 1997 when Drabinsky and his colleagues were scrambling to conceal the deteriorating financial condition of their company while, at the same time, attempting to raise much needed debt and equity capital.

Near the end of the 1996 audit, Deloitte & Touche, LLP, the U.S.-based branch of the firm, initially refused to allow its Canadian affiliate to issue an unqualified audit opinion on Livent's financial statements filed with the SEC. Deloitte's top technical partners in the United States believed that Livent had been much too aggressive in recognizing revenue on a few large transactions—transactions that, unknown to partners of both the firm's Canadian and U.S. affiliates, included fraudulent elements. After a series of meetings between Livent officials and representatives of Deloitte & Touche, LLP, a compromise was reached. Livent agreed to defer the recognition of revenue on one of the two large transactions in question until 1997. In return, Deloitte allowed the company to record the full amount of the revenue for the other disputed transaction.

During 1997, a major transaction with a real estate firm triggered another conflict between Deloitte and Livent management. In the second quarter of that year, the real estate firm purchased for $7.4 million the development rights to a valuable parcel of land owned by Livent. The contract between the two companies included a stipulation or "put agreement" allowing the real estate firm to cancel the transaction prior to the date that it began developing the property. When the Deloitte audit engagement partner learned of the put agreement, he insisted that no revenue could be recorded for the transaction. Complicating matters was the fact that the transaction involved a related party since Myron Gottlieb served on the board of directors of the real estate firm's parent company.

To quell the audit partner's concern, Gottlieb arranged to have an executive of the real estate firm send the partner a letter indicating that the put agreement had been cancelled—which it had not. After receiving the letter, the Deloitte partner told Gottlieb that the revenue resulting from the transaction could be recorded during Livent's third quarter when the put agreement had allegedly been cancelled. At this point, a frustrated Gottlieb ignored the partner's decision and included the disputed revenue in Livent's earnings press release for the second quarter of 1997.

When Deloitte officials learned of the press release, they demanded a meeting with Livent's board of directors. At this meeting, Deloitte threatened to resign. After considerable discussion, Livent's board and the Deloitte representatives reached a compromise. According to a subsequent legal transcript, the board agreed to reverse the journal entry for the $7.4 million transaction in the second quarter, recording it instead during the third quarter. The board also agreed to issue an amended earnings release for the second quarter. In exchange for these concessions, Deloitte

---

19. Securities and Exchange Commission, *Accounting and Auditing Enforcement Release No. 1097*, 19 May 1999.

officials purportedly agreed to allow Livent to reverse certain accrued liabilities that had been recorded at the end of the second quarter. The reversal of those accrued liabilities and the corresponding expenses reduced by approximately 20 percent the profit "correction" reported by Livent in the amended earnings press release for the second quarter.[20]

Another serious disagreement arose between Livent executives and Deloitte auditors shortly after the dispute just described was resolved. During the third quarter of 1997, Livent's management arranged to sell for $12.5 million the naming rights for one of its existing theaters and a new theater that the company was planning to build. Neither Maria Messina nor the Deloitte auditors assigned to the Livent engagement believed that the $12.5 million payment should be recorded immediately as revenue since the contract between Livent and the other party, AT&T, was strictly an oral agreement at the time and since one of the theaters was yet to be built. Gottlieb retained Ernst & Young (E&Y) to review the matter. The report E&Y submitted to Gottlieb did not take a firm position on the revenue recognition issue. Instead, E&Y's report simply suggested that the $12.5 million payment for the naming rights could be "considered" for recording during the third quarter. After receiving a copy of E&Y's report, Deloitte hired Price Waterhouse to review the transaction. When Price Waterhouse reached the same conclusion as E&Y, Deloitte allowed Livent to book the $12.5 million as revenue during the third quarter.

## Don't Blame Me, Blame . . .

Resolving the legal implications of a major accounting and financial reporting fraud can require years. However, one Canadian journalist suggested that in the Livent case the legal wrangling could continue even longer, possibly for decades.[21] From its inception, a key factor complicating the resolution of this case was its "cross-border" nature. Beginning in late 1998, officials from several federal agencies in Canada and the United States became embroiled in a tedious and often unfriendly struggle to determine which agency would be the first to prosecute the key parties involved in the Livent fraud. Those agencies include the Royal Canadian Mounted Police, the Ontario Securities Commission, the SEC, and the U.S. Department of Justice, among others. Law enforcement authorities in the United States failed to win the cooperation of their Canadian counterparts in attempting to extradite Garth Drabinsky and Myron Gottlieb to face a series of federal fraud charges filed against them in U.S. courts. Even more frustrating to U.S. authorities was the snail's pace at which Canadian authorities moved in pursuing legal action against the two alleged fraudsters.

While Canadian and U.S. law enforcement authorities tangled over jurisdictional matters, the leading actors in the final Livent "production" waged a public relations war against each other in major metropolitan newspapers and in the courts. Drabinsky and Gottlieb were the most vocal of these individuals. They repeatedly insisted that they were not responsible for the various fraudulent schemes that had been uncovered within Livent. At a press conference held in early 1999, Drabinsky suggested that he had been too busy overseeing Livent's creative operations to become involved in any creative bookkeeping.[22] In his typical Shakespearean manner, Drabinsky

---

20. *In re Livent, Inc. Noteholders Securities Litigation*. As a point of information, this legal transcript did not include any commentary from Deloitte's perspective regarding the nature and outcome of these negotiations.

21. Noble, "The Comeback King."

22. M. Lewyckyj, "Livent's Accounting Designed to Deceive," *Toronto Sun* (online), 15 January 1999.

declared: "The final act of this tragedy has yet to be played out and, when it is, Myron Gottlieb and I have complete confidence that we will be vindicated."[23]

In January 1999, Myron Gottlieb filed a civil lawsuit against Maria Messina, Christopher Craib, Gordon Eckstein, and three other former Livent accountants; the lawsuit charged those six individuals with responsibility for the Livent accounting fraud. In court documents filed with this lawsuit, Gottlieb alleged that he was not "an expert on accounting practices" and that he had relied on Livent's accounting staff to ensure that the company's financial statements were accurate.[24] In responding to that lawsuit, the six named defendants, with the exception of Eckstein, claimed that they had been coerced into participating in the fraud by its principal architects.[25] These defendants also rejected Gottlieb's assertion that he was unfamiliar with accounting practices. "Gottlieb was and remains an experienced businessman with a sophisticated and comprehensive grasp of accounting and auditing issues and intimate knowledge of the details of Livent's accounting practices."[26]

When Eckstein eventually responded to Gottlieb's lawsuit, he charged the Livent co-founder with being a key architect of the accounting fraud. "Gottlieb's denial of responsibility or knowledge of the accounting irregularities at Livent is in complete disregard to the facts as they existed . . . . [He] had the requisite expertise and business acumen to create and help foster the corporate culture at Livent, which ultimately resulted in the alteration of the books and records."[27] Eckstein also claimed that he was not involved in altering Livent's accounting records, although he did admit to relaying the changes demanded by Drabinsky and Gottlieb in those records to Livent's accounting staff. Finally, Eckstein maintained that Maria Messina had played an important role in the fraudulent scheme. "Messina relied on her former position as a partner at Deloitte in dealing with the field audit team . . . to ensure that the financial statements of Livent, as presented to the auditors, were approved."[28]

Messina answered Eckstein and other critics by maintaining that she had attempted to dissuade Livent's executives from using accounting gimmicks to boost the company's revenues and profits. She insisted that she had "begged" her former colleagues at Deloitte to crack down on the aggressive revenue recognition policies being used by Livent's management.[29] To support her claim that she had not been a willing member of the Livent conspiracy, Messina pointed out that she had refused to sign the letters of representations for the 1996 and 1997 audits, each of which indicated that there were no material inaccuracies in Livent's financial statements. In fact, near the end of the 1997 audit, Messina had redrafted Deloitte's pre-formatted letter of representations to remove her name from it.[30]

---

23. C. Brodesser and M. Peers, "U.S. Indicts Duo in Liventgate," *Variety*, 18 January 1999, 137.

24. *The Gazette* (online), "Livent Co-Founder Sues 6 Employees," 19 February 1999.

25. V. Menon, "Livent Whistle-Blowers File Defence," *The Toronto Star* (online), 1 April 1999.

26. B. Bouw, "Livent Employees Fight Back: 'Gottlieb to Blame,'" *National Post* (online), 1 April 1999.

27. B. Shecter, "Drabinsky's Assertions Refuted," *National Post* (online), 26 June 1999.

28. *Ibid.*

29. *Profit*, "Backstage at Livent." In a deposition filed in one of the many lawsuits triggered by the Livent fraud, Messina described Deloitte's audits of the company as "inadequate." See D. Francis, "Livent: A Bean Counter Scandal," *National Post* (online), 10 May 2001.

30. In a court document, Messina reported that she did not reveal the various Livent fraudulent schemes prior to August 1998 because she feared Drabinsky and Gottlieb and because she believed that she would be "implicated by association." See B. Bouw, "Livent Employees Fight Back: 'Gottlieb to Blame,'" *National Post* (online), 1 April 1999.

After firing Drabinsky and Gottlieb, Michael Ovitz and the members of the new management team he installed at Livent in June 1998 sued the company's co-founders for $325 million for their alleged role in the fraudulent accounting schemes. That lawsuit prompted Drabinsky and Gottlieb to file a $200 million defamation-of-character lawsuit against Ovitz and his colleagues.

In September 1998, Drabinsky sued KPMG, the accounting firm that Ovitz had retained to perform a due diligence investigation earlier in the year and the firm retained by Livent's board of directors in August 1998 to investigate the charges of accounting irregularities revealed by Maria Messina and her subordinates. That lawsuit, which requested damages of more than $26 million, was predicated on the fact that Drabinsky had been a client of KPMG over the past two decades. Drabinksy charged that by agreeing to perform the forensic audit requested by Livent's board in August 1998, KPMG had placed itself in a conflict of interest between two clients.[31]

Deloitte & Touche was a primary target of the various plaintiffs attempting to hold someone responsible for the Livent debacle and the resulting financial losses. In December 1999, a U.S. federal judge dismissed Deloitte as a defendant in one of those lawsuits filed by Livent's former stockholders. The judge concluded that the plaintiffs had not made a reasonable argument that Deloitte was at least "reckless" in auditing Livent. For lawsuits filed under the Securities and Exchange Act of 1934, as amended by the Private Securities Litigation Reform Act (PSLRA) of 1995, plaintiffs must allege or "plead" that the given defendant was at least "reckless."

In another class-action lawsuit filed by Livent creditors, a federal judge ruled in June 2001 that the plaintiffs had met the pleading standard of recklessness, meaning that the lawsuit could proceed. This judge observed that Livent's "accounting manipulations" were so flagrant that there was a reasonable likelihood Deloitte was reckless in failing to discover them. "Deloitte & Touche's actions and omissions in connection with Livent's manipulations of its books and records display acquiescence and passivity that, in this Court's reading of the pleadings, cross over the boundary of ordinary breaches of reasonable care into the zone of recklessness."[32]

## EPILOGUE

In July 1999, SFX Entertainment purchased the remaining assets of Livent, ending the company's dramatic and turbulent existence after only 10 years. In June 2000, the disciplinary committee of the Institute of Chartered Accountants of Ontario (ICAO) sanctioned the former Livent accountants who had publicly admitted some degree of involvement in the Livent fraud. Maria Messina, who pleaded guilty to three charges of professional misconduct, was fined $7,500 and suspended from practicing as a chartered accountant for two years. Christopher Craib received a six-month suspension and a $1,000 fine. In March 2007, this same body found three of the Deloitte auditors who had been assigned to the 1997 Livent audit engagement team guilty of professional misconduct and publicly reprimanded them. In October 2007, the ICAO announced that it had levied fines totaling $1.55 million against those three individuals and Deloitte.

31. Drabinsky and KPMG ultimately settled this lawsuit out of court. Although the settlement's financial terms were not disclosed, KPMG acknowledged that it had breached its "fiduciary duty" to Drabinsky by agreeing to perform the forensic audit requested by Livent's board.

32. Published reports indicate that Deloitte & Touche was dropped as a defendant in this case after agreeing to pay $5.5 million to a restitution fund established for Livent's former creditors.

The SEC sanctioned Craib and three other Livent accountants who had confessed to some role in the Livent accounting fraud. Craib received a three-year suspension from practicing before the SEC. The SEC has not yet formally sanctioned Maria Messina for her role in the Livent fraud. Likewise, federal prosecutors in the United States have yet to make a sentencing recommendation following Messina's guilty plea to one felony count of violating U.S. federal securities laws. A key factor that federal authorities in the United States will consider in determining Messina's punishment will be whether she continues cooperating with Canadian and U.S. authorities prosecuting the key architects of the fraud.

As predicted, Canadian law enforcement authorities were extremely methodical in pursuing their investigation and prosecution of Garth Drabinsky, Myron Gottlieb, and the other key individuals involved in the Livent scandal. In late 2002, the Royal Mounted Canadian Police finally filed a fraud indictment against Drabinsky and Gottlieb that contained 19 individual charges. Five years later, Gordon Eckstein pleaded guilty to one count of fraud and agreed to testify against Drabinsky and Gottlieb. Eckstein's testimony would prove to be pivotal evidence in the 11-month long criminal trial of Drabinsky and Gottlieb. That trial ended in late March 2009 with both Drabinsky and Gottlieb being convicted of fraud and forgery. The Canadian judge who presided over the lengthy trial rejected the two defendants' principal argument that they had been unaware of the massive accounting fraud and that it had been orchestrated by their subordinates. In handing down her verdict, the judge concluded that the two executives "had initiated the improper accounting system" that had "systemically manipulated" Livent's reported operating results and financial condition.[33,34] In August 2009, the judge sentenced Drabinsky and Gottlieb to prison sentences of seven years and six years, respectively.

The 2009 criminal convictions of Drabinsky and Gottlieb did not end the long-running Livent legal ordeal. Following those convictions, the two men still faced securities fraud charges in Canada and the unhappy prospect of eventually being extradited to face the litany of criminal charges pending against them for more than a decade in the United States.

---

## Questions

1. Identify common inherent risk factors that companies involved in the entertainment industry pose for their independent auditors. List and briefly describe specific audit procedures that would not be used on "typical" audit engagements but would be required for audits of companies involved in live theatrical productions, such as Livent.
2. Compare and contrast the responsibilities of an audit partner of a major accounting firm with those of a large public company's CFO. Which work role do you believe is more important? Which is more stressful? Which role would you prefer and why?
3. Explain why some corporate executives may perceive that their independent auditors are a "necessary evil." How can auditors combat or change that attitude?

---

33. Reuters (online), "Former Broadway Impresario Drabinsky Found Guilty," 25 March 2009.

34. Robert Topol, Livent's former COO, had faced charges similar to those for which Drabinsky and Gottlieb were prosecuted. However, those charges were dismissed in 2008 when his attorneys convinced the judge that he had been denied his right to a speedy trial.

4. When auditor-client disputes arise during an audit engagement, another accounting firm is sometimes retained by the client and/or the existing auditor to provide an objective report on the issue at the center of the dispute—as happened during Deloitte's 1997 audit of Livent. Discuss an accounting firm's responsibilities when it is retained to issue such a report.
5. Do you believe Deloitte & Touche should have approved Livent's decision to record the $12.5 million "naming rights" payment as revenue during the third quarter of 1997? Defend your answer. What broad accounting concepts should be considered in determining the proper accounting treatment for such transactions?
6. Maria Messina has testified that when she learned of the accounting irregularities at Livent shortly after becoming the company's CFO she felt "guilty by association," which prevented her from revealing the fraud to regulatory or law enforcement authorities. Explain what you believe she meant by that statement. Place yourself in Messina's position. What would you have done after discovering the fraudulent schemes affecting Livent's accounting records?
7. What professional standards apply to "due diligence" investigations performed by accounting firms?

## CASE 8.2

# Royal Ahold, N.V.

In 1887, a young Dutchman, Albert Heijn, entered the business world by purchasing a small grocery store from his father.[1] The store was located in Oostzaan, a village on the Dutch peninsula known as North Holland, which is also one of the Netherlands' 12 provinces. Unlike his father who was content to own and operate a small business, Albert had dreams of becoming an entrepreneur on a much larger scale. Within 10 years, the frugal and hard-working Heijn owned two dozen grocery stores scattered throughout the small country.

A key to the early success of Heijn's retail grocery chain was that he designed each of his new stores to meet the specific interests and needs of the community in which it was located. For example, the merchandise stocked by Heijn stores in fishing villages was quite different from the merchandise carried by stores located in farming communities. In metropolitan areas such as Amsterdam and The Hague, Heijn established large stores that stocked a complete range of food products and household merchandise. In fact, Heijn's company was credited with developing the supermarket concept in the Netherlands; in later years, his company popularized the convenience-store format in his home country.

In the early 1900s, Heijn launched his own brand of baked products including cookies and assorted pastries that he sold in his grocery stores. Over the years to come, the company would develop a wide range of its own products that it marketed under the Albert Heijn brand. In 1973, management changed the company's name to Ahold. The following decade, Queen Beatrix awarded the title "Royal" to the company, a designation reserved for Dutch companies that have operated continuously—and honorably—for one hundred years.[2]

By the early 1990s, Royal Ahold ranked among the most prominent and respected corporations in the Netherlands. For several years during that time frame, Royal Ahold was named the most desirable employer in the Netherlands and the company with the best reputation in that nation.[3] The company was also well known outside of its home country. In 1948, the Heijn family had taken the company public. By 2000, the company's stock was registered on stock exchanges around the world, including the New York Stock Exchange.

---

1. This case was originally published by the American Accounting Association in *Issues in Accounting Education*, Vol. 22 (November 2007) 641–660. The case was coauthored by Carol A. Knapp. I would like to thank Tracey Sutherland, Executive Director of the American Accounting Association, for granting permission to include this case in this edition of *Contemporary Auditing: Real Issues and Cases*. An instructional grant provided by Glen McLaughlin funded the development of this case. I would like to thank Mr. McLaughlin for his generous and continuing support of efforts to integrate ethics into business curricula.

2. "N.V." is an abbreviation for "naamloze vennootschap." This phrase indicates that Royal Ahold is a limited liability company under Dutch federal law whose ownership shares are publicly traded. Within the Netherlands, the company is known as Koninklijke Ahold, N.V.; in English-speaking countries, the company is referred to as Royal Ahold, N.V.

3. A. Kolk and J. Pinske, "Stakeholder Mismanagement and Corporate Social Responsibility Crisis," *European Management Journal*, Vol. 24 (February 2006), 59–72.

A financial scandal shortly after the turn of the century besmirched Royal Ahold's sterling reputation, prompted a consumer boycott of the company in the Netherlands, and resulted in many critics insisting that the Dutch royal family rescind the company's "royal" designation. In March 2003, *The Economist*, one of Europe's leading business publications, referred to the Royal Ahold scandal as "Europe's Enron."[4] The Royal Ahold scandal, along with the accounting fraud at the giant Italian firm Parmalat, caused the European Union (EU) to impose more extensive regulation on the financial reporting system and independent audit function within its member nations. The Royal Ahold debacle also focused more attention on the question of whether uniform accounting and auditing standards should be adopted around the globe.

## Going Global

By the mid-1970s, Royal Ahold's management realized that for the company to continue to grow it could not limit its operations to the Netherlands since it already dominated the retail grocery market in that country. At that point, the company's top executives, who had long been known for their conservative operating and financial policies, startled the Dutch business community by announcing that Royal Ahold would expand its operations into other countries.

Royal Ahold's expansion efforts got off to a slow start but then accelerated rapidly in the 1990s after the company hired a new management team. Until the late 1980s, members of the Heijn family had occupied the key management positions within the firm. In 1987, two grandsons of Albert Heijn, Ab Heijn and Gerrit-Jan Heijn, served as Royal Ahold's two top executives. In September 1987, Gerrit-Jan Heijn was kidnapped and murdered; shortly thereafter, his older brother retired from the company.[5] The professional management team hired to replace the Heijn brothers recognized that the quickest way for Royal Ahold to gain significant market share in the grocery retailing industry outside of the Netherlands was to purchase existing grocery chains in foreign countries. To finance their growth-by-acquisition policy, Royal Ahold's new executives raised large amounts of debt and equity capital during the 1990s.

By 2000, Royal Ahold had purchased retail grocery chains in Asia, Eastern Europe, Latin America, Portugal, Scandinavia, South America, and the United States. This aggressive expansion campaign made Royal Ahold the third-largest grocery retailer worldwide by the turn of the century. At the time, only U.S.-based Wal-Mart and the French firm Carrefour SA had larger annual retail grocery sales than Royal Ahold.

Royal Ahold completed its most ambitious acquisition in 2000 when it purchased U.S. Foodservice, a large food wholesaler headquartered in Columbia, Maryland, a suburb of Washington, D.C. Although Royal Ahold had previously purchased several retail grocery chains along the eastern seaboard of the United States, including New England-based Stop & Shop, U.S. Foodservice was easily the largest U.S. company it had acquired. The U.S. Foodservice acquisition was also important because it

4. *The Economist*, "Europe's Enron," 1 March 2003, 55–56.

5. *The Clearing*, a major motion picture released in 2004 that starred Robert Redford and Willem DaFoe, was based upon the kidnapping and murder of Gerrit-Jan Heijn, although the setting of the film was changed to the United States. Ironically, the perpetrator of the vicious crime was eventually apprehended when he attempted to purchase food in a grocery store with currency from the ransom that he had been paid by the Heijn family. After serving 12 years of a 20-year sentence, the kidnapper/murderer was released and returned to live with his family in The Netherlands. To protect the individual's privacy, the Dutch media insist on referring to him by his first name only.

signaled the company's commitment to becoming a significant participant in the food wholesaling industry.

In 2003, after purchasing two smaller U.S.-based food distributors, Royal Ahold ranked as the second-largest food wholesaler in the United States—Houston-based Sysco Corporation was the largest. In fact, the three U.S. acquisitions caused food wholesaling to be the company's largest source of revenue, accounting for slightly more than one-half of its annual sales. The company's more than 4,000 retail grocery stores located in 27 countries accounted for the remainder of its annual sales.

Royal Ahold's aggressive expansion plan created significant and largely unexpected challenges for company management. As Royal Ahold entered new markets, particularly markets outside of Western Europe and the United States, it encountered a wide range of laws, regulations, and cultural nuances that proved to be problematic for the company.

Human resource policies involving hiring practices, performance appraisal, and employee benefits that had been developed in the Netherlands were not necessarily well received by Royal Ahold's new managers and employees in Asia, Latin America, and South America. Likewise, because grocery shopping is a ritual significantly influenced by longstanding cultural norms across the globe, company officials found that customers in new markets often did not appreciate and sometimes flatly rejected the "Dutch" way of organizing and managing a grocery store. These and related problems convinced Royal Ahold's executives that the best strategy to use in managing their foreign grocery chains was to allow most major decisions to be made by the management personnel of those chains who were typically retained following an acquisition.

The headaches that Royal Ahold encountered due to its rapid expansion into retail grocery markets around the world were compounded by the company's decision to become a major player in the wholesaling segment of the huge food industry in the United States. Because company officials were largely unfamiliar with that segment of the industry, they applied their new hands-off mindset to that acquisition and relied almost exclusively on U.S. Foodservice's executives to oversee the subsidiary's day-to-day operations.

There was one key exception to the hands-off policy that Royal Ahold adopted with respect to its foreign operations. The company's top executives insisted that foreign operating units be held to the same rigorous performance standards that were imposed on the company's domestic operations. During the 1990s, the company's new management team established a goal of achieving a 15 percent annual growth rate in profits. That overall goal was then used by top management to establish annual earnings targets for each of the company's operating units in the Netherlands and elsewhere.

Royal Ahold's senior management pressured mid- and lower-level managers throughout the company's worldwide network to reach the earnings goal established for their individual operating units. According to a former Royal Ahold official, managers who met their unit's earnings target were rewarded with significant year-end bonuses. "Ahold was determined to maintain earnings growth of at least 15 percent annually. All of the operating units had difficult targets to meet, but the rewards [in the form of bonuses] were good if targets were met."[6] In retrospect, the earnings targets for many of Royal Ahold's newly acquired operating units were unrealistic. Intense competition and the historically modest profit margins within the food industry prevented many of those units from achieving their annual earnings goals.

6. A. Raghavan, A. Latour, and M. Schroeder, "Questioning the Books—A Global Journal Report: Ahold Faces Scrutiny over Accounting," *Wall Street Journal*, 26 February 2003, A2.

Similar to most major corporations, Royal Ahold had an ethical code that discouraged executives and employees from engaging in dishonest or otherwise unethical conduct. The company's "Code of Professional Conduct" included the following section that dealt specifically with accounting and financial reporting matters.

> *The integrity and completeness of record keeping is not only Ahold policy, but also law. We properly, accurately, and fairly record our financial transactions. Preventing fraud is an important priority at Ahold, both to protect Ahold's reputation and to prevent loss. Fraud is defined as committing illicit or illegal acts involving money and/or goods to achieve financial benefit, to benefit oneself or others, at a disadvantage to the company or others.*[7]

Despite such strong statements, beginning in the late 1990s, Royal Ahold's annual financial statements were distorted by a series of fraudulent accounting schemes perpetrated by self-interested executives and their subordinates. When the company's independent auditors discovered the misrepresentations in those financial statements, the prominent corporation suffered widespread embarrassment and condemnation as well as financial problems that threatened its ability to remain a going concern.

## Royal Problems

Deloitte Accountants, B.V., had served as Royal Ahold's "group auditor" since 1973.[8] The "group auditor" designation means that the Netherlands-based Deloitte Accountants oversaw the audits of the company's annual consolidated financial statements, although accounting firms in other countries, such as the United States, participated in those audits. Deloitte shocked Royal Ahold's top executives when the accounting firm announced in early 2003 that it was suspending its fiscal year 2002 audit of the company. According to Deloitte, auditors assigned to various operating units of Royal Ahold had uncovered questionable accounting and financial reporting practices that had to be thoroughly investigated before the audit could be completed.

Deloitte's announcement sent Royal Ahold's stock price into a nosedive. Over a short period of time in early 2003, the company's stock price plummeted by approximately 70 percent. During this same time frame, Standard & Poor's and Moody's slashed Royal Ahold's credit rating, which drove down the market price of the company's outstanding debt securities and made it difficult for the company to raise additional capital in either the debt or equity markets. The problems facing Royal Ahold caused one London-based financial analyst to suggest that there was a "very real risk" that the large firm would be forced into bankruptcy.[9]

Royal Ahold's board of directors responded quickly to the crisis that engulfed the company following Deloitte's decision to suspend its 2002 audit.[10] The board's first major decision was to fire Royal Ahold's chief executive officer (CEO) and chief financial officer (CFO), each of whom had been implicated in the company's accounting irregularities. The board also announced plans to raise much-needed capital by

---

7. Royal Ahold, *Code of Professional Conduct: The Basic Rules of the Game* (Zaandaam, the Netherlands: Royal Ahold), 2002.

8. "B.V." is an abbreviation for "besloten vennootschap." This phrase indicates that Deloitte Accountants is a limited liability company whose ownership shares are privately registered and thus not freely transferable.

9. V. de Boer, "Ahold Fires CEO, CFO over Inflated Profit," *Financial Post*, 25 February 2003, FP 12.

10. In fact, major Dutch companies typically have a two-tiered corporate governance structure that consists of a "supervisory board" and a "management board." For purposes of this case, Royal Ahold's two boards are simply referred to as the "board of directors."

selling several of its foreign subsidiaries. Finally, and most importantly, Royal Ahold's board pledged that it would fully cooperate with all law enforcement and regulatory agencies investigating the company's financial affairs and take the appropriate measures to ensure that the sources of the accounting problems were identified and eliminated. These measures served to bolster the flagging confidence of investors and lenders in the company.

## Accounting and Disclosure Issues at Royal Ahold

The investigative agencies that scrutinized Royal Ahold's accounting records identified three principal sources of the material misrepresentations in the company's financial statements. Royal Ahold had improperly included financial data of certain foreign joint ventures in its consolidated financial statements, which resulted in large overstatements of its consolidated revenues and assets. The company had also accounted improperly for the initial investments in many of those foreign joint ventures. Finally, a forensic investigation authorized by Royal Ahold's senior management uncovered extensive fraud in the accounting records of U.S. Foodservice, the company's large United States subsidiary.

Royal Ahold's 2001 financial statements were the final financial statements issued by the company for a complete fiscal year prior to the discovery of the accounting fraud. Exhibit 1 and Exhibit 2 present the comparative income statements and balance sheets, respectively, included in the Form 20-F registration statement filed by Royal Ahold with the Securities and Exchange Commission (SEC) for fiscal 2001. Foreign companies registered with the SEC file a Form 20-F annually with that federal agency, a registration statement comparable in most respects to the Form 10-K filed with the SEC by U.S.-based companies.

**EXHIBIT 1**

1999–2001 ROYAL AHOLD, N.V., CONSOLIDATED STATEMENTS OF EARNINGS

**Royal Ahold, N.V.**
**Consolidated Statements of Earnings**
**(expressed in thousands of euros, except share and per share amounts)**

| | Fiscal Year | | |
|---|---|---|---|
| | 2001 | 2000 | 1999 |
| **Net sales** | 66,593,065 | 51,541,601 | 32,824,327 |
| Cost of sales | (51,877,136) | (39,654,486) | (24,470,282) |
| **Gross profit** | 14,715,929 | 11,887,115 | 8,354,045 |
| Selling expenses | (9,650,092) | (7,905,310) | (5,806,134) |
| General and administrative expenses | (2,087,536) | (1,702,476) | (1,133,239) |
| Goodwill amortization | (166,496) | (5,236) | — |
| Exceptional results | (106,413) | — | — |
| **Operating results** | 2,705,392 | 2,274,093 | 1,414,672 |
| Interest income | 90,065 | 87,021 | 58,589 |
| Interest expenses | (1,020,853) | (808,990) | (420,820) |
| Exchange rate differences | (101,484) | 51,542 | (6,479) |
| Other financial income/expense | (961) | 1,162 | 2,516 |
| Net financial expense | (1,033,233) | (669,265) | (366,194) |

(continued)

**EXHIBIT 1—*continued***

1999–2001 ROYAL AHOLD, N.V., CONSOLIDATED STATEMENTS OF EARNINGS

**Royal Ahold, N.V.**
**Consolidated Statements of Earnings**
**(expressed in thousands of euros, except share and per share amounts)**

| | Fiscal Year | | |
|---|---|---|---|
| | **2001** | **2000** | **1999** |
| **Earnings before income taxes and minority interest** | 1,672,159 | 1,604,828 | 1,048,478 |
| Income taxes | (457,364) | (401,010) | (283,001) |
| **Earnings after income taxes and before minority interest** | 1,214,795 | 1,203,818 | 765,477 |
| Income from unconsolidated companies | 14,553 | 14,562 | 7,437 |
| Minority interests | (115,827) | (102,389) | (20,807) |
| **Net earnings** | 1,113,521 | 1,115,991 | 752,107 |
| Dividend cumulative preferred financing shares | 38,177 | 17,444 | 12,167 |
| **Net earnings after preferred dividends** | 1,075,344 | 1,098,547 | 739,940 |
| Weighted average number of common shares outstanding (× 1,000) | 857,509 | 737,403 | 657,230 |
| **Earnings per common share** | 1.25 | 1.49 | 1.13 |
| **Diluted earnings per common share** | 1.23 | 1.43 | 1.10 |

Source: Royal Ahold's 2001 Form 20-F filed with the Securities and Exchange Commission (SEC).

**EXHIBIT 2**

2000–2001 ROYAL AHOLD, N.V., CONSOLIDATED BALANCE SHEETS

**Royal Ahold, N.V.**
**Consolidated Balance Sheets**
**(expressed in thousands of euros)**

| | **December 30, 2001** | **December 31, 2000** |
|---|---|---|
| **Assets** | | |
| **Current assets:** | | |
| Cash and cash equivalents | 1,972,273 | 1,335,592 |
| Receivables | 3,453,869 | 2,849,275 |
| Inventories | 5,067,035 | 4,100,223 |
| Other current assets | 551,106 | 576,876 |
| **Total current assets** | 11,044,283 | 8,861,966 |
| **Non-current assets:** | | |
| Tangible fixed assets, net of depreciation: | | |
| Buildings and land | 7,659,768 | 6,855,938 |
| Machinery and equipment and other | 5,698,480 | 4,730,821 |
| Under construction | 713,581 | 645,892 |
| Total tangible fixed assets | 14,071,829 | 12,232,651 |

**EXHIBIT 2—*continued***

2000–2001 ROYAL AHOLD, N.V., CONSOLIDATED BALANCE SHEETS

**Royal Ahold, N.V.**
**Consolidated Balance Sheets**
**(expressed in thousands of euros)**

| | **December 30, 2001** | **December 31, 2000** |
|---|---|---|
| Intangible fixed assets, net of amortization | 5,648,679 | 3,152,688 |
| Investments in unconsolidated companies | 424,066 | 407,843 |
| Loans receivable | 534,157 | 414,055 |
| Deferred income taxes | 513,450 | 391,421 |
| **Total non-current assets** | 21,192,181 | 16,598,658 |
| **Total assets** | 32,236,464 | 25,460,624 |
| **Liabilities and shareholders' equity** | | |
| **Current liabilities:** | | |
| Loans payable | 1,848,912 | 2,335,345 |
| Taxes payable | 715,850 | 551,185 |
| Accounts payable | 6,029,505 | 5,185,432 |
| Accrued expenses | 1,530,520 | 1,418,778 |
| Other current liabilities | 945,799 | 710,120 |
| **Total current liabilities** | 11,070,586 | 10,220,860 |
| **Long-term liabilities:** | | |
| Subordinated loans | 1,779,684 | 1,779,907 |
| Other loans | 9,282,752 | 7,183,514 |
| Total subordinated loans & other | 11,062,436 | 8,963,421 |
| Capitalized lease commitments | 1,512,236 | 1,336,567 |
| Deferred income taxes | 437,982 | 362,949 |
| Other provisions | 1,576,570 | 1,396,882 |
| **Total long-term liabilities** | 14,589,224 | 12,059,819 |
| **Commitments and contingencies (note 20)** | | |
| **Minority interest** | 684,540 | 677,379 |
| **Shareholders' equity:** | | |
| Cumulative preferred shares | — | — |
| Cumulative preferred financing shares | 64,829 | 64,829 |
| Common shares | 230,245 | 204,213 |
| Additional paid-in capital | 11,218,491 | 8,675,969 |
| Revaluation reserve | 20,521 | 26,124 |
| Reserve shareholdings | 34,668 | 14,589 |
| Reserve for exchange rate differences | (189,714) | (85,270) |
| General reserve | (5,486,926) | (6,397,888) |
| **Total shareholders' equity** | 5,892,114 | 2,502,566 |
| **Total liabilities and shareholders' equity** | 32,236,464 | 25,460,624 |

Source: Royal Ahold's 2001 Form 20-F filed with the Securities and Exchange Commission (SEC).

Until late 2007, the SEC required a foreign company such as Royal Ahold to include in its annual Form 20-F a schedule that reconciled its net income determined by accounting principles applied in its home country to the net income that would have been produced by the application of U.S. generally accepted accounting principles (GAAP). Exhibit 3 presents those reconciliations for the three-year period 1999–2001.

**EXHIBIT 3**

RECONCILIATION OF ROYAL AHOLD'S NET EARNINGS BASED ON DUTCH GAAP TO ITS NET EARNINGS BASED ON U.S. GAAP

**Reconciliation of Royal Ahold's Net Earnings Based on Dutch GAAP to Its Net Earnings Based on U.S. GAAP (expressed in thousands of euros)**

| | | Fiscal Year | |
|---|---|---|---|
| | **2001** | **2000** | **1999** |
| Net earnings in accordance with Dutch GAAP | 1,113,521 | 1,115,991 | 752,107 |
| Items having the effect of increasing (decreasing) reported net earnings: | | | |
| a) Goodwill | (728,210) | (300,266) | (147,378) |
| b) Pensions | 23,811 | 16,596 | 6,552 |
| c) Revaluation of real estate | 1,882 | 2,175 | 2,263 |
| d) Restructuring costs | 33,219 | (1,143) | (19,202) |
| e) Other provisions | (57,556) | (21,434) | (28,630) |
| f) Sale-leaseback of property | (137,421) | — | — |
| g) Derivatives | (132,549) | — | — |
| h) Software costs | (5,360) | (5,360) | 10,109 |
| i) Deferred taxes | 46,648 | 4,494 | 9,825 |
| Subtotal | 157,985 | 811,053 | 585,646 |
| j) Dividends on cumulative preferred financing shares | (38,177) | (17,444) | (12,167) |
| Net earnings in accordance with U.S. GAAP applicable to common shares | 119,808 | 793,609 | 573,479 |

Source: Royal Ahold's 2001 Form 20-F filed with the Securities and Exchange Commission (SEC).

## *Joint Venture Accounting*

The growth-oriented policies of the management team hired to replace Ab and Gerrit-Jan Heijn stressed the importance of not only achieving an annual earnings growth rate of 15 percent but also placed a heavy emphasis on rapidly expanding the company's annual revenues. The new management team established a goal of doubling Royal Ahold's sales every five years. Royal Ahold's growth-through-acquisition strategy allowed the company to increase its reported sales from approximately 7.7 billion euros in 1990 to 62.7 billion euros in 2002. The impressive revenue growth gave Royal Ahold increasing credibility in the global equity and debt markets, which, in turn, allowed the company to raise the capital needed to finance its expansion program.

During the fiscal 2002 audit of Royal Ahold, Deloitte Accountants uncovered evidence suggesting that the company's consolidated revenues had been overstated. When Royal Ahold invested in a foreign company, it often acquired exactly a 50 percent ownership interest in the given company. Nevertheless, Royal Ahold would fully consolidate the company's financial data in its annual financial statements. Dutch accounting rules at the time permitted a parent company to fully consolidate the financial data of a joint venture company if the parent could control that firm's operations. Such control could be evidenced by a more than 50 percent ownership interest in the joint venture company or by other means.

Since Royal Ahold had exactly a 50 percent ownership interest in several foreign firms, the company's executives had to persuade the Deloitte auditors that they exercised effective control over those firms' operations to include their financial data in Royal Ahold's consolidated financial statements. To accomplish this goal, the company's top executives gave the auditors letters signed by key officials of the given joint venture companies. These letters informed the auditors that despite having only a 50 percent ownership interest in the company in question, Royal Ahold exercised effective control over the company's operations. In fact, Royal Ahold's management team had goaded officials of the joint venture companies to provide these letters to the Deloitte auditors. At the same time the "control letters" were forwarded to Deloitte, Royal Ahold's management signed "side letters" addressed to the executives of the joint venture companies that negated the control letters. The side letters indicated that major decisions affecting the joint venture companies would be made mutually by Royal Ahold executives and the other owners or executives of those companies.

Because Royal Ahold did not have effective control over the joint venture companies in which it had only a 50 percent ownership interest, those companies' financial data should not have been fully consolidated in the annual Royal Ahold financial statements. For Dutch accounting purposes, the joint ventures' financial data should have been "proportionately" consolidated. For example, 50 percent of the total revenues and expenses of the joint venture companies should have been included in Royal Ahold's annual consolidated income statement.

The decision to fully consolidate the financial data of the joint venture companies resulted in material errors in Royal Ahold's consolidated financial statements. In its 2001 consolidated balance sheet, Royal Ahold reported total assets of 32.2 billion euros. That figure included 4.4 billion euros of assets that Dutch regulatory authorities required Royal Ahold to "deconsolidate" when the company subsequently issued restated financial statements. Likewise, the improper joint venture accounting overstated Royal Ahold's reported consolidated revenues of 66.6 billion euros for 2001 by 12.2 billion euros.

Besides improperly accounting for its ownership interests in numerous joint venture companies, Royal Ahold failed to disclose that it had an obligation to purchase the ownership interests of certain investors in those companies. For example, Royal Ahold had committed itself to purchasing the residual ownership interest in a joint venture company based in Argentina if that company defaulted on its outstanding debt.

Because of poor economic conditions in South America, the Argentine company defaulted on its outstanding debt in 2002—resulting in Royal Ahold being required to buy out the company's other investors.

## *Initial Accounting for Investments in Foreign Joint Ventures*

In the late 1990s, Dutch accounting principles allowed companies to charge off against stockholders' equity goodwill arising from the acquisition of another company. Under U.S. GAAP at the time, companies were required to report goodwill resulting from an acquisition as an asset and to amortize that asset to expense over a time period not to exceed 40 years.

As Royal Ahold acquired ownership interests in an increasing number of companies during the late 1990s, the company became increasingly aggressive in accounting for the initial purchase transactions. Royal Ahold inflated the amount of goodwill arising from acquisitions of other companies and then promptly charged this goodwill against its stockholders' equity. The company also improperly charged off various acquisition-related expenses to stockholders' equity at the time of each acquisition. These abusive accounting practices helped Royal Ahold management meet or exceed its goal of achieving 15 percent earnings growth each year. The restated financial statements subsequently issued by Royal Ahold revealed that improper "acquisition accounting" had inflated the company's reported net income for 2001 and 2000 by 36 million euros and 8 million euros, respectively.

## *Fraudulent Accounting at U.S. Foodservice*

Deloitte Accountants' U.S. affiliate, Deloitte & Touche, audited the financial statements of U.S. Foodservice after that company was acquired by Royal Ahold in 2000. During the fiscal 2002 audit of U.S. Foodservice, the Deloitte auditors uncovered improper accounting decisions that had a material impact on the company's reported profit for that year. The improper accounting at U.S. Foodservice also materially distorted the consolidated net income of Royal Ahold. Deloitte's subsequent investigation revealed that U.S. Foodservice had been intentionally misrepresenting its financial statements for several years prior to its acquisition by Royal Ahold.

The accounting fraud at U.S. Foodservice involved "promotional allowances." Because the food wholesaling industry is intensely competitive, the companies operating in that industry have very small profit margins on their sales. In fact, the profit margins within the industry result principally from rebates, quantity discounts, "program money," and other promotional allowances paid to food wholesalers by their suppliers or vendors. For example, if U.S. Foodservice purchased $100 million of merchandise from General Mills during 2002, General Mills may have refunded 5 percent of that amount to U.S. Foodservice. Generally, the more merchandise purchased from a vendor by a food wholesaler, the larger the promotional allowance on a percentage basis.

U.S. Foodservice had various contractual agreements with its vendors regarding the volume of promotional allowances to which it was entitled and the timing of the related payments. A common agreement involved basing the prepayment of promotional allowances to U.S. Foodservice on an expected minimum amount of purchase volume over a multiyear period. Suppose, for example, that U.S. Foodservice expected to purchase $30 million from a given vendor over the three-year period 2000–2002. The vendor may have agreed to pay U.S. Foodservice $900,000, or 3 percent, of that amount as a promotional allowance. Most likely, the payment would have been made in early 2000, within the first few weeks of the period covered by the contractual agreement between the two parties.

Despite the material effect that promotional allowances had on U.S. Foodservice's operating results, the company did not have a systematic method of accounting for those allowances. "USF had no comprehensive, automated system for tracking the amounts owed by vendors pursuant to the promotional allowance agreements."[11] The absence of proper internal controls over promotional allowances provided an

11. Securities and Exchange Commission, *Complaint in re SEC vs. Resnick et al.*, July 2004. (Available at SEC website: www.sec.gov).

opportunity for dishonest employees to overstate those allowances for accounting purposes, which is exactly what occurred beginning in the late 1990s. When Royal Ahold acquired U.S. Foodservice in 2000, the improper accounting for promotional allowances escalated. Apparently, many U.S. Foodservice managers began overstating promotional allowances to ensure that their operating units reached the challenging earnings goals assigned to them by Royal Ahold.

Among the most common methods used by U.S. Foodservice managers to overstate their promotional allowances was to simply inflate the promotional allowance percentages allegedly being paid by given vendors. If a vendor had agreed to pay a 5 percent refund on purchases, U.S. Foodservice might record a promotional allowance equal to 7 percent of the purchases made from that vendor. Another common scheme was "front-loading" promotional allowances. For example, suppose that a vendor paid U.S. Foodservice a $2 million promotional allowance for the three-year period, 2000–2002. U.S. Foodservice might record the full amount of that allowance as a reduction in cost of sales for 2000 rather than prorating the allowance over the three-year period. Eventually, some U.S. Foodservice managers resorted to recording totally fictitious promotional allowances. These fictitious promotional allowances were typically recorded as "topside" adjustments to U.S. Foodservice's financial statements at the end of an accounting period.[12]

Of the three principal accounting frauds used by Royal Ahold to misrepresent its reported operating results, the improper accounting for promotional allowances at U.S. Foodservice easily had the most dramatic impact on the company's reported profits. In 2001, alone, the improper accounting for the promotional allowances overstated Royal Ahold's earnings by approximately 215 million euros. This amount accounted for 60 percent of the net overstatement of Royal Ahold's 2001 reported net income. As shown in Exhibit 1, the company reported a net income of 1.11 billion euros for 2001; the actual earnings figure for that year was 750 million euros.

## Pinpointing Responsibility for the Royal Ahold Fiasco

In the fall of 2003, Royal Ahold issued restated financial statements for 2000, 2001, and the first three quarters of 2002. The net income figures that Royal Ahold originally reported for those three periods had been overstated by 17.6 percent, 32.6 percent, and 88.1 percent, respectively. The corresponding overstatements of the company's reported revenues for those three periods were 20.8 percent, 18.6 percent, and 13.8 percent, respectively.

Similar to other recent accounting and financial reporting scandals, the public disclosure of the Royal Ahold fraud triggered a search by regulatory agencies, law enforcement authorities, the business press, and the investment community for the parties responsible for the fraud. Among the most culpable parties were the top executives of Royal Ahold. The new management team hired by the company's board to replace Ab and Gerrit-Jan Heijn created an environment in which fraud often develops and flourishes. The pressure exerted by that management team on their subordinates to achieve unrealistic earnings and revenue goals—when coupled with the significant incentive compensation that could be earned by reaching those goals—almost certainly prompted much of the self-serving behavior within Royal Ahold.

Despite the fact that Royal Ahold's Deloitte auditors were intentionally misled by the company's executives and the fact that those auditors were ultimately responsible for ending the fraud, many parties believed that Deloitte should have discovered and

12. "Topside" adjustments are made directly to a company's financial statements without first being recorded in its accounting records.

revealed the fraud earlier than it did. In fact, Deloitte was named as a defendant in several large class-action lawsuits filed subsequent to the first published reports of the fraud. In defense of the Deloitte auditors, they faced an onerous task each year in planning and coordinating an annual audit that was, in reality, audits of dozens of individual operating units loosely organized under the Royal Ahold corporate umbrella.

Many parties also held regulatory agencies and oversight bodies within the accounting profession at least partially responsible for the Royal Ahold debacle. The Royal Ahold case clearly confirmed the need for what the London-based *Financial Times* referred to as "cross-border cooperation" between and among the regulatory agencies and rule-making bodies that oversee financial reporting and independent auditing across the globe.[13] In recent years, a spirit of competition rather than cooperation has often prevailed between such organizations, particularly between those organizations in the United States and those in other developed countries.

The principal source of tension among international rule-making bodies in the accounting profession has been differing philosophies regarding what should be the fundamental nature of professional standards. The Financial Accounting Standards Board in the United States has generally insisted on issuing "prescriptive" or detailed accounting standards. On the other hand, the International Accounting Standards Board, which is responsible for issuing International Financial Reporting Standards that EU-based companies were required to adopt by 2005, believes that accounting standards should be general guidelines that are principles-based. This philosophical difference often results in financial statements prepared for a company under U.S. and EU accounting rules that are not comparable. Such lack of comparability can result in confusion on the part of financial statement users and, ultimately, in less-than-optimal decisions on their part.

Even more tension between international oversight bodies in the accounting and auditing disciplines was spawned by the Royal Ahold case when the U.S.-based Public Company Accounting Oversight Board (PCAOB) used the case to justify one of its most controversial policies. This policy required non-U.S. accounting firms to register with the PCAOB and be subject to the PCAOB's regulatory oversight. As the Royal Ahold scandal was unfolding, the PCAOB implied that the case demonstrated that foreign accounting and auditing regulatory bodies were failing to fulfill their oversight responsibilities.[14] The PCAOB's insinuation prompted indignant responses from professional organizations within several member nations of the EU and other nations as well. For example, the Japanese Institute of Certified Public Accountants (JICPA) sent an open letter to the SEC in which it criticized the PCAOB's policy. "We believe that the oversight system [for independent audits] in Japan should be relied upon without necessitating PCAOB inspection. Japan has an oversight system which is equivalent to the oversight required of professional accountants in the U.S."[15]

Finally, many parties charged that a large measure of responsibility for the recent series of audit failures involving multinational corporations such as Royal Ahold and Parmalat should be borne collectively by the small fraternity of international accounting firms that dominate the global auditing discipline. According to the *Financial*

---

13. P. Koster, "Europe's Auditors Should Give Us the Bad News," *Financial Times*, 19 January 2004, 13.

14. A. de Jong, D. DeJong, G. Mertens, and P. Roosenboom, "Royal Ahold: A Failure of Corporate Governance," Working paper presented at Erasmus University, Rotterdam, the Netherlands, 14 January 2005.

15. Letter addressed to Jonathan Katz, member of the SEC, dated June 27, 2003, from Akio Okuyama, President and CEO of the Japanese Institute of Certified Public Accountants. (Available at SEC website: www.sec.gov.)

*Times*, the major international accounting firms have "franchised their names like the McDonald's burger chain, but without its quality control."[16] The *Financial Times* went on to note that the major accounting firms are, in fact, only "loose confederal" organizations. As a result, users of audited financial statements of multinational corporations located across the globe have no basis for judging the quality of those audits even if they are performed by accounting firms within the same organization.

## EPILOGUE

Following the public disclosure of the Royal Ahold fraud in 2003 both Dutch and U.S. law enforcement authorities filed criminal charges against the company and several of its former executives. The *Financial Times* reported that the Royal Ahold case was the "most significant white-collar criminal case"[17] ever pursued by federal authorities in the Netherlands. Shortly after criminal charges were filed in the case, a Dutch prosecutor asked the SEC not to pursue the charges that it had filed against the company and its former Netherlands-based executives since doing so would raise a "double jeopardy" issue under Dutch law. In responding to the request, the SEC noted, "Because of the importance of the case in the Netherlands and the need for further cooperation between the SEC and regulatory authorities in other countries, the Commission has agreed to the Dutch prosecutor's request."[18]

In September 2004, the fraud charges filed against Royal Ahold by Dutch law enforcement authorities were settled. The settlement required Royal Ahold to pay a fine of approximately 8 million euros. In May 2006, a Dutch court found three of Royal Ahold's former executives guilty of fraud charges that had been filed against them. Those executives included the company's former CEO and CFO. The tribunal of judges that presided over the case gave the three former executives suspended prison sentences ranging from four to nine months. In addition, the three men received fines ranging from 120,000 euros to 225,000 euros—fines that were subsequently reduced by Dutch courts by as much as 90 percent. One of the judges who presided over the case defended the light sentences imposed on the three individuals. This judge maintained that although the Royal Ahold fraud was unfortunate and embarrassing to the Dutch business community and Dutch citizens, it was not nearly as serious as either the Enron scandal in the United States or the Parmalat scandal in Italy.[19]

A shareholders' activist group in the Netherlands was appalled by the minimal penalties imposed on the three former Royal Ahold executives. A spokesperson for that group noted, "The judgment sends a signal to managers that no matter what they do, the risk of a heavy punishment is minimal. In the United States, a conviction on the same facts would have led to a prison term of more than 10 years. This is Holland at its smallest."[20]

In July 2004, the SEC announced that it had filed fraud charges against four former executives of U.S. Foodservice. These individuals included the company's former CFO, former

16. J. Plender, "Problems at Ahold, Parmalat, and Now Adecco Raise New Questions about How Global Accounting Firms Work with Multinationals," *Financial Times*, 22 January 2004, 15.

17. I. Bickerton, "Four Ahold Directors Face Court Hearing in Accounting Scandal," *Financial Times*, 6 March 2006, 28.

18. Securities and Exchange Commission, *Accounting and Auditing Enforcement Release No. 2124*, 13 October 2004.

19. T. Sterling, "Royal Ahold Executives Fined after Conviction," *Associated Press Online*, 22 May 2006.

20. *Ibid.*

chief marketing officer, and two former executives in the company's purchasing division. The two former purchasing executives settled the charges by agreeing to permanent injunctions that prohibited them from being officers or directors of public companies and by forfeiting stock market gains they had earned on the sale of Royal Ahold's common stock during the course of the fraud. In September 2006, the former CFO pleaded guilty to one count of conspiracy and was given three years of probation by a federal judge. In November 2006, a federal jury found U.S. Foodservice's former chief marketing officer guilty of conspiracy and federal securities fraud. The following year he was sentenced to seven years in federal prison.[21]

In February 2006, the SEC filed charges against two former auditors of U.S. Foodservice, the audit engagement partner and senior audit manager who had been assigned to the company's 1999 audit engagement team. From 1996 through the conclusion of the 1999 audit in April 2000, KPMG had served as the independent audit firm of U.S. Foodservice. When the company was acquired by Royal Ahold in 2000, Deloitte Accountants, B.V., chose Deloitte & Touche to audit the U.S. Foodservice financial statements that were to be incorporated in Royal Ahold's consolidated financial statements.

The SEC alleged that the two former KPMG auditors violated numerous generally accepted auditing standards (GAAS) during the performance of the 1999 U.S. Foodservice audit. The SEC's most serious allegation was that the two auditors had identified several instances in which the company had improperly recorded promotional allowances and then later used white correction liquid to obscure the audit exceptions that documented those items. Those audit exceptions were allegedly masked with correction liquid before the U.S. Foodservice workpapers were turned over to the SEC—the federal agency had requested the workpapers during the course of its investigation of the U.S. Foodservice accounting fraud.

Among other allegations, the SEC charged that the two auditors frequently relied on implausible representations made to them by client officials. By failing to investigate those suspicious statements and other red flags apparent during the 1999 audit, the SEC maintained that the two auditors failed to exercise a proper degree of professional skepticism, failed to propose proper adjustments to U.S. Foodservice's financial statements, and failed to collect sufficient competent evidence to support the audit opinion rendered on those financial statements. In commenting on the case, an SEC spokesperson observed, "These auditors had evidence in their hands that could have stopped the fraud in its tracks. Instead, because they failed to exercise appropriate professional skepticism, the fraud was allowed to continue."[22,23]

In January 2008, a federal judge dismissed the allegations of improper professional conduct filed against the two former KPMG auditors by the SEC. Among other factors, the judge based her decision to dismiss those charges on the extreme degree of deception that U.S. Foodservice personnel used to mislead the two auditors and on the failure of the SEC to corroborate its allegations with appropriate evidence. For example, according to the judge, the SEC failed to provide any evidence to support its claim that the two auditors were the individuals who had used correction fluid to obscure the audit exceptions that documented improper accounting decisions by U.S. Foodservice.

In November 2005, the SEC announced that it had filed enforcement actions against several individuals who were employees or executives of major U.S. Foodservice vendors. According to the SEC, each of these individuals had signed false confirmations regarding the amount of promotional allowances owed to U.S. Foodservice by their given company. The SEC reported that several of these individuals had been pressured by U.S. Foodservice management personnel to sign and return the false confirmations to Deloitte. In one case, an executive of a food

21. In March 2007, Royal Ahold sold U.S. Foodservice to two U.S.-based private equity firms.

22. A. K. Walker, "SEC Faults KPMG Audits," *The Baltimore Sun*, 17 February 2006, 1E.

23. The SEC did not file any charges against members of the Deloitte & Touche audit engagement teams assigned to the 2000 and 2001 U.S. Foodservice audits.

vendor signed a confirmation indicating that his company owed U.S. Foodservice $3.2 million when the actual amount was only $68,000. Each of the individuals agreed to pay a $25,000 fine to the SEC to settle the charges filed against them. In commenting on the settlement of these charges, an SEC spokesperson observed, "The use of third-party confirmations is an important part of the audit process, and the Commission will hold accountable those who work to subvert it."[24]

Also in November 2005, Royal Ahold announced that it had reached an agreement to settle a large class-action lawsuit filed against it by the company's stockholders and former stockholders. Under the terms of the agreement, Royal Ahold contributed approximately 1.1 billion euros to a settlement pool that would be distributed to the class-action plaintiffs. Shortly after the announcement of this settlement, another class-action lawsuit was filed by Royal Ahold's U.S. stockholders against the company's Deloitte auditors. In January 2009, a federal judge dismissed this latter lawsuit when he concluded that the Deloitte auditors were "victims of Ahold's fraud rather than its enablers."[25]

In responding to the controversy generated by the Royal Ahold debacle, the European Parliament, which is the legislative body of the EU, amended the "8th Directive" that includes the various guidelines and rules to be followed by accounting firms performing independent audits of EU-based companies.[26] The new 8th Directive includes a requirement that foreign accounting firms involved in the audits of EU-based companies must be registered with regulatory authorities in the EU. A European publication noted that this new requirement was an apparent "tit-for-tat response" to the comparable requirement of the PCAOB.[27,28]

Among other changes, the revised 8th Directive imposes greater responsibility on group auditors to review and pass judgment on the overall quality of an independent audit and mandates that member nations of the EU establish "effective investigative and disciplinary systems" for accounting firms that perform independent audits. The revised directive also establishes common rules regarding the appointment and resignation of independent auditors, requires that auditors obtain appropriate training regarding International Financial Reporting Standards and International Standards of Auditing, and requires audit clients to disclose the fees paid to their independent auditors for both audit and nonaudit services.

---

24. S. Taub, "SEC Charges Seven in Ahold Fraud," *CFO.com*, 3 November 2005.

25. S. Andrussier, "4th Circuit Tosses Securities Fraud Class-Action Against Deloitte," North Carolina Appellate Blog (womblencappellate.blogspot.com), 7 January 2009.

26. When the European Parliament adopts a "directive," each member nation of the EU is committed to initiating legislation that, if enacted, would implement the requirements of that directive. However, the relevant legislative body within each EU nation may or may not fully adopt the stipulations of a new directive.

27. European Information Service, *European Report* (online), "Auditing: Commission Proposes Tough New Rules to Restore Market Confidence," 17 March 2004.

28. In May 2009, the PCAOB released a list of countries for which it intended to perform inspections of accounting firms that served as the auditors of one or more SEC registrants. Among others, these countries included Australia, Canada, France, Germany, Hong Kong, Israel, Mexico, the Netherlands, Norway, Russia, Sweden, Switzerland, and the United Kingdom. The release of that list created so much controversy that three months later the PCAOB announced that it was delaying the international inspections for up to three years.

## Questions

1. To arrive at the U.S. GAAP-based net income figures shown in Exhibit 3, Royal Ahold fully consolidated the operating results of the companies in which it held a 50 percent equity interest. For purposes of determining its U.S. GAAP-based net income figures, what accounting method should the company have applied to those investments? How would the application of this latter method have affected the U.S. GAAP-based net income amounts?
2. The application of Dutch GAAP and U.S. GAAP to Royal Ahold's financial data produced significantly different net earnings figures for the company each year. Explain what is meant by "earnings quality." Suppose that the application of IFRS to a company's financial data produces a higher net income for that company than the application of U.S. GAAP. Does this mean that the U.S. GAAP-based net income figure is of "higher quality" than the net income figure yielded by IFRS? Explain.
3. Accounting for promotional allowances in the retailing and wholesaling industries has long been a controversial topic. In 2002, the Emerging Issues Task Force (EITF) of the Financial Accounting Standards Board began studying that issue. What changes, if any, did the EITF make in the recommended accounting for such promotional allowances?
4. Identify the factors that complicate an independent audit of a multinational company. Explain how these factors affected the audits of Royal Ahold that were performed by Deloitte Accountants, B.V., and its affiliated firms.
5. Briefly describe the three elements of the "fraud triangle." Identify specific fraud risk factors that were present during the audits of Royal Ahold that were performed by Deloitte Accountants. How should those risk factors have affected Deloitte's audits?
6. What audit procedures would likely have been the most effective for detecting the fraudulent accounting for U.S. Foodservice's promotional allowances?
7. Royal Ahold's two major business segments were food wholesaling and retail grocery chains. Identify and briefly explain three key differences in the overall design of an audit for those two types of business segments.

## CASE 8.3

# *Kansayaku*

*Kokai saki ni tatazu [repentance never comes first]*

*Japanese proverb*

Satoshi Hirata served on the audit staff of Asahi, one of Japan's four largest public accounting firms.[1] Like its three principal rivals, Asahi was affiliated with one of the Big Four international accounting firms, namely, KPMG. Throughout the spring of 2003, Hirata had been assigned to the audit of Resona, a large metropolitan bank. The bank was being audited jointly by Asahi and Shin Nihon, the Japanese affiliate of Ernst & Young. On April 24, 2003, after completing his work for the day on the Resona engagement, Satoshi Hirata returned to his 12-story apartment building in central Tokyo, went to the roof of that building, and leaped to his death.

### Disloyal Auditors

Although Satoshi Hirata did not leave a note explaining his decision to take his life, law enforcement authorities subsequently learned that the young auditor was distressed by his job. At the time, Resona and Japan's other major banks were experiencing major financial problems. For well over a decade, Japan's handful of "megabanks" had routinely embellished their reported financial health by, among other means, refusing to provide adequate reserves for their expected loan losses. In the spring of 2003, Resona's financial condition had deteriorated to the point that its independent auditors doubted the bank could survive without a large infusion of capital from another bank or the federal government.

Hirata, one of the subordinate auditors on Resona's joint team of Asahi and Shin Nihon auditors, knew that Resona was technically insolvent and had been for years despite the fact the bank had received unqualified audit opinions each year on its annual financial statements. Hirata was apparently concerned that his superiors would issue a similar opinion at the conclusion of the audit to which he was assigned. According to one newspaper report, Mr. Hirata's suicide was intended as a "dramatic gesture to persuade his seniors that Japan could no longer afford to keep covering over the cracks."[2] The "cracks" referred to in this quotation were the huge and unreported financial problems facing Resona and Japan's other major banks.

Following Mr. Hirata's death, Asahi withdrew from the Resona audit engagement. Asahi's resignation meant that Shin Nihon would be forced to decide the large bank's future. Resona's president, Yasuhisa Katsuta, a prominent political power broker in Japan, never doubted that Shin Nihon would give his bank a clean bill of health. But he was wrong. When the Shin Nihon auditors insisted that the bank seek outside financing to remedy its financial problems, Katsuta accused them of "betraying" his firm.[3] A few days after the auditors refused to give Resona an unqualified audit opinion, Japan's federal government announced that an emergency infusion of government funds equivalent to $17 billion was necessary to rescue the bank from

1. "Kansayaku" is a generic term for "inspector" or "auditor" in the Japanese language.
2. M. Nakamoto and D. Pilling, "Resona's Downfall," *Financial Times*, 13 June 2003, 11.
3. *Ibid.*

imminent bankruptcy. To fully understand Mr. Katsuta's reaction to Shin Nihon's decision, it is necessary to study the history of Japan's banking system and its independent audit function.

## Okurasho

By the end of World War II, Japan's economy was practically destroyed. Over the following five years, General Douglas MacArthur of the U. S. Army supervised the post-war occupation of Japan by the Allied Powers. In carrying out his mission to convert the Japanese nation into a democracy and to establish a free market economic system within the country, General MacArthur largely succeeded in his attempt to dismantle Japan's ancient political and economic infrastructure. But one important feature of that infrastructure, the secretive and powerful Okurasho, was left largely unscathed by General MacArthur's purge.

From the seventh century A.D. through World War II, the Okurasho or "great storehouse ministry" was responsible for overseeing the economic development and well-being of the Japanese nation. Often referred to by political insiders as the "ministry of ministries," the Okurasho was a tightly knit group of powerful and wealthy individuals who advised the Japanese emperor on all major economic decisions facing the country and who effectively controlled the nation's banking system. In the Japanese economy, the banking system has historically been very powerful because the principal source of funds for private businesses has been debt rather than equity capital. The Okurasho also played a major role in overseeing Japan's stock market when it became a significant factor in the Japanese economy during the twentieth century.

Because senior members of the Okurasho chose each successive generation of the organization's leaders, the organization was self-perpetuating. In fact, the individuals who controlled the organization pressured their children to marry only members of other Okurasho families. Because General MacArthur was unaware of the Okurasho's far-reaching influence within Japan's social structure and economic system, members of the clandestine organization resurfaced following World War II and quickly took control of the Ministry of Finance (MOF), the government agency that would be responsible for managing the country's economy when the post-war occupation of Japan ended.

Despite the democratic political system imposed on Japan by General MacArthur, the country's elected officials had only minimal input into the post-war economic policies established by the MOF. Few of those officials ever questioned the MOF's heavy-handed, if not authoritarian, policies since those policies were responsible for the rapid modernization and recovery of the Japanese economy following World War II. Within four decades, the MOF's policies created the second-largest economy in the world and produced a level of economic prosperity surpassed only by the U.S. economy.

During the 1990s, President Clinton frequently criticized the MOF for its protectionist international trade policies that resulted in the United States having a huge and unfavorable trade imbalance with Japan. President Clinton charged that the secretive agency prevented Japan from becoming a "fully modern state with fair and open trade."[4] A *Business Week* report provided a similarly blunt assessment of the MOF's role in Japan's economy. "Japan's Ministry of Finance is much more than an office of

---

4. *BusinessWeek Online*, "The Ministry: How Japan's Most Powerful Institution Endangers World Markets," 25 September 2006.

government. It is a political, economic, and intellectual force without parallel in the developed world. It enjoys a greater concentration of powers, formal and informal, than any comparable body in any other industrialized democracy. In Japan, there is no institution with more power."[5]

By the early 1990s, Japan faced its first major financial crisis since World War II. Various economic factors and conditions prevented Japan from sustaining the impressive growth that it had experienced over the previous decades. Suddenly, Japan's economy faced many of the same problems that have frequently plagued the U.S. economy over the past century: volatile interest rates, inflation, and surging unemployment. These problems caused Japan's stock market to decline sharply and eventually led to a startling number of business failures.

The large number of business failures during the 1990s produced huge losses in the loan portfolios of the major metropolitan banks that were the principal source of Japan's investment capital. However, the extent of the loan losses was not reported in the audited financial statements released periodically by those banks. Pressure applied by MOF officials on the auditors of Japan's large banks resulted in those banks receiving clean audit opinions despite their massive financial problems. Eventually, both the MOF and the nation's major accounting firms would be held responsible for the huge government bailouts that were necessary to rescue Resona and other large Japanese banks.

## Japan's Independent Audit Function

A small number of large accounting firms have dominated Japan's accounting profession and independent audit function since World War II. In turn, the MOF effectively controlled those large accounting firms over most of that time frame, wielding power over them similar to the power that it wielded over the nation's major banks. In 1998, the founder of one of Japan's major accounting firms told a U.S. journalist that the large government agency "really controls the accounting profession in Japan."[6] So complete was the MOF's control of the accounting profession that it reportedly handpicked the individuals who were to serve in key executive positions at the country's largest accounting firms. In the late 1990s, the chief executives of four of Japan's six largest accounting firms had previously worked in some capacity with the MOF. The close ties between the MOF and the major accounting firms meant that the top executives of those firms routinely kowtowed to the wishes and demands of MOF officials.

Japan's public accounting profession is much smaller than that of the United States. In the United States, there is one CPA for approximately every 800 citizens, while in Japan there is one CPA for approximately every 9,600 citizens. In fact, Japan has fewer CPAs per capita by far than any other major industrialized country. The relatively small number of CPAs in Japan is due in large part to the onerous requirements for becoming a CPA. Until 2006, CPA candidates in Japan were required to pass three rigorous examinations and serve a three-year internship with an accounting firm before they could become a CPA.

The large accounting firms in Japan that dominate the nation's accounting profession also audit the great majority of the country's public companies, large private companies, and other important organizations in the private and public sector. Approximately 10,000 Japanese companies must be audited each year, including the approximately 4,000 companies that have securities listed on public stock exchanges. The remaining

5. *Ibid.*

6. L. Berton, "Japanese Accounting Bites Back," *Accounting Today* (online), 9 November 1998.

companies that must be audited include unlisted corporations that have total capital exceeding 500 million yen and corporations that receive government subsidies.

Similar to the United States, the number of major accounting firms within Japan has been declining in recent years, principally due to mergers. By 2006, Japan's Big Four included ChuoAoyama—an affiliate of PricewaterhouseCoopers, Deloitte Touche Tohmatsu, Ernst & Young Shin Nihon, and KPMG AZSA & Co. The latter firm was created in 2004 when Asahi, the firm that employed Satoshi Hirata, merged with another large Japanese accounting firm.

The nature, purpose, and structure of independent audits are generally very similar in Japan and the United States. However, there is one significant difference. Audit fees in Japan are dramatically lower than in the United States. The audit fee for a large Japanese company is generally one-tenth of the fee for a similar U.S. company. The much smaller audit fees charged by Japanese accounting firms impose severe restraints on the scope of independent audits and result in audit services being considerably less profitable for Japanese accounting firms than for their U.S. counterparts.

In the United States, the business press, financial analysts, and regulatory authorities maintain that an absence of auditor independence was a key factor that contributed to the series of high-profile audit failures of such companies as Enron, WorldCom, and Adelphia Communications, among others. Allegedly, the long tenure of auditors with their clients, personal relationships between individual auditors and client personnel, and the large consulting fees that clients paid their auditors for nonaudit services made it difficult for audit firms to objectively report on major clients' financial statements. However, parties familiar with auditing practices and norms around the world insist that Japanese auditors have historically had much closer ties to their clients than auditors in any other country, including the United States.

The cordial relationship between Japanese auditors and their clients is at least partially a cultural phenomenon because the Japanese business community "emphasizes relationships and harmonious working practices."[7] A critic of the Japanese public accounting profession suggested that this cultural norm results in Japanese auditors subordinating their judgment to the wishes or demands of their clients. "Even when corporate clients ask the auditors to do something that isn't allowed under the law, they just do it."[8]

By the late 1990s, Japan's independent audit function faced a growing credibility crisis. "In the late 1990s, problems with the current audit system started coming to light—exposed by a series of deplorable events at many corporations, including fraudulent accounting and the abrupt failure of financial institutions once considered healthy."[9] Worsening that credibility crisis was the fact that the principal regulatory authority for the public accounting profession, the MOF, rarely imposed sanctions of any kind on auditors who had failed to fulfill their professional responsibilities. In 1999, the MOF revoked a CPA's license to practice for the first time in more than 20 years.

Mounting frustration with the MOF's failure to take measures to strengthen Japan's independent audit function was one of several factors that resulted in the powerful agency being stripped of much of its regulatory authority near the turn of the century. The MOF lost even more of its authority following the election of Junichiro Koizumi as Japan's prime minister in 2001. The reform-minded Koizumi hoped to revitalize

7. D. Reilly and A. Morse, "Japan Leans On Auditors to Be More Independent," *post-gazette.com*, 18 May 2006.

8. *Ibid.*

9. *The Yomiuri Shimbun* (online), "CPA-Client Collusion Must Be Severed," 10 August 2006.

Japan's stagnant economy by enhancing the "transparency" of the nation's capital markets. To accomplish that objective, Koizumi realized that the arcane regulatory structure for those markets had to be overhauled.

Under Prime Minister Koizumi's leadership, a new federal agency, the Financial Services Agency (FSA), assumed most of the responsibility for monitoring Japan's capital markets—including the nation's banking and financial reporting systems. To assist the FSA in overseeing the independent audit function and accounting profession, the new federal agency was placed in charge of the newly created Certified Public Accountants and Auditing Oversight Board (CPAAOB), which is comparable to the Public Company Accounting and Oversight Board (PCAOB) in the United States. To police the securities markets, another new federal agency, the Securities and Exchange Surveillance Commission, was established and placed under the FSA's control.

In 2004, Japan's federal legislative body, the Diet, rewrote the Certified Public Accountants Law. A major purpose of revising this law was to increase the number of CPAs in Japan. Among other changes, the revised law requires CPA candidates to pass only one examination rather than three to become a CPA. The national organization of CPAs, the Japanese Institute of Certified Public Accountants (JICPA), also adopted a series of measures to strengthen the profession, many of which focused on the independent audit function. Among these latter measures was prohibiting independent auditors from having any direct financial interest in a public client. Previously, auditors of public companies had been allowed to own a limited number of shares of a public client's outstanding stock.

The first major test of Japan's new regulatory structure for the accounting profession and independent audit function was posed by a financial scandal involving a large manufacturing company, Kanebo, Ltd. The nation's business press often refers to the Kanebo fiasco as "Japan's Enron."[10]

## Kanebo, Ltd: Japan's Enron

The Tokyo Cotton Trading Company was founded in 1887 on the banks of the Sumida River that flows through Tokyo. Over the following decades, the company became a large and prosperous textile and apparel manufacturer—only to have its operating facilities totally destroyed during World War II. With the help of significant bank loans, the company, renamed Kanebo, Ltd., resumed operations on a much smaller scale in the late 1940s. By the late 1990s, the company ranked among Japan's largest public corporations. Kanebo's principal operations included the manufacture and sale of a long line of cosmetics, apparel, textiles, pharmaceuticals, toiletries, and food products.

In July 2005, Japanese law enforcement authorities arrested three former Kanebo executives, including Takashi Hoashi, the company's former president. The three individuals were charged with violating the Securities and Exchange Law, the principal federal statute that established the regulatory framework for Japan's securities markets, a statute comparable to the federal securities laws passed by the U.S. Congress in the early 1930s. Allegedly, the former Kanebo executives conspired to conceal their company's deteriorating financial health beginning in the 1990s. Throughout the time frame that the fraud was being perpetrated, Kanebo's audited financial statements indicated that the company was in reasonably good financial condition. However, a criminal investigation revealed that the company was hopelessly insolvent from 1995 through 2004.

10. *Accountancy* (accountancymagazine.com), "ChuoAoyama faces £100m Revenue Hit," 31 May 2005.

According to a representative of Tokyo's Public Prosecutor's Office, Hoashi ordered Kanebo's accounting staff to falsify the company's accounting records. Hoashi reportedly told the accountants that if they did not cooperate, the company would fail and its employees would lose their jobs. Hoashi's two subordinates (who were also indicted) gave the company's accountants specific instructions on how to distort Kanebo's reported financial data. The accountants were told to record fictitious sales and to understate various expenses to improve Kanebo's operating results and to make the company appear solvent.

In March 2006, Takashi Hoashi and one of his subordinates pleaded guilty to falsifying Kanebo's financial statements.[11] In commenting on the fraud, the judge who would ultimately sentence the two former executives noted, "It was a vicious and organizational crime committed by the leaders of a major Japanese company. It was also unprecedentedly cleverly devised."[12] Despite the judge's harsh remarks, he gave the two former executives suspended prison sentences.

ChuoAoyama, the second-largest CPA firm in Japan, served for decades as the audit firm of Kanebo Ltd. Tokyo's Public Prosecutor's Office filed fraud charges against three ChuoAoyama auditors who had been assigned to the Kanebo audit engagements. Each of those auditors had worked on the annual audits of that company for more than 15 years. One of the defendants had been assigned to the Kanebo engagement team for more than 30 years. In fact, it was common in post-World War II Japan for the same team of auditors to be assigned to an audit client indefinitely. According to the prosecutors, the three ChuoAoyama auditors had not only been aware of Kanebo's true financial condition but had also recommended additional methods for concealing the company's poor financial health. Among these methods was "deconsolidating" certain Kanebo subsidiaries that were posting large operating losses each year. The defendants never admitted as much, but the prosecutors speculated that the three auditors learned of this scheme from reading published reports of the Enron accounting fraud in the United States.

In the summer of 2006, the case against the ChuoAoyama auditors went to trial in Tokyo District Court. As one journalist noted, Japan's public accounting profession was "turned on its head"[13] by the case because it represented the first time in the country's history that auditors from a major CPA firm had faced criminal charges for allegedly falsifying or helping to falsify a client's financial statements. A few years earlier, ChuoAoyama had been involved in a precedent-setting civil lawsuit in Japan. ChuoAoyama had been the longtime auditor for Yamaichi Securities, a large brokerage firm that unexpectedly collapsed in late 1997. The following year, Yamaichi's former stockholders sued ChuoAoyama, charging that the firm had negligently audited Yamaichi. The lawsuit was the first of its kind filed by Japanese stockholders against an audit firm. In 2003, ChuoAoyama settled the lawsuit by agreeing to pay the Yamaichi bankruptcy administrator an amount equal to the total audit fees it had received for its final five annual audits of Yamaichi. Despite the settlement, ChuoAoyama officials insisted that the firm had properly performed those audits.

During the criminal trial of the three ChuoAoyama auditors, the defendants testified that shortly before the Kanebo fraud was uncovered by law enforcement authorities they had pleaded with Hoashi and his subordinates to make the proper correcting

11. No published report could be found regarding the resolution of the criminal charges filed against the third Kanebo executive.

12. *Associated Press* (online), "Ex-Kanebo Executives Sentenced for False Information," 27 March 2006.

13. *International Accounting Bulletin* (online), "Japan Confronts Its Audit Problem," 12 August 2006.

entries in the company's accounting records. According to the three auditors, the client executives refused to make those entries. When the auditors pressed the issue, the Kanebo executives "secured their cooperation by pointing out that ChuoAoyama had long overlooked the company's window dressing and said it was pointless to start complaining after taking a complacent stance for so long."[14]

In August 2006, the three ChuoAoyama auditors were convicted of the charges filed against them. Before sentencing the three individuals, the presiding judge noted that they had "damaged the social trust of certified public accountants" and that their "crimes deserve to be severely criticized."[15] The judge also observed, "It is shameful that they have failed to realize the high professional morality as certified accountants and lost the true aim of auditing, which is to protect investors."[16] After berating the three convicted auditors, the judge gave each of them suspended sentences ranging from one year to 18 months. The judge defended the suspended sentences by pointing out that Kanebo's executives, not the three auditors, were primarily responsible for the fraudulent scheme. The suspended prison sentences for the three auditors meant that no one involved in the large-scale Kanebo fraud would serve any time in prison for their misdeeds.

In May 2006, the FSA announced that the three ChuoAoyama auditors involved in the Kanebo fraud would have their CPA qualifications revoked. The FSA also announced that ChuoAoyama would be forced to suspend its operations for the two-month period July 1–August 31, 2006. The announcement of the suspension stunned Japan's public accounting profession. Japan's Securities and Exchange Law requires each listed company to have an independent audit firm at all times. The suspension of ChuoAoyama meant that the firm's approximately 800 clients that had securities listed on a stock exchange would be forced to either retain a temporary auditor for the two-month suspension period or dismiss ChuoAoyama and retain a new audit firm.

## EPILOGUE

To prevent Kanebo Ltd. from being forced to liquidate, the Japanese federal government placed the company in a "rehabilitation" program under the direction of the Industrial Revitalization Corporation of Japan (IRCJ). The government-sponsored and government-funded IRCJ had been created in April 2003 to help financially distressed companies obtain the capital they needed to survive and to provide them with "turnaround" advice from professional business consultants. Under the leadership of the IRCJ, Kanebo sold off its large cosmetics subsidiary and received more than $1 billion in government-guaranteed loans and waivers of outstanding loans. In 2006, a large investment fund purchased a majority of Kanebo's stock and took over control of the company from the IRCJ.

ChuoAoyama lost approximately one-third of its audit clients, including more than 200 publicly listed clients, during the two-month suspension imposed by the FSA. These companies included ChuoAoyama's two highest-profile audit clients, Sony Corporation and Toyota Motor Corporation. While serving the suspension, ChuoAoyama underwent an extensive internal review to strengthen its quality control functions and changed its name to the Misuzu Audit Corporation.[17]

14. *Japan Economic Newswire* (online), "Japanese Editorial Excerpts," 11 August 2006.

15. J. Hong, "CPAs in Kanebo Fraud Avoid Prison," *Japan Times* (online), 10 August 2006.

16. *Agence France Presse* (online), "Ex-Accountants Found Guilty in Japanese Fraud Case," 9 August 2006.

17. In February 2007, Misuzu announced that it was disbanding. The remaining three members of Japan's former Big Four hired the majority of Misuzu's employees.

**EXHIBIT 1**

EXCERPT FROM THE BUSINESS IMPROVEMENT ORDER ISSUED TO CHUOAOYAMA BY THE FINANCIAL SERVICES AGENCY (FSA)

As a result of inspecting ChuoAoyama PricewaterhouseCoopers, the firm-wide management to ensure audit quality control was deemed insufficient . . .

Specifically, its [measures for ensuring] compliance with laws/regulations and its implementation of auditors' independence [mandates] were found to be insufficient, and its system [for] training, etc. was deemed partially insufficient.

In addition, its risk assessments at the time of engagement acceptance/continuance, the performance of audit work by each audit team and the documentation/retention of audit working papers were deemed partially insufficient. In terms of internal reviews of audits, although a multi-tiered review system has been implemented, reviews rely on those [provided] by review partners and some are deemed to lack depth. In this context, its internal review system [for identifying problematic] issues of each audit and [for confirming] the appropriateness of the judgments and dispositions [with regard] to such issues were partially insufficient. Its monitoring of the quality control system was deemed partially insufficient, and joint audits were deemed insufficient.

Furthermore, its control system for branch offices was deemed insufficient.

Source: Financial Services Agency (www.fsa.go.jp).

Shortly after the FSA announced that it was suspending ChuoAoyama's operations for two months, the accounting firm's U.S. affiliate, PricewaterhouseCoopers, revealed that it would be creating a new Japanese accounting firm known as Aarata, a name that means "new and fresh" in Japanese. Aarata commenced operations on July 1, 2006, and in the subsequent weeks acquired dozens of ChuoAoyama's former clients, including Sony and Toyota. In addition, nearly one-fourth of ChuoAoyama's employees left that firm to join Aarata.

The Kanebo audit failure prompted the FSA to investigate the audit practices of each of Japan's four large accounting firms. These investigations were carried out by the newly created CPAAOB that had been placed under the authority of the FSA. The stated purpose of the investigations was to "regain public trust in certified public accountants damaged by ChuoAoyama auditors' involvement in Kanebo's falsification of its financial statements."[18] The CPAAOB issued a report on the six-month long investigations in July 2006. That report criticized the operating policies and procedures of the four accounting firms. As a result of the CPAAOB's report, the FSA issued "business improvement orders" to each of the four firms. Exhibit 1 includes an excerpt of the business improvement order issued to ChuoAoyama.

In the aftermath of the Kanebo audit failure, leaders of the Japanese accounting profession spoke out about the need for additional reforms to strengthen the nation's independent audit function. One such individual was Tsuguoki Fujinuma, the chairman and president of the JICPA. Fujinuma issued a public statement in which he compared the Kanebo incident to the Enron debacle in the United States.

> *The Enron affair was not an isolated problem of one accounting firm. To the contrary, it was regarded as a failure of the entire CPA system and provoked a barrage of criticism against audits and auditors in the U.S. public. This affair ultimately led to the passage of the Sarbanes-Oxley Act, legislation imposing severe controls on CPAs.*

18. *Japan Economic Newswire* (online), "FSA to Inspect 4 Biggest Auditing Firms," 25 October 2005.

*I urge all JICPA members engaged in audits to make efforts to ensure the public confidence in auditing practices, together with the JICPA itself. As they do so, I further urge them not to regard the Enron affair as a distant or unrelated failure to the accounting system, nor to regard the Kanebo incident as an isolated problem involving only one auditing firm.*[19]

Despite such statements and the actions of the FSA and other regulatory authorities in response to the Kanebo affair, many third parties doubted that there would be major changes in Japan's independent audit function. As one skeptic noted, "cultural mores" will likely prove to be "sand in the gears of change."[20]

## Questions

1. Research online news services to identify recent developments impacting the accounting and auditing profession in Japan. Briefly summarize these developments in a bullet format.
2. As noted in this case, Japanese companies typically rely more heavily on debt capital than U.S. companies. Explain how this fact may cause the independent audit functions in the two countries to differ.
3. The much higher barriers to enter the public accounting profession in Japan (as compared with other major industrialized countries) has resulted in a relatively small number of CPAs in that nation. Identify and briefly discuss the comparative advantages and disadvantages of high barriers to entry for a given profession.
4. In both Japan and the United States, a small number of accounting firms audit the great majority of large public companies. Identify the advantages and disadvantages of this "market structure" for independent audit services.
5. In both Japan and the United States, external auditors have frequently been accused of failing to maintain a proper degree of independence from their clients. What measures have and should be taken to promote the independence of auditors from their clients?

19. T. Fujinuma, "On the Alleged Fraudulent Accounting at Kanebo," website of Japanese Institute of Certified Public Accountants (www.hp.jicpa.or.jp/), 16 September 2005.

20. Reilly and Morse, "Japan Leans On Auditors."

## CASE 8.4

# Registered Auditors, South Africa

*Where the cattle stand together, the lion lies down hungry.*

*African Proverb*

After earning a law degree from the University of Capetown in 1988, 24-year-old Brett Kebble accepted an entry-level position with a prestigious Capetown law firm. The gregarious and impetuous Kebble soon realized that it would take years, if not decades, to achieve his personal goal of "making a name for himself" if he remained in the staid legal profession. So, Kebble decided to quit practicing law and join his father in the mining industry that has dominated the Republic of South Africa's economy throughout that nation's existence. Kebble's father, a successful mining engineer, had raised his family in the mining town of Springs in northwestern South Africa, 40 miles south of Pretoria, the nation's capital.

In 1991, Kebble and his father purchased a controlling interest in a small gold mining company. Three years later, Kebble, with the financial backing of his father and several other major investors, orchestrated the takeover of Randgold & Exploration Company Limited, one of South Africa's leading mining companies. Over the following decade, Brett Kebble would become the chief executive of Randgold and two other mining companies, all three of which were publicly owned firms.

By the turn of the century, Brett Kebble had accomplished his ultimate personal goal. Thanks to his role as the self-appointed spokesperson for South Africa's all-important mining industry, Kebble easily ranked among the nation's highest-profile corporate executives. Besides his prominent position in the South African business community, Kebble had close associations with several of South Africa's leading politicians and was a strong supporter of the arts. In 2002, Kebble, a large, heavyset man known for his quick wit and humor (and lack of modesty), established and funded the annual Brett Kebble Art Awards to recognize and reward leading South African artists, sculptors, and photographers.

## A Career Cut Short

Kebble's reputation and business career were severely damaged in 2004 when Randgold & Exploration Company Limited, the crown jewel of his large business empire, reported a huge cash shortage. The missing funds were equivalent to several hundred million U.S. dollars. Stockholder revolts forced Kebble to resign in August 2005 as the chief executive of Randgold and the other two public companies for which he served in that position. One month later, in September 2005, the 41-year-old Kebble was gunned down in a wealthy section of Johannesburg while on his way to a dinner engagement in his silver Mercedes.

Johannesburg police immediately concluded that Kebble's murder had been a well-planned "hit." The widely publicized murder of the controversial businessman reinforced Johannesburg's reputation as the murder capital of the world and served to bolster the prevailing view in the international business community that South Africa was a high-risk and dangerous place to do business. Even more damaging to the reputation of South Africa's business community were subsequent revelations of the underhanded and illegal methods that Kebble had used to build his massive empire. One journalist characterized the late Kebble as a "cheat, manipulator, corrupter, briber, and swindler."[1] South Africa's largest newspaper would add to that sentiment: "Brett Kebble was not a good South African. He was the great corrupter, a dirty businessman who had little respect for the law or codes of good business practice."[2]

South African law enforcement authorities were investigating Kebble and his business and political allies well before he was murdered in September 2005. Those investigations continued on a larger scale following his death. Among the parties targeted by the investigations was PricewaterhouseCoopers (PwC), the audit firm of Randgold & Exploration Company Limited. Throughout Kebble's tenure as Randgold's chief executive, PwC had issued clean opinions on the company's annual financial statements even as a huge amount of the company's funds were being siphoned off by Kebble and several of his top subordinates. Randgold's board of directors dismissed PwC and retained KPMG as the company's independent audit firm shortly after the public was apprised of the missing funds.

After Brett Kebble's death, Randgold's new management team hired a consulting firm to carry out a forensic investigation of the company's accounting records and financial affairs over the previous decade. Two dozen forensic auditors from the consulting firm spent months unraveling a series of complex and multilayered "Enron-style transactions" that Kebble and his subordinates had used to divert Randgold assets into related entities that they controlled.[3] In a lengthy report issued in November 2005, the consulting firm recommended that Randgold's new management team file civil and criminal charges against PwC. The consulting firm suggested that proper audits of Randgold would have led to the discovery and termination of the massive fraud engineered by Kebble.

## Doing Business, South Africa Style

In many ways, Brett Kebble's life and death epitomizes the turbulent nature of South Africa's business world following the collapse of apartheid in the early 1990s. In 1990, the South African federal government succumbed to immense international and domestic pressure when it lifted the ban on the African National Congress (ANC), the political party that had struggled for decades to eliminate apartheid in the country. The ANC drew its support from blacks who accounted for more than three-fourths of the nation's total population. The National Party, the political party of the nation's white minority that controlled most of South Africa's economic resources (including its crucial mining industry), had dominated South Africa's federal government since the 1940s. Shortly after World War II, the National Party had implemented the segregationist social and economic policies that formed the basis for what became known as apartheid.

When the first truly multiracial elections were held in South Africa in 1994, Nelson Mandela was elected the nation's president. Mandela, the leader of the ANC, had been imprisoned by the South African government from 1963 through 1990. The democratic elections also resulted in the ANC assuming control of South Africa's Parliament. After decades of a bitter and often extremely bloody struggle, South Africa's black majority had finally taken control of the country.

Since the collapse of apartheid and the takeover of the federal government by the ANC, South Africa's economy has been characterized by uncertainty and volatility.

1. S. Ulys, "The Mysterious Murder of Brett Kebble," www.ever-fasternews.com, 2 October 2005.

2. A. Meldrum, "Brett Kebble, Controversial Business Leader from the New South Africa," *The Guardian* (online), 7 October 2005.

3. "Massive Fraud Revealed at Randgold & Exploration," www.randgold.co.za, press release issued by Randgold & Exploration Company Limited, 1 November 2005.

Major institutional investors around the world have been reluctant to commit significant investment capital to South African business ventures because of that uncertainty and volatility. A related factor that has inhibited direct foreign investment in the South African economy has been corruption. In a recent study by Ernst & Young, corporate executives from nearly 70 countries around the world identified "corruption" as the principal factor that made them hesitant to do business in South Africa.[4] According to the Ernst & Young study, the corruption in South Africa's economy is manifested in widespread bribery, payroll fraud, inventory theft, and unauthorized expenditures by corporate executives, among other abuses.

South Africa's economy and capital markets have also suffered a loss of credibility as a result of a series of high-profile financial reporting scandals that have occurred in recent years. Those scandals have involved companies such as LeisureNet, MacMed, Regal Treasury, Saambou, and, most notably, Randgold & Exploration Company Limited. Critics of South Africa's accounting profession maintain that much of the responsibility for these scandals should be borne by the accounting firms that audited those companies' financial statements and failed to uncover the fraudulent schemes carried out by Brett Kebble and other self-interested corporate executives.

Numerous journalists and political adversaries of Brett Kebble believe that he used assets stolen from Randgold not only for his personal enrichment but also to buy political favors from leaders of the ANC. Since the early 1990s, Kebble, who was of western European descent, had been among the most vocal supporters of the black empowerment movement in South Africa and a leading figure in the ANC. One of his closest associates was Jacob Zuma who served for several years as South Africa's deputy president (vice president) before being forced to resign in June 2005 amid allegations of abuse of power. (Zuma resurrected his political career in 2009 when he was elected president of South Africa thanks to the support of the ANC.) The published reports of the missing funds within Randgold as well as Kebble's close ties and financial dealings with Zuma ignited the stockholder revolts that forced him to resign as the chief executive of Randgold and of the other two mining companies that he and his family had controlled since the mid-1990s.

South Africa's business press has referred to the financial scandal at Randgold & Exploration Company Limited as that nation's "Enron." Like the actual Enron debacle in the United States, the highly publicized Randgold scandal persuaded the South African Parliament to pass major legislation to combat financial fraud and strengthen the nation's financial reporting system. This new legislation was intended to convince the international investment community that South Africa's capital markets would be characterized by integrity in the future. The lynchpin of the legislative reforms was a new federal law that had pervasive implications for the nation's accounting profession.

## Overview of South Africa's Accounting Profession

South Africa's accounting discipline has several professional organizations. The two most important of these organizations are the South African Institute of Professional Accountants (SAIPA), which until recently was known as the Institute of Certified Public Accountants, and the South African Institute of Chartered Accountants (SAICA). Members of the SAIPA are certified public accountants (CPAs) who typically

4. M.S. Bayat, "Curbing Corruption in the Republic of South Africa," *Public Manager*, Summer 2005, 15. The results of a study by PricewaterhouseCoopers that was published in late 2007 identified South Africa as the "white-collar crime capital" of the world. (*Africa News* [online], "South Africa: Country is White-Collar Crime Capital," 16 October 2007.)

provide tax and bookkeeping services to small South African businesses. The dominant organization in the South African accounting profession is the SAICA, which issues the Chartered Accountant (CA) professional designation. The CA designation is equivalent to the CPA designation in the United States.

Unlike the United States, the accounting profession in South Africa is regulated almost exclusively at the federal level. Until recently, the federal agency overseeing that profession was the Public Accountants' and Auditors' Board (PAAB). PAAB delegated much of the responsibility for overseeing the South African accounting profession to the SAICA. The working relationship between the PAAB and the SAICA was analogous to the relationship that exists in the United States between state boards of accountancy and the American Institute of Certified Public Accountants (AICPA). For example, until recently, an internal SAICA committee developed and issued South Africa's professional auditing standards, which were then routinely endorsed by the PAAB. Similarly, the PAAB adopted a condensed version of the code of professional ethics developed by the SAICA.

The abrupt change of control in South Africa's federal government in the early 1990s presented major challenges for the nation's federal agencies, such as the PAAB, and its professional organizations, among them the SAICA. Throughout its history, South Africa's accounting profession, like other professions, had been dominated by the nation's white minority—principally white males. The ANC's takeover of the South African government in 1994 resulted in federal mandates calling for the integration of the nation's professions. Since that time, the SAICA and the nation's major accounting firms have spent considerable time and resources attempting to recruit black South Africans into the profession. Those efforts have generally produced discouraging results. In 2006, fewer than 9 percent of South Africa's 22,000 CAs were blacks and of those individuals fewer than 200 were black females. Ernst & Young reported in that same year that it was the first of the Big Four accounting firms in South Africa to have more than 25 percent black partners.

In the post-apartheid era, a large percentage of South Africa's white professionals have immigrated to other countries, including an estimated 20 to 25 percent of the nation's CAs. The emigration of white CAs and the continuing underrepresentation of blacks have resulted in a significant shortage of professional accountants within South Africa. In the United States, there is approximately one CPA for every 800 citizens. South Africa, on the other hand, has approximately one resident CA for every 3,000 citizens.

In April 2006, three Big Four firms—Deloitte, KPMG and PwC—asked the South African federal government to relax its restrictive immigration laws to make it easier for those firms to recruit accounting professionals from other countries. The three firms maintained that the significant shortage of skilled accountants within South Africa had made it increasingly difficult for the nation's accounting profession to provide the accounting, auditing, tax, and related services needed by South African citizens and businesses. The South African government never responded to that request. The federal government's position is that allowing skilled accounting professionals to immigrate to South Africa—even if those individuals are black—will only serve to continue the underrepresentation of native South African blacks within the profession.

The most significant challenge facing South Africa's accounting profession in the post-apartheid era has been the rash of accounting and financial reporting scandals involving major companies. Many parties internal and external to the profession have suggested that the most effective way to mitigate that problem is to strengthen the nation's professional accounting and auditing standards. After considerable debate, South Africa's accounting profession decided to adopt, as of January 1, 2005, the International Financial Reporting Standards (IFRS) issued by the International Accounting Standards Board (IASB). On that same date, the South African profession also adopted the International Standards on Auditing (ISA) issued by the International Federation of Accountants (IFAC).

The adoption of international accounting and auditing standards did not placate the most vocal critics of South Africa's accounting profession. Those critics became even more strident as the Randgold accounting and financial reporting scandal unfolded during 2005 and 2006. That scandal provided the impetus for South Africa's Parliament to pass a federal statute in 2006 that had been placed on the legislative agenda 10 years earlier. The Auditing Profession Act made sweeping changes to the nature of South Africa's financial reporting system, particularly the nation's independent audit function.

## Auditing Profession Act

South Africa's Auditing Profession Act (APA) went into effect on April 1, 2006. The new federal law eliminated the PAAB and replaced it with the Independent Regulatory Board for Auditors (IRBA). The term "independent" was included in the new agency's name because, unlike its predecessor, a majority of its governing board would not be accountants. Likewise, unlike the PAAB that had been financed exclusively by the accounting profession, the APA mandated that the IRBA be funded jointly by the profession and the federal government. These two stipulations were a direct response to criticism that the PAAB had been an ineffective oversight body for South Africa's accounting profession because it had been "captured" by that profession. In particular, critics suggested that the PAAB had been overly sensitive to the interests and demands of the Big Four international accounting firms, each of which has a strong presence in South Africa. The website of the IRBA identifies six "core values" that the new federal agency will embrace and promote: independence, integrity, objectivity, commitment, transparency, and accountability.

The APA also established a new professional designation in South Africa's accounting profession: Registered Auditor (RA). Under the APA, only CAs who also hold the RA credential can perform independent audits in South Africa. According to an official of the IRBA, the new RA designation was necessary because of the large number of audit failures and alleged audit failures that had occurred in South Africa over the previous several years. "Auditors have taken a huge knock in the past few years and we need to establish a brand locally that will restore integrity."[5]

The creation of the new professional designation was generally not welcomed by the SAICA and individual CAs who realized that the RA credential would almost certainly impair the prestige and prominence of the CA credential. In fact, officials of the IRBA candidly admitted that they hoped the public would impute more credibility to the new RA designation. "We're trying to tell people [existing CAs] that if you're an RA, it will have higher regard than a CA in South Africa because of the stringent new laws and examination. We want people to strive to be RAs not CAs."[6]

Prior to the passage of the APA, the SAICA had administered the CA examination. Under the APA, the SAICA continues to administer that examination; however, to become an RA a CA candidate must successfully complete a second examination administered by the IRBA. Before receiving the CA or RA credential, candidates must

---

5. S. Naidoo, "Auditors' Brand Set to Rival That of a CA," *Sunday Times* (online), 1 October 2006.

6. *Ibid.*

**EXHIBIT 1**

MISSION STATEMENTS OF THE SAICA AND THE IRBA

SAICA's mission is to serve the interests of the Chartered Accountancy profession and society, by upholding professional standards and integrity, and the pre-eminence of South African CAs nationally and internationally, through delivering competent entry level members, providing services to assist members to maintain and enhance their professional competence thereby enabling them to create value for their clients and employers, enhancing the quality of information used in the private and public sectors for measuring and enhancing organizational performance, running and facilitating programmes to transform the profession and to facilitate community upliftment and fulfilling a leadership role regarding relevant business related issues and providing reliable and respected public commentary.

The mission of the IRBA, on the other hand, is to protect the financial interest of the South African public and international investors in South Africa, through the effective regulation of audits conducted by registered auditors, and in accordance with internationally recognized standards and processes. This is achieved by providing the means and the regulatory framework for the education and training of adequate numbers of competent and disciplined accountants and auditors, to serve the needs of South Africa. The Board [IRBA] strives constantly toward the maintenance and improvement of standards of registered auditors. The Board protects the public who rely on the services of registered auditors and supports registered auditors who carry out their duties competently, fearlessly, and in good faith.

Source: SAICA website (www.saica.co.za).

complete a minimum three-year internship or "training program" within the accounting profession. This requirement had existed for CA candidates prior to the passage of the APA and the creation of the IRBA.

Leaders of the South African accounting profession were concerned that the creation of the IRBA and the new RA designation would lead to confusion on the part of the public regarding the nature of the CA and RA designations and the roles and responsibilities of the IRBA and the SAICA. To alleviate such confusion, the two organizations issued mission statements clarifying their roles and responsibilities and their relationship to the CA and RA credentials. Exhibit 1 presents summaries of those mission statements that were posted to the SAICA website.

The APA also made major changes in the regulatory infrastructure for South Africa's independent audit function. Under this new federal statute, the IRBA has far-reaching oversight responsibilities for that function. Individual RAs as well as accounting firms providing independent audits are required to register with the IRBA. Registered accounting firms must undergo an extensive quality review of their professional audit practices by the IRBA every three years.

The IRBA also has the statutory responsibility to establish ethical standards and rules for RAs. The APA required the IRBA to establish a "committee for auditor ethics" that will "determine what constitutes improper conduct by registered auditors by developing rules and guidelines for professional ethics, including a code of professional conduct."[7] The IRBA also requires RAs to engage in continuing professional development (CPD) each year. Organizations offering CPD courses or programs must be accredited by the IRBA.

7. *Government Gazette, The Republic of South Africa*, "Auditing Profession Act, 2005," Vol. 487, No. 28406 (16 January 2006), 26.

By far, the most controversial and important change in the nature of independent audits and auditors' professional responsibilities brought about by the APA is a requirement that RAs immediately inform the IRBA of any "reportable irregularities" relating to an audit client that come to their attention. Reportable irregularities are defined by the APA as

> *any unlawful act or omission committed by any person responsible for the management of an entity, which:*
>
> *—has caused or is likely to cause material financial loss to the entity or any partner, member, shareholder, creditor or investor of the entity in respect of his/her or its dealings with that entity; or*
>
> *—is fraudulent or amounts to theft; or*
>
> *—represents a material breach of any fiduciary duty owed by such person to the entity or any partner, member, shareholder, creditor or investor of the entity under any law applying to the entity or the conduct or management thereof.*[8]

RAs must disclose a reportable irregularity (RI) "without delay" to the IRBA, meaning that these matters are not to be discussed with client management before they are communicated to the federal agency. After an RI report has been submitted to the IRBA, an RA must discuss that report with client management within three days. Over the following 30 days, client management must be given an opportunity to respond to the report. At the end of this 30-day period, the RA must send a second report to the IRBA regarding the RI. In this second report, the RA must indicate whether in his or her opinion an actual irregularity has taken place or is taking place.

Reportable irregularities also have extensive implications for the audit reports prepared by South African RAs. The APA provides specific guidance for auditors to follow in determining whether and/or how to modify their audit reports for a wide range of circumstances involving RIs. For example, if an auditor reports a potential RI to the IRBA but then determines that an actual irregularity did not take place, no modification of the audit report is necessary. Management's failure to disclose an RI, whether or not the matter has been appropriately addressed, may require the auditor to issue an adverse opinion on the client's financial statements. If at the audit report date an auditor has not determined whether a potential RI is an actual RI, then the potential RI, at a minimum, must be disclosed in the audit report.

The APA mandates that RAs have a responsibility to report RIs regardless of how they became aware of them. For example, anonymous tips, statements made by disgruntled former employees, or confidential communications to the auditor by client employees could each trigger an RI report to the IRBA. Likewise, an RI discovered during the course of a nonaudit services engagement for a client must be disclosed to the IRBA. Under the APA, the reporting responsibility for RIs falls on individual RAs, not accounting firms. The RA on the engagement team who has the ultimate responsibility for the successful completion of the audit—typically, the audit engagement partner—has the obligation to report an RI to the IRBA. This stipulation of the law is very important given the serious criminal penalties for willfully choosing not to report an RI. An RA who has a responsibility to report an RI and fails to do so faces a large fine and a prison sentence of up to 10 years.

In addition to exposing RAs to criminal sanctions, the APA mandates that RAs who fail to fulfill their RI-related responsibilities will be subject to civil liability, as

---

8. *Ibid.*, 10.

well. This civil liability extends to any "partner, member, shareholder, creditor or investor of an entity" for which an RA fails to report a RI.[9] One of South Africa's leading corporate law firms reported that this provision of the APA "has potentially enormous consequences for auditors' liability claims."[10]

The stated purpose of the RI provisions of the APA was to "eradicate" the large-scale frauds, such as the Randgold & Exploration Company Limited scandal, that had undermined the integrity of South Africa's capital markets within the international community and resulted in large diversions of assets by dishonest corporate executives. Although certain parties, particularly South Africa's business press, welcomed the RI provisions of the APA, many corporate executives and members of the nation's accounting profession were startled, if not shocked, by those provisions. An audit partner with one of the Big Four accounting firms maintained that the RI disclosure rule would undermine the "relationship of confidentiality between auditor and client" and create an "atmosphere in which clients will be reluctant to discuss problems with their auditors."[11]

To minimize any confusion regarding the RI disclosure requirements imposed on auditors by the APA, the SAICA has recommended that accounting firms send each of their audit clients a letter describing in detail the nature of those requirements. Exhibit 2 includes a draft of such a letter prepared by the SAICA and distributed to its members.

**EXHIBIT 2**

DRAFT OF LETTER THAT THE SAICA SUGGESTED RAs SEND TO THEIR AUDIT CLIENTS REGARDING THE REPORTABLE IRREGULARITIES DISCLOSURE RULE

Dear Client:

You may be aware from press and other reports that new legislation regulating auditors has been enacted during 2006.

I have a statutory obligation to report matters to a regulatory oversight body or other person, such as the Independent Regulatory Board for Auditors (IRBA). Where permissible I shall endeavor to bring such circumstances to your attention.

Without detracting from the generality of such requirements, I am writing to you to provide a brief overview of the new reporting obligations imposed by the Auditing Profession Act 2005 (Act 26 of 2005).

The new legislation brings into existence a new regulator in the form of the IRBA which supersedes the Public Accountants' and Auditors' Board (PAAB).

Section 45 of the Auditing Profession Act places a legal requirement on the auditor to report to the IRBA, without delay, details of any reportable irregularity which comes to our attention, which we are satisfied or have reason to believe has taken place or is taking place in respect of [entity name].

The Auditing Profession Act defines a reportable irregularity as "any unlawful act or omission committed by any person responsible for the management of an entity, which:

9. *Ibid.*, 48.

10. K. Gawith, "Reportable Irregularities," www.deneysreitz.co.za.

11. *Africa News* (online), "Auditors Generally Welcome New Law despite Concerns about Education Roles," 7 April 2006.

**EXHIBIT 2—*continued***

DRAFT OF LETTER THAT THE SAICA SUGGESTED RAs SEND TO THEIR AUDIT CLIENTS REGARDING THE REPORTABLE IRREGULARITIES DISCLOSURE RULE

—has caused or is likely to cause material financial loss to the entity or any partner, member, shareholder, creditor or investor of the entity in respect of his/her or its dealings with that entity; or
—is fraudulent or amounts to theft; or
—represents a material breach of any fiduciary duty owed by such person to the entity or any partner, member, shareholder, creditor or investor of the entity under any law applying to the entity or the conduct or management thereof."

Matters which come to my attention and meet the definition above are clearly of a serious nature. In addition to reporting such matters to you and to those charged with governance of [entity name], I am obliged to report such matters to the IRBA.

Accordingly, the South African Institute of Chartered Accountants, of which I am a member, has advised its members who practice as auditors to write to their audit clients informing them of the requirements of the section dealing with reportable irregularities and what the implications can be.

**What must the auditor do?**

1. In terms of the legislation, if an auditor or an entity is satisfied, or has reason to believe that a reportable irregularity has taken place or is taking place, he or she must, without delay, send a written report to the IRBA.
2. The report must give particulars of the alleged irregularity.
3. The auditor must notify the members of the management board of the entity in writing within three (3) days of sending the report.
4. The auditor must take all reasonable measures to discuss the report with the management board of the entity.
5. The auditor must afford the members of the management board an opportunity to make representations in respect of the report. The auditor must send another report to the IRBA within 30 days of the initial report to the IRBA stating in his or her opinion whether or not a reportable irregularity has taken place or is taking place. This report should also deal with whether adequate steps have been taken for the prevention or recovery of any loss.
6. The auditor may carry out such investigations he or she may consider necessary to comply with the above requirements.
7. The auditor must refer to the alleged irregularity in his or her audit report attached to the annual financial statements.
8. It is important to note that the procedure described above must be carried out regardless of how the auditor came to know of the irregularity.

**What the regulator must do?**

The IRBA has a responsibility to report a reportable irregularity to the appropriate regulator (which includes any government agency) e.g. South African Revenue Services, South African Police Services, or the Financial Services Board.

**Possible Penalties**

I need to draw your attention to the fact that if the auditor fails to report a reportable irregularity, he or she may be guilty of an offense and may be liable to a fine of R10 million or imprisonment for a term not exceeding 10 years, or both a fine and imprisonment.

(*continued*)

**EXHIBIT 2—*continued***

DRAFT OF LETTER THAT THE SAICA SUGGESTED RAs SEND TO THEIR AUDIT CLIENTS REGARDING THE REPORTABLE IRREGULARITIES DISCLOSURE RULE

**Conclusion**

As mentioned previously, the auditors' responsibility with regard to reportable irregularities are well defined and can have serious consequences on the auditor if not followed appropriately.

While I am certain that you are committed to ensuring that such reportable irregularities do not exist, or if they do arise they are dealt with appropriately within applicable legal requirements, you may wish to further discuss the reporting obligations with me.

Yours Sincerely,
Registered Auditor, CA

Source: SAICA website (www.saica.co.za).

## EPILOGUE

Within the first five months that the APA was in effect, the IRBA received more than 200 RI reports from auditors. The majority of the RIs involved alleged violations of South African tax laws, apparent violations of the nation's federal securities laws, and a wide range of questionable accounting practices.[12] The regulatory agency also received informal reports from auditors that clients had threatened to dismiss them if they made an RI disclosure. These informal reports seemed to confirm that the RI reporting rule had created tension between auditors and their clients. In an interview with a newspaper reporter, the IRBA's senior executive, Kariem Hoosain, admitted that the new requirement had resulted in a "strained relationship" between auditors and their clients.[13] But Hoosain quickly added that was simply "tough luck." In the same article in which Hoosain was quoted, an officer of the SAICA indicated that the new RI rule was "onerous" for auditors and expressed his opinion that the criminal sanctions auditors faced under that rule were unfair.[14] The officer went on to note that "there's not much we can do now. It is the law and our members have to abide by [it]."[15]

As the details of the Randgold fraud were reported to the public, PwC, Randgold's former audit firm, became the target of increasing criticism for its role in that scandal. One reporter observed that "When the full tale of Brett Kebble's larceny is finally told, it would be something of a crime in itself if his auditors came off unscathed."[16] In October 2006, Karien Hoosain revealed that his agency was initiating an investigation of PwC's Randgold audits. Hoosain indicated that such an investigation was warranted given the report of the forensic consulting firm that had been retained by Randgold's board to scrutinize Kebble's fraudulent schemes. That report indicated that Randgold's fiscal 2003 financial statements (on which PwC had issued an unqualified opinion) "grossly misrepresented" the company's financial condition.[17] Hoosain reported that, because of the "complexities and sensitivities" of the Randgold

12. *Africa News* (online), "Auditors Reporting Dubious Clients," 29 August 2006.
13. Naidoo, "Auditors' Brand Set to Rival That of a CA."
14. *Ibid.*
15. *Ibid.*
16. B. Rose, "What About PwC's Role in Kebble Saga?" www.resourceinvestor.com, 13 March 2006.
17. Naidoo, "Auditors' Brand Set to Rival That of a CA."

case, the investigation of PwC's audits would likely take years to complete.[18]

In November 2006, South African police arrested a businessman on suspicion of involvement in the murder of Brett Kebble. The businessman, who was subsequently charged with murder and conspiracy to commit murder, is a close personal friend of the South African Police Commissioner and also reportedly a member of a South African crime syndicate. Several months after his arrest, the murder suspect confessed that he had been involved in Kebble's death *at Kebble's request.* According to the suspect, Kebble had arranged to have his "assisted suicide" appear as a murder so that his family could collect on large life insurance polices that he had purchased. Adding even more suspense to the case was an unconfirmed sighting of Brett Kebble on a remote Caribbean island by several South African citizens—Kebble's body, or what was allegedly Kebble's body, was cremated after his apparent murder. In any event, given the complexity of the case, South African law enforcement authorities believe that it may be years before it is ultimately solved.

---

## Questions

1. Research online and hardcopy databases to identify important recent developments within the South African accounting profession. Summarize these developments in a bullet format.
2. Over the history of the global accounting profession, political forces have often played a major role in the development of individual nations' independent audit function. Explain how political forces have influenced the development and evolution of the independent audit function in the United States.
3. Identify the advantages and disadvantages of having a professional credential or designation for independent auditors in addition to a professional credential for accountants.
4. In your opinion, should the United States adopt a rule similar to South Africa's "reportable irregularities" rule? Defend your answer. How do you believe such a requirement would affect the independent audit function and capital markets in the United States?
5. Identify strategies that the South African accounting profession could use to encourage young black men and women in that country to choose accounting as a career. In your opinion, what party or parties should take the lead in such recruiting efforts?

---

18. *Ibid.* In 2008, Randgold management filed a large civil lawsuit against PwC. Shortly thereafter, IRBA announced that it was suspending its investigation of PwC's Randgold audits pending the outcome of that lawsuit. Legal experts predict that, at the earliest, the case will go to trial sometime in 2011.

## CASE 8.5

# *Zuan Yan*

*Let China sleep, for when it wakes, it will shake the world.*

*Napoleon*

Every four years, the International Federation of Accountants (IFAC) organizes the World Congress of Accountants.[1] Accountants from across the globe attend this meeting to share their views on major issues and challenges facing their profession. In November 2002, the People's Republic of China hosted the World Congress of Accountants for the first time in the nation's history. Premier Zhu Rongji, the second-highest ranking official in the Chinese government, delivered the welcoming speech during the opening ceremonies. In his remarks, Premier Zhu, long known for his candid, if not blunt, manner, spoke openly of the embarrassing series of financial scandals that had created a major credibility crisis for the worldwide accounting profession over the previous decade. Premier Zhu pointed out that many of those accounting scandals had involved Chinese firms, a fact that Western journalists had largely ignored.

Similar to political leaders in many Western countries in recent years, Premier Zhu called on the accounting profession to reform itself and restore its credibility with the investing and lending public. He reminded the participants in the conference that "honesty and trustworthiness" are the lifeblood of the accounting profession.[2] Premier Zhu also assured those present that China was committed to "the cultivation of professional ethics among accountants" and, even more importantly, to creating a modern and transparent financial reporting system.[3]

### Then, Mao, and Now

For several millennia, a series of family dynasties ruled China; these included most notably the Han, Ming, and Qing Dynasties. The collapse of the Qing Dynasty in 1912 led to the creation of the Republic of China that was dominated by a political party known as the Kuomintang or National Party. For four years following the end of World War II, a bloody civil war ensued between forces loyal to Chiang Kai-shek, the leader of the National Party, and the increasingly popular Communist Party led by Mao Zedong and his top subordinate, Zhou Enlai. In 1949, the Communist Party gained control of the country, forcing Chiang Kai-shek and his followers into exile on the island of Taiwan. On October 1, 1949, the Communist country was renamed the People's Republic of China.

Mao immediately installed a Marxist regime in China under which the central government controlled practically all of the nation's economic resources. To revitalize China's economy that had been decimated by World War II and the Chinese civil war, Mao implemented a series of economic programs, most notably the "Great Leap Forward," that were intended to convert the nation's largely agricultural economy into a modern industrial economy. These programs were dismal failures, leaving China's economy in disarray and the country's citizens with a miserable standard of living.

---

1. "Zuan yan" is a Chinese phrase meaning "to search for the truth and hold fast to it."

2. *People's Daily*, "Cherish Integrity of Accounting Profession: Chinese Premier," english.peopledaily.com.cn, 21 November 2002.

3. *Ibid.*

In 1966, Mao launched the "Great Proletarian Cultural Revolution," more commonly referred to by historians as the "Cultural Revolution."[4] This sweeping set of social and economic reforms was intended to rid China of the "liberal bourgeoisie" that was allegedly undermining Mao's efforts to establish a utopian, Communistic society controlled by the working class. In reality, the Cultural Revolution was a desperate attempt by Mao to divert attention from his failed economic policies, while at the same time reaffirming his position as China's supreme leader. From 1966 through 1976, an estimated 500,000 Chinese citizens were executed and millions more exiled and persecuted at the hands of Mao's supporters.

Following Mao's death in 1976, several political figures wrestled for control of the country. Eventually, Deng Xiaoping established himself as China's unchallenged new leader, although he never officially held the top position in China's central government. Deng renounced the economic and social policies implemented by Mao during the Great Leap Forward and the Cultural Revolution. To raise China's standard of living, Deng replaced the nation's Soviet-style "command economy" with a "socialistic market economy."

Under China's new economic system, the nation's central government, which was still controlled by the Communist Party, would allow private enterprises to compete with state-owned enterprises (SOEs) across many sectors of the economy. Another critical element of Deng's economic blueprint was encouraging foreign companies to invest in China, a complete reversal of Mao's "closed door" policy. Deng especially encouraged large multinational corporations based in the United States and other Western countries to finance joint business ventures with Chinese SOEs.

In 1980, Deng emphatically endorsed his new economic plan for China, while at the same time shocking Communist allies and democratic societies around the world, when he proclaimed that "to be rich is to be glorious." Over the next three decades, Deng's economic policies, which remained in effect after his death in 1997, triggered an explosion of economic activity within China. By 2005, state-controlled enterprises accounted for only one-third of the nation's annual gross domestic product (GDP). Although still "poor" relative to common economic benchmarks, most Chinese citizens experienced a dramatic improvement in their standard of living under their nation's new "mixed" economy. Economists predict that by 2020 China's GDP will surpass that of Japan, making it the second-largest economy in the world. Those same economists project that by the midpoint of the twenty-first century, China's GDP will overtake that of the United States.

Deng Xiaoping's economic policies have impacted every facet of Chinese society, including the nation's professions, which had been largely discredited and debased during the three decades that Mao Zedong imposed his Marxist ideology on the country. Among the professional groups that have benefited the most from Deng's "revolution" is China's accounting profession. In recent years, China's political leaders have come to recognize that for their country to sustain its economic revival, a wide range of parties need reliable and comprehensive financial data regarding the nation's SOEs and other business enterprises. That data can only be provided if China develops a modern financial reporting system and an army of skilled accountants and auditors.

4. Wikipedia, "Cultural Revolution," en.wikipedia.org/wiki/Cultural_Revolution.

## Accounting for Profits

To fully appreciate the accounting and financial reporting issues facing the Chinese economy, it is first necessary to identify the major types of business organizations within China. Prior to 1980, SOEs were the overwhelmingly dominant form of business organization within China in terms of annual economic output. As a result of the economic reforms introduced by Deng Xiaoping, three additional types of business organizations have become well established within China: collectively-owned enterprises (COEs), individually-owned enterprises (IOEs), and enterprises with foreign investments (FOEs).[5] COEs are typically local cooperatives organized by the members of a small community, while IOEs are principally small businesses owned and operated by individual entrepreneurs. Because most COEs and IOEs do not obtain significant investment capital from third-party investors and lenders, external financial reporting is not a major concern or regulatory requirement of these two types of organizations.

FOEs are either joint business ventures involving Chinese companies—typically SOEs—and foreign multinational corporations, or China-based businesses that are wholly owned by foreign multinational corporations. As a result, the financial data of most FOEs are eventually integrated into the consolidated financial statements of a foreign multinational corporation domiciled in the United States, a member nation of the European Union, or another developed country, meaning that FOEs typically employ "Western-style" accounting and financial reporting systems.

Over the past three decades, the efforts to develop a modern accounting and financial reporting system within China have centered on SOEs. Although the annual economic output of SOEs as a percentage of China's GDP has been steadily decreasing over the past three decades, these organizations remain the most important business units in China. In recent years, the Chinese government has sold minority ownership interests in many SOEs to private investors, ownership interests that are traded on either the Shanghai or Shenzhen Stock Exchanges, China's two major stock exchanges. China's political leaders apparently have no intention of completely "privatizing" the large petrochemical, iron and steel, and other manufacturing enterprises that continue to make up the backbone of the nation's economic infrastructure.[6]

Despite the fact that SOEs remain under the control of China's central government, the organizational structure of these entities and their internal operating policies and procedures have changed dramatically under the economic system installed by Deng Xiaopeng. Likewise, the role of SOEs' accounting and financial reporting systems has changed radically.

> *Prior to 1978 . . . SOEs were essentially production units (factories). The managers of SOEs in the pre-reform era had little or no managerial autonomy. The state provided all financing to the factories and controlled virtually all the investment and operating decisions. . . . The factories simply served the purpose of fulfilling the production quota stipulated by the government. Consequently, the managers of these factories had neither the incentive nor the managerial authority to reduce costs and generate profits. In such a command economy, the main role of accounting was to assist the government in planning and controlling decisions.*[7]

---

5. X. Bing, "Institutional Factors Influencing China's Accounting Reforms and Standards," *Accounting Horizons*, June 1998, 107.

6. *Ibid.*, 109.

7. *Ibid.*

In China's present economic system, the central government has transferred the responsibility for the day-to-day operations and long-term strategic planning for most SOEs to professional management teams. So, despite being ultimately accountable to the central government, most SOEs "now significantly resemble modern corporations in the West in that they are characterized by a high degree of managerial autonomy and a separation of ownership from control."[8]

The dramatic change in the nature of SOEs over the past three decades has created a need for Western-style accounting systems for these organizations. Such accounting systems produce the data necessary to properly evaluate the operating decisions of professional management teams. Likewise, under China's new economic system, there is an explicit recognition on the part of the country's political leaders that individual SOEs are competing for a finite quantity of economic resources. Consequently, there is a need to regularly assess the extent to which individual SOEs are contributing to the overall economic productivity of the nation. Finally, the central government realizes that for SOEs to raise investment capital from external sources, they must provide those parties relevant financial data.

The Ministry of Finance (MOF) is the government agency responsible for overseeing China's economy, including the nation's financial reporting system. In 1993, the MOF adopted an accounting framework for China analogous to the "Conceptual Framework" developed by the U.S. accounting profession in the late 1980s. This framework was entitled "The Accounting Standards for Business Enterprises" (ASBE). Throughout the 1980s, the MOF and other Chinese government agencies had taken steps to revamp the outmoded accounting and financial reporting systems being used by SOEs. However, those measures had been largely ineffectual. The adoption of the ASBE suggested that China's central government was intent on requiring SOEs to adopt Western-style accounting and financial reporting practices. "The introduction of ASBE was considered the most significant achievement of China's accounting reforms since the 1980s in that it signaled the end of traditional accounting in China and brought China's accounting practices into close conformity with international standards."[9]

The ASBE required most SOEs and other large Chinese enterprises to adopt the fundamental accounting principles and financial reporting formats used in Western democracies. "Among the accounting characteristics specified in the standards [ASBE] are double-entry accrual records, consistency, conservatism, comparative financial statements . . . and explanatory disclosures."[10] Although the ASBE principally dealt with broad accounting and financial reporting issues, the pronouncement also introduced such specific accounting methods as LIFO/FIFO, the allowance method of accounting for bad debts, the percentage-of-completion approach to revenue recognition, accelerated depreciation methods, and consolidated financial statements. Following the issuance of the ASBE, the MOF retained Deloitte Touche Tohmatsu as a consultant to assist in developing a comprehensive set of accounting standards for the Chinese economy. Over the following decade, the MOF approved several dozen accounting standards proposed by Deloitte. These new standards were generally referred to as Chinese Accounting Standards (CAS).

8. *Ibid.*, 111.

9. T. Tang, B. Cooper, and P. Leung, "Accounting in China: Developments and Opportunities," in *Perspectives on Accounting and Finance in China*, edited by J.B. Black and S. Gao (London: Routledge, 1995).

10. G. M. Winkle, H. Fenwick, and X. Chen, "Accounting Standards in the People's Republic of China: Responding to Economic Reforms," *Accounting Horizons*, September 1994, 55.

As one would expect, there was almost no opposition to, or criticism of, the decision by China's authoritarian central government to adopt Western-style accounting standards. However, the MOF and other government agencies faced considerable challenges in executing that decision. The most intractable of these challenges stemmed from the fact that China's accounting profession had been dismantled under Mao Zedong's regime. As one journalist noted recently, "Grey hair and experience [in China's domestic accounting profession] are scarce because the Cultural Revolution wiped out the profession."[11]

Within Mao's Soviet-style economy, professional accountants who understood complex accounting and financial reporting issues were no longer needed and, in fact, were considered part and parcel of the "liberal bourgeoisie" that had to be eliminated. Instead of skilled accountants and auditors, China's state-controlled enterprises required only the services of bookkeepers and "bean counters" to accumulate production statistics and related data, which were then funneled to the proper authorities.

To help organize and promote China's accounting profession, the MOF created the Chinese Institute of Certified Public Accountants (CICPA) in 1988. This new government agency immediately began licensing CPAs; three years later, the agency began administering a CPA examination. In 1993, the "CPA Law" issued by China's central government provided a more coherent regulatory infrastructure for the new profession by documenting in detail the specific responsibilities of the CICPA. Although this law designated the CICPA as the principal regulatory body for the accounting profession, the powerful MOF retained the authority to override any decisions made by the CICPA.

Presently, China has approximately 150,000 CPAs; however, many of these individuals are retired government bureaucrats with minimal or even no formal training or experience in accounting. These latter individuals were granted CPA designations by the CICPA because they had administrative experience of some kind with an SOE or other significant government-related organization. Leaders of China's accounting profession estimate that the nation has fewer than 100,000 professional accountants who have formal accounting training of any kind. That figure is in contrast with the approximately 400,000 professional accountants in the United States, which has approximately one-fourth the population of China. Making matters worse, the educational programs completed by China's accountants are considerably less rigorous than the educational programs completed by professional accountants in Western economies. In fact, in 2000, fewer than 20 percent of China's CPAs held a university degree of any kind.[12]

Most of China's accounting firms were quickly organized in the early 1980s when the need for accounting services within the nation's new economy became evident. However, these new accounting firms were not equivalent to accounting firms in the United States and other developed economies. The largest and most prominent of China's new generation of accounting firms were created by various government agencies and, in reality, were simply appendages of those agencies. These "accounting firms" typically provided accounting services exclusively to the SOEs and other entities that were overseen by the agencies that had created the firms.

---

11. *The Asian Banker Journal* (online), "In Search of a Reliable Auditor," 31 August 2006.

12. Y. Tang, "Bumpy Road Leading to Internationalization: A Review of Accounting Development in China," *Accounting Horizons*, March 2000, 99.

Because the MOF and the CICPA recognized that the quality of services provided by the government agency-affiliated accounting firms was suspect, the two organizations launched a "clean-up" program in 1997 to force those firms to sever their relationships with the agencies that had created them. The MOF and CICPA also reviewed the operating policies and procedures of all Chinese accounting firms, including those not affiliated with government agencies. Over the course of the two-year clean-up program, approximately 10 percent of China's estimated 4,000 accounting firms were forced to disband, while another 30 percent were sanctioned and required to implement remedial measures of some kind.

Another principal objective of this clean-up program was to make accounting firms and individual accountants aware of their ethical responsibilities. One Chinese scholar observed that China's new accounting profession was created in a "moral vacuum" devoid of any consideration of ethical principles or issues.[13] In 1999, the CICPA issued a new authoritative pronouncement entitled "Professional Ethics" that identified the fundamental ethical responsibilities of Chinese CPAs, particularly their responsibility to perform accounting services with objectivity and integrity.

## Big Four Lead the Way in Chinese Audits

During the early 1980s, the major international accounting firms recognized that the robust economy emerging in China was creating a new and potentially huge market for professional accounting services. Over the following two decades, each of the major international accounting firms established a network of practice offices in China. PricewaterhouseCoopers (PwC) invested $200 million to staff 12 offices in China with a workforce of 5,500 accountants, while Deloitte spent approximately the same amount to establish 10 China-based offices with a staff of 3,000 accountants.[14] KPMG and Ernst & Young established China practice units of comparable size to those of PwC and Deloitte. As one Chinese news service noted, the Big Four firms suddenly developed an "insatiable interest" in the Chinese market.[15] Ernst & Young's global chief operating officer seemed to confirm that point of view when he observed, "There is no greater opportunity in the world than in China in terms of our business."[16]

By 2005, the Big Four accounting firms were operating the four largest accounting practices in China. The largest domestic firm, Shu Lun Pan Certified Public Accountants, based in Shanghai, had annual revenues equal to less than one-third of KPMG's China practice, which was the smallest of the Big Four accounting practices in terms of annual revenues. As could be expected, China's major domestic accounting firms felt threatened by the Big Four's rapid growth in their country.[17] Instead of choosing to compete with the Big Four, many of the large domestic firms developed working relationships with one or more Big Four firms.

Independent auditing was a principal focus of the Big Four's practice development activities in China. Prior to Deng Xiaoping's economic reforms, there was little need for an independent audit function in China similar to that of Western economies. The

13. *Ibid.*

14. *SinoCast China Financial Watch* (online), "Accounting Giants Load Up on China," 28 June 2005.

15. *Ibid.*

16. W. Davies, "China Accounting Sector Makes Gains amid IPO Drive," *Global News Wire—Asia Africa Intelligence Wire*, 6 February 2007.

17. T. LeeMaster, "Cleaner Regime for China Auditors," *Global News Wire—Asia Africa Intelligence Wire*, 18 April 2005.

SOEs that dominated China's economy did not prepare periodic financial reports comparable to those prepared by large corporations in the United States and other free market economies. In addition, the principal users of the financial data prepared by SOEs were government bureaucrats that had access to the accounting systems of SOEs and could "audit" that data directly if they questioned its authenticity.

As China's new economy began emerging, the need for an independent audit function became readily apparent. The large FOEs that were developing in China were typically required to have their financial data audited since those data would be consolidated into another reporting entity's financial statements. Likewise, China's political leaders quickly recognized that SOEs needed annual audits to encourage foreign investors to purchase minority ownership interests in them. Those officials also realized that annual audits of SOEs would establish an important measure of accountability for their professional management teams.

China's domestic independent audit function developed slowly and haphazardly during the 1980s. Unlike in the United States and other Western economies, China's accounting firms did not initially provide audit services. In the early 1980s, organizations offering audit-type services began appearing in China's major metropolitan areas. Similar to China's first-generation accounting firms, most of the nation's early audit firms were affiliated with, or sponsored by, a government agency. These audit firms—which were overseen by the State Audit Administration (SAA)—provided principally operational, compliance, and "social" audit services. Full-scope financial statement audits were rare, and when they were performed, they were not oriented around the rigorous professional standards used in Western economies. Eventually, many of China's larger domestic accounting firms began providing services similar to those provided by audit firms, resulting in significant competition between the two types of firms.

By the early 1990s, the Chinese audit market was a mishmash of various types of audit-type services and service providers. Adding to the confusion was an array of often conflicting auditing rules and regulations issued by the CICPA, MOF, SAA, and other government agencies that claimed some degree of regulatory oversight for the audit services market. This chaos was a contributing factor to several large-scale accounting and auditing scandals within China during the 1990s. Among the most notorious of these scandals was the Great Wall Fundraising fraud involving the Great Wall Electrical Engineering Science and Technology Company. This company's executives used financial statements "certified" by a local accounting firm to raise a large amount of funds from private investors across China, much of which they embezzled. A subsequent investigation revealed that the accounting firm had spent only one day auditing the company's financial statements. China's central government dealt quickly and harshly with the parties involved in the fraud. The chief architect of the fraud, the company president, was executed, while the company's accounting firm was disbanded.

The Great Wall Fundraising scandal and mounting criticism of China's chaotic audit services market by various parties, including the major international accounting firms, were key factors that persuaded the central government to issue the 1993 CPA Law. That statute consolidated the nation's accounting and auditing professions and placed them under the regulatory supervision of the CICPA, which remained ultimately accountable to the MOF. The CPA Law also mandated that the CICPA develop independent auditing standards that would be subject to the approval of the MOF.

In late 1994, the CICPA formed a task force to begin drafting Chinese Independent Auditing Standards (CIAS). Over the next several years, the CICPA issued auditing standards dealing with such topics as materiality, internal control risks, application of analytical procedures, computer-based auditing procedures, fraud detection, and "special considerations in the audit of state-owned companies."[18] Despite the promulgation of these standards, the quality of independent audits provided by domestic firms remained questionable. Many of China's domestic firms treated the new standards as guidelines rather than mandatory rules. Even more troubling, many audit clients routinely pressured their auditors to help them conceal material errors and fraudulent misrepresentations in their accounting records. "Some clients . . . expected their auditors to help them conceal their frauds. Many companies would not reappoint their auditors if the latter were unwilling to help them cover up their wrongdoings."[19]

As the Chinese audit discipline continued to evolve in the late 1990s and into the new century, the Big Four firms became increasingly important participants in that market. According to one Asian business publication, the Big Four's growing prominence in China's audit services market was due to those firms' reputation for "professionalism, technical ability, and their independence from clients."[20] By 2006, the Big Four firms audited a large majority of China's major business organizations. A Hong Kong brokerage firm surveyed 150 large companies listed on Chinese stock exchanges and found that only six did not employ Big Four auditors. The brokerage firm referred to those companies as the "suspicious six," implying that their financial statements were suspect.[21] A manager of a Hong Kong hedge fund expressed a similar point of view: "I don't think I'm comfortable with local [audit] firms. It's the professionalism of the people. It seems like they like to twist the rules. That bothers me."[22]

The most prized of all audit clients in China are the "Big Four" banks that serve as the cornerstones of the nation's economy. These banks include the Agricultural Bank of China, the Bank of China, the China Construction Bank, and the Industrial and Commercial Bank of China. Over the past several years, China's central government has used initial public offerings (IPOs) to sell minority ownership interests in these formerly wholly owned SOEs. For each of those IPOs, government officials retained a Big Four accounting firm to audit the given bank's financial statements. This "vote of confidence" in the Big Four accounting firms by China's political leaders suggested that those firms would likely play a significant role in the future development of the Chinese economy.

## EPILOGUE

In 2005, the MOF announced that it was working with the International Accounting Standards Board (IASB) to converge CAS with International Financial Reporting Standards (IFRS). Most Chinese business organizations would be required to adopt the revised CAS as of January 1, 2007, although several large SOEs were given an additional year to make the transition to the new standards. The IASB reported that it would help Chinese officials modify certain IFRS to meet the special needs of China's economic system. Among the latter IFRS was the standard requiring disclosure of material related-party transactions.

18. J. Z. Xiao, Y. Zhang, and Z. Xie, "The Making of Independent Auditing Standards in China," *Accounting Horizons*, March 2000, 77.

19. *Ibid.*

20. *The Asian Banker Journal*, "In Search of a Reliable Auditor."

21. *Ibid.*

22. *Ibid.*

> *This is a sound principle in general and particularly appropriate for companies in countries where the government owns a piece of everything, and presses companies to take steps that may be bad for them (such as buying from troubled suppliers to protect jobs). But because overlapping ownership is so common in China (the government still owns shares in almost every large company), detailing each [related-party] transaction would overwhelm the financial report.*[23]

At the same time that the MOF announced the plan to converge CAS with IFRS, the government agency also announced that as of January 1, 2007, CIAS would be converged with International Standards on Auditing (ISAs). These latter standards are issued by the International Auditing and Assurance Standards Board (IAASB), an entity sponsored by the IFAC. In February 2006, the MOF released 39 new accounting standards and 48 new auditing standards that had been converged with the respective international standards.

The decision by the MOF to converge Chinese accounting and auditing standards with international standards enhanced the already strong competitive position that the Big Four firms had established within the Chinese accounting and auditing services market. Because each of those firms had global accounting practices, they had extensive expertise in helping companies implement IFRS as well as significant experience in applying ISAs. As a result, the firms were ideally suited to help Chinese companies make the transition to the new accounting and auditing standards.

Despite the Big Four's bright prospects in China, the firms still face significant challenges in that market. These challenges include acquiring sufficient skilled accountants and auditors to staff their rapidly growing Chinese practices and coping with the nation's regulatory infrastructure that continues to be a cluttered maze of often conflicting regulations issued by several layers of the Communist bureaucracy. Two more serious and difficult-to-resolve problems facing Big Four firms are an increasing litigation risk within China and the need to deal with an authoritarian central government that influences every facet of the Chinese society and economy.

Since the 1970s, arguably the most important challenge faced by the Big Four accounting firms in the United States has been the large number of civil lawsuits filed against them. In recent years, the Big Four firms have begun experiencing litigation problems in China. Numerous accounting frauds, embezzlement schemes, and related scams have been perpetrated by opportunists hoping to take advantage of China's new economic system. Many private investors, institutional investors, government agencies, and other parties adversely affected by these subterfuges have begun adopting a Western-style strategy to recover their losses and/or mend their wounded pride, namely, filing lawsuits against parties even remotely associated with the fraudulent activities. At least in part because of their "deep pockets" and high public profiles, Big Four firms have increasingly found themselves targets of such lawsuits.

In 2003, KPMG became the first of the Big Four accounting firms to be named as a defendant in a major securities lawsuit filed by Chinese investors. The accounting firm issued a series of unqualified opinions on the financial statements of Jinzhou Port Company Limited, a company sanctioned by the MOF for intentionally overstating its revenues over the five-year period 1996–2000. The other Big Four firms have been ensnared in similar financial scandals involving Chinese companies: Deloitte (Guangdong Kelon Electrical Holdings Company), PwC (Shanghai Waigaoqiao Free Trade Zone Development Company Limited), and Ernst & Young (Global Trend Intelligent Technologies).

The Big Four firms insist that the complaints filed against them in these and other cases are unwarranted and that the engagements in question were completed with due professional care. Nevertheless, critics suggest that the quality of independent audits in China is generally weaker than in Western countries, an allegation seemingly confirmed by a Deloitte partner.

---

23. *The Economist* (online), "Cultural Revolution: New Accounting Rules Have Replaced the Little Red Book as China's Guide to Self-improvement; Can the State Handle the Truth?" 11 January 2007.

"Auditing is easier in an environment where all your clients have 25 accountants, internal controls, and independent boards. The audit process is the same in this part of the world; we follow the same methodology and document it in the same way. But, the material you're dealing with is different."[24] A KPMG partner voiced a similar opinion when he noted that within China, "the public expects too much of auditors. Audit work is one thing. The most important thing is the integrity of the owners and managers."[25]

An even more serious challenge than the increasing risk of civil litigation facing the Big Four accounting firms in China is how they will deal with their ultimate "client" in that market, namely, the authoritarian central government. No doubt, executives of the Big Four firms recognize that conflicts with officials of the Chinese government could damage their future opportunities in the lucrative Chinese market. These executives also realize that their credibility in other markets around the globe could be damaged if their firms are perceived as kowtowing or capitulating to Chinese governmental officials.

Ernst & Young was the first of the Big Four firms to have a highly publicized confrontation with China's Communist central government. In 2006, a Chinese government agency hired Ernst & Young to prepare a report on the "nonperforming loans" held by China's Big Four banks. Over the previous several years, the magnitude of China's nonperforming loans had become a major international issue. "The size of China's bad loans is a figure of immense importance, as it serves as a measure of the banking sector's financial health."[26] Many economists maintained that governmental officials routinely embellished the health of the Chinese economy by refusing to disclose that a large proportion of the Big Four banks' loan portfolios were uncollectible. Allegedly, those officials refused to recognize the magnitude of this problem because doing so would damage China's credit rating in international markets, discourage much-needed foreign investment, and undercut the impressive economic trends that the central government regularly touted in the global press.

In May 2006, Ernst & Young reported that China's Big Four banks had total nonperforming loans of more than $900 billion. That figure was several times higher than the $133 billion figure being reported by the Chinese government. Chinese officials reacted quickly and fiercely to the E&Y report, referring to it as "ridiculous and barely understandable."[27] Those officials went on to point out that if the nonperforming loans figure reported by E&Y was accurate, then the "clean" opinion E&Y had issued on a Big Four bank's financial statements was almost certainly wrong.

Within a few days of the harsh criticism by Chinese officials, Ernst & Young retracted its report. In the retraction, Ernst & Young stated that, "Upon further research, Ernst & Young Global finds that this number cannot be supported, and believes it to be factually erroneous."[28] The retraction went on to note that Ernst & Young believed that the nonperforming loans figure reported by the Chinese government of $133 billion was accurate. Skeptics immediately accused E&Y of capitulating to the Chinese government. Many economic analysts chimed in as well, insisting that the Chinese government's figure was only a fraction of the actual bad loans held by the Big Four banks.

The E&Y incident raised two concerns within the global investment and business community. First, the incident only added to widespread speculation that China's impressive economic data had been intentionally inflated by the nation's Communist government. "It has become an article of faith over the past quarter

---

24. *The Asian Banker Journal,* "In Search of a Reliable Auditor."

25. *Ibid.*

26. *Agence France Presse* (online), "Ernst & Young Withdraws 'Erroneous' Report on Bad Loans in China," 15 May 2006.

27. J. Manthorpe, "Accountants Backtrack on China Bad-Debt Report," *The Vancouver Sun*, 23 May 2006, E5.

28. *Ibid.*

of a century of China's economic opening up that numbers issued by the Beijing government are at best rose-tinted, and at worst politically motivated fabrications."[29] Second, the incident suggested that China's central government would not hesitate to use its authoritarian powers to stifle dissent or honest differences of opinion, even an objective opinion expressed by a respected international accounting firm.

Ernst & Young's unpleasant encounter with Chinese governmental officials angered many Western journalists. In commenting on that encounter, one such journalist suggested that those officials had not internalized the slogan adopted by Deng Xiaoping when he attempted to resurrect the Chinese economy after nearly 30 years of the failed policies of Mao Zedong. "'Truth from facts' was the slogan adopted by the Chinese government after Mao's death to strip away the lies that left China a wallowing giant. Thirty years on, this remains an elusive goal."[30]

## Questions

1. Research relevant databases to identify important recent developments within China's accounting profession, including the nation's independent audit function. Summarize these developments in a bullet format.
2. Since ethical and moral values vary from culture to culture and nation to nation, does this mean that a global profession, such as the accounting profession, cannot have a uniform ethical code? Explain.
3. How, if at all, do financial reporting objectives differ between a free market economy and a "socialistic market economy"? Explain. Are there specific accounting concepts or principles that are more or less relevant in a free market economy than in a socialistic market economy? If so, identify those concepts or principles and briefly explain your rationale.
4. Consider two organizations that require annual independent audits. Organization A is a Chinese SOE with a minority ownership interest of 20 percent, while Organization B is a U.S. company of similar size operating in the same industry. The common stock of both entities is traded on a domestic stock exchange and each is audited by a Big Four firm. List specific differences that you might expect in the independent audits of these two organizations. *Ceteris paribus*, would you expect more "audit failures" for SOE audit clients than for similar U.S. audit clients? Defend your answer.
5. What recommendations would you make to Big Four firms to help them (1) avoid confrontations with governmental officials in an authoritarian society and (2) deal effectively with such confrontations that do arise?

29. *Ibid.*

30. *The Economist*, "Truth from Facts," 13 January 2007, 14.

**CASE 8.6**

# Kaset Thai Sugar Company

The black Toyota minivan made slow but steady progress down the narrow, unpaved road as it approached the village of Takhli in south central Thailand, approximately 150 miles north of Bangkok. On either side of the bumpy road were fields of sugarcane, dense thickets of scrub brush, and an occasional rice paddy. Seated in a rear window seat of the minivan was Michael Wansley, a senior partner with Deloitte Touche Tohmatsu who was based in that firm's Melbourne, Australia, practice office. The vehicle's four other occupants were Thai nationals and employees of the Kaset Thai Sugar Company. No doubt, the five weary travelers who had spent several hours in the cramped minivan were overjoyed when they finally caught a glimpse of the large sugar mill in the distance that was their final destination. The sugar mill was one of many owned and operated by the Kaset Thai Sugar Company.

For the past several weeks, Michael Wansley had been supervising a debt-restructuring engagement for the company's banks and other lenders. Kaset Thai Sugar had defaulted on nearly $500 million of loans to those lenders. Wansley and the 14 subordinates on his engagement team were to study the company's accounting records and business operations and then make recommendations about how the lenders should proceed in attempting to collect all—or, at least, a significant portion—of the outstanding loans.

Wansley, a well known debt-restructuring expert, had become all too familiar with remote Thailand communities such as Takhli over the previous several months because the services of debt-restructuring specialists were much in demand within Thailand during the late 1990s. In March 1999 when Wansley visited the sugar mill on the outskirts of Takhli, the nation of Thailand was mired in a financial crisis. From 1985 through 1995, Thailand had boasted the highest economic growth rate in the world, averaging almost 9 percent annually over that time span. That trend prompted billions of dollars of foreign direct investment in Thailand companies, the bulk of which was in the form of loans.

Thailand's impressive economic growth came to a jarring halt in 1997, undercut by speculative investments, mismanagement, and extensive fraud on the part of business owners and corporate executives. According to one critic of Thailand's free-wheeling economic system, "cronyism, collusion, corruption, and complacency" had long been the "four modern horsemen of the apocalypse" in that economy.[1] By the late 1990s, hundreds of Thai companies faced bankruptcy, unable to pay back the loans they had secured over the previous decade. In 1999, nearly one-half of the $150 billion in outstanding loans to large Thai companies was classified as "nonperforming"—and it was estimated that $50 billion of that total would never be collected."[2]

As Thailand's financial crisis deepened, the foreign banks and other lenders that had pumped billions of dollars of debt capital into Thai companies began retaining

1. U. Parpart, "Restructuring East Asia: A Progress Report," *The Milken Institute Review*, Third Quarter 1999, 42.

2. *Ibid.*, 40.

debt-restructuring specialists in Australia, the United States, and other developed countries to help them determine how to best deal with their mounting portfolios of nonperforming loans. Among the major providers of these debt-restructuring services were the large international accounting firms, including Deloitte, Michael Wansley's firm.

The nature of debt-restructuring services varies significantly but such engagements often begin with an intense study or "audit" of the given entity's accounting records. This examination is intended to uncover any evidence of embezzlement or other malfeasance by management or other parties. These engagements also commonly include an in-depth analysis of the debtor company's business model to determine whether the entity appears to be economically viable. A debt-restructuring engagement typically concludes with the engagement team developing a series of recommendations intended to help the lenders of the financially troubled company minimize their loan losses. These recommendations may involve replacing the existing management team, having the lender or lenders forgive their outstanding loans in exchange for equity interests in the given company, or liquidating the company to raise funds that can be used to repay or partially repay its outstanding loans.

Not surprisingly given their nature and purpose, debt-restructuring engagements can be rife with tension. *Business Week* noted that Thailand's financial crisis spawned "Debt Wars" in that country that pitted representatives of the large international accounting firms, such as Michael Wansley, against Thai business owners and executives.[3] Thai business owners and executives resented the probing and relentless investigations of the "farangs" (foreigners) who did not appreciate or fully understand the informal and low-key culture of the Thai business community, a culture in which "handshake" contracts were common, disagreements were considered impolite, and face-to-face confrontations were rare. Making matters worse, Thai companies were not accustomed to having their financial records and business operations scrutinized by third parties since the nation's independent audit function was still evolving and was not nearly as rigorous as in developed countries around the world.

The investigative work of debt-restructuring specialists was particularly galling to members of the wealthy Thai families that had long dominated their nation's economy. Until the late 1990s, 15 Thai families controlled networks of businesses that accounted for more than one-half of Thailand's annual gross domestic product.[4] Among these families was the Siriviriyakul family that owned the Kaset Thai Sugar Company. For centuries, these families had operated their business empires with only minimal oversight or regulation by the Thai government or other parties. Suddenly, these prominent families found themselves being forced to respond to embarrassing questions and accusations posed by a small army of foreign accountants.

In January 1999, *Business Week* interviewed the 58-year-old Wansley regarding the difficult and stressful nature of his work in Thailand. Wansley noted that the most frustrating facet of debt-restructuring engagements in Thailand was the belligerent attitude of company owners. "Once you become grossly insolvent you're not supposed to be in a position of great strength, but here they think they are."[5] In a subsequent interview, Wansley also admitted that the hostile nature of the debt-restructuring engagements caused him to sometimes question his and his subordinates' safety. That concern was not unwarranted.

---

3. F. Balfour, "Fixing Thailand's Debt Mess," *Business Week* (www.businessweek.com), 12 February 2001.

4. Parpart, "Restructuring East Asia," 41.

5. R. Corben, M. Clifford, and B. Einhorn, "Thailand: Bring Your Spreadsheet—and Bulletproof Vest," *Business Week* (www.businessweek.com), 29 March 1999.

As the black minivan carrying Wansley and the four employees of Kaset Thai Sugar Company rolled to a stop outside the firm's Takhli sugar mill, two men on a motorcycle pulled up beside the vehicle. The man sitting on the rear of the motorcycle leaped off and within a matter of seconds fired eight bullets from an automatic pistol into the interior of the minivan. The bullets struck Michael Wansley in the head, killing him instantly. The four other passengers in the minivan were left unharmed as the gunman and his confederate sped away on the motorcycle.

The murder of Michael Wansley triggered outrage in Australia and the international business community. Australian government officials demanded that Thailand law enforcement authorities vigorously investigate the crime and apprehend those responsible. Eventually, six individuals would face criminal charges for Wansley's murder. These individuals included the gunman, the motorcyclist, the owner of the motorcycle, two employees of Kaset Thai Sugar Company who had allegedly been involved in the conspiracy to kill Wansley, and the owner of the Takhli sugar mill who was a member of the powerful Siriviriyakul family. This latter individual was charged with masterminding Wansley's murder.

The motorcyclist, who was arrested shortly after the incident, was convicted for his role in the crime and given a life sentence. A human resources manager of Kaset Thai Sugar and the owner of the motorcycle, a retired policeman, were convicted of conspiring to murder Wansley and received death sentences. The brother of the human resources manager, who was also a Kaset Thai Sugar employee, was convicted of conspiracy to commit murder but received a life sentence. In July 2008, the individual who allegedly shot Wansley was acquitted of that crime by a Thai court. The only witnesses who identified that individual as the gunman were two of his alleged co-conspirators; however, those witnesses' testimony was dismissed by the court. The court ruled that those witnesses were not credible since they were convicted felons.

The most controversial outcome in the criminal cases emanating from Wansley's death was the acquittal of the owner of the Takhli sugar mill despite seemingly strong evidence linking him to the crime. During this individual's trial, a witness testified that the defendant had paid him approximately $1,000 to dispose of the motorcycle used in the Wansley murder. Another individual, a senior law enforcement official, revealed that the sugar mill owner had offered him $4 million in exchange for not filing charges against him in the case. Phone records introduced as evidence during the trial documented that prior to the shooting the defendant had frequent telephone conversations with the three individuals convicted of conspiring to kill Wansley.

Court testimony also revealed that shortly before his death, Michael Wansley discovered that approximately $150 million loaned to the Kaset Thai Sugar Company had been secretly transferred to small companies controlled by the sugar mill owner and other members of his family. This testimony established that the defendant had a strong motive to harm Wansley. In fact, a Kaset Thai Sugar employee testified that following Wansley's death, the sugar mill owner had told him, "It's very good the farang is dead; now we can all live comfortably."[6] Despite such evidence, the three-judge tribunal that presided over the trial handed down a "not guilty" verdict, clearing the sugar mill owner of any involvement in Wansley's murder.[7,8]

---

6. J. Pollard, "Death Penalty for Aussie Auditor's Killers," *The Australian* (www.theaustralian.news.com.au), 6 September 2006.

7. One of the judges initially assigned to the case had been replaced when allegations surfaced that he had been paid a large bribe by the defendant's family.

8. The Siriviriyakul family maintained control of the Kaset Thai Sugar Company following Michael Wansley's death. When the debt-restructuring plan eventually developed by Deloitte was rejected by the company's creditors, a Thai court refused to liquidate the company and instead allowed the Siriviriyakul family to continue operating it.

The six individuals who faced criminal charges stemming from the murder of Michael Wansley were not the only parties blamed for his death. A journalist suggested that Wansley's employer, Deloitte, should shoulder some of the blame for his untimely death. Deloitte officials "should have known that they were sending the locally inexperienced Wansley into a dangerous situation without taking precautions."[9] The journalist pointed out that among the major international accounting firms, Deloitte had established a reputation as a leader in risk assessment and risk management. "These days, expertise in risk assessment—on which D. T. T. [Deloitte Touche Tohmatsu] prides itself—cannot be prudently limited to financial risk."[10]

Deloitte apparently did not respond directly to such criticism. However, several years later, Keith Skinner, the chief operating officer (COO) of Deloitte Touche Tohmatsu and a close friend of Michael Wansley, agreed to be interviewed regarding Wansley's death. In that interview, Skinner indicated that Wansley's murder "has had a lasting impact" on Deloitte's operations in regions of the world that are "culturally different."[11] When asked what specific changes Deloitte had made in response to the incident, Skinner reported that Deloitte was placing a higher priority on "security" issues for professional services engagements in high-risk countries. During this same interview, Skinner noted that his friend had not only been a well-respected professional but also an individual who was known for his extraordinary personal integrity and for being a devoted humanitarian. In particular, Wansley had devoted considerable time to working with the International Red Cross.

## Questions

1. Suppose in the future you are assigned to an audit engagement that requires you to travel to a foreign country openly hostile to the United States. Because of that hostility, you are uncomfortable with the assignment. What would you do? Before responding, identify the alternatives you have.
2. Do you believe it is appropriate for a professional services firm to ask employees to serve on engagements in which their personal safety is at risk? Defend your answer.

9. Parpart, "Restructuring East Asia," 39.

10. *Ibid.*

11. A. Caldwell, "Murdered Accountant's Son Welcomes Sentences," www.abc.net.au, 5 September 2006.

**CASE 8.7**

# Australian Wheat Board

The United States and the Commonwealth of Australia have long been strong and mutually supportive allies.[1] However, the two countries' close relationship was threatened recently by an international scandal referred to in the *Sydney Morning Herald*, Australia's oldest and most prominent newspaper, as the "worst corruption scandal in Australian history."[2] At the center of this scandal was AWB Limited, a large public company that had been granted a government monopoly over the export of all wheat from that country. During the United Nations embargo imposed on Iraq following that country's invasion of Kuwait, AWB became the largest supplier of wheat to Iraq. AWB's wheat sales to Iraq were made through the United Nations (U.N.) Oil-for-Food Program, a program intended to provide humanitarian relief to Iraqi citizens during the lengthy U.N. embargo.

Following the overthrow of Saddam Hussein's regime by U.S.-led coalition forces in 2003, allegations surfaced that AWB had secured the Iraqi wheat contracts by agreeing to pay bribes to the former dictator. The U.N. formed a task force headed by Paul Volcker, the former chairman of the United States' Federal Reserve System, to investigate those allegations. In late 2005, the task force reported that AWB had paid nearly $300 million in bribes to Saddam Hussein's regime beginning in the late 1990s. AWB management had been told by Iraqi governmental officials that if the bribes were not paid, the company would be denied the huge wheat contracts.

A former AWB officer testified that one of his superiors approved the payment of the Iraqi bribes. In defense of those illicit payments, the superior told this individual, "We are in the business of maximizing opportunities and sales returns" and, as a result, "we shouldn't jeopardize our business with Iraq"[3] [by refusing to pay the bribes demanded by Saddam Hussein]. After the fact, some AWB stockholders defended the company's decision to capitulate to Saddam Hussein's demands. "We have had enough of this free market bulls___. When you do business with Saddam, you do business the way he tells you."[4]

The AWB scandal created a brouhaha between Australia's two leading political parties, the Liberal Party and the Labor Party. Political opponents of Prime Minister John Howard, the leader of the Liberal Party, charged that he and his subordinates had approved AWB's decision to secretly funnel bribes to Saddam Hussein to secure the lucrative Iraqi wheat contracts. In referring to those bribes, a spokesperson for the Labor Party noted that, "This is the single biggest lump of money in the world paid to the Iraqi dictator, straight out of Australia, approved by the Australian government."[5]

---

1. I would like to thank Glen McLaughlin for his generous and continuing support of efforts to develop instructional cases for use in accounting and auditing courses that highlight important ethical issues.

2. *Sydney Morning Herald* (online), "AWB's World of Trouble," 25 November 2006.

3. Australian Government, Attorney-General's Department, "Inquiry into Certain Australian Companies in Relation to the UN Oil-for-Food Programme," Transcript 24, 2322, 9 February 2006.

4. H. Stringleman, "Aussie Farmers Fume over Single-Desk Loss," *The National Business Review*, 5 May 2006, 14.

5. *Associated Press* (online), "Australian Attorney General Defends Country's Stance on Bribery against OECD Criticism," 17 January 2006.

Criticism of Prime Minister Howard was not confined to Australia. U.S. wheat farmers and several large U.S. wheat exporters, such as Cargill, Inc., were incensed by the revelations of how AWB had obtained the Iraqi wheat contracts and insisted that the United States take appropriate measures to punish Australia. U.S. Senator Norm Coleman of Minnesota, a leading spokesperson for U.S. wheat producers, publicly criticized Prime Minister Howard and suggested that, at a minimum, the prime minister had been aware that AWB was paying the bribes. This accusation prompted an irate Prime Minister Howard, who had long been an ardent supporter of the United States and its Middle Eastern policies, to demand an apology from the U.S. government, an apology that the prime minister never received.

## Wheat Socialism

The Australian government created the Australian Wheat Board in 1939 to provide economic assistance to the country's wheat farmers. Many of the nation's wheat farmers had struggled to survive the Great Depression of the 1930s that had caused just as much, if not more, economic misery in Australia as it had in the United States. For the next five decades, all wheat grown in Australia had to be sold to the Australian Wheat Board at a price established by the federal agency. In 1989, Australia's federal government deregulated the nation's domestic wheat market, but any wheat that was to be exported, which was the bulk of the nation's annual harvest, still had to be sold to the Australian Wheat Board. The Australian Wheat Board pooled the wheat purchased each year for export and then marketed it principally to developing countries around the world. Proceeds from the sale of the wheat were then distributed on a pro rata basis to Australia's wheat farmers.

In 1999, Australia's federal government converted the Australian Wheat Board into AWB Limited, a private company with two classes of common stock. AWB's Class A common stock was distributed to the country's wheat farmers. This stock is nontransferable and must be sold back to AWB if an individual stops growing wheat. In 1991, AWB's Class B common stock was sold on the Australian Stock Exchange for the first time. Class B stock can be purchased by anyone, but Australian law prohibits any individual or institution from accumulating more than 10 percent of those shares. Since 9 of the 11 seats on AWB's board of directors are chosen by the Class A stockholders, Australia's wheat farmers exercise effective control over the company.

The so-called "single desk" system implemented for Australia's wheat industry was an economic boon for the nation's wheat farmers. That market structure allowed Australia to become a major player in the intensely competitive global wheat market. By the end of the century, Australia ranked second only to the United States in that market. Although Australia produced only 3 percent of the world's wheat harvest each year, the country accounted for 15 percent of annual wheat exports. Thanks to the AWB, Australian wheat was being sold to more than 50 countries by the late 1990s.

Many wheat exporters around the world, particularly major exporters in the United States, maintained that AWB achieved its lofty position in the global wheat market by relying on bribes, kickbacks, and other illicit payments to obtain major international wheat contracts. An Australian politician suggested that such payments were necessary to compete in the "corrupt" global wheat market.[6,7] That politician

6. D. Crawshaw, C. Brinsden, and P. Mulvey, "Tensions High as AWB Monopoly Crumbles," *Global News Wire* (online), 22 December 2006.

7. As a point of information, international wheat vendors outside of the United States have long maintained that government subsidies provide U.S. wheat growers with an unfair economic advantage over wheat exporters from other countries.

was referring to the fact that bribes, kickbacks, and similar payments have long characterized that market. Allegedly, governmental officials in the developing countries that are the principal buyers of exported wheat have historically demanded such payments from international wheat vendors in exchange for granting sales contracts to them.

Foreign competitors' use of bribes, kickbacks, and other illicit payments to acquire large wheat contracts was particularly galling to U.S. wheat exporters. In 1977, the U.S. Congress adopted the Foreign Corrupt Practices Act (FCPA) that prohibits U.S. companies from paying bribes or kickbacks to officials of foreign governments to initiate or maintain business relationships in those countries. The FCPA also requires U.S. companies to establish accounting and internal control systems that provide reasonable assurance of discovering such payments.[8] In the early 1990s, a member of President Bill Clinton's administration admitted that U.S. exporters were facing an "uneven playing field" in the markets in which they competed because the United States was the only country at the time that had "criminalized bribery of foreign officials."[9]

## Bribes vs. Facilitating Payments

The Organization of Economic Cooperation and Development (OECD) is an international organization of 30 democratic governments that assists its member countries in addressing a wide range of economic issues, including economic growth and development, the sharing of new technologies, and international trade disputes. Members of the OECD include, among other countries, Australia, Canada, France, Germany, Japan, Mexico, the United Kingdom, and the United States. Increasing concern over the integrity of international markets during the 1990s prompted the OECD to develop the *Convention Against the Bribery of Foreign Public Officials in International Business Transactions*, which was modeled after the FCPA. This convention, which the OECD adopted in 1996, obligated the organization's 30 member countries to "criminalize" bribes that are paid to foreign governmental officials by companies that wish to gain a competitive advantage.

Following the Australian Parliament's passage of legislation to adopt the OECD Convention, Australian companies involved in international trade realized that they could face criminal prosecution if they paid bribes to establish or sustain international business relationships. To address this issue, many companies, including AWB, modified their corporate codes of conduct to recognize the responsibilities imposed on them by the new law.

A major focus of AWB's effort to ensure compliance with the new law was to make their executives and employees aware of the important distinction between "bribes" and "facilitating payments." Generally, bribes are significant amounts paid to foreign governmental officials to secure or retain business, while facilitating payments are relatively modest and routine payments typically made to lower-ranking governmental officials to expedite or "facilitate" business transactions. For example, a small payment made to a government clerk to expedite the unloading of goods at a foreign port would be considered a facilitating payment and not a bribe. The OECD

8. Case 3.4, "Triton Energy Ltd.," summarizes the FCPA's key anti-bribery and internal control provisions and discusses one of the few cases prosecuted under that federal statute by U.S. law enforcement authorities.

9. A. Zipser, "A Rarely Enforced Law," *Barron's*, 25 May 1992, 14.

Convention did not require member countries to criminalize facilitating payments as long as those payments are legal in the countries in which they are made.[10]

AWB modified its Corporate Ethics and Code of Conduct Policy to acknowledge that bribes are illegal but facilitating payments are not. According to that document, facilitating payments are "used to smooth business deals or engender goodwill with customers" and thus "technically differ from bribes, which are solely associated with illegal practices."[11] More specifically, AWB defined a facilitating payment as a "small benefit to a foreign public official in order to facilitate routine government action of a minor nature."[12] AWB's corporate code also addressed hypothetical questions that employees might face regarding facilitating payments. Following is one such question and the company's response:

> Question: I am managing an operation in a country where it is accepted practice for government officials to receive facilitation fees to speed up government approvals. Should I work within the system?
>
> Answer: Where payment of these fees would break the law, AWB does not approve the making of the payments. If it is legal to pay facilitation fees and local business practice to pay them, you should review the matter with your line manager. You should consider if payment would be ethical if its disclosure would cause embarrassment to the company.[13]

## When in Rome

During the late 1990s and beyond, top AWB executives and their key subordinates ignored the new Australian law and their company's explicit policy prohibiting the payment of bribes to acquire international business contracts. Those conspirators realized that they had to disguise those payments so that they would not be uncovered by their independent auditors, internal auditors, or board of directors. In fact, according to subsequent statements made by a former Iraqi governmental official, representatives of international wheat vendors, such as AWB, often responded to requests for the payment of bribes by stating, "I can't do it. I've got a board. How do I get around my auditors?"[14] Saddam Hussein's subordinates would then explain to those executives how the payments could be made to avoid detection.

The U.N. investigation of the bribes linked to the Oil-for-Food Program was prompted by an Iraqi newspaper reporter who revealed the scheme in January 2004 following the collapse of Saddam Hussein's government the year before. In 2006, Kofi Annan, Secretary-General of the United Nations, demanded that Australia and other countries in which companies had made illicit payments to Saddam Hussein's regime take appropriate measures to punish the parties responsible for those payments. That same year, Prime Minister Howard appointed a former Australian judge, Terence Cole, to oversee a "royal commission," or task force, to investigate the AWB scandal.

---

10. The FCPA was initially unclear regarding whether or not facilitating payments qualified as bribes and thus were illegal under that federal statute. In 1988, the FCPA was amended to address that issue. As amended, "facilitating payments" made to encourage "routine governmental action" are not covered by the FCPA.

11. J. Barrett, "Policy on Payments Lost from AWB Site," *The Australian*, 25 February 2006, 4.

12. D. Uren, "Tax Law Change to Curb Crimes," *The Australian*, 9 February 2006, 8.

13. Barrett, "Policy on Payments Lost."

14. C. Overington, "Probe on Wheat Sales to Iraq," theage.com (www.theage.com.au), 29 April 2004.

Former AWB officials who testified before the Cole Commission explained that one of the biggest challenges they and other conspirators had faced was concealing the bribery payments from the United Nations. Under the U.N.'s Oil-for-Food Program, Iraq was permitted to sell a limited amount of oil each year during the U.N. embargo to provide the funds necessary to purchase food, medical supplies, and other necessities for Iraqi citizens. The proceeds from the sale of that oil were deposited in bank accounts controlled by the U.N. After Iraqi officials had negotiated to purchase goods from specific foreign companies, such as AWB, the U.N. disbursed payments to those companies from those bank accounts. AWB concealed the bribery payments from the U.N., as well as from its independent auditors and other parties, by funneling them through a Jordanian trucking company that was allegedly transporting the wheat to Iraq. The Jordanian company kept a small percentage of the bribes and then forwarded the balance to Hussein's regime in Baghdad.

AWB officials also devised a plan to recoup the bribes being paid to the Iraqi government. This scheme simply involved inflating the price of the wheat sold to Iraq to include those bribes. In an intracompany AWB correspondence obtained by the Cole Commission during its hearings, a company executive told one of his subordinates that because the bribe payments were being recouped from the U.N. Oil-for-Food bank accounts, they were "no skin off our nose."[15] A journalist for the *Sydney Morning Herald* berated the conspirators for this feature of the AWB fraud. "Extraordinary chutzpah was involved here. After all, the money [bribe payments] didn't even come out of AWB's pockets. It was siphoned by the wheat trader out of U.N.-held funds in New York. The defining detail of this scandal is that these bribes were free."[16] AWB also deducted the bribe payments as normal business expenses in its annual tax returns filed with the Australian Taxation Office, the Australian equivalent of the U.S. Internal Revenue Service.

The AWB official who had been responsible for overseeing wheat sales to Middle Eastern countries testified before the Cole Commission that by early 2000 there was "widespread" knowledge within AWB of the illicit payments being made to the Iraqi government.[17] Two other former AWB officials who were not involved in the decision to pay the bribes testified that they questioned the propriety of the payments to the Jordanian trucking company when they became aware of them and then retained Arthur Andersen & Co. to investigate the payments.

During the time frame that AWB was paying the bribes, Ernst & Young served as the company's independent audit firm and issued an unqualified opinion each year on the company's financial statements. Exhibit 1 presents the unqualified opinion Ernst & Young issued on AWB's fiscal year 2000 financial statements, while Exhibit 2 presents the mandatory "Directors' Declaration" that accompanied the 2000 audit opinion. Available sources do not reveal why the two AWB officials who questioned the payments being made by AWB to the Jordanian trucking company did not ask Ernst & Young to investigate those payments—or whether Ernst & Young discovered any evidence of the payments during their annual audits.

---

15. Australian Government, Attorney-General's Department, "Inquiry into Certain Australian Companies in Relation to the UN Oil-for-Food Programme," Transcript 24, 2333, 9 February 2006.

16. *Sydney Morning Herald*, "AWB's World of Trouble."

17. *Global Newswire* (online) "Zespri Boss Didn't Know about Kickbacks until Audit," 24 February 2006.

18. *The Risk Report*, "'Kickbacks' Inquiry Hones in on RM," www.services.thomson.com, Issue 222 (19 January 2006).

**EXHIBIT 1**

ERNST & YOUNG'S AUDIT OPINION ON AWB'S FISCAL 2000 FINANCIAL STATEMENTS

To the members of AWB Limited

**Scope**

We have audited the financial report of AWB Limited for the financial year ended 30 September 2000, as set out on pages 53 to 90, including the Directors' Declaration. The financial report includes the financial statements of AWB Limited, and the consolidated financial statements of the consolidated entity comprising the company and the entities it controlled at year's end or from time to time during the financial year. The company's directors are responsible for the financial report. We have conducted an independent audit of the financial report in order to express an opinion on it to the members of the company.

Our audit has been conducted in accordance with Australian Auditing Standards to provide reasonable assurance whether the financial report is free of material misstatement. Our procedures included examination, on a test basis, of evidence supporting the amounts and other disclosures in the financial report, and the evaluation of accounting policies and significant accounting estimates. These procedures have been undertaken to form an opinion whether, in all material respects, the financial report is presented fairly in accordance with Accounting Standards, other mandatory professional reporting requirements and statutory requirements, in Australia, so as to present a view which is consistent with our understanding of the company's and the consolidated entity's financial position and performance as represented by the results of their operations and their cash flows.

The audit opinion expressed in this report has been formed on the above basis.

**Audit Opinion**

In our opinion, the financial report of AWB Limited is in accordance with:

(a) the Corporations Law including:

(i) giving a true and fair view of the company's and consolidated entity's financial position as at 30 September 2000 and of their performance for the year ended on that date; and

(ii) complying with Accounting Standards and the Corporations Requirements; and

(b) other mandatory professional reporting requirements.

Ernst & Young
Melbourne
29 November 2000

**EXHIBIT 2**

DIRECTORS' DECLARATION ACCOMPANYING AWB'S FISCAL 2000 FINANCIAL STATEMENTS

In accordance with a resolution of the directors of AWB Limited, I state that:

In the opinion of the directors:

(a) the financial statements and notes of the company and of the consolidated entity are in accordance with the Corporations Law, including:

—giving a true and fair view of the company's and consolidated entity's financial position as at 30 September 2000 and of their performance for the year ended on that date; and

—complying with Accounting Standards and Corporations Regulations; and

(b) there are reasonable grounds to believe that the company will be able to pay its debts as and when they become due and payable.

This declaration is made in accordance with a resolution of the directors on behalf of the Board.

Andrew Lindberg
Executive Director

Melbourne
29 November 2000

**EXHIBIT 2—*continued***

DIRECTORS' DECLARATION ACCOMPANYING AWB'S FISCAL 2000 FINANCIAL STATEMENTS

The report filed by Arthur Andersen with AWB identified several "red flags" and "risk factors" associated with the suspicious payments.[18] In addition, the Andersen consulting team discovered similar payments being made to a Pakistani company. A subsequent investigation revealed that AWB had paid $12 million to a Pakistani governmental official to secure a grain contract with Pakistan. In its report, Andersen recommended that AWB assess its ethical culture and create a "transparent" environment in which employees "are encouraged to report incidents, risks, and improper conduct."[19]

Andrew Lindberg, AWB's former managing director (chief executive officer) testified before the Cole Commission for several days. During his testimony, more than 200 of Lindberg's responses to questions asked of him by commission members was one of the following statements: "I can't recall; I don't recall; I'm not sure I recall; I can't precisely recall; I have no recollection of that at all; I don't know."[20]

When asked what measures he and his subordinates had taken to address the allegations and recommendations included in the Andersen report, Lindberg responded that he had "left it up to the responsible management of the area . . . to see that things were done"[21] since he had a "million things to deal with" at the time.[22] The individual who oversaw AWB's wheat marketing operations during the period that the Iraqi bribes were being paid testified that he did not become "actively involved in investigating any of the issues that arose out of the Arthur Andersen report" because he had "heavy commitments in other areas"[23] at the time. This latter individual indicated that, rather than investigating the matters raised by the Andersen report, he had delegated that responsibility to one of his subordinates. An Australian journalist chided the former AWB executives for not only orchestrating the illicit scheme to acquire the Iraqi wheat contracts but also for refusing to take responsibility for that scheme *ex post* during the course of the Cole Commission hearings:

> *"When in Rome, do as the Romans do" appears to have been AWB's business credo. The company's line now and then was that it did what was necessary to protect the interests of its shareholders, though the bald truth was that it colluded in embezzling money from a fund set up to ensure that ordinary Iraqis had bread on their tables and medicines in their hospitals.*[24]

---

19. *Ibid.*

20. M. Vincent, "Ends Justifies the Means at AWB, Inquiry Told," www.abc.net.au, 19 January 2006.

21. *The Risk Report*, "'Kickbacks' Inquiry Hones in on RM."

22. M. Vincent, "Documents Reveal Discretionary Payments Made by AWB," www.abc.net.au, 20 January 2006.

23. *Global Newswire*, "Zespri Boss Didn't Know about Kickbacks."

24. *Canberra Times* (online), "Taxing Times for Corruption," 27 December 2006.

## Aftermath

The U.N. investigation of the Oil-for-Food Program chaired by Paul Volcker determined that Saddam Hussein's regime had received nearly $2 billion in illicit payments during the course of that program. Volcker's report indicated that more than 2,000 companies had paid bribes or kickbacks to the Iraqi government but that AWB was responsible for considerably more of those payments than any other company.

For several months after Paul Volcker publicly reported his task force's findings, AWB executives staunchly denied that they had secretly paid nearly $300 million to Saddam Hussein's regime to secure the Iraqi wheat contracts. In one press release, a company spokesperson stated that, "AWB did not knowingly pay or enter into any arrangements to benefit the former [Iraqi] regime."[25] In May 2006, the company's top management did a sudden and unexpected about-face by releasing a statement confirming that those payments had been made. The statement included a contrite apology from Andrew Lindberg, AWB's former chief executive, which noted in part that "we are truly sorry and deeply regret any damage this may have caused to Australia's trading reputation, the Australian government, or the United Nations."[26] During the nearly one-year long Cole Commission inquiry, evidence surfaced that a U.S.-based "crisis management guru" had advised the company to "over-apologize" for its misconduct, apparently in hopes of garnering sympathy from the public and law enforcement authorities.[27]

The Cole Commission report released in late November 2006, recommended that criminal charges be filed against 11 former AWB executives. Andrew Lindberg was not one of those individuals. Although the Cole Commission did not recommend that criminal charges be filed against Lindberg, the commission's report severely criticized AWB's former senior management team. In particular, the report noted that the management team had bred a "closed culture of superiority and impregnability" in which "no one asked, 'What is the right thing to do?' "[28]

The most shocking conclusion in the Cole Commission report was that the $300 million in payments made by AWB to Saddam Hussein's regime did not technically qualify as "bribes" since they were not unlawful in Iraq at the time. Critics of the Cole Commission report insisted that this conclusion was inconsistent with the Australian law prompted by the OECD Convention. Nevertheless, Australian law enforcement authorities relied upon the Cole Commission's conclusion in deciding that AWB's former executives could not be prosecuted under that Australian law. (Note: The charges that the Cole Commission recommended be filed against the 11 former AWB executives stemmed from their intentional violation of the U.N. trade embargo sanctions.) Likewise, because of the Cole Commission report, the Australian Taxation Office permitted AWB to treat the $300 million of payments as tax-deductible expenses, a ruling that saved the company approximately $400 million in back taxes, fines, and interest payments. The Cole Commission also reported that it found no incontrovertible evidence that Prime Minister John Howard or any of his subordinates had been expressly aware of the clandestine payments.

Not surprisingly, the Cole Commission report triggered charges of a government cover-up. An Australian critic of Prime Minister Howard's administration observed that, "For this, the worst corruption scandal in Australian history, the Cole

25. *Sydney Morning Herald*, "AWB's World of Trouble."

26. *Global Newswire* (online), "Dramatic Confession Presented at Australian Iraq Bribes Probe," 19 May 2006.

27. *Ibid.*

28. *The Economist* (online), "Australians Who Bribe: The Oil-for-Food Scandal," 2 December 2006.

Commission was effectively constructed as a ministerial cover-up."[29] Particularly incensed were representatives of the U.S. wheat industry. In 2006, a group of U.S. and Canadian wheat growers filed a civil lawsuit against AWB asking for more than $1 billion in damages. The plaintiffs alleged that AWB had used unfair trade practices to secure the Iraqi grain contracts. Ironically, the Canadian Wheat Board, a government agency similar to AWB before it became a private company, had negotiated to obtain the Iraqi wheat contracts. When Iraqi officials demanded bribes in exchange for granting those contracts, the Canadian Wheat Board refused, which resulted in an abrupt end to the contract negotiations.

Following the release of the Cole Commission report, Prime Minister Howard announced that he was revoking AWB's export monopoly for Australia's wheat market. A few weeks later, the U.S. Department of Agriculture banned AWB from seeking contracts with the U.S. government. Pressure applied by U.S. officials was apparently a factor in the decision of many other countries to prohibit AWB from receiving government contracts. These decisions angered Australian wheat farmers, many of whom, as noted earlier, believed that AWB had not acted improperly in making secret payments to obtain the Iraqi wheat contracts. Many Australian businessmen, politicians, and journalists expressed the same point of view. The *Canberra Times* noted that "many people sympathize with AWB's plight. Markets and cultures tainted by corruption and/or lax governance are the rule rather than the exception, and the competition to secure lucrative contracts is fierce."[30] In this same article, the newspaper took a swipe at what many Australians perceived as the self-righteous U.S. business community. "The view that corporations have no social responsibility beyond that of making profits for their shareholders is one which is well entrenched in certain boardrooms in Australia, and more particularly in the United States."[31]

## Questions

1. Many foreign companies sell securities on U.S. stock exchanges. Do the provisions of the Foreign Corrupt Practices Act apply to those companies?
2. Under current U.S. auditing standards, what responsibility, if any, does an audit firm of a multinational company have to discover bribes that are paid by the client to obtain or retain international business relationships? In a bullet format, list audit procedures that may be effective in uncovering such payments.
3. Suppose you discover during the course of an audit engagement that the audit client is routinely making "facilitating payments" in a foreign country. What are the key audit-related issues, if any, posed by this discovery?
4. A quote in this case from an Australian newspaper suggested that many corporate boards in the United States believe that they "have no social responsibility beyond that of making profits for their shareholders." In your opinion, what level of "social responsibility," if any, do corporate boards have? Defend your answer.
5. The audit report shown in Exhibit 1 refers to "Australian Auditing Standards." What organization issues Australian Auditing Standards? What is the relationship, if any, between Australian Auditing Standards and International Standards of Auditing?

---

29. *Sydney Morning Herald*, "AWB's World of Trouble."
30. *Canberra Times* (online), "Taxing Times for Corruption."
31. *Ibid.*

## CASE 8.8

# OAO Gazprom

In February 2002, a lengthy *Business Week* article examined a major financial scandal swirling around one of the large international accounting firms. Key features of the scandal included the accounting firm allegedly "overlooking wildly improper deals" in its audits of a huge client that ranked among the "country's biggest energy firms," a company that had become a symbol "for the evils of crony capitalism."[1] The opening prologue for the article went on to note that the scandal involved "billions and billions" of dollars of losses as well as "leaked documents, infuriated shareholders, and threatened lawsuits."[2] Several major political figures had been caught up in the scandal, including the president. No, the article was not dissecting the sudden collapse of Enron Corporation in December 2001. Instead, the article focused on the international controversy sparked by the relationship between the largest energy producer in Russia, OAO Gazprom, and that company's independent audit firm, PricewaterhouseCoopers (PwC).

The commotion surrounding PwC's audits of Gazprom was ignited by the accounting firm's alleged failure to report candidly on a series of huge transactions involving that company and several smaller firms owned or controlled by Gazprom executives or their family members. Principal among these entities was Itera, a secretive company with U.S. connections. Criticism of PwC's audits of Gazprom became so intense that the prominent accounting firm was forced to purchase full-page ads in the major Moscow newspapers to defend itself.

## Rogue Capitalism

Throughout the 1990s, the dominant international accounting firms pursued strategic initiatives to expand their worldwide operations. Many of these initiatives targeted Russia and the cluster of smaller countries carved out of the former Soviet Union when it suddenly disintegrated in 1991. *The New York Times* reported that the major accounting firms were among the first foreign firms to establish significant operations in Russia following the collapse of the Soviet Union.[3] In their "competitive rush" to establish an economic beachhead in Russia, these firms may have underestimated the many risks posed by that country's rapidly evolving business environment.

The massive reorganization of Russia's political, social, and economic infrastructure in the 1990s produced widespread chaos within the suddenly "new" country that had a proud history that was centuries old. Russia's political leaders wanted to quickly embrace capitalism. To accomplish this objective, Russia's new democratic government implemented a "privatization programme" intended to convert the country from communism to capitalism in a span of a few years. The first and most important phase of this enormous project gave Russian citizens the right to acquire

1. P. Starobin and C. Belton, "Russia's Enron?" *BusinessWeek Online*, 18 February 2002.

2. *Ibid.*

3. S. Tavernise, "U.S. Auditors Find Things Are Different in Russia," *The New York Times*, 12 March 2002, Section W, 1.

ownership interests in thousands of Russian firms at a nominal cost by using state-issued "privatization vouchers." These Russian firms were formerly state-owned companies or agencies that had established corporate governance structures equivalent to boards of directors to oversee their operations. From 1992 through 1999, more than 75 percent of Russian companies were handed over to the private sector, although the federal government retained a sizable minority ownership interest in the nation's largest and most important companies.

The privatization program succeeded in quickly converting Russia's controlled economy into a free market economy. However, the project was flawed in many respects. For example, more than one-half of the newly created companies were technically insolvent and able to survive only with subsidies and other economic support from the federal government. Complicating everyday life for these new firms and their managers was the rampant inflation in the Russian economy that exceeded 2000 percent annually.

Arguably the most pervasive weakness of the privatization program was that it allowed thousands of the individuals who had overseen the formerly state-owned businesses to acquire top management positions in the newly organized companies. The Russian press commonly referred to these individuals as "red directors," since most of them had been Communist Party "apparatchiks" or operatives. Not surprisingly, few of these corporate managers shared or even understood the capitalistic principles they were being asked to embrace. As *Business Week* noted, these individuals "cling to the view that the enterprise is an engine to generate wealth for themselves."[4] This pervasive attitude among the newly minted corporate executives spawned a rough-and-tumble version of capitalism in Russia that sparked widespread violence—including hundreds of murders and contract killings, kickbacks, bribes, and "organized robbery."[5] Critics of the privatization program often pointed to OAO Gazprom, a huge Russian company, as a prime example of this "rogue" capitalism.

Gazprom, a term that means "gas industry," was initially a privately owned company created by officials of the Soviet Union to assume control of the country's natural gas industry. The company's most important assets are enormous natural gas reserves discovered in Siberia following World War II. Gazprom was one of the first publicly owned firms created by Russia's privatization program. Fifteen percent of Gazprom's common stock was given to employees and 28 percent to customers, while the federal government retained a 40 percent ownership interest in the company. Most of Gazprom's remaining common stock was sold to foreign investors. To ensure that domestic investors maintained control of major Russian companies, foreign investors were permitted to buy only a small fraction of a Russian company's stock.

Gazprom's initial stockholders' meeting was held in 1995. At that meeting, the stockholders endorsed the board of directors' selection of PwC as the company's audit firm. Rem Vyakhirev, Gazprom's top executive at the time, reported that the world's largest audit firm had been chosen to enhance the credibility of his company's financial statements and financial disclosures.[6]

During the 1990s, Gazprom was arguably the most important Russian company and the largest by most standards. The massive company accounted for nearly 10 percent of Russia's gross domestic product and 20 percent of its exports and tax revenues. Gazprom had an estimated 400,000 employees and provided directly or indirectly a

4. P. Starobin, "Russia's World-Class Accounting Games," *BusinessWeek Online*, 5 March 2002.

5. Tavernise, "U.S. Auditors Find Things Are Different."

6. P. Kranz, "Boris' Young Turks," *Business Week*, 28 April 1997, 52.

livelihood for more than 6 million Russians. The company's influence stretched far beyond Russia's borders. Gazprom supplied more than one-half of the natural gas used in Europe and controlled one-third of the world's natural gas reserves.

## Gazzoviki

Victor Chernomyrdin was born 10 years following the Russian Revolution of 1917. Chernomyrdin's parents were peasants who worked on a Russian collective farm. As a young man faced with limited educational opportunities, Chernomyrdin decided to become a skilled craftsman, a machinist. Following World War II, he acquired a job working in his country's rapidly developing natural gas industry that was controlled by the Ministry of the Gas Industry. The Soviet Union citizens fortunate enough to have the relatively stable and lucrative jobs in this field became known as the gazzoviki.

Chernomyrdin gradually rose through the ranks of the gazzoviki. His career success was due to his hard work, dedication to the Communist Party to which he belonged, and, most important, his ability to foster mutually beneficial relationships with key superiors and subordinates. Chernomyrdin spent much of his long career with Gazprom in frigid Siberian oil and natural gas fields. For most of that time he worked side by side with Rem Vyakhirev, his most trusted ally and protégé whose first name was an acronym for "Revolution Engels-Marx," a common name given to Russian males in the years following the Russian Revolution. In a retrospective article examining the history of Gazprom, a British reporter commented on the company's culture and the close relationship that developed between Chernomyrdin and Vyakhirev, the two individuals who had the greatest impact on the company during its formative years.

> *Gazprom is a closed world obsessed by status and hierarchy, and disdainful of outsiders. It is dominated by the macho gazzoviki, lifelong gas workers, including Mr. Vyakhirev and Mr. Chernomyrdin, who speak an earthy slang. They are united by years of working and drinking together in production plants in Russia's most remote and inhospitable regions. "You can't believe how much they drank," says one company insider. "Life was simpler in Siberia. They knew what was expected of them."*[7]

In 1992, Boris Yeltsin became the new Russian republic's first president. Yeltsin chose Chernomyrdin, Gazprom's chief executive, to serve as the nation's prime minister, the second-highest-ranking position in the federal government. Before leaving Gazprom, Chernomyrdin appointed Rem Vyakhirev as the company's new chief executive. Despite being the senior member of Yeltsin's administration, Chernomyrdin kept a close watch on Gazprom's financial affairs and frequently communicated with Vyakhirev regarding the company's operations. Together, Chernomyrdin and Vyakhirev guided the company through its turbulent early years as a publicly owned company when it became known officially as OAO Gazprom. (The "OAO" prefix indicates that Gazprom is an open-stock or publicly owned company.)

During Yeltsin's administration, Russian journalists took advantage of their country's new freedoms to openly and harshly criticize top governmental officials. A common target of that criticism was Chernomyrdin. Gruff and terse by nature, Chernomyrdin was frequently derided by the Russian press for his unpolished social skills, his poor mastery of the Russian language, and his refusal to provide candid answers to questions posed to him by reporters.

---

7. A. Jack, "Is Time Up for the 'Secret State'?" *Financial Times* (London) 25 May 2001, 33.

Chernomyrdin's critics charged that he used his political power to grant large tax concessions and other economic benefits to Gazprom. These critics also maintained that Chernomyrdin and Vyakhirev diverted billions of dollars of Gazprom's assets to themselves and family members. Allegedly, the two men and their colleagues established a network of private companies and then channeled Gazprom assets to those companies through an array of complex and clandestine transactions. The Russian press also claimed that Chernomyrdin routinely used Gazprom funds to finance the election campaigns of political candidates in his Our Home Is Russia (NDR) political party. Likewise, although Chernomyrdin frequently insisted that he had cut all ties to his Communist background, he reportedly used Gazprom funds to finance the election campaigns of several longtime colleagues running for office under the banner of the still active and powerful Communist Party.

In responding to the persistent stream of allegations and innuendos directed at him by the Russian press, an indifferent Chernomyrdin typically resorted to a brief phrase that is the Russian equivalent of "that's nonsense."[8] Another tactic Chernomyrdin used to rebuff allegations that he and his former subordinates at Gazprom were misusing corporate funds was to point out that the company's financial affairs were being closely monitored by a prestigious CPA firm, namely, PwC.

Chernomyrdin's relationship with Boris Yeltsin deteriorated over the years. In 1998, Yeltsin forced Chernomyrdin to resign as prime minister. Later that year, Chernomyrdin failed in his bid to replace Yeltsin as Russia's president. Following Yeltsin's resignation in 2000, former KGB intelligence agent Vladimir Putin was elected the new Russian president. In the meantime, Chernomyrdin had returned to Gazprom, assuming the position of chairman of the board while his close friend Rem Vyakhirev remained the company's chief executive.

Putin had campaigned as a reform candidate, promising to clean up the fraud and bribery that pervaded Russian business. Putin realized that for the Russian economy to become viable, Russia's major companies had to raise large amounts of debt and equity capital from foreign investors. But as long as self-interested "red directors" were in charge of those companies, Putin knew that foreign investors were unlikely to make major financial commitments to the Russian economy.

Putin singled out Gazprom and its management team as prime examples of what was wrong with the Russian economic system. He was particularly offended that Gazprom's executives viewed themselves as being "above the law"[9] and not accountable to the Russian public or elected officials. In fact, while serving as Gazprom's chief executive, Vyakhirev had his company acquire Russia's only independent television network, ostensibly to silence his critics.

Vyakhirev took pleasure in bragging about the power that he exercised as Gazprom's top executive. Vyakhirev "liked to boast of dispatching flunkies in the company jet to pick special tundra grass to feed the reindeer on his private Moscow estate."[10] A British periodical claimed that such abusive practices were commonplace and carried out "under the noses" of the firm's independent auditors.

> *Under . . . Rem Vyakhirev, Gazprom resembled a badly run country more than it did a publicly traded energy company: it had its own intelligence service, fleet of aircraft, hotels, media outlets and even a yacht club. Under the noses of its Western auditors,*

---

8. *Global News Wire* (online), "Gazprom Denies Making Contributions to Election Campaigns," 24 January 2000.

9. *The Irish Times* (online), "Russian Gas Chieftain Pushed Out by Putin," 8 June 2001.

10. *Ibid.*

*billions of dollars of cash and assets leaked to companies where ownership was at best murky, at worst startlingly close to Gazprom's chiefs.*[11]

True to his word, shortly after becoming president, Putin began forcing large numbers of red directors of major Russian companies to resign. Among the first such executives to lose their lucrative positions with major Russian firms were Vyakhirev and Chernomyrdin who were allowed by Putin to voluntarily "retire" from Gazprom.[12] Unlike most Russian retirees, Chernomyrdin and Vyakhirev would not have to rely on a meager government pension for their retirement income. In 2001, *Forbes* reported that the two former Russian peasants were among the 500 richest individuals in the world. *Forbes* pegged Vyakhirev's personal wealth at $1.5 billion, while Chernomyrdin's more modest fortune was estimated at $1.1 billion.[13]

## Accounting and Auditing on the Fly

Banishing corrupt corporate executives was an important first step in Vladimir Putin's campaign to entice foreign investors to provide desperately needed debt and equity capital for large Russian companies. However, Putin also realized that his country's accounting and financial reporting practices had to be revamped before foreign investors would commit significant funds to those companies. The new country's existing financial reporting framework was a holdover from the system used in the Soviet Union, a system that was poorly suited for the needs of a free market economy.

*In the chaotic early years of new Russian capitalism, accounting standards here were poorly suited to market economics. They were built around reporting to tax authorities, not gauging a company's financial health for investors. Oversight was all but nonexistent and the legal system was undeveloped, leaving room for manipulation and theft.*[14]

Russia's move toward a Western-style accounting and financial reporting system actually began shortly after the creation of the new Russian republic in 1991, well before Putin became the nation's top elected official. In 1992, Russia's new federal government approved "Regulation on Accounting and Reporting in the Russian Federation," an administrative decree intended to provide a blueprint for radically changing the nation's accounting and financial reporting system. The primary responsibility for implementing this decree would rest with the Ministry of Finance, the government agency charged with overseeing the country's financial infrastructure. Several organizations, among them the United Nations, the European Union, and the World Bank, pledged to help the Ministry of Finance implement the decree. The international accounting community, including the major international accounting firms and professional accounting organizations in leading industrialized nations, also offered to help the Ministry of Finance in its effort.

The most important feature of the plan to overhaul Russia's accounting and financial reporting system was adopting the fundamental accounting concepts and procedures that had become generally accepted in major industrialized countries over the previous two centuries. Even before the break-up of the Soviet Union, Russian accountants had recognized the concept of "fair presentation." However, an entity's

11. *Economist.com*, "Last Night at the Gazprom," 31 May 2001.

12. Although Chernomyrdin had to give up his position with Gazprom in 2001, a few months later Putin appointed him Russia's ambassador to Ukraine. This appointment surprised foreign journalists since the two men had been fierce political rivals over the previous several years.

13. *The Russian Business Monitor* (online), "Eight Russians Put on Billionaires List," 22 June 2001.

14. Tavernise, "U.S. Auditors Find Things Are Different."

financial statements were considered to be "fairly presented" if they complied with the arcane taxation, reporting, and administrative requirements of the federal government. The new accounting framework introduced into Russia in the early 1990s required companies to adopt such revolutionary concepts as recognizing revenues when earned and realized, properly matching revenues and expenses each accounting period, invoking the historical cost principle for most assets, and applying the going-concern principle to discontinued operating units.

Because Russia did not have a rigorous rule-making process for the accounting domain, the major international accounting firms and other influential parties encouraged the Russian federal government to endorse the accounting standards being promulgated by international rule-making bodies. In 1999, the Ministry of Finance announced that Russian companies could apply either the loose amalgamation of "Russian accounting principles" that had developed over the previous several years or the much more comprehensive and logically consistent International Accounting Standards (IAS), which are now known as International Financial Reporting Standards (IFRS).[15] The latter standards are issued by the London-based International Accounting Standards Board (IASB), which was created in 1973 with the long-range goal of developing a uniform set of worldwide accounting and financial reporting standards. In 2001, the Ministry of Finance, with the full support of Vladimir Putin, made another bold and progressive decision when it announced that publicly owned Russian companies would be required to adopt IFRS over a transitional period running generally from 2001 through 2005.

In addition to higher-quality accounting and financial reporting practices, Putin and other leading reformers in Russia realized that their nation needed a rigorous independent audit function to enhance the credibility of publicly issued financial data. The large international accounting firms that established practice offices for the first time in Russia during the early 1990s found that most large Russian companies required so-called statutory audits. Statutory audits were effectively "compliance" audits intended to determine whether a given company's periodic financial reports and internal accounting functions complied with the various governmental decrees and regulations to which they were subject. (In the Soviet Union, "independent audits" intended to enhance the credibility of publicly released financial statements in the minds of investors and creditors had not been necessary since the federal government controlled practically all economic resources.) Exhibit 1 presents an example of a statutory audit report issued by PwC in April 2000 for one of its large Russian clients, the Joint-Stock Commercial Savings Bank of the Russian Federation.

**EXHIBIT 1**

EXAMPLE OF A RUSSIAN STATUTORY AUDIT REPORT ISSUED BY PRICEWATERHOUSE-COOPERS

To the Shareholders of Joint-Stock Commercial Savings Bank of the Russian Federation (an open joint-stock company):

1. We have audited the accompanying 1999 statutory accounting reports of Joint-Stock Commercial Savings Bank of the Russian Federation (open joint-stock company) (hereinafter—the Bank). These statutory accounting reports were prepared by the management of the Bank in accordance with the Chart of Accounts for credit institutions prescribed by the Bank of Russia and other regulatory documents. These statutory accounting reports differ significantly from financial statements prepared in accordance with International Accounting Standards mainly in areas of valuation of assets and capital, period of recognition of revenues and expenses, recognition of liabilities and disclosures.

15. The IASB adopted the phrase "International Financial Reporting Standards" in 2001.

**EXHIBIT 1—*continued***

EXAMPLE OF A RUSSIAN STATUTORY AUDIT REPORT ISSUED BY PRICEWATERHOUSE-COOPERS

2. Preparation of the statutory accounting reports is the responsibility of the management of the Bank. Our responsibility as statutory auditors is to express an opinion on the trustworthiness in all material respects of these statutory accounting reports based on our audit.

3. We conducted our statutory audit in accordance with:

   The Temporary Rules of Audit Activity in the Russian Federation adopted by Decree of the President of the Russian Federation of 22 December 1993, No. 2263;

   The Regulations on Audit Activity in the Banking System of the Russian Federation No. 64 approved by the Order of the Bank of Russia of 10 September 1997, No. 02-391;

   The Regulations of the Bank of Russia "On the order of compiling and presenting to the Bank of Russia the audit report on the results of checking the credit institution's activity for the reporting year" of 23 December 1997, No. 10-P;

   The rules and standards on auditing approved by the Commission on Audit Activity under the President of the Russian Federation;

   The standards of Banking Auditing approved by Expert Committee under the Bank of Russia;

   International Auditing Standards; and

   Internal standards of the firm.

   These standards require that we plan and perform the statutory audit to obtain reasonable assurance about whether the statutory accounting reports are free of material misstatement. An audit includes examining, on a test basis, evidence supporting the amounts and disclosures in the statutory accounting reports. An audit also includes assessing the accounting principles used and significant estimates made by management, as well as evaluating the overall presentation of the statutory accounting reports in order to assess compliance with laws and current regulations of the Russian Federation. We reviewed a sample of business transactions of the Bank for compliance with the effective legislation solely to obtain sufficient assurance that statutory accounting reports are free of material misstatements. We believe that our statutory audit provides a reasonable basis for our opinion.

4. In our opinion, the audited annual statutory accounting reports are prepared in all material aspects in accordance with legislation and statutory requirements regulating the procedure of accounting and preparation of statutory accounting reports in the Russian Federation and the principles of accounting accepted in the Russian Federation. On this basis, the proper preparation of the balance sheet and of the profit and loss account is confirmed.

5. Without qualifying our opinion, we draw attention to the fact that the operations of the Bank, and those of similar credit organisations in the Russian Federation, have been affected, and may be affected for the foreseeable future by the economic instability of the company.

PricewaterhouseCoopers
28 April 2000

Notice that the third section of the report indicates the various rules, regulations, and standards that PwC followed in performing the given audit.

International accounting firms encouraged Russian federal officials to adopt an audit model patterned after the independent audit function in Western countries. These firms generally supported a move toward the British audit model, which requires independent auditors to decide whether a given client's financial statements present a "true and fair" view of its operating results and financial condition. A Moscow-based PwC audit partner reported that his firm had encountered major resistance to this radical change.

> *Companies say, "I don't need this. I want you to check our compliance with the law and regulations and that is all." If the local law does not require something, it is difficult to persuade clients to buy it. They don't understand the process of [conforming] to a true and fair view.*[16]

In 1999, the Institute of Professional Accountants of Russia (IPAR), a leading professional organization roughly comparable to the American Institute of Certified Public Accountants (AICPA), applied for admission to the New York-based International Federation of Accountants (IFAC). The IFAC's website notes that it is "an organization of national professional accountancy organizations that represent accountants employed in public practice, business and industry, the public sector, and education." More than 150 professional accountancy organizations are IFAC members, including the AICPA. A major thrust of the IFAC is developing International Standards of Auditing (ISAs) that can be readily applied in developing countries without a formal rule-making body for the auditing domain. The IFAC's auditing standards tend to be broad conceptual guidelines rather than detailed rules. Nevertheless, ISAs are generally consistent with the professional auditing standards applied in the major free market economies, including Great Britain and the United States.

The IPAR became an IFAC member in 2000. In the fall of that year, the first official Russian translation of ISAs was made available to the Russian accounting profession and the foreign accounting firms with practice units in Russia. At that point, the Big Five accounting firms, each of which had a major presence in Russia, began encouraging their clients to obtain ISA-based audits and began lobbying government officials to formally endorse the ISAs.

A key factor that impeded the spread of Western-style auditing in Russia during the 1990s was the existence of so-called "pocket auditors." Many, if not most, new Russian companies created in the early 1990s retained accounting firms run by friends and relatives of their executives to audit their financial statements and provide related professional services. These accounting firms allegedly helped their clients "cook their books" and "evade taxes and disguise asset-stripping."[17] Executives of Russian companies feared that PwC and the other international accounting firms would not be as cooperative or compliant as pocket auditors. However, the controversy spawned by PwC's audits of Gazprom caused many critics to suggest that the prestigious accounting firm was firmly "in the pockets" of Gazprom's top executives.

---

16. PricewaterhouseCoopers, "Russia: Hammering Out Standards, Hitting a Mindset," *WorldWatch*, March 2000, 14–15.

17. Starobin, "Russia's World-Class Accounting Games."

## Wildest Dream or Worst Nightmare?

In July 1997, a reporter for the London-based *Financial Times* interviewed Bruce Edwards, the PwC audit partner who had just completed supervising his firm's first annual audit of Gazprom. The reporter noted that, "to most auditors, Gazprom would rank as their wildest dream—or their worst nightmare."[18] The "dream" feature of the engagement was that it provided instant credibility for PwC in the Russian audit market. Another "dream" feature of the engagement was the $12 million annual fee that the accounting firm earned for the audit. On the downside, the Gazprom audit required the 70 PwC personnel assigned to the engagement to travel the length and breadth of Russia. To accomplish their audit objectives, the PwC auditors had to inspect many of the company's more than 1,000 operating units, which included slaughterhouses, media outlets, hospitals, a yacht club, and dozens of other ventures unrelated to the company's primary line of business.

In the *Financial Times* interview, Edwards downplayed the suggestion that audits of large Russian companies were markedly different from audits of comparable U.S. firms. "There is nothing mystical about Russian accounts. There is a huge misconception that Russia is somehow different, but I do not see it being much different to anywhere else."[19] Edwards did admit that Gazprom executives and employees were initially reluctant to share information with PwC auditors. However, that reluctance was "short-lived," Edwards assured the newspaper reporter and then went on to maintain that the quality of financial information Gazprom personnel provided to PwC auditors "was extremely high."

One feature of the Gazprom audit on which Edwards did not comment was the company's extensive related-party transactions. During the late 1990s, major Russian newspapers and other media outlets charged that Gazprom's top executives were routinely siphoning off enormous amounts of assets to related-party entities that they or their family members controlled.

According to press reports, Gazprom officials sold a huge amount of natural gas at nominal prices to Itera, a privately owned company based in the Netherlands that has major operating units in Russia and the United States. Throughout the 1990s, Itera's top executive was Igor Makarov, a former Gazprom employee and Olympic biking champion for the Soviet Union. Makarov had been taught the intricacies of the natural gas industry by his close friend and mentor, Rem Vyakhirev. In one confirmed case, Gazprom sold a large volume of natural gas to Itera for $2 per cubic meter, which Itera then resold to European customers for more than $40 per cubic meter. In another transaction, Gazprom sold its 32 percent ownership interest in a gas-producing subsidiary, Purgas, to Itera for $1,200. Industry insiders estimated that the market price of that ownership interest was approximately $400 million. Thanks to such transactions, Itera grew from a small, unknown entity to the world's seventh-largest natural gas company in a span of only seven years during the 1990s.

Although Itera appears to be the company that has profited the most from Gazprom's generosity, several other firms have been the beneficiaries of similar sweetheart deals. Among these firms is Stroitransgaz, a pipeline construction company that landed a large number of lucrative contracts with Gazprom during the 1990s. According to the Russian press, Stroitransgaz's principal owners include Viktor Chernomyrdin's two sons and Rem Vyahkirev's daughter.

18. J. Thornhill, "Behind the High Walls at Gazprom," *Financial Times* (London), 11 July 1997, 24.
19. *Ibid.*

In 2001, Boris Fedorov, who had previously served as the head of the Ministry of Finance, was appointed to Gazprom's board of directors. Shortly after joining the board, Federov told the *Moscow Times* that Gazprom was losing the equivalent of $2 billion to $3 billion each year due to "corruption, nepotism, and simple theft."[20] That same newspaper went on to report that its own five-week investigation had uncovered evidence that Gazprom assets "have been systematically handed over to company managers—including Vyakhirev, his deputy Vyacheslav Sheremet, and former Prime Minister Viktor Chernomyrdin—throughout Vyakhirev's tenure."[21]

The increasingly revealing and hostile reports focusing on Gazprom's business dealings with Itera and other related companies outraged the international investment community and foreign political officials whose countries had provided billions of dollars of aid to jumpstart the fledgling Russian economy. Even more outraged were foreign investors who owned Gazprom stock. Among these investors were the stockholders of Hermitage Capital, Russia's largest private equity fund, which held a large minority ownership interest in Gazprom's outstanding stock. Most of Hermitage's stockholders were U.S. citizens.

William Browder, Hermitage's chairman and a former partner with the Wall Street investment banker Salomon Brothers, had begun accumulating Gazprom stock for Hermitage in the mid-1990s. Browder, an American citizen whose father had served decades earlier as a top official of the Communist Party in the United States, recognized that the huge natural gas reserves owned by the company were not properly impounded into Gazprom's stock market price. He expected that the stock's market price would rise dramatically when Western investors realized the massive resources controlled by the company. Unfortunately for Browder and his fellow Hermitage investors, Gazprom's stock price stubbornly refused to move higher.

A frustrated Browder reported in 2001 that if Gazprom's petroleum reserves were valued by the stock market on approximately the same basis as the comparable reserves of Exxon Mobil, the company's stock price would be 132 times higher.[22] Browder attributed the lack of interest in Gazprom's common stock to the fact that the company was literally "giving away" huge chunks of its natural gas reserves each year to Itera and other privately owned companies controlled by Gazprom executives, their family members, and their close friends and associates.

The growing controversy surrounding Gazprom's bizarre deals with Itera, which was fueled by the Russian press, forced the company's board to call for a "special audit" of the Gazprom-Itera transactions in January 2001. Ironically, that announcement sparked even more controversy and negative publicity for the company. When Gazprom's board announced that PwC had been retained to perform the Itera audit, critics immediately charged that PwC would effectively be auditing "itself," since the firm had given its implicit approval to the suspicious Itera transactions during its prior audits of Gazprom. Most galling to critics was that PwC had failed to even require Gazprom to disclose Itera as a related party in the footnotes to the company's financial statements over the previous several years.

Boris Fedorov, the sole Gazprom board member who voted to retain an accounting firm other than PwC to perform the special audit, publicly criticized the board's decision. "There is no way you can believe in an assignment which asks an auditor to check their own figures. It is spitting in the face of investors."[23] PwC's appointment

20. *Moscow Times*, "Time to Say Farewell to Vyakhirev," 22 May 2001, 12.

21. *Ibid.*

22. W. Browder, "Gazprom Investors Are Sold Short," *Moscow Times*, 30 July 2001, 8.

23. A. Jack and A. Ostrovsky, "Gazprom Vote Raises Concerns," *Financial Times* (London), 24 January 2001, 32.

to perform the special audit even caused dissension among the accounting firm's partners. *Business Week* reported that several senior PwC partners in the firm's Moscow office believed "that any self-review [of the Itera transactions] would lack credibility."[24]

Shortly after Gazprom's board hired PwC to investigate the company's business deals with Itera, a group of minority stockholders led by Federov appointed Deloitte & Touche to perform a parallel investigation of those same transactions. The other members of Gazprom's board squelched that effort by refusing to provide Deloitte access to the company's accounting records. Federov responded by claiming that the board's decision "showed that it [Gazprom's management] had something to hide."[25] Federov went on to demand that PwC rigorously interrogate Gazprom's executives and family members known to have ties to Itera. Within days, Federov found himself the target of anonymous threats by hostile adversaries. Accustomed to the often treacherous business environment of his country, Federov dismissed the threats and insisted that he would continue demanding that Gazprom provide more transparent and reliable financial reports to investors, creditors, and other third parties.

## No Smoking Guns

PwC completed its four-month investigation of Gazprom's business dealings with Itera in the summer of 2001 and filed a 67-page confidential report of its findings with Gazprom's board. Within days, much of PwC's report had been leaked to the press. According to the *Financial Times*, PwC did not identify any "deals in which Itera benefited at the expense of Gazprom."[26] Subsequent press reports undercut the credibility of PwC's investigation. These reports indicated that PwC's investigation had been severely hamstrung by a lack of cooperation on the part of both Itera and Gazprom officials. Itera's management had refused to provide documents requested by PwC auditors, while 19 executives and former executives of Gazprom, including Rem Vyakhirev, had refused to answer questions posed to them by the auditors.

Not surprisingly, the results of the PwC investigation failed to placate Boris Federov, William Browder, and other critics of Gazprom's management. Instead, the tepid PwC report served to focus increasingly harsh criticism on the large accounting firm. In early 2002, Gazprom's board announced a "contest" to retain an accounting firm to audit the company's financial statements for the fiscal year ending June 30, 2002. Although Gazprom invited PwC to prepare a bid for the 2002 audit, the Russian and international business press indicated that there was little chance PwC would be selected given the adverse publicity that continued to plague the firm. Diminishing even further PwC's chances to retain the Gazprom engagement was a recommendation issued in early 2002 by the Russian Securities Commission, a federal agency equivalent to the U.S. Securities and Exchange Commission. That agency strongly encouraged large Russian companies to change their auditors periodically.

A few days after Gazprom announced the auditor contest, PwC purchased full-page ads in major Russian newspapers. These ads attempted to rebut much of the criticism that had been directed at the firm over the previous two years for its Gazprom audits. The ads suggested that PwC had been singled out for criticism based on "an inaccurate understanding of the roles and responsibilities of auditors."[27]

24. Starobin and Belton, "Russia's Enron?"
25. "Gazprom Won't Permit Audit by Deloitte," *National Post*, 21 March 2001, C2.
26. A. Jack, "Auditors Find No Evidence of Deals That Aided Itera," *Financial Times*, 6 July 2001, 22.
27. A. Jack, "PwC Acts to Defend Itself in Russia," *Financial Times* (London), 28 February 2002, 20.

In April 2002, Hermitage Capital filed multiple civil lawsuits against PwC in Russian courts alleging, among other charges, that the accounting firm had performed "deliberately false" audits of Gazprom. At the same time, Hermitage filed a request with the Ministry of Finance to suspend PwC's license to practice in Russia. A PwC spokesperson maintained that the allegations in the lawsuits were "completely unfounded" and that the firm's audits had "met all applicable legal and professional standards."[28]

The Hermitage lawsuits were the first such lawsuits filed against a major international accounting firm in Russia. Many legal experts questioned whether there was a valid basis for the lawsuits under the emerging but scanty Russian securities laws and legal precedents. Nevertheless, the Hermitage lawsuits startled PwC and the other major accounting firms operating in Russia. The lawsuits raised in a new context a slew of "old" issues that had pestered audit firms since the inception of the independent audit function.

> *Whatever the truth, the audit profession in Russia faces the same difficulties as elsewhere in arguing that it is "watchdog not bloodhound"—with a remit to verify information, but not to actively sniff out fraud, and not to assume greater responsibility than management itself for errors they have committed. But the profession is also caught in a conflict of interest. Each firm is nominally charged with reporting to all shareholders whether a company's financial statements are "true and fair." In reality, it is appointed, paid by, and reports to executive management, which may be involved in activities to the detriment of outside investors.*[29]

The inherently problematic nature of the auditor-client relationship is made even more problematic within Russia by two key factors. *The New York Times* reported that "fierce competition" among the major accounting firms to acquire and retain the relatively few large and lucrative Russian audit clients had resulted in auditors feeling pressured to "sign off on questionable practices by such clients to avoid alienating them."[30] A former Ernst & Young employee who had been assigned to that firm's Moscow office was more blunt. "A big client [in Russia] is god. You do what they want and tell you to do. You can play straight-laced with minor clients, but you can't do it with the big guys. If you lose the account, no matter how justified you are, that's the end of a career."[31]

The second factor complicating the quality of independent audits in Russia has been the haphazard, if not ragtag, nature of the country's auditing rules. Critics of independent auditors in Western countries have long suggested that professional auditing standards are too "flexible," which ultimately results in less rigorous audits and lower-quality financial statements. This problem has been exacerbated in Russia over the past decade by the lack of consensus on what auditing rules should be applied.

The evolving nature of Russia's professional standards have allowed auditors in that country to interpret their mission too narrowly, according to one former governmental official. Auditors "check that the paperwork was done correctly, but look right past the corrupt heart of the matter."[32] One former PwC auditor provided an example of this mindset in an interview with *The New York Times*. This individual reported that a large automobile manufacturer that was a PwC audit client effectively gave away

28. S. Tavernise, "Shareholder in Gazprom of Russia Sues Auditor," *The New York Times*, 16 April 2002, W1.
29. A. Jack, "Testing Times for Auditors in Russia," *Financial Times* (London), 17 April 2002, 27.
30. Tavernise, "U.S. Auditors Find Things Are Different."
31. *Ibid.*
32. *Ibid.*

huge amounts of inventory by routinely shipping cars to supposed "dealers" who never paid for those shipments. The former PwC auditor recalled thinking, "'What's going on? You aren't getting paid—no guarantees, no nothing. Are you stupid?' It was clear to me that it was organized robbery."[33] In its audit report, PwC commented on the fact that the client was using different methods to account for certain domestic sales and sales made to foreign customers. But, according to *The New York Times*, the firm failed to convey in its audit report "what was actually going on at the company."[34]

A PwC spokesperson refused to respond directly to the charges made by his firm's former employee but did insist that PwC "stood by its audits" of the given client. *The New York Times* reporter then asked an audit partner with Arthur Andersen about an Andersen client that routinely sold merchandise to related parties at deeply discounted prices. The nature of these sales was not disclosed in the company's financial statements or in Andersen's audit reports on those financial statements. When asked why such disclosures were not made, the Andersen audit partner replied that Russian law did not require them. This attitude on the part of major international accounting firms operating in Russia has proven to be extremely detrimental to domestic and foreign investors.

> *In this environment, Western auditing firms could have and should have held their Russian clients to higher standards of behavior, investors in Russian companies are now saying. But, instead . . . the auditors chose to play by Russian rules, and in doing so sacrificed the transparency that investors were counting on them to ensure.*[35]

## Profit after Stealing and Subsidies

Despite earlier reports that Gazprom would likely retain a new audit firm, in May 2002 the company issued a press release indicating that PwC would remain its independent auditor. Of 29 accounting firms that had submitted bids for the Gazprom engagement, the company's board reported that PwC was the firm that best met its "requirements." Throughout the late spring and summer of 2002, PwC received more good news as one by one the Russian courts dismissed the lawsuits filed against the company by Hermitage Capital. The Russian courts ruled that under existing Russian law only the audited entity could sue its accounting firm for defective audits. Since the majority of Gazprom's board of directors and stockholders refused to side with the plaintiffs in the lawsuits, the courts' only alternative was to rule that the lawsuits were invalid. The Ministry of Finance also denied Hermitage's request that PwC's license to practice be rescinded.

William Browder reacted angrily to the dismissal of the lawsuits his firm had filed against PwC and the news that the accounting firm would remain Gazprom's auditor. Browder argued that, at a minimum, PwC and Gazprom officials should provide more detailed disclosures regarding the company's key operating results. For example, Browder suggested that in the future the company report in its income statements, "Profit after Stealing and Subsidies" and "Profit If Stealing and Subsidies Are Eliminated."[36]

---

33. *Ibid.*

34. *Ibid.*

35. *Ibid.*

36. M. Waller, "Fingered," *The Times* (London), 12 July 2002, 27.

## Questions

1. List the challenges that a major accounting firm faces when it establishes its first practice office in a foreign country. Identify the key factors that accounting firms should consider when deciding whether to establish a practice office in a new market.
2. Suppose that a U.S.-based accounting firm has a major audit client in a foreign country that routinely engages in business practices that are considered legal in that country but that would qualify as both illegal and unethical in the United States. What specific moral or ethical obligations, if any, would these circumstances impose on this accounting firm? Explain.
3. What responsibilities, if any, do you believe PwC had to Gazprom's minority investors?
4. In your opinion, should PwC have agreed to perform the "special audit" of the Itera transactions? Defend your answer. In your answer, identify the specific ethical issues or challenges that the engagement posed for PwC.
5. In the United States, what responsibility do auditors have to determine whether or not "related parties" exist for a given audit client? Explain.
6. Explain how the British "true and fair" audit approach or strategy differs from the audit philosophy applied in the United States. In your opinion, which of the two audit approaches is better or, at least, more defensible?
7. In recent years, there has been an ongoing debate in the accounting profession focusing on the quality of the accounting standards issued by the International Accounting Standards Board versus those issued by the Financial Accounting Standards Board. Research and briefly explain the key philosophical difference between those two important rule-making bodies that significantly affects the nature of the accounting standards promulgated by each.

# CASE 8.9

# Tata Finance Limited

*Whoever owns the stick owns the buffalo.*

*Indian proverb*

Prior to the Islamic conquest of the Middle East, the ancient Zoroastrian religion was the national religion of Persia. To escape persecution for their religious beliefs, a large band of Persian Zoroastrians migrated eastward during the eighth century A.D., eventually settling in modern-day India. Because of their Persian heritage, the new arrivals were referred to as *Parsis* by the Hindus who dominated the Indian subcontinent. Although warmly welcomed by the Hindus, the Parsis made every effort to retain and perpetuate their culture and religion. Largely by intermarrying within their own community and by discouraging native Indians from joining their sect, the Parsis have maintained their distinct cultural heritage and identity within India over the past 12 centuries. The Parsis' refusal to proselyte their religious beliefs, however, has resulted in their numbers gradually shrinking. By the dawn of the twenty-first century, there were fewer than 100,000 Parsis within India, most of whom lived in the city of Mumbai.

Despite their relatively small numbers, the Parsis have had a disproportionate impact on the history of India over the past millennium. The Parsis were among the most ardent supporters of India's long struggle to become independent of Great Britain. Several prominent Parsi families also contributed significantly to the development of the modern Indian economy. India's largest privately owned company is controlled by a Parsi family, as is the Tata Group, India's largest business conglomerate that consists of nearly 100 companies, two dozen of which are publicly owned.

The massive Tata business empire and the Parsi family of the same name that has overseen that empire since its inception have helped shape the economic and political history of India over the past century. In recent years, however, the Tata Group and its senior executives have faced a protracted and widely publicized accounting scandal that threatens to undercut the credibility and prestige of the prominent organization and its founding family. The scandal has already taken a toll on the reputation of India's largest accounting firm that is closely affiliated with the Tata Group.

## J.N. Tata: India's Business Pioneer

In the early 1870s, Jamsetjji Nusserwanji Tata founded the Central India Spinning, Weaving and Manufacturing Company. Over the following three decades, J. N. Tata would create one new company after another. Tata gave India its first steel company, hydroelectric plant, textile factory, shipping line, and cement factory. Later generations of the Tata family would found India's first automobile manufacturer, first domestically owned bank, first chemical company, and Air India, the nation's first airline, which was later nationalized by the Indian federal government.

Among the largest companies within the Tata Group are Tata Consultancy Services, Tata Finance, Tata Motors, and Tata Steel. Arguably, the best known of the public Tata companies is Tata Consultancy Services Limited, which is Asia's largest information technology consulting firm with more than 70,000 employees worldwide. In 2006, Tata Consultancy Services reported a profit of nearly $3 billion. Collectively, the publicly owned Tata companies make Tata Group the largest Indian corporate entity in terms of total market capitalization. Likewise, the member companies of the

Tata Group are India's largest employer in the private sector and account for nearly 3 percent of the nation's annual gross domestic product (GDP). Worldwide, the Tata companies have production or marketing facilities in 40 countries and export goods and services to more than 140 countries.

In addition to being India's first major business entrepreneur, J. N. Tata was an important figure in the Indian nationalistic movement. Tata believed that for his country to become independent of Great Britain, it had to first become economically self-sufficient. To achieve that goal, Tata realized that India had to develop home-grown engineers, architects, and scientists. So, late in his life, Tata founded India's first major scientific university.

J. N. Tata's dedication to achieving India's independence was surpassed only by his commitment to his religious ideals, which he integrated into each of the businesses that he founded. The crest of the Tata Group that commonly appears on the correspondence of Tata companies includes the three-word creed of the Zoroastrian religion: Humata, Hukhta, Hvarshta. That creed translates in English to "good thoughts, good words, and good deeds." Like other Zoroastrians, Tata fervently believed that one's principal purpose in life is to serve his fellow man. Because of that belief, Tata decreed that two-thirds of all the profits generated by his businesses would be contributed to charitable organizations. More than one century later, that policy is still in effect and has resulted in billions of dollars being donated by the Tata Group to a wide range of humanitarian causes.

## The Tainting of Tata

Corruption has long been a major problem within the Indian economy. Among 12 major Asian countries, one recent study found that only Indonesia has a higher level of business corruption than India.[1] Nevertheless, since the days of J. N. Tata, the Tata family has prided itself on maintaining a high level of ethics within the operations of each Tata company. The London-based *Financial Times* noted that the word "Tata" was for decades accepted as a byword for integrity" within the Indian economy and Indian society as a whole.[2] According to *Newsweek*, Tata's "rigid ethical standards are so well known that corrupt [government] officials typically don't even bother asking Tata for bribes."[3]

Tata's sterling reputation for integrity and for upholding the highest standards of ethical conduct was jeopardized in 2002 by a 900-page report issued by A. F. Ferguson & Company (AFF), India's largest accounting firm. AFF served as the independent or statutory auditor for dozens of the member companies of the Tata Group. One of the large Tata companies that AFF did not audit was Tata Finance Limited, a Tata affiliate engaged in automobile financing, mortgage lending, and consumer credit cards. Another of India's largest accounting firms, S. B. Billimoria & Co., served as Tata Finance's independent auditor.

In early 2001, senior executives of the Tata Group, which included its top officer, Ratan Tata, the corporate group's executive chairman and the great-great grandson of J. N. Tata, retained AFF to carry out an internal investigation of Tata Finance. The primary purpose of the investigation was to identify the individuals responsible for a series of fraudulent transactions that had produced large losses for Tata Finance and

1. *Reuters* (online), "India Second Only to Indonesia in Business Corruption," 2 March 2004.

2. K. Merchant, "Chairman on Defensive as Scandal Tarnishes Tata," *Financial Times*, 19 August 2002, 15.

3. G. Wehfritz, R. Moreau, and S. Chatterjee, "A New Kind of Company," *Newsweek International Edition* (online), 4 July 2006.

resulted in material misrepresentations in the company's publicly issued financial statements. The Tata Group executives suspected that Dilip Pendse, the former "managing director," or senior operating officer, of Tata Finance, was responsible for those transactions and believed that the results of the AFF investigation would confirm their suspicion.

## Enron Gimmicks: Indian Style

The accounting scandal at Tata Finance involved a little-known subsidiary of the company, Niskalp Investment & Trading Company. During the late 1990s, the stocks of technology companies soared in stock markets around the world but then suddenly collapsed when the "Internet Bubble" in those markets burst in early 2000. Niskalp earned substantial profits for Tata Finance in the late 1990s as a result of large investments made by Dilip Pendse in technology stocks. Executives of Tata Group would subsequently allege that Pendse's investments in technology stocks had not been authorized by Tata Finance's board.

When the stock prices of technology companies plunged in early 2000, Niskalp suffered huge losses on its portfolio of technology stocks. Niskalp's mounting losses throughout 2000 and into early 2001 posed a huge financial crisis for Tata Finance. The Reserve Bank of India (RBI), a federal regulatory agency for the nation's banking system, requires companies such as Tata Finance to maintain a minimum "capital adequacy ratio" (CAR). By early 2001, Tata Finance had breached the RBI's minimum CAR. Pendse initially used a series of intercompany investments, commonly referred to as intercorporate deposits or ICDs, from other companies in the Tata Group to shore up Tata Finance's capital structure. The RBI does not prohibit ICDs but it also does not allow financial institutions to consider them when computing their CAR. A subsequent investigation would reveal that many of the ICDs made to Tata Finance by its sister companies were not equity investments but rather loans. In either case, the ICDs should not have been considered by Tata Finance when computing its CAR.

As Niskalp's losses continued to rise in 2001, Tata Finance used one final measure in a desperate attempt to resolve, or at least conceal, its rapidly deteriorating financial condition. The company chose to "desubsidiarise Niskalp, allegedly to protect its own balance sheet by not having to disclose the losses of its subsidiary any more."[4] This stopgap measure failed to remedy Tata Finance's underlying financial problem, namely, its lack of adequate equity capital. Pendse then turned to his superiors at the Tata Group who provided the equity capital needed to rescue Tata Finance. Shortly after Tata Finance's true financial condition was revealed to the public, the Tata Group dismissed Dilip Pendse and four of his key subordinates. In August 2001, the Tata Group filed a complaint with law enforcement authorities charging Pendse with criminal breach of trust. Two months later, the remaining members of Tata Finance's board resigned as did the company's audit firm, S. B. Billimoria & Co.

When the details of the Tata accounting scandal were revealed, the Indian business press immediately pointed out that the accounting gimmicks used by Tata Finance were very similar to abusive accounting methods used by Enron in the United States. Like the Enron debacle, Tata Finance's independent audit firm faced heated criticism from the business press for failing to uncover and stop those abusive accounting methods. When asked to comment on the Tata scandal, S. B. Billimoria's managing partner noted, "Operating under the constraints of time and cost, we presume full honesty from our clients. After all, an audit is not an investigation."[5]

4. S. Vikraman, "Time to Regulate the Auditing Profession?" *Businessline*, 11 March 2002, 1.

5. "Financial Chicanery," *Flashpoint* (www.capitalmarket.com), 29 January 2002.

In interviews with the media, Ratan Tata maintained that he and his top subordinates at the Tata Group had not been aware of the fraudulent Tata Finance transactions. However, Dilip Pendse staunchly insisted that he had kept Ratan Tata and other Tata Group executives informed of those transactions. According to Pendse, who was employed by Tata Finance for nearly 25 years, he had met with Ratan Tata every Wednesday to discuss Tata Finance's financial affairs. Pendse also revealed that a financial report prepared for Tata Finance had included a candid discussion of the controversial ICD transactions and their impact on the company's financial condition. However, according to Pendse, a Tata Finance board member who had close ties to key Tata Group executives had deleted that discussion before the financial report was released to the public.

## "The Wrath of the Tatas"

One goal that the senior executives of the Tata Group hoped to achieve when they retained AFF to investigate the Tata Finance accounting scandal was to clear their own names. One of those executives reportedly requested that Y.M. Kale, a senior AFF partner who was in line to become the next managing partner of AFF, supervise that investigation. Kale was easily among the most respected members of India's accounting profession. An employee or partner of AFF for 30 years, Kale served on the International Accounting Standards Board, was a former president of the Institute of Chartered Accountants of India (ICAI), and had been elected to the ICAI's governing council five times—the ICAI is the Indian federal agency that oversees the nation's accounting profession, including its independent audit function.[6] Kale had also served as the chairman of the ICAI board responsible for issuing Indian accounting standards and at the time he was selected for the Tata Finance assignment was the chairman of the ICAI audit practices committee. Kale's prominent position within India's accounting profession and his reputation for integrity and candor were, no doubt, expected to add to the credibility of the AFF report.

AFF prepared the 900-page report on the Tata Finance accounting scandal exclusively for Ratan Tata and his top subordinates within the Tata Group. Nevertheless, by July 2002, two months after the report had been delivered by AFF to the Tata Group, large segments of the report, including AFF's major findings, had been leaked to the press. The public disclosure of AFF's principal findings reignited the Tata Finance accounting scandal and triggered a firestorm of criticism directed at the senior executives of the Tata Group. Instead of absolving those executives of any responsibility for the accounting scandal, the AFF report linked them to the fraud. One journalist relied on a sports idiom to describe the unexpected outcome of the AFF investigation when he noted that the Tata Group executives had "scored an own goal."[7]

The AFF report shocked Ratan Tata and the other senior executives of the Tata Group not only because it supported the allegation of Dilip Pendse that Mr. Tata and his subordinates had been aware of the fraudulent transactions—but also because the report criticized the quality of the Tata companies' corporate governance system. This unexpected criticism stemmed largely from the paternalistic nature of the organization's top management. Throughout the history of the organization, members of the Tata family and their close friends and business associates had dominated the operating management and boards of directors of the individual Tata companies.

---

6. Case 8.10, "Institute of Chartered Accountants of India," examines the ICAI's role in the development of India's accounting profession and independent audit function.

7. V. Law and M. Goyal, "Scoring an Own Goal," *India Today*, 26 August 2002, 49.

These individuals made protecting the jobs of Tata employees one of their primary objectives, even if that meant refusing to eliminate unprofitable businesses or business segments. This policy endeared the Tata family and organization to its employees but it also undermined the huge conglomerate's overall profitability. The "in-bred" corporate governance structure of the Tata Group also meant that the individual Tata companies typically did not have outside or independent board members who could provide objective analyses of the companies' operations, accounting and financial reporting decisions, and other important policies and procedures.

The AFF report and the ensuing controversy that erupted after much of the report was leaked to the press created a rift between the large accounting firm and Tata Group's senior management. On August 2, 2002, AFF startled the Indian business community and accounting profession by announcing that it was retracting the report because it was flawed. Even more startling was AFF's announcement six days later that it had dismissed the three partners responsible for writing the report, including its principal author, Y. M. Kale.

AFF's decision to retract its report and to dismiss Y. M. Kale only deepened the controversy swirling around the Tata Finance accounting fraud. A senior member of one of India's other large accounting firms suggested that Kale was being made the "scapegoat" in the unseemly affair and that the Tata organization was responsible for his dismissal.[8] The Indian business press also repeatedly implied that Kale had been fired as a result of pressure applied on AFF by the Tata Group. These media reports pointed out that the Tata Group had significant leverage on AFF because the accounting firm audited several of the largest Tata companies and because the close affiliation with the Tata organization enhanced AFF's stature and prestige within India's accounting profession.

The published reports connecting them to the firing of Y.M. Kale infuriated the senior executives of the Tata Group, including Ratan Tata. To respond to that allegation and other criticism they faced as a result of the Tata Finance accounting scandal, those executives issued a press release entitled "Tata Group Condemns Campaign of Vilification." The lengthy press release, which appeared in full-page advertisements purchased by the Tata Group in several major Indian newspapers, began with the following statement: "Sections of the media have been carrying deliberately distorted and sensationalized versions pertaining to the withdrawal of a private and confidential report prepared by A. F. Ferguson and Co. (AFF) for one of the Tata Group's companies . . . The Group's reputation and image are being sullied deliberately by the use of half truths and untruths."[9] Subsequent sections of the press release insisted that the senior executives of the Tata Group not only had nothing to do with the Tata Finance fraud, they also had not pressured AFF to either retract its report or dismiss Y. M. Kale.

The press release also charged that the AFF report, in fact, was flawed because Kale had excluded from the report important testimony provided by the former chief accountant of the Niskalp subsidiary of Tata Finance. According to that individual, Dilip Pendse had instructed him to enter fictitious transactions in Niskalp's accounting records and to prepare false accounting documents to corroborate those entries. The purpose of the fictitious transactions, according to the former accountant, was to mitigate the large investment losses being incurred by Niskalp. Four days after the Tata Group issued the August 10th press release, the former Niskalp accountant

8. V. Sridhar and A. Katakam, "L'affaire Tata Finance," *Frontline* (online), 31 August–13 September 2002.

9. Tata Group, "Tata Group Condemns Campaign of Vilification." Press release issued August 10, 2002.

recanted and insisted that he had made the false allegations against Pendse "under tremendous tension, with a disturbed frame of mind due to shock and also under threat of arrest."[10]

Following the release and retraction of the AFF report and his subsequent dismissal by AFF, Y. M. Kale refused to comment publicly on the controversy despite repeated interview requests from the media. As one journalist observed, everyone wanted to know how Kale could risk his 30-year career in public accounting by "incurring the wrath of the Tatas."[11] Many of Kale's colleagues in the accounting profession came to his defense and questioned why his former firm, AFF, did not "stand behind him" during the ordeal. The business press also berated AFF for apparently buckling to pressure applied by its largest and most important client.

> *This unprecedented withdrawal [of the AFF report] has raised the hackles of the entire accounting community. . . . The issue is—how can an accounting firm "withdraw" its observations just because the company was not happy with them? It is the duty of any auditing firm to point out the discrepancies; isn't that the basic objective of any auditing firm?*
>
> *What this issue highlights is that maybe auditing firms do indeed work for the companies for whom they audit. Independent views and observations are good in theory but not in practical life. Then this does nullify the entire purpose of any auditing agency, doesn't it?*[12]

Criticism of AFF within India's accounting profession became even more pointed when a subsequent investigation revealed that several AFF partners had performed a detailed review of, and approved, the AFF report on the Tata Finance accounting scandal before the report was forwarded to the Tata Group. As one journalist noted, "Trust and reputation are the two biggest assets for an audit firm. A. F. Ferguson & Co. (AFF) appears to have just mortgaged them in distress."[13]

## EPILOGUE

The white-collar crime unit of the Mumbai Police Department investigated the criminal complaint filed against Dilip Pendse by the Tata Group. In August 2002, that unit dropped the charges filed against Pendse, reporting that there was "insufficient evidence to support" them.[14] In a subsequent interview, a senior official of the Mumbai Police Department reported that the criminal investigation of the Tata Finance scandal had revealed that the "TFL [Tata Finance Limited] board knew everything that Pendse did. None of these transactions could have taken place without their connivance."[15] Since certain members of the Tata Finance board were close associates of Ratan Tata and other top Tata Group executives, this conclusion appeared to corroborate Pendse's testimony that Tata Group's senior management had been aware of the financial wrongdoing at Tata Finance.

10. Sridhar and Katakam, "L'affaire Tata Finance."

11. *Global News Wire* (online), "People in Glass Houses . . . A. F. Ferguson Report on Tata Finance Raises Storm," 26 August 2002.

12. R. Dubey, "Wave of Financial Scams Hits the Indian Shores," *Arab News* (online), 19 August 2002.

13. R. Srinivasan, "A. F. Ferguson Holding a Tiger by the Tail," *Businessline*, 11 August 2002, 1.

14. Merchant, "Chairman on Defensive as Scandal Tarnishes Tata."

15. Sridhar and Katakam, "L'affaire Tata Finance."

The Mumbai Police Department's decision to drop the criminal complaint filed against Dilip Pendse angered the senior executives of the Tata Group. Shortly after the charges were dropped, the Tata Group filed a legal appeal asking an Indian court to order the Mumbai Police Department to "reinvestigate" the matter.[16] Over the next several years, the Tata Group would doggedly pursue Pendse. As a result of additional criminal complaints filed by the Tata Group, Pendse was arrested for a second time by the Mumbai Police Department in December 2003. In August 2006, India's federal law enforcement agency, the Central Bureau of Investigation (CBI), filed criminal charges against Pendse, largely as a result of information provided to it by the Tata Group. These latter charges are still pending. To date, the principal criminal sanction that has been imposed on Pendse is a fine for insider trading levied against him in January 2007 by the Securities and Exchange Board of India, the Indian federal agency that is comparable to the U.S. Securities and Exchange Commission.

After retracting its report on the Tata Finance accounting scandal, AFF disclosed that it intended to reopen its investigation of the matter and file a revised report with the Tata Group. Apparently, the second report was never completed. According to an unnamed source within the Tata Group, the senior executives of that organization informed AFF in late 2002 that a revised report would not be necessary.[17]

Public criticism of AFF's decision to withdraw its report on the Tata Finance fraud prompted the ICAI to investigate that decision. The ICAI president at the time reported that his agency was considering filing charges of "gross negligence" against AFF.[18] The ICAI also announced that it would investigate allegations that AFF had shredded key documents pertaining to the Tata Finance investigation to prevent law enforcement and regulatory authorities from accessing those documents.

After a brief investigation in late 2002, the ICAI reported that it had not found any evidence of professional misconduct by AFF in connection with its investigation of the Tata Finance fraud or its subsequent decision to retract the report regarding that fraud. Over the previous several years, the ICAI had been criticized for being a lax and ineffective regulatory agency for India's accounting profession. In fact, several parties, including representatives of the major international accounting firms, had called for the ICAI to be replaced. The ICAI's finding that AFF was not guilty of any professional misconduct in the Tata Finance case reinforced the perception that the ICAI was lax in carrying out its regulatory responsibilities and resulted in even more criticism of the federal agency.

In November 2002, Y. M. Kale accepted a management position with a large consulting firm. To date, Kale has yet to comment publicly on the Tata Finance accounting scandal, his role in investigating that scandal, or AFF's decision to dismiss him. Within India's accounting profession and business community, Kale remains a respected figure. As one journalist noted, "In the entire TFL drama, only Kale appears to have come out unscathed."[19]

## Questions

1. Should the fact that a business entity or other organization embraces a specific ethical, moral, or religious code or framework be relevant in designing and carrying out an audit of that organization? Defend your answer.

---

16. *Global News Wire* (online), "Tata Rejoinder Seeks Criminal Charges against Dilip Pendse, Insists on Reinvestigation in TFL Case," 24 October 2002.

17. *Global News Wire* (online), "New Ferguson Report on TFL Any Time Now," 12 November 2002.

18. Sridhar and Katakam, "L'affaire Tata Finance."

19. *Ibid.*

2. Suppose that an accounting firm in the United States was retained to complete an engagement similar to the one performed by AFF for the Tata Group. What professional standards would be relevant to such an engagement? How do the latter standards differ, if at all, from those that apply to the performance of an independent audit?
3. In your opinion, why do you believe that Y. M. Kale chose not to comment publicly on the controversy that surrounded the retraction of the AFF report on the Tata Finance accounting scandal and his subsequent dismissal by AFF? Did he have an ethical or moral responsibility not to comment on those matters? Explain.

**CASE 8.10**

# Institute of Chartered Accountants of India

The spice trade first brought European explorers, most notably the Portuguese adventurer Vasco da Gama, to the shores of the Indian sub-continent in the late fifteenth century. In the mid-eighteenth century, Great Britain used a series of military excursions to gain control over several major Indian provinces and effectively made the country the largest colony within its far-flung empire. For almost a century, Britain's colonial rule of the country was administered through the infamous British East India Company. After Great Britain thwarted the bloody Indian Rebellion of 1857, the British East India Company was abolished and India became subject to direct rule by the British monarchy. Periodic rebellions, civil unrest, and ultimately the massive civil disobedience campaign orchestrated by Mahatma Gandhi culminated in India gaining its independence from Great Britain in August 1947.

Britain's colonial rule would leave a lasting imprint on all aspects of Indian society, including its economy, financial reporting system, and accounting profession. During the two centuries that Britain controlled India, a large number of British citizens immigrated to India seeking opportunities in banking, insurance, accounting, and other financial services industries and professions. Alexander Fletcher Ferguson arrived in India in the late 1880s. A few years later, he organized an accounting firm, A. F. Ferguson & Co., that would become one of India's most prominent professional services organizations and its largest accounting firm.

Native Indians typically did not welcome British immigrants who, like Ferguson, often took advantage of their British "connections" to further their careers and otherwise elevate their social status. Making matters worse, the new immigrants often treated Indians as second-class citizens in their own country. Not surprisingly, after India gained its independence, an isolationist mindset prevailed in the country. Because of that mindset, India's central government established protectionist policies to prevent foreign companies, professional firms, and other organizations from dominating the new nation's economy. These policies included significant tariffs on imported goods, limits on equity investments in Indian companies by foreign nationals, and, most important, the so-called "License Raj." The License Raj was an extensive set of government rules and regulations established by India's first Prime Minister, Jawaharlal Nehru, that gave India's central government effective control over the nation's economy.[1] Under the License Raj, any major business venture proposed by a domestic or foreign entity had to be approved by a central government planning commission.

India's protectionist economic policies discouraged the major international accounting firms from establishing significant operations in India. However, when India's central government announced that it planned to relax its protectionist policies in the early 1990s, those firms quickly began pursuing practice development opportunities in the world's second-largest nation. Over the following decade, a bitter controversy erupted regarding the aggressive expansion efforts of the major

1. Prime Minister Nehru, an admirer of Joseph Stalin, intended to develop an economy for India patterned after the Soviet economic system.

international accounting firms within India. Before examining that controversy, it will be helpful to review the recent history of the Indian accounting profession.

## Birth of a Profession

Shortly after India gained its independence from Great Britain, India's Parliament passed the Companies Act to set up a regulatory infrastructure for the new nation's capital markets. That infrastructure closely resembled the regulatory framework for Britain's capital markets that was created by the series of Companies Acts adopted by the British Parliament beginning in the mid-nineteenth century. Britain's Companies Acts also served as a blueprint for the federal securities laws enacted by the U.S. Congress in the 1930s. The regulatory agency charged with overseeing India's capital markets is the Securities and Exchange Board of India (SEBI), the equivalent of the Securities and Exchange Commission in the United States. Similar to the comparable federal statutes in Great Britain and the United States, India's Companies Act mandates that publicly owned companies issue periodic financial statements audited by an independent accounting firm.

In 1949, India's Parliament passed the Chartered Accountants Act. This statute created the New Delhi-based Institute of Chartered Accountants of India (ICAI) to oversee the nation's accounting profession. In carrying out its responsibilities, the ICAI works closely with the SEBI. Unlike such professional organizations as the American Institute of Certified Public Accountants (AICPA), the ICAI is a federal agency that has a wide range of statutory authority. The ICAI's regulatory mandate includes, among other responsibilities, issuing accounting standards and ethical rules of conduct for Chartered Accountants (CAs), overseeing India's independent audit function, administering the series of examinations that must be passed to become a CA, and sanctioning CAs and public accounting firms that violate their statutory, ethical, or other professional responsibilities.

Since its inception, the ICAI has embraced Great Britain's financial reporting model that requires public companies to prepare periodic financial statements providing a "true and fair" view of their financial condition and operating results. Although not expressly defined, "truth" and "fairness" in this context are generally determined in reference to the economic environment in which a company is operating, unique conditions or challenges facing the company, and accounting and financial reporting concepts relevant to the company's financial affairs.[2] Most important, the true and fair view demands that the economic substance of transactions prevails over their legal form. The true and fair reporting model is not nearly as "prescriptive" as the "fair presentation" model that underlies the U.S. financial reporting system. That is, the British and Indian financial reporting model relies more heavily on general concepts to guide financial reporting and accounting decisions rather than a large number of detailed accounting standards, such as those issued by the Financial Accounting Standards Board in the United States.

Shortly after its creation, the ICAI began issuing *Statements on Accounting Standards* to provide guidance for accounting and financial reporting decisions by Indian companies. Collectively, the ICAI's accounting standards were referred to as "Indian Accounting Standards" or IAS. In late 2007, the ICAI announced that it would "fully converge" IAS with International Financial Reporting Standards (IFRS) by 2011.

---

2. "While the term *true and fair view* originated in U.K. company law, U.K. law does not spell out what the term means" [D. Alexander and S. Archer, *Miller European Accounting Guide*, 2nd ed. (San Diego: Harcourt Brace, 1995), 24–25].

India's Parliament also vested the ICAI with the authority to establish or sanction professional auditing standards. Periodically, the ICAI issues *Statements on Auditing Practices* (SAPs), which are technical pronouncements that accounting firms must comply with when planning and performing independent audits. Although considerably fewer in number than the *Statements on Auditing Standards* issued by the United States' Auditing Standards Board, SAPs address the same general issues. Examples of specific SAPs include *SAP 1, Basic Principles Governing an Audit*; *SAP 3, Documentation*; *SAP 4, Fraud and Error*; and *SAP 6, Study and Evaluation of the Accounting System and Related Internal Audit Control in Connection with an Audit.* In addition to SAPs, the ICAI occasionally issues pronouncements to provide technical guidance to CAs and accounting firms on other important auditing topics. Representative of these latter items are the following ICAI publications: *Independence of Auditors*, *Control on the Quality of Audit Work*, *Audit Engagement Letters*, and *Audit of Banks*.

## Watchdogs vs. Bloodhounds

Despite the apparent similarities between India's independent audit function and that of Great Britain and, to a lesser extent, the United States, independent audits performed within India are widely viewed as being less rigorous than British or U.S. audits. One possible explanation for the less rigorous nature of Indian audits is the legal climate that Indian accounting firms face as compared with their counterparts in Great Britain and the United States.

Consider the following important legal precedent embraced by India's courts that addresses the nature of the independent auditor's role:

> *An auditor is not bound to be a detective or to approach his work with suspicion or with the foregone conclusion that something is wrong. He is a watchdog but not a bloodhound. He is justified in believing tried servants of the company, and is entitled to rely upon their representation, provided he takes reasonable care.*[3]

Because of this legal precedent, India's legal system seldom holds independent auditors responsible for failing to detect accounting and financial reporting frauds. No doubt, this legal precedent has influenced the audit policies and procedures of India's accounting firms. In commenting on the overall audit philosophy applied by his firm, the managing partner of one of India's largest accounting firms noted, "Operating under the constraints of time and cost, we presume full honesty from our clients. After all, an audit is not an investigation."[4]

As in the United States, independent auditors in India face criminal prosecution under various federal statutes and sanctions for unethical and otherwise unprofessional conduct by various law enforcement and regulatory authorities. The principal responsibility for punishing Indian auditors has been delegated to the ICAI. However, critics of the ICAI maintain that the federal agency historically has been reluctant to act on that responsibility. "The ICAI has been singularly lax in ensuring high standards of professionalism and conduct among auditors."[5]

In fact, the ICAI is the most common target of critics who claim that India's independent audit function has lagged far behind that of other countries in terms of professionalism, rigor, and overall effectiveness. Much of this criticism has been directed at the ICAI by representatives of the major international accounting

3. P. Ravindran, "Auditors and Fraud," *Financial Daily* (online), 11 October 2001.
4. *Flashpoint*, "Financial Chicanery," www.capitalmarket.com, 29 January 2002.
5. P. Ravidran, "Auditors and Fraud."

firms. In recent years, that criticism prompted a large-scale and highly publicized counterattack against those firms by parties defending the ICAI, including the ICAI itself. These parties maintained that the major problems facing India's accounting profession were not due to ineffective regulatory oversight by the ICAI but, instead, could be traced to the major international accounting firms.

## Barbarians at the Gate

A nationwide financial crisis in 1991 that threatened to bankrupt India prompted the so-called "liberalization movement" by the nation's central government. The principal thrust of the liberalization movement was ending the protectionist economic policies that had been the lynchpin of India's economy for the previous four decades. The opening of India's markets to the rest of the world resulted in record economic growth for the nation over the following decade. During the 1990s, hundreds of multinational companies invested heavily in a wide range of business ventures in India. The central government's abrupt change in its economic policy also resulted in billions of dollars of foreign direct investment (FDI) in India by individual and institutional investors around the world.

India's rapid economic growth during the 1990s triggered a significant increase in the demand for accounting, auditing, and other professional services offered by the major international accounting firms. The sudden increase in the demand for their services and the announced intention of India's central government to end its protectionist economic policies caused the Big Four accounting firms to begin vigorously pursuing expansion opportunities within India during the early 1990s.[6]

The enthusiasm of the Big Four accounting firms for the Indian market was soon blunted when they realized that the ICAI, unlike most other Indian regulatory agencies, had no intention of eliminating its protectionist policies. Over the previous four decades, the ICAI had erected numerous barriers to discourage foreign accounting firms from operating in India. The most problematic of these barriers was a regulation that prohibited foreign accounting firms from establishing branch offices in India. Two of the Big Eight firms—Deloitte, Haskins & Sells and Price Waterhouse—had established independent branch offices in India before this regulation went into effect. But those firms were limited to operating one practice office each with a maximum of 20 partners—a restriction imposed on domestic accounting firms as well. In addition, the two firms were not allowed to rename their Indian practice offices when each merged with another international accounting firm, which meant that those offices were required to operate under an out-of-date name for their firm.

Representatives of the Big Four firms reacted angrily to the ICAI's insistence on maintaining its protectionist policies even as most Indian markets were being opened to foreign competitors. In commenting on the regulation that prevented Big Four firms from establishing new practice offices in India, one Big Four spokesperson observed that the restriction was "part of a web of . . . protectionist restrictions that stifle foreign entrants and shield the indigenous audit profession from genuine competition."[7] An angry KPMG partner maintained that the ICAI was "outmoded" and suggested that its regulatory responsibilities should be assigned to other federal agencies.[8]

---

6. In fact, during the 1990s, each of the Big Five accounting firms, including Andersen & Co., pursued expansion opportunities within India. However, since Andersen effectively went out of business in 2002, "Big Four" will be used in this case when referring to the dominant international accounting firms.

7. B. Jopson and A. Yee, "Accountancy's Tangled Web," *Financial Times*, 26 July 2006, 6.

8. *Ibid.*

In the late 1990s and into the new century, the domestic business press in India also became critical of the ICAI, but for different reasons. An Indian business periodical maintained that the rising number of accounting frauds within the country was a direct consequence of the ICAI's lax regulatory attitude.[9] The business press also criticized the ICAI for allegedly being a "captive" of the profession that it regulated since the organization's governing council consisted of CAs from domestic accounting firms. One Indian journalist suggested that the ICAI should be eliminated and replaced by a regulatory agency similar to the United States' Public Company Accounting Oversight Board (PCAOB), which is controlled by a majority of nonaccountants.[10]

Mounting criticism of the ICAI greatly irritated, if not embarrassed, the members of the organization's governing council. Eventually, that criticism goaded the ICAI and its supporters to counterattack the agency's critics, principal among them the large international accounting firms. The ICAI and its supporters acknowledged that India's accounting profession was facing major challenges but contended that those problems were a direct consequence of the aggressive practice development activities of the international accounting firms within India. Despite those firms' harsh criticism of the ICAI's protectionist policies, the ICAI maintained that each of those firms, in fact, had established large-scale operations in India during the 1990s.

According to the ICAI, the so-called "MAFs" (multinational accounting firms) had used various subtle and, in some cases, covert methods to circumvent the laws and regulations intended to prevent those firms from wresting control of India's market for accounting, auditing, and related professional services from domestic accounting firms. As a direct result of those illicit methods, the MAFs had supposedly taken control of that market and, at the same time, undermined the credibility and integrity of India's accounting profession.

In 2002, the ICAI commissioned the Chartered Accountants' Action Committee for Level Playing Field (CAAC) to investigate the impact that the MAFs were having on India's accounting profession. Several months later, the CAAC issued its findings in a 141-page report entitled "White Paper on Multinational Accounting Firms Operating in India" ("White Paper"). The prologue to that report indicated that its principal purpose was to "inform the Indian business [community], Indian finance sector, Indian Government, Indian policy makers, Indian professionals, and also the general public about the correct facts about the Multinational Accounting Firms (MAFs) and about the state of the Indian accounting profession."[11,12] The prologue went on to note that it would demonstrate that the MAFs' presence in India was "illegitimate" and document that the MAFs had "illegally and surreptitiously taken over the attestation and audit functions of the [accounting] profession in India."[13]

The large international accounting firms have frequently found themselves the target of harsh criticism in recent years, primarily as a result of their link to such financial scandals as Enron and WorldCom in the United States, Kanebo Limited in Japan,

---

9. T. Ramanujam, "Checking the Explosion of Corporate Fraud," *Business Line*, 14 September 2002, 1.

10. S. Vikraman, "Time to Regulate the Auditing Profession?" *Business Line*, 11 March 2002, 1.

11. The "multinational accounting firms" specifically identified by the CAAC included Andersen & Co., Deloitte Touche Tohmatsu, Ernst & Young, KPMG, and PricewaterhouseCoopers.

12. The Group on White Paper on Multinational Accounting Firms, "White Paper on Multinational Accounting Firms Operating in India," The Chartered Accountants' Action Committee for Level Playing Field (New Delhi, 2003).

13. *Ibid.*, 3.

Parmalat in Italy, Royal Ahold in the Netherlands, and HIH in Australia. Easily the harshest criticism of those firms, however, can be found in the White Paper report issued by the CAAC.

## Dirty Business

Indian critics of the Big Four accounting firms maintained that the ultimate objective of those firms within India during the 1990s was to establish significant accounting and auditing practices that could then be used as a launching pad to market a wide range of consulting services to Indian businesses. Intensive marketing of such services had paid off handsomely for those accounting firms over the previous decade in the United States and Western Europe. By the early 1990s, the Big Four firms had developed large consulting divisions that provided a wide range of services, including systems design and implementation projects, cost containment studies, and internal audit outsourcing. Each of those firms' thousands of audit clients was the principal target market for such services.

The efforts of the Big Four firms to expand their consulting divisions was a direct consequence of the increasing competition within the audit market over the previous several decades that had resulted in paper-thin profit margins for audit services. Since the profit margins on consulting services were generally several times larger than those for audit services, the Big Four firms easily compensated for the declining profitability of their audit practices by selling a large volume of consulting services to their audit clients and other parties.[14]

The major roadblock that the Big Four firms faced in gaining broader access to the professional services markets in India during the 1990s was the ICAI's ban on those firms establishing their own branch offices in India. To overcome this problem, these firms began utilizing a two-pronged strategy to "invade" the India professional services markets. First, those firms began employing on a much larger scale a strategy that some of them had used to enter India in the first place, namely, aligning themselves with "surrogate" domestic accounting firms. Because ICAI regulations limited an accounting firm to a maximum of 20 partners and limited the number of independent audits that could be supervised by any one audit partner, the Big Four accounting firms found it necessary to establish alliances with multiple Indian accounting firms. "Each of the Big Four firms has created a messy agglomeration of Indian businesses [accounting firms] that are legally separate but in practice work together."[15]

The second tactic the Big Four firms used to establish themselves in India during the 1990s was to obtain a license to operate a business consulting firm within India. Such a license was readily available from the Reserve Bank of India (RBI), the Indian federal agency that issues those licenses. After obtaining this license, each of the Big Four firms could establish multiple practice offices within India under their global practice name—unlike the accounting profession, the consulting "profession" did not limit firms to having one practice office. These consulting practice offices then worked closely with the domestic accounting firms that were the Big Four's surrogates in the accounting and auditing services market.

Because the Big Four firms had considerably more economic resources than their surrogate firms, they reportedly dominated, if not controlled, the operations of those firms. As a result, the surrogate firms allegedly became "storefronts" through which the Big Four firms provided accounting and auditing services within India. In its

14. N. Lakshman, "Accounting Firms: Time to Redo the Numbers," *rediff.com*, 21 September 2002.

15. Jopson and Yee, "Accountancy's Tangled Web."

White Paper report, the CAAC suggested that many Indian accounting firms aligned themselves with MAFs during the 1990s because they believed that doing so was an economic necessity if they were to survive.

> *The traditional Indian [accounting] firms which had large audit and other professional presence felt too insecure about their capacity to retain their position and therefore many of them began thinking in terms of becoming [MAF] affiliates or surrogates to retain the very work they were handling and to access new work through the MAFs.*[16]

A major theme of the CAAC's White Paper report was that the MAFs use of surrogate firms to "colonize" the Indian market for accounting and auditing services was, in fact, illegal since that practice allowed those firms to provide accounting, auditing, and related professional services without being subject to the ICAI's regulatory oversight. "Because the MAFs are outside the scope of the discipline of the ICAI and for that matter any discipline, no such action [regulatory oversight] is possible."[17]

One of the most important ICAI regulations that the MAFs were able to sidestep was that agency's complete ban on advertising by accounting firms. Even though the MAFs were practicing in India under their "audit" names, they were not considered accounting or auditing firms within India. So, they could advertise and use, at will, the other marketing methods that Indian accounting firms were prohibited from using. Allegedly, the MAFs used large-scale advertising and marketing campaigns not only to lure consulting clients but also to attract audit and accounting services clients for their surrogate firms. The CAAC charged that the MAFs used a wide range of unprofessional and "dishonourable" marketing methods to sell those services and that those methods had greatly diminished the integrity and credibility of India's respected accounting profession.

> *While acting and operating through their surrogates in traditional areas where Indian CAs are subject to the discipline of the ICAI . . . the MAFs began and continue to merrily advertise and brand-build their own names, and take advantage of their brand value built in defiance of the Indian CA regulations established by law. . . . This snide and devious exercise extends from holding cricket matches—to high-cost advertisements—to even higher-cost events like instituting and giving Business Leadership and Entrepreneur Awards to squeeze themselves into the high-yielding corporate and financial market for professional work.*[18]

The marketing strategies and tactics used by the MAFs were reportedly so effective that those firms quickly persuaded most large Indian corporations and even government agencies that their services were superior to those offered by domestic accounting and consulting firms. As a result, in a little more than one decade, the MAFs captured the "high-end" market for business consulting services within India and, through their surrogate firms, became the *de facto* auditors for a large number of major Indian companies. According to the CAAC, the MAFs conquest of the accounting, auditing, and consulting services market within India "condemned" the country's domestic firms "to play a secondary role in their country, occupying just about the same position which Indian citizens occupied during the British rule in India."[19]

---

16. The Group on White Paper.
17. *Ibid.*, 35.
18. *Ibid.*, 34.
19. *Ibid.*, 37.

The CAAC maintained that the MAFs were anything but the "skilled" and "virtuous" professional services firms that they portrayed themselves to be in their elaborate marketing campaigns. Instead, the CAAC reported that over the previous few decades, the MAFs had engaged in a wide range of predatory and "dirty" business practices. Following are examples of such practices that the CAAC identified in its White Paper report, examples supported with dozens of references to specific litigation cases, news reports, and other anecdotal evidence.[20]

- "The MAFs have become skilled lobbyists and have become the tools in the hands of business to bribe the state and regulators."
- "They have become experts in money laundering."
- "The MAFs have been repeatedly caught in frauds and malpractices which have forced them to seek compromises at billions of dollars of cost."
- "Driven by their lust for money by any means, MAFs are now turning into experts in shredding evidence and in suppressing facts and evidence, to escape the consequences of their fraudulent actions."
- "The MAFs are guilty of thousands of violations of audit independence and ethical requirements."
- "The MAFs are experts in advising tax evasion and tax fraud to their clients on a global level, causing losses to governments in the billions of dollars."

The CAAC concluded its lengthy diatribe against the MAFs by declaring that the accounting profession in India was under a state of siege and that it was in the national interest that the profession be reclaimed by the nation's chartered accountants. "Finally, this is war. This cannot be won without high national spirit and without perceiving the confluence of national interest with the collective interest of the CA profession."[21] The CAAC hoped that it would be at the forefront of the effort to accomplish that goal. "This is the agenda of the CAAC. This is its goal. 'India First' is its mantra."[22]

The CAAC prepared an impressive list of action items to be considered by the ICAI and other relevant Indian regulatory authorities. Among these recommendations, two were particularly sweeping in nature. One proposal called for the ICAI to prohibit any additional multinational accounting firms from establishing practice units in India, either through an alliance with an existing Indian accounting firm or as an independent business consulting firm. For those MAFs already operating within India as consulting firms, the CAAC recommended that those firms' business licenses be revoked.

## Refutation & Denial

As could be expected, the CAAC's White Paper report prompted quick responses from representatives of the Big Four accounting firms. An Ernst & Young spokesperson defended his firm's alliances with India-based accounting firms by noting that "there is no bar on establishing an alliance with a foreign firm."[23] A few months later, the managing partner of Ernst & Young's India practice unit responded curtly to a journalist when asked why his firm should not be subject to the ICAI's regulatory oversight. "We don't even fall within the jurisdiction of the ICAI, since we are just another consulting firm like Boston Consulting Group, A. T. Kearney, or McKinsey & Co. So why us?"[24]

20. *Ibid.*, 54–56.

21. *Ibid.*, 139.

22. *Ibid.*, 141.

23. *Business India* (online), "This Ain't GATS," August 4, 2003.

24. *Business Today*, "Four Under Peril," *indiatodaygroup.com*, 23 November 2003.

In responding to the allegation that the Big Four controlled their surrogate firms, a PwC representative noted, "The Indian firms that are members of the PwC network are home-grown organizations wholly owned in India, and have built a brand name for more than 100 years."[25] In responding to a similar question, a KPMG spokesperson simply observed, "KPMG has been following domestic [Indian] laws."[26]

The Big Four firms also insisted that they were not providing accounting and auditing services within India. However, the CAAC's White Paper report had documented that the websites of the MAFs "proudly proclaim that they do accounting, audit, and assurance services through their Indian associates."[27] When questioned regarding the independent audits performed by one of Ernst & Young's Indian affiliates, an Ernst & Young partner reported that the affiliate was "100 percent Indian-owned and Indian-managed" and "does all the audit work" on its audit engagements.[28]

Parties other than the Big Four firms were angered and concerned by the CAAC White Paper report. In the United States, the National Association of State Boards of Accountancy (NASBA) collectively regulates the practice of accountancy. The NASBA reported that if the ICAI took action against the Big Four accounting firms, it might take measures to "retaliate" against Indian accounting firms.[29] Representatives of important international accounting organizations also voiced their opinion on the CAAC report. For example, the president of the International Federation of Accountants (IFAC) encouraged the ICAI to "refrain from embracing protectionist policies in the accountancy and auditing sector."[30]

Finally, not all Indian CAs and accounting firms joined with the CAAC in condemning the Big Four accounting firms. In particular, several executive partners of Big Four–affiliated firms came to the defense of their practice partners. A partner of an Indian accounting firm aligned with PricewaterhouseCoopers (PwC) reported that the staff members of his firm benefited greatly from working alongside PwC professionals and from being allowed to participate in PwC training programs.[31]

## EPILOGUE

The highly publicized release of the CAAC's White Paper report in July 2003 and the ensuing criticism of that report by a wide range of parties placed tremendous pressure on the ICAI. Both supporters and critics of the report expected the ICAI to respond quickly and decisively to the report's key findings and recommendations. But that did not happen.

At the time the White Paper report was released, the ICAI was mired in two controversies. First, the Indian business press had reported that the wife of the ICAI president was a part-owner of a private business that provided "coaching" courses for the series of examinations that had to be successfully completed to earn the CA designation within India. The press questioned whether the CA candidates enrolled in that business's coaching courses received an unfair advantage over other candidates. To quell that controversy, the ICAI purchased

25. *Business India* (online), "This Ain't GATS."
26. *Ibid.*
27. The Group on White Paper, 126.
28. *Business India* (online), "This Ain't GATS."
29. *Ibid.*
30. K. R. Srivats, "India Must Avoid Protectionism in Accountancy," *Business Line*, 16 March 2004, 1.
31. *Business India* (online), "This Ain't GATS."

newspaper advertisements insisting that the integrity of the CA examination process was not being compromised.

The second controversy facing the ICAI in the summer of 2003 involved what had become known as "India's Enron." India's largest business conglomerate is the Tata Group, which consists of approximately two dozen public companies and 80 privately owned businesses. Collectively, the Tata companies account for nearly 3 percent of India's gross domestic product and employ several hundred thousand Indian citizens. India's largest accounting firm, A. F. Ferguson & Co. (AFF), audits several of the largest Tata companies.

In 2001, the Tata Group hired AFF to complete an investigation of an alleged accounting and financial reporting fraud within Tata Finance Limited, a Tata company that was not audited by AFF. In 2002, AFF released a 900-page report documenting the results of its investigation of the Tata Finance fraud. That report shocked the Tata Group, the Indian business press, and the general public by implicating several of Tata's top executives, including the chairman of the Tata Group, Ratan Tata, in the fraud. Ratan Tata purchased full-page advertisements in major Indian newspapers insisting that the report was inaccurate. AFF eventually withdrew the report and dismissed the three partners responsible for writing it. One of those partners was Y. M. Kale, who was among the most prominent members of the Indian accounting profession. Kale served on the International Accounting Standards Board, was a former president of the ICAI, and reportedly was in line to become AFF's next managing partner.

The business press, leaders of the accounting profession, and various other parties demanded that the ICAI investigate the Tata scandal and the role of AFF within that scandal. After a brief investigation, the ICAI failed to file charges against anyone involved in the matter, which renewed allegations that the ICAI was a lax and ineffective watchdog agency for India's accounting profession.[32]

Finally, in late 2004, the ICAI responded to the CAAC White Paper report. The ICAI identified several proposals to strengthen the competitive position of Indian accounting firms that were not affiliated with MAFs. Among these proposals was a recommendation encouraging such firms to create cooperative networks that would allow them to pool their manpower, technological, and financial resources. The ICAI also announced that it planned to increase from 20 to 50 the maximum number of partners that accounting firms could have and that it would allow accounting firms to establish consulting divisions. Over the past decade, the so-called surrogate firms had established de facto consulting divisions as a result of their affiliations with MAFs. The ICAI's new policy meant that "nonaffiliated" firms would have an opportunity to participate in the booming business consulting market within India.

A major problem that nonaffiliated firms had faced during the 1990s was attracting qualified professionals. India's surging economy had resulted in a large increase in the demand for accounting and accounting-related services; however, there had not been a parallel increase in the number of CAs within India. In 2004, there were only 120,000 CAs in India, meaning that on a per capita basis India had considerably fewer professional accountants than any other major country, with the exception of Japan. Making matters worse for nonaffiliated firms was a large increase in the hiring of CAs by surrogate firms during the 1990s. Because the surrogate firms offered considerably higher salaries than other Indian firms, the nonaffiliated firms found it increasingly difficult to hire sufficient CAs to staff their professional engagements. To mitigate this problem, the ICAI shortened the minimum time required to obtain a CA license from nearly 5½ years to approximately 4 years.

Supporters of the CAAC's more radical proposals were disappointed by the ICAI's decision not to pursue the imposition of sanctions or other operating constraints on the MAFs or their surrogate firms. The ICAI did report that it would ask other Indian regulatory agencies to review MAFs' operations in India to ensure that those firms were not violating the terms of their business licenses or other relevant federal rules or regulations. In responding to the allegation that MAFs were indirectly providing audit and attestation services in India, the ICAI reported it had found no direct evidence supporting that allegation but would continue to investigate that possibility.

32. For a more complete discussion of the Tata Finance scandal, see Case 8.9, "Tata Finance Limited."

The most important policy initiative the ICAI pursued as a result of the CAAC White Paper report was seeking reciprocity agreements with regulatory agencies overseeing the accounting professions of other countries. The ICAI's president noted that, "while global [accounting] firms may be keen on becoming Indian, we at the ICAI are keen on making Indian firms global."[33] Reciprocity agreements with foreign countries that are signed by the ICAI would allow Indian CAs to be recognized as qualified professional accountants in those countries. For example, a reciprocity agreement with the United States would permit Indian CAs to practice public accounting in the United States—and U.S. CPAs to practice in India.

The ICAI's pursuit of reciprocity agreements was generally met with a lukewarm response by the relevant regulatory agencies of major developed countries. For decades, India had such a reciprocity agreement with Great Britain. However, Great Britain unilaterally canceled that agreement in the early 1990s, a decision that surprised and offended the ICAI. The United States has a reciprocity agreement that allows professionally registered accountants in certain countries to practice in the United States after successfully passing the International Uniform CPA Qualification (IQEX) examination administered by the NASBA. However, presently, the NASBA only allows certain professionally registered accountants from Australia, Canada, Ireland, Mexico, and New Zealand to sit for the IQEX examination.

A major reason that the ICAI decided to pursue reciprocity agreements with other nations was the large outsourcing industry for accounting services that quickly developed within India following the turn of the century. Thanks to the Internet, thousands of small Indian accounting firms found a new market for their services in other countries, in particular the United States. By 2004, an estimated 200,000 individual tax returns for U.S. citizens were being prepared by Indian accounting firms, a number that was expected to grow dramatically in the following years.[34] Indian accounting firms were also providing a large amount of rudimentary accounting services such as "write-up" work or bookkeeping for small U.S. businesses. U.S. accounting firms were outsourcing such work to India because Indian firms could perform that work much more cheaply. To make Indian accountants "globally competitive" and, in particular, better prepared to address accounting issues faced by their U.S. "clients," the ICAI added the study of U.S. generally accepted accounting principles (GAAP) to the required curriculum for the CA licensing program in 2006.[35]

Ironically, the sudden growth in the outsourcing of accounting and taxation services to India caused the AICPA to consider taking steps to protect the U.S. market for such services from Indian accounting firms. The AICPA was also troubled by the fact that U.S.-based accounting firms could not always ensure that outsourced services were being performed in compliance with the standards of the U.S. accounting profession. Many parties within the U.S. profession insisted that, at a minimum, U.S. accounting firms had an ethical responsibility to notify their clients when they were outsourcing the services for those clients to accounting firms in foreign countries. An article in *The CPA Journal* succinctly summarized this controversy.

> *Clearly, firms that outsource the preparation of income tax returns are likely to achieve significant cost savings. But at what cost? The profession does not need more scandals, and one must wonder why many CPA firms have an unspoken rule that the client does not need to know about outsourcing. Deep down, we know taxpayers entrusting their return with a CPA are likely to respond negatively if their tax returns are prepared in India without their knowledge or consent.*[36]

---

33. D. Murali, "ICAI Is Not Averse to Opening Up of the Accounting Sector," *Business Line* (online), 14 September 2006.

34. K. Vandruff, "Accounting for India," *Wichita Business Journal* (online), 23 June 2006.

35. *International Accounting Bulletin* (online), "The Price of Audit on Rise in India Again after Two Years," 12 August 2006.

36. R. Brody, M. Miller, and M. Rolleri, "Outsourcing Income Tax Returns to India: Legal, Ethical, and Professional Issues," *The CPA Journal* (online), December 2004.

## Questions

1. Research online and hardcopy databases to identify important recent developments within the Indian accounting profession. Summarize these developments in a bullet format.
2. In the United States, the accounting profession is regulated at the state level, while in India the accounting profession is regulated by a federal agency. Identify and briefly discuss the comparative advantages and disadvantages of each regulatory structure.
3. In India, independent auditors are considered to be "watchdogs" but not "bloodhounds." How, if at all, does that concept of the auditor's role differ from the prevailing concept of the independent auditor's role in the United States? Explain.
4. Do you believe it was appropriate for the major international accounting firms to establish networks of "surrogate" firms in India for the purpose of gaining wider access to the professional services markets in that country? Was that decision "ethical"? Defend your answers.
5. State boards of accountancy in the United States have allowed accounting firms and individual CPAs to advertise for approximately three decades. Identify the pros and cons of allowing professionals to advertise. In your opinion, should professional accountants be allowed to advertise and otherwise market their services?
6. In a bullet format, identify the parties impacted by regulatory policies designed to protect domestic professionals from foreign competitors. Briefly explain how each of these parties is affected by such policies. In your opinion, are such policies justified or appropriate? If so, under what circumstances?
7. What are the principal issues that organizations such as the ICAI and NASBA should consider in deciding whether or not to establish reciprocity agreements with other countries?
8. When CPAs outsource professional services to accountants in other countries do they have an ethical responsibility to disclose this fact to their clients? Does your answer change depending on the type of professional service being outsourced?

## CASE 8.11

# *Societe Generale*

*Qui seme le vent recolte la tempete.*
*(he who sows the wind shall reap the whirlwind)*

*French proverb*

Jerome Kerviel was born and raised in Pont-l'Abbe, a small coastal village in the Brittany region of northwestern France. His father was a blacksmith, while his mother worked as a hairdresser. Throughout his adolescent years, Kerviel dreamed of experiencing the excitement of nearby Paris, the City of Lights. Not surprisingly then, after completing undergraduate and graduate degrees in finance, the 23-year-old Kerviel accepted an entry-level position in Paris with Societe Generale, France's second largest bank.

Kerviel's job at Societe Generale involved working in the financial institution's "back office." For four years, Kerviel effectively served as an internal auditor ensuring that the bank's employees were complying with applicable company policies and procedures. His responsibilities included monitoring the bank's securities trades to identify unauthorized trades, for example, trades that exceeded the monetary limits that had been established for individual traders.

Although polite and well-mannered, the handsome Kerviel made few friends within the bank and was thought of as "loner" by most of his co-workers. In 2004, Kerviel accomplished his goal of being promoted to a securities trader. This new position provided Kerviel an opportunity to make better use of his educational background while at the same time allowing him to escape the relative anonymity and boredom of Societe Generale's back office.

Unlike Kerviel, Societe Generale's typical trader was a graduate of one of France's high profile universities and had been immediately assigned to the bank's trading staff when hired. In France's hierarchical society, one's educational background and socio-economic status tend to have a disproportionate influence on not only employment opportunities but also the ability to progress rapidly within an organization once hired. Reportedly, Kerviel wanted to prove that despite his modest credentials and lower-middle class upbringing, he could complete with his more blue-blooded colleagues when he finally landed a job in Societe Generale's trading division.

After joining the trading division, Kerviel worked hard to impress his superiors. Neighbors reported that he left his home in a Paris suburb early each morning and returned late every evening. Kerviel was so dedicated to his job that he refused to take advantage of the several weeks of vacation time that he was entitled to each year. By late 2007, Kerviel's annual salary was approximately 100,000 euros, an impressive sum by most standards but just a fraction of what many of his fellow traders earned.

In late January 2008, Daniel Bouton, Societe Generale's chief executive officer (CEO) and chairman of the board, startled the global financial markets by announcing that over a period of just three days his bank had suffered losses of more than six billion euros on a series of unauthorized securities trades made by a "rogue trader." According to Bouton, the trader had used his knowledge of the bank's computer and accounting systems to circumvent the labyrinth of internal control policies and procedures designed to prevent and detect unauthorized securities trades. That individual was none other than Jerome Kerviel.

Within two days of Bouton's announcement, Jerome Kerviel was arrested by France's gendarmes. For forty-eight hours, law enforcement and regulatory authorities grilled the young Parisian to uncover the details of the largest fraud in the history of the banking industry. According to his attorneys, Kerviel held up extremely well during the intense interrogations. At one point, the stoic Kerviel offered one of the greatest understatements in the sordid history of crime when he casually told his interrogators that, "I just got a bit carried away."[1]

## Fraud, French Style

Societe Generale was founded in 1864 during the reign of Napoleon III, the nephew of Napoleon Bonaparte and France's final monarch. The bank quickly became an important source of capital for the nation's rapidly growing economy during the final few decades of the nineteenth century. By the onset of World War II, Societe Generale operated 1,500 branches, including branches in the United States and dozens of other countries.

Following World War II, France's federal government nationalized Societe Generale to finance the reconstruction of the nation's economic infrastructure that had been decimated by the war. In 1987, the government returned the bank to the private sector. By the turn of the century, Societe Generale had reestablished itself as one of the world's largest and most important financial institutions. By 2007, the bank operated in almost ninety countries, had total assets of 1.1 trillion euros, and had more than 130,000 employees worldwide.

In the global banking industry, Societe Generale and several other large French banks are best known for developing a wide range of exotic financial instruments commonly referred to as derivatives. "Societe Generale pioneered equity derivatives, which allows investors to bet on future movements in stocks or markets."[2] Because of their leadership role in the development of financial derivatives, French banks control nearly one-third of the global market for those securities, a market that is measured in terms of hundreds of trillions of dollars. These same banks have also become well known for the "sophistication of their computer systems"[3] that are necessary to maintain control over their financial derivatives operations.

Societe Generale's 2007 annual report revealed that nearly 3,000 employees were assigned to control and manage the risks posed by the institution's around-the-clock and around-the-globe market trading activities. The most important of these activities are housed in the bank's equity derivatives division, the large bank's most profitable operating unit. The majority of the bank's control specialists work in Societe Generale's so-called "back office" where Jerome Kerviel began his career.

When he left Societe Generale's back office, Kerviel joined a relatively minor department within the bank's equity derivatives division. The mission of Kerviel's new department was to mitigate the risks that Societe Generale faced due to its high volume of derivatives trading. Kerviel's job involved making "plain vanilla hedges on European stock-market indices."[4]

Beginning in 2005, Kerviel began exceeding the maximum transaction size in euros that he had been assigned for individual securities trades as well as engaging in

1. P. Allen, "'I Just Got A Bit Carried Away,' says Trader Behind EUR5BN Fraud," *The Mirror* (online), 6 February 2008.

2. J. Eyal, "Breaking the Bank, French Style," *The Straits Times* (online), 2 February 2008.

3. *Ibid.*

4. S. Kennedy, "France's SocGen Hit By $7.1 Billion Alleged Fraud," *Marketwatch.com*, 24 January 2008.

other unauthorized transactions. Because he was very familiar with the electronic and manual control procedures used in the bank's back office to monitor trading activities, he was able to use a variety of means to circumvent those controls and thereby conceal his unauthorized trades. These measures included creating phony emails from superiors authorizing illicit transactions, intercepting and voiding warning messages triggered by unauthorized trades that he had made, and preparing false documents to corroborate such trades.

In the weeks following the disclosure of Kerviel's fraud, the bank's board of directors established a "Special Committee" to investigate the fraud—the board retained PricewaterhouseCoopers to assist this committee. The interim report of that committee revealed that Kerviel was particularly adept at manufacturing impromptu explanations for apparent irregularities discovered in his trading activities by back office personnel. Kerviel's explanations were laced with impressive but nonsensical jargon intended to confuse those personnel and discourage them from pursuing the given issues any further. In addition, the report suggested that back office personnel were intimidated by Kerviel and his trading colleagues, which caused them to be reluctant to vigorously investigate apparent trading irregularities.

The lynchpin of Kerviel's fraud was a technique that has been used in several previous stock market frauds, namely, recording fictitious transactions that appeared to be hedges or offsetting transactions for unauthorized securities trades that he had placed. For example, if Kerviel purchased a large block of securities, he would then record an offsetting but fictitious sale of similar securities. When he "shorted" a large block of securities, the fictitious hedge transaction that he recorded would be a "long" position in those securities or similar securities. These fictitious hedge transactions made it appear as if Societe Generale faced only minimal losses, at worst, on the large securities positions being taken by Kerviel.

The ease with which he could subterfuge Societe Generale's back office controls emboldened Kerviel. By 2007, he was placing what Societe Generale executives would later refer to as enormous "bets" on future near-term moves that he anticipated in major European stock market indices. At one point, Kerviel had outstanding positions that far exceeded the bank's stockholders' equity of 33 billion euros. In late 2007, he produced more than a one billion euro gain on a series of unauthorized transactions.

During the first few weeks of January 2008, Kerviel made several huge trades predicated on his belief that European stock market indices would turn sharply higher by late January. Instead, those markets declined, resulting in an unrealized loss of one billion euros for Societe Generale. On Friday, January 18, 2008, Kerviel's open positions were discovered and reported to Daniel Bouton. Over the weekend, Bouton decided that the positions should be closed to avoid potentially catastrophic losses for the bank.

Over the three-day period of January 21–23, the open positions on Kerviel's unauthorized trades were closed. Unfortunately for Societe Generale, European stock market prices fell sharply during that three-day period. Those falling stock prices caused the loss on Kerviel's January trades to sky to more than six billion euros, a figure that wiped out approximately twenty percent of the bank's equity capital.

After closing Kerviel's open positions, Societe Generale publicly reported the massive loss and the fraudulent scheme that had produced it. That disclosure unsettled stock markets worldwide, causing stock prices to fall around the globe. French president, Nicholas Sarkozy, reacted angrily to the announcement of the Kerviel fraud. "We have to put a stop to this financial system which is out of its mind and which has lost sight of its purpose."[5]

5. Eyal, "Breaking the Bank, French Style."

Jerome Kerviel's fraudulent scheme caused the international business press to shower Societe Generale's management team and independent auditors with a wide range of probing and embarrassing questions. Among these questions was how could Societe Generale's supposedly sophisticated internal control system be routinely and repeatedly undermined by one "rogue trader." Likewise, how could the bank's independent auditors fail to uncover what appeared to be pervasive deficiencies in that control system. Finally, the business press also questioned the auditors' decision to approve the highly unusual manner in which Societe Generale reported the massive fraud loss in its audited financial statements.

## Internal Controls, French Style

Shortly after the turn of the century, the Enron and WorldCom fiascoes in the United States undermined the confidence of the investing public in the nation's capital markets. Congress acted swiftly to restore that confidence by passing the Sarbanes-Oxley Act in the summer of 2002. This new federal statute forced public companies to spend enormous sums to overhaul and strengthen their financial reporting functions and internal control systems.

Each of the world's major economic powers closely monitored the reaction of the U.S. Congress and regulatory authorities to the Enron and WorldCom debacles. Many of these countries passed legislation intended to mimic the reforms embedded in the Sarbanes-Oxley statute. One such country was France.

Following the passage of the Sarbanes-Oxley Act in the United States, leaders of the French business community commissioned a study to determine what measures were necessary to strengthen financial reporting, internal controls, and corporate governance among France's large companies. Many of France's most respected business leaders were asked to serve on the committee that would carry out this study. Societe Generale's Daniel Bouton was chosen to chair the committee. In fact, the committee's lengthy report came to be referred to as simply the "Bouton Report."

According to the Bouton Report, many of the reforms included in the Sarbanes-Oxley legislation were unnecessary in France. "French companies find themselves in a very different situation from that of their U.S. counterparts. In many respects, French companies are better protected against the risks of excessive or misguided practices."[6] Despite that observation, the Bouton Report contained an impressive list of proposals. Many of these proposals were adopted by the French Parliament in 2003 when it modified the nation's federal securities laws that collectively are referred to as the French Commercial Code (*Code de Commerce*).

One of the Bouton Report recommendations incorporated into the French Commercial Code requires each public company's chairman of the board to include a report on his or her organization's internal controls in the company's annual financial report. Among other disclosures, this report should discuss a company's broad internal control objectives, key internal control procedures intended to accomplish those objectives, and factors that may limit the effectiveness of those procedures. In addition, the company's independent or "statutory" auditors must prepare an accompanying report that comments on the completeness and reliability of the chairman's internal control report. Statutory auditors are also required to disclose major control deficiencies that they discover during their annual audits to the chairman. The chairman must then include these items in his or her internal control report.

---

6. E. Didier, "Overview of Recent Corporate Governance Reforms," *globalcorporategovernance.com* (2003).

Exhibit 1 presents a brief excerpt from the seven-page internal control report included in Christian Dior's 2007 annual financial report. Christian Dior is a Paris-based company founded by the famous fashion designer of the same name. The company's many well-known brand names include Louis Vuitton, Givenchy, and, of course, Christian Dior. The excerpt in Exhibit 1 provides a concise summary of the internal control procedures employed by Christian Dior. Included in Exhibit 2 is the report issued by Christian Dior's statutory auditors on their client's 2007 internal control report.

The internal control report included in Societe Generale's 2006 annual financial report, the company's final annual report released prior to the discovery of Jerome Kerviel's fraud, included the following definition of internal control: "Those resources that enable the [bank's] management to ascertain whether the transactions carried out and the organization and procedures in place within the Company are compliant with the legal and regulatory provisions in force, professional and ethical practices, internal regulations and the policies defined by the Company's executive body." The report, which was the responsibility of Daniel Bouton, also identified the organization's three key internal control objectives:

- To detect and measure the risks borne by the Company, and ensure they are adequately controlled;
- To guarantee the reliability, integrity and availability of financial and managerial information;
- To verify the quality of the information and communication systems.

An important focus of the 2006 Societe Generale internal control report was the principal risks faced by the bank. These risks were intended to be mitigated by the large number of employees that staffed the bank's risk management functions, which included more than 1,100 internal auditors. A primary "operational" risk faced by the bank, according to the report, was the "risk of loss or fraud or of producing incorrect financial and accounting data due to inadequacies or failures in procedures and internal systems, human error or external events."

The 2006 internal control report provided no indication that the integrity of the bank's accounting data could by undermined by one employee.

**EXHIBIT 1**

EXCERPT FROM INTERNAL CONTROL REPORT INCLUDED IN CHRISTIAN DIOR'S 2007 ANNUAL FINANCIAL REPORT

II. Internal Control Procedures

The purpose of internal control procedures at Christian Dior is as follows:

- To ensure that management and operations-related measures, as well as the conduct of personnel, are consistent with the definitions contained in the guidelines applying to the Company's activities by its management bodies, applicable laws and regulations, and the Company's internal values, rules and regulations.
- To ensure that the accounting, financial, and management information communicated to the Company's management bodies reflect a fair view of the Company's activity and financial position.

One of the objectives of the internal control system is to prevent and control risks resulting from the Company's activity and the risk of error or fraud, particularly in the areas of accounting and finance. As with any control system, however, it cannot provide an absolute guarantee that these risks are completely eliminated.

Source: 2007 Annual Financial Report of Christian Dior.

**EXHIBIT 2**

Statutory Auditors' Report on Christian Dior's 2007 Internal Control Report

To the Shareholders,

As Statutory Auditors of Christian Dior and in accordance with Article L. 225-235 of the French Commercial Code (*Code de Commerce*), we hereby report to you on the report prepared by the chairman of your Company in accordance with Article L. 225-237 of the French Commercial Code for the year ended December 31, 2007.

In his Report, the Chairman reports, in particular, on the conditions for the preparation and organization of the Board of Directors' work and the internal control procedures implemented by the Company.

It is our responsibility to report to you our observations on the information set out in the Chairman's report on the internal control procedures relating to the preparation and treatment of financial and accounting information.

We have performed our work in accordance with the professional guidelines applicable to France. These guidelines require that we plan and perform procedures to assess the fairness of the information set out in the Chairman's report on the internal control procedures relating to the preparation and treatment of the financial and accounting information. These procedures notably consisted of:

- obtaining an understanding of the objectives and general organization of internal control as well as the internal control procedures relating to the preparation and treatment of financial and accounting information, as set out in the Chairman's Report;
- obtaining an understanding of the work underlying the information set out in the report;
- assessing whether major deficiencies related to internal control procedures and treatment of financial and accounting information have been appropriately reported in the Chairman's Report, if any.

On the basis of the procedures we have performed, we have nothing to report with regard to the information concerning the internal control procedures of the Company relating to the preparation and treatment of the financial and accounting information, as included in the Report of the Chairman of the Board of Directors, prepared in accordance with the Article L. 225-237 of the French Commercial Code.

Courbevoie and Paris-La Defense, March 10, 2008.
The Statutory Auditors:
Mazars & Guerard Ernst & Young

Source: 2007 Annual Financial Report of Christian Dior.

To the contrary, the report noted specifically that "accounting data" were compiled "independently" by the bank's accounting staff "thereby guaranteeing that information is both reliable and objective." The report went on to note that "the economic reality" of that data was subject to "daily verification" by the bank's internal control specialists. In their accompanying report, Societe Generale's statutory auditors did not challenge the accuracy of the bank's internal control report.

Following the public disclosure of Kerviel's fraud, the business press chastised Societe Generale's management team for failing to implement and maintain proper internal controls for the bank. Daniel Bouton responded to those critics by insisting that Societe Generale, in fact, had maintained strong internal controls. He then went on to suggest that Kerviel's fraud was so ingenious that even the most sophisticated internal controls would have been no match for the scheme. According to Bouton, Kerviel's fraudulent scheme had been comparable to a "mutating virus" since the nature of that scheme was constantly changing and evolving. "And when the controls detected an anomaly, he managed to convince control officers that nothing was wrong."[7]

Bouton's assertion that Societe Generale had strong internal controls was challenged by several parties. For example, the decision to allow Kerviel to transfer from the back office to the bank's trading division was questioned. "He [Kerviel] knew what the cops were looking for. That's what I find surprising about this—to let someone who knew how a fox might act, who knew the best way for a fox to act, get into the henhouse."[8] Another critic questioned why Societe Generale had neglected one of the most fundamental control procedures, namely, requiring employees in sensitive positions to take annual vacations.

> *A low-level French employee who declines to take his vacation entitlement is already an extraordinary anomaly, enough that Kerviel's superiors should have gone on immediate and full alert. As Kerviel himself acknowledged to French police investigators, "It's one of the elementary rules of internal control. A trader who doesn't take any days off is a trader who doesn't want to leave his book to another."*[9]

Several skeptics maintained that given the size of the trades made by Kerviel that someone other than him, possibly even top management, had to have been aware of them. Kerviel gave credence to this theory during his interrogation by law enforcement authorities shortly after he was arrested. The unfazed and self-assured Kerviel told those authorities that, "I accept my share of responsibility, but I will not be made a scapegoat for Societe Generale."[10] Kerviel testified that his superiors had "turned a blind eye" to his unauthorized trades "as long as he was in the black"[11] and only took exception to them when he incurred the huge loss in mid-January 2008. Kerviel went on to maintain that "his activities were part of a culture of lawlessness among other SocGen traders which had the bank's broad approval."[12]

Daniel Bouton and his fellow Societe Generale executives were not the only third parties who were held at least partially responsible for the massive loss incurred by Jerome Kerviel. Shortly after Kerviel's scheme was revealed, *The New York Times* questioned why Societe Generale's statutory auditors had not uncovered the fraud.[13] Throughout the time frame that Kerviel's fraud was ongoing, those auditors had issued unqualified opinions each year on the bank's annual financial statements.

The failure of Societe Generale's auditors to uncover the fraud was particularly perplexing to many parties since France's federal securities laws require that public companies retain not one but rather two independent accounting firms to audit their periodic financial statements. So called "joint-auditing" is not unique to France but the history of the nation's independent audit function is very different from that of other major economies. To better understand the role of Societe Generale's auditors

---

7. D. Jolly and N. Clark, "Greater Details Emerge of Bank's 4.9 Billion Loss," *International Herald Tribune*, 28 January 2008, 1.

8. A. Hanes, "Suspect 'A Fragile Being;' Trader's Best Intentions Can Go Wrong, Prof Says," *National Post*, 25 January 2008, A3.

9. J. Peterson, "Societe Generale's 2007 Annual Report—Jerome Kerviel is So Last Year," *jamespeterson.com*, 17 March 2008.

10. Allen, "'I Just Got A Bit Carried Away."

11. *Ibid.*

12. J. Lichfield, "'Rogue Trader' Freed on Bail after Judges Drop Fraud Charges," *The Independent*, 29 January 2008, 18.

13. N. Clark and K. Bennhold, "French Inquiry: Bank's Inaction Grows as Issue," *The New York Times* (online), 29 January 2008.

in the Kerviel affair it will be helpful to review the history of independent auditing in France with a particular focus on the nature of joint-auditing in that nation.

## Independent Audits, French Style

The accounting profession within France consists of two distinct disciplines. Statutory auditors (*commissaries aux comptes*) perform independent audits, while public accountants (*experts-comptables*) provide a wide range of accounting and related professional services. Most statutory auditors are also public accountants but these individuals cannot provide auditing and accounting services to the same client.

Although the accounting profession has existed in France for several hundred years, the nation's independent audit function was slow to evolve. A reputable independent auditing discipline was not firmly established until the late 1960s. According to a French academic, independent auditing was effectively a "laughing stock" in the country until that time because of the absence of any meaningful oversight by a regulatory body or professional organization.[14]

To help modernize the French economy and integrate it into the European Economic Community, now referred to as the European Union, the French government adopted several reform measures in the late 1960s. The goal of these reforms was to create a regulatory infrastructure for the nation's financial reporting function that was comparable to that of the United States and the United Kingdom. These reforms included the creation of the *Commission des Operations de Bourse* (COB), a federal agency equivalent to the U.S. Securities and Exchange Commission. The French government also established a federal agency to oversee the nation's independent audit function. This latter agency is *La Compagnie Nationales des Commissaires aux Comptes* (Institute of Statutory Auditors), which is commonly referred to as the CNCC.[15] The CNCC was given a wide range of responsibilities. These responsibilities include establishing standards of ethical conduct for statutory auditors, sanctioning auditors who violate those standards, establishing educational requirements for statutory auditors, and issuing professional auditing standards.[16]

Since the creation of the CNCC in 1969, the French government has periodically adopted measures to further strengthen the nation's independent audit function. The 2003 reforms prompted by the Sarbanes-Oxley Act included several new rules intended to strengthen the independence of statutory auditors. The French government now prohibits statutory auditors from providing public clients any services that are "unrelated" to the annual audit and requires such clients to have audit committees. Statutory auditors are also limited to one six-year "mandate" with each public client, that is, auditor rotation is mandatory after six years. During the term of the six-year mandate, audit clients can dismiss their auditors only under very rare circumstances.[17] When an auditor-client engagement terminates, five years must elapse before statutory auditors

---

14. C. Ramirez, "Exporting Professional Models: The Expansion of the Multinational Audit Firm and the Transformation of the French Accountancy Profession Since 1970." Working paper, HEC School of Management, Paris, January 2007, 23.

15. The comparable federal agency that regulates the practice of public accounting is the Order of Chartered Accountants or *l'Ordre des Experts-Comptables* (OEC).

16. In 2000, the CNCC began effectively requiring French auditors to apply International Standards of Auditing (ISAs). In May 2006, the European Parliament, which is the legislative arm of the European Union (EU), decreed that independent audits throughout the EU must be performed in compliance with ISAs. Member countries of the EU were required to adopt this new rule by 2010.

17. Likewise, statutory auditors are effectively prohibited from resigning during the term of a six-year mandate.

can accept employment with the former client. Finally, public companies must disclose in their annual reports the total fees paid to their statutory auditors each year. In 2007, Societe Generale paid its statutory auditors approximately 26 million euros.

In 2001, two years prior to the auditor independence reforms adopted by the French government, Societe Generale's board implemented several new policies to enhance the independence of its statutory auditors. These voluntary measures included prohibiting the bank from purchasing non-audit services from any member of its statutory auditors' worldwide networks.

When the French government initiated the reforms to modernize the nation's economy in the late 1960s, the U.S.-based Big Eight accounting firms targeted France as a potentially lucrative market. The aggressive client development activities of the Big Eight firms caused France's domestic accounting firms to feel threatened. To mitigate the impact of the Big Eight's intrusion into their market, the domestic accounting firms lobbied the government to require public companies to have joint audits.[18]

The lobbying efforts of the domestic firms were successful. The requirement that French public companies be jointly audited doubled the size of France's audit market for those companies and increased the domestic firms' chances of retaining a significant number of them as audit clients. Although the Big Four firms are easily France's largest audit firms in terms of annual revenues, most public companies in France have at least one French domestic accounting firm serving as their statutory auditors. By comparison, in Italy, which does not mandate joint audits, the Big Four accounting firms audit more than 95 percent of all public companies.

Christian Dior is an example of a major French company that retains a Big Four accounting firm and a domestic accounting firm to serve as its joint auditors. Mazars & Guerard, one of Christian Dior's joint auditors and France's largest domestic accounting firm, is a French accounting firm that has benefited significantly from the joint audit requirement.

Affiliates of two Big Four accounting firms, Ernst & Young Audit and Deloitte & Associes, served as Societe Generale's statutory auditors throughout the time period that Kerviel made unauthorized trades. The rule limiting audit engagements to one six-year mandate went into effect in August 2006. The previous year, Societe Generale agreed to a final six-year mandate with its auditors, meaning that Ernst & Young and Deloitte would serve as the bank's auditors through 2011.

France's joint audit requirement for public companies has been controversial. In fact, in 1984, the CNCC recommended that joint audits be voluntary rather than mandatory for public companies. The CNCC recommended the change because it believed that the joint audit rule unnecessarily increased the cost of independent audits for large French companies. That proposal was never enacted, largely because domestic accounting firms strongly objected to it.

Despite the CNCC's decision to retain the joint audit rule, critics of that rule continued to insist that it unnecessarily increased the cost of independent audits while having little impact on their overall quality. In recent years, academic researchers have addressed each of those issues. In terms of cost, one academic study demonstrated that joint audits performed in France are generally no more costly than comparable single-firm audits performed in other countries.[19]

---

18. Publicly, the domestic firms justified the proposal for joint audits as a measure to enhance the overall quality of independent audits.

19. J. Francis, C. Richard, and A. Vanstraelen, "Assessing France's Joint Audit Requirement: Are Two Heads Better than One?" Presented at the International Symposium on Audit Research, Sydney, Australia, 2006.

Another academic study found the surprising result that the quality of joint audits may actually be lower than that of single-firm audits, particularly when a company retains two Big Four firms, which was true of Societe Generale during the course of the Kerviel fraud.[20] The researcher in the latter study speculated that when both joint auditors are Big Four firms it is possible, if not likely, that neither firm will subordinate its judgment to the other firm. Such a lack of cooperation between the firms could impair the quality of an audit. An alternative explanation for the surprising result is that when Big Four firms serve as joint auditors, they may rely too heavily on each other, thus reducing audit quality.

The ongoing investigations of the Societe Generale fraud have provided few insights regarding the nature of the company's joint audits performed by Ernst & Young and Deloitte and whether the relationship between the two firms affected the quality of those audits. Despite being badgered and widely criticized by the press, neither firm has publicly commented on those audits. To date, a focal point of the criticism of Ernst & Young and Deloitte has been those firms' decision to endorse the unusual manner in which Societe Generale reported the massive loss due to Kerviel's fraud in its audited financial statements.

## Creative Accounting, French Style

When Societe Generale released its 2007 financial statements in March of 2008, the global investing community was shocked to discover that the 6.4 billion euro loss incurred by Kerviel in January 2008 had been recorded by the company's accountants in fiscal 2007, which ended December 31, 2007. Even more puzzling, Societe Generale's two audit firms had acquiesced to that financial statement treatment of the loss and issued an unqualified opinion on those financial statements.

As explained in Exhibit 3, which contains an excerpt from Note 40 to Societe Generale's 2007 financial statements, Societe Generale netted the 1.5 billion euro gain that it realized from Kerviel's unauthorized trades in 2007 against the 6.4 billion euro loss that his illicit trades produced in January 2008. Recognize that the 6.4 billion euro loss incurred by Kerviel in January 2008 resulted from the sale of securities that he had purchased that same month. None of that loss related to securities purchased by Kerviel during 2007.

In justifying its decision to shift the 6.4 billion euro loss from 2008 to 2007, Societe Generale invoked the "true and fair override" included in *International Accounting Standard No. 1 (IAS 1)*, "Presentation of Financial Statements." That override clause allows reporting entities to depart from an accounting or reporting standard if compliance with the given standard would result in misleading financial statements. Societe Generale maintained that Kerviel's January 2008 trades on which he incurred the 6.4 billion euro loss were a continuation of the "unauthorized activities" that resulted in a 1.5 billion gain in 2007. As a result, the bank concluded that the net gain or loss on those activities should be recorded in the year in which the unauthorized activities had been initiated. Note 40 failed to point out that Kerviel's unauthorized activities had actually extended back to 2005 when he joined the bank's securities trading division.

Exhibit 4 presents the audit report that Societe Generale's joint auditors issued on the bank's 2007 financial statements.

---

20. S. Marmousez, "Conservatism and Joint-Auditing: Evidence from French Listed Companies." Working paper, HEC School of Management, Paris, October 2006.

**EXHIBIT 3**

EXCERPT FROM NOTE 40 ACCOMPANYING SOCIETE GENERALE'S 2007 FINANCIAL STATEMENTS

The application of the provisions of IAS 10 "Events after the balance sheet date" and IAS 39 "Financial instruments: Recognition and Measurement," for the accounting of transactions related to those unauthorized activities and their unwinding would have led to recognizing a pre-tax gain of EUR 1,471 million in consolidated income for the 2007 financial year and only presenting the pre-tax loss of EUR 6,382 million ultimately incurred by the Group in January 2008 in the note to the 2007 consolidated financial statements.

For the information of its shareholders and the public, the Group considered that this presentation was inconsistent with the objective of the financial statements described in the framework of IFRS standards and that for the purpose of a fair presentation of its financial situation at December 31, 2007, it was more appropriate to record all the financial consequences of the unwinding of these unauthorized activities under a separate caption in consolidated income for the 2007 financial year. To this end in accordance with provision of paragraphs 17 and 18 of IAS 1 "Presentation of Financial Statements" the Group decided to depart from the provisions of IAS 10 "Events After the Balance Sheet Date" and IAS 37 "Provisions, Contingent Liabilities and Contingent Assets", by booking in estimated consolidated income for the 2007 financial year a provision for the total cost of the unauthorized activities.

Source: 2007 Annual Financial Report of Societe Generale.

**EXHIBIT 4**

STATUTORY AUDITORS' REPORT ON SOCIETE GENERALE'S 2007 FINANCIAL STATEMENTS

To the Shareholders,

In compliance with the assignment entrusted to us by your Annual General Meeting, we have audited the accompanying financial statements of Societe Generale for the year ended December 31, 2007.

These consolidated financial statements have been approved by the Board of Directors on February 20, 2008. Our role is to express an opinion on those financial statements based on our audit.

**I – OPINION ON THE CONSOLIDATED FINANCIAL STATEMENTS**

We conducted our audit in accordance with the professional standards applicable in France; those standards require that we plan and perform the audit to obtain reasonable assurance about whether the consolidated financial statements are free of material misstatement. An audit includes examining, on a test basis, evidence supporting the amounts and disclosures in the financial statements. An audit also includes assessing the accounting principles used by the management, as well as evaluating the overall financial statement presentation. We believe that our audit provides a reasonable basis for our opinion.

In our opinion, the consolidated financial statements give a true and fair view of the assets, liabilities, financial position and results of the consolidated group in accordance with IFRS as adopted by the European Union.

Without qualifying the opinion expressed above, we draw your attention to:

- notes 1 and 40 to the consolidated financial statements that describe the accounting and tax treatments of the net loss on unauthorized and concealed trading activities and the reasons which led the Group to make use of the exception under IAS 1 in order to present fairly its financial position as at December 31, 2007;

**EXHIBIT 4—*continued***

Statutory Auditors' Report on Societe Generale's 2007 Financial Statements

- note 40 to the consolidated financial statements that indicates that, on the date the accompanying financial statements are authorized for issue, Corporate and Investment Banking operations are currently the subject of various internal and external investigations as a result of which new facts, unknown to date may emerge.

**II – JUSTIFICATION OF ASSESSMENTS**

In accordance with the requirements of Article L. 823-9 of the French Commercial Code (*Code de Commerce*) relating to the justification of our assessments, we bring your attention to the following matters:

*BACKGROUND OF THE FINANCIAL STATEMENTS CLOSING PROCESS*

Following the uncovering of the unauthorized and concealed activities described in note 40, we have reconsidered and extended our audit procedures to be in a position to issue an opinion on the consolidated financial statements taken as a whole, keeping in mind that the purpose of these procedures is not to issue an opinion on the effectiveness of internal control over financial reporting. Accordingly, we have:

- extended the scope and nature of the audit procedures performed on Corporate and Investment Banking trading activities;
- reconsidered the General Inspector's intermediary conclusions and work performed following its assignment as of January 24, 2008, which was primarily intended to check that all unauthorized positions and related losses have been comprehensively identified and which conclusions have been endorsed by the Special Committee after receiving the comments of its advisor;
- reviewing the documentation supporting the amount of the recorded loss.

*ACCOUNTING POLICIES*

Note 1 to the financial statements describes the reasons that led the Group to depart from the application of IAS 10 and IAS 37 on the basis of the exception provided under IAS 1 for purpose of providing with a fair presentation of its financial position as at December 31, 2007, by recording a provision for net loss resulting from the unwinding on January 23, 2008, of the unauthorized and concealed activities. As part of our assessment of accounting principles applied, we have assessed the basis for applying these provisions of IAS 1 as well as whether appropriate disclosure is included in the notes.

*ACCOUNTING ESTIMATES*

- As detailed in Note 1 to the financial statements, the Group uses internal models to measure financial instruments that are not listed on liquid markets. Our procedures consisted in reviewing the control procedures related to the designed models, to assess the data and assumptions used as well as the inclusion of the risks and results related to these instruments.
- In the specific context of the current credit crisis, the Group discusses in note 3 its direct and indirect exposure to the US residential real estate market, the procedures implemented to assess this exposure as well as the process for measuring related financial instruments. We have reviewed the control procedures implemented to identify and measure such exposure, as well as whether appropriate disclosure is included in the notes with respect thereto.
- As mentioned in note 3, the Group assessed the impact relating to changes in its own credit risk on the measurement of certain financial liabilities measured at fair value through profit and loss. We have reviewed that appropriate data have been used for that purpose.
- For purpose of preparing the financial statements, the Group records impairments to cover the credit risks inherent to its activities and performs significant accounting estimates, as described in note 1 to the financial statements, related in particular to the assessment

**EXHIBIT 4—*continued***

STATUTORY AUDITORS' REPORT ON SOCIETE GENERALE'S 2007 FINANCIAL STATEMENTS

of the fair value of financial instruments accounted for at amortized cost, of goodwill and pension plans and other post-employment benefits. We have reviewed these processes, the underlying assumptions and valuation parameters and assessed whether these accounting estimates rely on documented procedures consistent with the accounting policies disclosed in note 1.

These assessments were performed as part of our audit approach for purpose of expressing the audit opinion on the consolidated financial statements taken as a whole that is stated above in the first part of this report.

**III – SPECIFIC VERIFICATION**

In accordance with professional standards applicable in France, we have also verified the information given in the Group management report. We have no matters relating to report regarding fair presentation and conformity with the consolidated financial statements.

Paris – La Defense and Neuilly-sur-Seine,
February 29, 2008
The Statutory Auditors
Ernst & Young Audit
Deloitte & Associes

Source: 2007 Annual Financial Report of Societe Generale.

That audit report contains the three standard sections of a French audit report; the actual audit opinion is included in Section I of that report. The audit opinion was unqualified, although the joint auditors included an explanatory paragraph relating to the Kerviel affair. In Section II of the 2007 audit report, "Justification of Assessments," the auditors reveal that they "reconsidered and extended our audit procedures" after learning of Kerviel's unauthorized activities. In that section, the auditors also note that they "assessed" Societe Generale's reliance on *IAS 1* as the justification for the accounting treatment applied to the net loss produced by Kerviel's unauthorized activities during 2007 and 2008.

Critics of Societe Generale's decision to backdate the 6.4 billion euro loss incurred in January 2008 speculated that the bank did so to "clear the decks," that is, to put the embarrassing incident behind it as quickly as possible. If the loss had been included in the bank's 2008 financial statements, the incident would have lingered and resurfaced again when the bank released those financial statements in March or April of 2009.

In commenting on Societe Generale's use of the "true and fair override" to justify its controversial decision, *The New York Times* reported that, "There is nothing true about reporting a loss in 2007 when it clearly occurred in 2008."[21] The newspaper went on to berate the bank's management team and auditors for apparently attempting to "appease" investors and other parties by backdating the January 2008 loss. A former member of the International Accounting Standards Board (IASB) and the Financial Accounting Standards Board (FASB) flatly stated that the bank's reporting of the 6.4 billion euro loss was "inappropriate" and that the prominent bank was "manipulating earnings."[22] A member of the IASB at the time added to that sentiment by noting that, "This raises a question as to just how creative they are in interpreting accounting rules in other areas."[23] Finally, another critic noted that, "What Societe

21. F. Norris, "Loophole Lets Bank Rewrite the Calendar," *The New York Times* (online), 7 March 2008.

22. F. Norris, "Societe Generale Invokes Special Accounting Rule to Absorb Kerviel Losses," *International Herald Tribune* (online), 6 March 2008.

23. *Ibid.*

and its auditors have perpetrated would be regarded here [the United States] as the accounting equivalent of pornography."[24]

Societe Generale's controversial decision was untimely and extremely embarrassing for the IASB, the London-based rule-making body that issues *International Financial Reporting Standards* (IFRS)—earlier versions of these standards were referred to as *International Accounting Standards.* Over the past two decades, the IASB had been involved in a contentious struggle with the FASB to determine whether IFRS or U.S. GAAP would emerge as the pre-eminent set of international accounting standards. Prior to the Societe Generale incident, the IASB had clearly gained the upper hand in that struggle. However, that incident made many parties question the wisdom of adopting IFRS as the worldwide standard for financial reporting.

A Canadian journalist suggested that the Societe Generale incident had exposed just one of many "tricks" that IFRS would make available to creative accountants around the globe and suggested that "there is mounting evidence that IFRS is a step backwards for financial comparability."[25] In the United States, the editor of an accounting periodical observed "Investors should be troubled by this in an IASB world"[26] and suggested that the range of accounting and financial reporting decisions permitted under IFRS encourages self-interested accounting and financial reporting decisions. The latter point was reinforced by another IASB critic who noted that, "Simply put, if you give management and auditors the opportunity to obfuscate, they will take it."[27]

*The New York Times* argued that the most troubling facet of the Societe Generale incident was not the IFRS loophole that permitted the bank to backdate the large trading loss incurred by Jerome Kerviel. Instead, the newspaper maintained that the primary issue raised by the incident was the absence of a worldwide international regulatory body for the accounting and financial reporting profession: "How well can international accounting standards be policed in a world with no international regulatory body?"[28]

## EPILOGUE

The Special Committee appointed by Societe Generale's board to investigate the Jerome Kerviel affair issued its final report in May 2008. That report largely contradicted Daniel Bouton's assertion that the bank had adequate internal controls but had been victimized by an ingenious fraud. *The New York Times* summarized the lengthy report by observing that "weak management and insufficient risk controls" permitted Kerviel to sustain his fraud for several years.[29] Shortly after this report was released, Bouton resigned as Societe Generale's CEO and Kerviel's two former supervisors were dismissed by the bank.

Civil and criminal litigation stemming from the Kerviel fraud will no doubt continue for many years to come. Charges pending against Kerviel include breach of trust, preparing false documents, and illegally accessing a computer. Kerviel faces a maximum prison sentence of three years if convicted of all of those charges.

24. *Accountingonion.typepad.com*, "IFRS Chaos in France: The Incredible Case of Societe Generale," 7 March 2008.

25. A. Rosen, "SocGen 'Rogues' Show Flaws in Accounting Rules," *National Post*, 9 April 2008, FP11.

26. F. Norris, "Loophole Lets Bank Rewrite the Calendar."

27. Rosen, "SocGen 'Rogues' Show Flaws in Accounting Rules."

28. Norris, "Loophole Lets Bank Rewrite the Calendar."

29. K. Bennhold, "Rogue Trader May Have Had Help, Audit Finds," *The New York Times* (online), 24 May 2008.

## Questions

1. Research relevant databases to identify important recent developments within France's accounting profession, including the nation's independent audit function. Summarize these developments in a bullet format.
2. Societe Generale maintained that because Jerome Kerviel's "unauthorized activities" were initiated in 2007, the 6.4 billion euro loss that he incurred in January 2008 should be recorded in 2007. Do you agree with that reasoning? Why or why not?
3. Societe Generale was criticized for invoking what is often referred to as the "true and fair override" in IFRS. Is there a comparable clause or rule in GAAP? If so, identify two scenarios under which a departure from GAAP would be necessary to prevent a set of financial statements from being misleading.
4. Compare the general format and content of the audit report shown in Exhibit 4 with the standard audit report issued under U.S. GAAS. What are the key differences between those two audit reports? Which report format is the most informative?
5. This case lists Societe Generale's three principal internal control objectives. Compare and contrast those objectives with the primary internal control objectives discussed in GAAS.
6. Identify countries in addition to France where joint audits are performed. What economic, political, geographic, or other characteristics are common to these countries?
7. Identify audit risk factors common to a bank client. Classify these risk factors into the following categories: inherent, control, and detection. Briefly explain your classification of each risk factor that you identified.

## CASE 8.12

# *Shari'a*

*Live together like brothers and do business like strangers.*

*Arabic proverb*

The surging demand for petroleum products in recent decades has produced a windfall of revenues for many oil-rich Islamic countries in the Middle East, including, among others, Kuwait, Saudi Arabia, and the United Arab Emirates. Because Islam limits the types of investments and business ventures in which the world's 1.2 billion Muslims can become involved, the Middle Eastern oil boom has resulted in the emergence of an Islamic economy that is largely distinct from the rest of the global economy.[1] In recognition of this new economy, which is the world's most rapidly growing economic sector, major business publications have established market indices devoted strictly to Islamic business enterprises. These indices include the Dow Jones Islamic Market World Index and the FTSE Global Islamic Index.

Banking ranks among the fastest growing and most important components of the burgeoning Islamic economy. In the early 1970s, only a few small Middle Eastern banks expressly embraced the restrictive conditions imposed on business transactions and relationships by the Islamic religion and thus qualified as "Islamic" banks. Collectively, the assets of those banks totaled less than $20 million. Four decades later, approximately three hundred major banks around the globe cater exclusively or primarily to devout Muslims. Those Islamic banks boast assets approaching one trillion dollars.

Although modern Islamic finance is still in its infancy, major Islamic banks have implemented most of the high-tech banking functions and practices used by their Western counterparts. The principal Islamic banking centers are Malaysia, the Middle East, and the United Kingdom, but financial institutions throughout the world have developed aggressive marketing campaigns to attract Muslim clients. By 2009, approximately two dozen banks in the United States offered financial services designed exclusively for the estimated five million Muslim-Americans.

Tenets of the Islamic religion dramatically influence the nature of banking practices within the Islamic economy. Easily the biggest difference between Islamic banking and Western banking is the prohibition against interest payments on capital within the Islamic world.

Islamic religious law or *Shari'a* forbids the payment or receipt of *riba* (interest) in personal or business relationships. Islamic banks have been forced to develop unique and elaborate profit and risk-sharing contracts known as *mudarahah* to allow them to provide financial services without paying interest on their depositors' funds or charging interest to their "borrowers."[2] As noted in a special report on Islamic finance published by the London-based *Financial Times*, "Islamic finance tries to replicate the conventional [banking] market, but in a structure that uses profits rather than interest."[3]

---

1. For example, Islam generally prohibits Muslims from being associated with companies whose lines of business involve alcoholic drinks, pork and pork products, gambling, tobacco, pornography, illicit drugs, and destructive weapons.

2. Western publications spell this term in several different ways. The most common spellings include *Shari'a*, *Sharia*, *Shari'ah*, and *Shariah*.

3. *Financial Times*, "Islamic Finance: An FT Special Report," ftalphaville.ft.com, 23 May 2007.

The literal interpretation of the term *Shari'a* in Arabic is "path to the water source." Wikipedia defines *Shari'a* as "the legal framework within which the public and private aspects of life are regulated for those living in a legal system based on Islamic principles of jurisprudence." Unlike legal codes in the United States and other Western countries, *Shari'a* is not a compendium of static laws but rather an evolving set of guiding principles and interpretations derived principally from the *Qur'an* and teachings of the Prophet Muhammad. The dynamic nature of *Shari'a* results from numerous religious opinions or *Fatwa* issued periodically by Islamic religious scholars on a wide range of contemporary issues facing Muslims.

*Shari'a* influences every aspect of day-to-day life in the Islamic world including politics, family issues, personal hygiene, and business relationships. Within the Islamic economy, the term "*Shari'a*-compliant" is used to refer to business practices, economic ventures, and individual transactions that have been sanctioned by Islamic religious scholars. An audit partner of Ernst & Young Global Limited recently observed that "*Shari'a* compliance is the essence of Islamic banking and finance."[4] In fact, only those banks that offer *Shari'a*-compliant financial services and products are considered to be Islamic banks.

The development of *mudarabah* and other *Shari'a*-compliant banking practices have contributed significantly to the growth of Islamic finance in recent years. Islamic banks presently account for less than five percent of the worldwide financial services market, but economic experts expect that market share to grow significantly in coming decades if the Islamic banking industry can overcome several major challenges that it faces. A major European financial publication has reported that "Islamic banking's long-term ambition" is to become a dominant force in international financial markets.[5] This same publication noted that among the biggest obstacles to accomplishing that goal is the "lack of uniform and consistent accounting and auditing standards" within the Islamic economy.[6]

## The Islamic View of Accounting

Since the inception of the accounting profession, cultural norms have influenced the development of accounting and auditing standards within every country, including the United States. Likewise, cultural differences across countries and regions of the world have complicated recent efforts to develop a common set of international accounting and auditing standards. Nowhere have cultural nuances had a greater impact on efforts to develop uniform accounting and auditing standards than in the Islamic world. Because of its growing size and prominence, the Islamic banking industry has been the principal focus of efforts within Islamic nations to develop domestic accounting and auditing standards that cohere with *Shari'a*, or, alternatively to modify international accounting and auditing standards to achieve the same goal.

Similar to every other aspect of Islamic life, accounting and auditing rules and principles are considered subordinate to the dictates of *Shari'a*. As one Islamic accounting scholar has noted, "Islam accepts the fact that accounting is a social construction and itself constructs social reality but this social reality which the accounting constructs must conform to the dictates of Islamic belief."[7]

4. O. Ansari, "Audit & Shari'a Compliance—Issues in Islamic Banking and Finance," www.icmap.com.pk/ppt/sem_asc_khi.pps, 20 September 2008.

5. N. Dudley, "Islamic Banks Aim for the Mainstream," *Euromoney* 349 (May 1998), 113–116.

6. *Ibid.*

7. B. Maurer, "Anthropological and Accounting Knowledge in Islamic Banking and Finance: Rethinking Critical Accounts," *Journal of Royal Anthropological Institute* 8 (2002), 660.

A more blunt point of view was expressed by another Islamic scholar who suggested that accounting principles can induce behavior inconsistent with fundamental tenets of his religion. "The problem with modern corporate accounting is not a matter of just numbers but a whole philosophy. Accounting can lead to perceptions of reality . . . Ultimately, what accounting tells us [is that] what makes more money is the best thing. Over time, people will become mesmerized with this infatuation and act accordingly."[8]

## Auditing in the Islamic World

Either because of governmental regulations in their home countries or because of economic necessity brought on by their growing size and involvement in international commerce, most Islamic banks have their annual financial statements audited by an independent accounting firm. In addition to annual financial statement audits, Islamic banks must also have their business activities "audited" each year to determine whether they are in compliance with *Shari'a*. An accounting professor provides the following description of *Shari'a* auditing:

> *We can define Shari'a auditing as a systematic process of objectively obtaining and evaluating evidence regarding assertions about socio-economic, religious and environmental actions and events in order to ascertain the degree of correspondence between those assertions and Shari'a (Islamic law), and communicating the results to users.*[9]

There is a wide divergence in *Shari'a* auditing practices across the nearly 60 Asian and African countries that are predominantly Muslim. This variance results principally from diverse interpretations and applications of *Shari'a* within individual Islamic countries that not only ultimately determine what business practices are acceptable in those nations but also influence how *Shari'a* audits are performed. Similar to Christianity, there are numerous factions or schools of thought within Islam, each of which share certain fundamental beliefs while disagreeing, often significantly, on other facets of their religion. For example, in certain Islamic countries, the *Qur'an* tends to be interpreted literally, while in other Islamic countries the *Qur'an*'s teachings are subject to more expansive or liberal interpretations.

The most common *Shari'a* auditing "model" applied presently is prevalent in the Middle East. Under this audit model, the principal responsibility for determining whether an Islamic bank has complied with *Shari'a* rests with the institution's *Shari'a* Supervisory Board (SSB). An SSB is typically composed of a minimum of three Islamic religious scholars who are independent of the given bank. When an Islamic bank is considering new business ventures, banking practices, or other major operational changes, its SSB will be asked to determine whether the changes are acceptable under *Shari'a*. Under the conventional *Shari'a* audit model, an SSB also reviews the given bank's financial statements and underlying transactions, accounting records, business contracts and other relationships at the conclusion of each year to determine that the institution has complied with *Shari'a* throughout that period.

8. *Ibid.*

9. S. Ibrahim, "The Case for Islamic Auditing," *International Accountant* 41 (2008), 21, 23.

Exhibit 1 presents a *Shari'a* audit or compliance report prepared by the SSB of Stehwaz Holding Company, a large Kuwaiti company that has significant investments in Islamic financial institutions.[10] This *Shari'a* report was included in Stehwaz's 2007 annual financial report, which was very comparable in terms of content and appearance to an annual report of a large U.S. company. For example, Stehwaz's annual report contained a standard set of financial statements—prepared in accordance with International Financial Reporting Standards (IFRS) rather than U.S. GAAP, an accompanying set of detailed financial statement footnotes, and traditional "front matter" including a letter to the company's shareholders from Stehwaz's chairman of the board.

An unqualified audit opinion issued by a Kuwaiti chartered accounting firm preceded Stehwaz's financial statements in the company's 2007 annual report. Stehwaz's audit report was comparable to unqualified audit reports issued in the United States with one principal exception—the report indicated that the audit had been performed in accordance with International Standards of Auditing (ISAs). Stehwaz's audit report did not explicitly address the question of whether the company had complied with *Shari'a* during the year under audit. Nevertheless, *Shari'a* compliance is an important issue for independent auditors of Islamic banks and other Islamic entities to consider whether or not they address that issue explicitly in their audit reports. Because violations of *Shari'a* could have serious financial consequences for an Islamic company, independent auditors in the Islamic economy must consider that possibility in designing and carrying out audit engagements.

**EXHIBIT 1**

*SHARI'A* COMPLIANCE AUDIT REPORT ON STEHWAZ HOLDING COMPANY'S 2007 FINANCIAL STATEMENTS

We have reviewed Stehwaz Holding Company's applied principles as well as its contracts and applications during the year ended December 31, 2007, and the company's compliance with *Shari'ah* guidelines and commitments to our *Fatwas*, decisions and instructions issued on our behalf. Stehwaz compliance with Islamic *Shari'ah* principles is the avowed responsibility of its Executive Management, where as our responsibility is restricted to forwarding an independent viewpoint based on our supervisory control of the company's transactions and to preparing this report. We have planned and executed our supervision targeting to get all necessary information and explanations deemed vital to support us with sufficient evidence to ascertain logically that Stehwaz Holding did not violate the Islamic *Shari'ah* principles. To the best of our knowledge, we hereby certify:

1. That Stehwaz Holding Company's activities, contracts as well as transactions till December 2007, submitted for our supervision, were practiced in compliance with Islamic *Shari'ah* Principles.

2. That the *Zakat* calculations were in compliance with the Islamic *Shari'ah* principles as well.

Sheikh Dr. Nayef Moh. Al-Ajmi, Board Member
Sheikh Dr. Issam Khalaf Al-Enizi, Board Member
Sheikh Dr. Issa Zaki, Chaqra, Chairman

Source: 2007 Annual Report of Stehwaz Holding Company.

10. Notice the reference to *zakat* in Exhibit 1. *Zakat* is one of the Five Pillars of Islam, that is, the five specific duties of devout Muslims. Under *Shari'a*, individual Muslims and Muslim businesses are required to contribute a certain percentage of their wealth each year to individuals less fortunate than themselves.

A second but less common *Shari'a* audit model results in a financial statement audit report that contains multiple references to *Shari'a*. Exhibit 2 presents the independent audit report issued by Ernst & Young on the financial statements of Dubai Islamic Bank, a large international bank based in the United Arab Emirates. Notice in this report that Ernst & Young's audit opinion includes an assertion that the bank's financial statements are in compliance with "*Shari'a* rules and principles" as determined by the bank's *Fatwa* and SSB.

In addition to approving new business ventures, banking practices, or other major operational changes, the Dubai Islamic Bank's SSB also periodically reviews or "audits" the bank's compliance with *Shari'a*, although a separate *Shari'a* audit report is not included in the company's annual financial reports. Consequently, under this *Shari'a* audit model, the *Shari'a*-related procedures performed during an entity's independent audit effectively provide a second layer of assurance that the given entity has complied with relevant Islamic religious principles during the year under audit.

The principal *Shari'a*-related procedures integrated into a financial statement audit under this second *Shari'a* audit model are performed by one or more Islamic religious scholars independent of the given audit client. These scholars are retained by the client's accounting firm. If an accounting firm does not have *Shari'a* scholars on its professional staff—which most firms do not, then the firm will retain the services of one or more such scholars on an engagement by engagement basis.

**EXHIBIT 2**

ERNST & YOUNG AUDIT REPORT ON DUBAI ISLAMIC BANK'S 2007 FINANCIAL STATEMENTS

**Auditors' Report to the Shareholders of Dubai Islamic Bank (Public Joint Stock Company)**

**Report on Financial Statements**

We have audited the accompanying financial statements of Dubai Islamic Bank Public Joint Stock Company and its subsidiaries (the 'Group'), which comprise the consolidated balance sheet as at 31 December 2007 and the consolidated income statement, consolidated cash flow statement and consolidated statement of changes in equity for the year then ended, and a summary of significant accounting policies and other explanatory notes.

**Management's Responsibility for the Financial Statements**

Management of the Bank is responsible for the preparation and fair presentation of these financial statements in accordance with International Financial Reporting Standards and the applicable provisions of the articles of association of the Bank, Federal Law No. 8 of 1984 (as amended), Federal Law No. 10 of 1980, Federal Law No. 6 of 1985 and Islamic *Sharia'a* rules and principles. This responsibility includes: designing, implementing and maintaining internal control relevant to the preparation and fair presentation of financial statements that are free from material misstatement, whether due to fraud or error; selecting and applying appropriate accounting policies; and making accounting estimates that are reasonable in the circumstances.

**Auditors' Responsibility**

Our responsibility is to express an opinion on these financial statements based on our audit. We conducted our audit in accordance with International Standards of Auditing. Those

*(continued)*

**EXHIBIT 2—*continued***

ERNST & YOUNG AUDIT REPORT ON DUBAI ISLAMIC BANK'S 2007 FINANCIAL STATEMENTS

standards require that we comply with ethical requirements and plan and perform the audit to obtain reasonable assurance whether the financial statements are free from material misstatement.

An audit involves performing procedures to obtain audit evidence about the amounts and disclosures in the financial statements. The procedures selected depend on the auditors' judgement, including the assessment of the risks of material misstatement of the financial statements, whether due to fraud or error. In making those risk assessments, the auditor considers internal control relevant to the entity's preparation and fair presentation of the financial statements in order to design audit procedures that are appropriate in the circumstances, but not for the purpose of expressing an opinion on the effectiveness of the entity's internal control. An audit also includes evaluating the appropriateness of accounting policies used and the reasonableness of accounting estimates made by management, as well as evaluating the overall presentation of the financial statements.

We believe that the audit evidence we have obtained is sufficient and appropriate to provide a basis for our audit opinion.

**Opinion**

In our opinion, the consolidated financial statements present fairly, in all material respects, the financial position of the Bank and its subsidiaries as of 31 December 2007, their financial performance and cash flows for the year then ended in accordance with International Financial Reporting Standards and comply, where appropriate, with the articles of association of the Bank, Federal Law No. 8 of 1984 (as amended), Federal Law No. 10 of 1980, Federal Law No. 6 of 1985 and the *Sharia'a* rules and principles as determined by the *Fatwa* and *Sharia'a* Supervisory Board of the Bank.

**Report on Other Legal and Regulatory Requirements**

We also confirm that, in our opinion, the financial statements include, in all material respects, the applicable requirements of Federal Law No. 8 of 1984 (as amended), Federal Law No. 10 of 1980, Federal Law No. 6 of 1985 and the articles of association of the Bank; proper books of account have been kept by the Bank and its subsidiaries, and the contents of the report of the Board of Directors relating to these consolidated financial statements are in agreement with the books of account. We have obtained all the information and explanations we required for the purpose of our audit and, to the best of our knowledge and belief, no violations of the articles of association of the Bank, Federal Law No. 8 of 1984 (as amended), Federal Law No. 10 of 1980, or Federal Law No. 6 of 1985 have occurred during the year which would have had a material effect on the business of the Bank or on its financial position.

Ernst & Young<br>
Signed by<br>
Edward B. Quinlan<br>
Partner<br>
Registration No. 93<br>
30 January 2008<br>
Dubai, United Arab Emirates

Just because an Islamic bank fails to issue a separate *Shari'a* audit report does not mean that the bank's independent auditors will necessarily refer to the issue of *Shari'a* compliance in their audit report on the bank's annual financial statements. Consider Arab National Bank, a large Islamic bank headquartered in Riyadh, Saudi Arabia. Although Arab National Bank has an internal *Shari'a* compliance function, the only reference to *Shari'a* compliance in a recent annual report released by the company was a brief narrative statement included in the letter to stockholders by the bank's chairman. That statement assured the bank's stockholders that all necessary procedures had been taken during the year in question to ensure that the institution complied with *Shari'a*.

## Enhancing the Uniformity of *Shari'a* Auditing

The wide disparity in *Shari'a* auditing practices has become an increasingly controversial issue within the Islamic economy in recent years. Many parties have suggested that the most effective way to eliminate this problem would be to establish a rule-making body that issues authoritative *Shari'a* auditing standards for all Islamic banks and other Islamic businesses. But the lack of consensus in interpreting and applying *Shari'a* across Islamic countries has so far prevented that goal from being accomplished.

To date, the most comprehensive effort to develop a body of consistent standards for *Shari'a* audits has been undertaken by the Accounting and Auditing Organization for Islamic Financial Institutions (AAOIFI). The AAOIFI was founded in 1991 in Bahrain by a cartel of large Islamic banks. By 2009, nearly 200 Islamic banks in more than forty countries were sponsoring members of the AAOIFI.

The AAOIFI employs approximately twenty Islamic religious scholars who review new transactions, contracts, and business structures being considered by Islamic banks. Periodically, the AAOIFI issues "*Shari'a* standards" to be used by SSBs and other parties, such as independent auditors, involved in the *Shari'a* compliance function of Islamic banks. These standards are intended to enhance the consistency of *Shari'a* compliance decisions across the Islamic banking industry. The AAOIFI also has a staff of professional accountants who monitor emerging accounting and independent auditing issues. When deemed appropriate, the AAOIFI releases "best practices" accounting and independent auditing standards for Islamic banks.

By late 2009, the AAOIFI had issued 35 *Shari'a* standards, 26 accounting standards, and five independent auditing standards. Presently, these standards are mandatory in Bahrain, the Dubai International Financial Centre within the United Arab Emirates, Jordan, Qatar, Sudan, and Syria. Although not mandatory in other Islamic countries, the AAOIFI's standards are consulted on a regular basis and considered an authoritative source by a large number of religious scholars, accountants, and independent auditors in those countries.[11]

Many Islamic academics have suggested that *Shari'a* compliance audits and financial statement audits should be merged. This proposal would leave intact SSBs and other oversight bodies who are charged with making initial decisions on which economic ventures, contracts, transactions, and other business practices are *Shari'a*-compliant. However, the responsibility for recurring periodic audits of *Shari'a* compliance by Islamic banks and other Islamic businesses would be delegated to professionally trained *Shari'a* auditors.

An Islamic academic who supports this proposal suggests that the effectiveness of the *Shari'a* compliance function is being undercut by the lack of formal training in auditing concepts and auditing methodologies on the part of the religious scholars principally responsible for that function. "While members of the *Shari'a* Supervisory

---

11. The Malaysia-based Islamic Financial Services Board (IFSB) functions in a role similar to that of the AAOIFI. The standards issued by the IFSB are principally directed to Islamic banks in Indonesia, Malaysia, and other predominantly Muslim countries in Southeast Asia.

Boards are pre-eminently qualified for their role of issuing *Fatwa* on the *Shari'a* permissibility of a financial product, they are not qualified auditors because they are not trained in the collecting and evaluating of evidence."[12,13]

This problem could be eliminated, according to the Islamic academic, by developing a "new breed" of Islamic accountants and auditors. "What is required is a new breed of Islamic accountants and auditors who would have both a Western accounting qualification and possibly a degree or certification in *Shari'a*."[14] To accomplish this goal, the scholar suggests that intervention by the Organization of the Islamic Conference (OIC) may be necessary.

The OIC is an organization sponsored by 57 Islamic countries that represents Islamic interests at the United Nations and other global tribunals. Because of its important position in the Islamic world and its financial resources, the OIC may be the only Islamic organization that could eventually persuade differing factions of the Islamic faith to adhere to a common body of *Shari'a* compliance standards, such as those issued by the AAOIFI. The OIC would also likely have the authority and ability to sponsor or oversee a certification program to train accountants capable of performing joint financial statement and *Shari'a* compliance audits.

## The Big Four: Gaining Access to the Islamic World

A spokesperson for KPMG recently acknowledged that auditors of Islamic banks require a unique skill set. "It has become evident that the role of the external auditor to Islamic financial institutions requires a different skill set and experience to that possessed by some accounting organizations today."[15] In fact, because of their international credibility and extensive resources, KPMG and the other Big Four accounting firms are well suited to develop accountants who have the skills necessary to perform joint financial statement and *Shari'a* audits.

In recent years, each of the Big Four firms has established an economic beachhead in the Islamic economy. In 2008, KPMG International issued a marketing brochure entitled *Islamic Finance Credentials* that identified the wide range of professional services the firm could offer Islamic banks. According to that brochure, "KPMG was one of the first accountancy organizations to meet the needs of Islamic financial institutions across national boundaries and we continue to be one of the industry's top international advisors."[16] At approximately the same time, PricewaterhouseCoopers (PwC) made a similar bid to attract clients in the Islamic banking sector.

> *PricewaterhouseCoopers in the Middle East has played an important role in the development of the [Islamic finance] industry . . . Our clients in the Islamic financial services sector include local, regional, and international banks, insurance companies, real estate investment trusts, mutual funds, as well as some of the major regulators and regulatory bodies.*[17]

12. Ibrahim, "The Case for Islamic Auditing," 25.

13. Another complicating factor is the lack of consensus within the Islamic world on exactly who qualifies as a "religious scholar" and is thus qualified to be involved in the *Shari'a* compliance function for Islamic banks and other organizations. Individuals recognized as religious scholars in one Islamic country may not necessarily be recognized as such in other Islamic nations.

14. Ibrahim, "The Case for Islamic Auditing," 25.

15. KPMG International, *Islamic Finance Credentials* (New York: KPMG International, 2008), 2.

16. *Ibid.*, 4.

17. PricewaterhouseCoopers, "Middle East Region: Industries—Islamic Banking & Takaful," www.pwc.com, September 2008.

Both Ernst & Young and Deloitte also claim to be leading providers of professional accounting, auditing, and consulting services to the Islamic finance sector. In late 2007, Deloitte became the first of the Big Four firms to appoint an Islamic religious scholar to its Middle Eastern professional staff. In commenting on this appointment, a Deloitte partner observed that, "We hope by this to create a gap big enough to make it difficult [for the other Big Four firms] to compete."[18]

An Ernst & Young partner downplayed the significance of Deloitte's hiring of an Islamic religious scholar. "We have good relationships with a number of scholars and a sound understanding of major *Shari'a* issues. There are variances of opinion among the scholars and, accordingly, the selection of scholars is particular to every organization."[19] In a subsequent press release, Ernst & Young "one-upped" Deloitte by announcing that it was the first of the Big Four firms to actually begin offering *Shari'a* audit services.

> *Ernst & Young was the first professional services firm to establish a dedicated team to service clients in this [Islamic finance] industry . . . and is the only professional services firm to offer Shari'a auditing. We have an unshakeable belief in the future of Islamic Finance. As a reflection of the changing needs of the industry, we currently offer more services in more markets and more industry segments in the Islamic financial services industry than any other professional services firm.*[20]

## Questions

1. Identify specific financial statement auditing concepts and procedures that could be applied in determining whether an Islamic bank has been *Shari'a*-compliant during a given financial reporting period. Would these concepts and procedures be applied differently in *Shari'a* compliance audits compared to conventional financial statement audits? Explain.
2. Do you believe that the proposal to merge *Shari'a* compliance audits with financial statement audits is feasible? Explain.
3. Do you agree with the assertion that "accounting can lead to perceptions of reality"? Explain. In deciding whether to adopt a proposed accounting standard, should accounting rule-making bodies consider whether that standard might induce socially irresponsible behavior on the part of economic decision makers? Defend your answer.
4. Identify the key challenges that the Big Four firms will likely face in their efforts to establish a major presence in the Islamic banking industry.

---

18. *Islamic Finance News* (online), "Deloitte 'First' with Shariah Scholar Post: Appoints Mufti Hassan Kaleem," islamicfinancenews.wordpress.com, 28 November 2007.

19. *Ibid.*

20. Ernst & Young, "Islamic Financial Services Group," www.ey.com/global/content.nsf/MiddleEast/services, September 2008.

## CASE 8.13

# Republic of the Sudan

*No investor should ever have to wonder whether his or her investments or retirement savings are indirectly subsidizing a terrorist haven or genocidal state.*

*Christopher Cox, SEC Chairman*

In 1956, Sudan obtained its independence from Great Britain. Although unified, Sudan was effectively two countries within one. Northern Sudan, home of the nation's capital, Khartoum, was controlled by Islamic fundamentalists, while southern Sudan was controlled by Christian fundamentalists. In 1989, a military coup led by General Omar Hassan al-Bashir, leader of the National Islamic Front, overthrew Sudan's central government and took control of Khartoum. Almost immediately, the new government imposed Islamic law or *Shari'a* on southern Sudan triggering widespread violence between the Islamic-controlled Sudanese military and rebel forces organized by Christian leaders in southern Sudan. By the early years of the 21st century, the primary battleground in Sudan was the large western region of the country known as Darfur.

Over the past several decades, various organizations, including the United Nations and the International Criminal Court, have documented atrocities on a massive scale that have been inflicted on the citizens of Sudan, principally residents of Darfur and southern Sudan. The *Christian Science Monitor* reported in 2008 that as many as two million Sudanese have died as a result of those atrocities, while four million other Sudanese have been displaced from their homes.[1] In June 2004, United Nations Secretary-General Kofi Annan and United States Secretary of State Colin Powell visited the war-torn country. During that visit, Annan referred to the ongoing civil war in Sudan as the worst humanitarian crisis facing the world, while Powell described the situation as a "humanitarian catastrophe."[2]

Government officials in numerous Western countries have insisted that the Sudanese government is responsible for the war crimes committed in Darfur and southern Sudan. Allegedly, the military dictatorship that has controlled the Sudanese government since 1989 has organized large bands of armed mercenaries or *janjaweed* to attack and wipe out entire villages in those regions of the country. The Sudanese government reportedly has used revenues produced by the nation's large oil industry to finance this campaign of terror against its own citizens.

In recent years, governmental authorities and private interest groups across the globe have undertaken initiatives to end the widespread suffering in Sudan. Many of these efforts have involved economic sanctions intended to limit the Sudanese government's ability to finance terrorist attacks on its own citizens. In 1998, President Bill Clinton imposed an economic embargo on Sudan that effectively prevented U.S. companies from engaging in commerce with Sudanese companies or the Sudanese government. During President Clinton's administration, Sudan was also included on the U.S. State Department's list of "state sponsors of terrorism" (SST), a list that

---

1. J. Adams, "Renewed Sudan Violence Raises Fears of Return to Civil War," *Christian Science Monitor* (online), 16 May 2008.
2. CNN.com, "U.S. Circulates U.N. Resolution on Sudan," 30 June 2004.

includes such countries as Cuba, Iran, and Syria.[3] More recently, several states have passed laws requiring state employee pension funds to divest themselves of investments linked to Sudan.

In 2004, a U.S. House of Representatives committee issued a report calling for the SEC to require companies with securities listed on U.S. stock exchanges to disclose any business operations within, or other relationships with, nations identified as SSTs. The House committee maintained that such information qualified as "material information" under the far-reaching "full and fair disclosure" regulatory mandate of the SEC and thus should be disclosed to investors.

> *A company's association with sponsors of terrorism and human rights abuses, no matter how large or small, can have a material adverse effect on a public company's operations, financial condition, earnings, and stock prices, all of which can affect the value of an investment.*[4]

The SEC responded to this directive by requiring public companies to disclose any and all ties to SST countries. To promote compliance with this new policy, the SEC established the Office of Global Security Risk (OGSR) within its Division of Corporation Finance. The OGSR monitors SEC filings to ensure that SEC registrants make all appropriate SST-related disclosures.

The most controversial measure to date to help investors identify companies with links to SSTs was an Internet search tool created by the SEC in June 2007. This search tool scanned the huge number of documents filed by SEC registrants on the agency's EDGAR (electronic data gathering and retrieval system) website and tagged companies with ties to one or more SSTs. After these companies were identified, they were included on a list that was posted to a Web page on the EDGAR website. The SEC reported that the intent of this new procedure was to provide investors and other parties with direct access to company disclosures involving "past, current or anticipated future business activities in one or more of these [SST] countries."[5] In fact, such disclosures were already available to investors and other parties who wanted to search for them by utilizing the existing search tool on the EDGAR website.

Nearly one hundred companies appeared on the initial SST "blacklist" that was generated by the SEC's Internet search tool. Because of the economic embargo imposed by the U.S. on Sudan, nearly all of these companies were foreign firms that had securities listed on U.S. stock exchanges. Among the more prominent of these companies were Alcatel, Benetton, Cadbury Schweppes, Credit Suisse, Deutsche Bank, HSBC, Nokia, Reuters, Siemens, and Unilever. The SEC reported "exceptional traffic" on the SST Web page. The agency also reported that individuals who visited that Web page typically "clicked" on individual company names to access the relevant financial statement disclosures made by those companies.[6]

Within a matter of days after the SEC initiated its new disclosure policy, the companies impacted by that policy began complaining bitterly to the federal agency. Executives of many of these companies insisted that it was unfair for them to be

---

3. According to the *Encyclopedia Brittanica Online*, terrorism is the "systematic use of violence to create a general climate of fear in a population and thereby to bring about a particular political objective."

4. Steptoe & Johnson, "International Law Advisory—SEC Disclosure for Operations in Sensitive Countries," 17 May 2004 (steptoe.com/publications-3091.html).

5. Securities and Exchange Commission, *Release Nos. 33-8860 & 34-56803*, "Concept Release on Mechanisms to Access Disclosures Relating to Business Activities in or with Countries Designated as State Sponsors of Terrorism," 23 November 2007.

6. A. Rappaport, "SEC Removes Terrorism Tool Amid Backlash," *CFO.com*, 23 July 2007.

singled out by the SEC since they had only minimal operations in, or some other tenuous connection to, one or more SST countries. For example, a major pharmaceutical company in India, Dr. Reddy's Laboratories, admitted that it marketed several of its products in Sudan. However, the company's CEO maintained that those sales were not "viewed as material to our business or our overall revenue."[7] Despite that point of view, under the SEC's disclosure policy any sales to an SST nation qualified as "material." As a result, when such information was disclosed in an SEC registration statement, the federal agency's search tool ensured that the given company appeared on the Web page listing registrants with SST ties.

Another common complaint voiced by executives of companies appearing on the SEC's SST list was that many firms avoided being included on that list by not disclosing links to terrorist countries in documents filed with the federal agency. One such company was the large U.S.-based investment firm Berkshire Hathaway. In its 2006 annual report, Berkshire Hathaway failed to disclose that it had a large investment in PetroChina, a company with extensive business operations in Sudan. When contacted about this matter, Berkshire Hathaway officials insisted that the PetroChina investment was not material to their company's financial statements and thus did not have to be disclosed as an SST-linked investment in its SEC registration statements. In late 2007, Berkshire Hathaway announced that it had liquidated its PetroChina investment. Warren Buffett, the company's chief executive officer, reported that the PetroChina investment was sold for economic reasons and not because of pressure to do so by parties who had criticized his company for having a Sudan-related investment.[8]

Other critics of the SST disclosure policy suggested that it was inappropriate for the SEC to "single out" registrants involved in one type of questionable business activity while ignoring companies involved in a wide range of other such activities. An officer of the National Foreign Trade Council noted that, "Providing enhanced access . . . in this particular case is selective and ignores the fact that there are a multitude of other social and political issues that do not receive similar treatment."[9] A similar point of view was expressed by an executive of the American Bankers Association—many large international banks appeared on the SEC's SST Web page. "Some investors feel strongly about activities supporting gambling enterprises, others oppose those businesses generating excessive greenhouse gases, still other investors avoid companies that are not unionized, while others avoid companies that are unionized . . . There is simply no basis for the Commission to dedicate special resources to a particular kind of taboo business activity."[10]

---

7. K. Datta and P.B. Jayakumar, "Dr. Reddy's in SEC List for Terrorist State Links," *Rediff India Abroad* (online), 30 June 2007.

8. In fact, Berkshire Hathaway's board of directors asked the company's shareholders to vote on whether the PetroChina investment should be sold. In presenting that proposal to the stockholders, the board indicated that it did not believe that "Berkshire should automatically divest shares of an investee because it disagrees with a specific activity of that investee" ("Shareholder Proposal Regarding Berkshire's Investment in PetroChina," www.berkshirehathaway.com/sudan.pdf). The stockholders voted not to require the board to sell the PetroChina shares by a margin of 97.5 percent to 2.5 percent.

9. W.A. Reinsch, Letter filed with the SEC in response to SEC *Release Nos. 33-8860 & 34-56803*, "Concept Release on Mechanisms to Access Disclosures Relating to Business Activities in or with Countries Designated as State Sponsors of Terrorism," 18 January 2008 (www.sec.gov).

10. S. Behram, Letter filed with the SEC in response to SEC *Release Nos. 33-8860 & 34-56803*, "Concept Release on Mechanisms to Access Disclosures Relating to Business Activities in or with Countries Designated as State Sponsors of Terrorism," 22 January 2008 (www.sec.gov).

Finally, two top executives of the Securities Industry and Financial Markets Association maintained that the SST disclosure policy went beyond the SEC's regulatory mandate by involving the federal agency in "foreign policy and national security matters."[11] These individuals went on to raise the issue that became a focal point of the controversy surrounding the SEC's new disclosure policy. That issue was whether the SEC should be allowed to decide what information in registration statements is particularly "material" and thus should be highlighted or otherwise brought specifically to the attention of the investing public.

> *We are not aware of the SEC having previously singled out companies based on disclosures that they have made, unless those disclosures were materially misleading or otherwise violated the law. With any website tool designed to draw attention to disclosures involving activities in countries designated as State Sponsors of Terrorism, however, the SEC in effect would determine what information should concern investors. Though this kind of judgment may be well-intentioned . . . it directly conflicts with the SEC's longstanding disclosure-based regulatory scheme, which is designed to elicit material information and then to let investors evaluate the disclosures for themselves.*[12]

## EPILOGUE

In July 2007, five weeks after the SEC instituted its new SST disclosure policy, the federal agency yielded to vocal critics of that policy by eliminating the Web page that contained the SST blacklist. At the time, the SEC reported that it would possibly re-institute the SST disclosure policy or an amended version of it in the future.[13]

Four months later, in November 2007, the SEC issued a "request for comment" release asking for public input regarding the issue of terrorism-linked financial disclosures. The key question raised by the SEC was whether such disclosures in SEC registration statements should be highlighted in some way on the EDGAR website. The large majority of the responses received by the SEC indicated that the federal agency should not bring special attention to such disclosures. To date, the SEC has taken no further action on this matter.

Sudan President al-Bashir bowed to international pressure in 2005 and accepted a peace agreement brokered by international mediators. The arrangement called for a ceasefire in all hostilities, established a semi-autonomous government for southern Sudan, and called for a nationwide referendum on independence for southern Sudan by 2011. Although the violence in Sudan has abated since the signing of the peace agreement, international peacekeepers in the country have reported frequent clashes between Sudanese military troops and rebel groups in Darfur and southern Sudan. Meanwhile, very few of the millions of Sudanese citizens uprooted by the civil warfare have returned to their former homes.

In March 2009, the International Criminal Court in The Hague, Netherlands, issued an arrest warrant for President al-Bashir. That court, which is recognized by nearly 150 nations worldwide, indicted al-Bashir for a series of war crimes and crimes against humanity. The arrest warrant was the first ever issued by the court to a national head of state. To date, al-Bashir has ignored the arrest warrant and insisted that the International Criminal Court has no jurisdiction over him.

11. D. Preston and D. Strongin, Letter filed with the SEC in response to SEC *Release Nos. 33-8860 & 34-56803*, "Concept Release on Mechanisms to Access Disclosures Relating to Business Activities in or with Countries Designated as State Sponsors of Terrorism," 22 January 2008 (www.sec.gov).

12. *Ibid.*

13. Despite closing the Web page that reported companies with links to SSTs, the SEC continues to require public companies to disclose in their SEC registration statements any relationships they have with SSTs.

## Questions

1. Do you agree with the assertion that any and all associations that SEC registrants have with SSTs qualify as "material information" for financial reporting purposes and thus should be disclosed in their SEC filings? Are there other "sensitive" or questionable business activities that SEC registrants should be required to disclose? Defend your answers.
2. Should the SEC have the authority to highlight or bring special attention to certain disclosures made by SEC registrants? Why or why not?
3. How does the SEC define "materiality"? How does that definition differ, if at all, from the definitions of materiality included in accounting and auditing standards?

## CASE 8.14

# Mohamed Salem El-Hadad, Internal Auditor

*The world is moved along, not only by the mighty shoves of its heroes, but also by the aggregate of the tiny pushes by each honest worker.*

*Helen Keller*

In 1976, Mohamed El-Hadad earned an undergraduate accounting degree in his native Egypt. Before he began his accounting career, El-Hadad completed his compulsory service in the Egyptian military forces. El-Hadad accepted an entry-level position with a large hotel in Alexandria after being honorably discharged from the military in 1979. Two years later, El-Hadad immigrated to Abu Dhabi, the capital of the United Arab Emirates (UAE), after he learned that there were excellent employment opportunities for accountants in that small Middle Eastern nation.[1]

The determined young accountant soon landed a job with the UAE's Ministry of Education. For ten years, El-Hadad worked as an auditor with that government agency. Throughout his tenure with the Ministry of Education, El-Hadad regularly received excellent performance appraisals from his superiors.

While on a vacation in the United States in 1992, El-Hadad visited the UAE's embassy in Washington, D.C. During that visit, he became acquainted with the embassy's cultural attaché and the deputy cultural attaché. The cultural attaché was impressed with El-Hadad and his employment history and encouraged him to apply for an open auditing position with the embassy. The position involved "the audit and review of all expenditures and accounting methods of the cultural attaché and the educational expenditures for UAE students in the United States, and reconciliation of all bank accounts."[2] The job would require El-Hadad to supervise eight other accountants. El-Hadad's immediate superior would be the cultural attaché.

El-Hadad was excited by the new job opportunity and the possibility of relocating to the United States. When he returned to the UAE, he informed his superiors in the Ministry of Education of his interest in the Washington, D.C., job. They encouraged him to apply for the position and gave him excellent personal references that were forwarded to the cultural attaché of the UAE's Washington, D.C., embassy. Among other complimentary remarks, the recommendations indicated that El-Hadad "was an exemplary employee who displayed seriousness and integrity."

In January 1993, El-Hadad accepted the supervisory audit position in Washington, D.C. El-Hadad enjoyed his new job and the relationships he developed with his superiors, his subordinates and the remainder of the embassy staff. He was certain that the increased scope of responsibilities he assumed in the new position would

1. Approximately 95 percent of UAE's workforce is made up of foreign nationals. For decades, the small, oil-rich country has actively encouraged immigration of foreign nationals to bolster its rapidly growing economy.

2. This and all subsequent quotes were taken from the following source: *Mohamed Salem El-Hadad v. The Embassy of the United Arab Emirates, et al.*, Civil Action No. 96-1943 (RWR), United States District Court for the District of Columbia, 2006. Much of the background information included in this case was drawn from other legal transcripts and news reports.

help him develop professionally. El-Hadad also realized that the cultural, educational, and recreational opportunities offered by the dynamic Washington, D.C., metropolitan area would be beneficial for himself and his family.

Unfortunately, within a matter of months, El-Hadad's American "adventure" turned bittersweet. During the performance of routine audit procedures in April 1993, El-Hadad discovered a secret bank account being used by the embassy. Upon further investigation, he determined that his new boss and friend, the embassy's cultural attaché, was maintaining the account with the assistance of the deputy cultural attaché and the embassy's chief accountant. He also determined that the three individuals were diverting UAE government funds into the secret account.

One method used by the conspirators to embezzle funds involved healthcare payments made by embassy employees. The embassy provided healthcare coverage for its employees but not for employee dependents. If an employee elected to have dependents covered by the embassy's healthcare plan, the employee was required to pay the monthly premiums directly to the embassy. The conspirators deposited these payments into the secret bank account and then used UAE government funds to pay the healthcare premiums for employees' dependents. In fact, the monthly amounts that El-Hadad paid to the embassy to provide healthcare coverage for his wife and children were included in the funds diverted into the secret bank account.

Another method used by the conspirators to misappropriate UAE government funds involved tuition refunds that the embassy received from a large number of U.S. universities. The UAE government had established an educational program that paid the college tuition of UAE citizens who chose to attend a U.S. university. The UAE embassy made these tuition payments directly to the given U.S. universities. Not unlike other college students, UAE students frequently "dropped" courses early in the semester for various reasons. The resulting tuition refunds remitted to the UAE embassy were funneled into the secret bank account discovered by El-Hadad.

Instead of informing top officials in the UAE embassy of the embezzlement scheme, El-Hadad chose to pass that information to a government official in the Ministry of Education, the agency for which he had worked the past ten years. This individual in turn notified UAE's Minister of Finance. The Minister of Finance promptly contacted El-Hadad to question him about the scheme and then traveled to the United States to discuss the matter with him in person. The Minister of Finance then sent a team of auditors from his agency to carry out a comprehensive and secret investigation of the fraud. This team of auditors discovered two additional secret bank accounts used by the conspirators and determined that the three individuals had stolen at least $2 million. In early 1994, the cultural attaché, his deputy, and the embassy's chief accountant were fired. Three other embassy employees who were aware of the embezzlement scheme were also dismissed.

Prior to learning that El-Hadad had uncovered his embezzlement scheme, the embassy's cultural attaché completed his annual performance appraisal of El-Hadad for 1993. The cultural attaché indicated that El-Hadad was an "excellent employee" and gave him 99 out of a possible 100 points on the scale used for the performance appraisal. El-Hadad received a similar performance appraisal near the end of 1994 by the embassy's new cultural attaché. The new cultural attaché also recommended that he be promoted, receive a salary increase, and a merit bonus for his excellent work. During 1994, El-Hadad also received plaudits from numerous UAE government officials, most notably the Minister of Finance, for his role in uncovering the embezzlement scheme.

Not surprisingly, the Minister of Finance, the new cultural attaché, and several other UAE government officials were stunned in late 1995 when the UAE State Audit

Division announced that Mohamed El-Hadad had been involved in the embezzlement scheme that he had reported. The State Audit Division, a government agency that provides audit services for other UAE government agencies, reported that El-Hadad had received several improper payments from the conspirators who had maintained the three secret bank accounts. These improper payments included compensation for overtime that he had not worked, expense reimbursements to which he was not entitled, and payment of healthcare premiums for his family.

The State Audit Division investigation that culminated in the charges being filed against El-Hadad had been initiated by another government agency, the Ministry of Higher Education and Scientific Research (HESR). Officials in the latter agency had been embarrassed when the embezzlement scheme at the UAE's Washington, D.C., embassy was publicly revealed in early 1994 since it involved an educational program that fell under the purview of their agency. These same officials also reportedly had an ongoing feud throughout 1994 and beyond with the embassy's new cultural attaché, who was a staunch supporter and ally of El-Hadad. Following the startling announcement that El-Hadad had been involved in the embezzlement scheme, a top official of the HESR Ministry traveled to the Washington, D.C., embassy and personally told several of El-Hadad's coworkers that he was dishonest and a poor employee.

In early 1996, the UAE cultural attaché capitulated to relentless pressure from government officials in Abu Dhabi and fired El-Hadad for his alleged role in the embezzlement scheme. El-Hadad, who had consistently and vehemently insisted that he was innocent of the charges, immediately appealed his dismissal. While his case was being reviewed, El-Hadad secured an entry-level auditing job for the UAE's military attaché in the Washington, D.C., embassy. When the HESR Minister learned of El-Hadad's new job, he notified government officials in Abu Dhabi. Within a matter of days, El-Hadad was fired once more.

In late 1996, El-Hadad's appeal of his dismissal from the supervisory audit position with the UAE embassy was denied. His appeal was denied despite several prominent individuals interceding on his behalf with the appellate tribunal. Among the individuals who wrote letters testifying to El-Hadad's work ethic and integrity was the cultural attaché who had been pressured to fire him, the UAE Minister of Finance, and the U.S. Ambassador to the UAE who was well acquainted with El-Hadad. Despite this impressive show of support for the Egyptian accountant, the appellate tribunal ruled that because El-Hadad's involvement in the fraudulent scheme had been well documented, his dismissal had been justified. The documents used to corroborate his role in the fraud had been provided by the Ministry of HESR.

Throughout the remainder of 1996 and much of 1997, El-Hadad searched for employment as an auditor or accountant in the Washington, D.C., area. Each time that he applied for a job, however, the prospective employer contacted the UAE embassy and learned that El-Hadad had been terminated because of his role in an embezzlement scheme. Economic necessity forced El-Hadad to return with his family to his native Egypt in late 1997 and seek employment there. Similar to his experience in Washington, D.C., each time that he applied for an accounting or auditing position, the prospective employer learned of his past history and refused to consider him any further.

Frustrated and disheartened, El-Hadad eventually realized that his career in auditing, a career that he had loved and a career to which he had devoted nearly two decades of his life, was over. El-Hadad then decided to pursue a new livelihood. For several years, he sold cosmetics through a small business that he organized. But in

2003 that business failed and El-Hadad was forced to rely on family members for economic support.

Prior to leaving the United States in 1997, El-Hadad had retained an attorney to file a lawsuit against the UAE's Washington, D.C., embassy. In this lawsuit, El-Hadad alleged that the embassy had wrongfully terminated him, that he had been defamed, and that his accounting career had been destroyed. Attorneys for the UAE attempted to have El-Hadad's lawsuit dismissed due to the concept of sovereign immunity. This concept generally prohibits criminal or civil lawsuits from being filed in U.S. courts against foreign embassies in the United States. However, the U.S. federal law that dictates the nature and scope of sovereign immunity, the Foreign Sovereign Immunities Act, includes an exception for lawsuits related to "commercial activity." Because the U.S. District Court in which El-Hadad filed his lawsuit ruled that his work as an auditor for the UAE embassy had qualified as "commercial activity," the federal court refused to dismiss the lawsuit.

During El-Hadad's civil trial in July 2001, his attorneys addressed one by one the allegations of dishonesty that had been filed against him by the UAE State Audit Division. The attorneys presented to the court the documents that had been used as the basis for those allegations and easily established that they had been forged. The attorneys also presented other documents and evidence that had been submitted to the State Audit Division during its investigation of El-Hadad that clearly demonstrated he had not been involved in any way in the embezzlement scheme. For whatever reason, the State Audit Division had ignored that exculpatory evidence. El-Hadad's attorneys went on to prove that not only had he not been involved in the fraud, he had been known for being scrupulously honest while employed by the UAE embassy. For example, evidence presented by his attorneys demonstrated that when filing for expense reimbursements, El-Hadad had understated the amounts to which he was entitled to reimbursement.

The federal judge who presided over El-Hadad's civil trial agreed with his attorneys that he had had been victimized by false and "trumped-up" charges intended to discredit him. The federal judge also ruled that El-Hadad had been defamed by his former employer and that the defamation had ended his career as an accountant and auditor. At the conclusion of the trial, the UAE was ordered to pay El-Hadad $1.25 million for lost wages, $500,000 of damages related to the defamation he had suffered, and accrued interest on both amounts since the date of his termination in 1996. The UAE's attorneys refused to accept the court's verdict and filed repeated appeals to have it overturned. At each level of the federal court system, the appeals filed by those attorneys were rejected. In 2007, the verdict was appealed to the U.S. Supreme Court. When the Supreme Court refused to review the case, Mohamed El-Hadad could finally claim victory. At last report, the UAE had yet to pay El-Hadad the more than $2 million that it owes him.

## Questions

1. Identify and briefly describe the legal protections that "whistleblowers" have in the United States.
2. Should U.S. companies integrate legal protections for internal whistleblowers into their internal control systems? Defend your answer.

3. Suppose that during your career you discover a fraud similar to that uncovered by Mohamed El-Hadad. List specific measures that you could take to protect yourself from recriminations by your employer or other parties.
4. Did El-Hadad face an ethical or moral dilemma when he discovered the fraud being perpetrated by his superior and friend? Before responding, define "ethical dilemma" and "moral dilemma."

## CASE 8.15

# *Tae Kwang Vina*

During the 1970s, the public accounting profession eliminated its bans on competitive bidding, advertising, direct solicitation, and related practices that the Federal Trade Commission maintained were restraints of trade. The decision to drop those restrictions contributed to the increasingly competitive nature of the market for independent audits over the following decades. That escalating competition was manifested by a rapid increase in the rate of auditor changes by public companies, "lowballing" on the part of certain accounting firms to obtain new clients, and stagnant or declining audit fees.

By the late 1990s, many leading accountants suggested that the independent audit "product" was diminishing in value. The American Institute of Certified Public Accountants (AICPA) concurred with that point of view in an article that appeared in its monthly newsletter. To counter the declining value of independent audits, the AICPA recommended that accounting firms begin developing and marketing other services.

> *The audit—the CPA profession's core assurance product—has been declining in value over the past few years, becoming a less marketable product. In fact, revenues from traditional accounting and auditing services have been flat for the past seven years . . . Where challenges exist, however, opportunities abound. . . [nontraditional] assurance services provide a lucrative opportunity to expand [accounting] practices. CPAs are singularly qualified as independent assurance providers to furnish businesses and their customers with the certainty they need to compete in today's marketplace.*[1]

To identify new professional services that accountants could begin providing the AICPA created the Assurance Services Special Committee that was chaired by Robert Elliott, a senior audit partner with KPMG. Elliott's committee recommended a wide range of new services that accounting practitioners could market. Specific examples of such services included the following: ascertaining the quality of home healthcare providers and assisted living (nursing home) facilities, identifying security breaches of Internet-linked information systems, and helping companies and other organizations identify and manage the economic risks they faced. The AICPA believed that these and other nontraditional services would provide accounting firms an opportunity to significantly increase their revenues while at the same time enhancing their overall stature and reputation within the business community.

Among the boldest initiatives taken by the AICPA in the late 1990s to expand the product line of services offered by CPAs was a proposal to create a new professional designation for accountants. This new credential would be awarded to individuals who passed a rigorous examination to demonstrate that they qualified as "multidisciplinary business advisers and strategic thinkers."[2] The AICPA believed this new professional designation would help existing CPAs strengthen their credibility as

1. American Institute of Certified Public Accountants, "Assurance Services: Transforming the Quality of Information," *The CPA Letter* (online), May 2001.

2. American Institute of Certified Public Accountants, "Internet Portal, Broad-Based Global Credential Discussed at Regional Council Meetings," *The CPA Letter* (online), May 2000.

general business consultants and thereby allow them to gain a larger share of the rapidly expanding market for business consulting services worldwide.

Throughout the 1990s and into the new century, the major international accounting firms began offering an extended product line of nontraditional services. These firms invested heavily in advertising programs and other promotional activities to market these new services. However, as these firms attempted to develop new markets and encroach on existing markets served by other professionals they encountered unexpected challenges and problems.

Nontraditional professional services marketed by the major accounting firms during the 1990s included "environmental and labor practices audits." These engagements were not financial statement audits but rather examinations intended to determine whether a given company, organization, or specific production facility was complying with state and federal laws, industry rules and regulations, and other predetermined criteria relevant to environmental issues and labor practices.

The accounting profession's dominant firms recognized that there was a growing demand for environmental and labor practices audits and similar engagements during the 1990s. This demand sprang from a social activism movement during the latter part of the twentieth century that targeted high profile companies in the United States that allegedly operated, or purchased goods from, "sweatshops" in foreign countries. Ernst & Young and PricewaterhouseCoopers (PwC) were the most prolific providers of environmental and labor practices audits within the accounting profession. In 1998 alone, PwC performed 1,500 such audits in China's Guangdong province, that nation's industrial epicenter.[3]

Wikipedia defines a sweatshop as a "working environment with very difficult or dangerous conditions, usually where the workers have few rights or ways to address the situation." These conditions may include "exposure to harmful materials, hazardous situations, extreme temperatures, or abuse from employers." Social activists claimed that many large U.S. companies were maximizing their profits by using sweatshops in third-world countries to minimize the production cost of the merchandise they sold.

In 1996, Wal-Mart was blindsided by a firestorm of unfavorable media attention ignited by a social activist organization. This organization revealed that Wal-Mart's popular line of Kathie Lee Gifford apparel was being manufactured under sweatshop conditions in the Central American nation of Honduras. Over the following several years, many other U.S. companies would face similar charges. The company targeted more than any other by the anti-sweatshop activists was Nike, Inc., the world's largest producer of athletic shoes.

Nike's critics insisted that the working conditions in the company's Far Eastern production facilities were harsh, hazardous, and in violation of the given countries' labor laws. Those production facilities were located principally in China, Indonesia, Taiwan, and Vietnam. The company's critics also lambasted the company for paying multi-million dollar endorsement fees to sports celebrities such as Michael Jordan and Tiger Woods while factory workers in its foreign production facilities received weekly wages of $10 or even less for working upwards of sixty hours.

In early 1997, threats of congressional investigations and consumer boycotts persuaded Nike to hire Andrew Young, a former U.S. congressman and leading civil rights advocate, to inspect production facilities in countries where the company's products were being manufactured. After visiting several of those factories, Young

3. *The Economist*, "Business Ethics: Sweatshop Wars," 27 February 1999, 62.

submitted a written report to Nike's board in which he indicated that the workers in those facilities were being treated well. To garner public support and quell its critics, Nike included favorable comments excerpted from Young's report in full-page ads that it purchased in several major metropolitan newspapers.

Andrew Young's report failed to placate Nike's critics. Those critics claimed that Young's visits had been brief and less than rigorous and that he was not qualified to assess the working conditions in the given facilities.

The next measure Nike took to silence its critics was to retain Ernst & Young to perform an environmental and labor practices audit of one of its major Far Eastern production facilities. The facility chosen for that audit was a Vietnamese factory operated by Tae Kwang Vina Industrial Company, Limited, one of Nike's largest manufacturing contractors. That factory, Nike's newest and most modern production facility in the Far East, employed 9,200 workers and produced 400,000 pairs of athletic shoes each month. During the 1990s, U.S. companies that outsourced production operations to Vietnam were responsible for much of that nation's impressive economic growth. In fact, by the late 1990s, Nike's Vietnamese factories accounted for more than five percent of that country's gross domestic product.

In the spring of 1997, Ernst & Young submitted a ten-page report to Nike management that summarized the principal findings of its Tae Kwang Vina audit. Only a brief excerpt from that confidential report was released to the press. That brief excerpt suggested that Ernst & Young's overall conclusion regarding the working conditions at the Tae Kwang Vina site was consistent with the conclusion reached by Andrew Young.

The excerpt from the Ernst & Young report provided to the press also indicated that the Tae Kwang Vina facility was complying with Nike's code of conduct. Among many other stipulations, that code required Nike's "business partners" to pay no less than the minimum wage mandated in a given country, to fully compensate workers for overtime hours, and to provide a safe working environment for those workers.

Ernst & Young's conclusion that the Tae Kwang Vina factory was operating in compliance with Nike's code of conduct infuriated the company's critics. In November 1997, several months after Ernst & Young submitted its final report to Nike, one of those critics covertly obtained a copy of the complete report and turned it over to *The New York Times*.

Ernst & Young's ten-page report painted a much different picture of the working conditions at the Tae Kwang Vina facility than the brief excerpt from that report initially provided to the press. The full Ernst & Young report documented numerous abusive labor practices and hazardous working conditions at that site. *The New York Times* summarized some of the more egregious of the deplorable working conditions that the accounting firm had found at the factory.

> *Ernst & Young wrote that workers at the factory near Ho Chi Minh City were exposed to carcinogens that exceeded local legal standards by 177 times in parts of the plant and that 77 percent of the employees suffered from respiratory problems. The report also said that employees at the site . . . were forced to work 65 hours a week, more than Vietnamese law allows, for $10 per week.*[4]

Other improper practices or incidents reported by Ernst & Young included inadequate ventilation systems, excessive noise levels and temperatures within the factory, insufficient safety equipment, inadequate training for employees required to work

---

4. S. Greenhouse, "Nike Shoe Plant in Vietnam is Called Unsafe for Workers," *The New York Times* (online), 8 November 1997.

with dangerous chemicals, failure to provide workers with sufficient water, refusal to pay wages owed to employees after they were terminated, and mistreatment of workers by supervisors.

The release of the complete Ernst & Young report to the press provoked an angry public outcry against Nike. In response, the company initially insisted that the problems identified in the report had been largely remedied over the more than six months that had elapsed since Ernst & Young completed its audit of the Tae Kwang Vina facility. That assertion was met with disbelief and ridicule by the company's critics. Several of those critics banded together and filed a lawsuit against Nike that charged the company with intentionally misrepresenting the working conditions within its foreign production facilities.

Ironically, the release of the full Ernst & Young report also resulted in heated criticism of the prominent accounting firm. Although Ernst & Young's report disclosed serious problems at the Tae Kwang Vina factory, a subsequent investigation by Dara O'Rourke, a consultant to the United Nations and a leader of the anti-sweatshop movement, revealed that the facility's working conditions were much worse than reported by Ernst & Young.

O'Rourke suggested that the Ernst & Young personnel involved in the Tae Kwang Vina engagement did not have the necessary qualifications and training to perform environmental and labor practices audits, which had resulted in the engagement being seriously flawed. Alleged deficiencies in Ernst & Young's Tae Kwang Vina engagement included, among others, relying heavily on the factory's management and other secondary sources for the information collected during the engagement, failing to properly test air quality and other working conditions in the factory, and failing to ensure that employees questioned during the engagement were free to respond candidly without any fear of reprisals from management.

Sweatshop activists also challenged Nike's claim that Ernst & Young performed the Tae Kwang Vina engagement as an "independent" third party. A governmental health and compliance officer for the state of California maintained that Nike's hiring of Ernst & Young to complete the Tae Kwang Vina "audit" was equivalent to "putting the fox's paid consultant in charge of the henhouse."[5] Corporate Watch, an international organization that monitors the social responsibility of multinational organizations, pointed out that rather than being independent of Nike, the Ernst & Young auditors had simply followed specific instructions given to them by Nike management in completing the Tae Kwang Vina engagement. To prove this point, the organization quoted the following statement directed to Nike by Ernst & Young it its ten-page report: "The procedures we have performed were those that you [Nike] specifically instructed us to perform. Accordingly, we make no comments as to the sufficiency of these procedures for your purposes."[6]

The Corporate Watch organization went on to suggest that accounting firms were not well suited to perform environmental and labor practices audits. "Indeed, Ernst & Young's incompetence as a social and environmental auditor, combined with Mr. O'Rourke's own findings inside the plant, present a strong argument against using accounting firms to conduct labor and environmental audits."[7] This latter opinion

5. D. Rourke, "Vietnam: Smoke from a Hired Gun," November 1997, www.corpwatch.org/article.php?id=966%20.

6. *Ibid.*

7. *Ibid.*

was seconded by the *New York Times* which called for companies such as Nike to use "truly independent monitors" to complete such engagements.[8]

## EPILOGUE

In 2003, the U.S. Supreme Court agreed to hear arguments in the lawsuit filed against Nike that charged the company with falsely denying that it used foreign sweatshops to produce the merchandise that it sold. However, the case was ultimately settled out of court when Nike agreed to pay $1.5 million to help monitor and improve factory working conditions in third-world countries. In 2005, Nike published a self-study of the working conditions in 700 factories scattered around the world that manufactured the merchandise it sold. The report documented that "widespread problems" still existed within those factories.[9] Nike executives pledged to work with social activist groups to resolve those problems.

In a nationwide vote in late 2001, the rank-and-file members of the AICPA rejected the proposal to create a new professional designation to recognize expertise in the field of general business consulting. Several months later, the U.S. Congress passed the Sarbanes-Oxley Act of 2002 in response to the massive losses imposed on investors by the Enron and WorldCom scandals. That statute included a wide range of reforms intended to strengthen independent audits. Sarbanes-Oxley served not only to enhance the perceived importance of the independent audit function in the United States but also refocused the attention of the major accounting firms on the "independent audit product." Thanks largely to the Sarbanes-Oxley reforms, the audit fees charged to public companies by the major accounting firms have risen steadily over the past several years.

## Questions

1. Define each of the following types of professional services: consulting services, attestation services, agreed-upon procedures engagements, and assurance services. Explain how, if at all, these services overlap.
2. Visit the websites of the major international accounting firms. Identify nontraditional services currently marketed by these firms. List several of these services and briefly describe their nature. Of the services you identified, are there any that you believe accounting firms should not provide? If so, explain.
3. On what types of engagements must CPAs be "independent"? Identify types of engagements on which CPAs are not required to be independent. What other traits should CPAs possess on professional services engagements?

8. *Ibid.*

9. *The Guardian* (online), "Nike Acknowledges Massive Labor Exploitation in its Overseas Markets," 14 April 2005.

# INDEX

## A

## B



## C

## S

## X



## Y



## Z

# SUMMARY OF TOPICS BY CASE

The following index lists the auditing-related topics addressed directly or indirectly in each case included in **Auditing Cases, Eighth Edition**. Those topics followed by the letter "Q" are the subject of a case question.

## Enron Corporation, Case 1.1, 3–22

1. "Scope of services" issue facing audit firms (Q)
2. Involvement of auditors in client accounting and financial reporting decisions (Q)
3. Preparation and retention of audit workpapers (Q)
4. Recent "crisis of confidence" facing the public accounting profession (Q)
5. Recent recommendations to strengthen the independent audit function (Q)
6. Evolution of concept of "professionalism" in public accounting discipline over past several decades (Q)
7. Auditors' responsibilities regarding a client's quarterly financial statements (Q)
8. History of public accounting profession in the United States
9. Roles and responsibilities of key regulatory and rule-making bodies in the public accounting profession
10. Corporate culture as a key determinant of an audit client's control environment
11. Criminal liability faced by auditors and audit firms

## Just for FEET, Inc., Case 1.2, 23–36

1. Use of analytical procedures to identify high-risk financial statement items (Q)
2. Identifying internal control risk factors (Q)
3. Determining impact of control risk factors on audit planning decisions (Q)
4. Identifying inherent risk factors (Q)
5. Determining impact of inherent risk factors on audit planning decisions (Q)
6. Identifying the most critical audit risk factors for a given audit engagement (Q)
7. Resolution of ethical dilemma faced by a corporate executive (Q)
8. Importance of considering economic health of client's industry in audit planning decisions
9. Nature, purpose, and importance of accounts receivable confirmation procedures
10. Role of the SEC in policing financial reporting process and independent audit function
11. Importance of investigating unusual and/or suspicious client transactions

## AMRE, Inc., Case 1.3, 37–46

1. Responsibility of corporate executives to investigate potential misrepresentations in their company's accounting records (Q)
2. Measures needed to encourage "whistleblowing" by corporate employees (Q)
3. Encouraging and rewarding ethical behavior by corporate executives and employees (Q)
4. Problems posed by close relationships between client personnel and independent auditors (Q)
5. Contractual arrangements between auditors and clients (Q)
6. Accounting firms' litigation resolution strategies (Q)
7. Need for auditors to thoroughly investigate suspicious items uncovered during an audit

## ESM Government Securities Inc., Case 1.4, 47–58

1. Problems posed by close relationships between client personnel and independent auditors (Q)
2. Audit-related implications of a job offer made by a client to one of its independent auditors during the course of an audit (Q)
3. Performance of inventory rollback and roll forward procedures (Q)
4. Weighing the cost of an audit procedure against the quantity and quality of audit evidence it yields (Q)
5. Documenting audit test results in audit workpapers (Q)
6. Identifying "red flag" fraud risk factors and determining their impact on each phase of an audit (Q)
7. Auditors' responsibilities for discovering and reporting illegal acts by clients (Q)
8. Historical overview of class-action lawsuits and their impact on public accounting firms
9. Impact of PSLRA of 1995 on auditors' legal exposure under the Securities Exchange Act of 1934
10. Proportionate vs. joint and several liability for auditors

11. Resolution of proposed audit adjustments
12. Nature of GAAS and the responsibilities they impose on independent auditors
13. Definition of "recklessness" and its implications for auditors' legal exposure under the Securities Exchange Act of 1934

### United States Surgical Corporation, Case 1.5, 59–68

1. Use of analytical procedures to identify high-risk financial statement items (Q)
2. Financial information needed for audit planning decisions (Q)
3. Non-financial information needed for audit planning decisions (Q)
4. Control environment issues pertinent to independent audits (Q)
5. Impact on auditor independence of litigation that names client and audit firm as co-defendants (Q)
6. Audit implications of important changes and developing trends in a client's industry
7. Identifying "red flag" fraud risk factors and determining their impact on each phase of an audit

### The Fund of Funds, Ltd., Case 1.6, 69–82

1. Importance of industry knowledge for auditors (Q)
2. Identification of high-risk financial statement items (Q)
3. Impact on audit planning decisions of a client's cash-flow data (Q)
4. Identifying violations of financial statement assertions (Q)
5. Financial statement classification and disclosure issues for liabilities (Q)
6. Nature and purpose of audit review process (Q)
7. Resolution of disagreements between members of an audit engagement team (Q)
8. Wrap-up phase of an audit engagement
9. Withdrawal of an audit opinion
10. Career advancement issues facing auditors

### Crazy Eddie, Inc., Case 1.7, 83–92

1. Use of financial ratios and other financial measures to identify high-risk financial statement items (Q)
2. Audit procedures used to detect fraudulent misstatements of inventory, accounts payable, and sales (Q)
3. Effect of important changes in a client's industry on audit planning decisions (Q)
4. Potential impact of "lowballing" on the quality of audit services (Q)
5. Objective of year-end inventory cutoff tests (Q)
6. Implications for the independent audit function of audit clients hiring former auditors (Q)
7. Impact of collusion among client executives and employees on auditors' ability to detect fraudulent misrepresentations in a client's accounting records
8. Importance of assessing the integrity of client management
9. Incentive for companies to retain large audit firms when going public

### ZZZZ Best Company, Inc., Case 1.8, 93–106

1. Key differences between audit and review engagements (Q)
2. Identification of critical management assertions (Q)
3. Audit evidence needed to support management assertions (Q)
4. Identifying appropriate audit procedures to collect desired types of audit evidence (Q)
5. Limitations of audit evidence (Q)
6. Predecessor-successor auditor communications (Q)
7. Auditors' responsibility for a client's earnings press release (Q)
8. Client-imposed restrictions on the scope of an audit (Q)
9. Content of an audit engagement letter
10. Overview of SEC's 8-K auditor change disclosure rules

## Gemstar-TV Guide International, Inc., Case 1.9 107–118

1. Audit procedures applied to asset retirements (Q)
2. Accounting for changes in estimates and the related disclosure requirements (Q)
3. Effect of changes in estimates and improper accounting changes on an audit opinion (Q)
4. Use of analytical procedures to identify high-risk financial statement items (Q)
5. Imbalance of power in the auditor-client relationship and its impact on audits (Q)
6. Key characteristics of audit evidence (Q)
7. Evaluation of conflicting audit evidence (Q)
8. Auditors' responsibility for detection of illegal acts (Q)
9. Client confidentiality when auditing two clients that transact business with each other (Q)
10. Criteria for determining when a sale is consummated
11. Effect of a management bonus plan on the inherent risk posed by an audit client
12. Chronology of an auditor-client conflict

## New Century Financial Corporation, Case 10, 119–136

1. Concentration of audit clients in specific industries (Q)
2. Quality control considerations for independent audits (Q)
3. Section 404 of the Sarbanes-Oxley Act (Q)
4. Auditors' responsibility to discover and report significant deficiencies and material weaknesses in internal controls (Q)
5. Auditing accounting estimates (Q)
6. Violations of generally accepted auditing standards (Q)
7. Mark-to-market rule for securities investments (Q)
8. Auditor independence
9. Impact of auditor-client conflicts on audit engagements
10. Audit implications of accounting changes
11. Auditor reviews of quarterly financial statements

## Madoff Securities, Case 1.11, 137–146

1. Audit procedures applied to client investments (Q)
2. Nature and purpose of peer reviews (Q)
3. Fraud triangle (Q)
4. Common fraud risk factors (Q)
5. Regulatory reforms necessary to improve auditors' fraud detection capabilities (Q)
6. Impairment of auditor independence
7. Criminal liability faced by auditors
8. Civil liability faced by auditors
9. Societal role of independent audit function
10. SEC's regulatory mandate

## Doughtie's Foods, Inc., Case 2.1, 149–152

1. Audit risk factors commonly posed by family-owned businesses (Q)
2. Key audit objectives for inventory (Q)
3. Quality of audit evidence yielded by internal versus external documents (Q)
4. Nature and purpose of a walk-through audit procedure (Q)
5. Auditors' responsibility to inform client management of significant internal control weaknesses (Q)
6. Whether or not auditors have a responsibility to insist that client management correct significant internal control deficiencies (Q)
7. Segregation of duties concept and its impact on a client's internal controls
8. Need for auditors to thoroughly investigate suspicious transactions and circumstances

## Golden Bear Golf, Inc., Case 2.2, 153–160

1. Identifying relevant management assertions for individual financial statement items (Q)
2. Choosing appropriate audit procedures to corroborate specific management assertions (Q)
3. Meaning of the phrase "audit failure" (Q)
4. Auditors' responsibilities on "high-risk" audit engagements (Q)
5. Nature and purpose of AICPA industry accounting and audit guides (Q)
6. Changes in accounting estimates versus changes in accounting principles (Q)
7. Proper application of the percentage-of-completion accounting method
8. Need for auditors to thoroughly investigate suspicious transactions and circumstances
9. Limitations of management representations as audit evidence

## Happiness Express, Inc., Case 2.3, 161–168

1. Audit objectives associated with receivables confirmation procedures and year-end sales cutoff tests (Q)
2. Selection of receivables for confirmation purposes (Q)
3. Alternative audit procedures for receivables selected for confirmation (Q)
4. Distinguishing between, and among, auditor negligence, recklessness, and fraud (Q)
5. Auditor responsibility to investigate the possibility of illegal acts perpetrated by client executives (Q)
6. Need for auditors to identify and consider impact of industry risk factors on a client's financial health
7. Need for auditors to document key changes in clients' business practices
8. Need for auditors to thoroughly investigate large and unusual year-end transactions

## SmarTalk Teleservices, Inc., Case 2.4, 169–174

1. Key management assertions related to cash (Q)
2. Audit procedures applied to cash maintained on a client's premises (Q)
3. Supervision of staff accountants assigned to an audit engagement
4. Internal auditor involvement in independent audits
5. Need to follow up on suspicious client transactions and implausible client representations

## Dollar General Stores, Inc., Case 2.5, 175–178

1. Audit objectives related to a restructuring reserve (Q)
2. Appropriate evidence to collect when auditing a restructuring reserve (Q)
3. Determining what pronouncements and other items are included in generally accepted accounting principles (Q)
4. Auditors' responsibility to preserve integrity of audit workpapers (Q)
5. Audit implications of earnings management by client executives

## CBI Holding Company, Inc., Case 2.6, 179–184

1. Key audit objectives for accounts payable (Q)
2. Proper application of the search for unrecorded liabilities and reconciliation of year-end payables balances to vendor statements (Q)
3. Differences and similarities in accounts payable and accounts receivable confirmation procedures (Q)
4. Responsibility of auditors when they identify mistakes or other oversights they made in prior year audits (Q)
5. Client requests to remove specific auditors from audit engagement team (Q)
6. Considerations relevant to the acceptance of "high-risk" audit clients
7. Need to identify critical audit risk factors and consider those factors in planning an audit engagement
8. Need to thoroughly investigate suspicious transactions and circumstances identified during an audit

## Flight Transportation Corporation, Case 2.7, 185–190

1. Methods that corporate executives can use to "manage" earnings (Q)
2. Ethical issues posed by earnings management by corporate executives (Q)
3. Audit implications of earnings management by client executives (Q)
4. Proper classification of key items in financial statements (Q)
5. Audit procedures appropriate to uncover potential violations of the revenue recognition rule (Q)
6. Distinguishing between auditor negligence and auditor recklessness (Q)
7. Impact of the Private Securities Litigation Reform Act on auditor-related litigation (Q)
8. Need for auditors to consider recent developments in a client's industry when planning an audit

## CapitalBanc Corporation, Case 2.8, 191–194

1. Assessing the materiality of financial statement errors (Q)
2. Audit procedures that may detect inventory overstatements (Q)
3. Factors affecting quality of audit evidence (Q)
4. Ethical responsibilities of accountants when being pressured to misrepresent their employer's financial data (Q)

## The Trolley Dodgers, Case 3.1, 197–198

1. Tests of controls and substantive tests for the payroll transaction cycle (Q)
2. Identifying internal control weaknesses in the payroll transaction cycle (Q)
3. Audit procedures useful in detecting payroll fraud (Q)
4. Control environment issues

## Howard Street Jewelers, Inc., Case 3.2, 199–200

1. Importance of internal controls for small retail businesses (Q)
2. Responsibility of a small business's CPA when alerted to potential control problems facing the client (Q)
3. Measures CPAs can take to acquire clients (Q)
4. Control environment issues

## United Way of America, Case 3.3, 201–206

1. Cost-effectiveness issues for internal controls (Q)
2. Scope of internal controls (Q)
3. Control objectives and related control activities in a retail environment (Q)
4. Audit implications of client control policies and procedures (Q)

## Triton Energy Ltd., Case 3.4, 207–216

1. Factors that complicate audits of multinational companies (Q)
2. Control activities intended to prevent violations of the Foreign Corrupt Practices Act (Q)
3. Effectiveness of control activities (Q)
4. Auditors' responsibility to detect violations of the Foreign Corrupt Practices Act (Q)
5. Impact on audit risk components of a client's high-risk business strategies (Q)
6. Accountants' responsibility when they discover illegal acts perpetrated by their employer (Q)
7. Auditors' responsibility when they discover illegal acts perpetrated by a client (Q)
8. Cultural differences in business practices and ethical issues posed by such differences for auditors and accountants (Q)
9. Regulatory policies and procedures of the Securities and Exchange Commission (Q)

### oodner Brothers, Inc., Case 3.5, 217–224

1. Identifying internal control objectives for a wholesale business (Q)
2. Identifying and remedying internal control weaknesses (Q)
3. Importance of an effective control environment for a business (Q)
4. Impact of management style and operating policies on an entity's internal controls
5. Role of internal auditors in an entity's internal control process
6. Need for auditors and client management to investigate suspicious transactions

### Saks Fifth Avenue, Case 3.6, 225–228

1. Scope of an entity's internal control process (Q)
2. Identifying control objectives and control activities for a retail business (Q)
3. Need to segregate key functional responsibilities within a small business (Q)
4. Compensating controls for a small business (Q)
5. Ethical responsibilities of management when subordinates are suspected of engaging in theft or other illicit activities (Q)
6. Impact of laws and other regulations on a business's internal control process (Q)
7. Control environment issues

### Creve Couer Pizza, Inc., Case 4.1, 231–234

1. CPAs serving as the moral conscience of small business clients (Q)
2. Conflict between auditors' responsibility to the public interest and the obligations imposed on them by the client confidentiality rule (Q)
3. Resolution of ethical dilemmas by auditors (Q)
4. Privileged communications between auditors and clients (Q)

### F&C International, Inc., Case 4.2, 235–238

1. Professional responsibilities of a business's financial executives and high-ranking accountants (Q)
2. Nature of the interaction between client management and independent auditors (Q)
3. Ethical responsibilities of management when they suspect subordinates are engaging in theft or other illicit activities (Q)
4. Need for an entity's executives and financial managers to thoroughly investigate suspicious transactions and events coming to their attention (Q)
5. Common methods used to misrepresent an entity's reported profits
6. SEC's oversight role for the accounting and financial reporting domain

### Suzette Washington, Accounting Major, Case 4.3, 239–240

1. Resolution of ethical dilemma faced by an accounting student (Q)
2. Ethical responsibilities of private accountants (Q)
3. Responsibility of accountants to report unethical conduct by their colleagues (Q)
4. Internal controls for a retail merchandiser (Q)

### Thomas Forehand, CPA, Case 4.4, 241–246

1. Intentional understatements of earnings by audit clients (Q)
2. Audit procedures intended to uncover revenue understatements and expense overstatements (Q)
3. Ethical responsibilities of accountants when being pressured to misrepresent their employer's financial data (Q)
4. Corporate accountants' responsibilities when interacting with independent auditors (Q)
5. Ethical responsibilities of non-CPAs (accountants) vs.CPAs (Q)
6. SEC's view regarding the responsibilities of corporate accountants who are aware of fraudulent misrepresentations in their employer's financial statements
7. Letter of representations as a form of audit evidence

## Oak Industries, Inc., Case 4.5, 247–252

1. Resolution of ethical dilemma by an accounting student (Q)
2. Proper disciplining of accountants who engage in unethical behavior (Q)
3. Responsibility of accountants to report unethical conduct by their colleagues (Q)

## Laurel Valley Estates, Case 4.6, 253–256

1. Resolution of an ethical dilemma by an accounting student (Q)
2. Ethical issues accounting majors may face when they have multiple job offers outstanding (Q)
3. Internship opportunities available to accounting majors

## Rocky Mount Undergarment Company, Inc., Case 4.7, 257–260

1. Nature and purpose of the client confidentiality rule (Q)
2. Identifying violations of the client confidentiality rule (Q)
3. Resolution of disputes with fellow professionals regarding ethical issues (Q)
4. Responsibility of accountants to report unethical conduct by their colleagues (Q)

## Cardillo Travel Systems, Inc., Case 5.1, 263–268

1. Ethical dilemmas that accountants and auditors must resolve (Q)
2. Parties affected by the resolution of ethical dilemmas facing accountants and auditors (Q)
3. Auditors' responsibilities when reviewing a client's interim financial statements (Q)
4. Importance of communication among members of an audit engagement team (Q)
5. Key characteristics of audit evidence (Q)
6. Evaluation of conflicting audit evidence by an auditor (Q)
7. SEC's 8-K auditor change disclosure rules (Q)
8. Importance of auditors' assessing the integrity of client management (Q)
9. Methods for assessing integrity of client management (Q)
10. Audit implications of significant auditor-client disputes

## American International Group, Inc., Case 5.2, 269–272

1. Auditor independence as the cornerstone of the auditing profession (Q)
2. Audit-related implications of an auditor discussing potential employment opportunities with an audit client during an ongoing audit (Q)
3. Ethical responsibilities of auditors who discuss and/or receive an employment offer from an audit client (Q)
4. SEC's oversight role for financial reporting and auditing domains

## The PTL Club, Case 5.3, 273–276

1. Proper treatment of proposed audit adjustments that have an immaterial effect on a client's financial statements (Q)
2. Preventing client from gaining access to materiality thresholds for an audit (Q)
3. Identifying violations of the revenue recognition principle (Q)
4. Principal objectives of audit workpapers (Q)
5. Whether competence of client management should affect planning and performance of independent audits (Q)
6. Role of a concurring audit partner on an SEC engagement

### Zaveral Boosalis Raisch, Case 5.4, 277–280

1. Auditors' consideration of a client's business model (Q)
2. Identifying fraud risk factors posed by a client (Q)
3. Objectives of audit workpapers (Q)
4. Identifying violations of generally accepted auditing standards (Q)
5. Responsibility of audit partners to serve as mentors for their subordinates (Q)
6. Ethical responsibilities of an auditor who is instructed to violate professional standards by his or her superior (Q)

### Koger Properties, Inc., Case 5.5, 281–284

1. Financial independence rules for auditors (Q)
2. Material vs. immaterial financial interests in audit clients (Q)
3. Rationale for financial independence rules (Q)
4. Audit practice implications of mergers between large accounting firms

### Ryden Trucking, Inc., Case 5.6, 285–288

1. Auditors' responsibilities regarding the "subsequent discovery of facts existing at audit report date" (Q)
2. Client confidentiality rule (Q)
3. Resolution of ethical dilemmas by the members of an audit engagement team (Q)
4. Disagreements between members of an audit engagement team

### Leigh Ann Walker, Staff Accountant, Case 6.1, 291–292

1. Need for auditors to possess personal integrity (Q)
2. Dealing with a lack of personal integrity on the part of staff accountants (Q)
3. Nature of staff accountant's work role and responsibilities

### Bill DeBurger, In-Charge Accountant, Case 6.2, 293–296

1. Nature of in-charge accountant's work role and responsibilities (Q)
2. Assimilation of audit evidence to reach an overall audit conclusion (Q)
3. Resolution of conflict between members of an audit engagement team (Q)
4. Performance of major audit assignments by relatively inexperienced auditors (Q)

### David Myers, WorldCom Controller, Case 6.3, 297–302

1. Ethical responsibilities of an accountant who is instructed to make false entries in his or her company's accounting records by a superior (Q)
2. Proper punishment of corporate accountants who intentionally misrepresent their employer's financial health (Q)
3. Role of regulatory authorities in policing the accounting and financial reporting domain (Q)
4. Nature of a corporate controller's work role and responsibilities
5. Impact of involvement in an accounting and financial reporting fraud on an individual's professional and personal life

### Tommy O'Connell, Audit Senior, Case 6.4, 303–306

1. Key differences between the professional roles of audit seniors and staff accountants (Q)
2. Implications for independent audits of interpersonal conflicts between members of an audit engagement team (Q)
3. Auditor's responsibility when he or she suspects that a colleague is not completing assigned audit procedures (Q)
4. Audit partner's responsibility when a subordinate reports that a member of the audit engagement team is not completing assigned audit procedures (Q)
5. Need for public accountants to achieve a proper balance between their personal and professional lives
6. Impact of a lack of client cooperation on the performance of an audit

## Avis Love, Staff Accountant, Case 6.5, 307–310

1. Parties potentially affected by ethical dilemmas facing auditors (Q)
2. Auditors' ethical obligations to third-party financial statement users (Q)
3. Auditors' responsibility to document and investigate errors revealed by audit procedures (Q)
4. Potential audit impact of personal relationships between auditors and client personnel (Q)
5. Audit objectives of year-end cash receipts and sales cutoff tests (Q)
6. Assessing materiality of financial statement errors (Q)

## Charles Tollison, Audit Manager, Case 6.6, 311–314

1. Requisite skills for promotion to partner in a major accounting firm (Q)
2. Partner promotion criteria in large vs. small accounting firms (Q)
3. "Up or out" promotion policy of many accounting firms (Q)
4. Need for public accountants to achieve a proper balance between their personal and professional lives
5. Need for a public accountant to actively plan and manage his or her professional career

## Hamilton Wong, In-Charge Accountant, Case 6.7, 315–318

1. Ethical issues related to the underreporting of time worked by auditors (Q)
2. Effect of underreporting time worked on quality of independent audits (Q)
3. Measures needed to mitigate the underreporting of time worked (Q)
4. Potentially dysfunctional effects of competitive promotion system within accounting firms on quality of independent audits (Q)
5. Nature of in-charge accountant's work role and responsibilities

## Ligand Pharmaceuticals, Case 7.1, 321–326

1. Nature and purpose of SEC sanctions imposed on accounting firms (Q)
2. Types of non-traditional services that accounting firms should be allowed to provide (Q)
3. Fee arrangements between accounting firms and their clients (Q)
4. Provision of services by accounting firms on a contingent fee basis

## HealthSouth Corporation, Case 7.2, 327–332

1. Purpose of professional codes of ethics (Q)
2. Dynamic nature of professional codes of ethics (Q)
3. Role of state boards of accountancy in regulating public accounting profession (Q)
4. Circumstances under which CPAs can accept commissions (Q)
5. Regulatory infrastructure of the public accounting profession (Q)

## Baan Company, N.V., Case 7.3, 333–340

1. Impact of existing ethical rules on CPAs' "commercial speech" (Q)
2. Economic barriers of entry created by a profession's code of ethics (Q)
3. Impact on independent audit function of competitive bidding for audit engagements (Q)
4. Impact of "lowballing" on independent audit function (Q)
5. Advantages and disadvantages of professions being regulated at the state rather than federal level (Q)
6. Impact of "creeping commercialization" on public accounting profession (Q)
7. Practice development activities used by CPAs
8. Regulatory infrastructure of the public accounting profession

## *Hopkins v. Price Waterhouse*, Case 7.4, 341–348

1. Responsibility of public accounting firms to facilitate the career success of their female employees (Q)
2. Informal employee networks within public accounting firms and related personnel and professional implications (Q)

3. Nepotism rules of public accounting firms (Q)
4. Acceptance of female and minority public accountants by clients (Q)
5. Governmental regulation of private partnerships (Q)
6. Partnership promotion process of large public accounting firms
7. Requisite skills for promotion to partner in a major public accounting firm

## Stock Option Mania, Case 7.5, 349–358

1. Interpersonal conflict between an employee and partner of a CPA firm (Q)
2. Responsibility of public accountants to respect personal rights of colleagues (Q)
3. Office managing partner's responsibility to protect the personal rights of each office member (Q)
4. Nature of staff accountant's work role and responsibilities

## National Medical Transportation Network, Case 7.6, 359–364

1. Client management effort to influence staffing of audit engagement team (Q)
2. Racial discrimination within the auditing discipline (Q)
3. Responsibility of senior members of an audit practice office and/or audit engagement team to protect the civil rights of their subordinates (Q)
4. Resolution of an ethical dilemma by an audit partner (Q)
5. Issues relevant to staffing of audit engagement teams

## Livent, Inc., Case 8.1, 367–380

1. Identification of inherent risk factors (Q)
2. Role and responsibilities of audit partners (Q)
3. Client attitudes toward auditors (Q)
4. Reports prepared by accounting firms on the application of accounting principles by non-audit clients (Q)
5. Revenue recognition issues (Q)
6. Responsibilities of corporate accounting personnel to investigate potential misrepresentations in their employer's accounting records (Q)
7. Potential conflict-of-interests faced by auditors who accept accounting positions with former clients (Q)
8. Accounting firms' responsibilities in due diligence investigations (Q)
9. Forensic investigations by accounting firms
10. Identifying "red flags" indicative of financial statement fraud
11. Audit firms' legal exposure under the Securities Exchange Act of 1934

## Royal Ahold, N.V., Case 8.2, 381–396

1. Impact on a multinational corporation's reported net income when applying accounting principles other than U.S. GAAP (Q)
2. U.S. GAAP vs. IFRS: impact on earnings quality (Q)
3. Accounting for promotional allowances (Q)
4. Factors that complicate audits of multinational corporations (Q)
5. Components of the fraud triangle (Q)
6. Identification of fraud risk factors (Q)
7. Audit procedures effective in uncovering fraudulent accounting (Q)
8. Nature of audit planning across different types of business operations (Q)
9. Accounting for intercorporate investments
10. Conflict between and among the accounting profession's international regulatory bodies
11. Need for major international accounting firms to enhance quality and consistency of their independent audits across the globe

## *Kansayaku*, Case 8.3, 397–406

1. Impact of macroeconomic variables on a nation's independent audit function (Q)
2. Impact of differing barriers to entry on the accounting professions of individual nations (Q)
3. Advantages and disadvantages of an oligopolistic market structure for independent audit services (Q)
4. Measures necessary to promote and protect auditor independence (Q)
5. Impact of cultural norms and nuances on the performance of independent audits and the overall nature of a nation's independent audit function
6. Common challenges and problems faced by independent auditors around the globe
7. Nature and structure of regulatory oversight for the accounting profession and auditing discipline across different nations
8. Criminal and civil liability of audit firms and auditors

## Registered Auditors, South Africa, Case 8.4, 407–418

1. Impact of political forces on the development of a nation's independent audit function (Q)
2. Advantages and disadvantages of a separate professional credential for independent auditors (Q)
3. Nature and purpose of South Africa's "reportable irregularities" rule (Q)
4. Impact of South Africa's reportable irregularities rule on that nation's independent audit function (Q)
5. Measures necessary to persuade individuals from underrepresented groups to pursue careers in the accounting profession (Q)
6. Impact of recurring audit failures on the international reputation and credibility of a nation's capital markets
7. Nature and structure of regulatory oversight for the accounting profession and auditing discipline across different nations
8. Criminal and civil liability of accounting firms and individual auditors

## *Zuan Yan*, Case 8.5, 419–430

1. Impact of differing cultural norms across the globe on the ability of the worldwide accounting profession to reach a consensus on important ethical principles (Q)
2. Impact of differing economic systems on the nature of financial reporting objectives (Q)
3. Relevance of fundamental accounting concepts and principles within differing economic systems across the globe (Q)
4. Impact of differing economic systems across the globe on the nature and purpose of independent audits (Q)
5. Challenges and problems faced by accounting firms when performing audits in countries with authoritarian central governments (Q)
6. Impact of political forces on the development and evolution of a nation's accounting profession and independent audit function
7. Unique challenges and problems faced by the accounting profession of the People's Republic of China
8. Nature and structure of regulatory oversight for the accounting profession and auditing discipline across different nations
9. Civil liability of accounting firms

## Kaset Thai Sugar Company, Case 8.6, 431–434

1. Problems faced by accountants when performing independent audits and other professional services in hostile countries (Q)
2. Responsibility of accounting firms to provide for the safety of their employees (Q)
3. Impact of a given nation's cultural norms and nuances on the performance of professional services engagements

## Australian Wheat Board, Case 8.7, 435–444

1. Relevance of Foreign Corrupt Practices Act to foreign companies that sell securities on U.S. stock exchanges (Q)
2. Responsibility of auditors to detect client bribes and related payments to obtain and retain international business relationships (Q)

3. Audit procedures designed to detect bribes and other fraudulent payments (Q)
4. Bribes vs. "facilitating payments" (Q)
5. "Social responsibility" mandate of corporate boards (Q)
6. Australian Auditing Standards vs. International Standards of Auditing (Q)
7. Professional and business risks posed for accounting firms by high-profile clients

## OAO Gazprom, Case 8.8, 445–458

1. Challenges that accounting firms face when they establish practice offices in foreign countries (Q)
2. Impact of cultural differences on business practices and ethical norms (Q)
3. Responsibilities of auditors to client stockholders (Q)
4. Threats to auditor independence (Q)
5. Auditors' responsibility to identify related parties and related-party transactions (Q)
6. British "true and fair" audit philosophy vs. the U.S. philosophy of "fairly presented" (Q)
7. Philosophical differences between IASB and FASB and resulting impact on standards promulgated by those two organizations (Q)
8. Impact of social and governmental influences on the development of accounting and auditing practices
9. Legal exposure faced by accounting firms in foreign countries
10. Professional and business risks faced by accounting firms that audit high-profile clients

## Tata Finance Limited, Case 8.9, 459–466

1. Impact on the design and performance of an independent audit when the client has a unique corporate culture and/or ethical code (Q)
2. Professional standards relevant to consulting engagements (Q)
3. Similarities and differences between auditing standards and standards for consulting engagements (Q)
4. Responsibilities imposed on professional accountants by the client confidentiality mandate (Q)
5. Auditor independence issues

## Institute of Chartered Accountants of India, Case 8.10, 467–478

1. Comparative advantages and disadvantages of a centralized vs. a decentralized regulatory infrastructure for a nation's public accounting profession (Q)
2. Philosophical differences regarding the purpose of the independent audit function that impact the nature of that function across different cultures (Q)
3. Strategic initiatives used by major international accounting firms to enter new markets (Q)
4. Ethical issues that the major international accounting firms have faced when entering new markets (Q)
5. Ethical and competitive issues posed by allowing accounting firms to advertise (Q)
6. Using economic policies to shield a nation's domestic accounting firms from foreign competition (Q)
7. Nature and purpose of reciprocity agreements between national regulatory organizations within the global accounting profession (Q)
8. Ethical, competitive, and regulatory issues posed by the outsourcing of professional accounting services (Q)
9. Impact of political and social forces on the development and evolution of a nation's accounting profession and independent audit function
10. International criticism of operating philosophy, policies, and procedures of major international accounting firms
11. Conflict between and among the accounting profession's international regulatory bodies

## *Societe Generale*, Case 8.11, 479–494

1. Timing of loss recognition for income statement purposes (Q)
2. Departures from GAAP necessary to prevent financial statements from being misleading (Q)
3. Similarities and differences between French and U.S. audit reports (Q)
4. Similarities and differences between internal control objectives in France and United States (Q)
5. Nature and purpose of "joint audits" (Q)

6. Audit risk factors common to bank clients (Q)
7. History of the independent audit function in France
8. Internal control reporting in France
9. Big Four firms' involvement in the French audit market
10. Key differences between IFRS and U.S. GAAP

### *Shari'a*, Case 8.12, 495–504

1. Financial statement audits vs. *Shari'a* compliance audits (Q)
2. Application of compliance audit procedures (Q)
3. Merging of financial statement and *Shari'a* compliance audits (Q)
4. Socially responsible accounting standards (Q)
5. Competitive conditions faced by Big Four firms in Islamic economy (Q)
6. Lack of uniformity in *Shari'a* audit practices
7. Promulgation of professional standards in Islamic economy
8. Financial statement audit report in Islamic economy vs. *Shari'a* compliance audit report

### Republic of the Sudan, Case 8.13, 505–510

1. Regulatory mandate of the SEC (Q)
2. Definition of "material information" for financial reporting purposes (Q)
3. Materiality standard applied by the SEC (Q)
4. Differences in materiality concept in accounting context vs. auditing context (Q)
5. SEC's concept of "full and fair disclosure"

### Mohamed Salem El-Hadad, Internal Auditor, Case 8.14, 511–516

1. Legal protections afforded whistleblowers in the United States (Q)
2. Integration of whistleblowing measures into internal control systems (Q)
3. Measures that whistleblowers can use to protect themselves from recriminations (Q)
4. Responsibility to report fraud (by organizational insiders) (Q)
5. Ethical dilemmas vs. moral dilemmas (Q)

### *Tae Kwang Vina*, Case 8.15, 517–522

1. Differences between and among: consulting services, assurance services, attestation services and agreed-upon procedures engagements (Q)
2. Nontraditional accounting services offered by major accounting firms (Q)
3. Services requiring CPAs to be independent (Q)
4. Required qualifications of CPAs on various professional service engagements (Q)
5. Commercialism within public accounting profession
6. Provision of environmental and labor practices audits by major accounting firms

# SUMMARY OF CASES BY TOPIC

## A

**Advertising by Accounting Firms:** Baan, ICAI.
**Analytical Procedures:** Crazy Eddie, Just for Feet, Royal Ahold, United States Surgical Corporation.
**Assessment of Client Management Competence:** Crazy Eddie, PTL Club, ZZZZ Best.
**Assurance Services:** Tae Kwang Vina.
**Audit Evidence—General:** Cardillo, Doughtie's Foods, ESM Government Securities, Golden Bear, Happiness Express, New Century.
**Audit Evidence—Limitations:** Bill DeBurger, CapitalBanc, CBI Holding, ESM Government Securities, Gemstar, Golden Bear, Ligand, Royal Ahold, ZZZZ Best.
**Audit Failures:** Gemstar, Golden Bear.
**Audit Implications of Control Deficiencies:** Crazy Eddie, Doughtie's Foods, ESM Government Securities, Goodner, New Century, United States Surgical Corporation, United Way.
**Audit Planning Issues:** Crazy Eddie, Just for Feet, New Century, Royal Ahold, United States Surgical Corporation, ZZZZ Best.
**Audit Review Process:** PTL Club, Tommy O'Connell.
**Audit Risk (and/or its components):** Livent, Triton.
**Audit Staffing Issues:** New Century.
**Audit Time Budgets/Audit Deadlines:** Charles Tollison, Hamilton Wong, Tommy O'Connell.
**Audit Workpapers:** Enron, ESM Government Securities, Fund of Funds, New Century, PTL Club, United States Surgical Corporation.
**Auditing a Multinational Company:** AWB, Gazprom, Livent, Royal Ahold, Societe Generale, Triton, Zuan Yan.
**Auditing Accounting Estimates:** ESM Government Securities, Just for Feet, Ligand, New Century.
**Auditing Accounts Payable (and other liabilities):** CBI, Crazy Eddie.
**Auditing Cash:** Avis Love, SmarTalk.
**Auditing Contingencies:** Cardillo.
**Auditing Contracts and Commitments:** Cardillo, Enron, Golden Bear, ZZZZ Best.
**Auditing Intercorporate Investments:** Madoff, Royal Ahold.
**Auditing Inventory:** CapitalBanc, Crazy Eddie, Doughtie's Foods, ESM Government Securities, F&C, Goodner, Just for Feet, United States Surgical Corporation.
**Auditing PP&E:** Dollar General.
**Auditing Receivables:** ESM Government Securities, Fund of Funds, Happiness Express, Just for Feet.
**Auditing Revenues:** Avis Love, Crazy Eddie, Flight Transportation, Gemstar, Golden Bear, Ligand, Livent, PTL Club.
**Auditor Independence:** AIG, AMRE, Avis Love, Crazy Eddie, Enron, ESM Government Securities, Gazprom, ICAI, Kansayaku, Koger, Madoff, New Century, Societe Generale, South Africa, Tae Kwang Vina, Tata Finance, United States Surgical Corporation, Zuan Yan.
**Auditor-Client Interaction Issues:** AIG, AMRE, Avis Love, Cardillo, CBI, Enron, ESM Government Securities, F&C, Doughtie's Foods, Howard Street, Kansayaku, Kaset Thai, Livent, National Medical, New Century, PTL Club, SmarTalk, South Africa, Tommy O'Connell, Zuan Yan.

## B

**Big Four Accounting Firms and International Practice Development Issues:** Gazprom, ICAI, Kansayaku, Kaset Thai, Shari'a, Societe Generale, South Africa, Tae Kwang Vina, Zuan Yan.

## C

**Career Development Issues:** Bill DeBurger, Charles Tollison, Fund of Funds, Hamilton Wong, Hopkins, Laurel Valley, Leigh Ann Walker, Livent, National Medical, Rocky Mount, Stock Option Mania, Thomas Forehand, Tommy O'Connell, Oak, Zaveral.
**Client Acceptance/Retention Issues:** CBI, Doughtie's Foods, Gazprom, Kansayaku, Kaset Thai, National Medical, Tata Finance, Thomas Forehand, Zuan Yan.
**Client Confidentiality:** Creve Couer, ICAI, South Africa, Rocky Mount, Ryden Trucking, Zaveral.
**Client Development Activities:** Baan, Charles Tollison, Hopkins, United Way.
**Client Management Integrity Issues:** AMRE, AWB, Cardillo, CBI, Crazy Eddie, David Myers, Doughtie's Foods, Enron, ESM Government Securities, Flight Transportation, Fund of Funds, F&C, Gazprom, Gemstar,

Golden Bear, Happiness Express, Kansayaku, Kaset Thai, Livent, Madoff, New Century, National Medical, SmarTalk, PTL Club, Royal Ahold, South Africa, Tata Finance, Tommy O'Connell, Triton, United States Surgical Corporation, Zuan Yan, ZZZZ Best.

**Client-imposed Audit Scope Limitations:** Doughtie's Foods, ESM Government Securities, ZZZZ Best.

**Collegial Responsibilities of Auditors:** Bill DeBurger, Charles Tollison, Fund of Funds, Gazprom, Hamilton Wong, ICAI, Leigh Ann Walker, National Medical, PTL Club, Rocky Mount, Societe Generale, Stock Option Mania, Tommy O'Connell, Zaveral, ZZZZ Best.

**Comfort Letter/Due Diligence Engagements:** Livent.

**Commercialism within Public Accounting Profession:** AIG, Baan, Enron, Gazprom, HealthSouth, ICAI, Kansayaku, Shari'a, Societe Generale, Tae Kwang Vina, Zuan Yan.

**Competition in U.S. Public Accounting Profession:** Baan.

**Compilation Engagements:** Howard Street.

**Compliance Audits:** Shari'a, Tae Kwang Vina.

**Confirmation Procedures:** CBI, Happiness Express, Just for Feet, Royal Ahold.

**Conflict in Auditor and Consultant Roles:** AIG, Enron, Gazprom, ICAI.

**Control Environment:** AMRE, AWB, Cardillo, CBI, Crazy Eddie, Dollar General, Doughtie's Foods, Enron, ESM Government Securities, Flight Transportation, F&C, Gazprom, Golden Bear, Goodner, Happiness Express, Howard Street, Kansayaku, Livent, New Century, PTL Club, Royal Ahold, SmarTalk, South Africa, Tata Finance, Triton, Trolley Dodgers, United States Surgical Corporation, United Way, Zuan Yan, ZZZZ Best.

**Convergence of International Accounting and/or Auditing Standards:** AWB, Gazprom, ICAI, Kansayaku, Royal Ahold, Shari'a, Societe Generale, South Africa, Zuan Yan.

**CPAs in Non-audit Roles**: AIG, AMRE, AWB, Creve Couer, ESM Government Securities, Gazprom, Howard Street, ICAI, Kaset Thai, Livent, Tae Kwang Vina, Tata Finance, Thomas Forehand.

## D

**Departures from GAAP (necessary):** Societe Generale.

**Detection, Disclosure, and Audit Implications of Illegal Acts:** AWB, Enron, ESM Government Securities, Gazprom, Happiness Express, South Africa, Tata Finance, Triton.

**Disagreements between Auditors:** Bill DeBurger, Gazprom, National Medical, Ryden Trucking.

## E

**Earnings Management:** AIG, Dollar General, Flight Transportation, Societe Generale.

**Engagement Letter:** AMRE, ZZZZ Best.

**Engagement Risk:** Ligand.

**Ethical Conduct vs. Legal Conduct:** Gemstar.

**Ethical Dilemma (definition of):** Mohamed Salem El-Hadad.

**Ethical Dilemmas vs. Moral Dilemmas:** Mohamed Salem El-Hadad.

**Ethical Dilemmas, Resolution of:** AMRE, Avis Love, Bill DeBurger, Cardillo, Creve Couer, David Myers, ESM Government Securities, Gazprom, Hamilton Wong, ICAI, Just for Feet, Kansayaku, Laurel Valley, Leigh Ann Walker, Livent, Mohamed Salem El-Hadad, National Medical, Oak, Rocky Mount, Ryden Trucking, Societe Generale, South Africa, Suzette Washington, Thomas Forehand, Tommy O'Connell, Triton, Zaveral.

**Ethical Issues Faced by U.S. Accounting Firms in International Markets:** AWB, Gazprom, ICAI, Kansayaku, Kaset Thai, Shari'a, South Africa, Tae Kwang Vina, Triton, Zuan Yan.

**Ethical Issues Involving Accounting Majors:** Laurel Valley, Oak, Suzette Washington.

**Ethical Responsibilities of Accountants in Private Industry:** AMRE, CapitalBanc, Cardillo, David Myers, Doughtie's Foods, Dollar General, Enron, ESM Government Securities, F&C, Golden Bear, Livent, New Century, Suzette Washington, Tata Finance, Triton, Trolley Dodgers, United States Surgical Corporation Zaveral.

**Expanding Product Line of Accounting Firms:** AIG, AWB, Enron, HealthSouth, ICAI, Kaset Thai, Shari'a, Tae Kwang Vina.

## F

**Foreign Corrupt Practices Act:** AWB, Triton.

**Fraud Detection and/or Disclosure:** AMRE, AWB, Cardillo, CBI, Crazy Eddie, Dollar General, Doughtie's Foods, Enron, ESM Government Securities, Fund of Funds, Gazprom, Gemstar, Golden Bear, Happiness Express, Kansayaku, Livent, Madoff, New Century, PTL Club, Royal Ahold, SmarTalk, South Africa, Tata Finance, Triton, United States Surgical Corporation, United Way, ZZZZ Best.

**Fraud Reporting Responsibility (by members of an organization):** AWB, Cardillo, F&C, Livent, Mohamed Salem El-Hadad, Triton Energy.
**"Full and Fair Disclosure" Doctrine (SEC):** Sudan.

## H

**Hiring of Auditors by Former Clients:** AMRE, Crazy Eddie, ESM Government Securities, Livent.
**History of Accounting Profession/Audit Function in Nations Other Than U.S.:** Gazprom, ICAI, Kansayaku, Shari'a, Societe Generale, South Africa, Zuan Yan.
**History of U.S. Public Accounting Profession:** Enron.

## I

**Identification of Inherent Risk Factors:** Crazy Eddie, Doughtie's Foods, Just for Feet, Livent, Royal Ahold, Societe Generale, United States Surgical Corporation.
**Identification of Internal Control Objectives:** Doughtie's Foods, Goodner, Howard Street, Trolley Dodgers.
**Identification of Internal Control Risk Factors:** Just for Feet, Societe Generale.
**Identification of Management Assertions:** Golden Bear, SmarTalk, ZZZZ Best.
**IFRS vs. U.S. GAAP:** Royal Ahold, Societe Generale.
**Impact of Cultural Norms and Values on Independent Audit Function:** Gazprom, ICAI, Kansayaku, Shari'a, Societe Generale, South Africa, Zuan Yan.
**Internal Auditors:** AMRE, Goodner, Mohamed Salem El-Hadad, SmarTalk, Triton.
**Internal Control Deficiencies:** Doughtie's Foods, ESM Government Securities, Goodner, Howard Street, New Century, Saks, Triton, Trolley Dodgers, United States Surgical Corporation, United Way.
**Internal Control Objectives:** Goodner, Howard Street, Mohamed Salem El-Hadad, Saks, Societe Generale, Triton, Trolley Dodgers, United Way.
**Internal Control Reporting:** Doughtie's Foods, New Century, Societe Generale.
**Internal Controls for Not-for-Profits:** Mohamed Salem El-Hadad, United Way.
**Internal Controls for Small Businesses:** Howard Street, Saks, Suzette Washington.
**International Accounting Issues:** Gazprom, Royal Ahold, Shari'a, Societe Generale, South Africa, Zuan Yan.
**International Audit Reports:** AWB, Gazprom, Shari'a, Societe Generale.
**International Auditing Practices:** Shari'a, Societe General.
**International Markets, Competitive Issues:** Gazprom, ICAI, Kansayaku, Shari'a, Societe Generale, Tae Kwang Vina, Zuan Yan.
**Issues Related to the Global Accounting Profession:** Gazprom, ICAI, Kansayaku, Kaset Thai, Royal Ahold, Shari'a, Societe Generale, South Africa, Sudan, Tae Kwang Vina, Zuan Yan.

## L

**Lack of Definitive Guidelines for Client Transactions:** Enron, Livent, Societe Generale.
**Legal Liability—Criminal:** Enron, Fund of Funds, Kansayaku, Madoff, Thomas Forehand.
**Legal Liability—General:** AMRE, Hopkins, Madoff, New Century, Ryden Trucking, United States Surgical Corporation, Zaveral.
**Legal Liability—International Markets:** Gazprom, ICAI, Kansayaku, Royal Ahold, South Africa, Zuan Yan.
**Legal Liability—1934 Act:** ESM Government Securities, Flight Transportation, Livent.
**Letter of Representations:** CapitalBanc, Livent.
**"Lowballing" Phenomenon:** Baan, Crazy Eddie, Tae Kwang Vina.

## M

**Materiality Issues**: Avis Love, CapitalBanc, Gemstar, New Century, PTL Club, Sudan.

## N

**Need to Follow-up on Suspicious or Unusual Client Transactions:** AIG, AMRE, Avis Love, Cardillo, CBI, David Myers, Enron, Flight Transportation, Fund of Funds, Gazprom, Gemstar, Golden Bear, Goodner, Happiness Express, Just for Feet, Livent, New Century, PTL Club, Royal Ahold, SmarTalk, Triton, ZZZZ Best.

## O

**Opinion Shopping:** Cardillo, Livent, Royal Ahold.
**Outsourcing of Accounting Services:** ICAI.

## P

**Peer Reviews:** Madoff.
**Personal Integrity of Auditors:** AMRE, Avis Love, Bill DeBurger, Cardillo, Enron, ESM Government Securities, Fund of Funds, Hamilton Wong, Kansayaku, Koger, Laurel Valley, Leigh Ann Walker, Madoff, National Medical, New Century, O'Connell, Oak, PTL Club, Rocky Mount, Royal Ahold, Stock Option Mania, South Africa, Tommy.
**Personal Lives vs. Professional Work Roles:** Avis Love, Bill DeBurger, Charles Tollison, David Myers, ESM Government Securities, Hamilton Wong, Hopkins, Kansayaku, Leigh Ann Walker, Ligand, Oak, Stock Option Mania, Thomas Forehand, Tommy O'Connell.
**Personnel Issues within Audit Firms:** Bill DeBurger, Charles Tollison, Fund of Funds, Hamilton Wong, Hopkins, Kaset Thai, Leigh AnnWalker, Ligand, National Medical, New Century, Stock Option Mania, South Africa, Tommy O'Connell.
**Practice Development Issues—International Markets:** Gazprom, ICAI, Kansayaku, Kaset Thai, Royal Ahold, Shari'a, Societe Generale, South Africa, Tae Kwang Vina, Zuan Yan.
**Predecessor-Successor Auditor Communications:** ZZZZ Best.
**Premature Signoff of Audit Procedures:** New Century, Tommy O'Connell.
**Privileged Communications for Auditors:** Creve Couer.
**Professional Roles of Auditors:** AMRE, Avis Love, Bill DeBurger, Charles Tollison, Enron, ESM Government Securities, Fund of Funds, Hamilton Wong, Leigh Ann Walker, Ligand, National Medical, New Century, Stock Option Mania, Tommy O'Connell.
**Professional Service Engagements Requiring Independence:** Tae Kwang Vina.
**Professional Skepticism:** AMRE, CBI, Enron, ESM Government Securities, Gemstar, Golden Bear, Happiness Express, Ligand, New Century, PTL Club.
**Public Company Accounting Oversight Board (PCAOB):** Ligand.

## Q

**Quality Control Issues for Audit Firms:** Bill DeBurger, Cardillo, CBI, Fund of Funds, Gemstar, Hamilton Wong, Hopkins, ICAI, Koger, Leigh Ann Walker, Ligand, National Medical, New Century, PTL Club, South Africa, Tae Kwang Vina, Tommy O'Connell, Zuan Yan.

## R

**Receipt of Commissions by CPAs:** HealthSouth.
**Reciprocity Agreements between International Regulatory Bodies:** ICAI.
**Regulation of the U.S. Accounting Profession:** Baan, Enron, Fund of Funds, Madoff, PTL Club, HealthSouth.
**Regulatory Issues Related to Global Accounting Profession:** AWB, Gazprom, ICAI, Kansayaku, Kaset Thai, Livent, Royal Ahold, Shari'a, Societe Generale, South Africa, Sudan, Zuan Yan.
**Related-Party Transactions:** Enron, Gazprom, Livent.
**Resolution of Ethical Dilemmas:** CapitalBanc.
**Review of Interim Financial Statements:** Cardillo, Enron, New Century, PTL Club, ZZZZ Best.
**Rule-Making Processes:** Baan, Gazprom, HealthSouth, ICAI, Kansayaku, Royal Ahold, Shari'a, South Africa, Zuan Yan.

## S

**Sarbanes-Oxley Act of 2002:** Fund of Funds, Ligand, New Century, Societe Generale, United Way.
***SAS No. 50* Reports:** AIG, Livent.
**Scope of Internal Controls:** Saks.
**Scope of Services (provision of non-audit services):** AIG, Enron, HealthSouth, Tata Finance.
**Securities and Exchange Commission:** AIG, AMRE, Cardillo, Crazy Eddie, Dollar General, Enron, ESM Government Securities, F&C, Fund of Funds, Gemstar, Just for Feet, Koger, Livent, Madoff, New Century, PTL Club, Royal Ahold, SmarTalk, Sudan, Triton, United States Surgical Corporation, ZZZZ Best.
**SEC's 8-K Auditor Change Rules:** Cardillo, ZZZZ Best.
**Societal Role of Audit Function:** Baan, Enron, Gazprom, ICAI, Kansayaku, Madoff, New Century, South Africa, Zuan Yan.
**Subsequent Discovery of Errors:** Ligand, New Century, PTL Club, Ryden Trucking.
**Substance over Form Concept:** AIG, Enron, Flight Transportation, Gazprom, Societe Generale.
**Supervision of Staff Accountants:** Leigh Ann Walker, SmarTalk, Tommy O'Connell.

## U

**Understanding the Client's Industry/Business Model:** Crazy Eddie, Doughtie's Foods, Enron, Flight Transportation, Fund of Funds, Gemstar, Happiness Express, Just for Feet, Livent, New Century, PTL Club, Royal Ahold, Triton, United States Surgical Corporation, ZZZZ Best.

## W

**Walk-through Audit Procedure:** Doughtie's Foods.
**Whistleblowing:** AMRE, Enron, Mohamed Salem El-Hadad.
**Withdrawal of an Audit Report:** CBI, ESM Government Securities, Happiness Express, Livent, New Century, Ryden Trucking, United States Surgical Corporation.